50 Years of The San Francisco Opera

Arthur Bloomfield

50 YEARS OF THE SAN FRANCISCO OPERA

SAN FRANCISCO BOOK COMPANY   *San Francisco*

First Printing

Copyright © 1972 by Arthur Bloomfield

All rights reserved. No part of this work may be reproduced or transmitted in any form by any means, electronic or mechanical, including photocopying and recording, or by any information storage or retrieval system, without permission in writing from the publisher.

ISBN: 0-913374-00-8

Library of Congress Catalog Card No.: 72-90014

Composed and printed in the United States of America by Science Press, Ephrata, Pa.

Photographs used in this volume were kindly furnished by the San Francisco Opera Association, Mrs. Horace B. Clifton, Madame Bianca Saroya, *The San Francisco Examiner*, Paul Tracy, the late Charles Kendrick and Clade Von Besser.

FOR ANNE—*and John, Cecily and Alison*

Contents

Preface

This is an *unofficial* history of the San Francisco Opera, a book which aims at an objective narrative and appraisal of the hits, misses, and points between, of the company. But it is a book born very much out of enthusiasm—enthusiasm especially for the vitality and spunk which propelled the company's early years under the colorful Gaetano Merola, and for the frequently high level of creativity in repertoire and production conspicuous during its recent two decades under Kurt Herbert Adler.

Although this volume is built on the "skeleton" of an earlier book, *The San Francisco Opera, 1923–61*, it is more than a simple updating. Thanks to newly-gained information from personal and phonographic sources, I've done considerable rewriting of the original chapters. Combining *these* new ingredients with an account of the interest-packed seasons of the past dozen years, *Fifty Years of the San Francisco Opera* is offered as a new history, essentially re-thought from the ground, or should one say stage-and-pit, up.

The San Francisco Opera hasn't missed a season in fifty years and it remains the company which can boast the greatest number of performances offered in the United States by an operatic organization outside New York. Bulk, of course, is not necessarily an index of quality. But San Francisco can probably claim, of the American companies outside the mammoth Metropolitan, the one which lately has offered the best combination of star singers (many in U.S. debuts), a thorough and well-balanced repertoire, and numerous home-grown new productions, with a consistent interest in staging values running parallel. Certainly its repertoire has often been more far-reaching than the Met's. Unique castings should be noted, too, and all this is not to mention the "up," on-the-toes quality which comes in part from the pressures of relatively compressed seasons and has often kept humdrum-ism at bay.

Furthermore, the San Francisco Opera has expanded its "empire" so that it must, in fact, be considered not only in light of the senior troupe but also as the producer of an experimental, low-budget Spring Opera season and the dispatcher of a grass roots touring subsidiary, Western Opera Theater, and the organizer of an auditions program and summer opera school, all feeding talent to the big brother of the complex.

Primary acknowledgments at the time of this new volume should go to *San Francisco Examiner* music critic Alexander Fried, with whom I have had numerous productive and amusing consultations on the performances of the early years of the company, and *Examiner* librarian Stuart Rasmussen who kindly led me into a warehouse where I could study bound volumes of newspapers from years long gone. Harold Rosenthal, editor of *Opera* in London, has continued to provide elusive biographical information with his usual efficiency.

The first chapter could not have been written without the help of Mrs. Horace Clifton, nor the second without the late Charles Kendrick and G. Albert Lansburgh. I have fond memories, too, of discussions with the late critic-collector Anthony Boucher, and more recent pleasure talking to such oldtime singers as Bianca Saroya and Frederick Jagel. Numerous collector friends have facilitated my hearing virtually all the extant sonic materials (a Fafnerian hoard) relating to the San Francisco Opera—that is to say private recordings of broadcasts and tapes made in the house.

Kurt Herbert Adler, general director of the San Francisco Opera, has helped clear up certain matters difficult to assess from the audience side of the footlights, as have company coordinator Matthew Farruggio and technical director John Priest. The various San Francisco Opera press officers of the past decade, Patrick Blake, Maryan Talbot, Richard Houdek, Margaret Norton, Kori Lockhart and Herbert Scholder, must all be credited for their friendly aid.

My thanks to Robert Messick, a student of opera who attends a mere thirty-five or forty performances a year, for reading the manuscript. And I am indebted to Kurt Binar for his keen observations. Last—but foremost in my acknowledgments—I want to cite the encouragement and editorial assistance of my publisher Ernest Scott, and the patience of my wife Anne!

Arthur Bloomfield
San Francisco
August 1972.

CHAPTER 1

The Beginnings

On September 26, 1923, 5000 persons made their way into the big, boxy and unaesthetic Civic Auditorium on Grove Street to attend the first night of the first season of the San Francisco Opera. The performance of Puccini's *La Bohème* starred Giovanni Martinelli as Rodolfo and Queena Mario as Mimi, and also on stage was a local girl, Anna Young, as Musetta. Top price was $4, the evening a near sellout. The auditorium, not basically a home for artistic events, had been modified and spruced up for the season: the stage was extended seventy-seven feet out toward the audience, the main floor seats were cushioned and arranged on a sloping platform, and an arc of so-called boxes was constructed at the rear. There was a big false proscenium, and curtains hid from view the empty sections of the huge balcony at each side of the stage.

The total effect was that of a theater within a theater (or perhaps barn is a better word), and if the transformation had elements of improvisation, it served.

On the conductor's podium that September night was a 44-year-old Neapolitan named Gaetano Merola. Son of a court violinist, he had arrived in the United States in 1899, fresh from the Conservatorio San Pietro a Majella in his home city where piano and conducting were his major studies. He was taken on as assistant to Luigi Mancinelli at the Metropolitan and, after a season, joined the Henry W. Savage Opera which plowed through the East and Midwest providing generous-lengthed engagements of opera in English—if this sounds unlikely, bear in mind that television had not yet been invented. It was in Buffalo that young Merola conducted his first opera, *Lucia di Lammermoor*. In February 1906 he came to San Francisco for the first time, as accompanist to Eugenia

1

Mantelli. The concert did not come off because an opera company starring Luisa Tetrazzini was having such a success at the Tivoli Theater there was no room in the city for anybody else. But the trip served a certain purpose. The city of San Francisco, with its bay as perfect as Naples' and Mount Tamalpais looming up in Marin County almost like Vesuvius, began to weave a spell over Merola. "If destiny wants me not to return to Italy," he was quoted as saying, "this is the place to settle down."

It took fifteen years, but Merola did settle in San Francisco. And it was he who provided the spark for the founding of a home opera company, an institution which, after troublesome birth pains, would emerge from its "experimental" first season in healthy shape, and, following some relatively adventurous early years, find a solid artistic place in the world of "international" opera.

After returning to New York in 1906 Merola went to work for Oscar Hammerstein's hell-raising Manhattan Opera as chorus master, and an unusually youthful, precise chorus it was. The summer of 1909 found him visiting San Francisco again, as conductor for the extensive engagement of W.A. Edwards' International Grand Opera Company at the Princess Theater on Ellis Street near Fillmore. *Otello, Fedora, La Gioconda* and *L'Amico Fritz* were offered, along with more basic fare. Between two San Francisco series of performances there were presentations in numerous other California cities and towns: Oakland, Sacramento, Stockton, Santa Cruz, Fresno, Bakersfield, Riverside, Los Angeles. Merola's nephew Armando Agnini, who was later to serve the San Francisco Opera for many years, was in charge of the stage. According to a newspaper clipping of the time, Merola resigned from the International while it was in San Francisco, and "the Italian quarter" interested itself in finding means whereby "Merola, the competent director from Rome, may be constrained to remain and be content."

The young Neapolitan was undoubtedly content to remain, but the means were apparently not there. His association with Hammerstein continued in New York where he led the premiere of Victor Herbert's *Naughty Marietta* in 1910, and in London where he conducted during the great Oscar's last operatic fling in the spring of 1912.

Work with the Schuberts followed, and for them Merola presided over *Maytime*. Then Fortune Gallo hired him as conductor of his spunky San Carlo, a touring aggregation that endured well into the middle years of the 20th century. The war was on and Gallo had lost Carlo Peroni, his regular maestro, to the U.S. Army. It's likely Merola would have spent more time in so-called grand opera prior to the San Carlo engagement had not Hammerstein's rivalry with the Metropolitan resulted in the impresario's 1910 agreement—for a $1,200,000 settlement —not to produce opera in New York, Boston, Philadelphia or Chicago for ten years.

At all events, the San Carlo provided Merola with several more trips to San Francisco, and the thread of destiny wound closer to the prime events of his career.

Merola returned in February 1919 for a well-attended two week season in the Curran Theater with such artists as Queena Mario, the Japanese-American soprano Haru Onuki and San Francisco's own Doria Fernanda. He was in the pit February 2, 1920 when the San Carlo returned to the Curran, the roster including Mario, Anna Fitziu, Alice Gentle, San Francisco's Maude Fay and the Spanish baritone Vicente Ballester. A special third week was added to take care of ticket demand. In January 1921, when he returned again, *Examiner* music critic Redfern Mason noted that "Merola conducted (the opening) and the audience greeted him like a friend." Again there was an added third week, and Merola had extra time to indulge his love for San Francisco, "my other Italy."

He not only liked San Francisco for its charms. He hoped he could benefit the city, and himself of course by producing opera by that famous Golden Gate. He knew San Franciscans paid a lot of money to hear visiting troupes—the Chicago Opera, the Scotti Opera, the San Carlo—and he figured there would be sufficient funds to give San Francisco what he thought it ought to have: its own company.[1] The fact that a new War Memorial Opera House was projected was of vital interest to him. Surely he thought, it ought to be opened by a locally organized troupe.

Following the San Carlo tour Merola went back to New York in the spring of 1921. Soon he was reminding his employer of an invitation from San Francisco. It was extended by Mrs. Oliver Stine, a music patron and something of a composer herself. She had developed an interest in Merola—she consulted him on a San Carlo visit regarding some music she'd written for an opera on a Japanese theme—and now she suggested he come West that summer. Mrs. Stine promised to get him voice pupils. Merola borrowed money from Gallo for transportation and, with his wife Rosa, set out for San Francisco. He left the door open for continued employment with the San Carlo, but, when Gallo corresponded with him about returning as a regular conductor the next season, Merola asked for a raise of $50 plus transportation. Gallo offered a $35 raise and no fares: this Merola refused. Obviously the possibilities which San Francisco offered were so favorable that he would not return to the San Carlo on other than his own terms.

The year 1921 found Merola becoming a permanent resident of San Francisco. He gave lessons to make a living, and, for recreation, played cards with friends he had made in the city's heavily Neapolitan Italian quarter. Meanwhile, remaining less active than during his touring days, he nursed his idea of producing opera "made in San Francisco." And then, in November of 1921, something happened which set Merola to thinking about the subject in more specific terms than previously.

The Merolas were invited to a football game—the "Big Game" between Stanford and the University of California—in Stanford Stadium, thirty miles south of San Francisco, and when he heard the band down on the field he was immensely stirred. The acoustics were surprisingly impressive. With tenors more on his mind than quarterbacks, Merola decided the stadium had excellent possibilities for opera. It reminded him of Verona's celebrated Arena, and the Baths of Caracalla in Rome. The idea was not the most practical in the world but, even if some thought it a romantic dream, he was determined to go ahead and try to execute it. A meeting was arranged with Dr. Ray Lyman Wilbur, Stanford's president, and Dr. Wilbur referred Merola to Dr. Williams, chairman of the Board of Athletic Control. Dr. Williams was won by the youthful, charming and enthusiastic Italian, and he granted him just the permission he wanted: the stadium would be available for opera.

So, ready to wear the hats of conductor, chorus master, impresario and even financial angel, Merola went ahead with plans for a short June season. Meanwhile, early 1922 found him guest conducting during the San Carlo engagement at San Francisco's Century Theater. The new chief conductor was the German Ernst Knoch, listed on the prospectus of the emphatically Latin San Carlo as Ernesto Knoch.

Funds for the Stanford season—singers, chorus and orchestra, not to mention the special stage—obviously posed a big problem. Merola was reluctant to ask for money from people he didn't know too well so he did not venture outside the Italian community for his support. Cashing in his own Italian bonds, he persuaded his North Beach friends—small businessmen, white collar workers, an artist—to contribute to his project. None of these men was particularly affluent, and some of them had just a little more than nothing salted away. But Merola was very convincing. The Italians put in their baptismal contributions, some $1000, some $500.

It was a handful of men who helped Merola set things in action: Guglielmo Torchia, Giuseppe Brucia, Antonio Farina, Giulio Stradi, Alfonso and Amedeo Napolitano, Milano Milani, Amedeo, Amalio and Anacleto Paoni.

Merola went East and engaged such well-known singers as Martinelli, Ballester, the bass Léon Rothier. For soprano roles he signed the tall, young Philadelphian Bianca Saroya,[2] whom he'd heard in opera and musical comedy in New York. He wired back that more guarantees were needed, and the more prosperous Italians found themselves at the bank arranging a note for several thousand dollars. San Francisco Symphony players were engaged, and Merola rounded up a chorus. It rehearsed in Frank Carroll Giffen's well-remembered Victorian house at the northeast corner of Hyde and Chestnut streets on Russian Hill. A visit to this corner in the spring of 1922 would have found Merola at the piano, playing with one hand, conducting with the other, working with a green but willing band of choristers. Outside, as the story goes, at least one gripman on the Hyde Street cable car line would call out Chestnut as Rue de l'Opéra.

Down the Peninsula preparations continued. A stage was constructed at the north end of the stadium, trees were set decoratively at each side of the playing area, and seats on the greensward and in the semicircular balcony formed by the End Zone were put on sale. Capacity was 17,000, the price scale $1 to $5. To accommodate patrons, special train service to Palo Alto was arranged. Meanwhile, the principal artists were whiling away their cross-country time on the Overland Limited, Rothier playing his cards for "blood," Ballester joining in in a more off-hand way, and Saroya winning in spite of the fact she would have rather been watching the scenery. When they arrived in Merola territory, stage rehearsals were set up in Scottish Rite Auditorium on Van Ness Avenue.

As if enough money hadn't been spent prior to the day of the first performance on June 3, an extra several hundred dollars had to be provided at the last minute for insurance because of a prediction it would rain. But there was no need for cancellation or postponement. The weather was balmy, and *Pagliacci*, followed by a ballet divertissement, was successfully presented. There were a number of vocal delights that night under the stars, none more memorable than the climactic A flat which the sure-voiced Ballester rolled out at the end of the Prologue, holding onto it as he sauntered across the stage. Only about 6000 were in the audience for *Pagliacci*, but 8000 came for *Carmen* on the 7th. *Faust* on the 10th had about 10,000 customers—and a natural assist from a full moon in the Garden Scene. For the second *Carmen* there was an even larger audience.

Despite the growth in attendance as the season progressed, hoped-for patronage by Shriners convening in San Francisco failed to materialize. And there was further loss of a sort due to the fact that some of the audience would buy cheap seats and then go sit in more expensive ones. Fog in San Francisco discouraged potential travelers, and that didn't help either. After the season one of the artists asked Merola, "Maestro, did you go in the hole?" and the answer, in characteristic Neapolitan accent was, "Yes, a beega hole!" Merola and his North Beach friends were liable for the stack of bills, and to say this group was happy about the financial outcome would not be accurate. At least one of the principal backers suggested Merola get help from wealthier men the next time.

Ballester, incidentally, joined the Metropolitan the season of 1924–25, singing several leading roles there. His career was unfortunately cut short by a fatal illness and that was his only season on 39th Street.

CASTS—STANFORD SEASON

JUNE 3: *I Pagliacci* (Leoncavallo)

Canio	Giovanni Martinelli
Tonio	Vicente Ballester
Nedda	Bianca Saroya
Silvio	Marsden Argall
Beppe	Aristide Neri

followed by:

Ballet Divertissement
    Conductor: Gaetano Merola

JUNE 7 and 16: *Carmen* (Bizet)

Carmen	Ina Bourskaya
Micaela	Bianca Saroya
Don José	Giovanni Martinelli
Escamillo	Vicente Ballester
Zuniga	Léon Rothier
Dancario	R. Agni
Remendado	Aristide Neri
Morales	U. Rovere
Frasquita	Constance Reese
Mercedes	Georgianna Strauss

    Conductor: Gaetano Merola

JUNE 10: *Faust* (Gounod)

Marguerite	Bianca Saroya
Faust	Giovanni Martinelli
Mephistopheles	Léon Rothier
Valentin	Vicente Ballester
Wagner	U. Rovere
Siebel	Doria Fernanda
Marthe	Georgianna Strauss

    Conductor: Gaetano Merola

Following the season, Mrs. Sigmund Stern, a philanthrop-ically-minded San Franciscan, gave an elaborate barbecue at her summer place in nearby Atherton. Since some wags had been wondering what happened to the bull from *Carmen*, an animal alleged to have been Escamillo's adversary found itself on the menu. A number of wealthy and influential people were at the affair, and in the warm afterglow of the season some of them offered Merola future help. Since he wanted very much to continue the summer seasons at Stanford—and initiate performances in San Francisco itself—he was extremely happy to acquire new and wealthier angels. One of his good friends, Horace Clifton, a San Francisco insurance man, made a note of those who had offered support, but back in the city after the festivities many prospective angels were suddenly much less interested.

A few staunch supporters, though, such as Mrs. Stine and Clifton, joined Merola in working toward his goal of a permanent San Francisco company—amidst rumors, by the way, that some San Franciscans wanted a company run by Giorgio Polacco, the distinguished Chicago Opera conductor. It was decided that approximately $75,000 was needed to prepare for a two week season in Civic Auditorium (there was no Opera House yet), and the idea was that seventy-five men would be found, each to contribute $1000. Robert I. Bentley, a prominent businessman, had a group of potential sponsors to lunch at the Pacific Union Club, Merola made a strong speech, and a committee was appointed to explore ways of getting the money.

But the memory of a visit by Mary Garden's Chicago Opera in the spring of '22 did not sit well with the moneyed men of San Francisco. The spendthrift Garden regime had brought the glamorous company to the West Coast with an expensive list of singers and a pretentious repertoire including *Tannhäuser, Lohengrin, Louise, Salome, L'Amore dei Tre Re, Monna Vanna, Girl of the Golden West* and several bread-and-butter items. San Francisco backers dropped $700 each on the venture.

On February 5, 1923, Bentley wrote a letter to Merola in which the Chicago fiasco was noted. "I have made inquiry of a number of the names we had under discussion the other day," the letter said. "Some have declined absolutely to come in at all and with all of them it was a case of being very reluctant about it."

Bentley's conclusion was that it certainly looked inadvisable to go ahead with the opera plan at that time. Merola was extremely depressed by the letter, but this seeming message of doom was simply the needed spark—a classic situation!—to set off the next, and most fruitful, stage in the progression of events toward realization of the goal. The evening of February 6 the Merolas dined with Clifton and his wife. While Merola sulked, Clifton thought. "I have it," he cried. "It's simply a matter of mathematics. If we can't get seventy-five to give $1000 each, we'll get 750 to give $100, and they'll get something in return. We'll give them a season ticket to the opera for each $50." The idea met with immediate favor, hope was renewed, and work toward the season started zipping along at tempo presto.

The first "executive committee" meeting was held February 7, with Mrs. Stine, Judge George Crothers, patron of the arts Albert Bender and impresario Selby Oppenheimer among those present. Solicitation of pledges was organized and almost daily meetings followed. A "party with a purpose" was given at Miss Edith Livermore's home February 13 with Merola offering a one-man preview of *Gianni Schicchi* at the piano. In March he went East to conclude negotiations with Martinelli, Beniamino Gigli, Giuseppe De Luca. Then came a climax, April 4, at the St. Francis Hotel, when a meeting attended by more than 100 persons was called to announce detailed plans for an autumn season. Merola told the assemblage that the Auditorium could be remodeled in a manner reducing acoustic faults to a minimum (there was an element of wishful thinking here), and the seating arrangement could be improved by raking the chairs like those in a conventional theater. Members of the San Francisco Symphony would be engaged, and a resident chorus would participate in the performances.

Governing officers were elected: Timothy Healy chairman, A. W. Widenham and Clifton vice chairmen, Mrs. James R. Miller secretary, and Edward F. Moffatt treasurer. Merola's title was general director, Oppenheimer was business manager. The executive committee consisted of Bender, Bentley, Crothers, Milton Esberg, Charles Field and B. F. Schlesinger; Mesdames William Fitzhugh, Marcus Koshland, W. H. Mills, M. C. Porter, William Sesnon, Ernest Simpson, M. C. Sloss and

Oliver Stine; and the Misses Louise Boyd, Mary Dunham, Edith Livermore and Sallie Maynard.

Work on ticket pledges continued through the spring, the chorus beginning its rehearsals in early May. At times the campaign seemed to be dragging, but actually a lot of quick activity was getting results. By the end of May solicitors could account for more than $30,000. Bentley, who had hoped as much as anyone that his February letter reflected too much caution, was at the head of the solicitors' list, accounting for thirty-six subscriptions. Next was Mrs. Sloss with thirty-one, Clifton with twenty-nine. The ticket money was just in promises, though, and a substantial bank loan had to be negotiated to assure building of scenery and the special stage.

By June the pledges had reached $40,000, suspense playing a key role in the year's operatic plot. The ultimate prospects were good enough to insure that the project would go on, but more cash was needed to make up for lack of a sufficient operating backlog. So Bentley, fully committed to the cause he earlier rejected, invited a group of men to dinner, took them to a chorus rehearsal at ballet master Natale Carossio's Sutter Street studio, and won additional backers. At the close of the season he was able to repay each of fifty underwriters $500.

When the idea of contributions was first broached there was some consternation at the size—reputedly $2000 per performance—of Martinelli's fee. But Merola turned that consternation into something approaching awe when he asked, "How many bankers are there in the world—and how many Martinellis?"[3]

Merola imported many of his artists from New York and Chicago. The aim of the company was to present the best international singers, and the program front billed "World Famous Principals and Leading California Artists." There was not sufficient talent in San Francisco, a musical city but hardly a highly developed opera-producing center by the standards of New York, Chicago and the musical meccas of Europe, to form the basis of the artist list. In this country, incidentally, Chicago held an especially high position in the operatic world during the 20's, maintaining as it did a winter season of approximately three months. Many important singers—Galli-Curci, Ruffo, Tito Schipa—sang for some years with the Chicago

10

Opera before joining the Metropolitan. And the heavily French-oriented repertoire, a heritage from Oscar Hammerstein, had its own character.

Merola's lineup in 1923 was thin, but he did have three of the greatest singers of the century, tenors Gigli and Martinelli and the baritone De Luca. The magnetic bass Adamo Didur was a force to be reckoned with, too. All of these, plus the up-and-coming tenor Armand Tokatyan, were from the Metropolitan. Merola also made much use of Alfredo Gandolfi, a rough-sounding but versatile bass-baritone who was then singing in Chicago and later went on to the Metropolitan where, in general, he sang roles less starry than those he was assigned in San Francisco. Figuring prominently, too, were well-routined comprimario performers from the Met: tenor Giordano Paltrinieri and basses Louis D'Angelo and Paolo Ananian.

The lack of reserves was especially noticeable (if not, as things turned out, a problem) in the stellar soprano list—it included only Bianca Saroya, the versatile spinto, and Queena Mario, an intimate-toned mini-Albanese. Saroya was called upon to follow a Giorgetta in *Il Tabarro* with a Suor Angelica the same evening, having sung Madeleine in *Andrea Chenier* two nights before, and with an appearance in *Mefistofele*—as both Margherita and Elena—scheduled for two nights later, and one in *Tosca* the evening after that! Doubling up also resulted in the bel canto De Luca taking on Scarpia, a relative roughie, in addition to more appropriate assignments.

Saroya had youth, and a Siegfriedian lack of fear, on her side. A marvelous trouper, she was taking on all her roles for the first time in her career. She arrived in San Francisco eight days before opening night—she was scheduled to sing the second night of the season—just as the orchestra was beginning its rehearsals at the Plaza Theater. But she didn't stay long. Elisabeth Rethberg cancelled two Aidas in Hollywood Bowl, and Saroya journeyed southward—Rosa Merola, a onetime Santuzza herself, accompanied her—to fill the bill. Rehearsals with the artists in San Francisco were not rigidly blocked out— there was, in any event, scant time, and some of the stars were not inclined to rehearse much—so Saroya's absence was taken in stride. Her "stage" preparation for a Martinelli *Tosca* consisted of going to the tenor's room with Merola and stage di-

11

rector Agnini and being told "at this point you stand here" and "then you stand there."

Puccini's complete *Trittico* (*Il Tabarro, Suor Angelica* and *Gianni Schicchi*) was a notable element in the far from insubstantial repertoire which, if almost exclusively Italian, did also include such a relatively rare item as Boito's *Mefistofele*—which the Met had revived in the 1922–23 season. The complete list was *Rigoletto, Bohème, Tosca, Pagliacci,* the *Trittico, Mefistofele, Andrea Chenier* and *Roméo et Juliette. Rigoletto* and *Bohème* proved the most popular at the box office, and *Mefistofele* trailed in last place, a scheduled second performance abandoned and replaced by a second *Chenier*. A generation later audience taste ranged wider and Boito's opera outsold some of the popular favorites when it was revived in 1952—of course the popularity of the basso Rossi-Lemeni did no harm.

Opening night of 1923 *Bohème* was on stage without benefit of dress rehearsal. The critics detected the chorus having some trouble getting together, and there were a few other reservations, but in general it was a night for rejoicing. Martinelli was in mellow form, and, according to Ray Brown in *The Chronicle:* "Although he was so deliberate in the delivery of 'Che gelida manina' as to lag a bit behind the orchestra at times, it was a deliberateness that served to accentuate the ease with which he sustained notes and linked them in unbroken sequence." Merola, Brown wrote, conducted "con amore."

The next night Gigli sang his favorite role, Andrea Chenier, and Saroya, who had probably seen the tenor more at parties than rehearsals, was so taken by the beauty of his voice that she almost forgot to sing. A couple days later she encountered some difficulty in getting the attention of tenor Tokatyan during the illicit love scene of *Il Tabarro:* it seems he had just become engaged to be married and his sweetheart insisted on watching from the wings. *Mefistofele* brought complicated scene changes and an evening which dragged overtime.

The *Rigoletto* at the end of the season was crowded and three "fishermen" reportedly paid $5 apiece for extra chairs which box-holders allowed to be placed in their boxes. And, if the story is to be believed, a young Italian in Senator James D. Phelan's box became so excited during a Gigli aria he fell off his seat and was knocked unconscious. It was after the first act of this performance, the last of the season, that Merola was feted with a tusch from the orchestra. He thanked all who had participated, citing especially the yoeman service of the choristers who had rehearsed spring and summer without remuneration.[4] There was also thanks to be given the women who had undertaken the finding of props for the operas.

One of them, who was assigned *Chenier*, remembers that the only item which gave her trouble was Marat's bust. All she could find in the junk shops was Dante's Beatrice, but when she brought her back to Agnini he took out a penknife, added various features, and soon Marat emerged. Pacific Heights mansions provided other more elegant props. For several years faithful subscribers helped out with furnishings as the company built up its stock. Mrs. X would proudly exclaim, "That was my best rug in the center of the last scene!" and Mrs. Y would shudder when it looked as if an impetuous prima donna might drop one of her treasured pieces of china or glassware.

Merola could be thankful that his first season was not only an artistic but a great financial success. The total seat sale was $124,000, and expenses being relatively small in those days he emerged with a tiny profit. There was one near-fatal postscript, however. Following the last performance the scenery was transported to a warehouse uninsured. And, while Horace Clifton tried to enjoy a post-season party, he couldn't help worrying about that lack of insurance. The following day he and his wife were to escort the De Lucas to Santa Rosa, fifty miles to the north, to visit Luther Burbank. They had to leave early. What to do? Clifton asked his friend Charles Christin to be sure to go to his office the next morning and ask his secretary to insure the sets.

When the party returned from Santa Rosa the next afternoon they reached the Sausalito ferry pier only to read headlines describing a fire which had seriously damaged the warehouse containing the opera scenery. The sets were gone. But, thanks be, the new policy had already gone into effect.

Merola was exhausted at the season's close—he had conducted all the performances. However, there was the happy occasion of returning the backers' money. As he told Bentley's contributors, "Gentlemen, I don't want your money. I just want your support—as subscribers, as boxholders." The busi-

13

nessmen, innately suspicious of artists' financial acumen, were impressed, and the relatively cloudless monetary picture created a warm, confident atmosphere. In 1924 about 2000 persons and firms were enrolled as "founders" of the company by buying one or more founderships at $50, and the company was incorporated under the laws of California as a non-profit organization with Merola as general director and Bentley as president. The new endowment of $120,000 enabled the company to operate until 1936 without resorting to elaborate annual campaigns for funds.

Notes

[1] In September 1921, 6313 persons paid $30,652 to hear Geraldine Farrar in *Butterfly* with the Scotti Opera in Civic Auditorium, and, according to the press of the day, this was the highest box office ever registered for a single performance of opera in the United States.

[2] A stage name—Saroya's extraction was actually German and English, and her German name was found unsuitable during World War I. Her early career in musicals included DeKoven's *The Highwayman* with John Charles Thomas. In the mid-30's she and her Rumanian tenor husband Dimitri Onofrei were pillars of the San Carlo on its late winter "dollar opera" visits to San Francisco.

[3] Speaking of top tenordom in those days in San Francisco, Gigli—according to his Memoirs—was escorted from the Ferry Building to his hotel by a squad of motorcycle policemen. The sirens whirred fortissimo.

[4] Chorus pay was minute and irregular in the early days. Less than $10 per performance was customary. In the mid-30's, with AGMA coming on the scene, rehearsal pay was added and there were other increases. Today the average tenured chorister can make $3000 or more per season. Many choristers have non-musical daytime jobs.

14

CHAPTER *2*

"Here Comes the War Memorial"

In a review of a *Tosca* performance midway through the first season Mason wrote that Merola "has proved to San Francisco that she can produce opera that will compare favorably with that of New York and Chicago. Now we must have an opera house and it is for the public to kindle new life in the dead bones of the trustees of the War Memorial." The need was more acute than ever as the successful new company was obviously ready to do more business in the years to come, and the prospect of more seasons in the Civic Auditorium, with its lack of permanent stage machinery, was not the happiest.

True, the huge building had been tamed somewhat for opera, but certain refinements were impossible. For instance, to anyone sitting in the side balconies near the stage an off-stage chorus would sound nearer than one on stage, because offstage in Civic Auditorium was simply behind a curtain rather than behind a wall.

Construction of an opera house was a major matter on the post-1906 earthquake agenda. San Francisco had always been an opera town—nearly 800 performances were registered in the 1860's, more than 1000 in the 1880's—and the operatic current by the Golden Gate, despite fluctuations of intensity, was not to be stopped.[1] The Grand Opera House which dentist Dr. Thomas Wade built on Mission Street near Third in 1873 went up in smoke in 1906, leaving a considerable void. The Tivoli, a former beer garden, had been a home to opera light and heavy in the years before 1906, but it was lost too. Although a new Tivoli opened in 1913 with performances of the Chicago Opera, it was soon turned into a movie palace.

In the years 1911–13 there was a campaign by the Musical

Association of San Francisco, sponsors of the newly founded San Francisco Symphony, to raise $1,000,000 for a grand music hall accommodating opera and symphony on a one-block site at the eastern end of Civic Center. A structure modeled somewhat on the Paris Opera was envisaged, with a grand staircase leading to the auditorium. A legal question arose as to whether the city could donate property to the Association, a private enterprise, and in settling a "friendly suit" testing the validity of the undertaking the California Supreme Court decided the city could not do so. Mayor James Rolph was obliged to veto the project, even though the Board of Supervisors had originally promised the land.

In 1918 a small group of prominent San Franciscans renewed efforts toward erection of a hall for symphony and opera. The project would further include an art museum,[2] and a small memorial court (8000 square feet or thereabouts in size) dedicated to peace and celebrating the termination of the World War. Leaders of the campaign were W. H. Crocker, Herbert Fleishhacker, John Drum, John D. McKee, Templeton Crocker, Milton Esberg, M. H. de Young and Walter Martin. During 1918 and 1919 they gathered pledges, and on September 1, 1919 an option was taken on the block bounded by Van Ness Avenue, Franklin, Hayes and Grove Streets, the former site of the St. Ignatius Church which had been destroyed in 1906. Their goal was $2,000,000 but by the end of 1919 they had less than half, and the great project appeared to be drying up.

Then, one day, Drum and Charles Kendrick, a young and cultured businessman, met by chance. Major Kendrick, recently home from the war, and influential in the American Legion, asked Drum how the fund-raising was going. Drum had to admit not so well. The matter remained in Kendrick's mind, and when he saw Drum a few days later he said to him, "You know, I think if you turn the whole project into a War Memorial I can get the veterans' support." So Drum's associates and Kendrick got together. The merging of private and veterans' fund-raising machinery seemed a hopeful prospect and the group gave Kendrick carte blanche to work out the alliance. He met with fifty representatives of veterans' posts, and they approved the intriguing idea. As far as the veterans were concerned, the suggestion that quarters be provided for their meeting purposes seemed a more practical plan than the memorial courtyard originally conceived.

The merger began smoothly but it was to run into very troubled waters later on. Plans went forward with representatives of the Musical and Art Associations getting together with veterans' officials on a bigger and better fund-raising committee. The St. Ignatius block on Van Ness Avenue was bought February 28, 1920 with $300,000 contributed by the Art Association. Forty thousand square feet of space for veterans' use was agreed upon. And on May 19, 1920 a mass meeting was staged in Civic Auditorium to arouse public interest in the War Memorial. The general architectural plan was for what today would be called a complex: a 3000-seat rectangular auditorium with a stage suitable for opera on the rear, or western, half of the block; a U-shaped structure to take care of the Art Museum and veterans' quarters in front of it; and an interior court in the center. There was also talk of a drama school and conservatory of music which never materialized. In retrospect the plan looks very, very squeezed.

The meeting was an inspirational event, complete with blare of brass band. Pledges were called out to "auctioneer" Lawrence Harris amid much happy tumult. Acting Mayor Ralph McLeran announced a $100,000 pledge from the city, and by the end of the meeting the kitty was swelled to, in round figures, $1,650,000. The drive was then taken into the streets, pup tents were set up on corners, and contributors dropped their money into cans with holes big enough for silver dollars. The hat was passed in theaters, too. After these and other activities were concluded the grand total take was approximately $2,150,000—not quite enough inasmuch as the needed figure had risen to $2,500,000 but a considerable total nevertheless. The cash and pledges were handed over to the care of the Regents of the University of California in nearby Berkeley and a board of trustees was appointed August 19, 1921 to administer it.

This board consisted of W. H. Crocker, Templeton Crocker, Drum, Esberg, Fleishhacker, E. S. Heller, Kendrick, Martin, McKee and Frank Kilsby.

It looked—in 1920—as if the War Memorial Opera House would soon be a reality, and there was a confident groundbreaking that year. Actually, however, it was twelve years before the building was ready. So from 1923 through 1931 the San Francisco Opera performed in Civic Auditorium, with the exception of 1928 and 1929 when the company was in Dreamland Auditorium (now Winterland).

Many factors contributed to the delay. The first stumbling block came when the attorneys for the regents determined that the pledges signed by the subscribers were legally insufficient! New signatures on new pledge forms were needed, and as there were several thousand subscribers the "bad dream" of re-signing took two years—some original subscribers cooling in the process. The trustees were specifically obligated by the regents not to enter into any expenditures or contracts for the War Memorial until at least $1,800,-000 in subscriptions had been signed up on the new form. And it was not until October 11, 1922 that an Architectural Advisory Committee was named—it consisted of Bernard Maybeck (Chairman), Arthur Brown Jr., Ernest Coxhead, Galen Howard, G. Albert Lansburgh, Fred Meyer, Willis Polk and John Reid, Jr. This committee soon reported unanimously that the St. Ignatius block was too small to carry out the War Memorial project with its variety of requirements. Besides, many were of the opinion that the buildings should have more nobility and greater pretensions than originally planned.

Meanwhile, a storage firm, the Lyon Fireproof Warehouse Company, bought a large lot on the southwest corner of Van Ness Avenue and McAllister Street across the wide avenue from City Hall, and proceeded to have plans drawn and building contracts executed for a warehouse thereon. A warehouse made no more aesthetic sense in that location than on Vienna's Ring across from the Staatsoper, but San Francisco was built, and rebuilt, by business rather than royalty or city planners.

Luckily some of the city fathers were concerned about aesthetics. Since the War Memorial was running over the sides of architects' drawing boards, Drum conceived a plan for buying out the Lyon people, and it won enthusiastic Supervisorial support. It had always been the hope of city authorities that the two blocks immediately west of City Hall be part of the Civic Center. Drum proposed that the trustees exchange their St. Ignatius block for one of the two west of City Hall if the city would purchase the other one. The War Memorial could then adorn two blocks. Mayor Rolph and the Supervisors' Finance Committee agreed that they could authorize the city to buy one of the blocks.

Numerous conferences were held with the Lyon firm, which finally agreed to accept $188,231 from the city for the property and damages accruing because of interrupted plans and cancelled contracts. Supervisor James B. McSheehy, a builder, thought the $140,000 asked for the lot itself "an elegant price," but discussion among the Supervisors brought out that the figure was not so outrageous. At the end of January 1923 the Supervisors ordered condemnation proceedings against the balance of the two blocks. The trustees advanced the money, and another long, slow process began as parcels of land were purchased. In the years 1923, 1924 and 1925, twenty-eight of these were bought by negotiation and suit. Meanwhile, on October 4, 1924, the trustees sold the St. Ignatius block to the Board of Education.

With a new working space of two blocks instead of one, original architectural plans were scrapped. But since the single block had obviously provided only a tight fit, the new elbow room facing City Hall was a blessing. A plan was put forward to expand the St. Ignatius format into a duplication in miniature of the City Hall, complete with dome in the center. This elaborate building or complex would have sat in the middle of the two blocks. An impressive staircase was part of this idea, and the conception also provided for museum facilities including the display of pictures in foyers adjacent to the auditorium itself. Naturally there were veterans' facilities, too, but influential men of that fraternity strongly opposed the plan and wanted to be off in their own grand and glorious building. So the architects returned to their drawing boards.

The two-building idea was developed, one, of course, being the Opera House, the other taking care of the veterans and the art museum. The buildings would be similar, the perimeter of the Opera House with its special stage and seating demands determining the perimeter of the second structure.

Polk and Lansburgh were put in charge of plans for the Opera House, Brown and his partner John Bakewell those for the Veterans Building. While the plans were still in their early stages Polk died and Bakewell withdrew, leaving Brown and Lansburgh as the War Memorial architects. Brown, who had designed the City Hall, with which the new structures would harmonize, was the overall chief. But Lansburgh was responsible for more of the design, including the interior of the Opera House, than his somewhat lesser fame in connection with the War Memorial would indicate. (Lansburgh's title was Collaborating Architect for the Opera House.)

An *Examiner* illustration of July 14, 1924 gives an idea of what the architects were considering in connection with San Francisco's War Memorial. It pictures idealized matching buildings on each side of a court, the buildings rectangular with seemingly endless rows of arches along the side facades, a tall column crowned with a sculptured figure emerging from a lagoon in the court. Stairs led to the court from each building. There were other and more grandiose ideas at this time—one of them to run a mall out Fulton Street from the War Memorial Court to Golden Gate Park. Interior studies continued, and a 1925 blueprint of the Opera House shows a semi-circular foyer wrapped around the auditorium, in distinction to the U-shaped, right-angled promenade area which ultimately emerged. In 1926 veterans' representatives examined plans of "their" building and space for their purposes was set at 65,000 square feet.

Two buildings on two blocks, obviously enough, were going to cost more than the contents of the one-block plan. By 1926 it was determined that the funds subscribed were entirely inadequate to construct a War Memorial of "the dignity and grandeur the people of San Francisco have a right to expect." Another ground-breaking took place—on Armistice Day, with Louise Homer singing *The Battle Hymn of the Republic*—but the trustees were about $4,000,000 short of the funds to go beyond symbolic shoveling. On February 18, 1927 the trustees informed the publishers of the five San Francisco newspapers that there were these alternatives: either the construction could go on piece-by-piece over the years Gothic cathedral-style, or, should the money be found more quickly, for instance by bond issue, then construction could proceed in the conventional manner.

The publishers felt that by all means the latter procedure was preferable. When the trustees mentioned the idea of building a usable "concrete shell" which could be finished later, Edmond Coblentz of *The Examiner* objected strenuously. He reminded them that the 1906 fiasco had furnished San Francisco with more than enough "ruins." A bond issue was carefully discussed, and the figure of $4,000,000 agreed upon.

In March 1927, City Attorney O'Toole advised the trustees he had eliminated from the resolution for the bond issue all direct mention of the Opera House and museum facilities, to make sure it conformed to California statutes. Remember the problem fifteen years earlier in connection with the city donating property to a private association? So when, on May 2, 1927, an ordinance was passed by the Supervisors submitting a proposition to the voters for the bond issue, it referred to the construction of "permanent buildings in or adjacent to the Civic Center to be used as a Memorial Hall for War Veterans and for educational, recreational, entertainment and other municipal purposes." A lawyer could have looked at that statement and not seen an opera house anywhere. As it happened, some of the veterans were to look at it and take only a very dim view of one.

In the arguments for Progress Bonds put out by the Civic League of Improvement Clubs and Associations of San Francisco, the following was set forth:

> "The utilitarian value of these buildings, alone, merits their construction. One of them will be the Veterans' Building, housing all the veterans' organizations in San Francisco. . . .
>
> "The other building will contain San Francisco's long-needed Symphony Hall and Opera Auditorium. . . . We have one of the finest Symphony Orchestras in the United States, and it should have a fitting place to perform. The San Francisco Opera Chorus, with the Municipal Chorus, foreshadow the day when the musical productions here will rank with those produced in Chicago and New York; and a home for all the future will be provided, second to none in beauty. . . . The War Memorial deserves unanimous support. Vote yes."

Despite this quaint description of the musical picture in San Francisco, with the opera company seemingly denuded of all but its chorus, this argument makes it obvious that an opera house was in the works.

In any event, the wording of the earlier-mentioned ordinance was unfortunate, and it was invoked many a time dur-

21

ing the several years of wrangling which followed the bond election. Bonds for the War Memorial were voted June 14, 1927, approximately 2000 persons more than the necessary two-thirds taking the affirmative view. But argument over plans and control consumed time into 1930, and the Opera House did not open until October 15, 1932. Several days before the election, Supervisor Frank Havenner had introduced a resolution that, should the bonds be voted, the Board of Supervisors would not appropriate money for construction of the War Memorial until plans received the formal approval of the majority of duly constituted representatives of all veterans' organizations in San Francisco. This was adopted 11 to 7. Now this was an entirely democratic resolution, but at the same time it strangled progress. It paved the way for the interminable bickering over details of the Veterans Building plans—bickering which almost turned the War Memorial into an unwieldy monster.

There were, of course, two ways of looking at the great project. There was the view from the board of trustees, mindful of its multipartite purpose, the original artistic emphasis, the fact that the original subscriptions were aimed at a project centered on a hall for symphonic and operatic purposes. The other view was that of some influential, outspoken veterans who were mindful of the wording of the ordinance, the dedication of the project as a War Memorial, and who vehemently sought maximum space for their organizations.

Trustee Drum reported at a public meeting in 1928 that plans had been discussed with veterans' representatives prior to the bond issue and there was no apparent dissatisfaction with the space allotted for their purposes. Lately however, he said, waves of indignation had resulted in a major enlargement of veterans' space. At first the vets had had a great area on the first floor and a number of impressively large rooms in the basement. The museum entrance was, logically enough, on Van Ness Avenue, leading into a multiple-story sculpture court, with galleries on the second and third floors. When the veterans demanded an auditorium, the sculpture court evaporated in a tug of war which consumed plan after plan.

Lansburgh threw in a handsome but perfunctory, ill-proportioned auditorium which, with its narrow stage and bad sight lines, plus portable seating (the veterans have occasion-

22

ally used it for dances), resulted in one of San Francisco's worst white elephants. The San Francisco Museum of Art was ultimately pushed up to the fourth floor where, as a matter of fact, it took on a pleasant feeling of intimacy, but access was, for many years, only by a single elevator from the McAllister street side.[3]

One aspect of the Veterans Building plans continued to irk representatives of the posts: this was a "temporary" indentation of 50 x 235 feet on the McAllister side, an indentation which would have made the building like an L with a fat vertical piece. It is certainly true that matching buildings— and matching buildings were ultimately constructed—are preferable to two not quite matched. On this point the veterans were right. But at the same time there were some extremely vocal veterans' officials who showed scant appreciation of the continuing growth in space awarded their "side." And those of them who were indignant that their building would cost less than the Opera House (in various planning stages the Veterans Building price tag remained $1,000,000 or so lower than the figure for its neighbor) failed to take into account the greater complexities of an opera house with its elaborate theatrical production demands.

Milton Sapiro, a prominent legionnaire, and later a San Francisco Superior Court judge, had the feeling as 1928 drew to a close that the history of the War Memorial should have taken an entirely different direction. "If we (the veterans) had gone out for a private War Memorial Building in 1920," he said, "we would have had a building and we would have secured subscriptions from the same groups that had provided the other million and a half for your musical purpose, because they are just as patriotic as we are."

Patriotism aside, some people interested in an opera house undoubtedly were not as interested in a veterans' building. As Sapiro continued, with a good deal less than complete appreciation of the trustees' charge, "You (the trustees) had money on hand all the time (from 1920). You had more than a million dollars. You could have put up a building to house us, and then gone out and put up the other building (the Opera House), or you could have started something that indicated there was going to be progress in the work."

Mayor Rolph, who appears through the War Memorial

battle smoke as an upstanding and principled public official, tended to favor the trustees. He rarely said things which didn't make sense, but there was a curious irony-to-come in his remark that the Opera House would be of more lasting value than the Veterans Building for the reason that the veterans would be gone in half a century or so. Perhaps he was thinking in terms of "the war to end all wars." Surely he cannot have foreseen that the rah-rah fraternalism and determined bingo playing of the vets would recede in popularity as the century wore on and Viet Nam set in. In any event, Rolph's remark brought an answer from Sapiro, who said: "An Opera House is *more apt to become a lodestone* on the back of the city than is a War Memorial." Obviously the good judge was not an opera buff.

Parallel to the argument over plans there ran another over control of the War Memorial! On September 18, 1928, Herbert Hall, attorney for the regents, issued an opinion to the effect that they could not turn over the privately-subscribed money to the Board of Supervisors as such, but they could to a group of trustees formed to carry out the terms of trust. A charter amendment was suggested, and at a special election on November 6 the people adopted an amendment providing for the appointment of a new group of trustees to watch over the composite War Memorial project. The strangulating item here was provided by a clause making nomination of the trustees by the mayor subject to confirmation by the supervisors. Rolph felt he was perfectly capable of selecting the men without outside review.

He submitted his eleven names on August 26, 1929. They were: General Hunter Liggett, U.S.A. retired; Frank N. Belgrano, state commander of the American Legion; James I. Herz, 363rd Infantry (San Francisco's own); Charles Kendrick; Herbert Fleishhacker, president of the Anglo and London-Paris National Bank; Kenneth R. Kingsbury, president of Standard Oil of California; Robert I. Bentley, president of California Packing Corporation; George Cameron, publisher of *The San Francisco Chronicle*; George Hearst, publisher of *The San Francisco Examiner*; Colonel Jesse Colman, a supervisor; and J. W. Mullen, publisher of *The Labor Clarion*.

This added up to only five veterans out of eleven, and a number of prominent veterans felt they should have a majority. A communication to the supervisors from the Advisory Board to Veterans' War Memorial Committees emphatically protested confirmation, warming up to the statement: "The veterans of San Francisco demand that the purposes for which the War Memorial Fund was created be carried out. The main purpose was to erect a building to house the veterans' organizations of San Francisco. Other uses and purposes were *incidental.* . . . If it is your intention to disregard the law and build an art museum and/or other buildings, leaving to the veterans such scraps of space as may be available and which some of their bodies can use, the best and most conclusive way for your board to manifest such intention is to confirm these appointments." The supervisors voted against confirmation 13 to 4.

Redfern Mason breathed some fresh air into the close situation in an *Examiner* piece of October 13, suggesting that the eleventh member of the new board be neither a veteran nor precisely a non-veteran, but a war worker, for instance a person with Red Cross or Salvation Army service. This person, he wrote, could act as a moderator, a harmonizer. Mason went on to say, with great rising-above-the-turmoil logic: "The museum is for the veterans as much as for the civilians. The same is true of the Opera House. But the Legion has this advantage over the Symphony—that, whereas the musical organizations will have to pay whenever they use the Memorial, the Legion gets its quarters for nothing.[4] The War Memorial's purpose is to honor the dead, but the best way to do that is to help the living. Its purpose is, through the gentle ministrations of art, to bring up a generation that shall have outgrown the brutalities of war."

On February 28, 1930, Rolph submitted his new nominations. They resulted in the same board, with the exception of the prominent Richard Montgomery Tobin, a Navy veteran, substituted for Fleishhacker. The new board was confirmed several days later and from then on the pace of constructive activity hastened. The unemployment problem had helped mellow some of the arguing, and by January 1931 actual construction began. Late in the month trucks bearing the words "Hello Prosperity! Here Comes the War Memorial" could be seen carrying materials to the long deserted site.

The cornerstones of the two buildings were laid on Armistice Day, 1931 and this was no premature ceremony like the ground-breakings five and eleven years before. *The Battle Hymn of the Republic* had its place again, this time voiced by Myrtle McLaughlin, a local singer. Sealed in the cornerstones were two boxes, including, among other things, a silver spade used in the 1926 ground-breaking, the Navy Cross awarded posthumously to the first San Franciscan killed in the war, the history and a file of programs of the San Francisco Symphony, and a copy of the charter amendment providing for the War Memorial board. Came October 15, 1932 and the Opera House opened with a performance of *Tosca* featuring Claudia Muzio.

Deflation had been a key factor in facilitating construction and furnishing of the War Memorial, which cost approximately $5,500,000—a figure considerably below architects' minimum estimates of 1929, excluding cost of land purchase. A five-figure sum was saved by postponing installation of an organ.[5] The happy ending of the story found the buildings matched: neither, actually, a rectangle as earlier conceived, but both with attractive lateral projections twenty-five and one half feet wide on each side near the fronts. Insufficient funds made it impossible to carry the Opera House all the way back to Franklin Street—and thus create useful extra backstage space—but the exterior look of the shorter form is, from the aesthetic point of view, more graceful.

Notes

[1] For the record, the first opera played in San Francisco was Bellini's *La Sonnambula*, at the Adelphi Theater February 12, 1851.

[2] The old museum of the San Francisco Art Association in the Hopkins mansion on Nob Hill had been destroyed in 1906. The Association carried on in the roofed-over foundation.

[3] Only recently has substantial classroom and office space on a lower floor been arranged for the Museum, with, for its public, a Van Ness Avenue entrance complete with a crisply modern first floor bookstore visible through a large window from the street. Ironically, the style of the bookstore is 1930-modern. The original War Memorial architects, working at that time, had no such thing in mind.

[4] A $15,000 subsidy from the city's Publicity and Advertising Fund helped the Opera Association substantially for many years in paying its rent to the city. It was succeeded in the early 60's by a Hotel Tax grant which brought in greater sums. The figure in 1970 was $225,000.

[5] It has never been installed.

CHAPTER 3

Making the Auditorium Do

1924

"It is hardly possible," an unidentified *Chronicle* writer said, "to expect a fashionable audience to arrive punctually for a performance that is plainly advertised to commence at 8:15 p.m. But after the initial disturbances of late and dilatory 'fashionables' there were several isolated instances of ranker vulgarity. Some minutes after the last act was in progress a youth, correctly attired in the habiliments of a gentleman, walked noisily down the center aisle accompanied by a brilliantly attired 'flapper,' both talking loudly and deliberately ignoring the feelings either of the performers or of the audience."

This rather dated-sounding but commendable knuckle-rapping was occasioned by an incident at the performance of *Madama Butterfly* on September 26, the musical side of which did not elicit any violent hosannas. Cio-Cio-San was to have been sung by the girlish-voiced but authoritative Toti Dal Monte, but Thalia Sabanieeva, a delicate Greek soprano, was her replacement, opposite the Pinkerton of José Mojica, a handsome Latin from the Chicago Opera who had a way of getting mixed reviews: sometimes, for instance, he was described as an ardent lover, at others he was rapped for being fussy and effeminate.[1]

The season had opened several days earlier with *Andrea Chenier*, Gigli repeating his favorite role and Claudia Muzio making her company debut as Madeleine. She sang her moving Tosca later in the '24 season, and also her equally memorable Violetta. Those who know her famous recording of the letter-reading scene and aria from the fourth act of *Traviata* have a good idea of the pathos she brought to this role. She had a way of throwing herself into a character so intensely she *became* the woman she was portraying, and when she clutched Teresina Monotti, the Annina in this San Francisco *Traviata*, she was trembling and crying as if she were indeed Violetta. Muzio also had a way of making her colleagues believe in *their* parts more than they might some other nights.

Gigli was busy in tenor leads, as was Tito Schipa, who came from the Chicago company for the first of several seasons in which he was a faithful, well-paid Merola employe. The patrician De Luca shone in the baritone register, offering a Rigoletto which brought from critic Redfern Mason this explanation: "His art is to begin in a rather subdued fashion and let the character unfold gradually." De Luca's voice was not so large, but the beauty of it, and his artistry, was. Meanwhile there was cause for lament over the lack of quality of some of the supporting performers, and Mason noted that whereas the leads tended to be excellent, the company was "adequate rather than inspiring in the assistants." This, of course, was a situation which would be rectified in the future, especially under Kurt Herbert Adler, but Merola deserves credit on that score, too.

The *Examiner* critic wrote a Sunday piece in which he pardoned the continuing emphasis on popular repertoire with the practical remark that "money is the sinews of opera." Therefore, he said, a hard-to-sell *Pelléas et Mélisande* is not to be expected. What, though, was to explain the inclusion in the repertoire of Mascagni's sweet, pale *L'Amico Fritz* which, even with the adored Schipa, and *Gianni Schicchi* on the double bill, brought relatively little into the box office?

The pure-voiced Myrtle Donnelly, a local girl, took over Mimi from Queena Mario in a *Bohème* repeat, but experience in smaller Italian towns didn't prevent Mason from declaring: "Of the art of acting Miss Donnelly is innocent as a pretty mannekin." Come to think of it, maybe Italy wasn't the place to learn. Margareta Bruntsch, another local, appeared as Maddalena in *Rigoletto* and Zita in *Schicchi*, and an unsigned article in *The Examiner* (the headline read: "San Francisco Girl Tops Opera Peak") reported that Madame Schumann-Heink had heard her and declared she was "the purest and greatest contralto in the world today." Her fame, alas, seems to have resided mainly in this exuberant article, although oldtimers in San Francisco remember that Miss Bruntsch had a voice to be reckoned with.

Came October 3, the penultimate night of the crowded season, and, on a few days' notice, a testimonial performance for Merola was arranged and presented before 4000 quick-to-respond souls at the Auditorium. Scenes and acts of operas from the repertoire were sung, and Merola was dragged before the footlights, crowned with flowers by the artists (who had a genuine affection for him), and applauded like a conqueror. The next night Muzio, Schipa and De Luca joined under the constant Merola to sing a *Traviata* which brought in the biggest box office gross to date, $19,615. Top price this year was up a dollar, and there was a modest profit on the season as a whole. Opera was expected, of course, to pay.

On October 6, Merola and his stars next established themselves in Los Angeles' Philharmonic Auditorium where a week's season got underway with Alexander Bevani in charge of the local chorus and Merle Armitage as business manager. The San Francisco-conceived productions were presented under the banner of the Los Angeles Grand Opera Association.

1925

With the main floor seating capacity reduced to allow more space between seats in the company's not especially comfortable home, the third season of the San Francisco Opera opened September 19. It was a particularly notable beginning for a particularly notable season. Rosina Torri of La Scala made her American debut as Massenet's Manon with Schipa as Des Grieux and Marcel Journet, that aging but still commanding bass, as the father. Antonio Nicolich of the Chicago Opera sang Lescaut, and the De Brétigny was a local baritone who had sung in the Stanford season, Marsden Argall. It was Argall who would have the first words to be officially sung from the new Opera House stage seven years later: the almost comically appropriate "Ah, finalmente" of Angelotti in *Tosca*.

Journet had not sung at the Metroplitan since 1908, at the Chicago since 1919. He was, of course, a regular in Paris, and a year earlier had sung in the premiere of Boito's *Nerone* at La Scala under Toscanini.

Torri's appearance marked the beginning of Merola's importation of singers directly from Europe. An artist who deserves to be better remembered, she possessed a pure lyric instrument which she used perfectly to convey a touching sense of fragility. She had a real Puccini voice—for Liu, Mimi and Butterfly. And she was, in fact, Rome's first Liu—in 1926. She continued at La Scala until 1934. Torri was also featured as Consuelo in *Anima Allegra*, a four-year-old opera by Franco Vittadini (1884–1948) which never made much of an impression. A sweetly tuneful, somewhat Puccinian work, disjointed and with a slim story, it had been produced at the Met two-and-a-half years earlier with Lucrezia Bori.

Other Merola catches were Muzio; coloratura Elvira De Hidalgo, the only teacher of Maria Callas; and Marguerite D'Alvarez, the highstrung mezzo. The tenor territory was populated by an especially starry group: there was, besides Schipa, the Belgian Fernand Ansseau and the Spaniard Antonio Cortis, both of whom were singing in Chicago and neither of whom ever joined the Metropolitan roster. Riccardo Stracciari and Cesare Formichi, also with Chicago associations, led the baritone contingent.

For the first time Merola shared the baton, his colleague being Pietro Cimini, a vigorous maestro who had conducted at the Chicago Opera. Cimini was a direct, capable conductor, a bit deficient in imagination but he got a good round sound from the orchestra. One veteran observer remembers him, in the middle of a peformance, taking out his handkerchief and waving it at the chorus to get them, for Heaven's sake, to look at HIM.

A large Opening Night audience greeted the Torri-Schipa-Journet *Manon*. The next day San Franciscans read in *The Examiner* that the young prima donna from Italy "had something of the charm of Pavlova and the spontaneity of Nazimova." Mason went on exultantly to say that "she charmed by the sustained delicacy of her cantilena. In moments of lyric rapture she has tones of pearly beauty." Schipa was awarded an encore for his singing of "Le Rêve." Two days later there were reports of Ansseau's debut in *Samson* and his vibrant, powerful voice, his impeccable French and handsome bearing. D'Alvarez was an intense Delilah. Ansseau was a relatively trumpety French-type tenor: some of his recordings remind a little of Bjoerling.

In those early days the press carried frequent reports of the box office status, and the box score after three performances (*Manon, Samson* and *Barber*) was: attendance, 14,781, and the take, $47,221. The performance of *Barber* was up to the season's vintage level and, as Mason noted, the Spanish De Hidalgo was "that rara avis among prima donne, a coloratura with brains and character . . . here is no female music box." Journet's "La Calunnia" began "like a breeze" and ended "like a storm."

Muzio was delayed in getting to San Francisco because the Buenos Aires season was extended for the Prince of Wales, but she did arrive in time for postponed *Aida* and *Tosca* performances. The Scarpia was Stracciari who, to Mason, showed "flinty hardness and Roman severity" as opposed to Scotti's "cold malignity and Machiavellian subtlety." (Take your pick.) Another end-of-season delight was the combination of Torri, Ansseau and Journet in Montemezzi's *L'Amore dei Tre Re.*

Besides being the most interesting of the company's first three seasons, Merola's 1925 effort resulted in the highest box office yield to date. Of the dozen shows in the large auditorium six were sold out, and the total receipts amounted to $154,058. In an atmosphere of prosperity it is not surprising that starry-eyed prophecies were made—prophecies which needed time for fulfillment. In one of Mason's editorials—they were often of a commendably crusading nature—he quoted Los Angeles impresario L.A. Behymer as predicting that within three years the West Coast would have twenty-four weeks of opera divided between the principal coast cities.[2]

"If we can," Mason wrote, "offer great artists a sufficient number of engagements to induce them to come and sing for us, we shall be able to compete for their services in the same field and on equal terms with the Metropolitan and Chicago." In the next forty-five years there was a gradual enlargement of the San Francisco Opera's activities, but the total length of time consumed by them in San Francisco, Los Angeles and elsewhere did not accelerate with Behymer speed.

During 1925 there was another Los Angeles season: a week's performances in the new Olympic Auditorium at 18th and Grand, a giant place hosting boxing, wrestling and home shows as well as the sweeter science of opera. Merola and Bevani collaborated again, this time under the name California Grand Opera Company. Behymer had replaced Armitage, who countered with his own autumn week of performances under the familiar title of Los Angeles Grand Opera. While Merola used the San Francisco casts (with slight changes in minor roles), Armitage hired Rosa Raisa, Maria Kurenko, Alice Gentle, Ulysses Lappas, Charles Hackett, Giacomo Rimini and Vicente Ballester for his innings at Philharmonic Auditorium. The repertoire included *Lakmé* and Massenet's *La Navarraise,* beside standard fare. Richard Hageman was the musical director. Merola's season brought, "by popular demand," a special *Butterfly* with Torri—and Schipa's little daughter Elena as Trouble. Rival seasons resulted, happily enough, in a February 1926 peace pact, and Los Angeles' operatic life became more harmonious. Los Angeles seasons with San Francisco and southland elements continued for several years, petering out during the Depression before the full Merola troupe embarked on southward journeys in 1937.

In the 1920's, with visits on and off of the Chicago Opera, the San Carlo and other companies, there were often five or six weeks of opera a year in San Francisco and sometimes more. Merola felt that his activities might well be expanded into two seasons a year, and late in 1925 he made preparations for a two-week season which took place the following January at the Columbia Theater. One of the special features of the season was an opera called *Fay-en-Fah,* the outgrowth of a 1917 Bohemian Club musical play, The *Land of Happiness,* with libretto by Templeton Crocker and music by Joseph D. Redding, prominent San Francisco socialites both. Their Orientalesque effort, an "only in San Francisco" sort of thing, had been premiered in Monte Carlo the year before, and three of the singers from that production, Lucy Berthrand, René Maison and Edmond Warnery,[3] were imported, the first two making American debuts in the San Francisco performances.

Toti Dal Monte was starred in *Lucia* and *Rigoletto*, the title role of the latter falling to Joseph Schwarz of the Chicago Opera (who died prematurely shortly thereafter) and Augusto Beuf, who was also the Enrico in *Lucia*. The repertoire also included *Tales of Hoffmann* with Berthrand as Olympia and Antonia, Maison as Hoffman, and Schwarz as Dr. Miracle. The season was not a great financial success, and this was the last winter series produced by Merola.

1926

Claudia Muzio was late again for her appearances with the company during the 1926 season, but she was, of course, worth waiting for. This time her ship, sailing from Rio de Janeiro to New York, was caught in hurricane territory and had to slow down for several days to avoid the worst of the storm. When her train from the East arrived September 27— the season was well on its way by that time—she was literally in good form. Slimmer than before, she told reporters that one meal a day was enough for her, a noon repast of chicken broth and vegetables, and she announced rather prematurely that "the day of the fat prima donna is over."

Muzio provided the expected passion in her performances as Mimi, Aida, Tosca, Leonora in *Trovatore* and Manon in the Puccini opera, all of these delivered within a space of eight days. And Louise Homer, mezzo and grandmother, was another dramatically convincing performer, her Delilah producing for Mason "a magnificent and perturbing (tonal) sensuality," even if the bloom sometimes wore thin and she didn't have the "purple richness" of D'Alvarez, the previous year's seductress.

But some of the other ladies seemed to be little more than self-conscious prima donne, dimly remembered now as hack birds of another era. On Opening Night Florence Macbeth looked to Mason "like a Romney portrait, but her atmosphere was a trifle mid-Victorian. Her Martha might have borrowed a little of the mercurial temperament of Elinor Marlo, the Nancy." The Marguerite in *Faust* originally scheduled for Luella Melius was handed over to local Myrtle Donnelly because Madame Melius "wants to make her debut as Gilda." That she did, and the pretty-voiced but slightly whoopy Australian soprano made merely a modest impression, drawing a surface image of the character. Miss Donnelly's Marguerite was dismissed as lacking in the flesh and blood of that unfortunate heroine.

The picture wasn't all dim, though. Marcel Journet sang his 1000th Mephistopheles during his 1926 engagement, and appeared with Muzio in *Tosca*—as Scarpia! The role had been planned for Formichi, whose suave baritone was not heard again as scheduled. But Journet, who straddled the bass-baritone border, was a Scarpia to be reckoned with. Interestingly enough, he never sang the role in his years at the Metropolitan (1900–1908) although he did sing Escamillo during that period. There was a light touch in *Tosca* when Vittorio Trevisan, the mellow Chicago Sacristan, bent over and picked up a pin while reciting the Angelus.

Even if Tito Schipa wasn't having the most vocally blessed season of his career his presence on Grove Street was highly welcome, and on Opening Night his "M'Appari" was successful enough to be sung twice. "One forgot it was opera, he sang with so touching a sincerity"—that from Mason with a tone of wistfulness which wouldn't be so necessary in the more drama-oriented 1970's. Other tenors in the lineup were the ardent-toned, aristocratic Cortis, Charles Marshall from Chicago, the experienced American Paul Althouse, and Aroldo Lindi.

Lindi, whose real name was Harold Lindau, was a Swede. Fate was to have him breathe his last on the stage of the War Memorial Opera House eighteen years later: he died just as he was finishing the first act of a San Carlo performance of *Pagliacci*. This sort of thing always happens at an especially dramatic point—the show, of course, *had to go on*! Lindi's ringing, light-colored voice was Italianate enough in sound to match his "nom de chant."

Schipa and Cortis were worked hard, the other leading tenors taking one opera each. Among the comprimario tenors was one Giuseppe Carcione, who, as a professional *Barber of San Francisco*, held down Chair No. 5 at the Safe Deposit Barber Shop on Montgomery Street in the financial district.

The 1926 repertoire was not adventurous. There was, however, a well-attended performance of Auber's *Fra Diavolo* which served as something of a lark in the midst of weightier considerations. Schipa had the title role. Florence Macbeth, whose engagement resulted form the non-appearance of Polish lyric soprano Claire Dux, was the Zerlina. Other happy news of the season was a box office tally of 55,000 admissions for twelve operas, the impressive local debut of baritone Richard Bonelli, the benedictory appearance of the Met's Otto Kahn at Opening Night, and the fact that the chorus was "no longer the assemblage of terrified amateurs it was two or three years ago." Scenic sophistication was, however, sometimes lacking. Mason pointedly remarked upon seeing *Martha*: "That was no English farmhouse."

The Los Angeles Grand Opera's 1926 season harmoniously combined former competitors Richard Hageman and Merola as, respectively, musical director and guest conductor. Merola then took over as general director in 1927 in association with L.A. Grand mainstay Merle Armitage. The 1926 season in the south actually began two nights before San Francisco's was finished, which meant that some of the principals in the Opening Night *Samson* could not be exactly duplicated. Thus, while Journet sang Scarpia in San Francisco, his High Priest in the Saint-Saens was taken over in Los Angeles by the Chicago Opera's Georges Baklanoff, no ordinary substitute. Antonio Cortis had the amusement of singing one Cavaradossi to Muzio's Tosca on the 4th, and, after a ride south on the Friendly Southern Pacific, another to Raisa's on the 6th.

1927

The 1927 season acquainted San Franciscans with several more-than-promising operatic youngsters: Ezio Pinza, Lawrence Tibbett and Puccini's *Turandot*. The repertoire, more interesting and mature than previously, also brought Wagner's *Tristan and Isolde* and Verdi's *Falstaff*—real caviar this. The *Tristan* was the first Wagner attempted by the company. The 35-year-old Pinza, veteran of one season at the Metropolitan, bowed in as Timur in *Turandot*, a plummy opportunity even if Mason dismissed it as a "minor role." Merola presented Puccini's last opera only a little less than a year following its American premiere (November 1926 at the Met) and indeed, only a year and a half after its world premiere (April of that year at La Scala). Tibbett,

30 going on 31, made his first appearance with the company in the role which had sealed his success at the Met, Ford in *Falstaff*. And the fat knight he clinked the coins at was the veteran Antonio Scotti, whose span of service at the New York house stretched from 1899 to 1933.

Another Tibbett special was Neri in the three-year-old *La Cena Delle Beffe*, Giordano's version of Sem Benelli's gruesome play. With a strong, if melodramatic, libretto, it was more compelling dramatically than musically, although it might be noted that the simple winding theme at the beginning of the fourth act is hard to forget. Gigli and Frances Alda's New York roles were taken by Armand Tokatyan and Frances Peralta (real name: Phyllis Partington), a big-voiced, California-raised soprano who had gone on to a middling career at the Met via the Scotti company. (She died in 1933.) Pinza and Tibbett were to have long records of San Francisco appearances. *Turandot*, however, disappeared for a generation, as it did in New York.[4]

The season opened September 15 as the city was preparing for Charles Lindbergh's arrival in his trusty "Spirit of St. Louis," an event which transpired at Mills Field two days later. The opera was Puccini's *Manon Lescaut*, repeated from the previous year. The urbane, rather flowery Mr. Mason found Peralta a Manon "of the Greuze type rather than the Watteau figure one usually associates with this most Parisian of idylls." Evidently conquered, he reported that "she appealed to more hearts than that of the Chevalier Des Grieux." The more heroic aspects of Des Grieux seemed the best in Martinelli's singing, Scotti was most comfortable in the "sinister, ironic" passages of Lescaut, and Louis D'Angelo did well as the aged roue Giullot, "albeit he was a little unduly mummified in the first act."

Tristan followed the next night at 7:45, and, while there were obvious imperfections, the audience gathered Wagner to its collective bosom like a long lost and highly respected friend. Alfred Hertz, bald and bearded conductor of the San Francisco Symphony—members of which have always formed the bulk of the opera orchestra—was on the podium. Elsa Alsen, a matronly but experienced Wagnerian (then associated with the Chicago Opera) was the Isolde, and Rudolf Laubenthal, gotten up as an unusually ascetic-looking knight, offered his relatively youthful-sounding but slightly strangulated Tristan. For a Latin touch there was Pasquale Amato, his voice somewhat faded, as Kurwenal. Quibbles aside, Wagner had arrived, and the audience cheered. Hertz dragged Merola on stage—he was, it seems, forever being dragged on—to share in the bows while Civic Auditorium went almost Lindbergh-mad for *Tristan*.

Anne Roselle, the young Hungarian soprano, undertook a Tosca and a Turandot with one day between—this was par for the stevedorian course in San Francisco during the 20's. Mason found her Tosca less subtle than Muzio's but an engaging, spontaneous portrayal. She sang "Vissi d'arte" with Scotti, the Scarpia, "panting over her shoulder"—a habit he had picked up, one supposes, when Miss Roselle was a member of the Scotti Opera Company. The new Cavaradossi was Mario Chamlee, a young American with an appealing spinto tenor not entirely unreminiscent of Richard Tauber or Gigli. Emphatically an above-average actor, Chamlee knew how to engage sympathy.

The *Turandot* cast was almost completely different from New York's, Roselle taking on the Principessa instead of Maria Jeritza, Myrtle Donnelly (and Marjorie Dodge in Los Angeles) the Liu rather than Martha Attwood, Tokatyan Calaf instead of Giacomo Lauri-Volpi, and Pinza rather than Pavel Ludikar as Timur.[5] Only Angelo Bada, the Pang, was in both productions. Roselle had sung the title role in Germany at Dresden. As demonstrated in her recording of "In questa reggia," she was a stunning Turandot, singing cleanly with a light, creamy tone and a relaxed manner stressing suavity over decibels. She sounded younger and less haughty than many later Turandots. So did Jeritza, San Francisco's 1928 Turandot—she was always completely taken with Calaf by the second riddle.

When the complex *Falstaff* arrived, helpfully toward the end of the season, it went quite well (there was also an announcement from Kendrick that the 1929 season would be performed in the new Opera House—he was only three years premature), but Verdi's shimmering opera didn't return for seventeen years. (More recently, however, despite some box office lag, *Falstaff* has been regularly revived.) Scotti's voice was well beyond its prime, but this mattered a

37

little less in *Falstaff* than in *Tosca*. Which is not to say that Sir John should not sing smoothly if possible.

As the season drew to a quick close Pinza was further exposed as Ramfis in *Aida* and Colline in *Bohème*, roles he continued to sing faithfully for a long time in San Francisco. *Carmen* reacquainted San Francisco with a protagonist, Ina Bourskaya, who had sung the role in Russian with a visiting troupe a decade earlier, and also at Stanford, in the accustomed French, during Merola's 1922 stadium season. Mason noted that "in point of sheer tonal beauty Miss Bourskaya's voice has its limitations, but the emotional suggestiveness, the tragic significance . . . recall Calvé at her best." On the minus side, stage director Agnini gave in to a bad idea and turned the street Arabs of the first act into "little dons and senoritas."

Notes

[1] When he turned up in San Francisco thirty years later, it was as a member of the Franciscan Order attending a religious conclave. He had joined the order in Peru in the early 40's, following a possibly not yet exhausted career on the operatic stage and in the films.

[2] Forty-five years later this figure was fairly accurate. The San Francisco Opera performed eleven weeks, and Spring Opera had another three or so. The New York City Opera (a visiting troupe, of course) played two weeks plus in Los Angeles. And the Seattle, Portland and San Diego companies put on several productions scattered over the season. Western Opera Theater, the San Francisco Opera's grass roots pocket touring troupe, was on the road as well.

[3] The Pelléas of the first London performance of Debussy's opera, at Covent Garden in 1909.

[4] Chicago played it in the seasons of 1933–34, 1934 and 1935. Turandots were Rosa Raisa and Maria Jeritza, Calafs Aroldo Lindi, Frederick Jagel, Armand Tokatyan and one Pane-Gasser. It was revived in 1938 with Eva Turner and Galliano Masini.

[5] The mischievous Jeritza used to make her chin shake when she sang with Ludikar, whose chin shook. But *he* couldn't help it.

CHAPTER 4

An Element of Reverie

1928

There was talk of "an atmosphere of intimacy" in describing Dreamland Auditorium, or Dreamland Rink (now Winterland), the large neighborhood arena which became the home of the San Francisco Opera in 1928—and almost that of Spring Opera in 1967. But the building, the San Francisco stand of the Ice Follies in recent years, was only slightly less of a barn than the Civic Auditorium as far as opera was concerned. A number of reasons were cited for the move to Post and Steiner streets: the capacity was smaller (4600), the setting up of the special stage less costly than at Civic Auditorium, and, as the press of the day reported, obviously from a publicity release, "the new hall has been built with a careful view to the housing of music . . . acoustics have been given much consideration." Redfern Mason thought the seats were more comfortable than those at the Civic Auditorium, but he also judged that the total situation was not ideal.

Although two seasons were played at Dreamland there was a distinct element of reverie in the optimism about the new home, which was not especially attractive or convenient, nor notable for sonic excellence. It was without reluctance that the company moved back to Grove Street following the 1929 performances.

An unusual aspect of the 1928 season was the large place held by composer Umberto Giordano in the repertoire. *Andrea Chenier*, *Fedora* and *La Cena delle Beffe* were all given. Considering that twelve operas were performed during the season, the traditional twins together, three out of eleven bills by Giordano seems undue consideration. He was a sometimes compelling puller of the heartstrings and a strong painter of atmosphere, but not the sort of consistently inspired composer who always makes his connecting passages as interesting as the arias on each side of them. Mason made the understatement of the year when he wrote: "Merola believes in Giordano."

Maria Jeritza, like Anja Silja nowadays, whose showmanship is more memorable than her voice, sang Fedora, Carmen and Turandot, also Tosca, this including her famous "Vissi d'arte" sung from a prone position. Elisabeth Rethberg began her long and happy association with the company during 1928, and the third of the hard-worked prima donne was Elda Vettori, an also-ran Met soprano. Backing them up was Myrtle Donnelly, recipient of a few crumbs of unstinting praise from the still dubious Mason.

The season opened September 15 with *Aida*—this was the first of a number of seasons to begin with this festive and classic opener. Rethberg was the Aida, and, for Mason, a subtle one ... not "orchidaceous" like Muzio, "nor serpentine in the Italian fashion, but impulsive with a Teutonic warmth of emotion." Wow! Opposite her was Edward Johnson, then a well-known tenor, later, of course, the Met's general manager. Mason described him as a flesh-and-blood Rhadames, not a stick.

But the hottest news of the evening had to do with Lawrence Tibbett's taking over for the indisposed Giuseppe Danise as Amonasro. Mason unloaded almost every adjective in the book—*primitive, virile, heroic, intense, impassioned, authoritative*—and summed up the situation thus: "It was so dramatic, so unlooked for, that suspicious ones will be inclined to accuse Merola of staging a Tibbett 'substitution' as the surest way of making the first night of the season a historic one. If such was the case—and of course it was not—it was a masterly bit of stage strategy." Only Marion Telva, a lackluster Amneris, refused to catch the histrionic fire engulfing the evening. The benched Danise recovered toward the end of the season, making his debut in *Fedora*.

Tosca brought Jeritza and her famous Floria—for which she was paid $3000 per evening—before an SRO crowd. She was described by Alexander Fried of *The Chronicle* as "a woman of royal beauty and magnetism." Her plan for the character, he continued, "could not be called subtle, but it was artistic and effectively credible throughout the story."

40

Jeritza, he said, "does not pretend to the perfection of bel canto," and her full voice was "rarely used with memorable beauty." It sometimes dropped to "dramatic prose speech, forced beyond mellifluousness." As Mason put it: "Jeritza made love to Tokatyan (the Cavaradossi) and the audience at one and the same time." Tibbett, he said, was not enough of a satyr and bigot as Scarpia, giving the impression, rather, of "one of the Puritan fathers gone wrong . . . he took no delight in his sensuality." Jeritza's Carmen he described as "a human panther."

Rethberg scored in *Butterfly*, singing opposite a new tenor, Gennaro Barra, who made a mixed impression in his U.S. debut. Pinza sang the first Archibaldo of his San Francisco career in *L'Amore dei Tre Re*, a role he was to repeat on Van Ness Avenue nineteen years later. Merola and Cimini did most of the conducting, but *L'Amore* and *Carmen* were taken over by Wilfred Pelletier, the young Metropolitan staffer. Throughout the season critics had cause to lament that choral action was not as spontaneous as it might be if there were more rehearsal time, and now and again there were complaints of a "bewildering diversity" of costume styles. But the day would come . . .

1929

The pre-Crash season was an unusually happy one: almost half the operas were comedies. *Barber of Seville*, *L'Elisir d'Amore*, *Don Pasquale*, *Gianni Schicchi*, *Martha* and *Hansel and Gretel* joined hands in a chain of merriment. Cutting through, of course, were a few bloodspillers and thunder-sounders, but never again was there to be such a large proportion of works whose leading characters live happily ever after. Tito Schipa, Giuseppe De Luca, Pompilio Malatesta and Nina Morgana were on hand to lend voice and charm to the comic proceedings—although the buffo Malatesta was chided by Mason for "gagging" an English phrase into the middle of the Italian in *Barber*. Rethberg, whose duties were all in the non-comic part of the list, sang Aida, Marguerite, Mimi and the *Trovatore* Leonora—a wide range.

The experienced bass Léon Rothier returned for the first

time since the Stanford season and was exceedingly "available" during a year missed by a company regular named Ezio Pinza. Rothier's assignments were Sparafucile, Ferrano, Basilio, Colline, Ramfis, Mephistopheles and Count Des Grieux—all within a nineteen-day period! Meanwhile, back East, Pinza was preparing for, among other things, the Met's overdue revival of *Don Giovanni*.

Opening night at Dreamland brought the super-tenor Giacomo Lauri-Volpi on stage and a traffic jam of customers, and gawkers, outside. The opera was *Rigoletto* and Lauri-Volpi's "La donna è mobile" stopped the show. The ovation remains one of the longest in company history and there was considerable expectation of an encore. But Merola, in the pit, played it straight. After a few minutes Lauri-Volpi, to whom a fiery petulance was not entirely foreign, turned his back on the audience and the performance continued, amidst a few boos of disappointment from the gallery.[1]

Some of the buffs were wondering just why this particular member of the Big Four of Italian tenors (Gigli, Martinelli and Schipa were the others) had been so long in coming to San Francisco. After all, he was about to go into his eighth season at the Metropolitan. As one member of the press reported it, De Luca innocently quoted Merola telling a patron that Lauri-Volpi was very expensive!

Opposite Lauri-Volpi as Gilda that Opening Night was Merola's old favorite Queena Mario, a pure lyric soprano whom some connoisseurs consider to have gone through her career with rather less than the acclaim she deserved. The well-worshipped tenor was back on stage four nights later, this time in *Trovatore* with Rethberg. This was one of those tremendously "with it" performances that come along now and again, and Mason was overjoyed at Lauri-Volpi's Manrico, its gamut ranging from "a clarion call to the dulcet utterances of love." Giuseppe Danise was a Di Luna "a little more human" than the average, and this was all to the good. Rethberg was in fine form and so was the Azucena, Kathryn Meisle. Even the chorus seemed to be moving better.

The season continued with Lauri-Volpi and Schipa alternating in each's particular repertoire, Gennaro Barra spelling them a bit, and Mason persisted in making copy out of a "war of the tenors" which had more of journalistic myth than reality about it. He was, in any event, probably kidding. The day he wrote about Schipa in *Barber* on page 11 of *The Examiner* there was another music story on page 19, this one about a local violin prodigy named Ruggiero Ricci. The headline asked: "Is San Francisco To Have Two Yehudi Menuhins?" Then there was a *Bohème* review which poured cold water on the Musetta of local Anna Young, whose "flauntings and diablerie" he compared to "those of a virtuous society lady who wants to appear bad for the amusement of her guests."

Merola and Cimini were again the conductors of the majority of performances, their interpretations not coming under heavy analysis. Lending aid on the podium were Met staffers Pelletier and Karl Riedel, and Antonio Dell'Orefice, Merola's chorus master. Merola's decision to employ a group of selected singers from San Francisco *and* Los Angeles as the chorus for performances in both cities met with strong favor.

Notes

[1]In the program for *L'Elisir d'Amore*—with Schipa!—two nights later there was a notice that there would be no encores.

CHAPTER 5

Jeritza, Gigli and Friends

1930

San Francisco gave an American premiere in the 1930 season. It was Ravel's wispy five year old, *L'Enfant et les Sortilèges*. Also on the boards was Puccini's *Girl of the Golden West* which had been revived at the Met the previous season. *Salome*, *Tannhäuser* and *Mignon* were other newcomers to the repertoire. Introduced to American audiences were Clara Clairbert, an elegant young Belgian coloratura with a dramatic edge to her ebullient, silvery vocalism, and Gaetono Viviani, an attractive-voiced, American-born and Italian-educated baritone.[1] Hope Hampton, a movie star ill-advised to try heavy opera, was also new to the company, and Sydney Rayner, a dark-toned, New Orleans tenor whose career took him to the Paris, Metropolitan and American San Carlo companies, joined the roster. Most of all, though, it was a Jeritza year, and a Gigli year.

Manon opened the season September 11 in Civic Auditorium. Merola conducted a performance which boasted the rare presence of the illustrious Gigli, and Mason wrote of his Des Grieux: "In place of the gently supersensitive young student of Schipa we were presented with a young Roman, robust, virile, almost severe in moments of deep emotion." Queena Mario was the Manon, and, said the *Examiner* critic,"(her) intensity and abandon in the scene in St. Sulpice outran expectations." The French diction, Fried reported in *The Chronicle*, would have raised many an eyebrow in Paris. But he added up some solid pluses for the evening, noting that "an excellent new seating arrangement, the lately provided canopy and an efficient stage all served to balm age-old wounds of disappointment at the lingering non-existence of the War Memorial Opera House." That canopy, alas, was fought over.

The "authentic pulsation of opera—a little lacking on the Opening Night" was very much in evidence, Mason reported, when the season's second evening brought the inflammable combination of Jeritza and Salome—for the first time in America. It was a performance which conductor-producer Merola "made organic and thrilling despite utterly inadequate preparation." Jeritza, Mason said, carried the last scene "to the white heat of horror," although perhaps some of the horror was subtracted with the covering of Jochanaan's head with an opaque veil, a concession to the Puritan ethic which even permissive San Francisco could not entirely extinguish.

Jeritza's first appearance, Mason wrote, was "rather a shock. Instead of being a lithe and orchidaceous Oriental she was a buxom Viennese . . . it jarred at first, especially in the colloquy with Jochanaan, which was one of sometimes crude physical reactions rather than the subtle witchery and weaving of moonlit spells to which we have grown accustomed through the art of Mary Garden. Perhaps Jeritza opened prosaically in order to develop a poetry of her own, a poetry of glorified and transcendent fleshliness."

That state of affairs arrived for Mason in a Dance of the Seven Veils which was "beautiful with sinister hints" and also "left too little to be imagined." The sheer authority of this Salome was such that Herod seemed "a poor human worm in the grip of a tigress." But "leaning over the cistern, waiting for the fall of the head, her art had not the silent fatalism of Garden's." Meanwhile there was praise for Rayner's Herod and John Charles Thomas' Jochanaan, but it was Jeritza's evening.

She repeated her Salome in Chicago in 1934—this was also the year *Salome* returned to the Metropolitan for the first time since the famous first performance in that house in 1907. By then Jeritza had left the Met and it was Gota Ljungberg who took the role on 39th Street. Jeritza's 1930 Salome in Los Angeles was conducted by L.A. Philharmonic musical director Artur Rodzinski.

A large crowd turned out for *Girl of the Golden West* September 15. "Minnie certainly, certainly never wore so expensive a 'nightie' as (Jeritza) donned," Mason proclaimed. "But when she forgot that she was supposed to be a Californian and only remembered that she was a woman loving, and fighting for her love, then she really impressed the audience." The Card Scene with Jack Rance (Viviani) was admirable except for "a crude bit of histrionics when the artist gyrated like a teetotum and fell spectacularly to the ground."[2]

An unintentionally funny bit of action occurred when the active prima donna knocked off Viviani's wig and he slapped it on again—backwards. The young attractive-toned Frederick Jagel was Dick Johnson, and he survived the evening to sing the role in San Francisco thirteen years later.

An even larger crowd visited Civic Auditorium for a September 17 *Bohème* in which Audrey Farncroft, a young local singer, sang creditably as Musetta among her famous colleagues Gigli and Mario. The artistic pièce de résistance of the season came two nights later with the Ravel premiere. The whimsical little opera was cleverly staged by Agnini with scenery by local artist Lucien Labaudt. The furnishings in the indoor scene—its walls were patterned with red apples and wide blue stripes—were exaggerated in size in an attempt to make Mario, as the *enfant*, look appropriately diminutive.

The Ladies' Committee on Props was commissioned by prop man "Happy" Adams to get a live lamb for *L'Enfant* but returned with a full-grown, matronly, sad-eyed sheep, which was, as a matter of fact, pregnant. This, alas, was not the only unsuccessful mission of the Committee: its attempt to get a big copper still, just the thing for the alchemist setting in *Faust*, came to naught when some Prohibitionistic spoilsport declared it was against the law to transport such an apparatus.

John Charles Thomas triumphed as Tonio on the 20th, an evening which saw the healthy and obliging Jeritza sing both Nedda and Santuzza. There was some disagreement as to just how good Madame Clairbert was as Philine in *Mignon* on the 22nd—the Civic Auditorium seemed to overwhelm her a bit—but Hope Hampton was judged simply not ready for such a pretentious part as Marguerite in *Faust*, which she was given on the 25th. (Even if her elderly, influential businessman husband thought otherwise!) Veteran observers remember that her entrance caught her literally voiceless.[3] Gigli sang in *Mignon* under the hardship of having just been informed of his mother's death in Italy. A performance of *Tannhäuser* on the 23rd included one of the most southerly-oriented Wagnerian casts ever assembled: the four knights were sung by Messrs. Paltrinieri, Sandrini, Oliviero and D'Angelo, and Pinza was the Landgrave.

On the 27th there was an afternoon *Salome* and an evening *Lucia* to close the season. Mason wrote in a curtain-lowering piece that, in spite of the Depression, fears of a deficit "have evaporated." The general public, he reported, attended the opera in larger numbers than ever. The title role in *Lucia* was taken by Clairbert. Her autumn schedule also included an engagement with the Philadelphia Opera and she sang at the Chicago Opera in 1931–32 but she never appeared at the Met. Some time later she managed a restaurant near the Monnaie, the opera house in Brussels, where she died in 1970. In San Francisco she also sang Violetta, ending "Sempre Libera" with a high E flat not in the score, but she was more than a simple songbird.

Cimini was absent in 1930 and Riedel, Pelletier and Dell'Orefice as Merola's podium partners were hardly the last word in conductorial elegance. He was slow to engage expensive conductors of great brilliance and obviously many top maestri were not interested in traveling such a long way to serve a company whose rehearsal schedule was skimpy—although top tenors were perfectly happy with this situation!

1931

Henri Rabaud's *Mârouf*, an ornate 1914 score campy by today's standards, was the opener for the 1931 season. That confection out of the way, Merola proceeded to more solid viands: *Tannhäuser, Lohengrin* and *Meistersinger*. *Mârouf* starred Yvonne Gall, the experienced Parisian soprano, and Mario Chamlee, the honey-toned Los Angeleno who went on to the Opéra Comique, Vienna's Volksoper and Prague's German Opera, and who had Metropolitan associations. Inspired by the Arabian Nights, Rabaud's opera tells of a poor cobbler cursed with a shrewish wife who passes himself off to a sultan as a rich merchant and wins the sultan's daughter's hand. Mason wrote of the "languor and sweetness and melancholy of it all." Also the poor donkey who "guffawed enthusiastically" at the dress rehearsal and had to be muzzled during the performance.

Merola's Wagnerian frontal attack was mounted predominantly with singers whose reputations were made north of the Alps. They were among the best available, and he was going to get plenty of mileage out of them. Wagner was in the San Francisco air, thanks in no small part to a couple of visits (in 1930 and 1931) by the German Grand Opera Company, a touring aggregation of Hurokian proportions which included such oldtime Wagnerians as Johanna Gadski (she died in 1932), Johannes Sembach and Carl Braun. Merola's choices were the mellow baritone Friedrich Schorr, the appealing soprano Maria Müller, the interesting heldentenor Gotthelf Pistor (he in his American debut), plus buffo tenor Marek Windheim and character baritone Arnold Gabor.

There was also the established San Francisco favorite Elisabeth Rethberg. Conductor of the Wagner performances was one Hans Blechschmidt, a well-schooled maestro who had appeared in Civic Auditorium the previous January conducting *The Flying Dutchman* for the German Grand Opera.

Müller managed the stylistic changes and summoned the vocal endurance to sing Mimi and Butterfly besides Elsa and Eva. Writing about her in *Lohengrin*, Mason pointed out an inward drama which, mixed with her lovely voice, called for the highest superlatives. Fried said of her Butterfly: "The deeply expressive quality of her song, and the conviction and logic of her acting, thrust from importance the question of whether a tall German soprano of heroic voice should impersonate a fragile, sad daughter of Japan." Pistor's voice was not the most consistently beautiful imaginable, nor was his production always effortless, but he was capable of producing a dark, suave tone, he was impressive-looking, and further, he was a man of no mean interpretative gifts. He had, as a matter of fact, begun as an actor and was "discovered" when he had to sing a song in a play. Mason said of Pistor in the title role of *Tannhäuser*: "(He) is essentially dramatic. In gesture,

48

in movement, in facial expression he suggested the mind processes of Tannhäuser."

Mason went on to note that Pistor sang to "the Venus of his imagination" because Maxine Castleton, the Los Angeles soprano who took that part, was "manifestly thinking more of tone production than what she way saying." Blechschmidt, he wrote, "brought virtues out of the brass which many people did not know were there."

The exuberant trio of Rethberg, Martinelli and that seductive-toned high baritone Giuseppe Danise carried the leads in *Aida, Chenier, Ballo* and *Traovatore.* There was a Gallic Tosca in Gall, a relatively dainty one who, one critic said, killed Scarpia "from impulse rather than with heroic desperation." Her soft tones were particularly lovely, her louder ones sometimes forced. Also new to the company was Faina Petrova, a portly Metropolitan mezzo from Moscow who made a big, if questionable, impression in *Carmen.* According to Mason "it was a *Bolshevik* Carmen that Faina Petrova gave us, a Carmen with the god of love left out, and, in his place, a divinity that was almost wholly animal. The audience marveled; they gasped; sometimes they laughed. Anything more different from the Carmen of their tradition they had never seen."

The veteran bass Andrès de Segurola, newly resident in filmland, was another addition—as Sharpless and Marcello —but not such a happy one since he was well past his prime.

Once launched, the San Francisco Opera had pursued a pleasant financial course, operating virtually without deficit. The Depression and diminished partronage now caught up with the company, however, and there was a spot of red ink adding up to approximately $18,000 in 1931. The Founders' Fund could take care of that, of course. At the same time Mason noted that repeats of *Lohengrin* and *Meister-singer,* had they been available, would have helped reduce the deficit. And, looking beyond the particular financial problem, he cited the obvious artistic advantages of repeat performances.

The visits of the German Grand Opera, in early 1930 and 1931, have already been mentioned. The winter of 1931 also saw a short visit of the Chicago Opera to Civic Auditorium. *Der Rosenkavalier* was given for the first time in

San Francisco, at a Saturday matinee, with Frida Leider as the Marschallin, Maria Olczewska as Octavian, Alexander Kipnis as Ochs, and Thelma Votipka, later known at the Met and in San Francisco for comprimario parts, as Sophie. Frank St. Leger conducted. The season was also interesting— in retrospect—for the presence, in small roles, of one Jenny Tourel. Other conductors were Roberto Moranzoni and Emil Cooper.

At this point the previous history of the Chicago's sporadic Bay Region activity following the 1922 "fiasco" might be recapitulated. The bulging troupe came to the Casino Theater at Ellis and Mason for four performances March 6–8, 1924. On this ground, now a parking lot across from the Hilton Hotel, there was *Boris Godounoff* with Chaliapin as Boris and Kipnis as Varlaam! Mary Garden did *her* thing in Massenet's *Cleopâtre*. When the characterful company appeared in Oakland Auditorium Theater across the Bay in 1928—there were four March performances—the diva-directa sang in Alfano's *Resurrection*. Rimsky-Korsakoff's *Snow Maiden* was also offered, and *Aida* and *Gioconda*. There were four more dates in March 1929: *Lohengrin*, *Thais*, *Faust* and *Norma*. Miss Garden had the title role in *Thais*, who else? The *Norma* went off with Rosa Raisa, but if she had been indisposed another Norma was not far away, because, on the night previous, Rosa Ponselle had made one of her fairly regular West Coast appearances in a Dreamland Auditorium recital, singing "Casta Diva" and other numbers to a rapturous audience. Ponselle never sang with the San Francisco Opera. Possibly because she tended to feel insecure away from the Met.

Notes

[1] Some record collectors may have noticed Viviani's presence as Barnaba on a "78" Italian Columbia recording of *Gioconda* with a young Ebe Stignani as Laura.

[2] Jeritza tended to be fall-happy, and, as Mason wrote re her Santuzza: "Who but she would have thought of having herself flung down the church steps at the end of the first act of *Cavalleria Rusticana*?" Tenor Frederick Jagel, who became a San Francisco resident in 1970, has told the author that Jeritza used to whisper to Turiddu: "Give me a big push!"

[3] Strong pressure seems to have been brought to bear to produce favorable reviews. In the case of at least one leading newspaper, the chief music critic bowed out while an assistant wrote a purple puff piece.

50

CHAPTER 6

A Dream Long Denied

1932

The great day came at last, on October 15, 1932—the first performance by the company in a home worthy of its best efforts: the War Memorial Opera House. The opera was *Tosca*, the cast headed by Muzio, Dino Borgioli and Alfredo Gandolfi. The first act was broadcast nationally over NBC's Red Network. The choice of opera reflected Merola's love of Puccini, his admiration of Muzio's art, the demand for a sure-fire hit, and then there was, of course, the joke about Angelotti's opening line, "Ah, finalmente."

Those who tuned in the broadcast on KPO heard an announcer—unlettered by today's standards—read a ten minute prepared script in which many of the hall's measurements and details of its decor were given. The night's musical fare, the man read in a sentence which dotted every i, would be "*Tosca*, an Italian opera in three acts by Giacomo Puccini, brilliant Italian composer of opera." And the evening, he said with complete accuracy, marked fulfillment of "a dream long denied."

Warm applause greeted Merola coming into the pit, and, before the announcer had quite finished his introduction, "The Star Spangled Banner" was struck up. It was a deliberate and highly moving performance of the anthem which carried through the house, the audience joining in fairly lustily. A short pause, and then the opera began.

Merola had a way with Puccini, and he was at the top of his form that night. The music was given a characteristically pliable, unrushed treatment, the rallentandos receiving all their due. Muzio brought to Tosca the combination of her warm, limpid voice and her strong, honest dramatic conviction. This was a Tosca who could be thoroughly imperious, but few have surpassed, or equalled, Muzio in the gentleness she brought to the part. The pianissimo effects were memorably finespun, witness the first act line: "Oh, innanzi la Madonna." Equally worthy of note was her magical handling of those three calls—"Mario, Mario, *Mario*", at her first entrance, the third given a particular emphasis which is entirely logical (and so marked in the score) but, for some reason, very rarely heard.

Borgioli (who reached the Met in 1934) was a dulcet-toned Cavardossi, and Gandolfi, if rather tight vocally, was at least a persuasively sinister Scarpia, cadaverous in look and dark in voice.[1] A versatile cross between leading man and comprimario, Gandolfi was making his first appearance with the San Francisco Opera since the first season in Civic Auditorium. He was in the opener that year, too, as Marcello in *La Bohème*.

Among those tuning in the broadcast were some of the thousands unable to obtain tickets. Some whose checks were returned were rather miffed to find seats available from brokers at premium prices. But that is a classic situation under such circumstances. Actually, a ticket problem applied to the whole season, offering as it did the usual dozen performances in a hall approximately 2000 seats smaller than the previous home. A rash of single ticket applications caused difficulties as 80% of the seats to the Regular Series were taken by subscribers.

The Opera House's first Opening Night—on an unusually warm night—brought out an audience fully cognizant of the festivity of the occasion. The *Examiner* writer who reported "an undercurrent of excitement that San Francisco society did not try to hide" wrote with fair accuracy, not just colorful wishful thinking. "Eyes sparkled," she said, "like the jewels the ladies in the audience wore." The elite were there, amidst numerous more anonymous. The boxholders included the George Camerons, William H. Crocker, the Sidney Ehrmans, the Mortimer Fleishhacker Srs, the A. P. Gianninis, the J. D. Grants, Mrs. I. W. Hellman Jr., two generations of Millers, C. O. G. and Robert Watt and their wives, Judge and Mrs. M. C. Sloss, Mrs. Sigmund Stern, two generations of Zellerbachs, I. and J. D. and wives. Conductor Alfred Hertz was in the audience, University of California president Sproul, and the Italian consul Signor Manzoni.

If the Depression was on, much of it was wafted away in the sea of "sable wraps, summer ermine, Manchurian ermine, and mink in simple but perfect lines of three-quarter length . . . there were any number of new ermine capes, some brief and flaring stiffly from the shoulders, others hip length and worn wrapped tightly about the figure."

After the broadcast, during the first intermission, there was a speech by Wallace M. Alexander, the new president of the Association—Bentley had just died without having the pleasure of seeing the company into its new home. "Italy has her Toscanini, New York her Gatti-Casazza, San Francisco her Gaetano Merola," said Alexander. He cited a mixture of "grasp of vocation, resourcefulness and indomitable perseverance" as the qualities which had enabled Merola to bring exciting opera to San Francisco for nine successive years. Armando Agnini, his "tireless co-worker," was also saluted. And then he concluded: "Ladies and gentlemen, this is *your* Opera House, your own rich heritage."

What was the new home like? Wider in its auditorium space than the typical large European opera house, but far from barn-like or inelegant. While some observers thought Chicago's recently-completed Civic Opera House suggested a movie palazzo, San Francisco's "dream" had more of an aristocratic feel, without being over-embellished. Few houses anywhere could boast a foyer as spacious, attractive and friendly as the great main floor oblong.

Browsers in souvenir booklets read that the building is 180 feet by 282 on the ground,[2] its external appearance similar to that of the neighboring Veterans Building except that the Opera House's stage block rises 150 feet above ground level, or higher than a twelve-story building. The exteriors of the two buildings, readers found, are in rusticated terra cotta, with granite bases and steps and free-standing columns of granite on the front facades.

The architecture of the Opera House and its near-twin is classic, harmonizing with that of other buildings in the light-colored Civic Center complex, notably the City Hall directly across Van Ness Avenue. It is not unreminiscent of Palladio's

Basilica in Vicenza. The main foyer has a marble floor, walls of cast stone, and a vaulted and coffered ceiling thirty-eight feet high. The auditorium itself is not completely traditional. There is a single golden horseshoe of boxes—twenty-five in all, each with a separate ante-room—but there are no other semicircular tiers.[3] Two wide, deep balconies cut across the hall, the lower one divided into Grand Tier and Dress Circle by a cross aisle, the upper similarly divided into Balcony Circle and Balcony. Total seating capacity is 3252. Had acoustics experts not discouraged it, the figure might have been closer to 4000.

The proscenium arch is fifty-two feet wide and fifty-one feet high in the center. Relief figures in the spandrels—two horses ridden by trim Amazons—are by sculptor Edgar Walter. The principal feature of the ceiling is the great star-like chandelier (twenty-seven feet in diameter), the color of which can be changed, to quote the 1932 program, "to suit the lighting of the stage or the mood of the music being played." Well, Hollywood wasn't far away.

The arches on the side walls above the boxes are faced with plaster grillwork concealing organ lofts. There is no organ and the lofts are almost never used, but Seiji Ozawa, the San Francisco Symphony's live-minded musical director, did place trumpeters therein to create dazzling stereophonic brass effects during 1969 performances of Respighi's *Pines of Rome*. There is a projection room behind the Dress Circle, and a loggia at the front of the building at the Grand Tier level which might conceivably be utilized on warm evenings. But large doors onto it were never provided, doubtless because the builders knew San Francisco's moderate but coolish climate only too well.

The stage itself is eighty-three feet deep and 131 feet wide, with 116 feet of usable height between stage level and overhead grid, this being a relatively generous amount. The four fly galleries at each side of the stage are helpful, too. But not the cumbersome arrangement which permits the stage floor to be set up with twenty-nine sections thereof at different heights. Portable levels have proven much more flexible.

The orchestra pit as customarily used seats about sixty-five in relative comfort, or seventy-five if sardine-packed, this with some percussion stuck away under the stage to the right of the prompter's box. The pit was constructed with an outer extension making possible the seating of a full symphony orchestra of 100 players. Alas, two rows of seats have to be taken out to make way for the extension, and the opera management has not seen fit, understandably enough, to forsake such revenue. How much better it would have been if the pit had been built with one total in mind—eighty five or ninety players, say—instead of two, one of them essentially inoperable. The normal complement of the San Francisco Opera Orchestra has been, in addition to the required winds, brass and percussion, twelve first violins, nine seconds, six or seven violas, six or seven cellos, five basses, with four or five added strings in some of the heavy German repertoire.

Meanwhile, an account of the Opera House is incomplete without mention of the fact that the old Mission Bay Creek from Hayes Valley runs underneath the War Memorial. There is continual sub-basement seepage, and a special drain gutter running along the underground passageway between the Opera House and the Veterans Building has been set up to deal with this persistent and not unhumorous liquid malady.

After Opening Night the 1932 season continued highly successfully at a $5 top, the Standing Room Only sign hung out for all performances but *Hansel and Gretel* and the second *Meistersinger*. The matinee of *Lucia* with Lily Pons was not only heard by an audience in the Opera House but another in City Hall Plaza which listened, thanks to the Art Commission, from a sound system al fresco. With Muzio, Pons, Schorr, Pinza and Bonelli kept busy, there were plenty of vocal delights as the season made its way. A visual low point was reached, however, with the mise-en-scène of *Lohengrin:* it was disturbed by such mishaps as a trumpeter taking a spill, a swan refusing to disappear, footlights going out, and four none-too-husky choristers almost toppling Maria Müller to the stage when they hoisted Elsa on the King's Shield. Not to mention the distraction of enormous peepholes in the nuptial chamber.

This particular evening reaffirmed the uncomfortable old truth that misadventures on stage usually happen cumulatively. Suffice to say that things never went quite so badly again.[4] In general, though, there was room for improvement of the visual element, especially since the company was in such an elegant new home. One thing Merola did was to ask for a permanent ballet school which could keep the company supplied with good dancers. Adolph Bolm of Diaghileff fame was secured as ballet chief and thus was launched the troupe which came to be known as the San Francisco Ballet. Officially established late in 1932, the company got into step the following year.

Francesco Merli, the vibrant-sounding tenore robusto known to many of today's record collectors from the pre-War Cetra/Parlophone *Turandot*, made a single appearance with the San Francisco Opera during the first Opera House season. *Lucia* found him out of voice as Edgardo, soft tones being a particular problem, and Merola reluctantly made substitutions in later performances for which Merli had been contracted. Tandy MacKenzie, a Scotch-Hawaiian tenor later associated with Fortune Gallo's San Carlo, was the replacement in *Trovatore*, gaining mixed reviews. Chamlee took over Turiddu, Borgioli the second Edgardo.

1933

Louis Gruenberg's somber and harrowing *Emperor Jones* was rather too much for some of the subscribers when it was unfolded November 17, ten months following its premiere at the Metropolitan. There were even some boos. But Lawrence Tibbett scored a personal hit in his tour de force role, and the second performance was better received than the first. The season brought two others works in English: Wolf-Ferrari's pleasant *The Secret of Suzanne*, which served as curtain-raiser for the Gruenberg, and Rimsky-Korsakoff's *Coq D'Or*, given as pantomime-cum-vocal accompaniment in a new and expensive production with a light scenic touch.

Fried provided a succinct estimate of *Emperor Jones*— "Eugene O'Neill's text is effectively curt, but at the same time it is prosaic and shallow . . . The success of Louis Gruenberg's modernistic music is that, added to the distant tireless drumbeat of the original play, it works well together with O'Neill's devices of theatrical tension. To build an opera for the ages, however, a composer has to conceive some musical eloquence of his own. Gruenberg's score is not eloquent. His use of voices in declamation heightens the vividness of speech a little, but it never glorifies diction into really thrilling utterance. His orchestra, for the most part, is energetically and cleverly busy with tight-lipped dissonant tricks of accompaniment. Only when Jones falls to his knees to sing the spiritual, 'It's Me, O Lawd,' does the music cast over the listeners' spirit a spell of large beauty."

How familiar much of that review sounds more than a generation later. Even the most promising composers are criticized, and often justly so, for failing to bring musical substance to a drama's high points. *Emperor Jones* seems to be forgotten, and nobody laments its passing, but Merola was right to try something new and provocative. When Richard Montgomery Tobin, president of the Musical Association of San Francisco, sponsor of the San Francisco Symphony, let out an irate broadside against the opera in *The Call-Bulletin*, Tibbett took time out from a *Pagliacci* rehearsal to remind Mr. Tobin, in another *Call-Bulletin* article, that "one can't live on sweets."

The 1933 season opened with the healthy-toned Cyrena Van Gordon in *Samson and Delilah*. Audiences listened not without appreciation to this and the *Coq D'Or* which came next on the subscription, but it was with the third bill, *Aida* with Muzio and Martinelli, that the customers found cause, understandably, for maximum excitement. There was lots of excitement over a subsequent *Bohème*, too—one which featured Lucrezia Bori, who was new to the company. While 3000-odd saw and heard her at the Opera House another several thousand listened to the performance as relayed to the Civic Auditorium. This was another public service of the Art Commission. Following the performance Bori was whisked from garret to auditorium, there to be presented with a bouquet by Mayor Angelo Rossi.

The precedent for the balletic *Coq D'Or* would be Fokine's version prepared for London and Paris in 1914 after the idea was voiced by Diaghileff's scenic collaborator Alexandre Benois. When Pierre Monteux conducted the Metropolitan premiere of this version in 1918 the part of the King was danced by Adolph Bolm. And so it was in San Francisco in 1933, Bolm, of course, being the director of the local ballet. He was credited with the choreography for this presentation, one which found the singers sitting in narrow double-decked grandstands at each side of the stage. The sets and costumes—delightful ones—were by Nicholas Remisoff of *Chauve-Souris* fame.

Anyone looking very closely might have noticed that tucked in there amidst the grandstand choristers one night was Merola himself, fully costumed and singing away in his strong basso. Conductor Pelletier had kicked up such a fuss at rehearsal that Merola figured he better get in there to help keep the tribe "right on."

Issay Dobrowen, the San Francisco Symphony's conductor, was engaged for *Tristan*, but he was indisposed, and Alfred Hertz, the orchestra's conductor emeritus, filled in. Paul Althouse was the Tristan, and his virile tenor, not unlike Jon Vickers' in timbre, was highly praised. Four months later he became the first American to sing the role at the Met. Gertrude Kappel's Isolde brought the advantage of an experienced artist's keen dramatic projection.

Another addition to the repertoire was Verdi's *La Forza del Destino*, destined, dare one use the word, to become one of the staple items on Merola's annual bill of fare. Its coming-in coincided, alas, with Claudia Muzio's going-out: December 1, 1933 marked her last appearance with the San Francisco Opera. Exactly a month later she returned to the Metropolitan from which she had been absent for nearly a dozen years, her affiliation having been switched to Chicago. She died in 1936, aged only 47, in the wake of much ill-health. Shortage of breath had been a persistent distraction, turned artfully to artistic advantage.

The relatively limited capacity of the Opera House, the expense of adapting old productions to the new theater, the cost of elaborate new productions of *Coq D'Or* and *Tristan*: these factors contributed to the whopping $36,000 deficit which the company recorded in its books for 1933. Actually, the ten performances of the Regular Series had been sold out, and the five repeats enjoyed a healthy sale, but a number of the most expensive seats for the repeats were not sold. Possibly the emphasis on Sunday matinees, plus a Thanksgiving matinee, proved a strategic error. At all events, $6000 of the losses were recouped at a post-season concert for which artists volunteered their services.

Meanwhile, a highly interesting resume of the season appeared, not in the daily press but in *The Argonaut*, a now-defunct San Francisco magazine which showed strong signs of life in the music criticism of one Covington Enderly. He suggested, in a magnificent wave of non-Establishment thinking, that the San Francisco Opera 1) hire fewer stars, 2) employ local conductors who were just as good as Metropolitan "hacks," 3) utilize economical modern scenic designs instead of expensive realistic sets, and 4) have more rehearsals, "toward which the visiting stars might contribute by arriving in town earlier."

Furthermore, he said with heroic optimism, "in the field of American opera it is time the San Francisco Opera created the precedent of including at least one premiere of a new American work each season."

For all the merits of Enderly's thinking it wasn't as simple as that to effect a revolution. His first point smacks of reverse snobbism because who would want to send Muzio, Bori, Kappel, Tibbett, Martinelli or Borgioli home without their having sung a note? On the matter of conductors—all right, one might do better than Pelletier and Dell'Orefice if the same effort put in on hiring Muzios and Boris were made. And it might well have been. But did San Francisco boast its own "paragons" of the podium, other, that is, than the resident Messrs. Merola and Hertz who did appear with the company.

Perhaps a very modern-minded general director would have initiated a consistent program of modern sets, economical or otherwise, but in 1933 there were still many opera managements that were conservative—not so much by design as habit. And a greater length of season was needed to facilitate Enderly's program. The fact that, in those days, the artists spent at least four nights on a train coming from New York, or three from Chicago, did not help.

As for those American opera premieres, idealistic Mr. Enderly wrote about one generation too soon. In 1959, the Ford Foundation announced a program whereby the San Francisco Opera, along with the Metropolitan, the New York City Opera, and the Chicago Lyric, was given financial aid to produce new American operas. Alas, this didn't produce what its sponsors had hoped, though it set up a situation whereby an Enderly program could be facilitated. It is probably safe to say that no supremely worthy American opera remained still-born because Merola wasn't looking hard enough in that direction.

Another intriguing point about Enderly's suggestions is that they are exactly the same ones that in 1960 were logically directed at the Cosmopolitan Opera, the rival troupe which performed in San Francisco for several years. In the mid-30's one didn't really expect modern sets in this country (although the crusading work of the Philadelphia Orchestra opera productions should be noted), but by 1960 the new visual aesthetic in opera staging had become a widespread living force. Certainly under Kurt Herbert Adler, Merola's successor, the "Enderlyzation" of the San Francisco Opera became virtually as complete as practicable. Stars and non-stars and stars-to-be were mixed together, the conducting level has been consistently high (without podium "superstars," however—they are rare and they tend to be mannered), staging has been definitely up-to-the-minute, and full casts have been arriving in town two and three and four weeks ahead. And there have been contemporary operas, and even an occasional premiere.

But one can hear newly-charged "Enderlys" of today loud and clear, wherever they may be mounting soapboxes. Obviously they would criticize the company for not producing new works as readily as the heavily state-supported Hamburg State Opera—or the Santa Fe Opera, which has few star fees to pay—and would wonder why Messrs. Bernstein, Karajan and Solti are not in the pit every week. Ah dreams!

1934

The 1934 season opened with a jolly *Bartered Bride*, continued with an estimable *Tosca*, let down briefly with a questionable *Carmen*, and caught its stride again with an exquisite *Manon*. And on through a total of fifteen performances a particularly high average was maintained.

The *Bride*, sung in German as an accommodation to Rethberg, was especially notable for the way Adolph Bolm integrated the dances with the stage movement. The Tosca was Lotte Lehmann, and an unusually interesting one. Redfern Mason wrote: "Her Tosca had not the sculptured beauty of a Muzio; she did not wallow as Jeritza had when she sang

'Vissi d'arte.' What she did was to give us a Tosca evolved out of her inner consciousness, and in that scene with Scarpia, she touched a note of beautiful humility which neither Bernhardt nor Muzio can give us." And from Fried: "She is a personality. Her voice, opulent and beautiful, but not necessarily restricted to the charm of honeyed tone, bespeaks a penetrating expressive intelligence. She constructs the role as it should be constructed with human conviction and with a controlled and flexible sense of its form."[5]

The *Carmen* suffered, the majority felt, from veteran Ninon Vallin's cool, intimate, straight-laced cigarette girl. She was not interested in being tough or vulgar. The celebrated French soprano—who, by the way, never sang at the Met or the Chicago Opera—also turned in a well-received Marguerite. It should be noted that she had Micaela besides Carmen in her repertoire, and very likely she was more a Micaela type, though not so starchy as to refuse a Paris music hall engagement. Richard Crooks made his company debut in *Manon* opposite Bori, his lyric voice, elegant phrasing and handsome appearance winning him warm applause. He was not, however, an imaginative actor.[6]

Lehmann continued her activities in the Italian repertoire with a Butterfly assigned more because of her presence in San Francisco than for her utter aptness for the role. Marjory Fisher in *The News* called it "more Italian than Japanese." The acting, she said, "verged on the melodramatic in tragic moments, but she was amazingly youthful and girlishly animated in the first act, and in the second, the matured woman who has known much agony." Others felt more strongly that this was a serious case of miscasting.

Besides adding Lehmann and Crooks to his roster Merola brought out Lauritz Melchior and offered him in both *Tannhäuser* and *Otello*. Verdi's opera, for no good reason, was missing from the Metropolitan repertoire from 1913 to 1937, so San Francisco was getting something of a scoop.[7] Melchior never sang the Moor on 39th Street. Rethberg, a more regular Otello-ite, was the touching Desdemona, and a good Elisabeth in the Wagner, too. Hertz was back in the pit for a lusty *Tannhäuser* plus *Bartered Bride*. In the second *Tannhäuser* Bonelli was succeeded as Wolfram by one Nelson Eddy, up from Hollywood for the Singing Contest. Although best known for his movie operetta appearances, Eddy's "serious" career was not without some distinction. Surprisingly enough, he had even sung the Drum Major in *Wozzeck*— hardly a *Chocolate Soldier* type—with the Philadelphia Opera.

Puccini's fluffy *La Rondine* was brought into the repertoire for Bori and had a minor success. This "afternoon off of a genius," as W. J. Henderson of *The New York Sun* once called it, waited many years before it returned to San Francisco, and, in truth, it has never found a firm place elsewhere. Bori was also welcomed in the title role of *Mignon*, a specialty of hers although a mezzo part. Transpositions were the rule of the evening.

Emily Hardy, a relatively inexperienced local lyric-coloratura, had a good starring opportunity in Delibes' candy-coated *Lakmé* which began a long association with the company in 1934. But the most serious opera lover might well have asked "Why *Lakmé*?" when the company had not even touched Mozart. What *had* the San Francisco Opera achieved in terms of repertoire in its first dozen years of operation? Well, one could credit Merola with the American premiere of Ravel's *L'Enfant et les Sortilèges*. One could thank him for keeping San Francisco informed of the later and less often played Puccini: *Turandot*, the complete *Trittico*, *Girl of the Golden West* and even *Rondine*. He could draw praise for bringing *Emperor Jones*, a provocative work at least, shortly after its world premiere. One could admire his ambition in performing Wagner.

At the same time, one had to question his scheduling *Anima Allegra* and *Mârouf* when the Strauss of *Ariadne*, the Bartok of *Bluebeard's Castle*, the Berg of *Wozzeck* and, above all, the Mozart of *Cosi Fan Tutte*, *Don Giovanni*, *Marriage of Figaro* and *Magic Flute* went untapped. Granted that some of these would have tossed almost insuperable rehearsal problems at his office door. The shortness of the season, the remoteness of San Francisco, the fact the Met was also slow in producing Mozart—all these factors cast shadows of limitation. Suffice to say that there was courage in San Francisco's operatic air, at least intermittently.

62

Notes

[1] Met customers used, in those days, to the vintage Antonio Scotti's Scarpia, did not expect voice so much as acting ability from a Scarpia.

[2] This figure does not include the lateral projections, which result in an overall front facade 231 feet wide.

[3] A number of the War Memorial trustees—Kendrick, Kingsbury and Tobin, for instance—were opposed to the idea of having boxes because they seemed like relics of bygone ages of aristocracy.

[4] Although, in one of the San Carlo's *Lohengrins* of the mid-30's, Lohengrin's helmet fell off—and the newspaper rolled up inside rolled out—when the skiff stopped too far from the stage "port" and the tenor had to jump for it.

[5] Madame Lehmann told the author in 1968: "I don't think I was a good Tosca. Because there's a kind of fireworks about her, and my way was more coming out of the heart."

[6] A generation later the white-haired, still handsome Mr. Crooks could be regularly found in the audience of the San Francisco Symphony's Thursday afternoon concerts. He had retired to the countryside west of Stanford.

[7] In Chicago, though, it was standard fare 1920–31. There was an especially formidable procession of Iagos: Titta Ruffo, Giacomo Rimini, Joseph Schwarz, Richard Bonelli, Cesare Formichi, Vanni-Marcoux!

CHAPTER 7

The Ring Achieved

1935

By far the most newsworthy event of the 1935 season, and the most ambitious project the company had yet undertaken, was the presentation of the complete *Ring* cycle of Wagner. For this impressive series of performances, exceedingly rare in the United States outside New York, Merola gathered a list of artists prominently associated with the Wagnerian realm. It included Kirsten Flagstad (then with only one Met season behind her), Elisabeth Rethberg, Lauritz Melchior, Friedrich Schorr, Emanuel List, Kathryn Meisle, Dorothee Manski, Marek Windheim, Hans Clemens and Gustav Schützendorf. There were also the American basses Chase Baromeo and Douglas Beattie, the latter from nearby San Jose with experience in Italy. Artur Bodanzky, who had presided over the Met's German wing since 1915 (he succeeded Hertz and became a fixture), was the conductor. The orchestra was beefed up a bit, and included four Wagner tubists from New York.[1]

Sets were, of course, in traditional style: they were designed by Julian Dove, who had worked for impresarios Conreid and Hammerstein in New York. The prop list included a large segmented aluminum-and-canvas dragon capable of some rather realistic thrashing about. And, sad to report, the Rhine Maidens looked like hula girls with leis about their necks.

The four operas were given consecutively as the first four performances of the Regular Series, and *Walküre* was repeated as a non-subscription event. *Rheingold* was the somewhat uncomfortable choice for Opening Night with its single long act, and an intermission was placed following the second scene—causing perfect Wagnerites to legitimately raise eyebrows. The cycle called forth many superlatives from the critics, Flagstad for instance being hailed by *The Chronicle's*

Alfred Frankenstein as "a kind of Nordic Winged Victory."
Melchior won the expected kudos although Frankenstein
cautioned about "an occasional touch of ponderous kittenish-
ness." Flagstad sang the *Siegfried* Brünnhilde for the first
time in her career November 6. Of the orchestra's performance on this occasion the *Chronicle* man wrote that it had
"fierce energy and subtle atmosphere." Bodanzky favored
fast tempos, conducting more with authority than the deepest
humanity and emotional conviction. His Wagner was more
brittle and highstrung than the glowing product offered by
Fritz Reiner in the seasons to follow, but he was capable on
occasion of highly moving effects, such as Brünnhilde seeming to cry out from the Magic Fire of *Walküre* via that
repeated falling phrase in the winds.[2]

From the box office view the *Ring* was a smashing success.
The complete package sold out a month in advance and a
second cycle doubtless would have done well, but the compressed season had to be pursued. The production of Wagner's epic symbolized more than any other effort the coming
of age of the company. The 1930's saw the San Francisco
Opera emerge from the cozy "family affair" status of its early
years to the more fully assured, more ambitious atmosphere
of its maturity. But, lest there be any concern that early
performances lacked the ultimate refinement, veteran followers remember a spontaneity which, in the best performances, was hard to beat. Some of the casts speak for themselves.

An unfortunate footnote to the *Ring* appeared after the
cycle was concluded. Back in New York, Bodanzky gave an
interview to *The Herald Tribune* which could easily be con-
strued as patronizing to San Francisco. The tremendous turn-
out and enthusiasm for the *Ring* in the western city was at-
tributed by Bodanzky to a lack of sophistication. Those who
felt San Francisco provincially chauvinistic clucked, but
others were disturbed by the conductor's remark, probably
an innocent one but not brilliantly tactful. In any event, some
San Franciscans were relieved when negotiations directed
toward reengagement of Bodanzky for the next season fell
through. He wanted a raise in fee, more rehearsal time, and
the pit expanded. There was certainly merit in his demand
about the pit; judging the rest of the matter is difficult from

this distance. Since he was succeeded by Reiner, San Francisco Wagner buffs were hardly shortchanged. Indeed, they prospered.

The non-Wagnerian repertory in '35 did not benefit from the presence of such variously slim fare as Massenet's *Werther*, Halévy's *La Juive* and Flotow's *Martha*. One in a season might do, but not all three! If there were any anti-Wagnerians around they had only *Aida, Rigoletto, La Bohème* and *Barber of Seville* as really solid consoling stuff. There remained the strange combination of *Coq D'Or* and *Suor Angelica*.

Helen Gahagan, actress and politician, made her American opera debut as Angelica. It was rather less than a complete success. Fried, now with *The Examiner*, wrote: "Miss Gahagan gave the title role some life because she is a seasoned actress. Her voice is strong and she sings feelingly. But neither in timbre nor in development is her soprano a first rate opera instrument." On to politics.

Martinelli, Schipa, Bonelli and Pinza gave obvious strength to the non-Wagner wing. Nelson Eddy made another excursion from Hollywood, and his Amonasro, *The Chronicle* said, was "vengeful, barbaric ... sung with a suave, aristocratic voice." Fried found his performance "beautifully, nobly sung." Even if his death fall was so realistic he required the services of a physician and masseuse, Schipa wasn't enough to make *Werther* really spring alive—especially since he sang in Italian to the rest of the cast's French. The Charlotte of Coe Glade, later a mainstay of Gallo's San Carlo, revealed a "contralto of beautiful dusky quality" but not a sufficiently forceful projection thereof.

It was a year for fledgling soprani (to help balance the budget?), and Josephine Tumminia, from San Francisco's Marina District, made a successful if unremarkable appearance as Rosina in *The Barber*. Fried said "she is young, pert, gay ... her voice is a natural coloratura... what it lacks in mellowness it balances in the sparkle and skill of its agility." The Gilda of San Francisco's Emily Hardy was uneven. She was more a lyric soprano than a coloratura and her handling of the traditional acrobatics was wanting. Helen Jepson, whose career had more mileage, was Lady Harriet in *Martha* to Schipa's Lionel.

At the repeat matinee of *Martha*, Schipa was something like a minute late for his third act entrance—thanks, the story goes, to an errant call boy.

A longer and more comic interlude came November 15 when a sort of variety show called "Opera-Tunities of 1935" was put on. It was staged to bolster the company's production fund, and it did so to the opera-tune of $7000. Emperor Jones, Aida and Madama Butterfly collected 50 cents apiece for souvenir programs in the foyer, Schipa conducted the Schipa Jazz Band, and the overture to *William Tell* was conducted by not one but two conductors. Shades of Charles Ives!

1936

The so-called endless melody of Wagner's *Ring* lingered on into the 1936 season, which offered performances, not in any particularly meaningful sequence—completely backwards, in fact—of *Rheingold, Walküre* and *Götterdämmerung*. While Wagner continued to flourish, Mozart finally was introduced into the repertoire, in the form of a single *Marriage of Figaro*. At least two artists of great Mozartian experience, Rethberg and Pinza, were in the cast, along with other principals—San Francisco's Perry Askam as the Count, Chicago's Gina Vanna as Cherubino—who were not quite so well versed in the Mozartian phrase. The handsome, strapping Askam had worked mainly in light opera.

Fritz Reiner began his three years' association with the company in 1936, taking over the Wagner and conducting it with distinction. An aircheck of Act 2 of the November 13 *Walküre* reveals a marvelous control, strong lyric propulsion, perfect tempos, and a lack of affectation. Possibly San Francisco had never experienced conducting of quite this class. The Wagner casts included familiar elements: Flagstad, Rethberg, Lehmann, Melchior, Schorr (who occasionally had to reach for a high note) and List. The *Walküre* performances mark the only times, so far as one can determine, that Flagstad (Brünnhilde) and Lehmann (Sieglinde) appeared in this particular combination—a remarkable one indeed! Lehmann, of course, was the Sieglinde of all time, tremendously warm and, in her harrowing second act scene, chillingly intense. Schorr's Wotan, while dignified, had about it an appropriate suggestion of an old tom-cat. Kathryn Meisle's light, "white" mezzo was heard in a cultivated, lieder-like Fricka, weak-topped but otherwise authoritative.

There was opera-in-English again in '36: Puccini's *Gianni Schicchi* in Percy Pitt's translation. Tibbett took the title role. The consensus was that the words could be understood about 85% of the time, but the presentation was coolly received all the same.

Tibbett also sang his first Iago anywhere during San Francisco's 1936 season, and Martinelli his first Otello. The lusty 51-year-old tenor won from Fried this praise: "In few of his roles is he so penetrating a histrion. Quickly in turn and by contrast he expressed Otello's imperiousness, his lovable sincerity and his maddened pathetic fury." When Martinelli became the Otello of the Met revival one season later he was highly praised again, and a generation later he was best remembered for his interpretation of the Moor. If, that is, one forgets his Canio.

The milky-voiced Grand Manner mezzo Bruna Castagna joined the company for Carmen and Azucena, making a particularly notable impression as Verdi's demonic hag. Marjory Fisher wrote in *The News* that "the vocal opulence she brought to the part seemed, at the time of hearing, unparalleled in local annals." Lotte Lehmann sang another Tosca, opposite the Cavaradossi of the young American tenor Charles Kullman, fresh from European successes. In those days his voice—which had real sex appeal—was in full bloom, but it was never a grandly-scaled instrument.

There were several abridged broadcasts over NBC during 1936, beautifully engineered with a single mike next to the prompter's box, and with Marcia Davenport, the popular author, an effusive but characterful commentator. Merola, she pronounced on Opening Night, "is a remarkable man, the powerhouse behind this thrilling operatic festival." Having just got back from Salzburg she had festivals on the mind, but in truth, there *was* a festive quality about Merola's stable of artists and most of what they were doing on the Opera House stage. Especially *after* Opening Night, when Martinelli bleated, and Merola simply beat time in *La Juive*.

Merola himself conducted only *Otello*, *Barber*, and *La Juive*, that "hair-raising" but insipid Martinelli vehicle which returned for the second year running, its heroine dispatched to a cauldron of boiling oil at the final curtain. The majority of the Franco-Italian repertoire went to Gennaro Papi, a diminutive maestro with long associations at the Met and in Chicago.

Papi is decried in Irving Kolodin's history of the Metropolitan as a sluggish routinier, but in San Francisco—possibly due to less exposure—he fared better with the critics. In general they found him an authoritative maestro, chiding him only occasionally for sacrificing the basic pace of a performance to make a questionable point. Airchecks from the Met and San Francisco indicate that Papi often had the punch, wit and lyrical feeling of a turned-on, imaginative opera conductor. Sometimes he did allow singers more than maximum leeway for virtuosic effects, and he could be reckless. His style tended to be looser than that of his colleague at the Met, Ettore Panizza—but he certainly wasn't dull.

Also new to the company was the elegant, forceful baritone Carlo Morelli, whose diverse background included Chilean birth, engineering study at the University of California, and vocal training in Italy.[3] German soprano Charlotte Boerner appeared with the troupe for the first time, singing Eudoxia in *La Juive* and Susanna in *Figaro*.

An important development in the makeup of the San Francisco Opera's seasons came in 1936 with the initiation of a special package in the form of a "popular" subscription series scaled at prices somewhat lower than those regularly charged. Instead of the $6 top asked for the main subscription performances, $4 was the highest price for a seat to one of the three events in the new series. *Barber, Trovatore* and *Rheingold* made up the list, and the experiment was a pronounced success. This sort of series was overdue, considering that some of the opera-loving public shied away from the formality and expense of the regular subscription performances.

The *Ring* having drained off what remained of the founders' fund—approximately $50,000 in 1935—it was necessary to provide some financial damming in '36. A new category of Guarantor Members of the Association was set up, each pledging assistance should a deficit materialize, and one of $20,000 was not unlikely. The original hope was for 200 guarantors, each pledging a maximum of $100. But about

400 signed up. The laudable idea was to broaden the base of support, only a relative handful of backers having wiped up 1935's red ink, and too few backers can be a dangerous thing.

Guarantor status became an obligation of season ticket holders to the Regular Series in the Orchestra, Boxes and Grand Tier. This was not accomplished without some grumbling—for a few it possibly meant financial hardship—but the bulk of the subscribers rallied, and the system has endured through the years without faltering.

1937

The 1937 season was the most generous to date, with fourteen bills in eighteen performances: *Fidelio, Tristan* and *Lohengrin* in German, *Norma, Aida, Ballo in Maschera, Traviata, Rigoletto, Bohème* and *Butterfly* in Italian, and *Roméo et Juliette, Faust, Manon* and *Lakmé* in French. There was, obviously, more dependence on experienced performers' knowhow than generous rehearsal time. Ticket demand ran high, spurring talk of enlarging the Opera House. Arms of the two balconies could extend over the boxes along the sides of the house, so the dreamers had it. This was not feasible, but an answer came with later years. It wasn't enlargement of the house, but rather, enlargement of the season's length, without increase in size of repertoire. In other words, more repeat performances.

Italy and France contributed important soprano talent for '37 in Gina Cigna and Vina Bovy, both of whom had been singing the previous season at the Met. Cigna, a powerful if variable artist, was the Norma (opposite Martinelli's cultivated Pollione) when Bellini's riot of bel canto was given for the first time in company history. (It did not, unfortunately, return until 1972.) In the Opening Night *Aida* her warm dramatic tones appealed, and her mezza voce made its expressive points, but full low tones could be tremulous, climactic high ones piercing. She made a healthy impression in *Ballo*, then went on to a Violetta which, while interesting, missed the ultimate in resilience. This part she did not sing in her two seasons at the Met.

Bovy, a warm, elegant-voiced lyric soprano of Belgian origin, was an unqualified hit in *Bohème*, singing, according to Fried, with "intelligent sensibility," and making, for Frankenstein, "*perhaps* the most successful debut of several seasons." With Flagstad a recent arrival one had, of course, to hedge. Bovy's other assignments were along expected lines: Juliet and Manon. Her Violetta would have made an interesting contrast with the heavier product of Cigna.

Progressive strides in scenery were noted in Agnini's clean-lined production of *Roméo*. But there was still a good deal that was old-fashioned—or becoming so. Herbert Graf joined Agnini in the stage direction and the massed movements he sent the prisoners through in *Fidelio* resulted in one of the best such effects in company history. Beethoven's opera—in its company debut—had a strong cast led by Flagstad and the Belgian tenor René Maison, with the smooth, villainy-colored bass of Ludwig Hofmann for Pizarro. *Fidelio*, a caviar-type opera, sold very well, but there was only one performance. The other Flagstad fare, *Tristan* and *Lohengrin*, appeared twice each.

Very likely the second *Lohengrin* was particularly well-patronized because of an announcement which reads strangely indeed today. Flagstad, it said, was planning curtailment of her career, would not appear in opera again in San Francisco following her last Elsa, and, further, would not sing at the Metropolitan after 1938–39. Well, as history says, she returned to San Francisco in 1939, was still at the Met in 1940–41, and returned triumphantly to the San Francisco Opera in 1949 and to the Met in 1951.

Following the home season a company of approximately 200 boarded a train for Los Angeles where they launched the first southland season under the name of the San Francisco Opera Association. The engagement of the complete troupe was guaranteed against loss by the Los Angeles Musical Foundation, a division of the Junior Chamber of Commerce. Five operas were given at Shrine Auditorium—four from the home repertoire plus a *Tosca* with the veteran Jeritza, Frank Forest and Bonelli. The charged opening was *Tristan* with Flagstad and Melchior (and List instead of Hofmann) conducted by Reiner, then came *Lakmé* with Pons, *Aida* with Cigna, and *Lohengrin* with the popular pair of Wagnerians. Ticket demand ran high and chartered buses from as far away as Phoenix and Tucson brought opera-hungry passengers. Los

Angeles seasons continued in the Shrine consecutively through 1964, with a visit to the new Music Center the following fall, this followed by a hiatus and another Shrine season in March 1969.

The Shrine is a cavernous building, like the Civic Auditorium of San Francisco's earlier operatic history, but its acoustics proved far better. Despite the far from elegant atmosphere and surroundings, in a south of downtown area, it saw openings not so much less gala than those at home. Movie stars, of course, were conspicuous.

The San Francisco Opera Association's new president in 1937 was Robert Watt Miller, an aristocratic businessman and opera lover who had served as first vice president for five years. He continued in the president's post until service in the Second World War, returning following hostilities as a director, and in 1952 again took the president's chair where he remained for fourteen years, keeping active after that as chairman of the board. Kenneth Monteagle, less of a personality, was president during and after the war.

1938

The 1938 season marked an advance, if an isolated one, in the direction of greater independence from the Metropolitan. Merola looked to Europe and garnered, despite war clouds, a large amount of talent imported directly from the continent. The great mezzo Ebe Stignani, whose 1938 voice was undiminished in freshness, made her American debut. So did Alessandro Ziliani, tenor of La Scala, and Mafalda Favero, remembered for her light, expressive soprano. Favero went on to sing a couple of Mimis at the Met on her way home, but the other two never appeared at that house. Two young artists, Janine Micheau and Georges Cathelat, were brought specially from Paris on recommendation of San Francisco Symphony conductor Pierre Monteux for the company's first encounter with Debussy's *Pelléas et Mélisande*.

Cathelat was called up for the French Army shortly before he was due, but things worked out so he did make it to San Francisco after all. *Pelléas* was conducted by Erich Leinsdorf, then only 26 and something of a wunderkind. Merola

72

cautiously scheduled only one performance of this subtle, fragile work, and it was not heard again until 1947.

Besides the singers new to America, Merola added to the roster Rose Pauly, Irene Jessner and Kerstin Thorborg, who formed the formidable trio hired for *Elektra* (new to the company); the lovable basso buffo Salvatore Baccaloni, who had sung in Chicago 1930–32 and was to join the Metropolitan in 1940–41; the tenor Galliano Masini, baritone Carlo Tagliabue and bass-baritone Carlton Gauld.

The tenor roster took on special lustre with the presence of Beniamino Gigli. He was making a brief return to the U.S., having left under rather disagreeable circumstances in 1932 after refusing to take a pay cut at the Depression-struck Metropolitan.[4] He was one of the Opening Night stars October 7, the chief one in fact, when *Andrea Chenier* was given with Rethberg and Bonelli, plus the elegant local baritone John Howell, who sang Fléville. Merola, who again relinquished most of the non-German works to Papi, was at the conductor's stand. In Chenier's famous first act aria Gigli and Merola collaborated to provide a deliberately-paced, tremendously intense account of the music. It began with a remarkable throb in the orchestra and ended with a bravo-launched ovation.

In *Martha*, several nights later, Gigli achieved one of the few encores in company history, repeating "M'Appari." And applause was so great following the third act of a *Forza* performance the the hero was roused from his dressing room to accept it. He appeared onstage in what one of the lady scribes thought might be a "nightie." At another performance Gigli allegedly got off the stretcher to accept applause for a vintage "Solenne in quest'ora," thereby leaving the bearers jobless.

Ex-stevedore Masini, the Rome tenor who had sung the previous season in Chicago and was to go on to the Metropolitan for a year, made a big impression with his stirringly passionate, decidedly Italianate performances. He was not a subtle artist—the sobs could be objectionable—but he was one of those singers who make an audience sit up and take notice.

Favero was the first major debutante of the season, appearing as Zerlina in a Reiner-conducted *Don Giovanni*. Rethberg was Donna Anna, and a contemporary aircheck reveals her as a marvelously impassioned if occasionally harsh Mozartian, suggesting vocal cousinship with the Elisabeth Schwarzkopf to come. Two nights later Favero was Lady Harriet in *Martha*, and she followed this with appearances as Norina in *Don Pasquale* and Mimi in *Bohème*. Her full lyric soprano and sensitive phrasing met with favor, but when she pushed her tones into harshness she was less than fine. The *Pasquale* was paired with *Cavalleria* to form what was surely one of the longer double bills ever devised.

It was in the latter that the copious Stignani made her only appearances of the season. Her debut was auspicious, Frankenstein finding her to have "a perfect grand opera voice." Although he felt she wasn't much of an actress, her singing, he said, "completely voiced Santuzza's sulphuric emotion, yet she tore no passion to tatters and never indulged in unmusical ranting for the sake of sensational effect." Ziliani's Turiddu met with a mixed press. The Alfio was Tagliabue, who demonstrated for Fisher "a commanding stage presence and a rugged baritone of excellent quality."

When *Pelléas* was given October 19, Micheau's performance as Mélisande was hailed by Fisher as "beautifully sensitive" and Frankenstein felt her portrayal had "just the right note of small, pathetic strangeness." Cathelat, he wrote, was "surely one of the great light tenor voices of the day." Cathelat, alas, faded out,[5] but Micheau had a long, long career. The American Gauld was a fine Golaud, and Leinsdorf conducted cleanly—also heavily, some said.

There was special praise for the sets of Jane Berlandina and William Gaskin which came to the Opera House stage as the result of a competition among local artists. They provided a dose of stylized modern theatricality not often seen during the company's early seasons.

A great find for 1938 was Baccaloni, the basso buffo broad in girth and action. He appeared as Leporello, Melitone and Pasquale. Baccaloni's inimitable services in roles of this sort won him a fond audience, and he reappeared with the company more or less regularly for a generation. He was with the Cosmopolitan for a short time between San Francisco Opera engagements. Incidentally, during his Chicago days he had sung Masetto to Virgilio Lazzari's Leporello in *Don Giovanni*. In the early part of Baccaloni's career, in the 20's, he sang serious roles. Records show, for instance, that he was Timur in *Turandot*—difficult as that might be to imagine—at Covent Garden in 1928.

The *Elektra* production used a generously augmented orchestra. Strauss' opera was one of the season's greatest hits, and so was the revival of *Meistersinger*, Schorr offering his autumnal Sachs (one of the performances was his 200th) with Reiner in the pit. The mellow-toned Rose Pauly should be credited with an heroic job of vigorously pursuing Elektra's wild course in the Los Angeles performance after falling and seriously hurting her ankle early in the proceedings. *Coq d'Or* was revived, too, as an opera with incidental dance rather than a pantomime with voices, and in French instead of English. The presence of Pons dictated the changes.

A plug for unused local talent was put in after the *Barber of Seville* matinee in which the dependable but hardly mellifluous comprimario from the Met, Lodovico Olivero, sang two small roles. It was entered by Marie Hicks Davidson of *The Call-Bulletin* who figured, with optimism and some accuracy, that better voices could be found in the company's backyard. The *Barber* performance was aimed at the children, and the reaction indicated that a regular program of Young People's Performances might be followed. The new Opera Guild pursued this matter.

The 1938 deficit—$88,000—came as something of a shock, although it was obvious that a "tomorrow we die" binge of *Elektra, Meistersinger* and imported stars doesn't come cheap. A big problem was that not as many seats were sold for the repeats as expected. The guarantors, who had been billed for 67% of the guarantee in 1936, and 31% in 1937, received 100% assessments. For the first time.

The Los Angeles season, November 5–11, brought at least two important cast changes: Rethberg sang Eva instead of Jessner, Gigli Rodolfo instead of Masini. The year 1938 also marked the company's first visit to the state capital Sacramento. Pasadena was added in 1939 as another brief stand.

A postscript might be added about a radio concert from San Francisco late in the season. One of the numbers was a trio from Verdi's *Don Carlo* with Stignani a sympathetic, glorious-toned Eboli, Borgioli a lightweight Don Carlo (did he ever sing the full role?) and Bonelli a forthright Rodrigo.

Also there was Stignani (joined by a noble-sounding Norman Cordon and a rather tattered small chorus) in "La Vergine degli Angeli" from *Forza*. Yes, Stignani as Leonora. She also sang the Habanera from *Carmen*—in Italian.

Notes

[1] Critic Fried remembers that the tubists out of the East not only sat in the pit in twos, one behind the other, but walked up the street in the same formation.

[2] Bodanzky, by the way, was an irascible, not precisely clean-mouthed personality at rehearsals. Shouting at Agnini to bring on the chorus, he'd yell out the sort of remark not designed to endear himself to rank and file performers. In any event, the orchestra tendered him a tusch when he received a standing ovation at the end of *Götterdämmerung*.

[3] He was the brother of Renato Zanelli, originally a baritone and later one of the great Otellos (Covent Garden 1928 and 1930). Zanelli died in 1935.

[4] In Gigli's early days in San Francisco he went to a party where a lady supporter cooed at him: "Oh Mr. Gigli, aren't you thrilled when you hear all that applause?" Whether or not he was putting her on, Gigli's hand-rubbing response was "Signora, I'm happy when I get the money."

[5] After singing Pelléas twice at the Met in March 1940.

CHAPTER *8*

The War Years

1939

Hitler and Mussolini were the leading villains of the 1939 season. And history was the most hapless tragedy presented. Merola had planned to show off his "Italian" company again: Favero, Stignani, Ziliani, Tagliabue and Baccaloni, plus the young and exciting dramatic soprano Maria Caniglia. But the state of world affairs decreed otherwise. None was available to San Francisco. Repertoire, of course, was thrown into a turmoil—Merola had planned, for instance, to use Favero, Stignani and Baccaloni, along with the long-familiar Schipa, in a Leinsdorf-conducted production of Cimarosa's *Matrimonio Segreto,* but this pleasant opera buffa didn't make its way into the program, in 1939 or any other year.

Caniglia had been slated for Desdemona, Tosca and Leonora in *Trovatore. Tosca,* planned with Caniglia, Ziliani and Tibbett, was dropped, and there was *Traviata* instead. There was a *Lucia* to make up for the *Matrimonio*—a much less happy wedding! Favero was replaced by the distinguished Brazilian soprano Bidu Sayao in the Opening Night *Manon* (her wistful Manon was a vintage portrayal) and by the lovely Jarmila Novotna in *Butterfly.* The Czech soprano made her American debut on this occasion, but it was an American debut which San Francisco won by default. Novotna had arrived in the U.S. earlier in the year in connection with a projected but unrealized series of operatic performances planned for the New York World's Fair.

Stignani's inevitable Santuzza—she sang it in each of the two seasons she did appear with the company, 1938 and 1948 —went to the technically crisp, plummy-toned American soprano Dusolina Giannini, a favorite of Toscanini. And her scheduled Azucena was assigned to Kathryn Meisle. Ziliani's

Pinkerton was taken over by a young American of Hollywood note, Michael Bartlett. He was to have sung in *Don Pasquale* on *that* double bill with *Cavalleria*, but with all the re-shuffling the projected *Pasquale*, to have starred Favero, was eliminated. *Cavalleria* appeared with its customary mate, *I Pagliacci*. Dezso Ernster, the Hungarian bass, was unable to fulfill his engagement, so King Marke in *Tristan* and Rocco in *Fidelio* were taken by Alexander Kipnis, Hunding in *Walküre* by Norman Cordon.[1] Julius Huehn, frequently associated with Wagner, took over Tagliabue's Sharpless.

Readers may now take a breath. All that juggling was more than Merola had ever had to contend with and he must be credited with quick work in more than salvaging the season. It opened only a month and a half after hostilities began. A mid-September opening would probably have been catastrophic.

Pagliacci brought with it the most newsy event of the year from the human interest point of view. This was the debut of "The Singing Cop," an erstwhile Highway Patrol officer named George Stinson. His move from patrol to *Pagliacci* was tailor-made for the press, and much was written about him. *Pagliacci* preceded *Cavalleria* the night of October 21, doubtless so the critics could hear him before deadline called them away.

Stinson was able to deliver some goods. Fried wrote that whereas his acting was green, his voice was "brilliant, power-ful, broad of range, thrilling in its top tones," and had "intrinsic emotional content." Frankenstein declared that Stinson's voice was "extremely large and powerful, fresh and youthful in its clarion ring ... he carried his assignment through to an ovation richly deserved." The new Canio was greeted with cheers, and a second *Pagliacci*, at popular prices, was scheduled with the ballet *Coppelia* rounding out the bill. On this occasion Stinson offered, following a nervous start, what was in sum a smoother performance than his first triumphant one.

As the story goes, several years earlier Stinson had been giving a traffic talk to some grammar school students in nearby Santa Rosa. The youngsters wouldn't settle down, so Stinson went to the piano, boomed out some songs, and all was quiet in the auditorium. Soon, all his traffic talks had musical accompaniments. Merola heard Stinson in 1937, coached him and saw him off to Italy for study. The reshuffling of the 1939 season in San Francisco precipitated his debut. He was heard again in 1940, but not thereafter. Well along in his 30's, Stinson realized he had started very late, and had a long way to go in acting, repertoire and calming of stage nerves. Eventually he returned to law enforcement.

The season's two *Walküres* brought an interesting switch. At the first, the young Australian soprano Marjorie Lawrence sang Brünnhilde and Flagstad Sieglinde. Then, at the repeat, their roles were reversed. It was generally agreed that the second combination was the better, for while Flagstad was a fine Sieglinde she was a great Brünnhilde. The first performance was conducted in excellent style by Leinsdorf; the second went to the baton of Edwin McArthur, Flagstad's accompanist and part of a "package deal" involving her services. Although neither the prosaic nor the bumptious were absent from his immature conducting, an aircheck of the October 24 *Walküre* indicates an ability to vitalize a performance in a not unengaging way. He was not the ideal choice, though, when Flagstad and Melchior recorded some ill-engineered, thrown-together Wagner excerpts with the San Francisco Opera Orchestra in a cramped Los Angeles studio. In that performance of the 24th, Fred Destal of Vienna Opera experience was a gutty, authoritative Wotan (his part woefully cut, however), Lawrence a spunky, unremarkable Sieglinde and Hertha Glaz a Fricka with a tough of Lehmann in her voice.

The sonically documented history of the San Francisco Opera also includes an aircheck of much of act 1 of the October 20 *Tristan*. Flagstad is glorious, Melchior remarkably poetic, Huehn a sonorous Kurwenal. But Meisle, while sympathetic, sounds vocally much too light by today's standards as Brangäne. McArthur's conducting, sometimes too blustery, settles into a not unpoetic, cogent account of the score—it's much better than his battered reputation would lead one to expect. The orchestra hardly sounds augmented, but plays quite well.

Novotna's Butterfly, opposite the well-schooled Pinkerton of Bartlett, was poignantly sung, and *The New York Times'* Olin Downes, in San Francisco at the time, wrote: "Miss Novotna has given proof of being not only a singer, but also a musician and interpreter of true dramatic instinct ... there is grace, warmth and communicative feeling in all that she does." He might have mentioned in particular the teeth-gritting quality she put into Cio-Cio-San's first lines after Sharpless tells her Pinkerton won't be coming back.

The afternoon of November 3 brought a special student matinee of *Butterfly*. Sponsor was the San Francisco Opera Guild, an outgrowth of the Women's Committee of the Opera Association founded in 1938 to develop wider public interest in opera. The Guild continued providing student performances at low prices in 1940 and 1941, and resumed the practice following the war. During hostilities it purchased tickets to the opera at box office prices and distributed them to members of the Armed Forces at greatly reduced rates. Five student performances are now given each season. During the 1950's an Opera Ball and Fol de Rol became an annual event, artists of the season engaging in humorous skits, proceeds going to the Guild's fund for new sets.

1940

The San Francisco Opera debuts of Strauss' *Der Rosenkavalier*, tenor Jussi Bjoerling and baritone Robert Weede—all to become more or less company staples—took place during the 1940 season. It was a rather light-textured one including no Wagner but two Mozart operas, *Figaro* and *Don Giovanni*. There was also *Manon, Carmen, Lakmé, Ballo, Aida, Rigoletto* and *Bohème*. A projected *Simon Boccanegra* was dropped because Tibbett had a throat ailment. *Girl of the Golden West* also went off the boards, for want of a Jack Rance.

It had been announced in the spring that *Rosenkavalier* would be given in English, a consummation much to be wished by those who found it troublesome to memorize the complete libretto in German, but the artists turned thumbs down on the idea. In the regular revivals of succeeding years the language has remained German, except for one interesting encounter with John Gutman's English translation in 1952. Lotte Lehmann was on hand in 1940 to sing her classic Marschallin, and Risë Stevens, still in her 20's, was a delightfully playful Octavian. Alexander Kipnis was the authoritative Ochs. The intricate prelude to the third act was omitted due to scant rehearsal time, and this unfortunate practice continued through several *Rosenkavalier* seasons, but the cut was later restored. Jane Berlandina's light, witty sets "danced to the music."

The *Don Giovanni* was to have had the services of that noted stylist Schipa but he was detained by bad weather on an air journey from Latin America. His place as Ottavio was taken by Alessio De Paolis, the exceedingly adept comprimario who delighted many an audience with such characterizations as his shifty-eyed Spoletta and his rickety, amiable Frantz in *Tales of Hoffman*. De Paolis omitted "Dalla Sua Pace," not because he didn't know it. At that stage of his career he simply wasn't trying to "do a Schipa." As a matter of fact, De Paolis was a leading lyric tenor as a young man, and recordings indicate he was a convincing one. Kipnis' Leporello was on the straight side: he portrayed a clever, attractive peasant trying to be a lower class replica of his master.

Bjoerling's debut occurred in *Bohème*, followed by his first ever *Ballo in Maschera*—in which he sang the third act aria he later cut at the Met. He was rightfully hailed as one of the most striking tenors heard in many years. Power, perfect intonation, and that floating freshness of youthful tone— all were gloriously in evidence to a happy audience. Backstage, Bjoerling quickly became the subject of good anecdotes. He was, of course, quite a tippler. In *Bohème* he liked to get on stage before the Act 2 curtain so he could put some real beer in his Cafe Momus mug. He was also partial to raw eggs—consumed in sherry!

Weede was the season's new Rigoletto, his large, beautiful voice and commanding presence bringing him one of the year's bigger ovations and some of the grandest critical praise. The Duke in *Rigoletto* was a Cuban tenor, Francisco Naya, who was good-looking and had a good natural voice but was hampered by stage ineptitude and faulty intonation. He did not go far. The Singing Cop's Rhadames on the Regular Series was cancelled when Stinson was found wanting at the dress rehearsal, but he did sing at a student performance later on.[2]

Marjorie Lawrence was the year's Carmen, warm-voiced but entirely too stolid in personality. If *Girl of the Golden West* had been staged she would have been the Minnie, and one who blended vocal and equestrian accomplishments. Meanwhile, there are no arguments to be registered about the tonal elegance and rhythmic persuasion which the Pinza of 1940 could bring to the Toreador Song. Three other local debuts during the season must be noted: the dry-voiced but musicianly Australian baritone John Brownlee, whose *Bohème* Marcello and *Figaro* Count were especially fine; character mezzo Irra Petina, whose Marcellina in *Figaro* set a very high standard; and Raoul Jobin, the reliable, sometimes exciting Canadian tenor. Leinsdorf's conducting of *Figaro*, preserved on an Opening Night aircheck, was crisp, ebullient, pointed, but not exactly resilient. The orchestra was very much on its toes.

1941

The 1941 season saw the first San Francisco Opera performance of Verdi's somber *Simon Boccanegra*, postponed from the year before, and Donizetti's *La Fille du Régiment*, an airy vehicle for Pons and Baccaloni. Italo Montemezzi, resident in southern California, conducted his own *L'Amore dei Tre Re*, not offered since 1928 but due for a new lease on California life during the 40's. Montemezzi returned in 1942 and 1947 to preside over his uneven but striking opus, an opera which, at the least, boasts a truly fine, literary libretto. *Rosenkavalier* with Lehmann was repeated while the repeating was good, and although world events eliminated a *Tristan* with Flagstad, there was *Tannhäuser* with Melchior.

The presence in minor roles of a 19-year-old southern California college student named Jerome Hines (Biterolf), Christina Carroll (Shepherd) and Wilma Spence (Page) should be noted because all went on to bigger things—notably Hines, of course, who became a leading bass at the Met and returned to San Francisco in the late 50's with the Cosmopolitan. In 1941 he also sang a Monterone, winning extremely favorable notices.

82

When the season was concluded, and the resumes were in, it was *L'Amore*, *Rosenkavalier*, *Tannhäuser* and *Boccanegra* which had made the outstanding impressions. But there were other pleasant things to report about the season, one which benefited from an out-of-town warmup by way of a Northwest tour including three performances each in Portland and Seattle.[3] Jan Peerce made a notable company debut in *Rigoletto*, and Licia Albanese conquered with her Cio-Cio-San.

Grace Moore was the Fiora of *L'Amore*, singing, according to Fried, with "impulsive fervor," but "her occasional stagey gestures were beneath the dignity of the opera." Schipa had originally been scheduled for 1941's Opening Night, singing Ernesto in *Don Pasquale*, but he wanted to cut things close coming from South America and his engagement was cancelled. Franco Perulli took his place. *La Fille du Régiment* was a generally happy presentation, with Agnini providing a bright comic setting although a conventional one. The "Marseillaise" was interpolated at the end by Lily Pons, but in light of the Nazi occupation of France it could hardly do other than cast a shadow.

Gennaro Papi's appearances with the company during '41 were his last. He died in New York in late November. In a sympathetic obituary Fried noted critical disagreements about him and went on to say: "Without being the exhibitionistic or arrogant type of conductor, he had an interpretative style that was consistently individual and scrupulous. Indeed, he conceived certain tempos in popular operas— zipping little vivacities in *Rigoletto*, for instance—that were so much his own that such stars as Lily Pons and Tibbett had to be very careful to blend in with them. . . .[4] People who did not care for Papi and who, for mysterious reasons, could not detect his finesse, considered him a routinier. No routinier ever loved music as Papi did."

On the lighter side, an anecdote about Papi is worth recording. One day a San Francisco critic met the conductor in the lobby, and said, "You know, maestro, I admire your conducting very much, but you haven't lost the habit of hissing at the orchestra. You'd be surprised how one can hear it even over the trombones." "All right, said Papi, "the nexa time I putta potato in my mouth."

1942

After the United States entered the war there was discussion as to whether or not the opera seasons should be continued. Thankfully the vote was against giving up. Merola felt that surely this was no time to expand—shortage of materials made new production unfeasible—and the 1942 and 1943 seasons were not especially adventurous. But he also felt that if the company stopped performing it would not start again easily. The Association pursued a cautious path through the spring, announcing tentative plans early in June. President Miller issued a statement that "by means of a series of economies in which all branches of the Association have cooperated, we are gratified to continue."

The tentative plans included the name of Pierre Monteux among the conductors. There had long been hope that the San Francisco Symphony's permanent conductor would lead performances of the city's other major musical organization, but as things turned out the public had to wait another twelve years. The more detailed plans announced late in July included mention of a *Werther* with Risë Stevens. This, too, failed to reach the Opera House.

At the same time it was reported that the city had agreed to finance the company's rental of the building, and that August 10 had been set as deadline in a drive to achieve $50,000 in season ticket sales, a supplement to the already purchased $75,000-worth. The implication was that if sales lagged too seriously the season would be abandoned. The season seat deadline had to be extended, but by mid-August, with Opening Night scheduled for October 9, the ticket situation was so encouraging that the season was assured. Transient servicemen swelled San Francisco's opera public, and all but three performances sold out.

There were three operas in English for '42: *The Bartered Bride, Die Fledermaus* and *Coq D'Or*. A lot of the diction was excellent thanks to the use of American talent, but sometimes the Europeans flavored the text beyond recognition. The productions were spirited, and some of the portrayals, for instance Douglas Beattie's brilliantly acted and richly voiced Kezal, were quite memorable.

Sayao's classic Violetta, Pinza's towering Archibaldo,

Irra Petina's coy, devilish Carmen—these were noteworthy performances. The lively, reliable Fausto Cleva began a long, although non-consecutive association with the company, conducting *Traviata, Faust, Ballo* and *Barber*. Montemezzi returned for *L'Amore*, this time with Jean Tennyson of radio's Celanese Hour as Fiora—and not one of the more successful ones. *Fledermaus* and *Bartered Bride* were conducted by Walter Herbert, at that time a member of the San Francisco Symphony's viola section and more recently a conductor of opera in New Orleans, Houston and San Diego.

1943

Puccini's *Girl of the Golden West* encountered labor pains taking hold in this country. After all, full-blown Puccinian melody is not necessarily the sort of music Americans associate with something as familiar and homespun as the Gold Rush in California. When *The Girl* finally made her way back to the War Memorial stage in 1943—she had been scheduled for 1940—the strange local color was too much for some of the patrons, especially as it was served up in English. The advance sale for the announced second performance was so slow that Merola withdrew it from the slate. This was unfortunate because the opera does boast some winning melody (the vagabond's nostalgic song in the first act, for instance, and Minnie's soulful, pre-Howard Hanson theme) and is shot through with the fascinatingly somber and edgy quality which comes from use of the whole tone scale and the questioning augmented triad, a harmonic cliff hanger.

Florence Kirk, a young veteran of the New Opera Company in New York, was praised for dramatic credibility and good diction in her portrayal of the heroine. But Jagel, about a head shorter, was not a romantic Dick Johnson. And some of the smaller parts were difficult to understand because of foreign accents. Weede took over Jack Rance, originally planned for Tibbett, and was a properly venomous sheriff. The R. H. Elkin translation was used, reworked into less British English by music critic Fried.[5]

Repertoire-wise this was an extremely pale, ill-balanced season, reflecting a certain wartime austerity. There was no

Wagner, no Strauss, and *Samson and Delilah* and Puccini's *Girl* were the only operas on the ration card outside the more or less normal Franco-Italian fare—although *Don Pasquale* might be added to the list of novelties. It is less performed today than it was in Baccaloni's day, which is not to say a later era hasn't produced excellent possibilities for the title role: Geraint Evans, Renato Capecchi, Herbert Beattie.

A special spark was provided, however, by the presence of Sir Thomas Beecham in the pit for *Carmen* and *Don Giovanni*. Beecham was an excellent opera conductor of seemingly unlimited versatility, and his appearances were a distinct boon to the season. If, on the night of his first performance, *Carmen*, there was any worry that his stiff, deliberate stroll to the podium indicated a lack of energy, such an idea was immediately banished by his immensely exuberant handling of the Star Spangled Banner, and by the almost impulsive vitality of his work the rest of the evening. Percussion effects in particular were explosively delightful.

The Carmen was Irra Petina, who offered what one critic described as an "apple-chewing, leg-scratching" version of the role. The elegant Escamillo was Pinza, who had a disagreement with Beecham about the timing of the toreador's entrance. The upshot was that the audience had a slight unscheduled wait.

The company's new chorus master, Kurt Herbert Adler, not to be confused with his counterpart Kurt Adler—sans middle name—at the Metropolitan, made his conducting debut at a performance of *Cavalleria Rusticana* which starred Dusolina Giannini, in fine form, as Santuzza. Fried wrote that Adler made the Intermezzo sound "truly expressive whereas it usually sounds maudlin." Adler was to build the chorus to a level not previously attained, and later became Merola's chief aide. Following Merola's death in 1953 Adler became the company's artistic director, and later, of course, general director. In the accompanying *Pagliacci* the Tonio was John Charles Thomas, reappearing after thirteen years.

The German tenor John Garris, whose fine reputation at the Metropolitan was built largely on supporting roles, was given the opportunity to do Ernesto in *Pasquale* and made the most of it, singing with a pleasingly lyric voice. In one of his more routine assignments, Arturo in *Lucia*, he made an excellent impression, eliciting from one critic the comment that "this was the only good Bucklaw in ten years."

Meanwhile, one George Burnson followed Hines as the year's Monterone. A few years later the same bass-baritone was singing the title role in *Don Giovanni* at the Vienna State Opera, Scarpia at the Met and the Dutchman at Bayreuth. By then, of course, he was called George London. The 1943 comments are especially interesting in light of what followed. Fried wrote: "George Burnson. . . . whose voice is excellent, though not of largest size, made a striking impression." From Fisher: "Another newcomer, George Burnson, made an unusually impressive Monterone with his commanding presence and excellent bass voice." And Frankenstein opined: "Burnson acted Monterone extremely well and has a very nice voice, but not a very powerful one. . . . If Burnson is the boy I think he is, the one who played the stuttering lawyer in *Fledermaus* (with the San Francisco Civic Light Opera), his voice has time to grow."

Tenor Kurt Baum made his company debut in a matinee repeat of *Forza*, arousing a huge ovation after the third act aria. His ringing, striking tone was good to hear, even if it lacked the ultimate in plasticity of handling. Baum's vocal power was an asset to a *Trovatore* which also boasted Thorborg as Azucena and Zinka Milanov as Leonora.[6] Thorborg, Frankenstein wrote, "swept through Azucena like a whirlwind attached to a rocket," showing off a luscious voice and commanding histrionics. This was Milanov's only season with the company and there were times in the years immediately following when her luxuriant tones would have bolstered the Italian dramatic soprano wing, mainly populated as it was by the intermittently handsome-voiced but phrase-chopping Stella Roman.

Ivan Petroff, a rather mellow-voiced baritone who had sung with the San Carlo, made his San Francisco Opera debut in one of the 1943 *Rigolettos*, initiating thereby a series of performances which had more than solidity to offer. The name of Petroff, on the roster for four seasons, evaporated from the San Francisco musical scene thereafter, but he was one of the more satisfying baritones Merola brought forth.[7] The 1943 season was also the first for baritone Leonard Warren, introduced as the High Priest in *Samson* on Opening Night. A Mexican bass, Robert Silva, joined the company, too, making several successful appearances. Also from south of the border, where Merola did some conducting during this period, came Irma Gonzalez, who sang an especially good Micaela.

1944

Two new conductors made outstanding contributions to the 1944 season: William Steinberg, who led the revival of *Falstaff*, and George Sebastian, in charge of the also long-absent *Salome*.

The 45-year-old Steinberg had come to the United States in the late 30's after vast experience—under the name Hans Wilhelm Steinberg—at Cologne, Prague and Berlin, and at Frankfurt, where he was general music director prior to Hitler's coming to power. He brought with him an especially crisp baton. Although his background might have typed him, for American impresarios, as a German repertoire man, Steinberg's assignments in this almost completely un-Germanic season were *Faust*, *Ballo in Maschera* and *Falstaff*. The casting worked exceedingly well: his *Falstaff* was as brilliant a piece of precision baton work as had ever come out of the Opera House pit, and the *Faust* had a sensitivity and dynamic control several notches above the average.

In later years Steinberg conducted much Wagner in San Francisco, but he never made a better impression than the fine one registered on the non-Teutonic side. Performances of *Aida* and *Otello* in seasons to come were bright, finespun, extremely rhythmic.

The more expansive Sebastian, a Hungarian who had worked under Strauss himself, not to mention Karl Muck and Bruno Walter, was responsible for the hair–raisingly exciting *Salome*. He also offered a rather bumptious *Carmen*. *Salome* marked Sebastian's debut as a conductor of stage-produced opera in America, although he had been an assistant conductor at the Metropolitan in the early 20's and had done considerable operatic work on a New York-based radio program.

For the first time in company history a full season of operas was broadcast in 1944. Evening transmissions began at 10 (after prime time?), matinee broadcasts at 4, each continuing from a midway point to the conclusion of the particular opera. Safeway Stores was the sponsor, KFRC the home station, and a number of outlets in California, Oregon, Washington and Idaho carried the fourteen operas. Safeway offered the last parts of fifteen the following year over KFRC; than, in 1946, time was arranged on KYA for the grocery chain to present ten operas complete. Following that season, union demand for a raise in the musicians' pay brought an early finale to this all-too-brief broadcasting history.

In *Falstaff* the title role was taken by Baccaloni.[8] Naturally he made much of the comedy, but he had a little trouble with some of the high notes. *Salome*, staged in an effectively icy, austere setting, was dramatically intense, notably well sung and orchestrally impressive—clearly a milestone in the annals. Lily Djanel, the Franco-Belgian soprano, was a rich, vibrant-voiced Salome, with a pronounced Lehmann-like quality in her singing, and Jagel offered one of the best performances of his career as Herod, throwing himself into the action with relish. John Shafer, a California baritone who worked in musicals, turned up as Jochanaan, singing the part in strong and noble fashion, if not quite with maximum roundness of tone.[9] In *Faust* the Marguerite was Vivian Della Chiesa, a plummy-sounding soprano well-known to radio audiences. Her fate was a mixed press.

Djanel also sang Giulietta when the company introduced a rather expensive but visually uneventful new production of Offenbach's *Tales of Hoffmann*. Virginia MacWatters, a young American soprano, was Olympia, Albanese sang Antonia. Claramae Turner, a member of the chorus who'd been singing in Gilbert and Sullivan at the Bush Street Musical Hall—where customers sat at tables and ate English muffins—had her first important assignment as the Voice of the Mother, this being a voice which had more to say than that in *L'Amore dei Tre Re*, her assignment two years previous. She went on to New York, becoming a leading performer in the title role of Menotti's *The Medium* and other character parts.

MacWatters was joined by baritone Hugh Thompson and

a mute Alessio De Paolis in Wolf-Ferrari's pleasant *Secret of Suzanne,* the curtain raiser for *Salome.* This confection, which blew in and out of the repertoire very quickly, was nicely conducted by new-man-in-town Adler. *Traviata,* with Lily Pons singing Violetta for the first time, was supposed to be a feature of 1944, but it was seven years more before the parties concerned got up the courage for this event.

Notes

[1] Kipnis, by the way, was possibly the most menacing, exuberantly snarling Hunding ever, as an old Met aircheck (December 6, 1941) demonstrates. Earlier in his career he sang Wotan.

[2] Frederick Jagel, sometimes dubbed "the minute man of the opera," was Stinson's replacement. Singing a concert in San Luis Obispo 200 miles away, he was quickly pressed into service. The San Francisco Opera people got him on the phone and told him he'd be picked up by an early morning United flight after his recital.

[3] *Manon,* not in the San Francisco repertoire, was heard in the Northland, with Grace Moore in the title role.

[4] There were also—in *Cavalleria Rusticana*—playful plinks in the opening chorus, prancing trumpets in Alfio's song, and a compassionately pensive tempo for "Voi lo Sapete," along with an admittedly over-boisterous Intermezzo.

[5] On the subject of GGW, there's an anecdote about the miners' shoes. They came from the costumers at the last minute—all brand new, and light yellow-brown! Some quick aging was indicated.

[6] Giannini sang Leonora in Los Angeles.

[7] Later Petroff taught in Los Angeles. He did appear briefly with the Pacific Opera in San Francisco in 1954. And he died in the mid-1960's.

[8] He also sang the role in Buenos Aires, but not in New York.

[9] Frankenstein thought his costume was horrid. He called it "rags fresh from the laundry."

90

CHAPTER 9

Crowded Schedules and a Threat from the East

1945

If wartime strictures had unduly lightened the weight of the 1942, 1943 and 1944 seasons, that which followed sought to bring things back to the earlier-established norm encompassing a fair share of the German along with the customary Verdi and Puccini. The list included *Tristan, Walküre, Rosenkavalier, Salome* and *Don Giovanni,* also *Boris Godounoff* which the critics had been calling for longingly and with reason for some years.

And then there was that finely-etched little work, Ravel's *L'Heure Espagnole,* which served as a curtain-raiser for *Salome.* Much of the dry verbal humor amid the hilarity of clockshop slapstick was missed without the benefit of English translation. At the same time one had to admit that some of the French puns would be difficult to capture in another tongue. From the tick-tock opening to the habanera finale, with Baccaloni squeezing into a grandfather clock in between, *L'Heure Espagnole* was still delightful fun. Albanese, Garris, De Paolis and the fine American baritone Mack Harrell were the others in an authoritative cast under Merola's direction. The production was something of a coup for the company as the Metropolitan had not played it since 1926.[1]

Heading the Wagner casts were soprano Helen Traubel, at her best a creamy-voiced, compassionate interpreter, and a vocally aging but still commanding Lauritz Melchior. Lorenzo Alvary, the Hungarian bass who, in his many years at the Metropolitan, had few opportunities to star, was the Hunding and Marke. In San Francisco's 1945 season he also did Pimen, Ochs, Sparafucile, the *Aida* King, Crespel, Masetto and Raymond, not to mention the First, and more important, Nazarene in *Salome*. Shades of Rothier! Alvary carried off his assignments with ample quality—his Ochs, for instance, while a trace low pressure, was genial and mellow-voiced.

The *Tristan* and *Walküre* baritone was Herbert Janssen, an experienced, lyric Wagnerian whose voice wasn't quite what it had been at Covent Garden in the '30's. Steinberg's conducting of these operas was lean, lithe, exciting, great spring and sizzle blended with a nice lyric touch. Djanel's Sieglinde approached the goose-flesh producing intensity of Lehmann, that being high praise indeed. An exceedingly interesting casting, it was never, so far as one can determine, available elsewhere in the U.S. outside the San Francisco Opera's territory.

Boris was introduced in Italian and minus Rangoni's part, but with the persuasive Pinza, a good-sounding if sometimes muddle-actioned chorus, and a strong cast conducted force-fully, if not always subtly, by Sebastian. The *Boris* production took on greater stylistic virtue later in company history as Rangoni was restored and the opera was sung in Russian, or English. Dimitri proved, like Herod, one of Jagel's best roles, Della Chiesa found one of her most apppropriate assignments as the imperious Marina, and little need be added here about De Paolis' incomparably oily, moth-eaten Shouisky and Baccaloni's uproarious Varlaam, both of them classics. John Garris was a memorable Simpleton, Claramae Turner had another good opportunity as the Innkeeper.

The part of the Frontier Guard Sergeant was entrusted to one Georg Spelvinski, whose name, for obvious reasons, does not appear in the roster at the back of this volume.

In *Rosenkavalier*, with Lehmann returning in great form for the Marschallin, the fanciful rococo-modern sets of Jane Berlandina again made a happy impression, although several of the principals brought along gorgeous costumes that did not precisely fit against them. (Berlandina's hand-painted costumes were never popular.) Sebastian's conducting of *Rosenkavalier* had an agreeably easygoing lilt, and the wistfulness at the end of Act 3 was perfectly paced.

Also worth remembering from 1945 would be Adler's rich-toned conducting of *Cavalleria* and *Pagliacci*, and an exceptionally lively *Traviata* with Albanese on stage, Merola in the pit. A notable feature of Agnini's direction was to move one scene usually played inside out, and one outside in. Evelynn Corvello, a local girl, made a modest impression as Olympia in the held-over *Tales of Hoffmann*. And there was good singing, if not the requisite power, from one Robert Mills, a bus driver (shades of the Singing Cop) who turned to opera, appearing as the *Don Giovanni* Commendatore and Monterone in *Rigoletto*, not to mention less elegant assignments.

A young lady named Lucy Armaganian joined the chorus in 1945 and remained in the ranks for two seasons. Mention of this affiliation might seem pointless, except that Lucy Armaganian later became well known under the name Lucine Amara. About this time another newcomer, a 190-lb. Greek girl from New York, auditioned for the San Francisco Opera —unsuccessfully. *Her* name was Maria Callas. A Callas biographer states that she was advised to build up a name, this causing her to vow: "When I make a name I shall not want you." Prophetic words considering the Callas-San Francisco Opera dispute of 1957.

1946

Lohengrin may have seemed an overly heavy dish for some of the Opening Night patrons in the War Memorial Opera House September 17, but many in the audience that evening were delighted to experience Astrid Varnay's good-looking, beautiful-sounding, movingly-interpreted Elsa. They could be happy, too, about the lyrical conducting of William Steinberg, and the special smoothness of ensemble thanks to pre-season stagings in Portland and Seattle. Set Svanholm, new from Sweden, was a better-than-average Lohengrin.

On the other side of the footlights, Opening Night was back to its peacetime atmosphere of full formality. The evening repeated a pre-curtain script played and played over the years with little variation but much fanfare, plenty of civic pride and lots of journalistic cliches, although *The Chronicle's* Vincent Mahoney was in inspired form when he wrote: "No one was let down. It was a collector's experience—the grandness of a bygone age kept alive by a complex and fascinating city. It was humanity with almost no suggestion of human dreariness, and that is a multiple dream walking."

During the fairly frantic half hour before the first note sounded the action was, as usual, most lively in the hallway by the Carriage Entrance on the north side of the house. The socially prominent, and some who are just ubiquitous First Nighters, enter there. Photographers collected their quota of shots to fill a page or more in each of the next day's papers, and society and fashion writers scampered around taking names and making notes on the gowns, which were, of course, stylish and impeccable in the San Francisco tradition.

Meanwhile, the central foyer was populated to the crushing point. Pity the man who tried to cross this mass of boiled shirt and ermine with any speed. And outside the glass front doors and those by the Carriage Entrance, faithful groups of relatively impecunious citizens came to press their noses, sometimes literally, against the barrier and see the "show." Singularly friendly, these assemblages sometimes suggest operatic choruses drifted through time, perhaps from a scene in *Boris Godounoff*.

A share of the San Francisco Opera's Opening Nighters usually spend the evening in one of the several bars—*Lohengrin* helped the bartenders of 1946 better than some other operas—but the audience is usually well-behaved. And the writers of color stories return to their offices with colorless stories because nobody provides a really good scandal. True, once there was a lady of questionable repute who wore a full-length cape of fresh carnation petals. Another patron of the fair sex "hung herself," as one opera chronicler remembers, with diamonds. And a gentleman came to the Opera House in white tie, tails *and* a ten gallon hat. But these were exceptions to conformity.

In recent years, of course, hippie dress (of a clean sort) has become unremarkable in the Opera House.

The men who brought transistor radios one Opening Night and listened to a crucial Giants game in the pennant race may be pardoned. But not the backstage employee who turned the lights up after a "Ritorna Vincitor" and sent a segment of the season's least informed audience toward the lobby at the wrong time.

But back to 1946: the schedule was the most elaborate to

94

date, and there were four performances each in Portland and Seattle, followed by twenty-seven at home along with three in Sacramento, these in turn followed by a dozen in Los Angeles, plus two in Pasadena. The total was fifty-two. Whereas there were five more performances than the previous season in San Francisco, they were crowded into a space of time only one day longer than that available during 1945. *Boris* and *Rosenkavalier* were successfully repeated from the previous year, Sebastian again in the pit. Kurt Baum was a huge-voiced and amusingly foppish Italian Tenor in the first performance of the Strauss, the local Kayton Nesbitt taking over in the second and making a modestly pleasant impression. With the season's *Rosenkavaliers* Lotte Lehmann bade farewell to the Marschallin, possibly her most famous role, and left the operatic stage.

The revival of *Fidelio*, in Theodore Baker's clumsy English translation, went a good deal less well than these other matters. The cast had some of the same weak elements apparent in the March 1945 revival at the Met: Regina Resnik's not completely pure-toned Fidelio and Kenneth Schon's mediocre Pizarro. Furthermore, there was no Bruno Walter to produce orchestral excellences to make up for insufficiencies on stage. Paul Breisach, who did much fine work during his several years with the company, notably in the French repertory, simply did not give *Fidelio* the monumental power it demands. The obituary of this event need further include only the Florestan of Mario Berini, which was not skimpy, but hard, in sound.

Breisach, along with an impassioned Sayao and Jobin, helped make the revival of Gounod's touching but saccharine *Roméo et Juliette* less pallid than it might have been. But the reappearance of Delibes' campy *Lakmé* was de trop. Thankfully her over-exposed form disappeared from the repertoire after 1946, presumably forever. The Lakmé, of course, was Pons. When she sang Gilda it was opposite the Rigoletto of Tibbett, returned after five years' absence for a single performance. His voice wasn't what it had been—hard drinking had not helped—but the portrayal was striking.

The season's first *Bohème* had not one but two Brazilian sopranos: Sayao singing her excellent Mimi and Maria Sa Earp, in her North American debut appearances, offering a shrill Musetta. There were three new Bohemians when the opera was repeated with Stella Roman as a dramatically interesting but vocally uneven Mimi, Bjoerling, Harrell and Nicola Moscona sub-letting the garret from the more familiar tenants Kullman, Francesco Valentino and Pinza. As usual, the Momus-bound Bohemians snickered lustily when, in the first act, Rodolfo calls down to say that "siamo in due" (I am not alone)—why has this delightful practice been abandoned?

Meanwhile, Lily Djanel's Carmen was a gaspy letdown after her final Salome, and George Czaplicki, the Polish baritone, was not a vocally suave Escamillo. Florence George, Bing Crosby's sister-in-law, was the uneventful Micaela in the year's second *Carmen*. Martina Zubiri, a young lady from the chorus, made a rather nice impression in smallish roles like Barbarina in *Figaro* and Ellen in *Lakmé*. Suffice it to say that 1946 was not one of those years notable for a barrage of new and exciting vocal talent. Or repertoire. With the possible exception of 1951 it was, thank Heaven, the last of the "Play Safe" seasons.

Shortly after the season was concluded a dark shadow was cast over the San Francisco operatic scene with the announcement that the Metropolitan would extend its annual tour to Los Angeles in the spring of '48. There was immediate concern that the appearance of the New York company in the southern California city would endanger the substantial Los Angeles season of the San Francisco Opera, a season of great financial importance because of the large capacity of Shrine Auditorium, which seated approximately 3000 more than the Opera House in San Francisco.

Furthermore, rumors were flying about that the Met would come right into San Francisco itself, and since the trip West was a long one, the stay at the end of the line would probably be of some length. When the musical press of San Francisco predicted that this could sink the home company, which operated on essentially the same scale as the Met—with, as a matter of fact, many of the same singers— and even capsize the San Francisco Symphony, sixty members of which traditionally derive helpful income from the opera performances, it was, very possibly, not being simply pessimistic.

The large guarantee for the Metropolitan's Los Angeles

season came from an organization called Greater Los Angeles Plans, Inc., or GLAP. One of its most conspicuous leaders, Dr. Charles H. Strub, vice president of the Los Angeles Turf Club, operators of Santa Anita racetrack, felt that Los Angeles had room for seasons by both companies, especially as GLAP was going to underwrite a 6000-seat opera house! Meanwhile, Fried was wondering in *The Examiner* about "the peculiar sponsorship the Met has accepted for its West Coast plans." How firm a foundation, he asked, would racetrack money, "shrewdly supplied for self-promotional and self-protective purposes," provide for the future of opera in Los Angeles?

On December 21 Strub conferred with officers of the San Francisco Opera. He told them he was authorized to offer the Metropolitan to San Francisco. Naturally, it was pointed out, the New York company would come to San Francisco only if a substantial guarantee was raised locally. San Francisco, not surprisingly, stuck by its own company, which was traveling full speed ahead with plans for its twenty-fifth season the following fall. Merola had already gone East, earlier than usual, to engage artists. He knew very well that new productions, lively revivals and strong new singers were of strategic importance to upcoming seasons.

Meanwhile, one could find some ominous chords in a statement issued in January 1947 by George A. Sloan, chairman of the Metropolitan board, when he arrived in Los Angeles for an inspection of the Goodyear Tire and Rubber plants in the area. "While the details of our Los Angeles engagements," it said, "other than for the spring of 1948, have not been worked out between our respective managements, Dr. Charles Strub, on behalf of Greater Los Angeles Plans, Inc., has indicated to Mr. Johnson (Met manager Edward Johnson) and to me the desirability of spending from six to eight weeks here each season after your new home is completed, and with the understanding that some of this time, perhaps, will include visits to other parts of the Pacific Coast. Later, when we discuss mutually satisfactory dates, it may be necessary to divide the time as between the early fall and late spring."

That talk of early fall was especially worrisome.

But the finale of this shadowy story was unpainful for San

Francisco: the Met gave fourteen performances in Los Angeles in the spring of '48 and '49, then withdrew from the Pacific. Neither the artistic quality nor—more critical, this—the financial reward of the venture was up to expectations. The touring Met was not generally superior to the San Francisco Opera, and occasionally it was quite inferior. The second season went less well than the first, and, as Quaintance Eaton puts it in *Opera Caravan*, her history of the Metropolitan tours, "the dream was over."

After the troupe turned Eastward, she writes, "Los Angeles expiated her feelings of guilt by turning her full loyalty to San Francisco." A new opera house in the southern city might have altered the situation, but it did not materialize, at least not until the Music Center opened sixteen years later.

1947

For his twenty-fifth season Merola offered a generous outlay of twenty-nine performances of seventeen operas. There was the customary Regular Series of ten performances, mostly on Tuesdays and Fridays; the Popular Series of five; plus a full dozen non-subscription performances, five of them tagged "extras" and seven "added performances." Not to mention two student matinees.[2] Productions new to the company were *Louise*, Charpentier's dreamy ode to Paris and its lovers, and Ponchielli's melodious melodrama *La Gioconda*. The important revivals were *Götterdämmerung*, not heard in eleven years; *Otello*, absent since 1939; *Pelléas et Mélisande*, which had been given only in 1938, and *L'Amore dei Tre Re*, last heard in 1942.

Of the revivals, only *Götterdämmerung* had two performances. The accent, as in 1946, was on quantity of operas rather than the chances for greater security of presentation which come with repeats. Very likely there was only one *Pelléas* because Merola remembered the hardly enthusiastic manner in which Debussy's model of musical understatement had been received nine years earlier. Times have changed sufficiently so that three performances by a good cast in one season are by no means unthinkable today.

Louise may not be a great opera, but it has a special warmth and deserves a certain place in the repertoire. When it arrived October 3 the performance served to introduce Dorothy Kirsten, a soprano whose pure lyric instrument and attractive appearance were prized assets in the title role—which, by the way, she was performing for the first time, having coached it with Charpentier himself.[3] Pinza was the father, Claramae Turner the mother, Raoul Jobin the Julien, and Breisach conducted.

Gioconda, strangely late in its appearance (it *does* require an expensive cast), was brought out with Stella Roman, later Regina Resnik (Gioconda), Blanche Thebom (Laura), Margaret Harshaw (Cieca), Kurt Baum (Enzo), Leonard Warren (Barnaba) and Nicola Moscona (Alvise). The conductor was a youngish maestro from Italy named Dick Marzollo. He conducted only *Gioconda*, returned in 1948, then vanished, his possibilities not exactly exhausted. While the cast was not thoroughly ideal, the show, crisply mounted in traditional style, did click. Certainly the individual timbre and soaring line of Warren's Barnaba were remarkable.

The single *Pelléas*, postponed from September 22 until October 10 because of "technical difficulties" (i.e., not ready), had a good pair of lovers in Sayao and Martial Singher, but the conducting of Wilfred Pelletier, returned after a long absence, was not as sensitive and mysterious as this halting, evanescent music demands. *L'Amore*, however, received a thrilling performance, with the white-maned Montemezzi himself in the pit. The climax of the second act, when Pinza as the blind Archibaldo choked his daughter-in-law (Kirsten) and carried her limp body over his shoulders across the stage, was so exciting that the oft-reserved Regular Series audience applauded vigorously and long.

Otello benefited from Steinberg's gripping conducting, and was interesting for Albanese's first Desdemona—she sang it a little over a year later at a Met Opening Night—and Svanholm's Otello. Albanese sang with generous tone and was honestly moving, if not supremely subtle. Svanholm was a fresh-sounding, intense Moor. Tibbett returned for his famous Iago, not in the voice to which his earlierday audiences were accustomed.

The 1947 season not only had its musical pleasures—and disappointments—but also provided much material under the headings of Human Interest and General News Value.

Before the Opening Night *Traviata*, for instance, Merola was presented with a scroll bearing the names of hundreds of San Franciscans tendering him a gift in commemoration of the twenty-fifth year of the company and his association with it. From the stage Merola responded with: "All I can say is, San Francisco knows how." At that the orchestra struck up Happy Birthday, and the onstage assemblage, the guests at Violetta's party, joined in.

Then there was the Pinza Family *Faust*, offered to a Sunday afternoon audience September 21. Ezio was Mephistopheles, daughter Claudia the Marguerite. Her Italianate soprano was fresh and appealing, but not a great instrument. The friendly audience, including many longtime followers of father Pinza, cheered the girl on. Giuseppe Valdengo, a baritone Toscanini liked, joined the company as Valentin.

There was also the Conquering Heroine's Return of Florence (or Fiorenza) Quartararo, a local girl who, rather to the San Francisco Opera's embarrassment, had sung at the Met but not with the company in her home city. Her debut at the New York house occurred January 18, 1946, at which time Howard Taubman, writing in *The New York Times*, opined that "she may be the find of the season." When she appeared as Donna Elvira in San Francisco her warm, generous spinto won her a major ovation, and her subsequent performance as the Countess in *Marriage of Figaro* was also enthusiastically welcomed. Alas, the Quartararo career was short-lived and she only returned to the San Francisco Opera in 1949 and 1950. She showed signs of having the spark to sustain a fruitful career, but she was plagued by a short range. She chose marriage—to Italo Tajo, who sang with her in San Francisco—and gave up singing as a profession. Lately she has been associated with the Pisani Printing Company (in San Francisco), as director of advertising sales.

Illness struck the company two sudden blows toward season's end. Nadine Conner sang the student matinee of *Traviata* October 17 suffering from a stomach ailment, and she fainted away—as if she were taking the libretto too seriously!—in the final scene. Simultaneously the company was making arrangements to go on with the evening's *Lucia*, threatened with cancellation since Lily Pons had come down with a bad cold. In one of those operatic scenes from real life

Josephine Tumminia, an alumnus of the company (1935–37) and a housewife in suburban San Mateo, rose to the occasion and subbed on extremely short notice.

That morning Merola called Nino Comel, Tumminia's teacher. "*Come sta* Josephina?" he asked, in his characteristic andante legato. "Does she know Lucia? . . . Have you heard her lately? . . . You know, Pons is quite sick, I don't think she can sing tonight." At that, Comel jumped: "Why, you know, maestro, Josephine's been retired for three years. You want her to sing TONIGHT?!" The upshot was that Comel gave Merola Tumminia's telephone number, then quickly called her himself to alert her. When Merola phoned she consented, rushed to San Francisco, and rehearsed briefly with Pietro Cimara, the evening's conductor. She had sung Lucia a few years earlier in Chicago—subbing for Pons on that occasion, too—and in South America. Considering the circumstances, she acquitted herself right well.

Following the 1947 season guarantors received their first assessment bill since 1941. Ever-growing production costs (*Louise* and *Gioconda* had been added to the repertoire in fairly elaborate guise) were given as the principal cause of the deficit. The San Francisco season's red ink, in round figures, spilled to $97,000, but profits on out-of-town performances, mostly in Los Angeles, and other income, including donations, brought the grand total down to $55,000. The concert activities which the Opera Association had initiated in 1939 ran, as usual, at a moderate profit. There was talk again of enlarging the Opera House as a curb against deficit, but such did not prove feasible, nor has it subsequently.

1948

Merola took his company into its second quarter century with another tightly-packed season: the 1948 schedule listed thirty performances of seventeen bills in thirty-four days. There were no new additions to the repertoire, but *Meistersinger* returned after ten years' absence, *Siegfried* after thirteen, and *L'Elisir d'Amore* after nineteen. The previous year's *Otello* was repeated, also *La Gioconda*—each in one performance. And *Boris* returned as a Pinza finale.

101

Obviously it wasn't a year of increased rehearsal, but it was the year in which Merola recommenced importation of singers on a big scale. Tito Gobbi, the young matinee idol baritone, made his American debut in San Francisco, a Swiss lyric tenor named Max Lichtegg also came to the U.S. especially for San Francisco appearances, and Ebe Stignani returned to the place of *her* American debut. Further luster shone on the roster thanks to the presence of tenor Ferruccio Tagliavini, bass Italo Tajo and contralto Cloe Elmo, all of whom had been singing in the U.S. only a short time, Tajo not yet at the Metropolitan.

Verdi's *Falstaff* is a great opera, Merola loved it, and he had the daring to put it on the Opening Night card, in an effort to make it more generally known. Signor Falstaff Baccaloni was, of course, one of the company's most beloved regulars. Naturally some of the tripping delicacies of the score were lost amid the first night festivities—for some the performance was part of a double bill, *A Day at the Races* and *A Night at the Opera*, racing at Golden Gate Fields having begun that afternoon. But the performance was first class. Steinberg's incisive conducting—without score, as usual—was a delight, and Stignani's warmly funny Dame Quickly was something special. Her voice wasn't quite as fresh as in 1938, but there was still some prime lusciousness in it. Her "Reverenzas" can still be heard in the mind's ear.

The company boasted another first-rate Quickly in Elmo, who took over at the second performance. She'd made a tremendous hit with her scenery-shaking, rich-toned Azucena at the Met the previous season, and it was in that role that she made her debut on the War Memorial stage September 30, 1948. She was awarded one of the biggest ovations of the season.

Gobbi's debut occurred in a Saturday matinee repeat of *Barber of Seville* October 2. His fame as a movie star had preceded him, and it was mentioned in the press that whereas he had never sung a note in the United States the Tito Gobbi International Fan Club of South Orange, New Jersey already existed. It's not surprising that the critics were on the suspicious side, and Gobbi's Figaro took a very secondary place at the bottom of the Monday reviews, which had some other news—from the Sunday matinee—to relate. This was the appearance of Astrid Varnay, hitherto associated with Wagner, in an important Italian assignment, the title role in *Gioconda*. With a silken, sexy spinto voice, dynamic phrasing, and impeccable musicianship, she seemed the best answer to the pressing problem of finding a really satisfying dramatic soprano for the Italian wing.

But the season's principal replacement for Roman, who had struggled with much of that repertoire for several years (not, of course, without some success), was an Argentine soprano who had sung in Rome and New Orleans named Sara Menkes. She appeared in *Forza* and *Trovatore* with some points in her favor but not enough to warrant a regular place on the roster.

Gobbi in 1948 was not quite the subtle artist he later became, and his Figaro was on the rough side. But in retrospect some of the reviews betray a certain bite.

Frankenstein wrote: "He was a Figaro straight off the cover of a candy box. His dapper little figure, his rolling eyes and his flash of beautiful teeth were accompanied by a light, deft and amusing style, tasteful singing, and a high baritone which is rather shallow in body though big enough in volume. He seemed, in short, like an extremely good musical comedy performer who was acceptable enough in opera without quite belonging there."

Fried wrote: "Despite his surprisingly brash, uninhibited manner of singing, the audience liked him immediately. True, he was an exceptionally agreeable Figaro to watch, for he was lively, merry and confident. Maybe when we hear him again he will give more thought to the quality of his tone and musical style." And this from Fisher: "Obviously young, attractive and blond, he may best be described by the teenagers' comment, 'He's cute!' While his voice was nothing to get excited about, it was pleasant, and his singing efficient."

The elegant-sounding Italo Tajo made a big impression in his introductory Basilio, and his inventive Leporello (in the season's second *Giovanni*) was very well received, too. The comparison with Baccaloni, the familiar servant of the earlier performance, was not unfavorable to either.

Tajo had a narrow escape when the company toured to Bakersfield, near Los Angeles, and the shade of a stage light fell on his head during the second act of *Bohème*. The theater was new and apparently not performance-worthy when the opera took the stage. Colin Harvey, who was playing a waiter, heard a pop as he opened the bottle of "Champagne" for Baccaloni, the Alcindoro. But the cork was still firmly in the bottle *after* the pop. What he had heard was the impact of the fixture on Tajo's head. Tajo continued singing through the act and there were no serious consequences. But at intermission time it was discovered that the instrument had cut full through his wig.

There were more problems that night in Bakersfield when, at one point, the motorized orchestra pit suddenly began to rise toward Heaven, and the musicians had to jump from this reverse version of a sinking ship.

If Tajo and Elmo won notably enthusiastic responses during the 1948 season it was Tagliavini who received the most prolonged ovation of all. It happened the night of October 11, at the only performance of *L'Elisir d'Amore*. After "Una furtiva lagrima" the applause was loud and persistent. While the audience clapped Tagliavini smiled anxiously, twisted his cap, shrugged his shoulders. Conductor Breisach knew that line in the program which reads "No encores permitted," but after five minutes something was needed to stop the flood. He looked up to Merola in his box, and the signal was given. The rule was broken that night—as it had been before and would be again, but not often. This "Una furtiva" was not necessarily the best thing that happened during the season, but Tagliavini's voice was unusually sweet and suave in lyric tone.

Another new Italian tenor was Mario Binci, with New York City Opera experience, who sang an undistinguished Turiddu opposite Stignani and never returned. Claudia Pinza was back for a couple of lightweight Elviras in *Don Giovanni*. The Ottavio was Lichtegg, whose Leharish voice had a slight Germanic hardness but was sure and pleasant.

One of the more important debuts of a local singer during this period was that of Dorothy Warenskjold, a young lady from Oakland, and a graduate of Mills College. She had sung in Jan Popper's Stanford University Workshop production of *Der Freischütz* a year and a half before, but her appearance as Nanetta in the San Francisco Opera's second *Falstaff* (October 7) marked her debut with a major company. Her charming lyric soprano won immediate favor, and a successful Micaela followed. *Carmen* starred Winifred Heidt, who was tall, good-looking, sensous in voice and relatively refined in interpretation. *Boris*, along with *Forza* and *Don Giovanni*, marked the outgoing of Pinza, who had sung with the company in twenty out of twenty-two seasons from 1927 onward. Next autumn found him well established on a *South Pacific* beachhead in New York.

The late Leonard Warren also departed from the company in 1948—at least for six years—and *his* leavetaking was considerably less warm than Pinza's. Warren was a top baritone and a conscientious artist, but he was not exactly popular backstage. He was, as everyone now knows, a headstrong, difficult man who sometimes pushed people around who happened to get in his way or went against his values. A particular bad habit was to step on choristers' toes. Before a *Rigoletto* he decided he didn't like certain aspects of the staging and made known his displeasure in no uncertain terms. In trying to smooth the argument between Warren and Agnini, Merola reminded Warren that his principal business was singing, not staging, and if he didn't like the staging in San Francisco he didn't have to come back. The result of this discussion was that Warren did not return as long as Merola was alive. Some are of the opinion that there was mutual regret, but the fact remains Merola never reengaged him. Certainly some of the choristers were almost ready to lynch the man.

Advancing costs, the "exceptional" effort made at brilliant productions because of Met competition in Los Angeles, and an unexpected recession in demand for tickets: these were the leading causes of the 1948 deficit, a larger one than the previous year's. A determined effort would be made, it was announced, to rectify the situation, and the number of operas, and performances, was cut down in 1949. The season in San Francisco remained the usual length (from 1946 through 1953 it was thirty-four days), so there

105

was more breathing space for performers and audience alike.

Notes

[1] It turned up at the New York City Center in 1952, and San Francisco's Spring Opera revived it in 1963.

[2] As in 1941 and 1946, there were performances in Portland and Seattle. The company did not return to the Northwest until 1959, when only Portland was visited. Problems of housing and guarantees, plus local pride, with its attendant home-grown products, have limited the San Francisco Opera's Northwest activities.

[3] Kirsten's actual debut with the company was in a 1945 Los Angeles *Bohème*, as Mimi.

CHAPTER 10

The Pacific Story

The year 1948 also saw the first spurt of growth in the re-organized Pacific Opera of Arturo Casiglia. Merola's chorus master during the first San Francisco Opera season in Civic Auditorium, Casiglia had struck out on his own, producing low-priced, low-budget opera off and on through the years with local talent. He was a sound musician, a spunky trouper, and many San Francisco singers remember him as a good friend to the youthful, local, non-star performer. Some of his charges went on to bigger things.

Following a considerable period of near-dormancy, tentative plans were announced in February for an economy season by the *New* Pacific Opera Company. "Putting on opera for a dollar a seat (orchestra seat!) plus tax is just like giving opera away," said Casiglia. "That's what we want to do."

Casiglia's advisory committee included Mrs. John Coghlan, Mrs. Thomas Carr Howe, Mrs. Leon Cuenin, Campbell McGregor, Karl Weber, William G. Merchant and Jack Pisani. At that time most of this group were guarantors of the San Francisco Opera, and the Pacific activities had the benediction of the San Francisco Opera Association, which termed the project a "valuable supplement" to its own performances. Local singers young and not-so-young had opportunities to sing major roles, and opera was introduced to people who couldn't afford the usual prices.

The projected season did not materialize, but there was an introductory performance in the Opera House July 29: *Rigoletto* with Splendora Merlitti, Ernest Lawrence and Vittorio Weinberg (Gilda, Duke and Jester respectively). Casiglia, of course, conducted. Many were turned away, but they were provided for when a season of nine performances did reach the boards November 5 through 26. The operas were *Carmen, Traviata, Rigoletto, Bohème, Cav* and *Pag, The Barber* and *Lucia.* Ina Souez, the onetime Glyndebourne great, was announced for Santuzza, but she did not appear.[1] The season was a great success, and another batch of nine presentations, at $1.80 top, was offered March 4–13, 1949.

At that time the Pacific was on relatively solid footing, and a happy adjunct to the city's operatic life. But, a few years later, the plot of this parallel story thickened. What Casiglia had never intended as a rival institution evolved into a company which had a good deal less than the most friendly attitude toward the San Francisco Opera. The feeling was mutual.

The path of the Pacific had never been precisely easy. When Casiglia, a Sicilian who had reached San Francisco via Boston, started his company in the mid-1920's, sporadic performances—not seasons—were all that could be achieved. The first show (December 17, 1925) was a *Butterfly* performed in a playhouse, the Capitol, which had been closed for some time. The original idea had been to call the troupe the Casiglia Civic Opera, but it was as the Pacific Coast Opera that it came to public light. The name must have seemed a bit cumbersome, and journalists took to shortening it to Pacific Opera: this name stuck. With local talent taking a commendably conspicuous part in the proceedings, the company reappeared June 16, 1926 in *Traviata*, Vera Didenco, Charles Bulotti and Albert Gillette taking the main roles, Max Lorenzini and Evaristo Alibertini among the supporting performers.

A *Cav* and *Pag* followed November 24, 1926, Bellini's *Norma* (not precisely standard fare) was given December 6, 1927, and the double bill was heard again February 28, 1928.

The second chapter of the Pacific history opens with its first full season, which began April 16, 1929 at the Capitol. Eight performances of *Norma, Carmen, Rigoletto, Traviata* and the double bill were given. Meanwhile, a group of "founders" was gathered, more than half of them already supporters of the Symphony Association and/or the San Francisco Opera. Seasons followed in 1930, 1931 and 1932, the repertoire largely standard but etched with some relatively offbeat items. Casiglia traveled from *Norma* to *Sonnambula* (1930), *Gioconda* (1931) and Catalani's not entirely

108

unviable *La Wally* (1932). The title role in *Norma* was sung by Florence Ringo, Amina in *Sonnambula* by Ione Pastori Rix. The avalanche at the end of *La Wally* has always been a staging problem, even in houses like La Scala. It was comically inadequate in Casiglia's production.

The first major instance of internal dissension within the Pacific came in 1932 when Hugo Newhouse, president of the Pacific Opera Foundation, urged that a subsidy from the City not be paid the company as he and his fellow officers had decided not to give a 1932 season. The municipal budget included an appropriation of $7500 from the old Welfare Fund, and $1600 had been paid, but $5900 was held up. The Supervisors honored the Newhouse request, but this was not the end of the matter. Casiglia went to court with a new set of officers headed by Ettore Patrizi, and in September 1933 Judge I. L. Harris decided in his favor.

But for the next fifteen years there was next to no Pacific activity in San Francisco. The records show a few wartime performances in North Beach's relatively minute Fugazi Hall, and a sprinkling of outdoor presentations at Stern Grove.

Following the rejuvenation of 1948 there were *two* seasons the following year, the first in March and the second in late November and early December—the two accounting for twenty-two Opera House performances. A series of eight San Francisco and three Berkeley performances was launched in late November 1950 with a *Bohème* starring Tomiko Kanazawa, the *Butterfly* soprano. Ticket prices by this time had risen to $2.40 in the orchestra.

If you looked closely, you would have seen Campbell McGregor, the Pacific's president and principal backer, blithely assuming the chores of a Cafe Momus waiter in the second act of a *Bohème* performance. McGregor, son of the head of the old Union Iron Works, had long been theater-struck.

Fortune Gallo's dying San Carlo troupe didn't come to San Francisco in 1951, and the Pacific, which hoped to concentrate its performances in the winter rather than the San Francisco Opera's autumn, secured four dates in the Opera House that February. The Pacific's history continues with six performances in March 1952—at the last one, a *Butterfly*, many persons were turned away—and six more in March 1953, the accent, as usual, on popular repertoire with local talent and young singers from other cities. The New York City Opera did not go unrepresented.

The 1953 season played to the usual good houses, but the house of the Pacific was not in order. The second major instance of internal dissension came to public light May 1 when it was reported that Casiglia was planning a season in November and "a Pacific Opera Company under a board of directors whose president is Campbell McGregor" was planning another season the following March. The Pacific board, headed by McGregor, had offered Casiglia a one year renewal on several conditions: 1) the directors have control of the Pacific name, 2) in out-of-town performances he use some other name than Pacific Opera, and 3) he surrender final say on singers and artistic policy to the directors. Casiglia insisted the name Pacific belonged to him. After all, he had been producing opera under that name on and off for almost thirty years. The bill-paying McGregor, on the other hand, subscribed to the opinion that the name belonged to the estate of the late Hugo Newhouse, one of Casiglia's former backers, and was lent to Casiglia by the trustees.

What had happened, really, was that some feeling had developed on Casiglia's board that he was on the provincial side as an artistic director. Dario Shindell, the dilettantish but ambitious company manager, wanted to hire singers in the East, but only Casiglia could sign the contracts. The determined Sicilian, who had always been the solo pilot of what had remained a spunky homegrown organization, felt squeezed, and he thought the character of the company might be changed. Casiglia now and then took a group of performers on the road almost on the spur of the moment. The more formal element in the Pacific directorate was not so sure these performances were on the level they were interested in maintaining. Furthermore, Casiglia would pack his troupe on a bus without insurance, and had there been an accident, McGregor, the moneybag man, could have found himself with some whopping bills he hadn't planned on.

The whole matter went to Superior Court May 7 when McGregor, with Angelo Scampini as legal counsel, filed a petition asking for an injunction preventing Casiglia from

110

using the Pacific name. His complaint stated that on September 29, 1950 Casiglia secretly incorporated a new society under the name Pacific Opera Company, without the knowledge of the New Pacific Grand Opera Association, that being the incorporated name of the company since 1948.

On August 20, 1953 Judge Harry J. Neubarth decided in favor of Casiglia. The Pacific would therefore go on under his aegis, and there was a Pacific season in February. McGregor, allied with Shindell, soon announced plans for *their* season, the first of the Cosmopolitan Opera, with an opening date in March.

What followed the winter of 1954 was one of the more curious spectacles in American operatic history, if hardly the first instance of a vigorous Battle of the Impresarios. It was tagged by columnists and critics the "Siamese Twin Opera Season" or the "Two Round Opera Season." Enter first the Pacific with four performances at $3 top in the Opera House from February 17 through 26. Enter second the Cosmopolitan with six performances at $3 top in the same house, from March 2 through 19. Both seasons opened with *Traviata*, and the same local comprimario crossed party lines to appear as Benoit and Alcindoro in both companies' *La Bohème*. No wonder the people in the ticket office at Sherman Clay were terribly confused: "Which *Traviata* will you have, sir?"

At all events, both troupes enjoyed box office success.[2] Casiglia contributed the one repertorial ace in *L'Oracolo*, Franco Leoni's Chinatown opera dating from 1905. An old vehicle of Scotti's, it had been last performed in San Francisco by the San Carlo a number of years earlier. The Cosmopolitan had the advantage of tenor Walter Fredericks, one of Casiglia's top talents, while Casiglia had a promising teenage Silvio in Ronald Dutro.[3]

By this point the Cosmopolitan Story is launched. And that is another story. The Pacific was finished. Casiglia died late in 1954, as if on some operatic timetable, now that his low-budget territory had been successfully invaded—by his own people! His company never performed after 1956.

Meanwhile, the Cosmopolitan proceeded to flourish. In the late 1950's McGregor and Shindell became more and more intensely competitive with the San Francisco Opera, offering big-name artists stupendous fees while the overall production values were not given anything like the same royal financial attention. By 1960 a dozen performances were scheduled. And the possibility of a serious collision between the San Francisco Opera and the Cosmopolitan was not to be ruled out.

Notes

[1] Performances by the Colorado-born Souez after her return from Europe in 1940 were rare. Her American career took on a checkered aspect, even including a tour with Spike Jones. She appeared successfully with the Werner Janssen Symphony (of Los Angeles) in San Francisco in 1945, singing excerpts from *Wozzeck*, and was again successful in a 1947 recital. She settled in San Francisco, took pupils, and there was reason to believe the San Francisco Opera might at some time value her services. But they made no overture in that direction. She made an unsuccessful "return" in an intimate production of *The Medium* in Berkeley in 1968, Christopher Keene conducting.

[2] It has subsequently come to light that during the early Cosmopolitan years Shindell on occasion gave away several hundred tickets—considerably more than the normal allotment of passes.

[3] A dozen years later Dutro was singing with the illustrious Walter Felsenstein's Komische Oper in East Berlin.

CHAPTER *11*

Personal Triumphs

1949

There was a long, suspenseful and unmusical overture to the 1949 season. And for a while it looked as if there would be no opera, or more specifically no season of operas, to follow it. This—was the Flagstad Affair.

On June 27 it was announced that Kirsten Flagstad would appear in two performances each of *Tristan* and *Walküre*. Her return to Norway during the Nazi occupation had been strongly questioned in some quarters, but there had been no incident when she appeared in an Oakland concert the year previous. Several weeks of rumors to the effect she would appear during the 1949 season resulted in absolutely no complaints from subscribers. But a stink bomb had been thrown at a Philadelphia appearance. And on July 11, in San Francisco, a verbal bomb was thrown: it came in the form of a resolution, submitted by Supervisor John J. Sullivan, aimed at preventing Flagstad from singing in the War Memorial Opera House.

Similar resolutions, hardly the soul of gentlemanliness, were adopted by the San Francisco County Council of the Veterans of Foreign Wars. The singer was labeled as one "whose sympathies and support were placed on the side of foes of freedom and democracy and with enemies of this country."

On July 14 the War Memorial Board of Trustees—a somewhat less sophisticated group than it is today—voted unanimously to officially "disapprove" Flagstad's Opera House performances because of the "highly controversial character of her public appearances elsewhere in the United States." Before the vote was taken, however, attorney Herman Phleger, representing the San Francisco Opera Association, warned that loss of the Wagner productions would be a terrible financial blow, and could result in cancellation of the season. Superior Judge Milton Sapiro, of the American Legion, countered with a point of view reminiscent of his peculiar reasoning in connection with the building of the Opera House twenty years earlier. "Her appearances," he proclaimed, "would desecrate the War Memorial and the ideals it stands for. We wouldn't want a Benedict Arnold to sing in the Opera House. It would be better for the Opera Association *to go out of business* than hire a traitor to Norway."

Phleger noted that the Association had made a thorough investigation of Flagstad's record during World War II, pointing out that she never sang in Norway or Germany or any German-occupied countries. She returned to Norway prior to the United States' entrance into the war, Phleger said, to be with her sick husband, lumberman Henry Johansen. This husband, Sapiro put in, "was one of the leading Quislings, and she should have stayed here to raise money for the Norwegian cause." The opera attorney countered that the King of Norway once gave Flagstad the highest decoration of that country, and had not recalled it after the war. (She went on, in fact, to become directress of the Norwegian National Opera.) Her son-in-law, Phleger added, was an American Air Force bomber pilot in the war.

Meanwhile, the demand for tickets to the Flagstad performances was far ahead of that for other operas on the announced list. And Flagstad herself was decidedly concerned when, in Salzburg, she read an erroneous news report that her San Francisco contract had been cancelled. On July 18 the San Francisco Opera made its commendable ploy very clear: the season, the directors said, must proceed as planned, without substitute for Flagstad, or substitute for the Opera House—there had been some talk of moving the Wagner to Oakland.

Mayor Elmer Robinson, who was on vacation, suggested a conference between the Opera Association directors and the War Memorial trustees. Such a meeting was called July 20 by Supervisor, and Acting Mayor, George Christopher. The directors served notice on the trustees that, should their ban not be lifted in a week, the season would most likely be called off.

The tide slowly began to turn. But the suspense remained

intense. Editorials in the newspapers criticized the trustees. The Mayor's Office queried the State Department and found nothing derogatory on the lady in question. The Junior Chamber of Commerce urged the trustees to reconsider. And the State Commander of the American Legion sent a telegram saying the local Legionnaires were "not acting for the Legion" in the matter. The American Guild of Musical Artists pointed out that the San Francisco Opera might be blacklisted by 95% of the world's greatest artists should the ban continue.

Another meeting in Christopher's office July 23 resulted in no remarkable progress, but the trustees were not far from an even split on their vote. The opera directors' deadline was postponed once, then a second time—to August 1. One of the trustees, the wealthy and cultivated Sidney Ehrman, a one-time patron of Yehudi Menuhin, was returning from Europe, and his vote took on critical importance. He reported by phone that he would cast his vote for Flagstad, and he did so in person at a short meeting held by the trustees August 1. As another trustee switched his vote to pro-Flagstad, a 6–4 "against" was turned into a 6–5 "for." The ban was lifted. The season would go on as planned.

Two months later, the night of September 30, Flagstad sang in *Tristan and Isolde*. There was a standing ovation, and no incident. In fact, a special third performance was added to the schedule. The three Isoldes and two Brünnhildes marked Flagstad's first U.S. opera performances after the war,[1] and they demonstrated that she still had plenty to offer.

Many of the elements in the Wagner casts were familiar. They also brought a Hungarian bass, Mihaly Szekely, who turned out to be one of the most distinguished Wagnerians in company history.[2] The Wagnerian wing was also the area in which the year's Horatio Alger story took place. Its protagonist was an heroic-sized but mortal-voiced young baritone named Richard Sharretts. He had come to California the year before with a road company of *Oklahoma* and, while in San Francisco, auditioned for the role of the Night Watchman in the 1948 *Meistersinger*. He won the part and was singled out for his handling of it. Then, for 1949, Merola gave him a Night to Day promotion—to Wotan! When Sharretts appeared in this extremely taxing role along with Flagstad,

Svanholm and Szekely, he sang gamely but without anything near the power and authority needed for the part, especially in a hall the size of San Francisco's Opera House. Janssen, possibly not so eager to take on the rigors of Wotan at an advanced stage in his career, was the seasoned replacement for Sharretts at the repeat.

The 1949 season calmed down from the previous year's thirty performances of seventeen bills in thirty-four days to twenty-five of twelve in the same amount of time. As an innovation, there were two Popular subscription series, and *Tristan* and *Tosca* both had unprecedented third performances. *Tosca*, strangely absent for eight years, returned as the Opening Night fare. One can only assume that Merola didn't have the soprano he wanted during the 40's, although Milanov was on the roster one year, and Della Chiesa and Varnay, who were present in others, had possibilities for the title role.

The choice in 1949 was a relatively obscure 26-year-old Italian, Elisabetta Barbato, who had gotten her "break" three years earlier when she substituted for Maria Caniglia in a Roma Opera *Aida*. San Francisco appearances marked her U.S. debut. If her performances as Tosca and Aida were not unqualified successes they had their points. Barbato's voice had warmth and beauty, and she tended to sing with an arresting passion, but the sound sometimes coarsened, and wobble wasn't absent. Youth enhanced the credibility of her performances, but she wasn't always at ease on stage.

This was a season unusually strong in tenors, and Merola offered two Cavaradossis of topmost rank: Bjoerling, who sang Opening Night, and Tagliavini. When the latter was called upon for heroic pronouncements his voice could lapse into mere loudness, but the lyrical aspects of the role were exceptionally well-voiced. Ramon Vinay, the dark-voiced Chilean—he was a tenor, then, between earlier and later stages as a baritone—made his company debut as Don José in *Carmen* opposite Heidt, and an impressive one it was. His acting had a conviction above the average, and his Rembrandtian tone quality was strikingly put forth, if not always with maximum freedom. Svanholm, Peerce and Jobin were also around, lending more strength to the tenor line. Giacinto Prandelli was supposed to make his American debut in San Francisco in 1949, but this didn't work out.

The major revival of the season was Puccini's *Manon Lescaut*, absent for twenty-two years. When it returned October 7 Albanese and Bjoerling sang the romantic leads, and Enzo Mascherini, an Italian import, was Lescaut. Baccaloni did Geronte. Fausto Cleva, absent for six years, led a performance which had a festive ring. Cesare Curzi of the chorus was a better-than-average comprimario talent in the role of Edmondo, subsequently going on to Nürnberg where he became well-established as a leading lyric tenor. Another chorister, Jo O'Connell, was a musically unpolished but spunky Olympia in the season's second *Tales of Hoffmann*.

Rose Bampton was heard with the company for the first time in 1949, singing Sieglinde and Donna Anna. In *Don Giovanni* Tajo switched from Leporello to the Don, and there was much feeling he was more the master of the servant's role.

1950

Again this year, Tristan and Isolde almost didn't get their night on stage. The circumstances were quite different.

The company admitted to the press on September 27 that Ramon Vinay just might not make it to San Francisco in time for needed rehearsals prior to his first performance ever in the role of Tristan, that performance being scheduled for October 3. And it looked as if some troublesome rearranging of the season might be in order. Vinay, it developed, had been delayed on his way from London to Chile, the plane having been grounded in Panama. As a result, he had missed two of his four announced performances in Santiago. Since Vinay retained something of the status of a national hero in Chile, his native land, pressure was put on him to stay long enough to make up the lost performances. Rumor even had it that the Chilean president had been persuaded to withhold Vinay's passport.

The tenor was reported as offering to repay the San Francisco Opera Association for any unfulfilled appearances, but the Association didn't consider that much help.

Luckily, this little comic opera did not play long. On September 29 it was reported that the situation had been resolved and Vinay would arrive in time for "adequate" preparation. The prized singer followed this news in person October 1, explaining to reporters that the management of the theater where he was appearing in Santiago had indeed sent his passport to the Secretary of Exterior Relations. On October 3 he sang as scheduled, proving to be one of the most moving Tristans of the modern operatic stage, his dark voice finding an especially appropriate home in the somberness and yearning of Wagner's score.

This performance also served to introduce the most impressive-voiced Wagnerian baritone the company had presented since Schorr, Sigurd Bjoerling—no relation to tenor Jussi.[3] And there was an experienced, authoritative Marke in Dezso Ernster, who had originally been scheduled for the roster in 1939. Flagstad was again the Isolde.

The new *Tristan* conductor was a goateed gentleman named Jonel Perlea, a Rumanian who had conducted in Italy and spent a short time at the Metropolitan. His interpretation was remarkably poetic, but not lacking in strong climax. With Perlea and the aforementioned advantages the 1950 edition of *Tristan* couldn't help being something special. But the year will probably be remembered most as the one in which Renata Tebaldi and Mario Del Monaco made their American debuts in San Francisco. Tebaldi, who was, of course, already well-established in Italy, had been enthusiastically recommended by Albanese. When the season's all-but-final plans were announced in March, they included her name, but that of Del Monaco, also on the rise in Italy, was not among the tenors. It did appear, however, in the revised roster released to the press in May—without any special fanfare. The name of Jussi Bjoerling, which had been in the earlier announcement, was absent.

That spring Merola had visited the office of Frank De Bellis, a patron of Italian arts, to listen to new recordings of Tebaldi, whom he had already engaged. Opera managers can never be too sure, and, although he was confident he was bringing a special singer to this country, he was happy to have documentary evidence. "Thank you," said Merola after a few records, "but you know, I'm not really worried about sopranos. Tenors are the problem. I know you buy a number of Italian recordings. If you hear a promising voice please call me." At that, De Bellis played him recordings by several tenors, but Merola was not aroused. The last tenor, however, brought the remark, "*Who* is this singing?"

It was not long before Del Monaco's engagement was announced.

The two debuts took place in a starry Opening Night *Aida* September 26 with Weede, Tajo and Elena Nikolaidi, the Greek mezzo from the Vienna Opera, also on stage. Cleva conducted—Merola was prevented by doctor's orders from being in the pit.

It was immediately apparent that Del Monaco was an exciting find. His little figure moved with brisk vigor. His eyes flashed. His voice cut through "Celeste Aida" without the early evening uncertainty that plagues many a Rhadames. As the season continued, and the succeeding *Andrea Chenier* and *Manon Lescaut* found Merola's prize bellowing and hamming things up now and then, it developed that some reservations could be registered about Signor Del Monaco. But there wasn't any question about the eclat of his presence— despite the personalized poses—and the free-ringing tone of his upper register, the dulcet seductiveness of his lower tones when he watched over them. In later seasons Canio and Manrico were notably apt vehicles for his robust talents—and Otello, of course.

The wistful beauty of Tebaldi's voice and her attractive personality won her a fond audience without delay. The new Renata Divina sometimes let her tone explode in forte passages, but this was usually a minor distraction. Merola had finally found a dramatic soprano for the Italian wing with a magnetic quality comparable to that of a Rethberg or Muzio. Tebaldi's Desdemona, which came a couple weeks later, was, in fact, harder to surpass than her Aida. Performances as the Countess in *Marriage of Figaro* were also scheduled, but ultimately taken over by Quartararo.

Rudolf Bing, the Met's new general manager, was interested enough in Tebaldi and Del Monaco to fly out from New York for the repeat of *Aida* on the Sunday matinee of October 1. At a press conference he said, of the total performance, "We shall have to pull up our socks to do better than that, or even match it."

The 1950 home season was another of relatively comfortable

proportions: twenty-five performances of thirteen operas within thirty-four days. The Mozart and Wagner statistics were enlarged by the delayed additions of *The Magic Flute* and *Parsifal*,[4] but Mozart's opera was not mounted with any great distinction; the genuine style which would have best reconciled its comic and serious elements was not in full supply. With its large amount of spoken dialogue it was wisely performed in English—in the Martins' translation. But the ragged ensemble and a hardly virtuoso cast took a lot of the natural shine out of this flute. Heavily literal sets didn't help.

Parsifal, presented on the last Friday evening of the Regular Series—beginning at 5 with a break for dinner—and the following Sunday beginning at 1, was conducted by Perlea with his customary sensitivity. Flagstad was the authoritative Kundry, almost unrecognizable in her black wig, and Kullman was, despite worries his voice would be inadequate, a strikingly forceful Parsifal. There may have been times that weekend when customers were reminded of the man who went up to the ticket window and asked for a lower berth for *Parsifal*, but the performances had their decided assets.

Among the lesser of these were the sets of Agnini and Eugene Dunkel, hardly revolutionary in design and only used for two seasons. They were contributed by the Opera Guild which raised money for the production at the first annual Opera Ball and Fol de Rol in Civic Auditorium. Many of the company's artists donated their services for this frivolous occasion on October 5, Lily Pons wiggling her hips to a recording of "Diamonds Are a Girl's Best Friend" and Baccaloni inintroducing the song "Some Unlikely Morning" from the musical "North Atlantic"—while an old colleague named Ezio Pinza sat at a table out front.

A note in the program pointed to the difficulty of building "new and necessary" productions without special financial aid. Ticket prices were not being raised, the note said, though production costs certainly were going up. Regular Series orchestra seats remained $7.20. In later years the Guild was to raise money for some "necessary new" productions which had more mileage in them than the company's first *Parsifal*.

The tenor department was exceptionally strong again in 1950. Besides Del Monaco, Vinay and Kullman (plus Jagel returning in his specialty, Herod), there were fine young additions in Giuseppe Di Stefano and Eugene Conley. Both sang Edgardo, and Di Stefano also took on Rodolfo, Conley Almaviva. Then there was a young man from Philadelphia, Walter Fredericks, who'd sung at the Ice Follies and been taken up by Casiglia for his Pacific Opera. His San Francisco Opera debut was as Narraboth in *Salome*—Brenda Lewis was the orgasmic, penetrating princess—and he carried the assignment off well, at least from the vocal point of view.

An unscheduled bit of business in *The Barber of Seville* occurred when Baccaloni, the Bartolo, sat down hard enough on a chair during the shaving scene to cave it in. This was a different kind of bend from the cute phrase-curling which Baccaloni employed through the years for comic (and more, or less, artistic) effect.

Del Monaco went to New York after his San Francisco appearances, singing a guest date at the Met November 27 in *Manon Lescaut*. He formally joined the New York company the following season, taking part in the Opening Night *Aida*. Tebaldi was not to appear at the Metropolitan until the 1954–55 season. Sigurd Bjoerling was on the roster there only in 1952–53. Perlea's first season on 39th Street, 1949–50, was also his last—according to Kolodin, he and Bing couldn't agree on repertoire.[5]

Deficit trouble rose in the wake of San Francisco's 1950 season. The guarantor assessment, a moderate 56% in 1949, soared to 100%. One unfortunate factor was a 6% drop in attendance at the Shrine Auditorium in Los Angeles—the proximity on the calendar of performances by the Sadler's Wells (now Royal) Ballet and the Civic Light Opera did not help. Meanwhile, the 20% entertainment tax was nearly paralyzing organizations like the San Francisco Opera in the face of rising costs. There's an interesting Los Angeles casting to be noted: San Francisco tenor James Schwabacher took over Tamino in *Magic Flute* for Kullman.

1951

A long postponed and not especially successful attempt at a new role by a celebrated artist very well known to San Francisco, and a rousing Boris by a young Russo-Italian bass-baritone in his "second American debut"—these were the newsiest events in a season which was more a reaffirmation of well-tasted items than one noted for unfolding of novel repertoire. Obviously the board of directors had spoken.

Lily Pons tried Violetta in *Traviata* for the first time October 5. Seldom has an individual casting received so much advance attention in the press, and there was much newspaper talk about it from late summer on. Pons arrived in San Francisco in late August after being coached in the role by Vincenzo Bellezza in Rome. She had, she said, lived with it for six months. And, it was prominently reported, the new Violetta had gone to Paris and ordered some expensive costumes from Balmain and Karinska.

Came the night of the first performance the audience was as dressy and social as that on Opening Night. Every important artist not singing in *Traviata* seemed to be there. Pons herself was extremely nervous at the start, and her tone became fluttery. But when she relaxed there were passages of intense feeling and beautiful singing. She seemed to identify herself with the role more and more as the evening progressed, but she couldn't persuade many listeners that Violetta is a role for such a light voice. All in all, a not uncommendable entrance into difficult coloratura-lyric (accent the lyric) territory, but ultimately an ill-advised one. Excepting a 1952 repeat, Pons did not pursue the role. Her Alfredo was Peerce, Giuseppe Valdengo the Germont, and Cleva conducted.

If the Pons *Traviata* was less than a hit there wasn't any question about the triumph of Nicola Rossi-Lemeni as Boris. With more than ample vocal resources, magnificent bearing, and lively dramatic ability, the young singer—only in his early 30's—elicited raves.

Rossi-Lemeni conceived the Czar as frantically racked with pangs of conscience, and his interpretation, vocally and visually, was intense enough to leave the audience limp. It was climaxed by a brilliant piece of showmanship skillfully wedded to his conception: a sensational corkscrew fall down a flight of steps—a fall so realistic that listeners greeted the tremendous thump on the stage floor with a collective gasp. This fall came at Boris' last words, as he rises from his throne at the top of the steps, clutching the arms of the chair, protesting he is still the Czar. A little earlier, after Pimen's narrative about the shepherd's vision of the child Dimitri, Rossi-Lemeni fell backwards freely and startlingly from the platform, to be caught by two choristers. The stage directions ask for a collapse here, but not necessarily one as daring as that employed in this instance.

There was unusual vividness in Rossi-Lemeni's Death Scene entrance, too, hurtling on as he did with a wild stare on his face, clutching a handkerchief.

The striking new artist had come to the United States shortly after the war to appear with a troupe of European singers recruited for a season in Chicago, the regular company there—or an incarnation of it—being temporarily defunct. Alas, the season did not come off, due to the shady doings of the impresario involved. Rossi-Lemeni did sing, however, at a concert given by the artists to earn money for their passage back to Europe. This, in reality, was his American debut, but the San Francisco Opera program-makers did not recognize it.

Son of an Italian father and a Russian mother, he had a law degree from Padua and, according to an interview, no formal vocal training. He also sang a Padre Guardiano in *Forza*,[6] and Colline in *Bohème*, and returned in 1952 and 1953. He was Merola's last great import, and his American career had a "made in San Francisco" stamp on it. Rossi-Lemeni appeared only briefly at the Met—in the first part of the 1953–54 season, opening it in *Faust* conducted by Monteux. After the Chicago Opera was relaunched in 1954 he sang there three seasons. Only San Franciscans saw his *Mefistofele*, in 1952 and 1953. He returned to San Francisco in 1967 and 1968, appearing as the father in *Louise* and Basilio in *Barber of Seville*.

There was, in 1951, another dose of that suspense which is an all too nerve-wracking prelude to many opera seasons. This time there was worry whether the Japanese Peace Treaty conference would vacate the Opera House on schedule, only several days before the commencement of the season. Russia's Andrei Gromyko had threatened to keep the meeting going for a month. Some wags suggested that perhaps the conference might be set to music and there could be opera after all. Ultimately everything went off as planned, the company moving its rehearsals from the Downtown (ex-Casino) Theater into the Opera House on schedule.

There were twenty-six performances of fourteen operas.

Nothing had been off the boards very long, witness *Rosenkavalier, Boris, Parsifal, Fidelio, Carmen, Manon, Roméo et Juliette, Traviata, Rigoletto, Forza, Otello, Bohème, Butterfly* and *Tosca.* There was, however, besides Pons' first Violetta, Dorothy Kirsten's first Tosca, Blanche Thebom's first Carmen and Octavian, and Astrid Varnay's first Leonore. Del Monaco was unavailable, but Bjoerling returned, in superb voice. Tebaldi didn't return either, and the Italian-born, American-trained Herva Nelli, favored by Toscanini, was a competent but not electrifying substitute.

Stella Roman came back to sing the Marschallin, which she had done at the Cincinnati Summer Opera, and this turned out to be one of the better things achieved by her in San Francisco. Anna-Lisa Bjoerling, the tenor's wife, sang opposite her spouse in the second *Roméo,* displaying a sweet if hardly exciting voice. An interesting addition to the tenor ranks was the Dutchman Frans Vroons whose Des Grieux was noteworthy for its style, handsome appearance and interpretative imagination. The voice was far from great, but the total effect meritorious. *Fidelio* was back in German, with Alfred Wallenstein, at that time conductor of the Los Angeles Philharmonic, making his operatic conducting debut—sans score. His baton work was not without authority, but suffered from insufficient rehearsal.

The 1951 guarantor assessment in this year of obvious retrenchment was down to 61%. But the entertainment tax continued to be a bother right up to November 1, when, too late to help the San Francisco Opera, it went out of effect. The Los Angeles picture was happier: five out of fourteen performances sold out, and the total gross was $225,000. Average attendance in the Shrine was almost 5000. For the record, the smallest houses were drawn by *Fidelio* and *Otello.*

Conspicuous cast changes in the southland included Ernster's Sparafucile (instead of Alvary) and Ralph Herbert's Iago (for Valdengo). Merola himself conducted *Traviata,* instead of Cleva.

Notes

[1]She returned to the Metropolitan, as Isolde, January 22, 1951.

[2]Non-Wagnerian assignments for him in San Francisco and Los Angeles were Ramfis and Sparafucile.

124

[3]Twenty years later, in his 60's, he was singing Wotan in the *Ring* cycle at Stockholm.

[4]*Parsifal* had last been staged in San Francisco by the Chicago Opera at the Tivoli in 1914. The Kundrys of the two performances were Minnie Saltzman-Stevens and Julia Claussen. Otto Marak sang Parsifal, Clarence Whitehill Amfortas, Allen Hinckley Gurnemanz, and Hector Dufranne Klingsor. Mabel Riegelman, a Californian and later a San Francisco voice teacher, was one of the Flower Maidens. Cleofonte Campanini conducted.

[5]Perlea was simply "joining the club." This was not the last time Bing and a top conductor on his roster couldn't get together.

[6]Those who know the Callas recording of *Forza* will notice the unusual intensity Rossi-Lemeni brought to this role: notice in particular the almost frenzied handling of the recognition that his visitor is Leonora di Vargas.

CHAPTER *12*

Reminiscences and Death

1952

An excusably nostalgic Merola decided, to the great benefit of those attending the thirtieth anniversary season, to re-
vive two operas not heard since the company's first year. They
were Boito's *Mefistofele*, with its cataclysmic Prologue and
wild Witches' Sabbath, and Puccini's *Il Tabarro*, with its
poignant, punchy verismo. The Boito was brought back
thanks to the availability of Rossi-Lemeni; *Tabarro* returned
as part of the complete *Trittico*, the other two parts being the
Suor Angelica and *Gianni Schicchi* which had been given
now and then as parts of double bills following their original presentation with *Tabarro* in 1923. While there was great
point in the reminders of how far the company had come
since the first performances of these operas there was also
pathos. For this, it turned out, was Merola's last season.

Veteran buffs remembered a cooler reception for *Mefistofele* in 1923 when lengthy scene changes in the technically
ill-equipped Civic Auditorium dragged the performance on
beyond midnight. During that season a projected repeat had
to be dropped because of insufficient interest, but the total
impact of the first performance in 1952 was so shattering that
a special third performance had to be added to the two originally scheduled.

What caused the excitement? Undoubtedly at the heart of
the matter was the score itself, a refreshing change from
Gounod's perennial with its high sugar content. The music
is not all good, but much of it is very good, and students of
operatic history can be fascinated by the echoes of Berlioz
and Liszt, the foreshadowings of late Verdi, the hints of
Mahler. Cleva conducted with great spirit and authority, and
Rossi-Lemeni, catlike in his fluid movements, was a sonorous

menace from his first emergence, bat-winged, out of the scenery. Bidu Sayao and Tagliavini were the lyrically well-endowed Margherita and Faust.[1] Visual effects served up by Agnini and Dunkel were appropriate if traditional, and the staging of the Witches' Sabbath was notably fast, vivid and applause-stimulating.

On one occasion a gremlin turned on the steam too soon and the chorus lost Cleva's beat for a bit, but that was a minor disturbance. This scene is supposed to have a nightmarish effect on the audience; it can, alas, also provide nightmares for the stage director.

No less exciting, really, than *Mefistofele* was *Tabarro*, conducted with high intensity by Glauco Curiel, a young maestro who died prematurely a few years later. The prompter's box was his usual working place during his several years with the company, but out on the podium he did some fine things—notably with Puccini, for whose music he obviously had tender feelings. At times in this *Tabarro* he let the orchestra well up over the voices, but it was a flood of sound difficult to argue with. Brenda Lewis, Del Monaco and Weede were excellent in the main roles, and Claramae Turner made much of the cameo part of Frugola. In the second performance Fredericks replaced Del Monaco as Luigi and the comparison was not too unfavorable.

One of the more worthwhile "experiments" in company history was the 1952 *Rosenkavalier* presented, at Lorenzo Alvary's suggestion, in an English translation (by Met assistant manager John Gutman). If understanding of it depended on where one sat, well-placed members of the audience heard a lot of the words and found the talky parts less so than usual. But it cannot be reported that the production was received with great enthusiasm. Brenda Lewis was the Marschallin, Blanche Thebom Octavian, Dorothy Warenskjold Sophie, Alvary the Ochs, and Breisach—who died a couple months later—conducted. The baroque-surrealist sets "suggested" by Tony Duquette were serviceable but not the ultimate answer to the company's needs for this opera.

Another experiment took place with *Don Giovanni*. It consisted of scenery painted onto slides and projected from backstage machines onto translucent screens placed behind three archways. This system, reportedly being used in opera for the first time in America, was the work of Richard Rychtarik, a CBS art director in New York. He was brought to San Francisco by Herbert Graf, returning after several years' absence to share staging duties with Agnini and Carlo Piccinato. Much of the action was played in and out of archways which were approached by stairs and platforms, there being ample space downstage for props but not for the ballroom crowd.

The main problem was that the lighting had to be very subdued to allow the projections to shine forth, and it was hard to see what was going on in what *Chronicle* critic R. H. Hagan so aptly termed the "twilight zone." The new staging facilitated speedy moves from scene to scene, but the price of pace was high.

Merola evidently toyed with the idea of producing Alban Berg's *Wozzeck* in 1952, and there was report of a Los Angeles patron of the arts offering to subsidize the production, but this did not come to pass. One wonders if a little more daring on Merola's and the board's part would have made *Wozzeck* possible in the early 50's. The schedule of new productions after the wartime austerity period could have been rather more adventurous. *Louise, Parsifal, Gioconda* and *Magic Flute* came into the repertoire, but nothing really new. Merola, aging and in frail health, had clearly lost some of his early fire, and he was, of course, a man of the so-called old school.

Very likely if Robert Watt Miller had come back to the presidency immediately after the war things might have picked up faster. Miller had a way of thinking big.

Rossi-Lemeni was the year's Don Giovanni, blond and effective—even if perfectionists worried about his "playing" the mandolin with gloves on. He delved further into the old Pinza repertory with a compelling Archibaldo in *L'Amore dei Tre Re*, worthily revived after five years' absence. But he didn't do the Philip II in *Don Carlo* and the Scarpia which strong rumor had predicted for him. Composer Montemezzi had planned to be in the audience for his *L'Amore*, but he died early in the year. Cleva conducted, Kirsten repeated her excellent Fiora, and Brian Sullivan, a young, ultimately ill-fated Met tenor of California origin,[2] made his company debut as Avito. He revealed a not fully matured but excitingly romantic tenor. At times he put forth a sort of sublimated whine which made its point in this chilling, highly charged score.

Lily Pons repeated her Violetta in a non-subscription performance, but the role still wasn't really right for her. She was, in fact, not as sure of her part as she might have been—Curiel practically sang a duet with her from the prompter's box. A much happier vehicle was the revived *Fille du Régiment*. Only there was a transportation problem here. In the matinee repeat the horse drawing Pons' carriage charged from its resting place on stage and crashed out into the wings, knocking into a side flat which some choristers promptly propped up before greater damage could result. The horse had been fidgeting and backing off, and at one point the man holding the reins let go and the driver urged the animal forward. Pons was supposed to get in the carriage, but, minus it, she went off in a huff instead. And who could blame her?

The biggest new vocal sensation of the year was Fedora Barbieri, who took over where Ebe Stignani and Cloe Elmo had left off. She was introduced as Azucena in the second *Trovatore*, winning warm applause, and later, like Stignani, sang Santuzza. Del Monaco returned, finding outlets for his lusty talents not only in *Mefistofele* and *Tabarro* but also *Tosca*, *Aida*, *Trovatore* and *Pagliacci*. Americans filled out the tenor department: Conley, who sang Cavaradossi in the second *Tosca*; Peerce, who sang the first Turiddu of his career at a student matinee; Sullivan, Fredericks, and a reedy-voiced local tenor, Ernest Lawrence, who took over for the unavailable Vroons in *Fille du Régiment*.

A *Bohème* with Tagliavini saw Brenda Lewis moving convincingly from Giorgetta's barge to Musetta's Latin Quarter only a few Parisian blocks away. Merola presided over the Regular Series *Bohème*, following a heartwarming standing ovation. President Miller made a speech before the curtain rose, citing the genial director's guiding force through three decades. Nobody knew, of course, that this was the last evening Merola would ever enter the Opera House pit.

Although 1952 was a challenging season, the guarantor assessment managed to slip down to 36%. Breaking of attendance records in Los Angeles helped soften financial blows.

The total patronage there was 72,119, marking an increase of 7613 over the previous year. *Tosca*, as a matter of fact, captured the all-time box office record for opera in Los Angeles. *Bohème*, *Aida*, *Cav* and *Pag*, and also the attentively-witnessed Opening Night *L'Amore*, were other favorites, with *Don Giovanni* and *Traviata* not far behind. Weakest in public interest were *Fille du Régiment* and Puccini's *Trittico*.

1953

It was a cold Sunday morning at Stern Grove August 30, 1953. Heavy dew dripped from the eucalyptus trees as musicians from the San Francisco Symphony shivered in their seats on the outdoor stage. It was so cold, in fact, that there was talk of moving the rehearsal for the afternoon's concert to some indoor place—Merola, who was to conduct, was not in good health. But the gaunt maestro said no, don't fuss, we will carry on in the usual manner.

And they did. That was the afternoon Gaetano Merola died.

He conducted the first half of the "pops" program. Then, after intermission, he was accompanying Brunetta Mazzolini, a Portland soprano, in "Un bel di" from *Butterfly*. She sang the beginning of a sentence: "Io, senza dar risposta me ne starò nascosta un po' per celia, e un po' per non . . . ("I, without answering, will stay hidden partly for fun, and partly so as not . . .) At this point there is a downbeat, on the second syllable of *"morire* al primo incontro" ("to die at the first meeting"). Merola's baton was upheld, and in a moment the downbeat should have come. But it never came. His baton remained upheld, and a strange, dazed look came into his face. It seemed as if he might spring into the air. Suddenly he fell forward, and onto the stage floor. There was dead silence. Orchestra and audience arose, standing motionless. A doctor in the audience rushed on stage, but there was no commotion. Everyone knew what had happened.

Merola died conducting the music of one of his favorite composers, leading the musicians he had known so well. It was, after all, a death that perhaps he might have chosen for himself, had he been given the opportunity. As a kind fate would have it, Merola died honoring an old Italian superstition which decrees that a man should not die with his feet on the ground. Falling from the conductor's stand he turned around and landed with his feet up on the podium.

Although Merola's health had been poor for several years his generalship of the company had not basically faltered. And he had, in fact, constructed for 1953 a season of strong variety and freshness. But a major problem beset him just a few days before his death: the cancellation of Del Monaco, who did not feel well enough to come for his assignments. The season had been built, if not around him, at least in an adjacent semi-circle. He was slated to sing in *Turandot, Manon Lescaut, Otello, Ballo in Maschera* and *Carmen.*

When word from Del Monaco's manager arrived, several days before the Stern Grove concert, Merola wanted to make doubly sure that what the notification said was irrevocable. The manager was called, but this proved unproductive. So Merola attempted to get in touch with the tenor himself. He thought he might be able to persuade him to come. Meanwhile, all possibilities of replacement and rearrangement were considered, and necessary machinery set in action. The night of August 29—the night before Merola's death—a cable was received at the Opera House by his chief aide, Kurt Adler. It was from Del Monaco. He would not come. This was the ultimate answer. Adler, knowing how much Merola was depending on a yes from Del Monaco, decided not to show him the communication until after the Stern Grove concert. So at least Merola never knew—even though he may have suspected the outcome.

Otello tenors are as rare as *Turandot* sopranos, and when an international search proved fruitless, Verdi's opera left the schedule. *Manon Lescaut* was also scratched—but this was the last time the company batted out to the point of having to change its repertoire at the last moment. Preparations for the September 15 opening were carried on expeditiously, and meanwhile, messages from old Merola artists flowed in. They came from Lotte Lehmann, Lily Pons, many others. The official announcement of Del Monaco's indisposition was in the papers September 2 and it was further announced that *Bohème* and *Traviata* would be inserted for *Otello* and *Manon Lescaut.*

What was not spelled out was the fact that the chorus had

already spent lots of time on *Otello* and *Manon Lescaut* and had not looked at the other operas. This was not a problem for old-timers, but every year there's turnover in choral personnel. Substitution of an opera at the last minute would be even more of a problem today than twenty years ago because individualized choral action has become an artistic necessity. The days of "throwing together" a *Traviata* are over in San Francisco.

The September 2 announcement also informed the public that David Poleri, a young tenor who had sung with the Pacific company, would appear in *Carmen*, *Traviata* and *Bohème*. Kenneth Neate, an Australian, was to take over Calaf in *Turandot*—there would have been a Revolution had Puccini's long-rested opera gone unrevived—and Riccardo in *Ballo in Maschera*. The Neate story was full of ironies. Some months earlier, en route from Sydney to Ottawa, he had stopped over in San Francisco. Since he was interested in singing with the company, an audition was arranged. Merola liked him, but had no spot for him on the roster. Later, after the unhappy Del Monaco cancellation, Neate was contacted and engaged. But illness forced him in turn to regretfully withdraw. Ultimately it was Roberto Turrini, a lusty if not especially elegant tenor, who took on Calaf and Riccardo.

There was no eulogy for Merola on Opening Night. This was as he would have preferred it. The company which he had created—and whose growth was largely due to him—could speak for itself. One of his major successes, *Mefistofele*, was the evening's fare. That was Merola's choice, and a good one. With Rossi-Lemeni starred it was received with a good deal more enthusiasm than Opening Night audiences had been able to muster for many other operas. There was no official talk yet of a successor: it had been announced after Merola's death that all consideration of a new director would wait until the season was over. There was a mission to accomplish, a trust to fulfill.

Speculators, of course, speculated. Some figured the new man would be Kurt Herbert Adler, assistant to the general director. There was also talk of Agnini, or Cleva, or Carl Ebert, the noted producer of Glyndebourne fame.

Merola had liked importing fresh talent from Europe, and

he had enjoyed encouraging young Americans. Both enthusiasms were strongly reflected in the 1953 season. Six singers were introduced to the U.S.: sopranos Inge Borkh and Gertrude Grob-Prandl, mezzos Giulietta Simionato and Margarete Klose, and tenors Cesare Valletti and Ludwig Suthaus. Also, and it's a big also, conductor Georg Solti. Three young Americans, Ellen Faull, Beverly Sills and Barbara Gibson, had good opportunities, forming together the trio of ladies in *Don Giovanni*. Faull was to have been the Desdemona. Of the imports, only Valletti went immediately on to the Met.

At that time Beverly Sills was a relative unknown, just a new soprano with flaming red hair. She was, of course, to emerge thirteen years later as a star coloratura when she triumphed as Cleopatra in Handel's *Julius Caesar* at the New York City Opera. She proceeded, in superstar steps, to La Scala, the Teatro Colon, Covent Garden, etc., continuing, however, to give prime time to the City Opera. Merola had hired her in 1953 (at $175 per week) as a sort of protege, and she was to have lived with the Merolas—but he died a day or two before she arrived. She reached San Francisco with only $10 in her purse. When no Merola appeared at the airport she looked up his address in the phone book and made her way there by various buses and streetcars. She got a room at the Whitcomb, the singers' hotel on upper Market Street where, she recalls, she cooked frankfurters on the radiator.

Except for a Cosmopolitan Musetta and Micaela in March 1958 Sills did not appear in San Francisco again until a happy, triumphant recital in April 1970—although there had been a visit with the City Opera to Stanford in the summer of '65. Following her performance as Donna Elvira in 1953— she had never, by the way, seen a performance of *Don Giovanni*—Alexander Fried wrote in *The Examiner*: "Beverly Sills did well in the Elvira role, *but she needs to become surer of everything about it.*"

Valletti's elegant style was introduced in *Werther*, revived after eighteen years, and there wasn't much question he carried on the Schipa tradition quite nicely. His soft and medium-loud singing was beautifully suave, well-rounded and delicate. His fortissimos may occasionally have sounded

133

like cultured yells, but lusty tones have been something of a hazard for singers of his leggiero type. Valletti also appeared in *Barber of Seville*, demonstrating again his talents as singer *and* actor.

Simionato's gifts were most brilliantly put forth in Rossini's opera, which she sang in the original mezzo key. The virtuosity of her cleanly executed fioriture and the spirit of her presence made a marvelous impression. She also appeared as Charlotte in *Werther* and Marina in *Boris*. Her projected Carmen went to Turner.

Inge Borkh was one of the chief powderkegs in the brilliantly revived—and cheered—*Elektra*, in which she had the title role. The young soprano, large but not bulky in figure, had vocal resources to burn and vivid dramatic accents to spare. Solti's conducting was on the same high level of commitment, his highstrung style suiting the Straussian violence only too well. The rich-toned Berlin veteran Margarete Klose was a striking Klytemnestra, and Paul Schoeffler, the Viennese bass-baritone (then at the Met) a mellow Orestes. Furthermore, Harry Horner's granitic set from 1938 wore well.

Curtain-raiser for *Elektra* was a shortened version of Beethoven's ballet *The Creatures of Prometheus*. To the best of the company's knowledge San Francisco was giving it its American premiere. As a matter of fact, the records showed only two major performances since the Vienna premiere in 1801.

Another, more elaborate new production was the Puccini *Turandot*, an opera which Merola had been thinking about wistfully for some time. Yet a quarter of a century was allowed to pass between performances.[3] Casting had not been easy, although one wonders why Cigna, Martinelli and Pinza didn't have a go at it in 1937. At all events, Merola found in Borkh a striking Principessa, and Turrini was a gutsy Calaf. Albanese and Warenskjold shared the Lius, the latter singing this poignant role the day after her father's sudden death.

The Opera Guild donated new sets by Horner which mixed realism and fantasy to reasonably good effect but created problems for the stage director by placing the royal steps in a head-on rather than the diagonal position which permits more flexibility of movement. Obviously a new production was indicated—although, as a matter of fact, a by no means bare effect had been created in 1927 when decorative rigging, curtaining, banners, lanterns and high steps were the ingredients of a "field expedient" treatment of the big choral scene in the second act.

Rossi-Lemeni conquered again in *Boris* in the 1953 season. In December 1952 he had sung a concert version in Russian with Stokowski and the San Francisco Opera Chorus at the regular concerts of the San Francisco Symphony (RCA recorded it), but Italian was the language again when *Boris* returned to the Opera. Tullio Serafin, that authoritative veteran, was on the podium, not in very dynamic form.

A new departure in the staging of *Traviata* was Piccinato's setting the first act on two levels, minus the clutter of dining tables of old. "Champagne" was served on the upper deck, the guests sauntering back and forth between the two. Poleri was an Alfredo of conviction, but more subtlety and shading were in order. A lively, strong-headed personality, Poleri would fight with conductors and act rough with leading ladies, but there was more youthful impetuosity than meanness in his temperament.[4]

Wagner was unusually well served with Solti at the helm of *Tristan* and *Walküre*. Grob-Prandl's matronly looks and old-fashioned acting were not ideal, but there was vocal power and some exquisite quiet singing to be savored in her Isolde and Brünnhilde. Borkh was a warm Sieglinde, Suthaus in his prime for Tristan and Siegmund, and Schoeffler's beautiful voice and intelligent stage manner were assets for Wotan and Kurwenal. Klose and Ernster lent further authority to the Wagnerian wing.[5]

Grob-Prandl and the dramatically keen Klose crossed the Italian border into *Ballo in Maschera* to close the Regular Series—it was at this performance, during the second intermission, that a small ceremony in Merola's honor took place. A plaque bearing a bas relief portrait done by Spero Anagyros was unveiled at the west end of the south corridor of the Opera House.[6] The portrait might well have smiled, for this had been a season which included much that was exciting. It was an expensive one for the guarantors—the assessment was 100%, partly because Los Angeles box office was down—but eminently well worth it.

135

Those who watched the unveiling could remember an essentially warm, just and loyal man, a unique figure, more magnetic than systematic but with many fine qualities of personality. He was, indisputably, a personality, but not a flamboyant one. To the stranger on the street his trim moustache, well-tailored clothes and the expansively but tastefully draped handkerchief in the breast pocket would have indicated the urbane man he was: a continental gourmet of selective taste (when he entered a restaurant he usually headed straight for the kitchen), an enthusiastic traveler (especially in planes), a good raconteur, and above all, a gentleman through and through, even if one distinguished colleague termed him a picaresque character.

His manners were impeccable, and as one of his students from the early days in San Francisco remembers, he accompanied her down the street after a lesson only after solicitously inquiring if she minded that he wore no hat. Merola liked the artists to act like ladies and gentlemen—most did, although some definitely did not—and they in turn recognized his courtly mixture of fairness, firmness and friendliness.

One singer recalls: "He was such a gentleman I didn't feel I needed a contract."

Merola's acute feeling of how to handle his artists kept the backstage atmosphere warmer and more easygoing than in some other houses. There are those who might say his disinclination to take sides smacked of evasiveness, but he knew as well as any director ever did how to get what he needed artistically from his charges without letting them know he might be strongly displeased with them at heart. He knew the power of time as a great settler, and when his secretary worried how a duel of two artists for the same role would turn out, Merola simply said: "Don't worry. Justa let the pot boil." He could be very understanding, and when one of his most reliable violinists reached a Los Angeles performance late he didn't bawl out the musician. He simply asked, in a benign manner, "You sleepa too much?" He knew it wouldn't happen again.

Tantrum was a word Merola didn't seem to know, and although he could be irritated—after a long conversation with an admirer he once said: "In the hands of a woman a telephone is a terrible instrument!"—his impatience rarely turned to rage. Actually, some of his most characteristic actions were silent ones: he had a way of walking out from the wings at a rehearsal, slowly taking out his watch, putting it away, and walking off without a word. No one needed to be told that overtime was creeping up. He sometimes added the visual prop of an overcoat to complete the pantomime. His manner of speaking, when he did speak, was musical and Neapolitan. An expressive face and hands, and mastery of the shoulder shrug, amplified his vibrant speech.

Perhaps no better picture of Merola's warmth—and practicality—can be offered than that revealed in a speech he addressed one afternoon to the audience at a student matinee. "Good afternoon, young people," he said, "This is a beautiful opera house. It's here for your enjoyment. We are going to play nice music for you ... Please don't put gum under the seats."[7]

Merola played a lot of nice music for a lot of people, young and old. He was not a great conductor, being on the permissive side, but he was a sensitive musician nonetheless. His fond touch with Gounod and Massenet should not go unremembered, and he was by all means a remarkably warm and idiomatic interpreter of Puccini. As a general director he was on occasion more conservative than he might have been. But there was much in his planning that was creative.

Had the war and ill health not plagued him and the company his record of achievement might have been greater in specific accomplishment, but the grand sweep of it remains impressive. It is very likely that, without him, San Francisco would have long remained only a host to touring troupes.

Notes

1 Sayao sang this role, and also Nedda, only with the San Francisco company.

2 He did away with himself in Lake Geneva in 1969.

3 The Met shelved *Turandot* from 1930 to 1961. But New York did hear it in the 50's at the City Center. And Chicago played it in the 30's.

4 Another ill-fated tenor, Poleri was killed in an Hawaiian helicopter accident in 1967 at the age of 40. He had just remarried his estranged wife after fourteen proposals—not surprising spunk from the man who once walked off the stage in a New

York City Opera performance of *Carmen* in Chicago, telling the conductor, Joseph Rosenstock, to "finish the opera yourself."

[5]A sorry footnote to the Wagnerian doings took place when the stagehands, as if playing Donner, got the beefy Grob-Prandl to sit in their mildly-charged "electric" chair, a backstage gimmick which, happy to say, has been banished.

[6]And subsequently moved to a fittingly more conspicuous place in the main part of the foyer.

[7]Another instance of that practicality: when conducting he would admonish the double basses, "I want to hear you bassi. I'm paying for you!"

CHAPTER *13*

The Adler Years Begin

1954

Kurt Herbert Adler, Assistant to the General Director, became Artistic Director in November 1953. As such, he was the chief architect of the 1954 season. This was his season to show what he could do—no General Director had yet been named to succeed Merola—and the 49–year-old Viennese provided enough freshness in approach to make a very convincing case. He was, in effect, launching a new era, one in which staging had greater importance than ever as a basic rather than incidental factor in performance, and one in which productions of contemporary operas became a more or less regular event.

To introduce Adler more specifically, he had studied at the University of Vienna and the Vienna State Academy of Music, served as a coach, accompanist and conductor for Max Reinhardt in that city, and in the mid-30's conducted at the Volksoper. He was an assistant to Toscanini at the 1936 Salzburg Festival, came to the U.S. in 1938 and joined the Chicago Opera, serving there as chorus director, and then, in 1943, summoned by a Merola telegram asking if he could be out in San Francisco in a week's time (it took a little longer), he began his highly efficient work with the San Francisco Opera Chorus. In Merola's last years he was the first lieutenant in the command post, and in that capacity he had become thoroughly familiar with the problems of constructing an opera season, an occupation which might be likened to putting a jigsaw puzzle together with a few pieces missing.

Mixing this experience with ideas definitely his own, plus some unrealized Merola plans, Adler came up with one of the top seasons in the annals. It began, however, not precisely on a sour note but on a high one which had more altitude than artistry. Mado Robin, the late French coloratura, made her American debut in *Rigoletto* the first night. It was well-known backstage that a B above high C was a specialty of hers, and Cleva, the evening's conductor, was against her using it. But came the end of "Caro Nome" and, without warning, a loud, pointed alarm was sounded. B-stung Cleva restrained himself from walking out of the pit then and there as the audience gasped, but he refused to conduct the repeat. Karl Kritz took over, and as things turned out Robin arrived at the crucial point during the second performance and didn't offend.

Opening Night was also the night Leonard Warren returned to the company, after a long period of persona non grata status, and the night Richard Tucker joined it. The baritone's portrayal of the jester needs no further comment from this source; the tenor's fresh, facile vocalism was very welcome, despite the negative visual factor. The season then proceeded to its various pièces de résistance.

There was the company's first performance of Wagner's *Flying Dutchman*, a Merola pet project and not played in San Francisco since the German Grand Opera Company visited Civic Auditorium in 1931; the American premiere of Cherubini's 1798 opera buffa, *The Portuguese Inn*; and the first fully staged presentation in the U.S. of Honegger's *Joan of Arc at the Stake*. There was also *Turandot, Salome, Fidelio, Marriage of Figaro* and *Il Tabarro*, not to mention bread-and-butter items. The Cherubini was curtain-raiser for *Salome*, *Tabarro* for the Honegger.

Perhaps the major coup of all was Adler's procuring the services of Pierre Monteux in the pit. As the 79-year old conductor emeritus of the San Francisco Symphony told the press, he had not felt that the conductor of the Symphony should also conduct the Opera, but now that he had retired from his old post (in 1952), he was ready to join up. His assignments were *Fidelio, Joan,* and *Manon*, which he propelled lustily and engagingly without letting the tension in this fragile score lag. *Manon*, of course, he had conducted innumerable times. *Fidelio* he had led on only three occasions, but the Monteux Beethoven needed no apology. The score of *Joan* he learned for the San Francisco production.

Adler entrusted the stage direction to three men: Piccinato,

Horner, and Paul Hager, a 28-year-old German who had assisted Wieland Wagner at Bayreuth and spent some of his early years as Intendant at Heidelberg. Hager quickly became a regular, indeed, the most favored member of the staging department, coming up with some good ideas and some too somnolent, seldom reaching heights of utter magnetism but only occasionally descending to the goofy or making detours from a reasonably stylish level.

The new spirit of production which henceforth would be a central ingredient in the company's modus operandi was a neat answer to Horner's press conference remark that "operas in San Francisco and at the Met are still being staged in the style of the 1890's. This is a style in which scenery and direction is based on providing a background for whatever opera star is in the foreground."[1]

The state of affairs on Van Ness Avenue wasn't quite as antiquated as Horner's statement might have indicated. The Met was taking on something of a new lease on visual life in the Bing regime, by that time four years old, and Agnini, although of the old school, had succumbed a little to the contemporary spirit in San Francisco. But a major overhaul of scenic ideas *was* necessary, and it was begun in earnest at this time. Agnini was not in the best of health and had gone on to the New Orleans Opera with its less concentrated schedule. Much can be said for his pioneering work in facilitating the production of opera in San Francisco. He was a very hard worker, and although Graf, William Wymetal and Dino Yannopoulos came now and again to work at the San Francisco Opera, he always liked to carry a big load. He was efficient—he could, for instance, rehearse *Meistersinger* singing most of the roles—and he was quite inventive within the context of traditionalism. Frankly, though, the new regime could not fit him in as a central figure.

The Flying Dutchman came to the Opera House stage October 5 with the great Hans Hotter in the title role. The new production gave a prominent place to a projection system devised by the Viennese electrical engineer Paul Planer. Whereas the *Don Giovanni* projections came from behind the stage, Planer's machines were set up high on the bridge behind the asbestos curtain. The slides in this production were exact copies of Horner designs transferred to glass. The system permitted stationary *and* moving effects, so the Dutchman's ship could be seen sweeping to the shore. The "wide screen" views were altogether more vivid than those of the earlier experiment.

Hotter's dark, haunting voice sounding forth from a towering frame was absolutely first class. Inge Borkh's Senta was lively, but her agitational-gyrational acting effects were more appropriate to Elektra. Alvary's Daland and Curzi's Steersman were likeable, and Brian Sullivan added Erik to his San Francisco credits. The well-schooled but somewhat ponderous conductor was Eugen Szenkar of the Düsseldorf Opera, in his first U.S. opera engagement.

In *Salome* Borkh was more convincing—especially when she casually asked for the head of Jochanaan while primping and freshening up her face! Kullman's Herod, a far cry from his oldtime romantic parts, was hair-raising.

Joan of Arc at the Stake, Honegger's dramatic oratorio from 1938, is sometimes performed in concert version and sometimes as an "opera." There's an urge on the concert platform for the Joan to act out her role, and, conversely, there's a need in staging *Joan* for a certain amount of stylization. Horner handled the chorus Greek-fashion and heightened moods of the drama with projections of the Planer variety. The ballet also had a prominent part in the action. Dorothy McGuire of the movies, replacing Greer Garson, was a touching Joan, and Lee Marvin, future Academy Award winner, was Friar Dominic.

The Portuguese Inn came into the repertoire on the hearty recommendation of Alvary, who had sung it in Europe. Composed in 1798, the score had been left in somewhat fragmentary form, but arrived in San Francisco sewn up by Giulio Confalonieri, an Italian composer and critic. It turned out to be a rather Mozartean buffo charmer, by no means great but more than serviceable, capped with a polonaise finale. The story, about a young woman who flees the amorous attentions of her guardian, has points of similarity with Rossini's *Barber* and almost every other 19th century comic opera. It was set by Horner and staged by Piccinato in the commedia dell'arte manner with, as one critic put it, "some of the tallest hats and most extravagant wigs, plumes and noses ever seen on the Opera House stage." The cast included, besides Alvary and Curzi, a handsome Italian soprano named

142

Rosanna Carteri. This warm-voiced singer had made her U.S. debut at the season's first matinee as Mimi, and by the time, a few days later, she appeared in the Cherubini, the word had gotten around that she was one of the best lyrics in company history. The thought of her sustained pianissimi still brings chills.

There were sixteen calls after the Cherubini. The applause meter also rang up a standing ovation for Monteux when he entered the pit for *Manon*, his first opera of the season. Although his permissiveness had not brought requisite discipline to the San Francisco Symphony during his long period at its helm, the warmth and transparency of his unsensational interpretations, plus his paternal nature and evident joie de vivre, had endeared him to the public with good reason. Massenet's opera was performed, according to his wish, with the rarely-given Cours la Reine Scene, a restoration which gave the story better continuity and provided the ballet with a good opportunity.

Kirsten and Carteri shared the Manons, Giacinto Prandelli was Des Grieux, and not surprisingly, with such an Italian emphasis, there were departures from ideal French diction.

Although in this and the following season there were three French operas, there were casting problems in the Gallic wing. The lack of a large population of top-flight native French singers has long been a factor in the soft-pedalling of this repertoire during the Adler regime. Of course the Austro-German taste in opera tends to run north and south of the Alps and not west of them. *Carmen* is popular in German-speaking countries, and *Tales of Hoffmann* has its chance, but to say that the Gounod-Massenet-Saint-Saens sugar factory is run at full operating force in Vienna, Berlin—or San Francisco—is certainly not true.

A new dramatic soprano for 1954 was the big-voiced, Yugoslavian-born Carla Martinis, a Milanov type who had experience at New York's City Center. She made an uneven impression as Leonora in *Forza*, and her Turandot—she shared the role with Borkh—was not one of the super best. Another name to mention is Franca Duval, who sang one of the better Musettas. An innovation, not repeated since, although programs at the Fol de Rols have resembled it somewhat, was an extra performance in the Opera House titled

Gala Night at the Opera. Scenes and acts from several operas were presented. Altogether there were twenty-six San Francisco performances of thirteen bills during 1954—an average number during the 50's.

Between the 1953 and 1954 seasons a vital, independent arm of the San Francisco Opera Association commenced its work. This was the Merola Memorial Fund. It was christened with a benefit performance of Verdi's Requiem conducted by Cleva on April 2. Proceeds went to the Fund, which set up, in conjunction with the Association, the San Francisco Opera Debut Auditions. This operation has proved a great boon to young singers from the Western states and Canada.

A summer training program sponsored by the Fund was initiated in 1957, and a number of Auditions participants have taken advantage of the coaching which the program offers in numerous phases of opera performance.[2] Some of the productions mounted at Paul Masson Vineyards (near Saratoga) featuring talent from the Program have been really distinguished—Lotfi Mansouri's 1965 *Cenerentola,* for instance, and Dennis Rosa's 1970 *Four Saints in Three Acts.* Auditions alumni—Jess Thomas, Robert Thomas, Janis Martin, Heather Thomson, Judith Beckman, etc.—have gone on to bigger things.

1955

On September 8, 1955, a week before the season would open, it was announced that the company was seeking financial support through a public fund campaign supplementing the guarantor system. The appeal for $100,000 was not being made in sudden desperation, President Miller said, but in the cool light of cold facts: even after a full guarantor assessment, the 1954 deficit was only lowered from $157,420 to $89,635, and a small surplus built up over the years had had to be tapped. In order to stem the tide of rising costs and at the same time maintain, and indeed, extend the range of artistic accomplishment of the company, a fairly agonizing financial reappraisal was necessary.

There would be similar drives every year, Miller said, but he was able to remind guarantors that contributions would be deducted from their normal assessment.

Assessments in general were maximum during the second half of the 1950's, but this was a period which saw the company developing its repertoire to the point where it could be termed a truly important international theater. Sir William Walton's *Troilus and Cressida* had its American premiere in 1955, Francis Poulenc's *Dialogues of the Carmelites* was given for the first time in the United States in 1957, and Richard Strauss' *Die Frau Ohne Schatten* reached the American stage in 1959—all at the San Francisco Opera. Carl Orff's *Die Kluge* had its American premiere in San Francisco in 1958 on a double bill with the same composer's *Carmina Burana*, which had previously been done in the U.S. only in concert version. And Berg's *Wozzeck* did join the repertoire in 1960, in its West Coast premiere.

Meanwhile, Verdi's *Macbeth* was added in 1955, Mozart's *Cosi Fan Tutte* in 1956, Strauss' *Ariadne auf Naxos* in 1957, Cherubini's *Medea* and Verdi's *Don Carlo* in 1958, Gluck's *Orfeo* in 1959. Not to mention Zandonai's *Francesca da Rimini* in 1956, surely an opera Adler did not consider basic repertory material. No season was allowed to pass without two or more operas new to the company. To report these additions is not to take away from the vital groundwork laid by Merola himself. But Adler was especially aggressive in expanding the company's horizons, and Miller was right with him.

Troilus, which had been introduced to the world at Covent Garden the previous December, came to the War Memorial stage October 7, Leinsdorf conducting, and the composer in attendance.[3] Here was a new opera which could really be called grand. Its music was full-bloodedly amorous and sumptuous, its text—Christopher Hassall's "original dramatic variation on the theme Chaucer borrowed from Boccaccio"—nobly rhetorical and poetic. Not all the score is of prime interest, but a fair amount of it, notably the love music, is worth remembering. An arching lyrical line embroidered with ecstatic floridities captures the lovers' desires very nicely.

Richard Lewis, the English tenor who created the role of

Troilus, was brought over for the San Francisco production and began what was to become a long association—his principal operatic one in the U.S.—with the company. Kirsten was Cressida, Weede Diomede and Giorgio Tozzi Calkas. Ernest McChesney of the New York City Opera took over Pandarus, a role originally planned for Kullman, who was rounding off his career as a character tenor. Airy settings did not burden the viewers with heavy literality, nor the accountants with bulging bills. Sir William's opera was received with fair enthusiasm, and there have been some requests for its revival, but it's not exactly "in" today.

Verdi's *Macbeth*—absent from New York between the early 40's and 1957—arrived September 27 and proved one of the most interesting novelties in company history. It revealed, for all its earthy, elementally exuberant, and not displeasing, early Verdiism, pages and pages of strong imagination and pointed ironic touches. Some of the most effective music is already in the score of the original version dating from 1847, four years before *Rigoletto*, when Verdi was turning out considerable hack work.

Obviously a realistic approach would have underlined the cornyness of some of the music, and the designer, Berlin-born Leo Kerz, wisely took another tack. The sets were bare and awesome, nicely suggestive of a dank, barren old castle, with a long curving staircase a recurrent ingredient. Changes of scene were accomplished in large part by projections. To heighten the sense of chilling spaciousness, the stage opening was literally higher and broader than usual, and the projections seemed to be reaching for the top of the house.[4]

Barrenness was an asset to *Macbeth*, but the lean Kerzian style was rather over-applied during the early days of the Adler regime—a not surprising backlash (conscious or not) following the Agnini era.

Weede and Borkh combined the vocal strength and histrionic punch for bringing the Macbeths to life. Tozzi, American but whith Italian experience, and one Met season behind him, made an excellent impression as Banquo, and Cleva conducted strongly. As a matter of fact, everything Tozzi did during his first San Francisco season—Ramfis was another assignment—was very successful. Here was a lyric bass of the highest class. He did not return during the following two seasons, except in one pre-season concert, but later he became a regular, and distinguished, member of the roster, especially in the lyric repertory for which he is best fitted.

A revival of *Louise* with Kirsten and Sullivan was coolly received, as if Charpentier's love letter to Paris was sealed with too much sentiment. The two performances were conducted with the appropriate subdued ecstasy by Jean Morel, but this didn't fill seats. Morel's *Carmen* was disappointingly ultra-refined, bloodless and clipped. Nor did Bizet's opera get a fair account on stage. Worst of all was Lewis' tiptoeing vocalism as Don José. One could be thankful for a tastefully quiet conclusion to the Flower Song, but too often the lack of full weight of tone color was extremely tantalizing. Luckily this demonstration—at Lewis' debut—was not typical, and almost everything he did afterwards was infinitely more effective.

The Carmen, Nell Rankin, was so straight-laced she rejected amorous byplay from the male chorus. The Escamillo was not particularly convincing from the dramatic point of view, but his voice had the ring of great promise. This was a gentleman named Cornell MacNeil.[5]

A *Lohengrin* revival had no swan and an Italian conductor (Cleva). A vertical shaft of Herr Kerz' light signified the presence of the swan, in accordance with his timely interest in painting "with light" rather than "on scenery." Brian Sullivan's lyrical performance in the title role (at a fee of $800) was one of the best things he did in San Francisco, and MacNeil was a truly trumpety Herald. Borkh was the intense Elsa, her husband Alexander Welitsch a less than vintage Telramund. Nell Rankin sang Ortrud, Otto Edelmann King Henry. Edelmann was engaged principally for his well-regarded Baron Ochs in *Rosenkavalier*. Certainly his buffo-cantate singing, authoritative jollity and perfect Viennese dialect produced a fine one.

The Marschallin was sung by Elisabeth Schwarzkopf, who made her American operatic debut on the Opera House stage September 20. In an interview the 39-year old soprano, an early starter, noted that she did not sing so much in opera anymore, and indeed, she had something resembling a phobia about the supposed pressures of opera engagements in the U.S. But Adler had met her after a concert in Los

147

Angeles and persuaded her to come. His persuasion was San Francisco's gain; her highly inflected and near-youthful interpretation of the Marschallin was, if not agreeable to all, on a very high plane of distinction. With Frances Bible an excellent Octavian, Dorothy Warenskjold a charming Sophie, and Leinsdorf in the pit, this was a *Rosenkavalier* which set a standard for seasons to come.

Schwarzkopf also sang Donna Elvira in a Leinsdorf-conducted *Don Giovanni* which concluded without the jocose final ensemble. There was a new series of projections designed by Kerz, but the slides were too bright, the lighting in front of the three arches from 1952 too dark. Albanese switched from Zerlina to Donna Anna, and this was one of the more controversial assignments of the season. Opinions ranged from extremely favorable to a good deal less than that. Cesare Siepi was the Don.

If *Don Giovanni* lacked only its finale, *Coq D'Or*, revived after thirteen years, was stitched together with a number of its parts missing, the abridgement allowing a pairing with *Pagliacci*. The production used the vintage Remisoff sets. Mattiwilda Dobbs, the first black to join the roster, was a good if not remarkable Queen, Alvary an agreeable Dodon, and Raymond Manton, a local lyric tenor, handled the Astrologer's tricky part well.

Renata Tebaldi finally returned after a five year absence—meanwhile she had joined the Met—and conquered as Aida, Tosca, and Madeleine in *Chenier*. The partnership of Tebaldi, Tucker and Warren in the Giordano set off a healthy lot of sparks. She was less fortunate in her *Aida* tenor, on Opening Night and in two subsequent performances, this being the robust but ordinary Roberto Turrini. *Tosca* had only a single performance as a non-subscription event October 19, and it was a night to remember. The first act ended with an under-par Te Deum, and Curiel, the evening's conductor, was fuming backstage. But then something happened which stamped the evening as memorable. In excellent voice, and with superb control, Tebaldi put across a "Vissi d'arte" which seemed to hypnotize the audience, and when they recovered from its spell they broke into wild applause. After several minutes Curiel was faced with a decision on an encore. Adler was not in his box at that point, so it was up to the conductor to decide. He opted for the repeat, and Weede, the Scarpia, politely turned his back to the audience as Tebaldi began the aria again.

In the years to follow, Adler insisted more than once that she sang it less well the second time.

The encore brought the usual scoldings in the press, talk of a claque and ruined continuity, and a backstage scolding for Curiel by Adler—while Tebaldi walked serenely by. Yes, there is a No Encore rule, and for good reason, but every few years the bonds have to be broken. To say that many in the audience were worried about the continuity would be pedantic in the extreme. As for the claque, there has been no such thing, the management insists, in recent years. A claque leader who came from the East was politely but firmly told not to operate.

Aida was performed in "revised" settings (that means *not* a new production) with projections by the busy Kerz. The vast figure of a Sphinx projected in the Temple Scene was a notable artistic addition. The Triumphal Scene was less gaudy and gala than usual; more modern, rather, and stylized. The effect was neat and imposing, but there's a good deal to be said for old-fashioned pomp in this context.

The Los Angeles season added *Butterfly* to the repertoire, with an interesting cast including Lewis as Pinkerton along with Kirsten and MacNeil. Curiel conducted. In nearby Pasadena a "gala evening" of operatic scenes included, among other things, the second act of *Rigoletto* with Dobbs, Peerce and MacNeil, and Act 2 of *Traviata* with Albanese, Fredericks and Weede. The visit to the south was financially triumphant, the fourteen performances in Los Angeles taking in $316,000 as opposed to the $228,000 which thirteen shows had brought the previous season. At home, too, attendance was up.

Following the 1954 and 1955 seasons it was obvious that Adler was carrying the ball without any serious directorial fumbles. Indeed, he was bringing a freshness and excitement to the repertoire and staging which was commendable. There were instances of over-emphasis in one direction or another, and perpetuations of certain routines, but the basic impulses were sound and encouraging. So, in 1956, Adler's title was lengthened to Artistic and Musical Director, and in 1957

149

he became General Director, that being the title Merola held for so many years.

1956

If a production can be said to be lovable such was the San Francisco Opera's first *Cosi Fan Tutte*—until, that is, it became tacky and had to be replaced. It was unveiled October 2, 1956 in George Jenkins' admirably light and tasteful rococo-modern settings and immediately found a place in the hearts of the patrons. The genius of Mozart was well served by an enthusiastic cast consisting of Schwarzkopf, Nell Rankin, Patrice Munsel, Richard Lewis, Frank Guarrera and Alvary, with Hans Schwieger conducting, and Paul Hager in charge of the stage. The comedy of the piece came through with a mixture of laughs and style, and while cuteness had more of an upper hand than Da Pontean cynicism, this was a production that, in total spirit, really clicked—as Mozart productions, it must be said, had not always done in San Francisco. Ticket demand was high enough a third performance was added to the scheduled two.

There was no contemporary opera in 1956, but there were new stagings—controversial ones, too—of *Walküre* and *Boris*, plus the first *Boccanegra* in fifteen years, and the first *Falstaff* in eight. Not to mention the American debuts of sopranos Leonie Rysanek, Birgit Nilsson and Leyla Gencer, mezzo Oralia Dominguez, baritone Anselmo Colzani, bass Boris Christoff and conductor Oliviero De Fabritiis.

Furthermore, soprano Eileen Farrell sang for the first time with a "major" operatic organization, and an expatriate tenor named Richard Martell was given special opportunities to shine. La Scala baritone Rolando Panerai and the Yugoslavian conductor Lovro von Matacic were also supposed to be on the roster, but didn't make it to San Francisco. Nor did Cleva, busy at the Met.

Reappearance of *The Flying Dutchman* served to introduce Vienna's warm-voiced Rysanek in one of her best roles—the one that opens with that haunting pianissimo. Following the *Dutchman*, which was solidly, perhaps too solidly conducted by Steinberg, she sang Aida and her impassioned Sieglinde, the latter in a Kerz-designed *Walküre* with Nilsson as Brünnhilde and Hotter as Wotan, Schwieger conducting. Needless to say, it was full of vocal splendors, but at the same time it offered some visual curiosities. Modern man need not worry much over Wotan's having given up his big eyepatch, but did Brünnhilde have to wear that dowdy, institutional dress? And did the rocks of the third act have to be reached by pink onyx steps? The Valkyries had ponytail haircuts which were not unattractive, and Hunding's hut, if it did have touches of the contemporary suburban tract home, had its decorative points. But one came away with the feeling of much visual distraction. The production was replaced, following an altered 1963 repeat, when the handsome new *Ring* came into being in the late '60's. Comparisons would be unkind.

The new *Boris*, another effort by the briefly ubiquitous Kerz—it was sung by Christoff and associates in Russian—was even more problematical. Actually there were some strokes of great artistic beauty (the simple Revolutionary Scene with its stark downward daggers had visual merits beyond the fairy tale literalism of the older version), but removing the pomp and glitter from the Coronation Scene coldly negated the point of the matter. It had been thought that the music and costumes would provide enough of the requisite peasant color, and that the stern daggers, lowered to different levels in various scenes, would have strong symbolic value. But all the open space worked against the best acoustic interests of the chorus, and when Christoff insisted on certain trappings, they collided with the aesthetic of the production.

As far as Christoff's interests were concerned, the company had specifically inquired of the Hurok office whether the basso would be offended by an untraditional staging. The answer was in the negative, but it was also incorrect. When the Bulgarian basso arrived, he didn't like the production at all. Furthermore, he had an argument with Steinberg, who had replaced Von Matacic as conductor, and left a rehearsal to go off and sulk in his dressing room. Swallowing his dissatisfaction somewhat, he ultimately did perform as advertised. The relatively lyric, formal approach was a change from the frenzied Rossi-Lemeni manner with its near-Sprechstimme. Both interpretations, of course, had much to offer. Elsewhere in the cast Lewis was a vivid Dimitri, Curzi a pointed Shouisky, Hotter a powerful Rangoni, and Alvary a Varlaam who didn't overdo the clowning.

151

The *Francesca* project stemmed from the fact that Tebaldi was learning the role for the Maggio Musicale in Florence. When that festival dropped the work she was less interested in doing it for San Francisco. It was more feasible for Adler to go ahead with a substitute soprano than a substitute opera—the production was already built when the unwooable Tebaldi made her decision—so Leyla Gencer, a Turkish soprano with Italian opera experience, was imported. She turned out to be an exceptionally interesting if uneven artist. Her physical beauty at that time was marked, her poise sure, her pianissimi exquisite, and her voice in general, when well-projected, remarkably warm in tone. Whether she made more or less of *Francesca* than Tebaldi might have done is one of history's little question marks.

In any event, the opera—which dates from 1914 and has not been done at the Met since 1918—was not really worth doing. It has some sweeping love music of a Richard Straussian sort, and the end of the first act, with the solo viola and lute providing a nice medieval color, is especially felicitous. But much of the score, related to Puccini, Giordano, Montemezzi, Wagner, Debussy, is derivative and not very interesting. Zandonai's opera, which might, incidentally, be called *L'Amore dei Tre Fratelli*, is akin to Montemezzi's *L'Amore dei Tre Re* in that both are romantic-medieval tales set to music at a time when verismo was at its height in the Italian lyric theater.[6] Colzani and Curzi as the two disagreeable brothers offered particularly vivid portrayals, the uninhibited Colzani almost chewing the scenery in the fiery finale.

Tebaldi's roles for '56 were Tosca, which she sang beautifully, sans encore, and Amelia in *Boccanegra*, a part she did learn for San Francisco. She sang much of it well, but there was a disconcerting lack of volume control: the tone could get hard and explosive. Martell, an American from Paris, was the Cavaradossi of the first *Tosca*. His compact voice was not of ideal size for the house, but there was some nice dulcet vocalism along the way, and his handsome appearance and lively acting acility were points in favor. Bjoerling, absent for five years, was the second Mario. Warren and Colzani shared the Scarpias, indicating that the Roman police department was well-staffed.

Eileen Farrell was introduced as Leonora in *Trovatore* at a

152

Sunday matinee, and, barring some shrill tones while warming up, the heroically-scaled soprano sang in the Grand Manner. She acted hardly at all, but her stage experience was limited. Most of her impressive career had, of course, been in radio and concert. The Mexican Dominguez (with La Scala performances to her credit) was a relatively refined but vocally distinguished Azucena. Bjoerling and Colzani helped make this 1956 *Trovatore* an afternoon's entertainment which the buffs still talk about fondly.[7]

Dominguez was also a young-looking Quickly in *Falstaff*. Warren took over the title role, singing it sonorously and pointedly, and making more of the joviality than one might have expected—although, at a rehearsal, he snapped at Schwarzkopf, the Mistress Ford, when she got in his way as he perched in the laundry basket. Schwarzkopf was, of course, the sort of prima donna who could put *him* in his place. Audrey Schuh, a young soprano who had sung in New Orleans, was an attractive Nanetta, and the Fenton was Giuseppe Campora of the Met, who displayed an extremely attractive voice and an occasional coarseness of style. He was also heard in a dismal stepchild revival of *L'Elisir d'Amore* with Munsel as Adina and Tajo Dulcamara. The latter was in particularly bad voice and Curiel had trouble holding the ensemble together. Some of the magic of 1948 was needed. Panerai's replacement, as Belcore in *L'Elisir* and as Lescaut in the *Manon Lescaut* which opened the season, was Louis Quilico, a highly promising young Canadian who'd sung at New York's City Center.[8]

Most of the Italian repertory was conducted by Oliviero De Fabritiis, the well-known Rome Opera maestro. His conducting was authoritative but tended toward the phlegmatic. With Met openings moving up into late October Cleva was no longer available, and a strong replacement was needed. De Fabritiis didn't seem to be quite the man.

The Los Angeles season was more profitable than ever, eight of the fifteen performances in the 6500-seat Shrine being sold out. Average attendance approached 6000! The southerly proceedings began with a *Manon Lescaut* which had better pace and fewer kinks than the one which had opened the home season. The dressy audience which crossed a red carpet into the exotico-prosaic, unfashionably located

153

Shrine knew they were hearing a good show. Kirsten and Bjoerling were joined on this occasion by Frank Guarrera, a new Lescaut, and there was plenty of applause for all. But the enthusiasm meter in Los Angeles oscillated with special brio at the end of the first act of a *Bohème* with Albanese and Peerce. The fact that the Shrine's resonant acoustics result in a situation wherein applause tends to breed applause did no harm.

Productions in the Shrine could suffer from the toy look of a normal-sized stage picture set inside an overly large proscenium, but audiences and singers alike found the acoustics suprisingly good for such a cavernous hall—many singers, in fact, admitted that they could feel their voices floating out to the audience better than they could in San Francisco's Opera House. Another Los Angeles asset was the advantage of operas having been performed once, twice or three times before in San Francisco. It's not an infallible rule that succeeding performances are better than earlier ones, but, to give one instance, Tebaldi caught the stride of Amelia in a *Boccanegra* that was more flexibly sung than those which San Francisco heard. The overly open-voiced Turrini, ending an inexplicably long attachment with the company, repeated his San Francisco Adorno and added Cavaradossi in Los Angeles.

1957

Contemporary opera returned with the American premiere of Francis Poulenc's finespun *Dialogues of the Carmelites* September 20, eight months following the work's world premiere at La Scala. Leinsdorf conducted the triadic-beatific score with conviction, and the strong cast sang clear English. Harry Horner's sets were placed on a revolving stage and could be swung into place without unduly long waits between scenes.[9] Introduced to San Francisco as Mme. Lidoine, the new Prioress, was a young black soprano with *Porgy and Bess* and NBC Television Opera experience. Her name: Leontyne Price. She sang the role with rare charm and lovely tone, but there was no clear indication this girl would turn into one of the great Aidas. In San Francisco her opportunities were to grow, as indeed her voice itself evolved into a big dramatic instrument.

154

Another debutante was Sylvia Stahlman,[10] a pure-toned lyric soprano with just the right sort of light-textured sound for Sister Constance. Dorothy Kirsten was in the central role, Blanche de la Force.

These ladies and their colleagues projected movingly the story of a band of nuns sentenced to the guillotine during the French Revolution. Set against their collective story is that of the timid, confused Blanche, who joins the Carmelite order as a refuge from her fear of life and finally wins over her fear of death (the same thing?) by going, in her moment of truth, to the guillotine with equanimity. Poulenc's score, which is sweet but chilling too, is dedicated to Debussy, Monteverdi, Moussorgsky and Verdi, and there's no question that Debussy and Moussorgsky were strong influences. But in spirit the music is descended, most of all, from a long line of French composers including Couperin, Berlioz, Fauré. It is not derivative, but simply a logical and unhurrying followup to an old tradition of tastefully sugared musical expression.

The *Carmelites* was received with moderate to warm enthusiasm—Claramae Turner, the First Prioress, had a big success with her death scene, and Price won prolonged applause for her beautifully spun-out lyric passage in the prison. The show was entertaining enough that a third performance was added, a special attraction presented in connection with an International Industrial Development Conference under *Time-Life* auspices. In the last analysis, *The Carmelites* provided a theatrical experience so freshly moving that some of the conventional operas which followed seemed rather more melodramatic and deficient in thought than usual. The passage of time has underlined the tepidities and monochrome aspects of the score, but the first flush of *The Carmelites* was really appealing.

The elusive Maria Callas had been signed for the 1957 season January 3, and when September arrived the public was anticipating with great interest her scheduled appearances in Verdi's *Macbeth* and Donizetti's *Lucia*. But in the papers of September 13—Opening Night was four days off—San Franciscans read that Adler was checking into indications Callas planned to cancel her engagement with the company. She had withdrawn from an "extra" performance with La Scala at the Edinburgh Festival after an August 29 *Sonnam-*

bula because the cold air in that city, not to mention a bothersome case of nervous exhaustion, was giving her serious trouble. The report in the San Francisco papers on September 17 was this: the diva's husband Meneghini said Madame Callas would be happy to sing four performances with the San Francisco Opera beginning October 15. But her first *Lucia* was scheduled for September 27, her second October 5, and her first *Macbeth* October 11!

The report continued with a statement of the position of the San Francisco Opera, which was, not surprisingly, that Madame Callas was fired, and that a complaint, furthermore, was being sent off to the American Guild of Musical Artists (AGMA). The fact that a recording of Cherubini's *Medea* was on the ailing Callas' September schedule—sessions took place from the 12th to the 19th—did not sit exactly well with Adler and Miller. Nor the fact that she "rested up" by going to an early September ball tossed for her in Venice by Elsa Maxwell. Callas had wired Adler September 1 that he should have a sub on hand "in case." But Callas' logical followup, in Adler's estimation, would have been either to come on schedule and *try* to perform, or to cancel outright, and stay home. Most subscribers felt Adler and Miller were to be commended for their uncompromising action, and after Leonie Rysanek's Lady Macbeth and Leyla Gencer's Lucia— both highly successful—Maria Callas was, if not forgotten, hardly missed.

AGMA ultimately released a reprimand in which it was concluded that Callas was "not wholly justified" in her failure to fulfill the contract. "There is reason to believe," it said, "on the basis of medical statements submitted, that Maria Meneghini Callas would have been justified in not performing because of her physical and emotional condition at the time. But the board further finds that, in fact, Maria Meneghini Callas did not rely entirely upon the medical advice, and, in fact, indicated to the San Francisco Opera Association her willingness to perform during a portion of the period covered by the contract. In view of these circumstances and other incidents testified to before the Board demonstrating that she did not rely entirely upon medical advice, the Board concludes, and is of the opinion that she was under an obligation to come to the United States at the time called for by her contract with the San Francisco Opera."

156

On the heels of the Callas affair came Antonietta Stella's cancellation for an appendectomy—she'd been slated for Aida and Amelia in *Ballo*. Rysanek, originally engaged for title roles in *Turandot* and *Ariadne*, took on not only Callas' two San Francisco Lady Macbeths but one each of Stella's Aidas and Amelias in addition. The Amelia she sang in German to the rest of the cast's Italian, the opera becoming monolingual again when Herva Nelli came out for the second performance.

Turandot opened the season September 17 and also served to introduce to America the well-liked little maestro who became the chief conductor of the Italian wing for nine seasons, Francesco Molinari-Pradelli. His dependability, his musicality, the grace and punch of his phrasing, and his feeling for overall continuity: all stamped him as a sensible man to have around. With Molinari there could be evenings of less than ultimate involvement, and a tendency to shy away from capital I Interpretation made now and then for disappointment. But often he proved a stylish, satisfying pilot, especially in Verdi.[11]

There were three *Aidas* at home in '57. Two were taken by the new Miss Price who'd been planning to sing her first Nile Scene at a later date in Vienna. *Turandot* was not only played in the Opera House but taken across the bay to Hearst Greek Theater on the University of California's Berkeley campus, the performance initiating a custom of one open-air Sunday matinee per year which lasted through 1969, when financial problems intervened. The Bay Area's customary Indian Summer stamped many of these performances as sun-baked affairs. Always they were pleasantly al fresco.

Ariadne joined the repertoire October 8 in a charming production with scenery by Jenkins, the *Cosi* man, stage direction by the regularly reappearing Hager, and Steinberg in the pit prior to his annual return to the Pittsburgh Symphony podium. The prologue, with its long stretches of marvelously unctuous spoken pronouncements from the Major Domo, was wisely given in English (a custom not presently followed at the Met), the more lyrical opera itself in German. The silvery light vocalism of Rita Streich, a German lyric coloratura making her first U.S. appearances, was capital in the role of Zerbinetta. On the other hand, her Sophie in *Rosenkavalier* was not as romantic-looking or spontaneously acted as it might have been. The 1955 combination of Schwarzkopf-Bible-Edelmann-Leinsdorf was back in this opera, as was the Schwarzkopf-Lewis-Alvary lineup in the rerun of the 1956 *Cosi*. Nan Merriman, the noted mezzo, was a good-looking, vocally superb Dorabella, and Southern California's Heinz Blankenburg—moving up in the operatic world—a thoroughly first-rate Guglielmo. Streich was Despina, Leinsdorf conducted.

Gencer's Lucia was not of the pretty-pretty pyrotechnical variety. Here was a warm spinto soprano who simply happened to have coloratura flexibility as well. The richness of her voice which, like Callas', had a certain sonic sex appeal, helped produce an adult Lucia. Also the vivid acting: she conveyed a real sense of derangement in the Mad Scene. All in all this was the most memorable portrayal offered in San Francisco by a sometimes remarkable artist. Her success in the part indicated that another reengagement was in order, and she returned in 1958. Her other '57 assignments were Violetta and Liu, the latter only in Los Angeles.

The impressive baritone Giuseppe Taddei made his American debut on Van Ness Avenue as Macbeth, following this with Scarpia. In Los Angeles he added two Enricos in *Lucia*. Taddei was a fine addition to the roster, but why an obscure, rough-sounding colleague named Umberto Borghi was imported made little sense. Robert Merrill, the Met stalwart, was also among the baritones.

The tenor register went through a crisis in the late 50's. Tucker did not return after 1955, and Del Monaco was absent from 1952 to 1959. When Bjoerling did come—in '56 and '58—it was, by design or not, only for a few performances. Interesting tenors appeared, for instance Lewis and Martell, but there was a need during the seasons 1956–58 for at least one big-league Italian dramatic or spinto tenor who combined suavity and fire in equal proportions. Eugene Tobin, an American in Stuttgart, was the Calaf and Rhadames in 1957, and while he had solid merits—Adler's bringing back experienced American singers from Europe has sometimes proved a highly rewarding policy—he was not the ultra-magnetic and polished singer needed to take on all the season's performances of *Turandot* and *Aida*. The following year Piero Miranda Ferrero was less good. And Jon Crain, who sang Cavaradossi during the 1957 season, didn't have the vocal strength for an Opera House *Tosca*. Gianni Raimondi, the estimable La Scala tenor, appeared in '57 and '58, evidently not at his best.

In *Tosca*, by the way, Leinsdorf's relatively Germanic approach caused at least one member of the orchestra to relabel his part *Das Tosca*.

The Achilles Heel aspect of the somewhat lackluster tenor rosters lay, aside from purely musical considerations, in the fact that some of the customers are especially conscious of "name" singers and the absence thereof. It must be stressed that numerous singers who have appeared in San Francisco have shown themselves to be important artists despite their lack of star fame. But Adler did need more glamor than he brought into the tenor department, and he left himself open to possible sniping. Sniping there was—indeed, cries for impeachment—when the situation piled up in 1958.

1958

After the war the San Francisco Opera seasons were usually five weeks long, give or take a day or two. In 1957 the length rose to thirty-eight days, and in 1958 home activities were leveled off at six weeks. The Regular Series grew from ten to eleven performances, and each of the popular series from five to six. The schedule remained highly concentrated, but by no means as squeezed as some of the early five week ones in the 40's when non-subscription performances were piled high within thirty-four days. The increase in the proportion of Thursday and Saturday Evening Series performances— slightly cheaper and less dressy than those of the Regular Series—was a distinct boon to the public.

Not since the *Ring* year of 1935 had there been so many additions to the repertoire as in 1958. Verdi's *Don Carlo*, Cherubini's *Medea* and a Carl Orff double bill, consisting of *Die Kluge* (1942) and *Carmina Burana* (1937), were all new. *Medea* and *Carmina* received their first staged performances in America—the American premiere of *Carmina*, in concert version, had taken place in San Francisco in 1954— and *Die Kluge*, presented in English as *The Wise Maiden*, was given its first American performance in any guise. There were also revivals of two long withdrawn operas: *Bartered Bride*, last heard in 1942 and offered in a new production, and *Tannhäuser*, silent since 1941. In line with the theory that standard rep should be visually freshened, *Bohème* was given in a new production financed by the Guild.

Singers in American debuts included soprano Eugenia Ratti, tenor Sebastian Feiersinger, baritone Rolando Panerai and basses Giuseppe Modesti and Arnold Van Mill. Conductors new to the U.S. were Leopold Ludwig and Jean Fournet. San Francisco favorites Rysanek, Schwarzkopf, Price and Farrell were on hand,[12] and sopranos Lisa Della Casa and Christel Goltz, and mezzos Grace Hoffman and Irene Dalis—the latter from nearby San Jose—joined the roster.

Dalis appeared first in one of her best roles, Eboli in *Don Carlo*. She swung into it with a fiery regality and sang it warmly, winning friends who would welcome her back in many seasons to come. She shared top honors in the first two performances with Tozzi, whose limping, swaggering Philip was a stage portrait drawn with great imagination and style, certainly one of the best all-around characterizations he offered through the years of personages more interesting than the stock Ramfis and Zaccaria types. Frank Guarrera was a vivid Rodrigo, Piero Miranda Ferraro a so-so Don Carlo. No soprano has ever known better than Leyla Gencer how to stand about looking noble, but her vocal projection in the role of Elisabetta was spotty. As Molinari-Pradelli was unable to return this particular year—there was illness in his family—George Sebastian was brought back for the Italian wing.[13] In general this proved a mistake—Adler's alternate thought was the well-remembered Perlea, who was not in the best of health—but Sebastian did understand well the somber atmosphere of *Don Carlo* and put it over with grip and thrust. Especially at the first performance, when tempos were on the slow side, and effective in a brooding sort of way.

There were some interesting additions and subtractions when a new cast took over at an added third performance—proof, this "encore," that the subtleties of *Don Carlo* can take hold at the box office. Van Mill was a more stolid Philip than Tozzi but his formidable approach made sense. Grace Hoffman sang well as Eboli but didn't provide the electricity

160

Dalis put into the role. Goltz was a matronly, tremulous Elisabetta, and one preferred to remember her stupendous Elektra of a few days before. In Strauss' opera she sounded like the owner of the world's richest, creamiest voice, and she romped up and down the Horner set in the approved manner.

Elektra provided Van Mill with his entry music, and his rock-like, grandly sonorous Orestes goes down as one of the more commanding things in San Francisco Opera history. The *Don Carlo* sets, a mixture of fact and fancy striking for their vastness, were borrowed from the Chicago Lyric Opera, thanks to a new—if briefly invoked—agreement which sent San Francisco's *Turandot*, and later its *Cosi*, eastward.

Medea was the Opening Night fare, and not ideal material for that evening: starch is all right in tired businessmen's boiled shirts but not on stage when the season's curtain is rung up. But there were some cheers for Eileen Farrell, who portrayed the heroine, that tigress on a hot tin operatic roof. At first her sustained tones were thin and tremulous, but as the evening progressed, her beautiful voice became more lustrous and secure, its huge tone under control. She didn't move around much, but there was action in her singing. Sylvia Stahlman was an excellent Glauce, and Richard Lewis, if not ideally suited to the role vocally, was a lively, stylish Jason.

Modesti showed off a truly beautiful lyric bass as Creon, displayed it well during the rest of the season, but regrettably did not return.

Medea dates from 1797, its modern revival from a series of performances with Callas in Italy, the first at the Florence May Festival of 1953. Farrell had sung it in a concert version in New York with the American Opera Society. The score is reminiscent of Cherubini's older contemporaries Gluck and Mozart in the fragile elegance and poignant expressiveness of much of its melody. For all its formality, magnified by the Lachner recitatives replacing original spoken dialogue, *Medea* still lives as a viable musico-dramatic experience and is certainly worth reviving occasionally. Waldemar Johansen provided the starkly simple, lightweight sets.

Carl Orff remains something of a controversial figure, paradoxically because his music is written in the simplest of styles. The oft-repeated rhythm is his trademark, the diatonic scale his favorite. Some people relish his music, others can't stand its unsubtle insistence. There doesn't seem to be much question, though, about the Bavarian composer's vivid orchestration: the Orffian orchestra tinkles with ravishing delicacy and thumps with terrific vigor. Judging by the exuberant applause which followed *Carmina*, the public in large part voted for Orff. *Die Kluge*, with its large percentage of spoken dialogue, would have been a dead loss in German, but in the English of Jane Mayhall and Otto Guth its rustic and rather roguish fairy tale spirit came through.[14]

The charming sets by Jean-Pierre Ponnelle, a precocious 26-year-old French designer with a light romantic-surrealist bent—and some mature triumphs as a director-designer in his San Francisco future—helped a lot.

Die Kluge was staged in "peasant theater" style with boards on barrels and three long-nosed, puffed-cheek puppet musicians sitting on a rope-hung ladder above the stage. Aptly enough, *Carmina* was done up more elegantly, with the all-important choristers placed in small groups around a semicircle and plenty of space in front for soloists and ballet. Orff intended his *Carmina* to be staged and it is eminently worthwhile to do so, but this "scenic cantata" is more a pageant than an opera of action. So Hager's problem was a big one. He solved it reasonably well: the movements seemed neither unduly forced and cluttered nor static. The lighting was magnificent, and the way the costumes were spotlighted at the end of the scene in the Court of Love will long be remembered. Incidentally, Adler, Hager and Ponnelle conferred with Orff on this production in Munich.

Leontyne Price and Lawrence Winters, a Hamburg-based black baritone who died prematurely in 1965, had the leading roles in *Die Kluge*. She was altogether enchanting as the wise maiden, and he acted superbly the role of the inept, lecherous king. The sympathetic conductor of the double bill was Hamburg's general music director Leopold Ludwig, a musician who made a good initial impression but whose San Francisco career, extending to 1968, proved *over*extended. One of the year's Auditions winners, Robert Thomas, a bright, strong-voiced tenor, formed a third of the Ping-Pang-Pongish trio of vagabonds in *Kluge*. Following his namesake Jess, he went on to major roles, at Zurich and Düsseldorf.

162

Schwarzkopf, Lewis, Tozzi and Howard Fried, an amusing Vashek from New York, were the leads in a new and pleasant production of *Bartered Bride*, sung in English. *Tannhäuser* provided the first real opportunity to hear Feiersinger, the new Austrain heldentenor—he had been introduced as Aegisthus in *Elektra*, not a character who has much to do, telling as that little can be. Although his projection was not always ideal, the relatively lyrical phrasing and suave sound he put forth were superior to that of some of the available brethren. (This was before the heyday of Messrs. King, Thomas and Vickers in the Wagnerian realm.) With Rysanek, Hoffman and Van Mill on stage, this *Tannhäuser* gave scant opportunities to those old gremlins Wobble and Shriek.

Demonstrating that it was by no means simply a friend of the ultra-standard repertoire, the public registered sufficient interest to allow third performances of *Bartered Bride* and *Tannhäuser*. *Bohème*, the popularity of which never surprises anybody, was offered in all three series, with new scenery by Jenkins. He was especially successful in the second act, providing a set which really looked like a Parisian cafe, complete with tables outside and an interior bar. The first and fourth acts were problematical because the action was put on a puppet platform several feet above the stage with lots of empty space on each side. A lowering and spreading of the set was indicated, and the appropriate changes were made the following season. Della Casa was surprising casting for Mimi, but her velvety voice and meaningful acting were clear assets. Certainly she brought out the fact that the frail embroideress has in her character a touch of Manon Lescaut.

Jean Fournet, the well-known French conductor, was by no means out of his element in *Bohème*—a mixture of shimmering precision, symphonic sweep and warm emotion came out of the pit—but in his home territory of Massenet's *Manon* he was strangely ineffective. Gallic neatness and clarity ruled, and the passion was left singularly untattered. Come to think of it, one hears this sort of over-mild performance in Paris often. Gencer's Manon was argued over, and Lewis sang Des Grieux with the same maddening tonal tiptoeing he employed in *Carmen* in '55. But his "Le Rêve" was one of the finest in the history of the War Memorial.

Leontyne Price sang her first *Trovatore* Leonora September

163

26, and once warmed up she performed with a special elegance and radiance of tone. Bjoerling, who was scheduled for *Don Carlo* earlier in the season, pleaded delay from Europe but did arrive in time for this performance. He seemed distracted and at times bumbled about the stage absentmindedly. Furthermore, his voice sounded tired. But a few days later at the Fol de Rol he was in much better shape. *Trovatore* and *Forza* both suffered from the soggy, bumpy conducting of Sebastian: the ill-phrased overture to *Forza* was surely one of the worst-judged things to happen in a San Francisco Opera autumn.

Weede, who had been on Broadway in *Most Happy Fella*, returned as Don Carlo in *Forza* and as Rigoletto, singing beautifully some of the time, and growling now and again. Obviously his voice needed a rest following the Broadway grind.

Taddei returned, too, but only in the title role of *Gianni Schicchi*, nicely tossed off as a curtain-raiser to *Elektra*. The modestly successful Rinuccio was one Richard Miller, an American who had appeared at the Zurich Opera. He was hired as a replacement for Curzi, who couldn't obtain a release from German obligations. He was rather out of his element singing Almaviva in an Opera House *Barber of Seville*, his delicate diminuendos into something close to silence being altogether too negative for that auditorium if not without some style. Eugenia Ratti's Rosina was marred by dainty shrieks for top tones but otherwise commendable.

Panerai was a large-voiced and exceptionally lively Figaro who raced to and fro like a kitten intrigued by everything around him. The portrayal looked like a delightfully impulsive improvisation, but the consensus of press reaction to Panerai's spontaneity was negative.

In Los Angeles there were a few noteworthy changes from the San Francisco casts. Bjoerling did sing Don Carlo, Tozzi took over Guardiano from Modesti, Alvary the Rossini Basilio from Tozzi, and Dorothy Kirsten, who didn't appear at all in San Francisco, was heard as Mimi in her city of residence. Farrell was indisposed for her *Trovatore* Leonora, so Price flew back from the East to do it.

While the company was in Los Angeles, a number of San Franciscans were grumbling about their 1958 season. The absence of Molinari-Pradelli, the late arrival of Bjoerling, the fact that the thriving San Francisco Ballet was off on a foreign tour and had to be replaced—all these things hurt. Following a post-season board meeting Robert Watt Miller announced that the Association fully recognized, and regretted, certain artistic weaknesses which resulted from these factors. Still, the nagging continued in some quarters. There had, as a matter of fact, been a strong current of discredit campaigning during the 1958 season. The morning after the new *Bartered Bride* was unveiled, newspaper critics received anonymously dispatched telegrams telling them if they had any courage they would condemn the show as a hopeless waste of time and money. Meanwhile, a rather squelchy critique of the San Francisco Opera by Roger Dettmer, the informed but acerbic critic of *Chicago's American*, was being circulated to the press.

Actually, *Don Carlo*, *Medea*, *Carmina Burana*, *Die Kluge*, *Tannhäuser*, *Bohème*, *Elektra* and *Schicchi* (six complete bills, that is) all received performances which in many, if not all, respects would have been difficult to surpass. It's true there were real problems in the *Trovatore*, *Forza*, *Barber*, *Marriage of Figaro* (inflexibly conducted by Adler himself) and *Manon*. And it may be granted that some Janacek would have been more engrossing than *Bartered Bride*. All this is why 1958 does not add up as one of the great all-around seasons. But there were fine things in it.

Miller and Adler were sufficiently concerned to make sure they hired a top tenor like Del Monaco for 1959. Presumably the statute of limitations had run out over his problematical cancellation in 1953. With Jon Vickers and Giuseppe Zampieri also on hand, not to mention Lewis, the tenor department revived markedly. As if to set the right mood, the gentlemen running the company decided to open the next season with a strongly-cast, sure-fire *Aida*.

1959

One of the company's greater coups came September 18, 1959 with the U.S. premiere of Richard Strauss' 40-year-old *Die Frau Ohne Schatten*, an opera Adler had become fond of as a young man in Vienna. This is an opera which is supposed to be almost impossible to produce, but there it was on the stage of the War Memorial, a bouncing strapping wonderchild delayed in its American birth until a day when Strauss' style was already that of another era, but also a day when the best of the once-scorned later operas of Strauss were gaining the attention they deserve. Fate had tried to trip up the production: three of the principal singers cancelled their engagements and the scenic designer was drafted into the French Army before the company had all the designs in hand. But obstacles were hurdled, the performances took place, and they reaffirmed the fact that the San Francisco Opera could take on a great challenge and succeed.

There was, in place of the popular Rysanek, who regretfully had to cancel because of illness, a Hamburg-based American named Edith Lang as the Empress. One of the handful of sopranos who had taken up this taxing part, she turned out to be an eminently satisfactory if not ideal substitute. Eleanor Steber, who had been learning the role of Barak's Wife for San Francisco, also bowed out, so Marianne Schech was brought in from Munich. Edelmann, too—not the most logical choice for Barak anyway—was indisposed, and Mino Yahia, an Egyptian-born, New York-raised, German-based psychiatrist-turned-opera singer, got the part. He'd been engaged for some important but less elaborate roles than this and the Don Giovanni he assumed for George London later in the season. Yahia's attractively lyric bass-baritone came in handy. Irene Dalis was the Nurse, Feiersinger the Emperor, young Mary Costa the Guardian of the Temple Gates.

Reading the libretto of *Frau*, with all of Hofmannsthal's elaborate verbal baggage surrounding the essentially simple message, one couldn't help worrying that the opera in performance would sag under all the weight. But in the Opera House, under the spell of the ravishing score and a handsome (if not grandly scaled) production, such dim thoughts could be forgotten. The reception was very enthusiastic, local raves echoed by those from Eastern critics.

At his best, Leopold Ludwig shaped the music with a nice lyrical glow. Jean-Pierre Ponnelle's decoratively spooky sets were handsome, and their lightness enhanced the production's fairy tale touch. Two-level staging was used

166

throughout to accommodate the various worlds of action, and, thanks to a scrim curtain and expert lighting, the vision of the Emperor turning to stone appeared really to be taking place in midair. The third of the five scenes in the second act was omitted, but this small sacrifice was an anti-fatigue factor. After the season was over there was no question about it: *Frau Ohne Schatten* would return in 1960, and with Rysanek herself.

The year's second addition to the repertoire was Gluck's *Orfeo*, the first opera by this composer to be performed by the company. It was greeted with a great deal less enthusiasm than the Strauss, partly because of Gluck's inherent starchiness, and also because of a rather dour, if not unbeautiful production. Invoking the original spirit of the legend, stage director Yannopoulos decided to let Orfeo kill himself after Euridice's second death, thereby avoiding the incongruously happy denouement of the opera as customarily presented. In principle a composer's work should not be tampered with, but Yannopoulos had a point. Orfeo and Euridice were ill-starred lovers, and the prevailing mood of the opera is sorrowful and wistful. Perhaps an 18th century court demanded a happy ending, but does the story?

After "Che faro" and Orfeo's death the Furies rushed in and scooped up the dead lover, to exciting effect. Then, after a pause which was distracting, the audience was taken back to Euridice's tomb and the opening chorus was repeated. Barring the pause, all of this seemed logical and inevitable. Of course the basic problem with *Orfeo* is its static, ceremonial quality, and it's not surprising that after a while the choristers seemed to be posturing self-consciously as if they'd been told to avoid being dull. There was a somber beauty about Waldmar Johansen's basic set, with its Stonehenge effect of rock above an impressive doorway, and the visual symphony of light and shadow was another plus. Silvio Varviso, a young conductor from Basel,[15] presided with great warmth and dignity, but the musical atmosphere was a shade too solemn.

Considering the fact *Orfeo* is not exactly sure-fire entertainment, it's scarcely surprising that Gluck's opera was at the bottom of the box office ladder—along with the fading *L'Amore dei Tre Re*. In the late 1960's Adler considered mounting *Iphigénie en Tauride* for Crespin, but that lady's vocal problems, and other obstacles, perhaps some Glucko-phobia, nixed the project.

The visual freshening of the standard repertoire continuing, the Opera Guild donated a new production of *Carmen* which arrived September 29. When the prelude was struck up, the curtain rose to reveal a special show curtain of fierce waves of red, pink and black. That it looked like an Abstract Ex-pressionist view of a can-can is beside the point because at the same time it suggested all the energy, blood and tension of the story. Although it augured extremely well for the evening, the rest of the scenery was not devoid of problems. Architects of the production were Howard Bay—like Jenkins a veteran of Broadway—who designed the sets and costumes, and Yannopoulos, who did the staging. Their intent was to create a more realistic atmosphere than one often encounters in this opera, and they took *Carmen* back from the standard 1840 to the war-ravaged 1820's where she really belongs. The grisly shadows of Goya's Spain hung over Bay's costumes, and Yannopoulos populated the stage with a wider variety of "real" people than one sometimes sees. The ragamuffins were more rowdy and disheveled than ever.

But Bay's sets were not in the same vein of realism: devilish fancy, instead, was the thing, the scenery providing a rather fantastic counterpart to the action. The effect was extremely brilliant in the first act with its tall clock tower, somewhat questionable in the last with its arena taking off like a slow rocket. Possibly this leavetaking was designed to heighten Don José's derangement, but Jon Vickers, the José in this production, did not emphasize derangement. He remained quite stalwart to the end.

Gloria Lane was a superb Carmen who seemed less a prod-uct of the dressing room than of life itself. Short, extremely bosomy and not made up to look wildly attractive, here was a Carmen who could sing beautifully the evening through without resorting to that self-consciously throaty sexiness of voice some Carmens love.

The Carmen—and the Orfeo—was to have been Risë Stevens. But when, a few months before the season, she de-manded $100 more per evening than anyone else would get, including that anyone's travel expenses, the company refused.

168

A $1,000,000 suit resulted, but it never got to court. Blanche Thebom was the vocally worn but reasonably effective substitute in the Gluck.

The Opening Night *Aida* was a smash. Molinari-Pradelli was back in the pit, and Leontyne Price was in great form on stage. Vickers' Rhadames was velvety in voice and thoughtful in interpretation. His "Celeste Aida," for instance, was more lyrical and deliberate than usual, suggesting that hardhat Rhadames was not a complete extrovert. Vickers didn't quite offer the ultra-liberated top tones of Del Monaco, but there were other advantages. Dalis, Weede and Tozzi also contributed to the evening's sonic pleasures, as did three of the best California talents, Carl Palangi, Robert Thomas and Katherine Hilgenberg (King, Messenger and Priestess, respectively).

Two performances of *Aida* were on the original schedule, but with box office demand high, and Del Monaco in the mood for a Rhadames, a third was added. It served also as the occasion of San Franciscan Lucine Amara's first Aida in a major house. She almost made her listeners believe that a strictly lyric soprano can fill the role satisfactorily: in a dolcissimo passage like that of the third act, wherein Aida tells Rhadames of the appeal of life in Ethiopia, her liquid voice was just right. But often she was overwhelmed and one yearned for more weight.

Del Monaco's first appearance of the season had already occurred in *Andrea Chenier* a few days earlier, and he later came on as Otello. The Madeleine and Desdemona were to have been Rysanek—a big season for her with the Empress, too! Her replacement in the Italian roles was the young Gabriella Tucci, who came on Del Monaco's recommendation— they had sung with Gobbi in Tokyo—and made successful if not epical American debut appearances. The pure, warm tone of her middle register cut through not unlike Tebaldi's, but her voice thinned out somewhat on top and her temperament thinned out, too, at dramatic points where more was needed.

Weede had to give up Iago when personal matters called him away. His place was taken by Mario Zanasi, a lightish baritone from the Met who had offered a pleasant Sharpless and a lackluster Escamillo. His Iago, on the other hand, turned out to be something special: here was a slender, youthful villain who, praise the change, looked and acted like a real schemer instead of a stock heavy. *Otello* audiences are used to darker, richer, heavier voices in the role, but Zanasi put lots of dramatic vocal strength into his performance, and emerged as a meaningful addition to the company.

Tucci was not the only singer to make an American debut during '59. Three important artists, soprano Sena Jurinac, baritone Geraint Evans and tenor Giuseppe Zampieri, were added to the roster. All were successful and all were re-engaged.

Jurinac, for more than a decade a leading soprano light of the Vienna State Opera, was long overdue. She was introduced September 22 in a *Butterfly* which began unpromisingly for Cio-Cio-San with a shrill entrance. But once she found her stride she sang the evening through with a lyric soprano of melting richness. Her Donna Anna, her *Meistersinger* Eva, her Composer in *Ariadne*—all were of high quality. All one could have asked was that she had come a little sooner, before the youthful freshness in her voice had hardened a bit.

Welsh-born Evans came to San Francisco virtually unknown. Possibly a few customers had heard him on one or another Gilbert and Sullivan recording released in the U.S. But his biography included appearances in the title role of *Falstaff* at Glyndebourne and Rodrigo in *Don Carlo* at Covent Garden. He carried the further distinction of being a Commander of the Order of the British Empire. Some of the German aficionados were wondering how an Englishman could be a good Beckmesser, but they needn't have worried. The newcomer triumphed as the man with the slate. Beckmesser is not exactly a lovable character, but Evans made such an impression that the audience applauded him as if he were the conquering hero himself. His characterization recalled an old time movie villain, except that no matter how hard this villain tried to be snakes and daggers he was so engagingly inept one couldn't help feeling sympathetic.

The *Meistersinger* revival boasted the presence of Paul Schoeffler, the reigning Sachs of the post-Schorr generation.[16] There was a fine pair of Pogners in Tozzi and Yahia, a quite lyric Stolzing from Feiersinger, an appealing if vocally

170

Italianate David from Curzi. Ludwig conducted, following a humdrum overture, with fair warmth and style.

Zampieri had begun as a comprimario, going on to leading roles in Italy and Vienna. But few knew about him when he came to San Francisco. His first dulcet pianissimi in *L'Amore dei Tre Re* indicated he would make a fine protagonist of lyric roles like Fenton and Massenet's Des Grieux. But later, when he let go with ringing, dramatic tones, one was almost tempted to think in terms of a ruggeder character like Otello. Pinkerton and Cassio were his other assignments, well served, except for detours into unfocused notes and graceless phrases.

Don Giovanni, thanks to a superior cast, had a vintage year. Price sang her first Elvira on the operatic stage and she sang it with opulence and charm. George London was late in arriving for his duties as the Don, a case of jaundice having gotten in the way. His place was taken by Yahia, who needed to energize his stage movement but sang with mellifluous tone and good style. Tozzi replaced *him* as the Commendatore in the first performance, but Yahia went back to the part of Don Pedro—who can afford to act like a statue—in the second, London having arrived. Local boy Theodor Uppman returned after eleven years with his beautifully sung, jellyfish-gaited Masetto. Pierrette Alarie (Zerlina), Alvary (Leporello) and Lewis (Ottavio) completed the cast. The staging was somewhat more successful than the immediately preceding tries.

Evans was the Music Master and Uppman the Arlecchino in *Ariadne*. Robert Symonds, of the local Actors' Workshop, was an excellent Major Domo, using a snippy, mincing English accent, but it made no sense to have the others perform in German while he spoke in English. Adler was trying to have his cake and eat it too, which is to say Jurinac's Composer, which didn't come in English, along with the advantage of having the talky stretches understandable to the audience. Farrell was the Ariadne this time, and had considerable trouble managing her booming voice. There was some talk of her doing Isolde in 1959—it would have been her first—but this was not to be.

Albanese returned for a remarkably fresh Mimi, in a non-subscription *Bohème*, to round off her two decades of faithful service to the company on Van Ness Avenue. (She filled in for

171

Price in *Butterfly* in Los Angeles two years later.) Mary Costa, a bright girl with a young and varied career spanning TV commercials and a tour of Bernstein's *Candide*, was an impressively spunky, big-toned Musetta. She also appeared in *Carmina Burana*, happily repeated from the previous season and newly paired with *Pagliacci*. In Los Angeles, where houses averaged close to 6000 persons, Tucci took over Donna Anna from Jurinac and Del Monaco the Canio from Vickers.

When all the activities of 1959 were done, there was little question that the year, despite some inevitable disappointments, had been particularly successful. An aura of good feeling hung over the Opera House, not the atmosphere of dissatisfaction which had shadowed 1958.

1960

Having shown in 1959 that *Frau Ohne Schatten* was not too burdensome a production within a tight schedule, the company went on in 1960 to *Wozzeck*, which Adler had long wanted to do. The West Coast premiere took place October 4 —the preparation had included more than two dozen hours of orchestra rehearsal—and it was, on virtually all counts, a great success. The performance went smoothly and attendance was encouraging, if not capacity. If a handful of patrons walked out during the first scenes there *was* a tremendous ovation for conductor Ludwig and the orchestra following the sole intermission (after the second act) and the musicians answered the flood of applause with two collective bows. After the performance word of the achievement spread. The second *Wozzeck* was crowded, and a third showing put on the bill.

Ludwig conducted with obvious love for the score, balancing its details in crystalline fashion and shattering responsive listeners with the inexorable cumulative sweep of its anguished chromaticism. On stage, Leni Bauer-Ecsy's expressionistic sets and Hager's tight direction captured the oppressive, crazed atmosphere of the story. The second scene sun was right out of late Van Gogh, a tall skeleton eavesdropped overbearingly on Wozzeck and the doctor, and the endlessly windowed barracks seemed to be falling in on the bunks at the end of the second act.

Evans, pale-faced in drab fatigues, sang the title role for

172

the first time in his career and was enormously sympathetic—
a poor clod who walked the stage with the heaviness of a
man who is crushed just a little more each day. The haunting
pathos of his beaten, plaintive voicing of Berg-and-Büch-
ner's trampled man doesn't leave the memory easily.

Some of the less even-keel characters in *Wozzeck* resemble
puppets of a contorted world, and the lethargy of Evans' step
heightened this resemblance. So did the creaky jerkiness of
Richard Lewis' superbly etched Captain, a role new to
him, too.[17] One couldn't help thinking of the versatility of
these two Britons, both so adept in Mozart, Berg—and Sir
Arthur Seymour Sullivan. Marilyn Horne, a young Los Angeles soprano with more than a dozen German performances of
Marie behind her—she'd been based in Gelsenkirchen—was
as sympathetic in her way as Evans in his. Horne's opportunity to appear in San Francisco, her first major "house" in
the U.S., followed Brenda Lewis' cancellation during the
summer for reasons of health.

Alvary, looking like a character out of an old Fritz Lang
movie, was a spooky doctor with an appropriate Mittel-
Europa accent. And Ticho Parly, while vocally unsatisfying,
was a histrionically convincing Drum Major. With the exception of the Danish-American Parly, all the cast made themselves well understood in the Eric Blackall-Vida Hartford
English translation. A plain black curtain was lowered for
scene changes, and these were executed with a nearly cinematic speed. The production, in sum, looked like something
from the most stylish legitimate theater. Although this wasn't
exactly the sort of production which had been the rule in
Merola's era, surely he would have approved.[18]

Wozzeck was closely succeeded on the season's schedule by
Bellini's *Sonnambula*, the year's other opera new to the repertoire. This fragile flood of bel canto and tinkly melody
might have been completely overwhelmed by the grip and
thrust of the Berg, but it was played with a helpfully fresh
slant. The chosen direction was straight into comedy. Nobody
can be expected to take *Sonnambula* very seriously these days,
and Yannopoulos turned it into a satirical buffo plaything.
Elemer Nagy's glorified comic strip sets, complete with seven-
towered castle up on the hill, fitted the treatment perfectly—a
treatment which found the choristers sitting on spectator

benches, sniffing into handkerchiefs, and nodding their heads in unison at appropriate moments.

Doubtless there were some in the audience who would have preferred to have the period of the piece stand out. After all, the pathos, such as it is, of the Sleepwalking Scene is a serious matter, and, when the audience is in a laughing mood as Amina makes her doubtful way across the set, some adjustment of emotional sights is necessary. At all events, Anna Moffo was a first rate Amina, providing a model of what beautifully floated lyric tone should be. Her characterization was not too mannered: a frail, Giselle-like Amina would not have added up in this *Sonnambula*. Nicola Monti, who had sung in Dallas and Chicago, came from Italy to help San Franciscans recall the best traditions of light liquid tenorism as Elvino. Giorgio Tozzi was an ebullient Rodolfo, looking like Dr. Dulcamara's brother.

Also newsworthy in 1960 was the revival of an opera returning after a long absence with a few alterations, and what might be called a certain protective covering. This was *The Girl of the Golden West*, reappearing as *La Fanciulla del West*. In 1943 the language had been English, the Dick Johnson a head shorter than the Minnie, and too many of the audience thought it was all just too funny. But people remained —and Adler was one of them—who felt that if the local references were played down, the corn quotient reduced, and the cast exceptionally strong, Puccini's problematical western could be revived successfully. As much a gamble as that second act card game perhaps, but worth trying. Because, after all, there's a wealth of exciting music in the score, and the story has an elemental appeal.

Adler's highest hopes for this lovable soap (and horse) opera were vindicated, and the show went over nicely. Yes, there were some titters (the tossing of snowflakes outside the second act cabin door reminded of W.C. Fields' classic line: "T'aint a fit night out for man nor beast"), but the second and third act curtains brought warmly enthusiastic applause.

The sets were basically those of 1930 and 1943, perfectly appropriate, one must say, in their homey realism. A new and happy scenic touch lent a bit of sophistication to the beginning of the opera: a show curtain with an old photo of a snowy 49'er scene set in a postmark oval. The language of

174

the production was, of course, Italian. The reference in the first act to Agenzia Wells Fargo was deleted, that being the name of an established San Francisco bank, and the Indians in the second act sensibly refrained from saying their Ughs. There were several horses in the last act, and some of them were so speedily and efficiently ridden across stage that the audience cheered. But the equine character who chose to shatter the calm of the third act opening summoned unsolicited laughter by neighing from behind the curtain just before it went up.

The *Fanciulla* revival served to introduce Sandor Konya, the new Hungarian tenor, to America. A tallish, sturdy Johnson, he put forth a spinto voice with a pulsating emotional quality. The fact that he tended to lumber about the stage (there are roles more comfortable than Johnson), and the fact that his projection was occasionally a bit insecure or grainy—these mattered not so much in earshot of Konya's lyric charms. He followed the Johnson with a superior Lohengrin, a fresh Rodolfo, and a Rhadames which, while stiff in movement, intermittently called to mind the singing of Lauri-Volpi. He was immediately reengaged, and returned to San Francisco numerous seasons, but not always singing with the best taste and the clearest projection, nor acting with keen dramatic sense.

Minnie provided another role which the versatile Dorothy Kirsten could, as some more celebrated sopranos could not, make visually and vocally believable. Tito Gobbi, returning to the scene of his American debut a dozen seasons and lots of seasoning later,[19] was an absolutely perfect Jack Rance, master of the suave snarl. He looked like a lecherous old cattle baron, and when he threw that chair across the room after Minnie *won* the card game you knew this was one of the angriest, most despicable villains who ever trod the War Memorial boards.

Gobbi's first appearance of the season was in the Opening Night *Tosca*. Tebaldi, absent for four seasons, was due back in the title role, but an indisposition kept her from fulfilling her engagement. She was suffering from an arthritic condition, and was advised in August to rest for 60 days. There was reason to believe she might arrive in time for two *Bohèmes* late in the San Francisco season, but she did not. Kirsten, scheduled only for Minnie, undertook the opening Tosca—as she would ten years later for an ailing Régine Crespin—and Lucine Amara the second. There was concern about the advisability of casting Amara in this role, but her first Floria in Italian—she had sung the part in English at Central City—had points of merit. It was, to be sure, small-scale in approach, and there was little sense of Tosca as an impressive personality. But Tosca is, above all, a woman, and Amara's performance was supremely feminine.

It's too bad the second act close was ruined by the encore curtains suddenly rushing prematurely to the center of the stage. When before has a Tosca had to agonizingly stage whisper "Aspetta, aspetta!" And agonizingly enough she was heard in the last row of the orchestra!

The rest of the repertoire was mainly composed of proven recent successes: the *Cosi* and *Rosenkavalier* last heard in 1957—these, of course, for Schwarzkopf; *Aida* and *Frau Ohne Schatten* for Rysanek; and the newly set *Bohème* and *Carmen*. *Lohengrin* returned after five seasons, *Boccanegra* after four, *Traviata* after three. Paul Schoeffler, the Vienna State Opera's genial Don Alfonso, was new in the *Cosi* cast, as was Katherine Hilgenberg, the Los Angeles mezzo, who had her biggest opportunity to date as Dorabella, performing gamely while Schwarzkopf upstaged her. Mary Costa's spunky comic style produced a delightful Despina. But those who might have thought comedy was this artist's strongest suit had not yet heard her Violetta, a commodity which arrived October 20. Costa handled the coloratura brilliantly, and she gave the role a touching, incisive sort of characterization which brought it fully to life.

As if one superior Violetta were not enough, Adler offered yet another at the Regular Series *Traviata* the following week when Anna Moffo took over. Rarely in company history had two such interesting and authoritative, yet wholly different, versions of a role been delivered in such close succession. Moffo emphasized the mature, introspective nature of Violetta while Costa played up the ebullience.

Rosenkavalier brought a new Ochs in Kurt Boehme, the distinguished Munich bass. Here was a Lerchenau with a battering ram belly and cheeks that shook like bowls full of jelly, a giggly, bumptious, overgrown boy of an Ochs. He missed the pathos that lies in the part, but he did sing it gorgeously besides being a barrel of fun. Varviso's warm lyric touch in the pit was a big asset. It was also a boon to *Tosca*, *Bohème* and *Traviata*—along with occasional deficiencies in continuity which were not.

Although Adler was tending to make conducting assignments on a nationalistic basis—the Swiss Varviso was treated more internationally than his more northerly and southerly colleagues—there *was* a major exchange in 1960 when Molinari-Pradelli took over *Lohengrin* (following in the steps of Cleva) and Leopold Ludwig assumed responsibility for *Boccanegra*. The Italian Wagner was immensely vibrant, spontaneous and to the point, the German Verdi more elegantly controlled but forceful.[20]

Evans took on Paolo in *Boccanegra*, and was also the season's dashing, quick-witted, non-buffo Gianni Schicchi at the season's student matinees.

Frau Ohne Schatten returned in large part because Rysanek, the queen of the world's Empresses, could renew her San Francisco association in 1960. She did so with a new slim beauty of face and figure. Schoeffler's vintage Barak was another plus, but not Parly's garbled Emperor. Dalis and Schech were in their accustomed positions. Ludwig conducted effectively at the first performance, sloppily at the second. Attendance in general was somewhat disappointing. The Rysanek *Aida* was a sellout and Adler added an extra performance to give San Franciscans a look at Floriana Cavalli, Tebaldi's replacement for Los Angeles performances of *Tosca*, *Bohème* and *Boccanegra*. (Amara, the substitute in San Francisco, had to return to the Met.)

The handsome Cavalli came to the American stage with starring engagements in Rome and Naples behind her. Certain refinements were in order—her low tones could be rather raw, her phrasing graceless, and she slithered around the stage registering the most self-conscious sort of agony—but her voice was so large and limpid and full of rich beauty that an exciting performance resulted.

Rysanek's Aida was not only vocally elegant but intensely dramatic. Exhibit A: operating in a highly-charged climate heated up by Molinari, and with a determined Amonasro (Weede) singing at her, she let out a blood-curdlingly realistic cry when Father says "you are no longer my daughter."

Originally Konya was the only singer scheduled for a U.S. debut, but the non-appearance of Tebaldi precipitated Cavalli's arrival in this country, and the cancellation of Jurinac, scheduled for Octavian and Elsa, resulted in the engagements of Hertha Toepper and Ingrid Bjoner, both new to America. The first, a valued member of the Munich Opera, was a fine Octavian in the second and third *Rosenkavaliers*. Frances Bible returned for the first. Bjoner, a young Norwegian saved from the fate of a pharmacological career, and based then at the Düsseldorf Opera, broke short her honeymoon to take over the Elsas—nicely, too.

Meanwhile Adler was bringing back some more unknown Americans from Europe. In 1960 there was Robert Anderson of the Augsburg Opera who made a successful entry in a variety of roles including Telramund, Ramfis and Pietro in *Boccanegra*. Presence as a weekly salaried hand brought him smaller assignments, too. Janis Martin, a very young mezzo from Dick Johnson's Sacramento—she was not yet of age and her parents had to sign her contract—made an exceptionally good impression in such bits as the *Aida* priestess, Annina in *Traviata* and Teresa in *Sonnambula*.[21] And Frances McCann, a Los Angeles soprano, was a superior Frasquita in *Carmen*.[22]

Altogether there were eighteen Californians on the roster. Another of them, a likeable and vocally competent L.A. baritone named Ned Romero, took over the old Cehanovsky roles.

The year's Carmen was Jean Madeira, who had sung the role with the Cosmopolitan. Her deep voice, rich as the Philadelphia Orchestra string section, sounded beautiful, but the portrayal was too healthy, good-natured and two dimensional. Why Adler recast Zanasi as Escamillo, a role in which he was vocally uncomfortable, is a good question. Possibly because he was a handsome toreador who looked rather like a young Bruce Cabot. Zanasi also shared Amonasro with Weede, returned in his best post-Broadway form.

The revival of Leo Kerz' 1955 *Lohengrin* (hardly a full-dress production) brought some lovely projections and misty lighting effects. The swan was now a stationary emblem-like object behind a scrim. Even though it looked, as Alfred Frankenstein put it, like a Mexican postage stamp, a fairly satisfactory compromise was struck between the creaky old-fashioned swan boat and ultra-modern invisibility.

The 1960 season also brought a couple of productions from the San Francisco Ballet's repertoire: Lew Christensen's riotous *Con Amore*, which followed *Schicchi* at the student matinees, and *Variations de Ballet*, a Balanchine-Christensen concoction appended to *Sonnambula*—unfortunately as an anti-climax thanks to the flimsy music by Glazounoff.

The highly successful visit to the south brought some alterations from the San Francisco casts, Cavalli and Kirsten sharing Tosca, Weede and Gobbi Scarpia, Cavalli and Moffo Mimi, Evans and Romero Schaunard. Zampieri, who had added Don José in Sacramento, was the Rodolfo in one Los Angeles *Bohème* and the Pinkerton of *Madama Butterfly*, given only in that city. Pressure of engagements had kept Leontyne Price from availability except during the southern series, but she did sing the second Cio-Cio-San of her career in Los Angeles November 8—her first was in Vienna. Rysanek was indisposed for her L.A. Aida and replaced by Mary Curtis-Verna, the Mary Curtis of 1952. Tozzi was unable to sing his Rodolfo in the San Diego *Sonnambula* and was replaced by Ferruccio Mazzoli, summoned from the Chicago Opera. Konya took over the Italian Singer in *Rosenkavalier*.

One of the remarkable deceptions of operatic history took place in a *Cosi* performance at the Shrine. The Act I quintet, "Sento o Dio," was turned into a quartet when Guarrera, the Guglielmo, missed his entrance. But Lewis (Ferrando) played ventriloquist for his absent partner at the beginning, singing Guglielmo's lines, and later on, when Ferrando and Guglielmo are supposed to sing together, Schoeffler took over the missing baritone's part. When Guarrera saw an unobtrusive opportunity to go on stage he cheerily did so and the performance continued at full complement.

Notes

[1]One is reminded here of a soprano who sang with the San Francisco Opera in the 20's. The local singer who was playing her lady-in-waiting asked, "Madame X,

179

what would you like me to do in this scene?" Madame X replied: "I don't care, as long as you stay at the rear of the stage." Agnini was furious.

[2] A favorite has been Matthew Farruggio's afternoon workshop in the art of dying—by slow poison, consumption, stab-in-the-back. There are almost 57 varieties.

[3] The New York City Opera performed it soon thereafter.

[4] Thanks to the Opera Guild, the company had acquired three projectors of its own.

[5] His "Avant des quitter" brought a big round of spontaneous applause from the chorus at a *Faust* rehearsal.

[6] Neither is without some of the shock tactics of verismo within its period regal setting.

[7] Farrell, by the way, had a good sense of humor about her bulk. As she announced backstage: "They're shipping my costume out in a boxcar."

[8] Quilico became a staunch advocate of California red wine—not Dulcamara's "Bordeaux"—when he found out, before the nerve-wracking opening, that a careful dosage of same loosened up his voice as nothing else could.

[9] The curtain was not lowered during the changes, and the pit lights, which tend to spill over onto the stage, were turned out for the scene shifts from a dimmer by the conductor's stand. When Leinsdorf was sure the orchestra could play the last few bars of a scene from memory, he pushed the button.

[10] Hailing from Tennessee, Stahlman had sung with the Brussels Opera under the name Giulia Bardi.

[11] In *Otello*, for instance, one could detail a lively opening storm, a delightfully lacy "Fuoco di gioia" chorus and a Drinking Song full of swagger. The confrontation of Aida and Amneris in the second act of *Aida* could be staggering in its intense urgency. And so on . . .

[12] Price and Farrell didn't join the Met until 1960–61. Rysanek went on the New York roster in 1958–59. Schwarzkopf reached 39th Street only in 1965. Farrell first sang at the Chicago Opera in '57, Rysanek in '58, Price and Schwarzkopf in '59.

[13] Now Georges, he had been conducting a great deal at the Paris Opera since his earlier San Francisco days.

[14] With, at the second performance, ten minutes of the score cut.

[15] Varviso went on to the Met, where he did not fare especially well, and later became musical director of Stockholm's thriving Royal Opera and a regular guest at the Vienna State Opera.

[16] Actually, Schoeffler was 62 in 1959 and only about ten years younger than his illustrious predecessor would have been if alive. Edelmann was the originally scheduled Sachs. When he couldn't come, a Czech, Ladislav Mraz, was engaged. He in turn was indisposed. Schoeffler couldn't have been a happier solution—he should have been selected in the first place.

[17] Lewis' Captain remains far and away the best seen in the U.S.

[18] Ten years later Evans, a veteran of many *Wozzeck* productions, including that at the Salzburg Festival, told the author that he felt San Francisco's was the best.

[19] He first sang at the Met in 1955–56, and then became a fixture at the Chicago Opera, singing very little in New York.

[20] Molinari is considered a major Wagnerian in Italy and it was he who presided over *Lohengrin* at the Teatro Communale in Bologna when the centenary of Wagner's official introduction to Italy was celebrated with an Italian-language performance in the autumn of 1971.

[21] Ten years later she was cast as Eva at Bayreuth.

[22] Her future was less happy—she was shot to death in a Rome hotel two and a half years later.

180

Gaetano Merola, general director 1923–53.

Kurt Herbert Adler, Merola's successor.

Bianca Saroya, busy soprano
of 1923

Rosina Torri made her U.S. debut as
Manon in San Francisco, 1925.

Queena Mario and Beniamino Gigli arrive at the Ferry
Building, 1923; Captain Quinn of S.F. Police at left.

Baritone Vicente Ballester, who held a long A flat in the Stanford Stadium *Pagliacci*, 1922.

The first season over, S.F. Opera backers sat down to this celebratory fare at the Fairmont Hotel, October 9, 1923.

Opening Night 1930, in Civic Auditorium.

Ezio Pinza as Archibaldo,
L'Amore dei Tre Re, 1928.

Arriving 1929: Giuseppe
De Luca, Giuseppe Danise,
Léon Rothier, Giacomo
Lauri-Volpi.

Antonio Cortis, San Francisco's Rhadames in 1926, shown here as Don José in *Carmen*.

Fernand Ansseau kneels
into the role of Avito,
L'Amore dei Tre Re, 1925.

Pietro Cimini helped Merola
with conducting chores
during the early days.

Hope Hampton, onetime
beauty contestant and movie
star, sang in *Faust*, 1930.

Soprano Maria Müller, Wagnerian and Puccinian of 1931.

Soprano Elisabeth Rethberg and friend.

Maria Jeritza as Salome, 1930.

Lawrence Tibbett, the great American baritone, in the early days.

Ticket to opening performance
in the Opera House: *Tosca*, 1932.

Alfredo Gandolfi and Claudia Muzio in *Tosca*, 1932.

Ninon Vallin made a
rare U.S. appearance
in *Carmen*, with Mario
Chamlee, 1934.

San Francisco's
Josephine Tumminia
with Tito Schipa
in *The Barber of
Seville*, 1935.

Ebe Stignani made her U.S. debut
as Santuzza in *Cavalleria
Rusticana*, 1938.

Francesco Merli,
tenore robusto of 1932.

Richard Crooks in
the St. Sulpice Scene,
Manon, 1934.

Giovanni Martinelli in *La Forza del Destino*, 1936, with Carlo Morelli.

Traditional: *Tosca*, Act 1, 1932.

Jane Berlandina's lightweight *Der Rosenkavalier*, 1940.

Early Adler Minimalism:
The Revolutionary Scene
of *Boris Godounoff*, 1956.

Several Generations of Sets

Post War Contemporary: Alfred Siercke's
Hamburg-style *Barber of Seville*, 1963.

More of Same: Gunther Schuller's *The Visitation*;
set by Leni Bauer-Ecsy, 1967.

The one-block War Memorial project incorporating an Opera House, 1920.

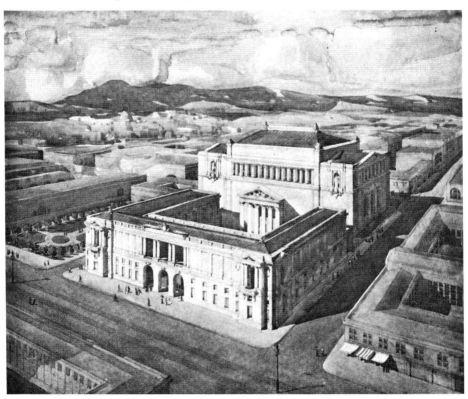

The War Memorial Opera House, one of a pair of buildings on Van Ness Avenue.

CHAPTER 14

The Cosmopolitan Story—
and a Spring Song

At the end of the chapter titled *The Pacific Story* it was suggested that a collision between the San Francisco Opera and the Cosmopolitan was not impossible. Stars became increasingly important to the Shindell-managed operation. In 1956 some older singers of large fame such as Sayao, Baccaloni and Baum were on the roster, along with Resnik, Herva Nelli, Brenda Lewis and the baritone Cesare Bardelli. With these artists the Cosmopolitan filled houses at a $3.50 top—or at least appeared to do so—while the Pacific, with less lustre at $2.50, suffered along. Obviously there wasn't room for *three* companies in town, and the Pacific died. Cosmopolitan continued on its course of bigger and better stars, the production aspects remaining at a generally unimaginative, old-fashioned, low-budget level.

Eccentricites of production, like a real trained bear in *Bohème,* were sometimes thrown in as extras, but dubious ones they were.

Milanov, Valletti and Vinay came in 1957, and *Turandot,* planned for that year's fall season by the San Francisco Opera, was scooped off the shelf and placed in the Cosmopolitan's late winter repertoire. Cornell MacNeil appeared in 1958, Richard Tucker the following year—at $2500 per performance. This was $750 more than the San Francisco's top price at the time. There was, of course, the problem of inducing singers of Tucker's repute to appear with a company of small reputation, but this sheer financial abandon reached fairly wild proportions in 1960 when Bjoerling was allegedly paid $4000 a night.

There were eight performances in 1959, a dozen in 1960, and plans for 1961 called for more than that. A fantastic list of tenors was lined up by Shindell, as if to rub in an old Adler failing; it contained the names of Bjoerling, Tucker, Del Monaco, Di Stefano and Carlo Bergonzi! Other visitors would be Birgit Nilsson, Giulietta Simionato, Risë Stevens and Fausto Cleva, all with previous San Francsico Opera associations. Nilsson was to get $5000, Del Monaco $3500, Stevens $3000, Bergonzi $2500.

This season, however, never came to pass. It was almost too starry to be true.

Shindell repeatedly tried to persuade others from Adler's stable (Rysanek, for instance) to run in his league at stratospheric fees. Repertoire remained almost totally standard, and, since the budget was not weighted in favor of much rehearsal time, no operas outside the San Francisco's repertoire —barring *Hansel and Gretel* (with Anna Russell, that famous *Ring* analyst, as the witch)—were presented. Members of the San Francisco Opera Chorus formed the Cosmopolitan choral force, and the new company had to stick to what it knew.

Miller and Adler were suspicious of Shindell's aspirations and not about to let the new troupe use its scenery as some Cosmopolites suggested. Obviously the mixture of big stars, small prices, and Big Company scenery was a danger. As Miller said, when his company was accused of trying to stifle the Cosmopolitan, "It's necessary to protect our interests since low-priced opera comes into direct competition with our lower scale seats."

While Shindell continued to raise his fees, and the top ticket price rose to $4.90, Campbell McGregor, holder of the Cosmopolitan purse strings, left the purse wide open. The deficit was approximately $70,000 in 1959, and more in 1960. Mr. McGregor picked up the tab, as he liked to do. Shortly after the 1948 rejuvenation of the Pacific company McGregor had discouraged a broad base of support, and the single angel idea continued when he founded the Cosmopolitan. Without him, the Cosmopolitan could not exist, short of drastic reorganization.

On April 11, 1960 the explosion came—just after the season's close. McGregor announced he was withdrawing his support. The decision came as a surprise to just about everybody, probably even to Shindell.[1]

Members of the board met April 26 and rubber stamped the liquidation. There was really not much choice. But soon, one of the more concerned directors, Mrs. Leon Cuenin, was talking about reorganizing. Neither the name of the company nor the scenery, it developed, would be available to her. Mrs. Cuenin, a spunky little woman, told the press: "Early last season I tried to organize a group of sponsors to assume some of the financial responsibility. But when Mr. McGregor heard about it, why he hit the ceiling. He said 'When I die, Cosmopolitan dies.'"

When Mrs. Cuenin and her friend Mrs. William Woods Adams called a meeting of persons interested in opera June 16, 1960, the purpose was to form a company to succeed the Cosmopolitan in offering springtime opera, albeit on a more modest scale than had become the rule. But at least two persons—William Kent III, a young businessman and opera lover, and the author—left the meeting with the feeling that San Francisco could afford more opera performances, but not more opera companies and the possible attendant rivalry. James Schwabacher, San Francisco business executive, professional singer and music commentator, felt the same way. As a result of discussion among the three, Schwabacher suggested that a sponsoring group be formed to raise money, and that the San Francisco Opera be asked to "produce" for it a spring season of appropriate character—one that is, which would be a foil rather than competition to the senior company's activities. At the same time, scenic and administrative facilities of the San Francisco Opera could be used because they were already on hand.

Kent approached Miller, who said he'd been interested in the idea of a spring season but hadn't wanted to saddle his guarantors with any new financial burdens. But what if the money were raised independently by a new group? Kent asked. After a long cautionary pause, Miller agreed that if a new groupd raised $40,000—$30,000 of it to cover the deficit of six performances in 1961 and $10,000 as a headstart for 1962, or a cushion against budgeting error in 1961—well, then, the matter could probably be worked out.

Meanwhile Schwabacher talked to Adler, who had long been interested in producing spring seasons. And Mrs. Cuenin was persuaded to forget old rivalries and join in a united operatic front for San Francisco.

By July 13 the official announcement was ready. Spring

183

Opera of San Francisco—the name was Mrs. Cuenin's—had been organized. Kent was named chairman of the executive committee, and a small artistic advisory committee was set up to consult with Adler in maintaining the appropriate policy for the spring. The repertoire would mix standards, revivals and hopefully some new materials, the accent being more toward Opéra Comique or Volksoper fare than Grand Opera. The budget was low, but artistic aspirations ran high. Productions, however slight, would be all-around affairs, not thrown together. Singers on the rise would be featured.

Meanwhile, Shindell was not through. In August he launched a surprise solicitation for funds to start a *Cosmos* Opera featuring big stars, and the literature, sent out through the Jack Shelton mailing machinery, implied that the Spring Opera program was doomed to failure. But a promised report of financial status did not materialize, and no Cosmos season came to pass. Much as the Spring people considered Shindell a sort of Rothbart among the Swans, a slight tear can perhaps be shed for the passing of the Cosmopolitan-and-Cosmos because the emphasis on vocal stars reflected a genuine enthusiasm of the operatic public.

On December 19, 1960 the directors of the San Francisco Opera Association unanimously approved collaboration with Spring Opera—which had already raised three-fifths of the $40,000. As the year ended, the future was not sure, but it seemed likely that Spring Opera seasons would grow in size, possibly providing the San Francisco Opera with a way of rescuing worthy productions from the warehouse at an unprecedented rate. This was misplaced optimism because, while there were some worthwhile materials beautifully fit for Spring, the San Francisco Opera's storehouse was loaded down with productions which had gone out of date, no matter what the budgetary level.

At any rate, Spring Opera opened a six-opera, seven-performance season at the Opera House May 2, 1961.[2] The opera of the festive evening was Gounod's *Roméo et Juliette*, a viable piece which Adler was not likely to be reviving in fall seasons, and one which sounded the note of a heightened interest in French opera which would become a Spring Opera trademark. *Roméo*, thankfully, was available in one of the more durable of Agnini's remaining productions. The performance, while not exactly high-powered (a state of affairs which can actually be detrimental to this opera), pleased a a near-capacity crowd and realized the hopes of the company's founders.

The utter believability and girlish charm of Lee Venora as Juliet, the elegant, free-topped lyricism of Roméo Richard Verreau, and the glowingly sonorous bass of John Macurdy[3] as Friar Lawrence: these were notable elements in a performance crisply conducted by the veteran Joseph Rosenstock. The tight, suspenseful, mood-catching direction of Allen Fletcher was possibly the most brilliant element of all. Six West Coast singers were on stage—Janis Martin (Gertrude), Margot Blum (Stephano) and Donald Drain (Gregorio) were the most conspicuous—and the season as a whole stressed opportunities for young singers from the U.S., East and West.

It continued with a youthful *Bohème* freshly staged by Adler's stage manager Matthew Farruggio in the pre-Jenkins San Francisco Opera sets. Venora was Mimi, and the Rodolfo a young dark-voiced tenor named George Shirley.[4] *Martha*, surprisingly well-attended, came next, in English, with next to no scenery but at least staged by Fletcher. *Traviata* brought home local girl Mary Gray (once Mary Jane Gray) from Germany for Violetta, and Henry Lewis, a young Los Angeles bass player-turned-conductor,[5] offered one of the most sensitive and sparkling accounts of Verdi's music ever heard at the War Memorial.

The possibilities of continuity between Fall and Spring were stressed in Marilyn Horne's assignment as Carmen, opposite a young and then unknown tenor named James King[6] in a generally vivid performance staged by Irving Guttman of Vancouver.

Possibly the pièce de résistance of the season was a new and untraditional production of Mozart's *Magic Flute* by San Francisco's Vincent Porcaro. Working with a unit set including steps, a smiling scrim and a central pavilion, and utilizing a wide range of lighting effects, he kept the show moving well. Eighteenth century court costuming was used to escape the exotic mishmash suggested by the libretto. Boys replaced the customary adult women as the genii, and there was even a dragon from Chinatown. Rosenstock conducted authoritatively, Shirley was Tamino, Doris Yarick Pamina and Macurdy

Sarastro. Without much voice, Donald Drain managed nevertheless to make an appealing Papageno.

The season came to a happy conclusion May 19, four houses sold out, another almost. To be sure, Spring Opera was only attempting to sell one performance of each opera, as opposed to the San Francisco Opera's two or three performances (at that time). But well-balanced, stylish low-budget opera, with stars of the future rather than the present (or maybe the past!) was not exactly driving people away. Spring Opera seasons were to expand. And there would be problems, too, and resolutions. More of that later.

Notes

[1] Who, after 1960, went more or less into limbo. A clipping from *The San Francisco Examiner* of February 1, 1967 reports that Shindell was arraigned for burglary and grand theft in Los Angeles in connection with several losses of art works from Beverly Hills homes.

[2] It could be said that, for some of the founders, Spring Opera became a palpable reality from the moment, one April morning, when live singers from the East emerged from a car outside Fugazi Hall in North Beach and walked inside for the first staging rehearsal with cast.

[3] Destined to become a leading bass at the Metropolitan.

[4] Also to be a Met star. Spring Opera engaged him a few months *before* he won the Met Auditions.

[5] Marilyn Horne's husband, yet another future celebrity.

[6] King was tentative in the first two acts, but built to a memorably striking account of Don Jose's pathetic final scene.

CHAPTER 15

A World Premiere and Other Newsmakers

1961

Artistic matters aside, the 1961 season can take its place in the annals as one of the more precious, its realization having been cast into an early spring shadow. During the month of April the company went through one of the more agonizing crises in its history: a protracted union-management dispute which, while it wasn't quite the cliff hanger which came along in 1964, was suspenseful enough.

Now it's certainly true that the deficit after the *Ring* cycle of 1935 had stirred up a scare, the 1939 artists' list was notably altered by European events, the entrance of the United States into the Second World War brought doubts about going on, the Metropolitan invasion of Los Angeles in the late '40's was difficult, and the Flagstad Affair seriously threatened the 1949 season. Producing opera is, in short, a kind of hell. But somehow the company had never missed its date with a fond audience. In April 1961 one began to wonder, though, if its capacity for weathering storms had not reached the breaking point.

The company had hoped to announce its plans for the autumn about the first of April. But negotiations with the American Guild of Musical Artists (AGMA), representing the chorus, ballet and salaried singers, resulted in no contract even after three months of intermittent talks. The association was willing to grant salary increases, but not the union's demand for unemployment insurance. Repeatedly AGMA demanded the insurance. Just as assertively the Association repeated its stand. Such coverage, optional according to state law for a non-profit corporation, must be paid to all company employes if it is paid to one, and, as president Miller stated in a letter to the Board of Governors March 29: "Our current income and potential resources of all sorts could not meet an increase of expenditure of this magnitude." Furthermore, he noted, "Only a small number of AGMA members and other opera employes would benefit from this insurance coverage since most are protected through employment elsewhere."

The president told the governors AGMA had held up necessary rehearsals during the negotiations and, he concluded, if the demands were not promptly and substantially reduced, he would be forced to recommend, most reluctantly, the suspension of operations for 1961.

The cloud hung over the Opera House for three-and-a-half weeks. The talks stopped for several days, an editorial called for Mayor Christopher, a savior in the 1949 Flagstad crisis, to move in, and the agony continued. Talks resumed, were fruitless again. Symphony men started worrying about the fate of their autumn employment, which gave them a vital income for almost three months' work outside the orchestra's concert season. And a society editor wondered in print what would happen to the social season: it would be impossible to decide when it began if there was no opera to open it.

Miller had set April 20 as deadline. The April 21 papers carried dismal stories of the talks having broken down on the insurance argument, and cancellation seemed sure. Miller, characteristically firm, called in his board and the season was officially cancelled by unanimous vote. More than that, if a contract for 1962 were not negotiated by September 1, 1961 the San Francisco Opera would be dissolved. Ah, brinkmanship.

San Franciscans considered what seemed to be happening impossible, unthinkable. After all, they said, San Francisco is "The City That Knows How." At least that's what they read in the columns. The cliché proved as meaningful as ever when Mayor Christopher went into action. The announcement of the board's decision had come in the morning. The same afternoon, Christopher called Miller and Adler into his office, then AGMA representatives. The following day, Saturday April 22, a meeting of both sides began at 12:15 p.m. in the Mayor's Office. There was discussion until about 3, then the negotiators suggested a recess until the following day. Christopher answered, in effect, "Keep Talking." And at 5:15 he emerged, weary but happy, to announce that an agreement had been reached. The Association had raised its salary increase offer from 5.5 to 6% and the union had waived the unemployment insurance demand.

The crisis was over, the resolution reaffirming the deep belief of San Francisco's many opera fans that the death, or indisposition, of the company was unthinkable. Thirty-eight and still growing with a pioneering vitality, the San Francisco Opera pulled itself together and faced the future with confidence. The immediate future included a world premiere—of Norman Dello Joio's *Blood Moon*—which didn't exactly bring the company a bushel of critical praise. But if this opera didn't survive, the company certainly did.

Dello Joio set out to write an attractive piece, to communicate with his audience. The only trouble was that he made it so "attractive" the opera came out wishy washy. Actually it was sagging inspiration that tripped him up. He didn't have to go twelve-tone to achieve a major artistic effect, far from it, but he could have given his score more color, variety and pace. Not to mention a few lumps less of Broadway/Hollywood sugar.

The opera opened well, with an arching little love motif still hummable a decade later, and indeed, the whole first scene was a reasonably compact, engrossing musical statement. But the route was downhill from there, with a few helpful peaks and scant gold in the valleys between.

Despite Dello Joio's failure, one can still salute his intentions. They were healthy. As he stated before the premiere: "The time is at hand for the human voice to reassert itself as the most compelling instrument to convey meaning to the musical public." But there was too much verbosity, Dello Joio's tired recitative and Gale Hoffman's contrived libretto producing a high sogginess quotient. If the audiences really liked anything about *Blood Moon*, it was the gauzy-mossy wedding cake production of Reuben ter-Arutunian, a thing of grander and more gorgeous scope than Dello Joio had himself imagined, but a visual symphony which didn't do any harm under the circumstances. The San Francisco Opera did not take undue advantage of the Ford Foundation's helping financial hand in this production—the sets were not as expensive as they looked—but the foundation's benign presence may have been reassuring when the withering reviews came in.

In 1961, Ford's $950,000 appropriation to the country's four largest companies, the Metropolitan, the New York City, the Chicago Lyric and the San Francisco, was a new and hopeful element in American operatic life. Under its terms the companies set out to produce a dozen or more operas during the eight years ahead. The money, one hastens to add, was not a mindless gift but an allotment, to be used for extra rehearsal costs, stage production needs and to compensate the box office for revenue it might lose by performing a new and unknown work instead of a sure-fire grosser.

Alas, the program was not as productive as hoped, in any of the cities involved, although the New York City Opera did a lot with it. In the mid-60's the San Francisco Opera commissioned a *Sappho* from Peggy Glanville-Hicks and an *Of Mice and Men* from Carlisle Floyd as possible Ford program material. But stung by *Blood Moon*, Adler was armed with extreme caution, and found neither work anything to rush into production. The Seattle Opera did produce *Of Mice and Men* in 1970, and with some success.

The story of *Blood Moon* takes its audience to New Orleans in 1859 where they meet Cleo Lafont, a quadroon who loved a white man only to be deserted, and Ninette, the product of that union. She is, by easy mathematical calculation, an octaroon. Ninette bursts into Cleo's cottage with scintillating brio to report she has just been awarded a contract in the theater. But the mother breaks the girl's jubilant mood by reminding her she cannot hide her partly black identity. There's a new law that women with any degree of Negro blood must wear a yellow scarf in public, and Cleo hands her one. Ninette tosses it aside.

At a fashionable ball Ninette and Raymond Bardac, a wealthy gentleman, pledge their love. But a rival actress, Edmée Le Blanc, overhears Cleo when she slips onto the scene to tell Ninette she's wanted by the police. Naturally she threatens to expose Ninette, and our heroine accepts defeat, retreating to New York with a bewildered Raymond left standing on his southern soil. Raymond follows Ninette to New York, where they redeclare their love, agreeing to meet in Paris.

190

The final act, in Ninette's Paris apartment, brings her into discussion with a philosophically-minded Alexandre Dumas. Raymond duly arrives, eager to marry Ninette as the Civil War is threatening and he must return to fight for his way of life. Cleo, who has hung on as her daughter's maid (!), baits him, and he answers by calling her a "black witch." This brings on a Third Act Revelation: Ninette's admission of her relationship to Cleo. Raymond bows out gracefully, and Ninette puts on a yellow scarf. But Cleo, perhaps guilty at the thought of her meddling, tells her daughter she needs it no longer.

Does sound corny, doesn't it? Well, the cast did what it could. Mary Costa had the right panache for Ninette, the new Australian tenor Albert Lance sang Raymond with a boyishly bright-voiced sound, and Kieth Engen, a young Berkeleyan already on the rise at the Munich Opera, was a memorably sonorous Dumas. Ludwig was the conductor.

Blood Moon was not the only contemporary opera on Adler's ambitious 1961 schedule; there was also Britten's *A Midsummer Night's Dream*, which produced the kind of artistic success Dello Joio's effort couldn't muster. *Dream* remains an oasis in today's desert of operatic inspiration because Britten's melodic sense is so fertile and his capacity for quick comic comment so nimble. These assets go hand-in-glove with a painting-in-sound technique worthy of Wagner. The opera is a tour de force of evanescence because rarely has such an airy touch been so warmly sustained throughout an extended score.

There are, of course, three categories of character: the fairies, the lovers and the rustics. The lovers get in some gritty bits, and the rustics have their moments of lumbering, but that airiness—the magic of the wood, if you will—dominates everything. Nowhere better than in the prelude to Act 2, a wistful, delicate sound picture of the void of sleep, with characteristic disposition of the orchestral commentary in diverse ranges and colors, harp sprinkles played off against sound of distant brass. When, a little later, Bottom finds himself alone, and sings bluffly like a Winnie-the-Pooh to show he's not afraid, Titania wakes and answers him with the most beguiling foil: repeated sustained tones amidst an ardent,

191

quiet floridity. And then the fairies rush to roll call as winds in the orchestra scamper.

Repeated notes lyrically employed are a trademark in Britten's score, and time does not erase that gripping phrase, "I swear to thee," which Hermia and Lysander weave emphatically from a possibly unpromising collection of tones in the first act. When the lovers get untangled in Act 3, Britten uses an equally simple device, a weaving of upward scales which results in a marvelous spirit of amorous affirmation.

The rustics are treated to chuckling music of an engagingly post-Falstaffian sort, and Britten drops comic asides with a near-compulsive but unassailable wit. In the rustics' play one can find sly helpings of Verdian passion, Rossinian patter, Handelian vigor and Expressionistic wayward chromaticism, not to mention the bass viol recitative which, before the play, suggests—as in Beethoven's Ninth—important things to come.

Evans added a lovable Bottom to his growing gallery of San Francisco portrayals, and the rest of the cast, including a delightful quartet of juveniles, performed with style. Russell Oberlin, the counter-tenor, sounded rather too spongy and distant as Oberon, but Britten's opera does ideally ask for a smaller hall than San Francisco's Opera House. Adler imported Harry Horner's turntable-centered production designed for the 1961 Vancouver Festival, and brought England's Basil Coleman to direct. The first San Francisco performance, on October 10, constituted the U.S. premiere of a work which had met its first public only sixteen months earlier, at Aldeburgh.

New productions were also made for *Lucia* (to launch the season) and *Marriage of Figaro*, and Verdi's *Nabucco* joined the repertory. Bauer-Ecsy gave Donizetti's warhorse a new saddle of visual sophistication, putting much emphasis on the fallen fortune and impending doom motifs hanging over the libretto. The Opening Night audience was presented with a stark, chilly landscape tossed by nature and circumstance, and a recurrent element was a strange piece of architecture halfway upstage which suggested the remains of a bombed-out castle. One of the circular openings took on a Rose Window look in the last scene.

Joan Sutherland was to have made her San Francisco debut

192

at the opening, but a case of abscessed ears in Edinburgh delayed her arrival, and Anna Moffo was flown in for the first performance, Sutherland taking the second and third. Sutherland's, of course, was the more mannered interpretation, but her coloratura command was unarguable, and brought down the house. The season's opening threw a lot of new talent at the subscribers, Engen making his sonorous debut as Raymond,[1] Renato Cioni calling a nice truce between refinement and vocal abandon in his exhilarating assumption of Edgardo, and Vladimir Ruzdak, the Yugoslav baritone of the Hamburg Opera, turning on a big, open, Italianate sound for his American debut as Lord Henry.

To cap his parade of novelty, Adler put the usually-cut Wolf Crag Scene back in the script. It's barren music, really, although style detectives can take note of some prophecies of an early Verdian vigor. At the third performance Ruzdak was succeeded by Claude Heater, a lightweight American baritone who, several years later, was to turn in up in rather important places as a "heldentenor."

There was one unscheduled novelty at the third performance which must have set Adler shuddering. Richard Bonynge, Sutherland's conductor husband, was sitting in Box A when something about Molinari-Pradelli's conducting so bothered him he leaned over the side and cried "Porco" (Pig)—an expression reserved in a later day for the police force. Apparently the maestro and the soprano had not conferred quite long enough on details of her ornamentation of the score, and Molinari failed to pause sufficiently for an embellishment. Suffice it to say that Bonynge was on the stand when his wife returned in future seasons.

Nabucco was unveiled in a near-Cinemascopic production by Andreas Nomikos which mixed spaciousness (a diagonal shaft of columns backing off toward the cyc here, a painted backdrop path flowing into infinity there) with the immediacy which came from the then-novel use of a raked stage. One could also say that Nomikos' sets flowed toward the gaudy, but as time passes they are assuming a nicely Camp aspect which suits the opera's oom-pah-pah breast beatings. Hager had a field day, tumbling terrified Hebrews from the wings onto the sloping temple floor as the first act battle spilled to the stage.

Cornell MacNeil returned as a fully-matured star (Cosmopolitan patrons had seen him in this form in 1959) in the title role, Tozzi was a superb Zaccaria, and the chorus was inspired—*Nabucco* choruses usually are. Lucille Udovick, who'd grown up in San Francisco but spent most of her career in Europe, usually singing voice-killing parts like Abigaille in *Nabucco* and Puccini's Turandot, turned up in both these assignments. She revealed a gutty dramatic soprano of some beauty and richness which tended to become shrieky on top. A competent trouper, but not always refined enough for San Francisco, she was at her best after the debut pressure was off, witness the last performance of *Nabucco*.

The ill-fated Ettore Bastianini, one of the more mellifluous-sounding baritones to grace the San Francisco Opera's history, took over the title role at the third performance, when Janis Martin, the blossoming "baby of the opera," took over Fenena from Stuttgart mezzo Margarethe Bence. Adler also offered *Rigoletto* patrons the choice of MacNeil or Bastianini, and quite a heady one it was, too. At first Bastianini's jester seemed overly busy and fidgety in the light of the less studied (or under-studied) approach of MacNeil, but he went on to give a vivid, believable performance amidst all his seeming infatuation with tone and audience.

The *Nabucco* premiere was an unusually festive event, celebration of the 100th anniversary of Italy's unification being a central element in the evening. The national anthems of Italy and the U.S. were played, there was a talk by Sergio Fenoaltea, the Italian Ambassador, and flags of the U.S., Italy and Italian provinces adorned the boxes. Financial help making the production possible came from the America-Italy Society and the National Festival of Faith and Freedom Foundation.

Something else to be celebrated was the American debut of Graziella Sciutti, a scintillating artist who, rumor had it, had turned down a Met offer which, curiously enough, asked her to make her debut as Despina in *Cosi* in English. Her roles in San Francisco, in her native tongue, were Susanna in *Figaro* and Oscar in *Ballo*, and what a lovely impression she made. Her Susanna was worldly, experienced, practical, quick to hit the ceiling but loaded with charm, her Oscar pixyish, sung with a spankingly crisp tone and acted

194

with a winning smile. There was a strong desire on the part of the management to reengage her, but personal circumstances made her unavailable in 1962, and unfortunately she vanished from the roster for almost a decade. As a matter of fact, her category was quickly filled by Reri Grist, an equally delectable but very different artist.

Bauer-Ecsy's new *Figaro* was an elegant, handsome addition to the scenic assets of the company. Hardly in the same class was the last scene of an ancient *Ballo* which looked as if one good puff would blow it over. Gré Brouwenstijn, the haunting-voiced Dutch soprano, made a warm impression as Amelia in the *Ballo* and in the title role of *Fidelio*. The latter opera brought the unusual casting of Marilyn Horne, hardly a typical soubrette, as Marzelline. Adler told the press he felt the character was substantial enough to take the relatively gutty sound which was a Horne trademark.

Horne and Irene Dalis shared Marina in *Boris*, which returned five years following the Christoff Affair in the original Agnini-Dunkel production. The lighting was more dramatic than in the 40's but it was not until the third production arrived in 1966 that the *Boris* question was settled, at least insofar as the visual side is concerned. Tozzi offered a lyric but reasonably gripping Boris, minus rugged Slavic vocalism but not prettified. Yannopoulos went for broke, practically crucifying our tragic protagonist at the end of the Clock Scene as he fell back, arms outstreched, against a fallen table. At another point in the show Herbert Handt, the Shouisky, could be caught peering over the back of Boris' chair like some Charles Addams character who'd just come out of a manhole.

The busy Mr. Engen was an unusually boozy Varlaam who reeled more vigorously than his predecessors. He turned up in *Meistersinger* too, as a red-haired, bread-munching Kothner. The David of the '61 *Meistersinger* was another American from Munich, the stage-wise, boyish-voiced tenor David Thaw. Gottlob Frick, the great German bass, was to have been the Pogner and Rocco, but dental problems kept him abroad. His replacements were Tozzi and the Stuttgart bass Otto Von Rohr in the Wagner, the American-in-Stuttgart William Wildermann and Von Rohr in *Fidelio*.

The Los Angeles season saw the addition of *Aida* to the card, Brouwenstijn taking one performance, Elinor Ross replacing an ailing Price in another. Mary Costa missed a performance, too—her promising Gilda—and Eva Likova was *her* sub. Albert Lance was the *Ballo* tenor in Sacramento, in place of Zampieri. Janis Martin was Ulrica (she has never sung it since) in her hometown, and it was on the evening of that *Ballo* performance that Adler requested she take over Fenena in a San Francisco *Nabucco* scheduled only a few days later. She carried it off well, thanks in part to coaching with assistant conductor Otto Guth which continued right into the intermissions!

A 1961 postscript: Promising negotiations were made with George Szell to conduct the *Figaro*, but ultimately the plan fell through. Varviso was a middling "second," breezy but crude.

1962

The fortieth anniversary season added a pair of Verdi productions which would provide the company with lots of future mileage: a *Don Carlo* designed by Nomikos, and a *Falstaff* from Elemer Nagy. The San Francisco Opera had long wanted its own *Carlo*—in 1958 the Chicago Lyric production was borrowed—and Nomikos, in association with Yannopoulos, delivered nicely. The partnership put forth a strikingly somber show which revelled in beautiful lighting in the spirit of baroque chiaroscuro. There was some help from a fellow named El Greco, a selection of whose paintings were projected onto the cyclorama. Yannopoulos had his taut innings, witness the breathless first entrance of Philip preceded by intent guards who rushed in with frightening determination.

Nagy's *Falstaff* was another winner, one of those rare productions, in fact—like the '63 *Barber* and '67 *Elisir*—which are so captivating one wants to take the whole confection, stuff it in a pocket, and take it home. Nagy dressed the stage Elizabethan-fashion with a dual-level unit set including an upper central balcony reached by comically precipitous stairs. Changes of scene and related announcements conveyed via signs (carried by the company's faithful retainer Colin Harvey) denoted "An Inn," "Ford's House,"

"Intermission," "The End," and, ultimately, "Good Night."

No such happiness was found in the new *Faust*, one of the few productions in company history to be banished from sight after one year's exposure. Designer Marciano Longarini and director Tito Capobianco betrayed an obvious confusion about just how Gounod's stripped-down Goethe should be played, and, as a result, there was a distressing lack of unity about their show. The first and second acts were cute and tricky, with Hansel and Gretel architecture which might well have been sent back to the drawing board, and up-and-down lighting for Mephisto which was overdone. The taste level improved in the dignified Cathedral Scene with its stained glass effects. And the Prison, with three sets of impressive bars jutting out at the audience, brought a progressive touch. But the traffic jam of styles was alarming.

Much of the blame can be put on the opera itself, a dated and sentimental confection lost somewhere between Walt Disney and High Camp. The best theatrical minds have tripped on it.

A "bomb" fell, too, in the *Carmen*, which had more miscastings than Adler was likely to offer under the worst of circumstances. Del Monaco, the Don José, wandered through the sets showing only remote identification with the proceedings around him. His acting—until a convincingly desperate final scene (how many Don Josés miss *this* chance?)—was dangerously similar to that in a Grade B silent movie. And worse, there was a shameful lack of shading in his singing. Poor Bizet's careful indications of loud and soft went out the tavern window in an outrageously bellowed Flower Song.

Wilma Lipp, the redoubtable but fading Viennese soprano, was the Micaela, singing with a quick wobble in her top tones. One could only wonder why some talented young American wasn't assigned the part. Escamillo was taken by Thomas Stewart, an interesting baritone with major Bayreuth experience, and promise of becoming a lightweight Hotter, less vibrant but on his best nights hardly less intense. He was, however, neither svelte enough in look nor resilient enough in vocalism for this killer assignment. It was no help that the schedule found him singing three big roles—Rodrigo, Valentin and Escamillo—at the beginning of the season.

This leaves Sona Cervena's Carmen, an interpretation mixing finesse and caprice in interesting proportions. Cervena, a migrant from Czechoslovakia to West Germany, was to find her San Francisco form as an exceedingly vivid character mezzo, with one week's battleaxe-washerwoman Bertha in *Barber* followed by an effete Countess in *Lulu* the next. A real repertory performer, in the central European tradition.

That the *Carmen* remained on the track amidst inadequacies and misjudgings was largely due to Janos Ferencsik, Kleiber disciple, teacher of Kertesz, and musical director of the Budapest Opera. He didn't miss one opportunity to make the score sing, sparkle and glow; his beat was crisp, his sense of phrase sophisticated. "In art, and love, you musn't lie"— this was a forthright statement from the genial Ferencsik, and it says something about the spark which his baton ignited. Swinging around the repertoire—how do you type a Hungarian?—he was also in charge of *Rosenkavalier*, and the *Falstaff* which brought Geraint Evans' prime interpretation of the fat knight for the first time in the U.S.

Giulietta Simionato, returning after nine years, carried on the great Stignani tradition with a stentorian and heartwarmingly wise Quickly. And Stewart made a fine impression with his determined Ford. His glowing, focused, large-scale Rodrigo in the Saturday repeat of *Don Carlo* demonstrated the ability which must have won him his contract. The cast for this opera also boasted three well-assigned basses: Tozzi (Philip), Michael Langdon of Covent Garden (Inquisitor) and John Macurdy, Spring Opera veteran and a later Met stalwart (Friar). Irene Dalis reacquainted San Francisco with her Eboli and Sandor Konya was dramatically more at home as Carlo than in a number of other parts. Elisabetta, however, remained a stepsister role: this time it went to Consuelo Rubio, a Spanish soprano who did not demonstrate the necessary evenness of projection.

In Faust Mary Costa was an appealing Marguerite, stressing by her temperament the worldy aspect of this maiden. The Jewel Song was not entirely unfamiliar, thanks to her touring in Bernstein's *Candide*. Tozzi's playful Mephisto wasn't ideally spontaneous.

That area of repertoire loosely referred to as "contemporary opera" was represented not only by *Wozzeck*, repeated from 1960 to somewhat less than capacity but hugely enthusiastic aduiences, but also Stravinsky's *The Rake's Progress*. The spacious, pointed, richly-colored sets borrowed (and later acquired) from the Graz Opera were by Wolfram Skalicki, a man with a talent for buoyant, nonponderous scene design—his continued presence on Adler's production team would be a decided boon to the company. His *Rake* was an essay in seemingly endless imagination, witness for instance the collection of props constructed to convey the loony taste of the Bearded Lady. When she became angry and took a swat at the dinosaur skeleton one witnessed what was perhaps the most delightfully bizarre bit of business ever played in the Opera House.

Richard Lewis was monumental as Tom Rakewell, arrogant, blustering and profoundly anguished by turns. Kerstin Meyer, the versatile Swedish mezzo, was a magnificently vampish Bearded Lady, and Nick Shadow, that mop-haired sneak, was well-served by the exuberant style of Thomas Tipton, a bulldog-voiced American baritone from Mannheim (later Munich). Costa's Anne, however, was bothered somewhat by a dark, diction-swallowing projection which later put her exceedingly promising career briefly off the track. And conductor Ludwig made a serious mistake in softening Stravinsky's sharp accents and contours.

By coincidence, *Rake* came close on the heels of *Don Giovanni* in the schedule, making a juxtaposition which couldn't help underscoring Stravinsky's delight in speaking someone else's language (Mozart's) in his own accent. The production was the international one by Franco Zeffirelli, borrowed in this case from the Dallas Opera, with costumes made in San Francisco after sketches by Skalicki. Zeffirelli's show—not, however, directed by him—was massive and old-fashioned, complete with long waits between scenes, and sounds of determined hammering on stage. The space in the ballroom scene came in handy, but the exterior for Elvira's entrance demonstrated what happens when a set tries to copy extravagant reality and runs out of theatrical square footage.

The first Don of Tozzi's career was another of his not-quite assumptions in the classic Pinza repertoire. Evans' Leporello was, at this stage, something of a gangster type.

Later he softened that emphasis. Schwarzkopf was an epical, near-Camp Elvira, playing the part with a touch of high melodrama. Victoria de los Angeles, finally on the roster after years of intermission chatter in her cause, was a light but incisive Anna. Lewis' ethereal pianissimo in the reprise of "Dalla Sua Pace" was something to remember for a long time to come.

An earlier-day Leporello, Mr. Baccaloni, came back to cap his quarter century of more or less regular San Francisco appearances with some turns at Sergeant Sulpice in *Daughter of the Regiment*. It was presented this time in Italian. Graziella Sciutti was to have returned as Marie (plus Zerlina and Nanetta), but she had to cancel, and Jolanda Meneguzzer, a pretty Italian lyric soprano with coloratura agility and a warm lower range, took over. She made a snappy impression in *Reggimento*, and, in the classic San Francisco tradition of rewards for show-rescuers, she was awarded reengagements in a couple of seasons to follow. But, as often happens with members of the rescue squad, the charm wore thin. Meneguzzer's tendency to shrillness became more bothersome with repeated exposure.

Capobianco, a bright future awaiting him at the New York City Opera, scene of his enchanting 1967 *Manon* and *Coq D'Or*, retrieved his sagging press after the *Faust* with a marvelously sly and stylish job of direction in Donizetti's behalf. There was no undue slapstick but plenty of material for laughs, like the dry pantomime of the bored guests at the Countess' salon. Cervena was a superbly comic Countess, and she and Joshua Hecht, her attendant, pranced around like a couple of associates of *The New Yorker*'s famed Eustace Tilley.

Renato Cioni was an exuberant Tonio, enjoying himself mightily even with, for a while, slipping suspenders! Oliviero De Fabritiis, hanging over the score in a Merola stance, returned to conduct the *Reggimento*, *Faust* and *Cav* and *Pag* with a high degree of elegance, and some of the familiar deficiency in momentum, although his *Pagliacci* was enormously turned on. It was in *Pagliacci* that Bastianini, after glibly sauntering through Di Luna in *Trovatore*, proved he could really act. His Tonio was one of the most sympathetic ever seen on the War Memorial stage: a forlorn, moronic, shuffling, grownup delinquent. The double bill brought a variety of interpretations, Dalis and Simionato sharing Santuzza (the first electric and non-shrewish, the second unleashing a Fluid Drive vocalism), while Lipp and Horne took on Nedda (the first hard as nails, the second much more appealing). Naturally the pirated tape recording of the Horne performance is a collector's item, since she later left Nedda behind.

Cast changes in the three performances of *Bohème* brought Horne in succession to Costa's Musetta—both were spunky, spitfire, better-than-average accomplishments— and de los Angeles as a Mimi to follow Kirsten. The fabled Victoria sang with beautiful style, but there was a touch of polished aloofness, too. Horne's Musetta lengthened the list of her wide-dimensioned San Francisco repertoire, prior to her becoming a bel canto expert, mostly, alas, in other cities.

The Leonora in *Trovatore* was to have been the young black soprano Ella Lee, but pregnancy held back her arrival until a later season. Elinor Ross, a performer of less than high fascination, took over.

There was plenty of fascination, however, in the Manrico of James McCracken, a lusty new talent who, as everyone knows, left bit roles at the Met for a European career which gradually mushroomed into top stardom. His Otello followed, opposite de los Angeles' touching Desdemona. When a sub was required to ease de los Angeles' crowded schedule (she was not in the best health), Raina Kabaiwanska, the Bulgarian soprano, flew out from New York (where she was preparing for her American debut at the Met) and made a vivid dramatic impression in the season's second *Otello*. Gobbi was the oily, almost larger-than-life Iago.

Spring Opera's second season, running from May 8 to 26, 1962, soothed the restless breasts of a lusty battalion of San Francisco opera buffs who wanted to hear Bizet's melody-bathed *Pearl Fishers*. The opera had been out of the Met repertoire for forty-five years, although it was given at the Empire State Music Festival in 1961, and no one in San Francisco had record of a performance within living memory. Lee Venora, Richard Verreau, Chester Ludgin and John Macurdy made for a strong cast, but the less than ideally flexible conducting of Victor Alessandro, conductor of the San Antonio Symphony—whom Adler was trying out untested—was a detriment. And it was Alessandro's glum, hard approach which made Spring Opera's try at *Manon* a failure. A pity, since Massenet's worthy opera had fared ill in the senior troupe's most recent attempt.

Marilyn Horne did have a bel canto chance as Rosina in a *Barber* amusingly staged by Elemer Nagy, and there was a quite charming cut-rate production of Mozart's *Abduction from the Seraglio* designed by Vincent Porcaro, with Herbert Beattie a notably crisp Osmin. Another asset to the middlingly successful season was a *Tosca* conducted in distinguished fashion by Henry Lewis. A move to appease a faction calling for hiring of local singers in top roles brought the casting of Raymond Manton, an inimitable comprimario, as Alfredo in *Traviata*. It simply didn't work out that Manton, superb in so many character assignments, could impress as the romantic lover type.

1963

1963 was one of the most fascinating seasons in the annals. It introduced two off-the-beaten-path operas to the repertoire: Tchaikovsky's harrowing, hyper-romantic *Queen of Spades* and Strauss' elegant, creamy *Capriccio*; it brought two handsome new productions of standard fare: *Forza del Destino* and *Barber of Seville*; and it offered revivals of such long unplayed material as *Mefistofele* and *Samson and Delilah*. There was also a revival of Poulenc's *Dialogues of the Carmelites*, continuing evidence of Adler's wish to test the endurance of relatively viable items in his contemporary repertoire.

Traviata and *Aida* were not treated to totally new productions, but they were rearranged (Mickey Moused, to use a Farruggio phrase) and freshened up. And Joan Sutherland, this time with husband Bonynge in the pit, shone new brilliance on *Sonnambula*. *Falstaff* was repeated from the previous season, principally as the Guild matinee fare for young people (Evans was keen on playing it for *them*), and the meaty rep also included *Walküre* and *Tosca*, plus *Cosi*, home from a 1961 loan to the Chicago Lyric.

The 1963 season also marked the local debut of Reri Grist, the inimitable lyric coloratura who was to become a company fixture in a range of roles including Susanna, Rosina, Oscar, Sophie, Zerbinetta, etc. long before reaching the Met. And it should also be remembered as the season which brought back a new, more interesting, Regina Resnik after fifteen years' absence from the company (she had appeared briefly with the Cosmopolitan in the interim). The new visit found her a mezzo, not a soprano, and a brilliantly mature actress.

German baritone Hermann Prey, Cockney soprano Amy Shuard, French conductor Georges Prêtre—they were important personalities on the scene, too.

Skalicki designed a sprawlingly somber *Spades*, counterpointing massive statuary with lots of airspace, and causing one to wonder, is this an aching hollow of panic through which the players move so elegantly? In line with his expressionistic-surrealistic approach, director Hager subtracted a sizeable amount of local color (the children's chorus at the beginning, the extended Mozartean masque and entrance of the Empress in Act 2) and focused on the tormented central characters. Some charming music was lost in the cutting, but the show was laudably tight. *Spades* IS a very long opera, and a bit diffuse. Suffice to say it made a difficult problem for the scissoring department.

Resnik, a prober of character unsurpassed on the operatic stage, cast a rare spell as the sinister old Countess. Who isn't chilled by the memory of her drowsy nostalgia as she sat in that high-backed chair, musing over life as it used to be, with Herman hovering in the shadows. McCracken took this part, giving it the ideal blend of driven emotionalism and vocal suavity—the latter even while singing with his head dangling backward over the edge of a bench. John Shaw of Covent Garden was a dashing Tomsky, Dorothy Kirsten a fairly effective Lisa, and Leopold Ludwig's conducting was exceptionally taut. The opera was sung in English, and with predominantly clean diction.

Spades, to no one's surprise, emerged as a gripping piece of theater. *Capriccio* looked to be more of a problem, what with its conversational emphasis, and all that talk in German. But thanks to the poised, plastic, affectionate conducting of

Prêtre, and a superior cast led by Schwarzkopf as the Countess, the show went over nicely. It was played with pillars from the second act of Bauer-Ecsy's 1961 *Figaro*, redraped for the occasion. Schwarzkopf never sang this Countess elsewhere in the U.S., and very little in Europe, although she did record it. Relatively early in her career she sang it at the Paris Opéra-Comique, in French.

Leonardo Wolovsky, an American bass-baritone with Frankfurt and Hanover associations, was the La Roche, turning in a commanding performance which registered better than his lethargic Alfonso in *Cosi*. Prey's handsome Olivier was top class, and Thomas Stewart was in good form as the Count, drawing him as a stumbling silly. Two memorable comic vignettes must be listed: Glade Peterson, as an Italian Singer, eyeing his reward for musicmaking, a piece of splendiferous cake, and Joshua Hecht, a servant, patting a foldup horse and chariot brought in as a theatrical prop.

The new *Forza* was launched in memory of Merola, who had died a decade earlier. It was one of his favorite operas, but had been given no special production treatment during his long regime. The second act set, for instance, was interchangeable with *Suor Angelica*. Stark Spanish atmosphere under a recurrently fateful sky—this was the predominant note of the new show, with Bauer-Ecsy eschewing, as usual, undue massiveness. The opera was played, according to San Francisco *Forza* tradition, as close to uncut as an 8 p.m. curtain permitted.

Of course the new *Forza*'s most meaningful asset from the audience point of view was the Leonora of Leontyne Price. She was taking on the role for the first time. With her soaring line, smooth from a light, sweet top down to those velvety chest tones, she had no trouble establishing the happy inevitability of her assignment. McCracken was the heroic, plaintive-voiced Alvaro.

The *Barber*, designed by Alfred Siercke and directed by the celebrated Günther Rennert (who had the cast to himself for a couple weeks' rehearsal at Nourse Auditorium near the Opera House) turned out to be one of those intoxicatingly lovable productions stirring affection of the same sort as the previously welcomed *Cosi* and *Falstaff*. Siercke's tour de force unit set, employed before in Europe but new to San Francisco, brought a three-story, multi-chambered, life-size house (doll house?) which was set quite close to the proscenium.[2] With a spiral staircase affording vertical transport, the characters moved up and down besides in and out, shutters opening and closing to reveal particular rooms at particular points in the action. Stairs from the pit allowed a further degree of mobility, and characters sang on occasion with their feet dangling into the pit. The business was all very carefully worked out, and there *was* a lot of it, but it flowed nimbly, spontaneously.

As if the production itself weren't captivating enough, the premiere offered the local debut of Grist, an exceedingly bright, stylish performer whose wistful-sounding, girlish soprano defied critical analysis. Prey was a huge-toned, magnetic Figaro, Cesare Valletti an experienced Almaviva. Elfego Esparza, a pug-faced American bass from Düsseldorf, took on Bartolo, suggesting a new model, somewhat less broad Baccaloni. Peter Van Der Bilt, a young and first-class Dutch bass, was a comically dour Basilio. And Sona Cervena made an hilarious impression as Bertha. Ferencsik's conducting was elegant, radiant, fun-conscious, though sometimes a little heavy.

A red-faced, scratch-happy creature with red hair tied into an apple bun on the top of her head, and a loony, vacant expression down below, Cervena seemed a mixture of washerwoman and battleaxe. There were a number of delicious antics in her script, but perhaps the most memorable bit was that determined shaking-out of a rug from the third floor balcony, dust set flying without thought of creatures down below. That dust provided motivation, perhaps, for subsequent Rossinian sneezes. The ubiquitous Colin Harvey was Cervena's companion in slovenly servantship, playing a mesmerized Ambrosio.

Mefistofele came back, after a decade, under something of a cloud. It's an opera which has a way of falling apart now and again due to a lack of tight organization. But repeatedly it picks itself up with inspired snatches of melody and fascinating shocks of vivid harmonic and instrumental coloring. The skimpily-rehearsed revival fit Boito's problematical work only too well, which is to say the show fell apart now

205

and again, only to prop itself up with glorious singing and convincing stage pictures.

The most stable and praiseworthy elements were Costa's moving Margherita and Molinari-Pradelli's affectionate conducting. Konya trod through Faust's part with the gingerly attitudes of a man who's afraid his shoes might squeak. And wrongly-typed Tozzi, while he looked an impressive devil, had neither the coal black bass a No. 1 demon demands, nor the abandon.

Remember those pictures of sets in the ancient editions of the Victor Book of the Opera? Well, the San Francisco Opera's "production" of *Samson and Delilah*, not seen since 1949, belonged in that company. The scenery was out of the dim past—including the jungle for Delilah's home in the valley at the top of the mountain. But there was nothing dim about the passionate, characterful conducting of Prêtre, nor the trumpety Samson of McCracken. His wife, Sandra Warfield, was the Delilah, singing with less magnetism, but, especially in the second performance, making some lovely sounds. The High Priest, new to the U.S., was Belgium's Julien Haas, a baritone with a vibrant, gutty, anti-bel canto style which sometimes forced him out of tune.

The vivid temple-toppling finale was, dare one say it, a smash, nicely cooked up by Lotfi Mansouri, the new Persian-American, Zurich-based director, a protege of Herbert Graf. He and Lew Christensen worked out a magnificently Hollywoodesque ballet in which they said, in effect, there's no sense trying to hide the hokum.

Carmelites is a fragile opera, difficult to bring off because of its bare minimum of musical contrasts, its emphasis on talk rather than action, and its exceedingly refined tone. However, if a production finds the right key, this instrument can unlock some beatific expression which grips mightily and gives an audience the shivers. The 1963 revival was something of a paradox because a number of the leading performers were decidely in the room of success, but the key was still, in certain basic respects, left unturned in the lock. Scanty rehearsal didn't help. Lee Venora, a Spring Opera alumna, conveyed the fragility of the fearful Blanche most eloquently with her light, sensual soprano. Nor could one fault Grist's bright, pure Sister Constance. And Resnik was, expectedly, a remarkable First Prioress. But all this wasn't enough. The logical choice for conductor would have been Prêtre, but he was busy with *Capriccio,* so the task fell to Ludwig, a man to whom the special Gallicism of Poulenc was less than ideally clear. The sentiment, the wonderment, the halting, ecstatic quality of the score—these eluded him, and without them the opera's latent monotony became too real. Furthermore, a more consistent treatment of the time between scenes was needed. Sometimes the curtain came down, sometimes it stayed up while the audience waited beyond the psychological moment.

But there were only kudos for the staging of *Traviata,* another Mansouri-Christensen collaboration. There were delightful touches: Flora's putting on a top hat, a cackling card player, and the girl who ran after the handsome dancer in the third act party scene. Speaking of Flora, rarely has this lady had as much personality as Cervena gave her. And rarely, too, had a portrayal of Douphol emerged as vividly as Esparza's. This *Traviata* was a tribute to Adler's "depth casting." Costa was again the extrovert Violetta; Stewart's rather cloudy Germont disappointed.

The company did not go so far as to label the latest *Aida* a new production, but it did boast beautiful new projections, handsome new costumes, and, in the Triumphal and Nile scenes, a laudable switch to diagonal rather than head-on arrangement of the building-block platforms. There was a real march of triumph in the second act, a tradition which could be welcomed back with an armful of palmleaves. Perhaps the projection of magnificent portals didn't need to resemble the opening of a 20th Century Fox movie, but that is a coincidence which can go unnoticed in the light of the "interim" production's basic success.

There was a king on each side of the footlights when Verdi's perennial opened the season September 13—a season which ran seven weeks instead of the established six. Ancient Egypt was represented on stage, contemporary Afghanistan in Kurt Adler's box. A royal performance is what you'd expect under such circumstances and, in certain respects, this was what the audience got. The biggest news in the starry cast was the unforced, sophisticated and tellingly musical Amneris of Resnik. To have Resnik *and* Price's ever-growing Aida on stage at the same time was more exciting than ten toy fire trucks at a five-year-old boy's birthday. Konya and McCracken were the season's Rhadames, Shaw and Haas the Amonasros.

Sonnambula found La Sutherland abandoning in large degree the arch, mannered approach which has vitiated the effect of so many of her recordings. There was a further asset in the Rodolfo of young Richard Cross. His swaggering, slyly melodramatic impersonation of this dashing playboy indicated a true feeling for the stage. In *Walküre* Shuard was a zesty, sympathetic Brünnhilde, Wolovsky a woolly Wotan and Siw Ericsdotter a fair Sieglinde. Vickers' Siegmund was the main asset.

The Los Angeles season involved the cancellation of *Spades*—and a gross of $25,000—on the night following President Kennedy's assassination. Sandra Warfield, beset by bronchitis, was replaced by Nell Rankin as Delilah and Amneris, and by Blanche Thebom as Mother Marie in *Carmelites*. Poulenc's opera had the least success at the box office, *Aida* and *Forza* the most. The *Mefistofele* audience, if not capacity, went wild. Another substitute was Otto Edelmann, the Wotan for San Diego after Wolovsky lost his voice. The total Los Angeles gross was an encouraging $577,000, with average attendance in the Shrine 5544 persons.

Spring Opera's 1963 season, from April 30 to June 8, brought at least two very stylish programs: a double bill of Bartok's *Bluebeard's Castle* (in a new production designed by Archie Sharp) and Ravel's *Spanish Hour* (in the still viable 1945 set from the parent company), and a single one of Donizetti's indefensibly neglected *Don Pasquale*, an opera Adler was convinced wouldn't sell. This one also came from Merola's warehouse, and was done in English. Charles Bressler, a crisp, musicianly tenor best known for his oratorio and antique music performances, joined the familiar Venora, Beattie and Richard Fredricks to propel the Ravel and Donizetti to captivating triumphs. Beverly Wolff and Peter Harrower were the Judith and Bluebeard in the Bartok.

Porcaro's latest, and last, contribution to Spring Opera's growing list of new productions was a *Tales of Hoffmann*

208

which, while not perfectly brought off, included some of his customary bits of whimsy—a sample would be the cable car lever worked by Cochenille to get the doll into action. Robert Moulson, a tenor who graduated to East Berlin, was a Hoffmann of more than promise, and Beverly Wolff an enticing Giulietta. A re-do of the Porcaro *Magic Flute* went awry because insufficient rehearsal made it impossible for Henry Lewis, the idealistic conductor, to get his broad, serene, Olympian interpretation through to the cast. There were gaffs, too, like costuming Monostatos as a cross between Chaplin and Hitler, then changing his makeup halfway through the evening.

On October 15, 1963 it was announced that the Ford Foundation had granted Spring Opera a five-year grant of $125,000, the amount to be matched by the company raising its annual base of support $12,500 by the third year, and $25,000 by the end of the grant. The money was not aimed at providing basic operating expenses; the purpose, rather, was to allow the company—along with twelve other U.S. organizations—to lengthen its season and expand its repertoire. The immediate result was that the 1964 season brought seven instead of six different operatic bills.

1964

Harrowing as the spring prelude to the 1961 season was, 1964 can claim the record in terms of pre-season tribulation. The year's performances were literally snatched from just inside the gates of cancellation. Protracted negotiations between the Opera Association and the Musicians' Union reached the "final" point of non-resolution August 26 and the season was formally cancelled. That means telegrams sent to artists in the East and abroad telling them not to come. And since the season was little more than two weeks away, many were about to step on a jet.

There was, however, another installment of that familiar drama *The Mayor to the Rescue*, and John F. Shelley banged the heads of the warring parties together in a marathon "last chance" negotiation the following day.

The end may have been nearing in a long tug of war involving controversy over orchestra salary figures, length of contract, hiring of extra musicians, and reenstatement of those laid off. But at about noon on August 27 catastrophe at City Hall appeared certain. Both the union and Miller had rejected a final Shelley appeal for arbitration of the remaining issues. Miller had actually grabbed his hat and was on his way out of the room when Shelley prevailed on him to stay "just another ten minutes." Then the Mayor went back to union representatives and pulled out the stops. And he got the modification that meant resolution: the union would accept a two-year contract instead of holding out for three, in return for establishment of a $180 weekly minimum in the second rather than the third year.[3] When he took this back to Miller he made it plain this was the "final" proposal. Miller accepted it.

At times the air had been pretty strained between Miller and Shelley. Once during the sessions the Mayor told the Opera's steel-faced president he had a cavalier attitude. But now the air was clearing. At 1:50 p.m. Adler flashed the word to his staff that agreement had been reached and ratification seemed assured. The musicians did approve it, 47 to 19, that night. Within minutes, secretaries, publicity staff and other administrative personnel were on the phone and sending wires to Germany, Switzerland, Paris, London, New York, Los Angeles, notifying singers, conductors and stage directors that the cancellation was off.

Meanwhile, Adler, tired but relieved, walked over to the Opera House from City Hall. Hager and other staff greeted him. There were embraces, and solemn handshakes. The whole scene was quite emotional. And then—to business. At 6:45 that evening the chorus was arriving at the stage door, with conductor Prêtre, in flaming red sport shirt, ready to go to work. "Happy?" chorus master Vincenzo Giannini asked one of his charges. "Yes, sir!" came the answer. And another put in, in a mood of jest: "But we only had one night off."

There were not to be many more for a while. The 1964 season marked another increase in length, the playing time having grown from seven to eight weeks. This permitted the company to put on a number of operas three times instead of two in San Francisco, thereby reducing individual performance costs through pro-rating of a production's expenses.

210

Although the average attendance per performance dropped slightly, a total of 114,909 persons took in thirty-seven performances during 1964 as opposed to 104,528 admissions for thirty-two performances in 1963. Meanwhile, the price scale had risen from $4–10 to $4.50–11.50.

The season brought a number of interesting new singers, a new opera for the repertory (Shostakovich's *Katerina Ismailova*) and long-needed new productions of *Fidelio*, *Parsifal* and *Rosenkavalier*. Among the new singers were several of considerably more than routine interest: Pilar Lorengar, a Spanish lirico-spinto who reminded somewhat of Rethberg; Marie Collier, the high voltage Australian soprano (she was Katerina) and Eberhard Waechter, that immensely poised, versatile Austrian baritone.

Robert Ilosfalvy, a Budapest tenor rarely permitted to leave his country (he did ultimately settle in Cologne) made a nice impression with Alfredo, a sort of dress rehearsal for the truly thrilling performances he sang three years later in *Manon Lescaut*. Irmgard Seefried made a belated company debut as a somewhat over-bumptious Octavian, but she calmed down after the first performance. And there were valuable contributions from sopranos Ella Lee and Gladys Kuchta.

Franco Tagliavini, a tall young tenor, no relation to Ferruccio, showed off a pretty voice in *Turandot*. It wasn't quite big enough, however, to match that of Birgit Nilsson, returned after eight years (too long!) as the Principessa. Raymond Wolansky, an American lyric baritone stationed in Stuttgart, began an extended association with the company: his big, open, fairly bel canto baritone was an asset to a number of performances (Exhibit A would be *Carmina Burana*), but a tendency toward uniform coloration became too obvious when Adler used him frequently. Chester Ludgin, an old Spring Opera and New York City Opera hand, moved into the fall season, launching a series of performances which would peg him more as a rugged character baritone than, say, the Germont type.

Katerina, the revised version of Shostakovich's 32-year-old *Lady Macbeth of Mtsensk District* (the revisions, principally involving changes in the texts of the bedroom scenes, are not very extensive) was given its American premiere

October 23. It turned out to be a hypnotically theatrical affair, even if not completely laugh-proof. In a superficial way its characters—the deceitful Katerina, her fatuous husband, her bullying father-in-law, her ambitious lover—are not sympathetic. And yet one can't help feeling they are all caught in a pathetic vortex. They are like life itself, even if treated like figures in a dream. The atmosphere is real, the passions and crimes are real, and there are passages of wrenching pathos. Meanwhile the element of wild, loony mockery and consuming irony is never far away.

Examples are easily citable: when Boris Timofeyevich, the brutish merchant, and father-in-law to Katerina, enters, he does so to a bizarrely bouncy bassoon. It doesn't so much "represent" Boris as it makes fun of his pretensions, his strutting, swaggering conception of himself as a great lover. When Katerina's husband Zinovy goes off on a trip he asks her not to forget him, but the irreverently jocular trombone section indicates she probably will. Zinovy's return—he has been supplanted by Katerina's lover Sergei—is accompanied by a most outrageously mock heroic trumpet call. When Katerina, angry at Boris for flogging her lover, serves him a plate of poisoned mushrooms, he eats them to the accompaniment of a syrupy, wistful, heart-rending violin solo. No simple snack music this, it becomes a powerful, sympathy-inducing requiem.

San Francisco's *Katerina* had style, and a coruscating nervous tension which fits the work very well. At the first performance there was, as a matter of fact, too much nervous laughter from the audience, although one can hardly blame the customers for breaking up when Sergei, surprised by Zinovy in the presence of Katerina, proclaimed: "What a mess we're in!" At the second performance this redundant line was omitted. And another one—Sergei's "That's enough" as Zinovy lies dead, strangled *and* bludgeoned—was soft-pedaled.

The production could be described as stark but colorful. Skalicki put together a collection of fragmented sets which worked well in various combinations. While there was an expressionistic tinge to the coloring of the backdrop, the settings were basically realistic, as a subsequent Russian film of *Katerina* made on "location" confirmed, and the lack

212

of any visual tricks helped intensify Katerina's nightmare. One could argue with Hager's Brechtian direction which set the old convict so far apart from his hapless fellows on the road to Siberia. But the trance-like immobility of Katerina herself—at the very beginning of the opera, and also when she finds herself, in the fourth act, in a sort of transfixed agony—was most effective. Much of the credit belonged to Collier, who made a strong impression in her American debut. There were high marks for Ludwig, too, whose conducting extracted maximum poetry from Katerina's soliloquys, and the last ounce of abandon from the racy spots. Vickers caught Sergei's suavely slimey opportunism perfectly, Ludgin was a solid enough Boris, Tozzi a striking Convict.

Vickers' Florestan (he looked like Beethoven himself) was a commanding contribution to *Fidelio*, newly viewable in a Skalicki production which, on first sight, seemed one of the most succinct and satisfying in company history. Gone was the building blocks-in-a-cave look of the 1937 set. Instead, the audience beheld a huge grillwork cutting across the stage diagonally, separating imprisonment from freedom and making a most authoritative barrier. Additions and subtractions of minimal props helped achieve scene changes. The lighting effects, particularly the chiaroscuro of soldiers lined up inside the grill (they came to attention with chilling Nazi efficiency), were most dramatic. Hager wisely cut out the silly parade during the first act march music, and indeed, his general call for restrained movement heightened the sobriety of the story and lessened the melodramatics. Nilsson was the Fidelio, great in voice but lacking in warmth. Evans took on Pizarro for the first time, dispatching his first act aria from the footlights in an unflinchingly granitic-hypnotic position.

Parsifal was another Skalicki-Hager collaboration. The action took place between scrim and cyclorama, the latter busy with projections, and in the filmy middleworld there were frozen, subtly lighted knights suggesting Gothic statuary set free from cathedral niches. The producers aimed at creating a state of half-waking, half-sleeping, and to a large extent the suspended feeling they sought was achieved. Projections were employed to mirror the characters' moods and thinking, the visual comment varying from expressionistic to rococo. There was some feeling the parade of projections was too busy, and there was a reduction in number at the repeats; a pity that this house-cleaning meant the loss of that spinning cathedral which fitted the transformation music so well in the middle of the first act, even if it did jerk a bit.[4]

Prêtre conducted with the continence which had marked his *Capriccio*, and if the choral forces were not as sumptuous as those to be found in Bayreuth or Berlin, the cast *was* better than some of the distributions an opera buff might encounter on leading European stages. Dalis was a vivid Kundry, Konya gave up his gulps and plods for a beautifully-done Parsifal, Waechter presented an Amfortas who knew the value of understatement, and Tozzi, although he was not into the notes until after the first performance, was an elegant, sympathetic Gurnemanz. The Klingsor of Joshua Hecht, the company's lively utility bass, seemed to show promise of more important Wagnerian roles to come.

The new Bauer-Ecsy *Rosenkavalier* succeeded in underlining the social distinctions of the various acts notably well, although the honest fade of the Marschallin's correctly elegant palace took the shade of a rather gruesome lavender. Completely satisfying was the spanking brilliance of Faninal's mansion with its nouveau riche confectioner's green. As usual, the first act bed was well-hidden, strange this in view of the classic permissiveness of San Francisco.

Schwarzkopf and Edelmann were familiar elements in the cast, while Ferdinand Leitner, general music director at Stuttgart, was new on the podium. Barring a couple prosaic moments his baton work was extremely rewarding—for the plasticity of phrase, the tender piloting of slow tempi, the sweet sound he drew from the strings. The Los Angeles performance had a substitute Marschallin, the Munich soprano Hildegard Hillebrecht, summoned for an unscheduled American debut, and on her birthday, too! Régine Crespin was the first choice sub, but she was ill in Chicago. Hillebrecht had just arrived in Munich from Buenos Aires when Adler contacted her, and it was a case of Back to the Airport for her.

The Bartered Bride returned, in English again, but without much special fascination, most of the rehearsal time having gone to new productions. There was, however, another role freshly taken on by Evans, Kezal the marriage broker. This character is a boor pure and simple, and even Evans couldn't make him sympathetic, as he had that delightful other boor, Beckmesser. But he made him entertaining. A paunchy, red nosed creature he presented, crudely pompous and not quite respectable.

Frau Ohne Schatten, virtually standard repertoire in San Francisco, was on the boards again, with Waechter offering the first Barak of his career. Ella Lee, arriving a few seasons late, showed off an ethereal spinto in the Empress role, and Kuchta wowed the public with her luminous powerhouse of a voice as the Dyer's Wife. Dalis repeated her success as the Nurse. The Emperor was Richard Martell, a tenor who had made a nice impression in the 1956 *Tosca*. The interim found him graduating, if that's the word, to such heavier fare as Siegfried. The voice did sound bigger than before, but less sweet. Martell was also Don José, opposite Resnik's authoritative but rather campy Carmen.

In the exit music from Carmen's *Habanera* there was reason to worry over Prêtre's hustling the tempo. Earlier he had rushed Micaela out for sound dramatic reasons—she's afraid of those wolves! But the sum effect of his conducting was an overdose of impulsiveness. Leitner took over when engagements elsewhere called Prêtre away in mid-season; his interpretation was more circumspect, which is not to say placid. Hecht was promoted to Escamillo, offering what was very likely the best toreador San Francisco had seen since Norman Treigle appeared in the role with the Cosmopolitan. The voice was suave and dark, his first entrance had an interestingly macabre flavor, and his super-confidence in the face of Don José's taunts in the third act was delightful.

Carmina Burana returned, paired twice with *Gianni Schicchi* (Gobbi was a twinkly rogue) and once with *Pagliacci*, this the occasion of Robert Weede's return, and farewell, to the San Francisco Opera stage, as Tonio. In his 60's, and with a forty-year career behind him, Weede was establishing himself in the Bay Area as a sought-after teacher.

Speaking of baritones, Waechter left a very attractive impression, not only with his Amfortas and Barak but also those aristocrats Germont and Almaviva. In *Traviata* the Viennese charmer made most Papa Germonts look stiff in comparison, and as for the Count in *Figaro*, this character who can be

215

such a stuffy stick emerged, in the Waechter portrayal, as the confident, amorous, easy-going socialite he is. It was just another case of Waechter going beyond acting and turning into the character portrayed. Possibly the fact that Waechter is a real-life nobleman helped.

Sutherland was the year's Violetta, producing great queues for Standing Room along the Van Ness Avenue sidewalk, and playing the part with a stock sort of wistfulness. Bonynge conducted, restoring some cuts (Alfredo sang his second act cabaletta), and much of Mansouri's lively direction from 1963 went out the window.

Meanwhile, Harold Rosenthal, editor of *Opera Magazine* in London, was in San Francisco and Chicago for several performances and gave the informed outsider's view as follows: ". . . Some of the results achieved, with what many a European would consider the bare minimum of rehearsal, do great credit to both organizations. For a parallel one turns back to the famous annual eight weeks of International Opera at Covent Garden in the inter-war years. For a more modern parallel, one could compare Chicago to an Italian house, like the San Carlo at Naples or the Teatro Massimo in Palermo, and the San Francisco to a first rate German or Austrian house. Indeed there is a flavor of Vienna or Hamburg about San Francisco under the Vienna-born Kurt Adler, with Paul Hager as chief producer and Leopold Ludwig as chief conductor of the German works . . . with some of the settings designed by Leni Bauer-Ecsy and Jean-Pierre Ponnelle. They are assisted by the gifted young producer Lotfi Mansouri . . . By bringing back this team Mr. Adler has established an artistic continuity.

"Nor is Mr. Adler afraid of engaging promising young American artists, and some of the best performances I heard in California came from some of the young singers in small roles . . . The small-part singers who in San Francisco had been so distinguished, were not so good in Chicago.

"The auditorium of the War Memorial Theater in San Francisco is large and comfortable, and the proscenium arch very much like that of the San Carlo, Naples. But the atmosphere both in San Francisco and Chicago has something of the enormous super-cinema about it . . . In San Francisco the audience behavior was excellent; Chicago's audiences were more Italianate, and broke into every aria with applause drowning the orchestra."

Following a troubled midseason amid the snares of French opera, Spring Opera ended its 1964 season with two blazes of success—both taking place inside a harem. There was an affectionate revisiting of *Abduction*, and a welcome production, completely new, of Rossini's *Italian Girl in Algiers*, the latter given twice. Patricia Brooks, a spunky mainstay of the New York City Opera, was the bombshell Blonde in *Abduction;* Herbert Beattie was the memorable Mustapha in the Rossini. Beattie earned the description of "adult basso buffo" because his mugging was always inextricably bound up with a genuinely musical and accurate account of the score. This Mustapha had real dignity, and was immensely funny into the bargain.

Director Bliss Hebert and designer Allen Klein propelled their Rossini audiences to a never-never land of rabbit-suited eunuchs, a Viking-styled getaway boat, and sets that looked like cardboard cutouts for a children's puppet show. Marilyn Horne, happier with the bel canto coloratura mezzo repertory than the rugged female types Adler had been offering her, was the sumptuous-sounding, bubblingly comic Isabella. Husband Henry Lewis' conducting was full of rhythmic impetus and elegant phrasing, and he unscrambled those complex ensembles with a razor-sharp transparency.

Pearl Fishers and *Faust*, unevenly cast, did not further Spring Opera's ideals. But Carlisle Floyd's *Susannah*, in a new production, and with that important singing actor Norman Treigle as the preacher, was something of a milestone. A pithy opera, rushing firmly to its conclusion with music easy on the ears but integral to the drama, it could hardly help making a rather strong impression, and it attracted about 4000 customers, divided over two performances.

Thanks to the helping financial hands of the Ford Foundation, there was yet another new production, Weber's highly melodious, rustically mystical and hard-to-translate *Der Freischütz*, bravely put into English, including a line, "Pull yourself together, Max" (that being Richard Cassilly) which sent the Opening Night audience into gales of laughter. But the capacity crowd was indulgent and when the lead singers were on stage there was quite a bit to be happy about. The score, of course, has some gems of melody and belongs on the main line from Beethoven to Wagner. Elisabeth Mosher, a local girl who'd been singing abroad, was the Agathe, phrasing aristocratically and showing off a silvery soprano of promise. Gwen Curatilo, a resident local, surpassed all previous efforts with a deft, cute, cozy Aennchen. Jan Popper of UCLA, who had conducted the last Bay Area *Freischütz* at Stanford University in 1946, was on the podium. Dino Yannopoulos had some of his customary trouble with choral movement, but he concocted a chilling Wolf Glen Scene. Wolfgang Roth's setting made marvelous use of airspace and threatening silhouettes, and Yannopoulos trained a symphony of light and shade upon it.

1965

An inflated, ill-conceived *Fledermaus*, and a *Pelléas et Mélisande* with much magic: these were leading contrasts of the 1965 season. The *Fledermaus* (in English) was especially surprising because it was so blatantly a contradiction of the typical San Francisco Opera style—a style in which lightness and buoyancy of scenic design are the rule. This *Fledermaus*, with all its cumbersome grandeur, couldn't have been more off the track.

Thank Heaven, at least, for the third act, in which the cast, rather than the props, was allowed to do the moving around in Herr Frank's delightful prison. It followed a lethargic ballroom scene in which the characters were all but buried in a dreary choreography for furniture. The whole point of the party at Orlofsky's is gaiety, and in a buoyant production the facile flow of the cast through the glitter can be exhilarating. But designer Oliver Smith, used to providing visual distractions for tiresome Broadway musicals, joined Hager in a massive choking of humanity. There were more moving parts than in a giant factory. Exotic couches, with paintings or mirrors attached to them like huge windshields for horseless carriages, kept moving itchily back and forth. Pieces of scenery flew up and down like elevators in a busy department store. Tiers of boxes on each side of the stage turned this way and that. And the lights went up and down as if there were trouble at the nearest PG&E substation.

218

As some one asked during an intermission, "Well, are you overwhelmed?" And that seemed to be the point of the production, to clobber the audience. When, five years later, the possibility of a *Fledermaus* revival was mentioned, one buff suggested, with much point, that the management be sure to "nail down" the show.

Very likely the production would not have gone so awry if Adler hadn't been convinced that *Fledermaus* in the Opera House had to be BIG. A pity it did misfire because there were excellent performers in the cast who didn't need such heavy framing: Reri Grist, for instance, who made a radiant Adele; Richard Lewis, a most agreeable Eisenstein; and Raymond Wolansky, ingeniously made up to suggest a doltish public official, as Frank. Scott Beach from The Committee, that band of local cabaret satirists, was a Frosch comparable to the tipsy best, and he slid down a challenging fire pole with delightful abandon.

Jean Martinon, then conductor of the Chicago Symphony, received a major ovation for his work in *Pelléas*. He produced a succession of the most glorious pianissimi to fall gently, but pointedly, on San Francisco Opera patrons' ears, and his luminous, vibrant interpretation was eminently satisfying. Much that transpired on stage was highly successful, too, although there were inconsistencies to be noted. Skalicki set the players down in a great Parsifalian space between scrim and cyc which suggested the amorphous reaches of Arkel's never-never castle, and, at the same time, the claustrophobia which tends to make its inhabitants sad.

In line with the muted orchestration, and his usual way of direction, Hager sought to keep the action subdued and the number of literal details at a minimum. But the question did arise, where is the line drawn, and is there really a clear one between important visual symbols and useless trappings? Mélisande carried no flowers, but did throw a ring into the air at the fountain, while Pelléas was not given the chance to fondle her long hair. The last tragic love duet was not played at the fountain, as prescribed, but this gave Skalicki and Hager a chance to set the couple in a symbolically appropriate crown of thorns.

The tragedy of *Pelléas et Mélisande* is, of course, as much Golaud's as that of the title players because he simply cannot tune in on the same love-death wave length. They remain airy, he is literal. Thomas Stewart met the challenge of the role with penetration, although Hager's restriction of his action at the beginning was not convincing. André Jobin, son of Raoul, was an attractively ardent Pelléas, and his lack of affectation went a long way toward excusing a bad habit of carelessly draping off-pitch notes into a phrase. Pilar Lorengar had the right trembly warmth for Mélisande, if not the fragile figure.

Two of the other new productions, *Don Giovanni* designed by Smith, and a Boston *Ballo in Maschera* by Lloyd Burlingame, suffered from casts which left more or less to be desired. And with that low score for *Fledermaus*, plus a few other disappointments, the 1965 record must stand as somewhat less fine that that of the immediately preceding years. The *Don* was argued over heatedly, many customers feeling it lacked the grandeur and sobriety requisite for Mozart's opera. However, in terms of the work's subtitle, *dramma giocoso*, the lightness of the show was not entirely inapropos. Smith and Hager's general plan involved the juggling of several chunks of scenery which suggested chess pieces. It's not easy to give an exact count because they turned up pointed in different directions. They were conceived to turn in front of the audience and facilitate a lightning-quick pace of production. But an insufficiency of time and money (the errant *Fledermaus* siphoned off more than its share) prevented full realization of what might have been an ingenious solution to a classic problem.[5] Even so, a compact and fairly agreeable stylization was achieved. And miracle of miracles, Smith and Hager devised the first truly convincing demise of the Don to be seen in San Francisco. Usually he seems to sneak off all too obviously behind some furniture, but this time he was magnetized right into the mausoleum housing the dead Commendatore's statue. And the doors clamped shut behind him!

Weaknesses in the cast were Lucine Amara's bright but wooden Elvira, Meneguzzer's shrill Zerlina, and the weary Commendatore of Thomas O'Leary, an American bass from the Nürnberg Opera and Vienna Volksoper who could do better, witness his beautiful-sounding Pogner. Ugo Trama, another new bass, was an exceptionally nimble and tasteful

220

Leporello, with a nice point on his coal black tone. Stewart was a suave-sounding but not mercurial Don, Lewis still an elegant Ottavio and Price a stunning Anna (succeeded at the third *Giovanni* by Lorengar in one of her greatest performances).

The *Ballo* came on lackluster with Konya's insufficiently characterized Riccardo, Wolansky's dullish Renato, Meneguzzer's unstylish Oscar, Claramae Turner's less than mellifluous Ulrica, and Molinari's heavy conducting, a letdown after his buoyant *Chenier*. This leaves Price, who sang the first Amelia of her career in this dubious atmosphere, and a fairly gorgeous-sounding one it was, too. Burlingame's sets put much emphasis on heavy Jacobean wood—"Puritanical meat and potatoes architecture," he called it, "because New England wasn't really affluent in those days."

Alban Berg's *Lulu* was the year's new addition to the repertoire. Hager and Bauer-Ecsy gave it a skillful production, the characters emerging from a Jungle Gym-like apparatus. But the opera, compared to *Wozzeck*, is grossly unsympathetic. In *Lulu* one never loses the sense of the title figure's lack of humanity. It's in some of the other characters that one finds people who might arouse some sympathy. The situation in *Wozzeck*, generally speaking, is the reverse. The dreary main protagonist is drenched with humanity, and he comes to epically dramatic grief because he *has* feelings. In *Wozzeck* it's the fleeting figures, not the dominating one, who are maddeningly lacking in understanding.

The animalistically mindless Lulu was Evelyn Lear, and the possessed, helpless Dr. Schoen Ramon Vinay, who was returning—as a baritone—to the company after many years. He also made a cheerful Bartolo (it was his first) in Rennert's *Barber*, and a superb Scarpia, bestial and unctuous, cunning yet spontaneous. Stage manager Matthew Farruggio was caretaker of Rennert's production, providing a touch or two of his own, for instance Bartolo's magnificent yawn which found his mouth wide open just as Rosina opened hers for a high note in the Lesson Scene. An unintentional bit of humor overtook *Lulu* in Los Angeles when Evelyn Lear's gun failed to go off at the point when she kills Dr. Schoen. Prompter Philip Eisenberg happened to have a spare pistol in his box, and he quickly shot it off virtually on cue. He almost went up in smoke in the process.

Marie Collier was 1965's Tosca, arousing argument over her high-strung first moments on stage. They are justified to a degree by the directions in the score, but this Tosca came dangerously close to being downright unattractive in her all-out irritation. Collier's second act, however, was wonderful, with marvelous details like her obvious distaste at prying the safe-conduct out of the dead Scarpia's hand. And it took a couple of tugs, too.

There were three different Cavaradossis: Konya, Jess Thomas and Franco Corelli. The most intelligent and consistently characterized was that of Conquering Hero Thomas, returning to his home city eight years after winning the San Francisco Opera Auditions. In the interim he had, of course, gone abroad to forge an important career. Piero Bellugi's conducting in *Tosca* was rather low pressure, lyrical, intimate.

Corelli had been the intended Chenier on the Opening Night card, with *Fanciulla* also on his agenda, but an orthopedic problem kept him benched until a *Tosca* late in the season. Richard Tucker flew out for two Cheniers, opposite an all-there Renata Tebaldi, and Giovanni Gibin, the Brazilian tenor, took over two Dick Johnsons (Corelli did the part in Los Angeles) and one Chenier. Renato Cioni took Corelli's place in the third *Bohème*. When Corelli finally arrived he sounded glorious enough, but his "acting" was like a series of poses while he marked time waiting for his Moments.

Bastianini sang Gerard in *Chenier* knowing he was incurably ill, and advised that he might live longer if he didn't sing.

One of the joys of the season was Collier's first assumption anywhere of that pistol-packing assignment, Minnie in *Fanciulla*. The powderkeg soprano played the part as if the inconsistencies of the lady simply did not exist. The heroine is, of course, the owner of a saloon in the Wild West, but she has never kissed a man. The result is a sort of tomboy, and that is what Collier made of her. The vocalism was warm and pulsating, with a true Puccini voice clearly marked for Minnie and the Giorgetta of *Tabarro*. The tall, handsome Gibin made a commanding Dick Johnson, singing with a grand old-fashioned tenor which suggested the nasal coloration of Pertile in mid-range and soared gloriously on top. Chester Ludgin was a sonorous Rance (less malevolent than Gobbi) and Molinari-Pradelli the immensely congenial conductor.

Extended playing time meant that more and more singers were coming and going platoon-fashion while the season progressed, but Thomas did stay for the full eight weeks[6] and sang four parts: Lohengrin, Stolzing, Bacchus in *Ariadne* and the Cavaradossi. Pleasure from his performances was matched, in *Lohengrin* and *Ariadne*, by the conducting of Horst Stein, a Kleiber disciple who had served conspicuously at the State Opera in East Berlin, left the "East" for Hamburg, and who, following a stint as general music director in Mannheim, would become first conductor at the Vienna State Opera and be appointed g.m.d. back in Hamburg. A rock-like control and a suave lyric touch: this combination made him a decided asset, and he was quickly reengaged. Time proved him to be a more consistent man for the German wing than Ludwig, whose work was showing a pattern of variance from taut to tepid. If Stein's Wagner was sometimes a trifle light, his *Elektra* (1966) and *Salome* (1968) had a tremendous long-range suspense and intensity, and, when appropriate, a special kind of poetry, too—witness, for instance, the very slow and tastefully soulful orchestral interlude in Elektra's opening monologue. Stein's intensity, it must be stressed, was never blatant, only inexorable.

The *Meistersinger* revival benefited from the first David of Alexander Young, the light but firm-voiced English tenor. Toni Blankenheim of the Hamburg Opera was a chair-straightening, smile-producing Beckmesser. Heinz Imdahl, a young German, offered a Sachs that was likeable but lacked the grand arches of phrase which create a magnificently wise, autumnal atmosphere around this figure. *Lohengrin* was hampered by the dull, dowdy, unethereal singing of Elsa by Hildegard Hillebrecht. Another case of a show-saver (the Los Angeles *Rosenkavalier* of the year previous) who was gratefully reengaged and failed to deliver. In an unusual switch, due to the indisposition of Hillebrecht, the *Lohengrin* scheduled for October 8 was reassigned to October 12, this putting one *Barber* on the heels of another October 7 and 8.

The home season ending November 3 with *Pelléas*, the troupe went on to Los Angeles, but not to the Shrine. On

November 5 the San Francisco Opera opened its first, and only, season at the Dorothy Chandler Pavilion of the as yet uncompleted Music Center up the hill north of Pershing Square. Capacity, at 3250 seats, was approximately half the Shrine figure, but this didn't mean the house was jammed. With a $50 maximum price, there were several hundred upper scale seats unwarmed, and as the season progressed at a top of $12.50, a considerable hike over the Shrine asking price ($8 in 1964), there were some box office problems. With no permanent guarantee in sight, the company obviously wasn't going to reduce its deficit in the manner to which it was accustomed on Figueroa Street.

Opening Night at Mrs. Chandler's crowning achievement, the result of some very intensive, democratic fund-raising in the southern California manner (as opposed to the more delicate, inbred method traditional in San Francisco), found a number of stage, screen and TV stars among the Beautiful People on hand. And one could admire the delightful chandeliers in the open, curving foyer, the exquisite crystal work over the exits leading from the almost austere wood-dominated auditorium. Raked continental seating produced a more intimate feeling than the heavily-aisled Opera House San Franciscans were used to.

But Martin Bernheimer of Mrs. Chandler's *Times* found occasion to complain vigorously about ill-timed applause, undue chatter, long-distance greetings to friends, and "intramural arguments as to who the characters on stage (in *Ballo in Maschera*) were supposed to be." The admittedly somewhat less sophisticated atmosphere of San Francisco's more populous neighbor to the south was reflected in the abandon with which one customer, following Wolansky's "Eri Tu," cried out: "Sing it again!"[7]

Meanwhile, on November 2, in San Francisco, the voters turned down Proposition B by a vote of 126,000 NO to 60,000 YES. Proposition B was a much-paraded but ill-written plan for a whopping $29 million package to include: 1) construction of a large building behind the existing War Memorial which would include a 2200-seat hall housing performances of "ballet, incidental concerts, recitals and repertory groups," plus a large rehearsal stage and offices for the Opera, Symphony and Ballet, 2) a 700-car garage, 3) a Franklin Street underpass since there would be a corridor from the Opera House to the new building at the rear, 4) rehabilitation of the Opera House, with twenty-nine items listed in reference to this subject in the official brochure, and 5) rehabilitation of the Veterans Building, including a spruce-up of the dowdy, un-theatrically-oriented Auditorium therein.

The people who drew up Proposition B failed to establish a significant enough need for such a huge expenditure. Although there had been discussions in the direction of a Symphony Hall, a 2600 to 2800-seater freeing the Opera House for such theatrical endeavors as opera and ballet, they didn't jell into a definite proposal to the public. It is conceivable that such a proposal, unsaddled by such accoutrements as the underpass and garage, might have made some headway.

San Francisco's cultural leaders were to admit in the years immediately following the sinking of Proposition B that the Symphony Hall idea was the one that really made sense. Just how the various repertory groups—professional, semi-professional and amateur—were going to share the space in the Proposition B theater was never explained. And thankfully not tested. The professional, and exciting, American Conservatory Theater came to San Francisco in 1966 piloted by sometime opera director William Ball. A.C.T. settled in the old but serviceable Geary and Marines Theaters down-town, making do with buckets of paint, showmanship and artistry.

With Proposition B dumped unceremoniously, the trustees set about convincing City Hall that rehabilitation of the Opera House and Veterans Building would have to be effected at least on a year-to-year basis. Improvements were made in that manner, and by June 1968 board chairman Wilson Meyer could take the press on an Opera House tour, pointing out a new gold curtain (the old one was cut up for souvenir neckties etc.), the cleaning of layers of dust from the proscenium and 200-bulb chandelier, and the dressing up of the foyer, lobby and bar areas. Dowdy old dressing rooms had been trans-formed into bright new ones—not lavish but attractive. And the Opera House administration was getting ready to move into relatively spacious quarters at the north side of the house where a high-ceilinged scene shop had been remade into two floors of offices. This meant, among other things, that Company Coordinator Matthew Farruggio would no longer have to work in a closet!

The approximately $750,000 spent on the Opera House between Prop. B and mid-1968 (another $250,000 went to the Veterans Building next door) also included renovation of backstage elevators, an electronic call system to all dressing rooms, and closed-circuit TV linking stage, pit and backstage. Yes, the days of the faithful peep hole were numbered.

Before the 1965 L.A. season of twenty-one performances was over, Zubin Mehta, the new young musical director of the Los Angeles Philharmonic, let drop the information that the San Francisco Opera's current L.A. visit would be its last. Mehta had only revealed what seemed inevitable, ironic as a desertion of the handsome new Music Center might be. A Los Angeles guarantee had been necessary for the '65 visit, and such would be an uncomfortable financial hurdle to be jumped every year. Furthermore, with San Francisco about to lengthen its home season to ten weeks there would be scant time between opera and symphony seasons to allow the orchestra, common to both, to travel to Los Angeles.

While some observers muttered suspensefully about Mehta's alleged ambitions as a producer of opera, the unperturbed Robert Watt Miller, questioned about the Los Angeles situation, commented a bit cavalierly that "If we have a nine or ten week season, and don't go to Los Angeles en masse, it will certainly not diminish the appeal of our company to the big artists. Many of them are happy to come and sing with us for two or three weeks and then move on to the next important point on their itinerary, which may be as distant as Vienna or Buenos Aires."

Heretofore, he pointed out, the San Francisco Opera had had to pay double travel expenses for many artists because they came to San Francisco for a few weeks, returned East or abroad, and then had to be brought back again for the Los Angeles season.

Miller noted that "they have that beautiful new theater down there and we would have been very bad neighbors indeed if we didn't help christen it," but it was obvious to him that San Francisco would not be paying much attention to Los Angeles from then on, unless, that is, Los Angeles pitched in with more resources of its own. Mehta said that L.A. had been negotiating for some of San Francisco's productions to be played in the spring with a southland orchestra. Miller said "there's nothing definite on that yet," but there would be later.

Meanwhile, a move to launch and stabilize the Los Angeles Opera Company, a modest-budget operation presided over by conductor Henry Lewis and director Peter Ebert, came to naught, partly because of internal disagreements and partly because the Music Center people didn't consider it grand enough.

Spring Opera's 1965 season, running from May 25 to June 22, repeated the double bill of *Bluebeard's Castle* (well-conducted by the Oakland Symphony's Gerhard Samuel) and *The Spanish Hour*. The novelty was Robert Ward's *The Crucible*, taking up the same material as Arthur Miller, and like *Susannah* a New York City Opera familiar. It was in approximately the same quasi-folksy style, but less succinct. Only one performance was scheduled by the necessarily cautious Spring forces, but the near-capacity crowd that attended showed honest enthusiasm. There was one performance of the double bill, and two each of *Cosi, Butterfly* and *Rigoletto*. The *Cosi* was done in English, sensitively directed by Bliss Hebert and played in the "fall season" sets banished to the spring—they were beginning to look a little tacky. The *Butterfly* was beautifully conducted by Herbert Grossman. *Rigoletto* offered Linda Newman, the most pulchritudinous but also the most sophomorically giggly Gilda in local memory.

In the *Butterfly*, resident director Farruggio, always intelligent, hit on a memorable bit of business during the touching third act trio. Pinkerton, distraught and remorseful, is pacing around the room. And in this version he picked up, and threw down, a doll, symbol of the child he's about to take away from Cio-Cio-San against his better judgment. In tossing down the doll Pinkerton appeared to be renouncing the child—as well he might.

Although the winter had brought the usual wintry rumors that Spring Opera was about to capsize in a sea of financial trouble, the organization emerged from the 1965 season in healthy shape. Average capacity was only 85%—the lateness of the season didn't help, nor playing *Cosi* the same night

Sviatoslav Richter was at the keyboard up on Nob Hill—but there was an extra dose of energy in the fund-raising, and the operating expenses were less than usual because the season had to be sandwiched between the Symphony's finale and the UN's twentieth birthday observance. The result: a happy burying of a deficit stretching back three seasons.

1966

The management almost hoped the purse string-holding board wouldn't notice, because there were six, count 'em, six new productions for 1966: an *Elektra* from Alfred (*Barber*) Siercke, a *Tannhäuser* by Skalicki, a *Butterfly* by the young Zurich designer Toni Businger, a low-budget *Boris* put together by Dino Yannopoulos, and new to the company two important rarities: Berlioz' *Les Troyens* (Skalicki) and Janacek's *Makropulos Case* (Bauer-Ecsy). Bellini's *Puritani* was also added to the repertoire, but in sets borrowed from Genoa as regular San Francisco performances in the future seemed unlikely.

Other newsworthy features were Marilyn Horne's first Eboli, Ramon Vinay's first American Falstaff, Jess Thomas' first American Tannhäuser, and the belated company debuts of soprano Régine Crespin, mezzo Grace Bumbry and tenor Alfredo Kraus, plus the advent of British baritone Peter Glossop, a relative stranger on the American scene.

The season was, on the whole, one of the best planned and executed in company history. It's too bad the almost perfect record was spoiled by the near-catastrophe which struck the American premiere of the Janacek opera, a worthy addition to the repertoire. Came November 20 it was as if the company offered half a performance of this highly-charged fare. No, the score wasn't cut, but the net effect of the evening was half-baked because stage and pit simply weren't correlated. This is a sorry state of affairs in *Makropulos* because Janacek's orchestra spins the musical thread. The singers, to be sure, have their lyrical moments, but in general they carry on a conversational sort of speech song, and it's the orchestra which picks up and magnifies the emotions.

Marie Collier was magnetic in the central role of Elina Makropulos, and she had a congenial cast around her—literally around her because they repeatedly gathered in a frozen circle with Elina in the center. But in the pit Jascha Horenstein was not running a tight ship. In fact, in his role as captain of the performance the veteran and well-reputed Russian maestro didn't seem to have much idea what his course should be. Momentum was lost, grievous intonation problems arose, and the orchestra sounded as if it were participating in a first reading rehearsal rather than a public presentation.

The score of *Makropulos* is a fascinating example of motivic unity, literally dozens of thematic figures built from the same intervals to show some aspect or relationship of Elina. Any conductor who takes baton to this opera must keep these themes distinct, give them mood, not just run them together into a puny, unphrased mass. Surely if Charles Mackerras, the London and Hamburg-based Janacek expert, had been available to San Francisco—he was the first choice of Collier and Adler—there would have been no cause for complaint. As a matter of fact, Mackerras did visit Horenstein at the Savoy Hotel in London to discuss the score, but evidently to small avail.

The story of *Makropulos*, somewhat better known in the U.S. now because the New York City Opera took it up in 1970, is that of a woman fed a life-giving elixir against her will. By the time the curtain rises she's 342 years old and she's had more than enough. But she's so used to living she can't help searching tenaciously for a recipe refill, and in the process her bizarre, extended past is discovered. The opera is part detective story, part philosophical question-poser, a fantasy clothed in real emotion. The audience has to believe in it, but an ethereal rather than an earnest style would seem to fit better, and this was the route taken by Hager and Bauer-Ecsy.

Gregory Dempsey, a versatile tenor from Sadler's Wells, was an ardent Gregor, Chester Ludgin a magnificently stuffy Prus, New York's Leon Lishner a sonorous lawyer Kolenaty (if not as fussy and wonder-struck as the admirable Eric Shilling at London's Sadler's Wells), and character tenor Robert Glover, a recent Auditions winner, turned in one of his cozy little portraits as Vitek the clerk.

At least three things were certain about the new production of *Les Troyens*, brought out in an "American professional stage premiere." One, that Madame Crespin found the dual

229

assignment of Dido and Cassandra immensely congenial. Another, that the sets, lighting and special effects were exceedingly handsome and dramatic. Yet another, that Louis Erlo's direction kept the action well-controlled and to the point—which is to say suspensefully static, or cataclysmically sudden.

These points established, a touch of chaos sets in because it isn't easy to make capsule decisions about this episodic pageant of an opera, especially as regards the problem of how much to cut and how much to leave in. How to slice Berlioz' five hour behemoth (comprising *The Capture of Troy* and *The Trojans at Carthage*) while serving the composer's best interests: that is a question which the San Francisco Opera did not answer with finality.[8] The three hour show concocted by Erlo and associates was essentially a vehicle for Madame Crespin. It made a reasonably neat package, most of the highlights were there, and some indubitably dull padding was banished. But there were still some serious musical losses, not to mention a few loose ends.

The evening would have been more symmetrical if the scene from the first part of the opera involving the ghost of Hector and Aeneas had been left in. The vital point of Aeneas' being fatefully directed to the shores of Italy was soft-pedalled, not only with the abandonment of this episode but also the elimination of Mercury's "Italie, Italie" later on, which Erlo felt might sound ludicrous.[9]

After Crespin's loud, shrill Elisabeth in *Tannhäuser* (the role of her San Francisco debut) it was a pleasure to salute her magnificent work in *Troyens*. Dido and Cassandra are more heroically pitched, and that state of affairs seemed to suit her better. She offered meltingly beautiful tone, and a genuinely coruscating intensity. Vickers' Aeneas was a stalwart characterization, although his costume, a cross between a Santa Claus and a Superman suit, did him small justice. His soft singing tended to be softer than the Crespin pianissimo, and one could quibble that their blend was less than ideal, but, when both singers were so much in the mood of what they were singing, it seems beside the point to fuss.

Troyens, even truncated (which is not to say that a completely uncut version would be so palatable), was one of the season's biggest hits. But the most memorable event of all was the *Elektra*, strongly cast, beautifully conducted (by Stein) and intelligently staged. Siercke's production centered on a tholos, a beehive Mycenean tomb modelled after archaeologist Schliemann's Treasury of Atreus and affectionately known around the Opera House as the "igloo." It created the right sort of claustrophobic atmosphere, and to have Elektra spending her time so close to Agamemnon's resting place made good dramatic sense.

Amy Shuard registered Elektra's seething discontent only too well. The fresh, springlike Chrysothemis of Enriqueta Tarrés, a young Spanish soprano, provided just the right foil, and the intensity and subtle coloring in Regina Resnik's Klytemnestra were spellbinding. Thomas Stewart's introspective, Bayreuthized Orestes proved one of his best achievements, as appropriate a measure of his mature style as his Salzburg Wotan with Karajan. Richard Cassilly's Aegisthus was appropriately foppish.

Jess Thomas sang his first American Tannhäuser in the new production launched October 18. Not very many weeks before, he had sung the first of his career at Bayreuth. The night of October 18 he sang with a particular person on his mind: Wieland Wagner, the genius without whom Bayreuth would have been a much less interesting place in the post-War years. Wieland died in Munich October 17, aged 49.[10] His death was a special jolt for San Francisco because, after ten years of discussions, he had finally accepted an invitation to make a production or two on Van Ness Avenue. He was slated to stage *Tristan* and/or *Salome* in 1967. The *Tannhäuser* cast happened to include two other singers with considerable Bayreuth associations, Crespin and Stewart, and a conductor (Stein) and a stage director (Hager) who worked at the famous festival early in their careers. There must have been a lot of grieving, but the show went on.

Skalicki's production included a marvelously smooth transformation from the nebulous rosy glow of the Venusberg (and a labored ballet) to the mountain valley, although this healthy pastoral scene was not bathed in enough light. After a second act Hall of Song with flown vaulting suggesting Memling, the sequence of events brought the audience back to the valley, and Tannhäuser lying dead in Scarpia position, which is exactly how they found him at the beginning of the

Venusberg Scene. Evidently his life there was a kind of death, too. That's how the Wielandized Hager appeared to see it.

A new production of *Butterfly* was unveiled a few days later with Teresa Stratas in the title role. Plants and flowers were everywhere, and Businger's love nest had a nice blossomy look to it, although it didn't escape the criticism that it resembled a Hallmark card. The diminutive Miss Stratas was made up with a very pale face, she colored her intimate soprano with just the right touch of girlish sound, and the result was as fragile, sad and wistful a Cio-Cio-San as San Francisco is likely to ever experience. She really looked 15, and how often can one say that about a Butterfly? Not often, except that two years later Jeannette Pilou *did* duplicate the effect—minus the semaphoric Japanese gestures prescribed by director Nathaniel Merrill.[11]

The new *Butterfly* replaced an adequate, attractive enough veteran from the warehouse. *Boris '66*, on the other hand, provided an answer to a nagging visual problem. Adler and producer Yannopoulos were only too keenly aware that an earlier "new production" in 1956 had been a dismal flop. Just about everyone, including the Boris himself, Boris Christoff, thought it too bare and stark. In 1961 the company reverted to the 1945 sets in old-fashioned realistic style, relit, of course. But Adler preferred in 1966 to modernize *Boris* rather than continue presenting it in olden style. So Yannopoulos devised a setting in which the dominant feature was a triptych; three drops, that is, on which huge high-rise projections of ikons were shown. As he put it, "We want to create a feeling of Imperial Russia, and when you think of old Russia you think of ikons."

The projections hung over a raked stage, Yannopoulos' palette suggesting the earth colors of veteran Bay Area painter Louis Siegriest as they unfolded a changing exhibit of various churchly motifs. Working with the projections, a few props, and lighting, Yannopoulos managed an economical but rich-looking stylization.

Although it's possible that certain vignettes of the staging were due to the inventiveness of various individual performers, Yannopoulos can be credited with embracing a host of good ideas. Perhaps the most notable was the perpendicular procession in the Coronation Scene. The usual procedure finds a great troop of personages crossing the stage from wing to wing. But in the new San Francisco look there was simply a terse runway from upstage center down to the prompter's box, and some of the dignitaries ran down it with a kind of Police State desperation. Chilling!

A little list of fine points would also include the marvelous treatment of the nurse (Dorothy Cole) in the second act. Instead of bouncing around like a jack-in-the-box she spent much of her stage time bogged down in a chair, a picture of cheerful but drab and arthritic antiquity. And there was David Thaw's gaping, plaintive death-face look as he played the fool at the end of the moving Basiliki scene, the scene of confrontation between Boris and the holy idiot which had never before been done in San Francisco.

Also worth mentioning: Raymond (Missail) Manton's hilarious stacking of wine cups as if he were a child playing with building blocks, and Sona Cervena's comically furious table wiping at the beginning of the Inn Scene.

Chester Ludgin, one of Adler's "minute men," replaced the ailing George London as Boris, rising to the occasion well. The Shostakovich orchestration was used, Stein conducted most effectively, and the opera was wisely sung, as in 1961, in English. Thanks to the intelligent direction and lively cast (Lord Harewood, writing from San Francisco in *Opera*, thought Vinay's Varlaam the best characterized he had ever seen), this was a *Boris* dominated by a sense of realism—the sort which takes opera out of the world of songbirds and puppets and makes it a vivid dramatic experience.

Songbird and Puppetland is, of course, the territory of Bellini's *I Puritani*, which was the season's Opening Night fare. This is the sort of opera that made Gilbert and Sullivan possible. The plot, if such you could call it, is the essence of silliness, and it hangs by a very slender thread. But that thread happens to hang above a veritable Niagara of melody, and that is what *Puritani* is all about. Joan Sutherland, the Elvira, was in characteristic form, which is to say that ebullient, magnetic coloratura vocalism was bothered now and then by covered tones and dropped syllables. Sutherland proved expert, for instance, at turning "secoli" into "sei."

The great news of the *Puritani* was Alfredo Kraus, possessor of Pinza profile and Schipa tenor, or at least a cousin thereto.

233

Kraus' bright lyric timbre, crisp articulation and impeccable taste—all these in company of a sound not strictly gorgeous —were also available in *Rigoletto:* he and Reri Grist made a most sophisticated team, and their duets were real acts of musical togetherness, not competitions.

A jarring foreign note—a fortissimo boo—came sailing down from the upper reaches of the house the night of October 14, the first *Rigoletto.* This blemish on the often exuberant but usually tasteful atmosphere inside the Opera House couldn't have been more out of place. It was directed at Molinari-Pradelli as he took to the podium for the third act. As a matter of fact the previous act had proceeded with considerable impact. The little maestro may have been too sober in his approach to the opening scene, but there was method, and elegance, in his work. The following season he was unavailable to San Francisco, having given himself over to the mercies of the gallery at the Metropolitan. Audience reaction aside, he has been less successful at Lincoln Center than in San Francisco.

Peter Glossop was the Rodrigo in *Don Carlo*, presenting a good case for the argument that this is the opera's central figure. Newsworthy, too, if less successful, was Marilyn Horne's first encounter with Eboli. It marked a complete change from the standard, more aggressive approach. She took the bel canto route, emphasizing an even, creamy tone of Golden Age purity, and building "O don fatale" introspectively. Alas, she went too far, passing by Stignani Land and going on to something else which was a little too refined—with a curious detour into chesty, almost night-clubby fioriture in the Veil Song. There were intonation problems, too, and suffice to say that Horne did not vigorously embrace a role about which she obviously felt some reservations, though she did sing it again in San Antonio a couple of years later.

Claire Watson, the Munich-based American soprano, joined the roster, making a less than ideal entrance as Elisabetta in the *Don Carlo.* Those who knew her recordings as Ellen Orford and Gutrune, and had heard her Elsa, knew how enchanting and supremely feminine her finespun lyricism could be. These qualities were on short rations, however, as she offered an Elisabetta which suffered from mechanical phrasing and too aloof a posture in the first scene. Possibly a case of a fine artist who, like a fragile wine, doesn't travel well.

Other Verdian activities included the first American Falstaff of Vinay, a conception which held its own in the glaring light of Evans' well-known portrait. Vinay's tipsy cavalier was a personage who contrived to be altogether hilarious and still preserve a definite sense of aristocracy. There was a naturalness about his Falstaff which came from the fact he didn't move about too much. The old guy doesn't have to be a jack-in-the-box, and Vinay reminded his audience of that fact without sacrificing a bit of jollity. Furthermore, his dark, well-aged baritone suited the character, even if the sound was a bit less free than Evans'.

The congenial *Falstaff* cast included a new Pistol in Federico Davia, an exuberant and creative character bass with Glyndebourne credits,[12] and the rich-toned Raina Kabaiwanska returned—not as a replacement this time—to propel Alicia's soaring lines. Frank Guarrera was back after six years as Ford: his portrayal was unusually mercurial, a veritable Merry Husband of Windsor, at least up to a certain point in the story. Meg was Janis Martin, also the year's *Tannhäuser* Venus, that being a role she was booked to perform at La Scala and the Paris Opera. About this time, "old pro" Martin, still in her early 20's, fled from minor roles at the Met to sign a contract as leading mezzo with the Nürnberg Opera, subsequently graduating to Cologne.

New as Fenton was Ottavio Garaventa, a young Italian who made an agreeable impression in *Rigoletto* and *Butterfly*. He phrased cleanly and with taste, showing the kind of style which suggested he might make a respectable Des Grieux in the Massenet *Manon*. The Nanetta was Lee Venora, a natural for the assignment. Opposite Garaventa she had taken on Gilda in the second *Rigoletto*, and while her "Caro Nome" had its gingerly moments she looked adorable and sang for the most part with haunting tone. Davia was a notably scruffy Sparafucile, lounging about his pad with foot on table and slobbering into his wine. Ludgin, taking over the hunchback from Glossop, sounded worn and colorless, thereby giving a clue to the unhappy state in which the 1967 season found his voice.

Grace Bumbry's entrance into the company—she had

sung a good deal in San Francisco seven and eight years earlier as she was emerging from Lotte Lehmann's tutelage at Santa Barbara—was in the role of Carmen. There had not been such a richly sung Carmen in some time, and that was unarguable, but there was disagreement over the degree of warmth, or coolness, in her interpretation.

Nothing about the reappearance of *Carmen* was better than Erlo's anti-cobweb campaign aimed at freshening up the less than universally accepted 1959 production. His most practical stroke was to put the fourth act procession out of view, thus staving off the choral movement problem, and there was the dramatic bonus of seeing Don José out front alone with some beggars. Erlo also turned the Toreador into an almost satirically fatuous extrovert and got Zuniga well smashed before he returns to the tavern.

Jean Périsson, the sensitive new French conductor, a veteran of several years as musical director of the busy Nice Opera, provided an interpretation which was suave, balletic, conscious of the score's inner caprices. Recommended by Crespin, he was also in charge of *Troyens*, conducting musically but not always producing an ideal cohesiveness. He caught his stride the following season and became a regular asset to the company.

Horenstein's lack of resilience damaged *Figaro* badly. An especially ironic state of affairs considering the superior cast: Grist as Susanna, Evans (who seemed at times to be conducting the performance in an effort to save it) as Figaro, Stewart as the Count and Watson as the Countess. David Thaw's Basilio made news by being the most hilariously antique incarnation of that fuddy-duddy to be seen by San Francisco in modern times.

You can't win 'em all, and the old saw certainly applied to the revival of *L'Amore dei Tre Re*, a problematical entertainment at best. This is an opera that seethes and swims with a feverish ecstasy, and to play it lukewarm is fatal. Dorothy Kirsten, that experienced trouper, did her best, bringing a genuine conviction, not to mention strong, pleasant tone, to her Fiora. But that wasn't enough. Molinari gave small evidence he relished the pseudo-Tristanesque music. Indeed, he even made fun of it at rehearsal. Matters proceeded without the aura of amorous desperation which permeates this ripe

236

entertainment, not only because of Molinari's coldness but also the less than magnetic Archibaldo of Nicola Ghiuselev, the latest Bulgarian bass to reach American shores.

Ghiuselev could offer a dark, haunting Slavic tone quality which gave him a certain potential for the role. But his first try at the tricky assignment—following in the path of Journet, Pinza and Rossi-Lemeni—found him minus the needed authority. Archibaldo is a character practically eaten away with frustration, and there's an incrustation of morbidity on him which no costume department can issue like a suit of armor. Sufficient to say that young Ghiuselev, a good musician with a less than huge voice, needed to collect a lot more cobwebs. Adler had approached Rossi-Lemeni to return for the role. That was an excellent idea, but Rossi-Lemeni did not relish Adler's companion offer of the Inquisitor in *Don Carlo* rather than Philip.

Marilyn Horne bowed out for a time after her Eboli, but if she was not contracted by the San Francisco Opera for any of the seasons between 1966 and 1973, it was not, as some would have it, because Kurt Adler "doesn't like her." Problems relating to dates (scarce) and fees (high) would be the real reasons for her absence.

The morning of November 22, as the fall season was drawing to a close, somebody rang the prizefight bell at Winterland (remember Dreamland, where Lauri-Volpi sang in '29?) and Spring Opera came dashing out of the corner with a press preview of unusual things to come. A new "thrust stage" concept of opera-in-the-round, or, to be more precise, opera-in-the-three quarter, would be tried in the Fillmore District arena come April or May. If, that is, $100,000 were raised for the basic expenses of the move. Not from the public, mind you, but from foundations which help establish worthy causes.

"Our idea," said SPO president Robert Mackenzie, "is to put opera right in your lap, and we think that's pretty exciting." Kurt Adler chimed in that he'd just been talking to Leonard Bernstein and Lennie thought the idea was great. The slightly raked stage, it was explained, would jut out from the west end of the hall to a midway point. The audience would be draped around three sides of the stage, with people in the first row twelve feet from the action. Stage entrances would be controlled to a great extent by lighting, and the orchestra would be concealed in a loft behind the stage, with closed circuit TV contact. Capacity would be 4442 vs. the Opera House's 3252, which meant that ticket prices could be lowered from a $2.75–$5.50 scale to $1.50–$5.

"With this range," Mackenzie said, "we can *really* put on Popular Opera. We want people to come in their shirtsleeves and sandals. And we want people from this district (the heavily black Fillmore) to come."

Spring Opera did have genuine motives of public spiritedness, but the idea of the move to Winterland was generated to a large extent by the fact that lengthening Symphony seasons were pushing SPO into June at the Opera House—a time when the important student segment of the audience is busy with final exams and taking off on vacation. The 1966 season, running from May 24 to June 28, had been particularly disastrous at the box office.

It could be argued, though, that this season was far from ideally structured in terms of repertoire, casting and scheduling. And there was still reason to believe that a strongly conceived and executed June season in the Opera House could succeed (the one in 1967 almost did). Critics of Winterland, worried over its less than elegant atmosphere, and dubious about its location in the middle of an only partly redeveloped quasi-slum area, might have invoked the statement of David Clatworthy, an engaging new baritone who, when interviewed during the 1966 season, remarked that for a young singer the whole point of Spring Opera was to be able to sing important roles in a great opera house. At all events, the moving-money was not raised—dissension on the board surely didn't help—and Opera House champions breathed more easily.

Bonelli-disciple Clatworthy sang the Lord Henry, and an incisive new tenor, Nicholas di Virgilio, the Edgar in one of the better shows of the 1966 spring season, a *Lucia* intently conducted by Gerhard Samuel. The opener was the long absent *Mignon*, pleasant but pale, and in Adler's mind a jinx opera. A re-do of *Italian Girl* minus Horne and Lewis was a weak sister, the attempt at a robust piece like *Trovatore* came to grief with possibly the weakest cast in SPO history (excepting the viable Azucena of Betty Allen, the experienced concert mezzo), and a new opera, Douglas Moore's *Carry Nation* (previously given only in a midwestern college presentation), turned out to be less than an absorbing affair. The director was Frank Corsaro, later to be celebrated for his daring interpretations of such classics as *Faust* (complete with cadavers in the good doctor's study) and *Butterfly* (with drunk comrades at Pinkerton's wedding) at the New York City Opera.

Moore and his librettist, William North Jayme, attempted to explore why Carry, the famous bar smasher, took to the hatchet in her later years. In doing so, however, they simply stirred the suds of a tiresome soap opera.

Finally, at the end of a season in search of a winner, Spring Opera did strike gold in a very keen, ethereal production of Britten's *Turn of the Screw*, an opera which, with its chamber orchestration, might suggest a need for a smaller hall, only it's a singularly bright orchestration, and it carried. Conductor Grossman and director Thomas Skelton, a wizard at vaporous stage effects, shared honors with Patricia Neway, a splintering, choked-up governess, and Raymond Martinez and Elizabeth Lantz were both disarming in the juvenile parts.

Screw might even have pleased the pickets who paraded outside the Opera House on Opening Night when *Mignon*, that rear-guard rather than avant-garde opera, was set to take the stage. "Is the Musical Establishment Turning the San Francisco Opera Into a Metropolitan Mausoleum?" one of the placards asked, with an added punch aimed in the direction of a certain Eastern opera company. Just how, a reporter asked signholder Robert Moran, a professional composer of far-out "theater pieces," could the Opera House be rescued from the tomb-like atmosphere he and his dozen or so compatriots found hanging over Mr. Brown's magnificent pile of rusticated terra cotta. By putting on operas by such as Berio, Nono, Pousseur, Schoenberg, Krenek and Haubenstock-Ramati, he said, to be played off against the old hat stuff.

Kurt Adler was not worried by the pickets. He enjoyed their interest. And he told the press he was interested in Schoenberg's *Moses and Aaron*. He had, as a matter of fact, invited the Deutsche Oper from West Berlin to do it in San Francisco en route to or from the company's Japan appearances in the fall of 1966. But a visit could not be arranged to fit the Berliners' schedule.

Adler might have reminded the pickets that San Francisco doesn't do as much avant-garde contemporary opera as, say, Hamburg, because it doesn't have the virtually unlimited funds available to that state supported house. Nor, when a season runs approximately eleven weeks (fall) or three (spring), is the ideal sort of rehearsal time available for highly complex works of an "experimental" nature. *Moses*, Adler noted, is considerably more difficult to rehearse than *Lulu*, presented in the fall season of 1965. Spring Opera, he said, could be more flexible if it didn't have to contend with working around the Symphony's schedule in the Opera House.

There was a glimmer of hope for the avant-gardists in Spring Opera's future history—more on that later.

Meanwhile, late in the summer of 1966 came the birth announcement of Western Opera Theater, a grass roots arm of the San Francisco Opera created with the impetus of a $105,-877 grant from the National Endowment for the Arts. Supervised by the parent company, WOT drew together a pocket ensemble of young singers and proceeded to tour them around the hinterlands of the western United States, introducing opera to small communities. In-school performances in San Francisco and evenings sponsored by various unions were also placed high on the agenda.

Notes

[1] Engen had actually made his first appearance in a San Francisco Opera production in 1948 when he sang in *Meistersinger* in the auxiliary chorus provided by the Loring Club.

[2] Actually, this sort of set had originally been a "field expedient" because of the truncated facilities of the partly-destroyed Hamburg opera house.

[3] The orchestra had been making $159.50, and the opening bid in negotiations was $230.

[4] Houses with better technical resources sometimes duck the challenge of the Transformation Scene altogether.

[5] Reportedly Smith had better luck with a similar *Don Giovanni* done for Sarah Caldwell's Boston Opera.

[6] He subsequently bought a house in the Tiburon hills of Marin County overlooking San Francisco Bay.

240

[7] It must be admitted that, at the opening of the San Francisco Symphony's 1968–69 season, Josef Krips concluded The Star Spangled Banner only to hear a voice shout out from an Opera House upper region: "Play Ball!"

[8] Berlioz once compared his bulging *Troyens* with Robinson Crusoe's dugout canoe which was so heavy and far from the water it could not be launched.

[9] At a press conference Vickers pointed out that the opera is really the story of Aeneas (Aha, said Madame Crespin with a smile) and that in the San Francisco version it becomes more the story of Dido. "Of course I'm very jealous (lots of group laughter here), but I couldn't think of a nicer soprano to get the advantage."

[10] More or less exactly the age of such other opera figures as Caruso, Bjoerling and Warren when they died prematurely.

[11] Miss Stratas qualified for some sort of Hero Medal after slipping a disc during the first act love duet of a subsequent performance. Flat on the floor of her dressing room during a long intermission, she insisted on continuing, and did so, under the heavy influence of a painkiller. After the show she went to the hospital—and into traction.

[12] At a rehearsal Davia mugged so hard he stumbled and broke his foot, but he appeared in the *Falstaff* performances anyway—on crutches.

CHAPTER *16*

Longer Operatic Autumns

1967

The 1967 season was, like that of 1966, ten weeks long, with thirteen operas rather than the fourteen (performed in eight weeks) which had been the previous distribution. Three or four performances of each opera had become the rule. And there were, in fact, five *Magic Flutes* in 1967, not including student performances.

For his new season Adler scrutinized past repertory lists and came up with a flock of revivals. Eight of the operas had been absent for ten or more years. *Das Rheingold*, set to launch a new one-opera-a-year *Ring* cycle, was the longest off the boards, not having been given since 1936. *La Gioconda* (1948) and *Magic Flute* (1950) were next in rarity, and the long-postponed *Tristan* (at least once rumored with Farrell) had not been seen since 1953. *Louise*, last done in 1955, was also a novelty. There were two non-standards last heard in 1956, *Manon Lescaut* and *L'Elisir d'Amore*, plus *Macbeth*, silent since 1957.

The *Rheingold*, *Tristan*, *Elisir* and *Flute* were treated to new productions, as was *Faust*, while *Louise*, *Gioconda* and *Manon Lescaut* survived in serviceable settings from the Agnini era. *Macbeth* had been new in 1955. The year's remaining new production was Gunther Schuller's new opera *The Visitation*, previously performed only by the Hamburg Opera (in Hamburg and New York). The *Tristan* brought the first Isolde anywhere of Irene Dalis, whom Wieland Wagner had thought appropriate for the role, and the first Tristan of that regular Wagnerian Jess Thomas. Not for the first time was San Francisco happy to be a "tryout town"—artists have rarely regarded its Opera as a mere utility company to be used and discarded.

242

Lots of interesting new talent appeared on the roster. Covent Garden's Stuart Burrows, a honey-voiced tenor, and Delme Bryn-Jones, a mellifluous baritone, joined the well-established Mr. Evans to make up Adler's Gift Package from Wales. Mirella Freni, the adorable soprano of Karajan's *Bohème* movie, arrived on the scene along with Luciano Pavarotti, a tall tenor with a beefy lyric voice. Basso Nicolai Ghiaurov made his long-awaited, and expensive, entrance. Swedish baritone Ingvar Wixell, in his U.S. debut, launched a happy association with the company, making San Francisco another pin on his map along with Stockholm and West Berlin. And Wixell's Norwegian colleague Ragnar Ulfung, a distinguished member of the Stockholm Opera roster, showed off his rare gifts as a very turned-on character tenor.

Sesto Bruscantini, better known in Chicago than New York, joined up for Dr. Dulcamara in *Elisir*, and Jane Marsh, the 24-year-old all-American Marin County soprano (she had won the Tchaikovsky vocal contest in Moscow) made her first major appearances on an American operatic stage as Pamina in *Magic Flute*.

Elisir was the year's opera to take to a "desert island," the comic heir to the throne previously achieved by *Cosi Fan Tutte, Falstaff* and *Barber of Seville*. Just about everybody who saw the premiere October 21 fell in love with Lotfi Mansouri's production, and its reward was a ten-minute ovation.

One could start the good news about this happy event by mentioning the delightful puppet horse which blinked in time to the music and pawed the air heatedly as Dulcamara fed him some elixir in the grand finale—when Mansouri did *Elisir* at La Scala three years later the stuffy management wouldn't go for such an animal! Or that scene worthy of W. C. Fields in which the good doctor repeatedly tried to get his spaghetti into mouth but was interrupted time and time again by the excited Nemorino. But the show was more than a bundle of gags. As masterminded by Mansouri and designer Robert Darling (an Oakland boy with experience in New York), this was a production of *Elisir* more sensible, attractive and mercurial than is often the case. Adina was not played as a shrew, but a warm lass who wants to be romanced. Nemorino, while shy, was not a complete bumbler. Movement of the chorus was individualized, and the three components of the set (a central one which turned, and two which came in from the sides) provided enough flexibility to keep the action from getting frozen in the center of the piazza.

Having spent his three previous seasons (1963–65) in San Francisco mostly as a house doctor for Agnini-age productions, Mansouri deserved something new, and *Elisir* proved his worthiness. Most new productions were going to Hager, whose ubiquitousness might have bothered some critics a little less if he'd been given a title to match his duties as "chief" stage director.

Bruscantini, capped in a shocking wig of red hair, made his belated local debut as Dulcamara, mixing mirth and intelligence with just the right prescription. He looked monumentally sly, impish and disreputable, and credit him with a thousand subtle little winks and shrugs. Wixell's Belcore revealed a natural comic flair in his everstrutting, swaggering account of this narcissistic non-com. For quickness he could equal Bruscantini, and his smooth (if not always ideally open) baritone, a bulldog instrument, suggested he'd make a good Amonasro in the next *Aida*.

Reri Grist was the last word as Adina, similarly Alfredo Kraus as Nemorino. Giuseppe Patane, the Berlin-based conductor chosen as Molinari's probable successor (the little maestro was giving the Met prime autumn time) offered gracious and propulsive if slightly sober leadership from the pit. As is his custom, he used no score. In the 1967–69 period Patane conducted a lot in San Francisco, impressing, especially in blood and thunder pieces, with a mix of sizzle and style reminiscent of Ettore Panizza. The touch was light, his sense of continuity exemplary.

The revival of *Louise* stands out as another 1967 special, in particular because of the "coming of age" of conductor Jean Périsson and the return of the long-absent Nicola Rossi-Lemeni as the father. In the previous season Périsson had made his musicality clear but had trouble establishing rapport with the orchestra. His return visit found him on surer ground and he was able to realize his potential. He conducted *Louise* in the most tender, supple fashion, gently pushing and pulling poetic voices from the instrumental texture, never forcing the sound, and maintaining a feeling of conversational intimacy. He got into the heart and soul of the characters, building an atmosphere of brooding ecstasy in which the people on stage could really live, instead of simply performing.

Rossi-Lemeni, after fourteen years, was still a magnetic personality. His performance as the father was a perfect mixture of burning spontaneity and steely control, laying much stress, by the way, on the less than completely innocent nature of this character's affection for Louise.

John Alexander looked a rather square and prosperous bohemian, but his Julien was ardently sung with a rich, well-produced, French-timbred tenor. Arlene Saunders (from the Hamburg Opera) let some primness get in the way of her Louise, but she also offered some nice ethereal singing. Sona Cervena was a stoical, grippingly imperious mother, convincingly French but a little too spooky, her soup pot having a slight touch of the witch's cauldron. Louis Erlo made the most of Charpentier's sure-fire heart twisters like the silent episode of the evening meal ("La soupe est prête?") and he caught the period atmosphere of the scene in the seamstresses' sweatshop, lighting the occupants to suggest an old lithograph.

The Conquering Welsh had a field day in Toni Businger's new production of *The Magic Flute* (in English), a tremendous improvement on the abortive 1950 try. While patrons at the Met were being blinded by Marc Chagall's riot of pattern and color Businger came up with an airy mise-en-scène which had poise and profile, charm but not excess cuteness. Geraint Evans' Papageno proved an inimitable product from that first, beautifully-timed entrance which was a resolute march across the stage, into the wings, and right out again —as if he hadn't been on the stage in the first place. This was a quick, hearty and stentorian Papageno, a bluff but delightful workingman.

Harold Rosenthal from London caught the fifth performance, and wrote that Evans' Papageno "has never been so cheeky ... his cleverly calculated ad-libbing would surely have delighted Mozart himself."

As the busy caretaker of coincidence would have it, a new tenor named Stuart Burrows had grown up on the same block of the small Welsh town which Evans calls home. Burrows was the Tamino in *Flute*, singing his U.S. debut with a tenor which caressed the air in suave arching phrases all tone and no forcing. Other assignments like Edmondo in *Manon Lescaut* revealed that Burrows had a lesson or two to learn in terms of limber, imaginative stage action, but the voice was heavenly and one could wait.

Delme Bryn-Jones, the third Welshman of the season, turned up first at the Fol de Rol singing the famous *Pearl Fishers* duet with Burrows. The portly, genial Bryn-Jones revealed a handsome baritone voice and made of Lescaut (and Schaunard) characters of some distinction.

Faust, traditionally as much a problem to stage as *Magic Flute*, was adequately served by Erlo and Skalicki's new production, a thing of pleasant fantasy. Erlo neither reached for non-existent Goethe nor tried as wide a range of novelty as the New York City Opera's Frank Corsaro. Ghiaurov's hardly prompt San Francisco debut (his fee was devilish) brought a Grand Manner Mephisto in the free-wheeling Chaliapin tradition. The accent was away from cornball sinister and he played the devil with a devil-may-care sense of fun. He bent the rhythm and pitch as he went his spontaneous way, but one had to forgive him—it was all too convincing. Kraus was a vintage Faust, Arlene Saunders a prim but gradually unwinding Marguerite. Périsson's conducting was springy, elegant, affectionate, far above the French norm.

Wagner, ever sure of a sizeable San Francisco audience although Adler had been rationing him out at the rate of one opera a year—he needed time and money to build new productions—was especially conspicuous during 1967. *Tristan*, long unavailable due to casting problems, almost ran aground again on the drawing board because of the death (in October 1966) of Wieland Wagner, but substitutions were made. And *Rheingold* went off on schedule.

Wieland had been slated to make his American debut producing one or two operas in the fall of '67. There had been a plan whereby Jess Thomas would do his first Tristan in a Wieland production in Japan conducted by Pierre Boulez, the increasingly prestgious composer-conductor, and the production could be repeated in San Francisco with certain local variations. This was not to be, but Adler still wanted a *Tristan* with Thomas. So he commissioned Hager and Bauer-Ecsy to produce one.

Thomas' Tristan was fresh and youthful in look and sound, with optimum use of a suavely arching and compassionate head tone, and an excusable minimum of unsteadily sustained sound. Despite the vigor and point of Melchior's portrayal a generation earlier (including an admirably "worn out" third act), Thomas emerged as the more romantically appealing figure. A major pity that about fifteen minutes of his third act was cut.

A number of people were dubious about Dalis as Isolde, although there was precedent for a mezzo Isolde in, for instance, Margarete Matzenauer. The first performance came, as it happened, only a few days after her father's death, and Dalis, obviously steeling herself, treated the range above the staff in gingerly fashion. Her high mezzo came through steady but subdued, and one had to admit that her Isolde, while appealing, simply wasn't complete. At subsequent performances she was much more confident, sang out more, and restored some, if not all, of the previously missing high notes. Since she looked attractive, and sang with elegance and a fair amount of passion—although she didn't make some of the textual points Flagstad had—Dalis had to be reckoned with as a major Isolde. But, feeling as she did that she was attacking the role from below rather than above, she did not undertake it again.

If, she later mused, she had approached Isolde via Sieglinde, she might have felt better about it.

Mignon Dunn, an equally attractive Met veteran, was an excellent Brangäne, and Rod MacWherter, the new Melot, sounded like a Tristan-in-the making. Kurwenal provided the vocally troubled Ludgin with his most likely role of the season, but the aging Josef Greindl from Berlin was a wobbly King Marke. (He was hired basically for a Baron Ochs which sounded a good deal better.)

Stein's *Tristan* was characteristically springy and suave, if not quite on the Reiner plane with its coiled-spring stateliness and grand rhetorical thrust. Bauer-Ecsy's sets were simple and handsome, more or less in the Bayreuth mold. Hager's notion of Isolde dying standing up, and in the dark, seemed contrived and "fashionable." But when

Marke confronted the lovers in Act 2 there was a beautifully spaced arrangement of six unhappy characters in search of a resolution.

Placement was handsome and dignified, too, in the *Rheingold*. Especially when the Gods, about to wither due to loss of the Golden Apples, stood stationed around the raked disc like live numbers on a clock face. Skalicki managed modern but uneccentric settings, amorphous enough to have the right fantastic air of legend. But the silly flying-Rhinemaiden dolls didn't look good, and they were deleted a year and a half later when the production turned up in Los Angeles.

Despite a basically handsome production, and a strong if not ideal cast, the cycle got off on the wrong foot thanks to Leopold Ludwig's pedestrian conducting. He flattened the score into a tepidity surprising even from this inconsistent conductor. David Ward's young Wotan was a bumptious, almost jolly figure, sensibly humanized but lacking some of the requisite nobility. Thomas was a less slinkily balletic Loge than, say, Gerhard Stolze, but his portrayal had a lot of presence. Robert Glover had his best opportunity to date as Mime and made much of it. Arlene Saunders seemed more at home as Freia than in the French repertory.

The Visitation, which had its unveiling on a late October Saturday night—this was thought to be a more friendly audience for contemporary scores than the more conservative Tuesday night Regular Series customers—was the closest to a hot-off-the-griddle opera since *Blood Moon*. It was more successful than that, but generally considered to have its own share of embarrassing cliches. Its world premiere had taken place (in English) in Hamburg the previous autumn, and the work had received several dozen curtain calls, spurring on Kenneth Rexroth, *The San Francisco Examiner*'s critic-at-large, to exult that "this is the only really good, large scale American opera and the only one likely to stay in the world repertoire."

But Arthur Jacobs, writing for *Opera Magazine* from San Francisco a year later, had cooler and doubtless more accurate remarks to make when he said: "One is left wondering whether the enthusiasm apparently evoked in some quarters (i.e: Hamburg) is not in part dependent on inverted race prejudice ('How marvelous to see black people sympathetically portrayed on the opera stage! And with all those black singers in the cast, too!').''

Schuller, as his own librettist, had taken what he called a ''motive'' from Kafka's *The Trial* and applied it to the situation of the Negro in America. Jacobs was not the only observer to feel that ''the depiction of the Negro as a passive victim in a faceless society has a slightly out-of-date air in the new era of Black Power.'' The story tells of Carter Jones, a black student who becomes a victim of persecution. The aim, in scene after scene, is to parallel Kafka's haunting surrealistic novel. But in Kafka the victimization of a Mittel-Europa bank clerk is always mysterious, and profound—such was not the case in the opera. As Alexander Fried succinctly put it in *The Examiner*, at times there is a ''troubling crack between what is surreal in the opera and what is superficially real, with moments of banality.''

A mundane, prosaic libretto, in effect a prose play couched in deliberately colloquial language, and a recitative-like vocal line with complex orchestral weavings: these took the fascination out of what might have been a really gripping experience. Schuller concocted a *Wozzeck*-like peroration for his non-hero toward the final curtain, but somehow one couldn't have cared less.

Totally objective views from outside critics having their particular force, Jacobs' estimate of San Francisco's production was heartening to fans of the company. He liked it better than the opera itself, writing: ''The production by Paul Hager, with scenery by Leni Bauer-Escy, stunningly depicted the 'faceless' city by a structure of scaffolding which yielded various 'acting areas' for interior and exterior scenes. Gaudy yet cold, neon-lighted yet fundamentally dark, this staging was masterly. The end of the first act, when the interrogating tribunal suddenly turns its attention from Carter Jones to the theater audience with the help of a very powerful light projector, is a real theatrical stroke on Schuller's part and came off perfectly.''

San Francisco's cast was notable for distinguished vignettes, especially Ragnar Ulfung's Chuck, a possessed bully who sprang like a monkey from pole to pole of Bauer-Ecsy's apparatus; Bryn-Jones' glazed Claiborne, a broken-down lawyer; the rotund Canadian tenor Alan Crofoot's night club boss; and Jeannette Scovotti's giggly Miss Hampton, that being Carter Jones' rooming house neighbor.

Simon Estes, the young black bass-baritone who played Jones' uncle in Hamburg, had the central role in San Francisco. McHenry Boatwright, Hamburg's Jones, had batted out in a Spring Opera *Trovatore* (as Di Luna) in 1966 and it was thought wise to use someone else. Estes was not sufficiently experienced and gutsy a performer to make a monumental figure, but he did reasonably well with material which was, in any event, somewhat trying.

Opening Night 1967 brought a revival of *Gioconda*, not seen in nineteen years. Adler had waited until he had the whopping sort of cast that can make this over-climaxed but irresistible warhorse run. Up through the summer of '67 there were problems, two of his choices agreeing to the job and then backing off. Crespin was to do her first Gioconda, and she had coaching with Zinka Milanov in Yugoslavia on her agenda, but indisposition made it impossible for her to learn the role in time, and Peter Glossop defected from Barnaba for Falstaff with Sarah Caldwell's American National Company which toured the U.S. in the wake of the prematurely-hatcheted Met National troupe.

Crespin was ably enough replaced by Leyla Gencer, absent for nearly a decade from the San Francisco scene. For Barnaba there were the parched tones of Chester Ludgin, the man-of-all-work baritone who was encountering vocal problems especially inconvenient for such a draftable singer. With Patane an exceedingly crisp, cultivated man on the podium, Grace Bumbry an ideally handsome, mellifluous Laura, Maureen Forrester (a rare figure on the operatic stage) a plummy Cieca, and Cioni a pingy Enzo, this was, despite problems, a *Gioconda* lineup not to be dismissed.

Gencer's dramatic handling of the title role made one respect her artistic integrity even as one worried over instances of vocal abandon. Especially after Opening Night, a traditionally troublesome time for voices, she achieved a fairly even effect, alway using her voice, according to her habit, as a piece of highly charged equipment. There have been more brilliant-sounding sopranos of the Gioconda type, but none more resourceful. Gioconda being the sort of character who turns up from everybody's woodwork, she tends to be more than a bit tiresome, but Gencer put you on her side.

Rosenkavalier, the most in-the-rep of the German works performed by the San Francisco Opera, returned again in 1967, not with Schwarzkopf, whose exclusive property the Marschallin had been since 1955, but Crespin, a less up-tight princess for whom advancing age, and a receding Octavian, proved less threatening. Crespin was moved by the loss of the doting boy, but more realistic. The new Octavian was Sylvia Anderson, a Denver girl based at the Frankfurt Opera. Excellent bearing, a keen acting talent, and a warm, finespun if not epical high mezzo—all added up to a viable sum. The veteran Greindl played Ochs as a happy oaf, with at least a solid degree of dignity amidst the animal passions.

But possibly the biggest news of the year's *Rosenkavalier* was the first really exciting Italian Tenor since the earlier day when Kurt Baum would stride out and do magnificent battle with "Di Rigori Armato." The new man was Robert Ilosfalvy, the Hungarian who had made a very nice impression as Alfredo in 1964 and had become a member of the Cologne Opera. His tone was so big, sweet and ringing one's breath felt swept away. And the glorious sound was no sonic mirage, as subsequent performances of *Manon Lescaut* were to prove. During intermissions at the Puccini opera everybody seemed to be talking about a vocal likeness to Bjoerling. And sure enough, Bjoerling had been an inspiration to Ilosfalvy.

The Geronte in *Manon Lescaut* was Federico Davia, a magnificently lean, rickety, sinister type, an arthritic-demonic roué who used his eyes and chin as much as his voice to create a man who was surely born sneering. Puccini's opera was conducted by Herbert Grossman, a Spring Opera veteran who was most attentive to the situations transpiring on stage.

Out, damned spot, cries Lady Macbeth, but there were a lot of troublesome spots which didn't go out in the *Macbeth* revival. When Grace Bumbry was on stage the sparks flew, but much of the rest of the time things were pushing toward rock bottom—and sometimes even getting there. Bumbry took the fearsome lady's unwieldy but rewarding music and tossed it off with brio, fluidity and unforced tone. The histrionics were good, too, and she capped the show with a truly mad Sleepwalking Scene in which she fell, most realistically, into a limp mass of destroyed ambition. But Ludgin's pressing vocal problems seriously hurt his Macbeth. Thomas O'Leary, still unable to recapture the success of his 1965 Pogner, was a weak Banquo. And Daniele Barioni, an ex-Met tenor with a gorgeous voice and small style, was a painfully lachrymose Macduff. (Adler had tried to get Glade Peterson for the part but he was unavailable.)

The 1967 *Ballo* proved an ill-balanced affair because Adler was trying to have his cake and eat it, too. For Amelia he hired Leontyne Price, a *singer* extraordinaire. For Riccardo he hired Ragnar Ulfung, a very creative singing *actor*, and one used to appearing in the Stockholm Opera's historically accurate, Swedish-set production in which the Riccardo (Gustav III) gives off a homosexual air. In San Francisco's woody Boston setting the combination was doomed, as indeed it probably would have been in Stockholm. Ulfung, although a highly experienced artist, became nervous about the discrepancies between what he was used to doing and what would fit with stellar sopranoism, and the result was he sang distressingly off pitch at the first performance.

A pity that this admittedly unappealing state of affairs kept many in the audience from appreciating Ulfung's acute dramatic abilities. For the record, his death scene was so graphically convulsive and pitiable it caused empathetic chest pains in at least one observer. Ulfung was willing to withdraw, but Adler stood by him, suggesting a toning down of the prissyness which fought the production, and the Norwegian visitor remained, eliminating, however, the third act aria.

Otherwise there was Reri Grist's delightful Oscar, Cornell MacNeil's not always focused Renato, and some extremely crisp, characterful conducting from Mario Bernardi of London's Sadler's Wells.

Spring Opera opened its seventh season—possibly the best yet—on June 2, 1967 with *Traviata*. The performance turned Verdi's perennial from a mellifluous but often soapy potboiler into a searingly dramatic experience. Much of the credit can be divided between Patricia Brooks, a scintillating and poignant Violetta, and James de Blasis, a young Syracuse-based director who had done *Carmen* for the New York City Opera. Brooks played the heroine as a real woman, not a cardboard soprano, and rarely have Violetta's conflicts between the demi-monde and life with Alfredo been so acutely registered. The keen direction knit up the story superbly, letting Violetta lapse into forced coquetry before she leaves the second act lovenest, and allowing Alfredo to shower her with kisses in the next scene even as he's bawling her out. Karl Kritz conducted most effectively, producing as intimate and conversational a musico-dramatic atmosphere in the second act as any San Francisco *Traviata* ever boasted.

Pearl Fishers, virtually a Spring Opera theme song, returned on its third visit with the usual less than ideal cast but one which was graced by New York City Opera baritone Dominic Cossa, a high lyric rather in the De Luca tradition. In a revival of *Cavalleria* and *Pagliacci*, Ghita Hager's direction scored many pluses. In *Cav* she filled up empty spaces (Turiddu, for instance, sang the Siciliana on stage, an altar boy, late for his chores, scampering by him and into the church before the crowd congregates), and she kept the pace taut. Good touches in *Pag* included Nedda's throwing Canio his costume off the wash line just before "Vesti la giubba." That, for sure, is unvarnished verismo. To close the season, the Porcaro *Tales of Hoffmann* from 1963 returned under the directorial hand of Byron Ringland of the American Conservatory Theater. A conspicuous advantage was having Nicklausse sung by a tenor instead of a mezzo.

1968

Early winter is traditionally a time when opera buffs around San Francisco can be found comparing notes over the latest rumors about the fall season to come. Early in 1968 they were talking, with some authority, about a new production of *Coq D'Or* with Reri Grist and Rossi-Lemeni, *Daughter of the Regiment* with Sutherland, and what would be the company's first experience with Handel, a production of *Semele*. None of these plans, however, came to fruition. Grist's pregnancy eliminated the *Coq*,[1] a switch in Sutherland (and husband Bonynge's) plans involving a recording of *Don Giovanni* disbanded the *Regiment*, and *Semele* entered the realm of fantasy since Nicolai Gedda turned down Adler's suggestion that he learn Handel's score.

What ultimately resulted was a repertoire including several curious novelties, period pieces from the 19th and 20th centuries. *Fra Diavolo* (1830) was revived for Gedda —this was an assignment which really intrigued him—and, on a triple bill, there was the didactic *Discovery of America* from Darius Milhaud's *Christopher Columbus* (1930), Schoenberg's monodrama *Erwartung* (1909), and a ballet with voices based on a lost one-act opera by Kurt Weill, *Royal Palace* (1927). Verdi was unsatisfactorily represented by only two oom-pah operas, *Ernani* and *Trovatore*, the latter, of course, a vastly more mature creation than the former. There was some consolation in the fact that *Trovatore* was treated to a marvelously thoughtful production, the most genuinely dramatic in many an opera-goer's experience.

Those who hoped the Rossini centennial might be celebrated by something other than the perennial *Barber* were disappointed, but surely some of the disappointment disappeared when beguiling performances arrived in September with Teresa Berganza—and *Cenerentola* did follow in 1969.

The most important production of 1968 was the posthumous Wieland Wagner *Salome* with Anja Silja, Wieland's protege, making her American debut in a show which the lamented producer was to have staged himself. Wieland conceived at least three distinct *Salome* productions—for Stuttgart, Vienna and Geneva, the last being the model for San Francisco. He was not, of course, a man to pass off an old suit out of his inspirational closet when a new one would reflect his latest thoughts. What makes the Wieland *Salome* story especially interesting is that the three productions reflect a cumulative direction toward a dramatic essence. *Salome* A, B and C would seem to form a plot of their own, and it goes like this: at Stuttgart the scene was dominated by a huge wall, a great textured thing of blocks of stone which sheltered Herod's wicked court and wrapped around the cistern holding the prophet Jochanaan. In Vienna the wall disintegrated Dorian Gray-fashion, becoming tattered and morbid. And then, in the Geneva production, there was no longer any wall at all. Only a huge moon set in a great, swirling sky.

The moon, remember, is a symbolic football tossed around by the various pre-Neil Armstrong characters: to the love-sick Narraboth it resembles a dancing princess, to the worried page it's a woman rising from the grave. The Geneva version, as San Franciscans found out, not only gives the moon elevated billing, it lets the cistern overwhelm the stage in a swirling floor which answers swirling sky. Best to forget that the cistern resembles a great waffle iron.

There was some equivocation over the "premiere" status of the show. The Geneva production had been put on at the Grand Théâtre in the Swiss city, but posthumously also, and with Wieland's widow Gertrude, not considered the greatest interpreter of his wants, in charge. Silja, of course, knew his wants and communicated them in the Swiss performances. In San Francisco one of Wieland's most trusted assistants, Renate Ebermann, was the official stage director. And Silja did her thing. Designer Robert Darling, charged with inspecting the Geneva setup, came back from Switzerland unsatisfied because the huge cistern at the Grand Théâtre could not be opened manually by the soldiers. In San Francisco the technical staff made this maneuver possible.

Silja's Salome seemed the final answer to how this character should be played. No stock seductress she, she was, rather, a completely willful, monomaniacal sex kitten. The sort who open-mouthedly beckons a man in a "come with me" attitude, then pushes him away. And the sort who throws her lean body into a fourteen-minute pout in a prone position, with hands on chin, while the orchestra launches an orgiastic heap of crescendos.

Some patrons complained about her several obviously wobbly notes, but surely they were incidental to the dramatic effectiveness of her coloratura-based but amply-supported baby-doll sound, not to mention her informed phrasing. Too much fussing of this sort would have consigned such performers as Mary Garden and Maria Jeritza to an early scrap heap.

There were also arguments that Silja didn't dance enough in the Dance of the Seven Veils, in which, by the way, she only dropped one veil, ending up in bra and tights from the hips. But the point is this: after beginning to dance for Herod, as requested, this Salome lay down and wallowed in her own sexual desire, and the self-indulgent tossing about was perfectly consistent with her animal nature. The majority of the audience at the first performance was obviously won over. When the opera was finished, Silja and her collaborators (including Richard Lewis in the first Herod of his career, and Austrian Franz Mazura, a sonorous Jochanaan) were awarded a full ten minutes' applause.[2]

Wieland Wagner's style depended a great deal on acting which conveys intensity from a stationary position—the page's rubbing her right arm with the left hand, for instance, as she reacts nervously to the unfolding drama. It also put much stress on capturing a concentrated essence of pure crude horror. The San Francisco *Salome* did have the Wieland feel in these departments, and will long be talked about.

Anyone who might have been dreaming over the years about encountering a really adult *Trovatore* had reason to rejoice come October 11 when a new production by Hager and Skalicki had its premiere. For once Verdi's tattered melodrama emerged as decent theater. Everyone looked right—the singers, that is, were the right shapes, and they all reacted when the situation called for a show of emotion. Furthermore, they appeared in moody, coppery sets of an appropriately menacing nature—as Skalicki observed to an interviewer, *Trovatore* characters are forever being hemmed in by walls. Played German-style with only a single intermission (board chairman Robert Watt Miller objected strenuously, one member of the administration remembers), the evening sped to a final curtain with zest. Helped, by the way, by Patane's crisp, urgent, staccato conducting. Rarely has the Anvil Chorus been so ebullient, so un-banal.

Act 1 began interestingly with Hager's placing Ferrando (Ara Berberian) on a balcony and giving him a whip, as if to suggest he was several notches in authority above the run-of-the-rabble soldiers. Scene 2 introduced Radmila Bakocevic, a slim Yugoslavian soprano to whom looking noble came easily. And she clutched the tenor (trumpety Ilosfalvy) as if she meant it. Her voice turned out to be a finespun spinto, as light-timbred an instrument as one ever hears in the role of Leonora—she almost seemed a Gilda—but of a character which made a great deal of sense considering all the passages calling for a fragile maiden's floating head tone. Some explosive notes limited her success, but in sum she satisfied. Victor Braun, the Canadian bel canto baritone, was a Di Luna who seemed driven to nastiness not so much out of empty villainy as lovesick jealousy. But a cold unfortunately gripped him most of the season and it hurt his Luna as it did other roles.[3]

Hager had another good idea in the final scene when several *Fidelio*-like prisoners came in view to watch the principals' dungeon despair. Inspired by a spikey medieval torture rig he'd observed as a child in an Austrian castle, Skalicki devised a semi-circular central grillwork which enclosed Azucena and Manrico in separate cells.

There was a line in the San Francisco Opera's 1969 souvenir picture album which referred to the company as "ceaselessly inventive." Well, much invention there has been, but it all went out the window, and into a sea of banality, when the season opened with *Ernani*. The evening marked a perfect example of the tyranny of the star system, the choice of potboiler having stemmed principally from the fact that Leontyne Price was going through an Elvira period, singing the role all around her circuit. Maybe some directors have the imagination and tenacity to transcend the hapless deficiency of meaningful motivation in the libretto, but Yannopoulos appeared to have given up after a few self-conscious tries at moving bodies about the stage. Lighting of any point or distinction was, to put it kindly, virtually nil. What held the performance together was Patane's admirably secure beat, his sense of purpose, his keen ear for underplaying the dramatics.

Price sang "Ernani, Involami" over-vehemently and spent the evening parading in fancy costumes rather than creating a sympathetic character. It was sad to see, because in earlier seasons she had struck one as so sincere an artist. Glossop, back as Carlo, was not in good form, so this left laurels mainly for Renato Cioni's valiant, pingy Ernani and Met bass Ezio Flagello's dependable Silva. Subsequent performances ran somewhat more smoothly, but not enough. The sets, borrowed from Italy, were Ercole Sormani copies of Nicola Benois' La Scala originals.

Gunther (*Visitation*) Schuller conducted the Triple Bill, which might have been titled "A Night in Old Berlin," or "Schuller's Choice." First on the list was *Royal Palace*, originally given in Berlin in 1927 by Erich Kleiber and the Staatsoper forces at the Kroll Opera. It failed, and the full score was lost during the Nazi period. Adler and friends felt that the text, which survived, would strike a dated note in 1968, so Schuller changed the opera into a ballet, with only a bit of vocal commentary (hardly audible in performance). Also, of course, he re-orchestrated. The bittersweet music didn't reveal much of the expected Weill vinegar (conceivably Schuller had somewhat changed Weill's emphasis) but it did show some exquisite lyricism revealing a cousinship with Hindemith.

Choreography by Alan Johnson of *West Side Story* developed an alienation story which matched the score in lyrical quality. And Skalicki's beautiful projections on elegant cloudlands served, like leitmotifs, to tell the story. The heroine's face, first shown in a Cocteau-like line drawing, was all purity; then it wept bitter tears like a hangman's noose.

The second segment of the bill was a highly overwrought production of *Erwartung* by Hager. Although Hager had been a target in certain critical circles which did not welcome his ubiquitousness, it must be said that only in the ill-fated *Fledermaus* of 1965 (and perhaps the *Jenufa* of 1969) had he failed as he did in this *Erwartung*. To be sure, Schoenberg's vague, over-ripe piece is almost beyond production, but the simplicity which might have made it stronger was avoided in favor of a fussyness which accentuated its pretensions. What, one wonders, would Wieland Wagner have done?

Part of the blame can be put on Hans Aeberli, who constructed a large, creaky labyrinth which moved laboriously across the stage. The protagonist, Marie Collier, enacted her role zombie-fashion in garbled, covered German, entwining herself self-consciously in Aeberli's construction, according to the Hager prescription.

The infinitely more exhilarating finale was *The Discovery of America*, a self-sufficient half—the better one, by all accounts, including the composer's—of Milhaud's *Chris-*

258

topher Columbus. Originally produced in 1930 in Berlin, it came to San Francisco in the wake of long years of critical comment that Milhaud's regular presence at nearby Mills College should be recognized on a big operatic scale. More oratorio than opera, the spectacle was treated to an imaginative visual unfolding which is just what it requires to come off. A perfect sealing up of its rather segmented structure was missing—perhaps it could have been achieved had Milhaud supplied new filler material—but failing that there was much to excite in the brilliant staging by Adolf Rott of the Vienna Burgteater.

Pages in the book of Columbus' life came into vivid focus with sudden appearances of startling scenes, picture book freezes of the characters, and the nimble visual counterpoint of actor-singers on the move. The human tower of Babel oppressively holding up a giant image of Spanish royalty was a particular masterstroke. On the musical side it was the stirring choruses, sung from platforms straddling each end of the orchestra pit at stage level, which made the strongest effect.

"Modern" opera was also represented by a revival of the vintage Hager/Bauer-Ecsy *Wozzeck*, the Evans-Lewis-Ludwig combine functioning again in its behalf. Adler was pleased to observe that the third performance, on a Saturday night, played to Standing Room Only. Box office for the Triple Bill, however, produced an accountant's (and Adlerian) nightmare.

At the other end of the emotional scale could be found *Fra Diavolo*, standard fare in Germany but well over the hill in America. Auber's pretty, pre-Johann Strauss tunes and snappy march rhythms (not to mention passages of only workmanlike quality) add up to a kind of "family entertainment" asking little of the audience except to relax and travel into fantasy land. The place is inhabited by wooden soldiers, village idiots, sniffy tourists, bumpkin robbers, and, at the crest of this rustic romp, a Robin Hood bandit who masquerades as an honest gentleman while he goes about his business "stealing ladies' hearts, and their silverware." The script, much of it revealed in spoken dialogue, is pure operetta drivel, sometimes so silly one can't help laughing lustily. Scribe's text had been translated by the Met's John

Gutman and was doctored for San Francisco by the local producers.

Fra Diavolo has to be done with finesse and pace or the soufflé will flatten fast. Lotfi (*L'Elisir*) Mansouri has an enchanting sense of humor and he poured it into the show, occasionally overdoing but most of the time achieving just the right happy-happy feeling. His "in" joke on a *Salome* theme was capital, playing on the fact that Silja, earlier in the season, had dropped only one veil instead of the classic seven. Mary Costa, the Zerlina, prepared for bed at the village inn by taking off seven skirts.

The Gilbert and Sullivanesque first act duet between Lady Pamela and Lord Plimpton, Diavolo's expensive prey, was highly amusing as one, then the other, bobbed up from his, and her, seat at the innkeeper's table. Mansouri also deserved bouquets for arranging a trick ending (it favored the bandit who's sometimes shot at the end) which was impossible to predict. His choreography of the overture (in collaboration with Nancy Johnson) was less successsful because the music was composed by the yard with material for inches.

In an interview Mansouri said the title role requires "an Errol Flynn with a voice," and this is what Nicolai Gedda provided. Costa was an agreeable Zerlina, but at the first performance she had a slight cold and sang somewhat discreetly. By the second she was unable to sing, but decided to go on and pantomime the role, speaking the dialogue and turning over the singing to Sheila Marks, a recent Auditions winner, who made *her* contribution from the pit!

There's an old story about the Chinese waiter who, when asked the difference between the 50 cent and 75 cent dinners, answered: "75 cent more, and better." The San Francisco Opera's *Les Troyens* returned in 1968, and it was definitely a case of "more, and better"—even if some of the buffs were growling, not unreasonably, for more pounds of Berliozian meat. Several cuts were opened, the cast was more aptly chosen, and Jean Périsson conducted with more authority than before, joining his basic musicality with a great finesse.

About twenty minutes were new: the doom-laden and effectively doleful scene of Hector's widow and son appearing before Priam and Hecuba, followed by Aeneas' grisly account of Laocoon's death, and, in the second part of the opera, Iopas' quite charming aria, and Mercury's intrusion on the Dido-Aeneas love duet with the call to Italy. The first additions help pave the path of dread which is the whole point of Berlioz' opening half, and the Mercury call is necessary for another building job, the cumulative campaign of the gods to get Aeneas moving on to his destiny.

Guy Chauvet, the trumpety French tenor, took over Aeneas from Vickers, his more extroverted style doing no harm. Margarita Lilova, a Bulgarian mezzo from Vienna, was the new Anna, offering an appropriately dulcet sort of voice unavailable to her predecessor, Sona Cervena. Crespin, of course, was on deck, and in good form.

But the question of the cutting remains. A central reason for it, naturally, was the double casting of Crespin. Few if any soprani would have the vocal and emotional endurance to do both Cassandra and Dido complete. But, at root, the management chose the path it did because a five-hour evening of Berlioz seemed like bad box office. Should it? Well, *Les Troyens* is an uneven work. Certainly the subtraction of the musically weak and anti-climactic final duet between Dido and Aeneas was no great loss. Since the opera is written quite sectionally, cutting can be handled with relative ease. But there were lost gems, like Cassandra's duet with Chorebus in which he sings an untroubled melody while his girl friend frets. And surely the scene with the ghost of Hector in the first part of the opera is vital. Given the presence of an extremely viable physical production, the answer seemed to be this: the third time around why not open thirty or forty minutes more, using a separate Dido and Cassandra—possibly Silja and Crespin.

Speaking of cuts, the barbarous seven-minute hole traditionally punched into Wotan's second act monologue in San Francisco performances of *Walküre* was as gaping as ever in 1968, except that one hardly cared because the Wotan, the Hamburg Opera's Hubert Hofmann, was so lackluster. Originally Adler had made an "arrangement" with Thomas Stewart to sing the role, but ultimately he was contracted elsewhere. The continuing absence of Birgit Nilsson resulted in a Brünnhilde, Nadezda Kniplova, who scooped, wobbled and

261

missed vital points of interpretative subtlety while producing a big-voiced, occasionally beautiful and ultimately provincial account of the role.

With sympathetic but growingly sloppy conducting from Ludwig there were really too many minuses in connection with the second production of the new *Ring*. Thankfully there were strong pluses, too: Crespin's authoritative Sieglinde, Jess Thomas' highly musical Siegmund, William Wildermann's superbly black-toned Hunding and Lilova's unshrewish Fricka. The Skalicki-Hager production was sensible and handsome, and especially effective in the first act with its genuinely woodsy hut of helpfully intimate dimensions (the traditional hearth and table and chairs were merged into a primeval campfire area with tree stumps) and a stunning light script which turned the scene from a golden redwood glow to a graveyard grey as the light on the sword went out.

The second performance, on the Regular Series, was given in honor of Lotte Lehmann, former Wagnerian extraordinaire and undoubtedly the greatest Sieglinde of all time. Interviewed after arriving from her Santa Barbara home, she bubbled as follows: "To be 80 and having so many plans, it's almost ridiculous. But I love life so. I saw a man on TV the other day who is 112 years old, and I think I would like to reach 112, too." She went on to say she had only one regret, that she never sang Isolde. "I always hesitated, but now I know I should have done it."

The incompletely realized *Don Giovanni* from 1965 returned with its original plan of "turning scenic pieces" abandoned. Instead, the pieces were spaced out, and Skalicki designed a big central backdrop which focused, as an in-joke, on Prague's Tyl Theater, place of the original *Don Giovanni* premiere. Somehow the effect was makeshift. But, although the handwriting on the wall seemed to say let's start again from the ground up, the performances still benefited from such assets as Cesare Siepi's suave Giovanni, Enriqueta Tarrés' brilliant-sounding Anna, and the luxuriously creamy and resilient Elvira of Teresa Zylis-Gara, a Polish soprano on the way to the Met. Allan Monk, an Auditions winner from Western Opera Theater, showed his high professional ability as Masetto.

262

Teresa Berganza's belated entrance into the company came with a gorgeously scintillating Rosina in the centennial *Barber*. She looked as cute as your daughter's best doll, she bathed the audience in creamy tone, she phrased aristocratically, she controlled dynamics perfectly, she floated the fioriture with ease, and she exhibited a lovability which doesn't come across on her *Barber* recording. Wixell was a very lively Figaro, even playing his own guitar, and Rossi-Lemeni's Basilio was grand in the Chaliapin (and Rossi-Lemeni) tradition: he strutted, careened, and mopped himself after his aria, not with one but two large pocket handkerchiefs. Pietro Bottazzo, fresh from a Rome Opera visit to New York, was the stylish Almaviva.

And Renato Capecchi, favorably remembered from the Cosmopolitan, was a non-hammy Bartolo, a more than ordinary substitute for Geraint Evans who had been advised by his doctor to rest up between Salzburg and his San Francisco Wozzeck later in the fall.

The tenor lineup also included Luciano Pavarotti, who sealed his selling power in San Francisco with an heroic, cultivated Edgardo in *Lucia*, and Ludovic Spiess, a beefy Rumanian who registered the right ring for Calaf in *Turandot*, although he tended to strut, and push his attractive voice. One *Lucia* performance brought Nicholas di Virgilio, Spring Opera's 1966 Edgardo, as a sub for the ailing Pavarotti. With only eight hours notice to brush up on a role he hadn't sung for more than a year, di Virgilio was nervous, naturally enough, in the early acts. But his Tomb Scene was distinguished. In *Lucia*, Margherita Rinaldi was a sincere protagonist, rather in the Pagliughi tradition. In *Turandot* Jane Marsh's Liu was less successful than her Pamina of the previous season.

There were some interesting points to Yannopoulos' *Lucia* direction. The governess was played blind, as in Sir Walter Scott's story, which meant she could do grandly dramatic things like stamp her cane at an anguished turn of events. And it made sense to have Lucia pick up Edgardo's sword at the end of Act 2. But there was also some extremely muddled choral movement.

Came late February 1969 and Lord Henry Ashton's castle, Dr. Bartolo's house, 2000 costumes, six miles of electric cable,

600 light bulbs, a closed-circuit TV system with eleven monitors, and a lot of other things, too, were packed into a fleet of piggyback trucks and put on the Southern Pacific for a trip to Los Angeles. After a three-year-plus hiatus the San Francisco Opera was going back to the southland—not to Mrs. Chandler's Pavilion but the faithful old Shrine Auditorium. And it was taking the bulk of its 1968 San Francisco season under the terms of a long-range agreement which, if realized, would bring opera in California into a new and different balance.

'Twas not to be.

Actually it had been in the summer of 1967 when a momentous announcement to the press was made, as follows:

"The cities of San Francisco and Los Angeles have entered into a new operatic agreement . . . The first phase calls for the Los Angeles Music Center Opera Association to present a Los Angeles opera season produced by the San Francisco Opera Company in March of 1969 and annually thereafter. In addition, the two associations have it as their aim within five years to begin a permanent and equal partnership. This would result in the formation of a San Francisco-Los Angeles Opera Association that would produce opera for Northern California as the San Francisco Opera Association and for Southern California as the Los Angeles Music Center Opera Association. . . .

"Kurt Herbert Adler, general director of the San Francisco Opera Association, will have the same responsibilities in the new company when it is formed. The 1969 Los Angeles season will last four weeks and will take place in the Shrine Auditorium, with the intent to bring future seasons into the Dorothy Chandler Pavilion of the Music Center when it becomes available . . . The resources thus united will enable the company to undertake new projects and maintain the present artistic level . . . It is expected that in 1970 Los Angeles (financing) will contribute a new production to be premiered in the south and included in that autumn's San Francisco repertoire. Additional Los Angeles productions will follow in succeeding years."

But financial problems within the camp of the Los Angeles sponsors attendant on that March 1969 season were monumental, and, as *The Saturday Review's* Irving Kolodin observed, after visiting the Shrine for three performances: "As a proposition, the idea of combining San Francisco's operatic resources of properties and people with the new impulses to expansion in Los Angeles, thus conferring long-term benefits on both, has much to commend it. As a practicality, its first manifestation in a March season just completed in the Shrine Auditorium suggests that a successful outcome for the scheme may challenge the best brain power, financial as well as artistic, in both communities."

Opening Night, with *Turandot*, came March 1, and the next day Martin Bernheimer wrote in *The Los Angeles Times*: "After three years of negotiating, buck-passing, hat-passing, worrying and manipulating, Northern and Southern California have resumed their long-standing operatic interrelationship (which resembles) a merger-to-be . . . During the inevitable, self-congratulatory intermission speeches, John A. McCone, president of the Music Center Opera Association, and Joseph Alioto, Mayor of San Francisco, tried desperately to put an end to the concept of rivalry between Los Angeles and San Francisco. Instead, both gentlemen introduced a would-be rivalry with New York, stressing the notion that 'our' opera company 'will be second to none, not even the Metropolitan.'"

Bernheimer suggested, with some point, that the promoters of the season get an audience first, and worry about being the "last word" later. Because it was only a half-full Shrine which greeted the *Turandot*, and there were many more half houses to go before the troupe packed up at the end of the month. Although, in truth, a half-filled Shrine equalled a full Chandler Pavilion.

Everyone tried to figure out why the season wasn't a smash. And there were plenty of reasons given. For one, Los Angeleans had gotten out of the habit of taking their opera in the unprepossessing and ill-located Shrine. Furthermore, the San Francisco Opera hadn't been around for a while and there is nothing like continuity for box office success. Publicity efforts prior to the season were not what they might have been, either—no stops could be pulled out until the New York City Opera had left town in December. Meanwhile, the expense of rehearsing a new Los Angeles orchestra, the San Francisco Symphony being occupied with its regular subscription season, raised the bill, and there was the expense of bringing back the artists who had been in San Francisco a few months earlier, or bringing in different ones.

The makeup of the Los Angeles season was somewhat different, and artistically less exciting, than that of the autumn innings in 1968. Transportation and casting problems, plus fears of small box office, nixed the trip for the Triple Bill, *Wozzeck* and *Fra Diavolo*. And the *Salome* originally intended for the Shrine had to be given up when it developed that Silja was due in Palermo on the same dates. A *Rheingold* was thrown in, to give Los Angeleans a mini-*Ring* since there were also two performances of *Walküre*, but under the circumstance of late preparation, a repertory rather than festival cast was all that could be assembled.

Turandot went well, with Delme Bryn-Jones taking over Ping from the otherwise occupied Wixell. *Ernani* came more into its own (such as that is) because Glossop was in better voice than in San Francisco, and Tozzi took over Silva, giving it a little more pizzazz than Ezio Flagello. *Barber* brought several honorable changes of cast, Mary Costa offering a Rosina of great charm, Enzo Sordello an ingratiating Figaro and Ramon Vinay his authoritative Bartolo.

In *Walküre* the Siegmund of Vickers (for Thomas) and especially the Wotan of David Ward (instead of Hubert Hofmann) were considerable assets, but other debits remained. *Troyens* continued as one of the company's proudest achievements, even with the cuts, and there were successful *Butterfly* performances with Kirsten and Pilou. Like Glossop, baritone Victor Braun was in better shape in Los Angeles and this helped the *Trovatore*. There was also the Rinaldi *Lucia* with Cioni and Bryn-Jones for Pavarotti and Braun. One performance of the Siepi *Don Giovanni* was troubled by a strange electronic buzz which hummed away distractingly for about an hour.

The *Rheingold* cast, which did have some points, listed Franz Mazura as Wotan, Glade Peterson as Loge, William Wildermann as Fasolt, Ara Berberian as Fafner, Robert Glover as Mime, Rudolf Knoll as Alberich, Bryn-Jones as Donner, William Cochran as Froh, Margarita Lilova as Erda, Sona Cervena as Fricka, Jeanne Cook as Freia, and the Misses

266

Marks, Anderson and Nadler as the Rhine Maidens. Horst Stein conducted.

Kolodin saw *Butterfly, Ernani* and *Barber* and was quite happy. He thought Adler deserved credit for "seeing in Pilou, whose assignments at the Met have run to Juliette, Micaela, etc., not only a potential but a present Butterfly, with the strong middle sound to support an affecting characterization." Of the *Barber* he glowed: "Quite the most satisfying of the productions offered in this period was the company's famously amusing treatment of *Il Barbiere* . . . With the action adroitly controlled by director Ghita Hager, and Aldo Faldi an admirable conductor both for Rossini and singers, a sense of the fun and the froth in this score was conveyed to a sizeable audience."

Midway in the season there was a benefit concert involving the services of ten principals of the troupe, but funds (not considerable) raised at this event had small effect in countering a six-figure deficit accosting the less than homogeneous Los Angeles sponsorship. After this debacle the Music Center Opera Association virtually abandoned the San Francisco-Los Angeles "partnership" idea and continued to sponsor late November-early December visits (begun in 1967) of the New York City Opera, an organization whose somewhat more intimate scale of production and de-emphasis on stars—except for the important Beverly Sills and Norman Treigle—made it available to Los Angeles for less than the San Francisco Opera.

There was talk of San Francisco's company "commuting" to Los Angeles on Monday nights of the regular fall season, but that idea proved cumbersome. The San Francisco Opera was, of course, quite busy at home. The enthusiasm (financial, as well as otherwise) of Los Angeles sponsor Lawrence E. Deutsch for the City Opera proved a notable factor in the continued visits of that company. These visits have created a varied opera diet for California, so long as Angelenos could fly north for their Silja *Salome* and San Franciscans go south for their Treigle *Mefistofele,* or perhaps Ginastera's *Bomarzo.*

The 1968 Spring Opera season took place in April because the San Francisco Symphony was on tour in Japan and the

Opera House was available. As the Oakland Symphony from across the Bay was also occupied, a pickup group was used in the pit, with hardly magnificent results. *La Rondine* was brought back in a new production with sets by Robert Darling, and had a surprising success with the public. There was also special interest in a *Carmen* with the original spoken dialogue. *Abduction and Rigoletto* filled out the repertoire.

1969

The 1969 season proved one of Adler's best, but it would have made its mark if only because of the immensely stylish and mercurial production of Rossini's *La Cenerentola*, staged and designed by the long-absent, now-celebrated Jean-Pierre Ponnelle and conducted by London's Charles Mackerras. Rarely do all components come together in such inspired fashion: stage direction so musical, musical direction so stage-conscious, a cast which sings, and acts, so well, and scenery which keeps one guessing as to what it's going to do next. Ponnelle's staging was characteristically French in its discriminating elegance, but this didn't keep the show from being full of fun. Things were lively, never rowdy.

There were many lovely visual details, like the rolling out of an extremely long red carpet, in time to the music, just before Dandini's entrance as the prince. The quasi-rococo sets were merry visual romps loaded, not with in-jokes but what might be called on-jokes: a winking mask and cuddly lovers, for instance, who graced a "formal" sculptured facade. There was also a "rain curtain" during the second act storm—with real water. Originally estimated at a lamentable $2000 cost, the rain effect ultimately came in for about $50. Some backstage genius figured that a simple "soaker" garden hose with numerous outlets would do. All these "Ponnellites" were seen again when Ponnelle did the show for the Florence and Edinburgh festivals in 1971.

Mackerras, the versatile musical director of Sadler's Wells (and a frequent guest at Hamburg), conducted a highly intelligent and satisfying *Magic Flute* during 1969—but his *Cenerentola* was a revelation. From the playful-suspenseful phrasing of the overture's introduction, under which the allegro stole in like a determined urchin, one had the feeling the music was being invented on the spot, rather than simply read from score. It was a puckish, springy interpretation, delicate but firm. The cast boasted Teresa Berganza's creamy-toned, adorable Cinderella, Paolo Montarsolo's winningly helpless Don Magnifico, Pietro Bottazzo's handsome Ramiro, and Clifford Grant's tactful, sonorous Alidoro. But there was something extra special about Renato Capecchi's Dandini.

The assignment calls for a valet to pretend he's a prince, and Capecchi made it only too clear that the butler is a bit embarrassed by the chore, and that, since princely bearing is not his natural state, he must indulge in an over-effusive exaggeration of regal pomp. Capecchi not only mugged with relish but subtly suggested the pathos of Dandini's situation.

Cenerentola was new to the company's repertoire. So was Janacek's *Jenufa*, which the Chicago Opera had done a decade earlier but the Met has not taken on for fifty years. Felicia Weathers' Jenufa and Hager's direction were problem points but other elements were just right—especially the conducting of Bohumil Gregor, a Prague maestro (based in Hamburg) who provided all the soul and suavity one could want. The problem, of course, with operas as intense as Janacek's is that performances must proceed with a strong electric charge taking hold of everyone involved. At the first performance Weathers was cold and stagey, more a figurine than a flesh-and-blood country girl. Hager seemed determined to get some Bayreuthian trances into the act, and a high stairway in Bauer-Ecsy's first act set cut up the playing area uncomfortably. But Irene Dalis' Kostelnicka was forceful and sympathetic, Glade Peterson's newly robust tenor served Laca well, and Ragnar Ulfung was a lusty, pingy Steva. Although Hager unaccountably obscured his boozy first act entrance, Ulfung executed those same cartwheels which had awed Lincoln Center patrons when the Hamburg Opera brought *its* production of *Jenufa* to the Met in 1967.

The season opened September 16 with another from a healthy batch of five new productions, this a much-needed and impeccably-rehearsed *Traviata* devised by August Everding, a highly-regarded legitimate theater director from Munich's Kammerspiele, and Toni Businger, author of sets for the 1967 *Magic Flute*. If the evening had a somewhat Germanic *ganz organiziert* quality there was no reason to complain because the string of new ideas was so logical, realistic and amusing. The list was a long one, beginning with the party laughter heard even before the curtain went up, on to the ironic background vision of Violetta's hoped-for ballroom future as she fell dead of consumption.

The first act alone was chock full of good bits: the marvelously imperious finger-snapping of a precious headwaiter,[4] the ceremonial popping of three champagne corks timed to the chords before the 'Libiamo,' Violetta's claustrophobic request for the lights to be turned up at 'Sempre Libera,' and so on. The scene at Flora's, set in shocking red, included a spicy ballet which looked more integral to the action than is sometimes the case and which built to a fun climax with the 'matador' quickly dispatching five bulls, or ballet boys, to the floor—where they rested like so many railway ties.

Possibly Everding overdid his cinematic dim-the stage-and-spotlight-a-character effects, but they can be defended. It makes theatrical sense, for instance, to mirror Alfredo's dark mood when he sings 'Oh infamy' in the rarely-performed second act cabaletta. Jeannette Pilou, the Butterfly of 1968, returned as Violetta. She was dry-voiced on Opening Night, that traditionally nerve-wracking time for singers, but three evenings later the sensuously silvery quality of her soprano emerged. In all performances one could enjoy the conversationally realistic phrasing she employed most gracefully for dramatic effect. Franco Bonisolli, tall, handsome and a good actor, was the smooth Alfredo, and Ingvar Wixell an unusually sympathetic Germont.

This was not quite a Golden Age *Traviata* in terms of vocalism per se, but a very moving, theatrically vivid one. Giuseppe Patane's conducting was a bit methodical, but zippy, and well-correlated with the stage. A $43,000 grant from the Charles E. Merrill Trust helped make it all possible.

Whatever the effect of Adler's *Traviata* offering, most of the customers had forgotten, or never registered, that Maria Callas was supposed to relaunch her long-dormant operatic career as San Francisco's Violetta, going on from there to Chicago and Dallas—San Francisco being, of course, "the diamond" on her "chain" of opera houses which had never come to be. Callas asked of Adler two conditions, and he

270

agreed. One was that, since she had been away from the operatic stage for a while, she wished to have three weeks of rehearsal prior to the opening. No problem. The other was that she hoped to sing no more than two performances a week. Fine.

Inasmuch as six *Traviatas* were scheduled, that meant she would stay in San Francisco for a total of six weeks, three of rehearsals and three of performances. But her manager, S. A. Gorlinsky in London, told her: "You don't want to spend as long as six weeks of your valuable time in a dump like San Francisco—especially since you're only rehearsing in Dallas for ten days." What Gorlinsky failed to take into account is that the Dallas season comes later in the fall when, presumably, Callas would have felt more "warmed up." At all events, Callas sang—not unpredictably—at none of the three opera houses on her theoretical itinerary.

If Everding's U.S. debut was a grand success, the next evening brought another impressive achievement in Gunther Schuller's world debut as a conductor of normal repertory in a major house (he had presided over his own *Visitation* in 1967 and the recherché Triple Bill of 1968). This time Adler, in one of his greatest inspirations, assigned Schuller Strauss's *Ariadne.* The task proved immensely congenial and Schuller produced an interpretation that must have had confirmed Straussians like Karl Böhm looking to their laurels. One of his prime objectives was to savor the colors and shapes of Strauss's phrases in all their richness and piquancy without dropping a stitch in terms of overall flow. Another was to retain the chamber orchestration's intimacy while projecting the score with a highly charged intensity. That intensity reached a magnificent peak in the slow, suspensefully ecstatic build-up in the long Bacchus-Ariadne duet, Schuller wrapping organ-like sonorities around the Naiad-Dryad-Echo trio as they sang the ethereal "Töne, Töne, Süsse Stimme."

Janis Martin, with a contract for Eva at the 1970 Bayreuth Festival in her pocket, was a radiant Composer, and Ludmila Dvorakova, the Czech dramatic soprano, one of the more sympathetic Ariadnes. Grist repeated her remarkable Zerbinetta at the first two performances, being succeeded at the third by the splashy, unrefined Colette Boky (subbing for indisposed Jenifer Eddy) when a Deutsche Grammophon recording date in Munich—for *Ariadne* under Böhm—called her away.

The jets also had the business of Jess Thomas, a participant in the same recording, who was available to San Francisco for Bacchus in the *first* and *third* performances, showing some evidence of jet lag on his return. James King, returning to the scene of his 1961 Spring Opera Don José, took over the middle performance. King sounded more trumpety, Thomas phrased more dreamily. The prissily unctuous and hilarious Major Domo—the best in company history—was Walter Matthes, a San Francisco banker(!) and a regular in local Gilbert and Sullivan productions.

Work on the *Ring* continued in 1970 with, for no immensely plausible reason, *Götterdämmerung* rather than *Siegfried.* In any event, the production was visually no less beautiful and nimbly fluid than its predecessors in the cycle. Particularly noteworthy were the coppery, sky-reaching central tower, one of three, depicting the Gibichung Hall, and—in the third act—the light withheld except from Siegfried's face as his body is borne aloft. Whether or not the idea was uniquely Hager's, it was fascinating to see Gunther fall to the floor in a Wielandesque heap of despair after the vassals leave in Act 2.

Neatly-made cuts held the show down from 7:00 to approximately 11:40, and some of them, like the chunk toward the end of the Norn Scene, were helpful, but not the curtailment of the harrowing final scene of Act 1 and Gutrune's tortured awakening in Act 3—even if Wieland Wagner had been in the habit of cutting that passage. Several buffs were highly indignant about the excisions, and their complaints were sympathetically received by conductor Otmar Suitner—who announced he was writing a book on the ticklish subject of cuts! With some of the performances on week-day nights the management felt, naturally enough, that it had to accomodate the numerous patrons not affluent enough to abandon their jobs in favor of full-time festivalizing. But it might have pondered how Londoners manage to fill the Coliseum for 5 p.m. Wednesday *Götterdämmerungs.* Adler made it clear that, no matter when the circumstance, he didn't want to risk going beyond the psychological point of endurance—wherever that lies.

Suitner, general music director of East Berlin's tradition-steeped Deutsche Staatsoper (he was, in that position, the titular descendant of Kleiber and Blech) took over the Wagner since Stein, newly appointed first conductor at Vienna's Staatsoper, was unable to return. Although at least one *Götterdämmerung* was less intensely sustained than others, Suitner brought a knowing baton to his task, keeping the orchestral tone luminous and spinning a prevailing web of compassionate sadness which was quite remarkable. Amy Shuard was the slightly matronly but crisp, warm Brünnhilde, and Jess Thomas continued as anchor man of San Francisco's *Ring* with an ardently-phrased Siegfried.

If anyone stole the show—he didn't quite win the other things he wanted—it was the Hagen, Peter Lagger. Hired after Wildermann backed out, the Swiss-born, Berlin-based Lagger offered an immensely baleful, debauched, overbearing portrayal. He looked at times like the most offensive sort of headwaiter, waiting, as it were, for the other characters to spill the soup. Lagger's Rocco in *Fidelio* (his U.S. debut) was not so interesting.

The fifth new production of the season was *Aida*, absent for a surprising six years while it lined up behind other candiates for new sets. Skalicki's sun-bathed, clean-lined show (based on memories of a trip to Egypt and researches into Egyptian art) was conceived on a huge if not weighty scale. Crowd scenes stretched from pit to Franklin Street, and heavenward, too. A characteristic Egyptian monumentality was stressed—suggesting, by the way, the pitiful fragility of characters caught under the relentless tread of a governmental conformity which seems particularly uptight by today's standards.[5]

At least one theatrically keen observer—he was singing in another production—made the valid point that Anthony Besch's staging of the Triumphal Scene would have been more realistic, and considerably more effective, if all the processionists were sturdy soldier types rather than relatively emaciated extras, and if they had shown signs of sweaty exhaustion while carrying the assorted heavy trophies and idols. But barring the absence of this sort of imagination, which *Aida* needs less than some other operas, Besch's direction was sensible and uncluttered.

Gwyneth Jones, one of the better-established Welsh singers to join the roster, was, in her best performances, a notably liquid-toned Aida, possibly the finest in the annals. *Aida* had a record six performances in San Francisco (and one in Sacramento), and since Jones had to move on she was succeeded at the last three by a new Yugoslavian soprano named Ljiljana Molnar-Talajic. Credits included a very clean, powerful light spinto, not inherently beautiful because of a certain girlish nasality, but capable of some lovely sounds, especially in the Tomb Scene. Both in acting and vocal characterization, however, she was too placid. She made up, by the way, in blacker face than any other recent Aida.

Guy Chauvet's Rhadames gave way, in the second cast, to Jon Vickers' vigorous and more mannered performance. James Farrar, an American from Germany, was the season's only Amonasro, displaying an attractive if somewhat small-scaled voice, at times reminiscent in timbre of Leonard Warren. He obviously wasn't Adler's first choice, but—in this role at least—he got by quite nicely. Jean Périsson, liberated briefly from the French repertoire, conducted Verdi's music suavely. Often there was an Italianate-enough impact, but sometimes the effect was rather too courtly. The Ballet Music was sinuous, racy, and nothing short of superbly stylish.

San Francisco was, in 1969, more than ever the chief U.S. outpost of the Welsh Army of Opera Singers. Close on the heels of Gwyneth Jones' company bow came the U.S. debut of Margaret Price, a remarkably cultivated soprano still in her '20's who had sung at Covent Garden as Marzelline in Klemperer's *Fidelio*. Jane Marsh had been Adler's intended Pamina for the re-run of *Magic Flute* but Düsseldorf wouldn't release her. This paved the way for Miss Price who, boasting a dark yet silvery, full but intimate soprano, broke numerous hearts with an expressive, Elisabeth Schumann-like warmth. She needed to watch her figure, but she gave off just the right appearance of a girl in Wonderland. And when she returned in 1970, in *Falstaff* and *Cosi*, people were talking about "Price" and meaning Margaret, not Leontyne. Also new to the *Flute* cast was the athletic Ulfung's impish, giggling, waddling, darting, clicking Monostatos.

Local color got into the act at the Greek Theater in Berkeley when *Magic Flute* went to college, that being the University of California's main campus across the Bay. Evans, now Sir Geraint, went for broke with his Papagenan opportunities for improvised dialogue, and when Tamino asked, "What is this land, and who rules over it?" he waved his arm at the surroundings and pronounced: "Ronald Reagan." This convulsed the huge and spirited audience, few of them happy with the Governor of California's conservative policies, and Evans broke up in turn, almost bringing the show to a halt. This was not the last, because later on the irrepressible Welshman asked a mysteriously garbed priest, "Say, are you from the board of regents?"—that being the university's governing body.

Along with his second act glass of wine Papageno munched on a hot dog from a nearby stand, commenting: "This restaurant has an excellent chef." He also had a remark for the trombones as they intoned a recurrent solemn motif: "If I don't go now, they'll never change their tune."

The Verdi quotient was filled out in 1969 with *Forza*, this serving as occasion for the belated company debut of Carlo Bergonzi. When he arrived on stage he looked more like the proprietor of a fine Italian restaurant (which he is) than a romantic hero, and he acted as if the semaphore were his own invention, but his spinto tenor was possibly the most fluidly "Italianate" and freshly blooming instrument heard since the departure of Tucker. Capecchi's punchy, shuffling, bookish Melitone was way above the routine,[6] and Patane's everurgent conducting indicated that *Forza*, which he had not conducted before, was very much his meat.

Casting Leonora proved a stumbling block. Quite late the word got around that it would be Raina Kabaiwanska, but then she was invited to open La Scala in *Ernani* in December and she pleaded she needed November, the time of the San Francisco *Forza*, to prepare. The role went to Nancy Tatum, a large and cheerful soprano who offered gorgeous head tone and less than ideally jelled phrasing. Ingvar Wixell's Don Carlo was the first of his career.

By "popular demand" as it were, the 1967 *L'Elisir d'Amore* was brought back with the same cast except that Pavarotti took over for Alfredo Kraus. Pavarotti had his points, but Stuart Burrows' sweet, silken, seamless singing of Nemorino in the student performances (these in English) was something very special. Too bad that some unbelievably uptight parents and teachers wouldn't let their charges attend because they thought the *elixir* might be a dangerous drug!

Pavarotti encountered something potentially more dangerous when, during the October 1 performance of *Bohème*, one of San Francisco's better earthquakes rocked the Opera House. Dorothy Kirsten and Pavarotti had just begun the wistful third act duet after Mimi's Addio and, as the tenor began his phrase "Addio Sognante Vita" (Ricordi score, page 217) a tremendous hubbub welled up from the audience. Pavarotti went right on, finishing his four bar phrase resolutely enough although with a certain questioning sag at the end of it. By this time the audience was applauding his (and their) refusal to be completely panicked, and Kirsten entered with her answering phrase smack on the beat. Conductor Anton Coppola was obviously not about to give in to the ponderous budgings which, wrote Alexander Fried, had "an odd side-to-side softness" about them. Dozens of people in the audience stood up startled and uncertain. Some moved briskly up the aisles or to side walls and exits. But there was no pervasive exodus. Pavarotti stepped out of character sufficiently to demand of prompter Gianfranco Cauzzi, when he had the chance: "What the ---- was that?"

"Just an earthquake," said the man in the box.

Curiously enough the performance had just struck interest earlier in the third act after lackluster preceding acts. And naturally, when the No. 1 critic spoke, it continued to the final curtain with an only too evident dedication. How strange, and typical, that the great shake came on the line "Farewell to the life of our dreams."

Pavarotti had a happier experience at the October 12 *Bohème* when Adler, no less, put on Colin Harvey's waiter's jacket and suddenly appeared on stage during Act 2, and, his back to the audience, poured real Champagne for the Bohemians. It was the tenor's birthday. The secret had been well kept, and the performers just about broke up.

Late season performances of *Bohème* were conducted with great verve, good humor and humanity by Périsson, obviously a very congenial Puccinian. There had been some criticism that Adler was type-casting his conductors too much by nationality, and Périsson's Puccini had the effect of answering

276

this criticism not only on paper but with good results, too. Placido Domingo, the important new Spanish tenor, turned up for one of the November *Bohèmes*, giving great pleasure with his mellifluous vocalism and excellent style. Périsson was also in charge of a surprisingly early return of *Pelléas et Mélisande*, presented because Pilou had gone over well the year before and Mélisande was an ideal role for her particular talents.

It remains to mention the season's least happy offering, a series of performances of *Fidelio* conducted with neither the requisite radiance nor consistency by the nervous-batoned Sixten Ehrling, conductor of the Detroit Symphony. Jones was a starry-class but uneven Leonore. Franz Mazura's stark, taut Pizarro (seen the following summer at Salzburg) was more memorable, also King's heroic Florestan. Sheila Marks of Western Opera Theater took over Jane Marsh's Marzellines most creditably.

Spring Opera's 1969 season was back in the troublesome month of June. Although there was a rather distinguished revival of Gounod's *Roméo et Juliette*, staged with contemporary theatrical perceptions by Martial Singher (San Francisco's Pelléas in 1947), and a *Figaro* in English charmingly directed by Ghita Hager, there were serious problems, too. *Rondine* was unaccountably repeated before renewed demand could catch up with it, and Adler, looking for a "modern" work not too complex, hit on Menotti's *The Consul*, an entertainment which many people considered passé. Even if, one might add, police states are not passé. Friday night performances in general sold well, but Tuesdays were disastrous. One had to ask, was Adler making as crisp and efficient decisions for the Spring Opera board as he was for his own?

More and more there came the realization that Spring Opera was reading as a cheap carbon copy of Fall Opera. So, ever pressed by the increased usage of the Opera House by the Symphony, the Spring Opera people decided the time had come to make a Big Change or Fold the Tent. The result, announced to the public in January 1970, was a plan to skip the 1970 season, work out details of an agonizing reappraisal, and come back on the scene March 1971 with a four-week season in the 1700-seat Curran Theater, downtown scene of

San Carlo visits fifty years earlier. As president J. Peter Cahill put it: "Imaginative changes in format and a more adventurous approach are needed for Spring Opera to fulfill its function, develop the art form of opera and the audiences supporting it."

With the summer of 1970, Spring's new president, a brilliantly efficient, opera-loving attorney named William Godward, could announce details of the first Curran season. The stage would be run out over the pit and the orchestra would play hidden behind the scenes (as in the Winterland plan), and all operas—even *Rigoletto*—would be in English. Immediacy would be the thing. A revival of *Don Pasquale* was also promised, and two extremely interesting novelties: the first San Francisco production of Mozart's *Clemenza da Tito* and the local premiere of an experimental new "collage opera" on the Faust theme by John Gessner and H. Wesley Balk, this production to be brought in on a fee basis from Minneapolis' progressive Center Theater.

1970

There must be a bit of magic in the number eleven. By 1970 the number of operas for the season had gradually been whittled down from thirteen (1968) to twelve (1969) to eleven, the length of season remaining more or less eleven weeks. The number proved more than an empty statistic because the company came up with what might well be termed its best season in modern times. Granted that Adler chose his repertoire and casts well, and luck—even in the face of cancellations—was on his side in terms of artist availability, but eleven operas (each performed from three to seven times) in as many weeks seemed a truly manageable number. Only one production proved less than festive in its general tone, and that was not the fault of a lack of time. Gone were the days when, in the midst of bread-and-butter performances and five or six well-treated new productions, interesting revivals (one thinks of the *Carmelites* of 1963, the *Bartered Bride* of 1964) received very short preparation indeed.

As a matter of fact, the decision to mount only eleven shows stemmed from financial pressures. Fiscal stresses reaching back to such dubious matters as the 1968 Triple Bill made themselves so apparent during planning stages of the 1970 season that sails had to be trimmed. But the Adlerian flagship hardly looked denuded. While there were only three new productions for the year, they were all impressive (Ponnelle's *Cosi Fan Tutte* and *Otello*, and the Hager-Skalicki *Siegfried*), and numerous recent productions (for instance the 1967 *Tristan*, the 1962 *Rake's Progress* and *Falstaff*, the 1968 *Salome*) were available to fill in the other eight slots.

The 1970 season boasted a lot of blessed events: the first instance of a grand-scale individual corporate gift, the first live stereo opera broadcast in U.S. radio, the first U.S. Tristan of Wolfgang Windgassen, the first ever Sacristan of Renato Capecchi, the first King Marke of Giorgio Tozzi, the first Fiordiligi of Margaret Price, the first Carmen in French of Brigitte Fassbaender. It was also the first season in several years in which average capacity attendance shot up from a 90-or-below figure to a solid 95%.

Various theories were propounded as to why the box office was so socko. One gave prime thanks to p.r. director Patrick Blake's season-describing insert distributed to one day's full circulation of *The Sunday Examiner-Chronicle*. Another took note of the fact that, with the exception of Stravinsky's *Rake*, all operas on the list were works of unimpeachable popularity or long-established quality.

The corporate gift came from Crocker-Citizens National Bank, to the tune of $41,200 for production costs of *Cosi Fan Tutte*, the choice of opera possibly reflecting a thought that the title "Thus Do They All" could be directed at San Francisco's banking concerns—*thus do they all make a corporate gift!*[7] The broadcast, on November 28, marked Dorothy Kirsten's twenty-fifth anniversary performance with the company, and the first live broadcast of a San Francisco Opera performance since the last Safeway transmission twenty-four years earlier. Sounds permanently captured during the 1947–70 interim issued only from well-placed portable tape recorders.

In a season deserving many superlatives perhaps the most monumental event of all was the *Tristan* served forth in five handsome helpings[8] with the impressive lineup of Birgit Nilsson, Windgassen, Tozzi, and, for Brangäne, Janis Martin. Suitner was in the pit, carrying on from the best impulses of his *Götterdämmerung*. He took the score slowly, suavely, grippingly, balancing instrumental lines in telling fashion and, most significantly, creating a sense of total immersion in a drama of sadness and resignation. Magnetized, perhaps, by the heady cast, and certainly possessed by a special love of the score, he kept up the same intensity throughout the series of performances, establishing himself on equal standing with the Reiner (or a Kleiber) of a generation earlier.

Jon Vickers was to have done his first Tristan in San Francisco—like Vinay and Thomas before him. The arrangement had been made back in 1968. But upon arriving for rehearsals he developed throat trouble, and, after seeing three doctors, accepted a verdict proclaiming rest for up to two months. Sticky rumors went the rounds that the problem was not strictly medical: investigation reveals that Vickers had complained to Adler that the five full orchestra rehearsals he wanted were not available, but Adler in turn reminded Vickers that the agreement had been for four. Perhaps Vickers was getting cold feet about his Herculean assignment—although certainly his temperament and style suited the role well, and he'd coached it with the great Reginald Goodall in London. In any event, he departed amicably enough, and sang in the Met's new *Fidelio* a couple months later.

Curiously enough, when, only three weeks after the *Tristan* opening, James McCracken lost his voice in the midst of a series of *Otello* performances, Vickers was sounded out by phone and he conceded that he could return to San Francisco if necessary to play the Moor. McCracken recovered sufficiently and this proved unnecessary.

Vickers' *Tristan* replacement was the 56-year-old Windgassen who, by 1965, had sung the role 179 times and passed the world's record. Windgassen had retired from Bayreuth following performances in the summer of 1970—he would continue to accept engagements elsewhere—and there had been quite an emotional atmosphere at Bayreuth's final dress rehearsal of *Tristan*. Would this be the last ever series of *Tristans* with the essentially ultimate pair, Nilsson and Windgassen? That was the feeling at the German shrine. Thus the San Francisco performances had a certain "stolen goodies" quality about them—as if they were some special unplanned bonus. Windgassen had sung briefly at the Met in the 50's, and his stay at that house was, according to Kolodin, not exactly joyful. But for San Francisco he bent every effort, cancelling a Munich *Tristan* to make the trip possible.

No one claimed that Windgassen's voice was a big as Nilsson's almost unnecessarily Niagaran instrument—and at least one patron indulged in the discourtesy of booing the visitor from Stuttgart—but the lyricism of his singing, his poise, his immersion in the drama: all added up to an impressive sum. The timbre of his voice even suggested a certain youthfulness.

At the second performance, when the generally magnificent Nilsson was feeling under par during the first act, the experienced Windgassen came to the rescue, rubbing Nilsson's back during the post-potion encounter—the action fit the clinch—in order to loosen up the troubled soprano's voice. The classic prescription worked.

Tozzi's Marke had the advantage of more generous and smooth vocalism than is often available for this role. Janis Martin's soprano-like Brangäne may have been a trifle light in sound, but it was so sweet, so legato, so compassionate, so full of effortless thrust that only a foolish impresario would have looked elsewhere. Meanwhile, Hager's mellowed direction eschewed the tired Bayreuthism of Isolde dying standing up. After the first performance there was seven minutes' applause, and there would have been more, but the march of overtime required the pit to be cleared—it's a San Francisco custom for the musicians to remain in the pit during the calls so the bowing conductor, if so disposed, can point toward them with a smile and clapping of the hands.

It was a year of Standing Ovations, and one of the bigger ones came at the premiere of the Ponnelle-designed and directed *Cosi*. Lightning, they say, never strikes twice in the same place, but the artistic electricity generated by the quick-minded Frenchman evidently could, because he came up with a production thoroughly the equal of the 1969 *Cenerentola* in terms of impeccable style and theatrical ingenuity. And then, when he donned his two hats in the service of *Otello*, he quickly settled the question as to whether or not he was only a sophisticated comedy man. Ponnelle, make no mistake, could handle realistic tragedy with equal ease.

Of course it did no harm that Adler awarded him great casts.

The lineup in *Cosi* was Margaret Price (her voice grown into a generous near-spinto soprano) as Fiordiligi; Teresa Berganza—and later Rosalind Elias—as Dorabella; Graziella Sciutti (her return called for the cry, "Ah, finalmente!") as Despina; sweet-voiced Ryland Davies, the newest Welsh import, as Ferrando; Alberto Rinaldi, a livewire from Italy, as Guglielmo; and the eversharp Renato Capecchi as Don Alfonso, with Glyndebourne's John Pritchard a courtly, affectionate Mozartean in the pit. In *Otello* there was Raina Kabaiwanska (Desdemona), James McCracken (Otello), Kostas Paskalis (Iago), and Davies (Cassio), Bohumil Gregor conducting.

The Ponnelle view emphasized the "serious" nature of the *Cosi* libretto, and, while he struck an excellent balance between merriment and cynicism, there was an especially keen accent on the latter. The production was definitely drier and more tart than what San Francisco was used to. Alfonso was played by Capecchi as a rather genial but quasi-Mephistophelean character who directs the business of deception (behind unsuspecting backs) with an imperious walking stick. He was a self-satisfied type all right, playing most of the first scene settled back in a deep dish tavern terrace chair—a nice touch of conversational realism. Ponnelle's daggers of irony were deftly applied when, in the next scene, a relatively darkened stage gave way to an almost blindingly bright light to show the two ladies in all their "innocence."

Rosalind Elias, who had done Dorabella with Ponnelle at the Salzburg Festival, got into the act when Berganza became indisposed after the first two performances. Telephoned one night in New York at 10, she got a plane at 11:30, arrived in the early morning hours, slept, went to the opera house at 4 p.m., rehearsed, asked for a cot and a sandwich, stayed in her dressing room, and went on that night—approximately one day after her life was disrupted 3000 miles away. Capecchi noted to a colleague that she fitted into the show perfectly. The only adjustment was lengthening Berganza's dress.

Reality was the rule in Ponnelle's staging of *Otello*. Masts jerked on the quai during the storm, Cassio fell flat on his face after getting drunk, his duel with an unusually young-looking Montano was a dust-biting, blade-to-blade wrestling match, and there was "cold fire," an old magicians' technique (unknown to the San Francisco Fire Department, the property master says) which was used to simulate flames in the "Fuoco di Gioia." But Ponnelle's greatest stroke was the way he played the arrival of the Venetian ambassador and his entourage in Act 3, the scruffy local soldiery rushing into place as the white-as-snow Venetians moved delicately onto the scene, all frills. The sociological contrast was devastating.

Ponnelle's rearrangeable styrofoam wall pieces worked well in general, but the setup for the last act, with only a realistic bed against a giant stylized wall, was jolting. The crunchiness—plainly audible—of the styrofoam (little pieces chipped off when impassioned players "chewed the scenery") made for minor comic footnotes. But sobriety was ascendant when, at the November 20 performance, McCracken lost his voice after the second act, continuing the performance at a high dramatic pitch but sotto voce, or lower.

McCracken's vivid Moor was played off against Paskalis' exuberant, natural, non-oily Iago. Kabaiwanska's radiant Desdemona boasted not only an exquisite vibrant warmth (she reminded somewhat of Magda Olivero) but the sort of technique which permits a thoroughly accurate rendering of such Verdi directions as the "con una voce *lontana*"[9] of the first act duet. Davies was probably the best Cassio in the annals, acting with great conviction besides singing with a strikingly dulcet tenor. Gregor's nervy, springy, suspenseful conducting helped create performances which seemed to be happening fresh rather than just following a ritualistic groundplan. Few conductors dare take such a contemplative tempo for the first act duet—suffice to say Gregor made his choice convincing.

Siegfried completed the year's list of new productions, and a handsome one it was, too, fluid but not self-consciously modern. Skalicki effected a marvelous transformation scene in the third act with his circling, soaring projections of the magic fire. The fishy, flat-topped dragon was more endearing a creature than he should have been, but by the second performance he at least got his mouth open wide enough to put a good bite on a weaker, less agile hero than Siegfried. Jess Thomas (Siegfried) and Thomas Stewart (Wanderer) were familiar Wagnerian elements. New in town was Berit Lind-

283

holm, a Varnay-like Brünnhilde from Sweden with stellar Bayreuth experience—she came in place of the originally envisaged Dvorakova. Ragnar Ulfung continued his activities as a character tenor with the first Mime of his career. Surely he must have gone to the zoo and observed the monkeys, so animal-like was his crouching, tumbling, swaying gnome. And it was nice to have a change from the Gerhard Stolze whine so well known on recordings. Offers soon poured in to Ulfung to repeat his Mime at Bayreuth, La Scala and the Met.

An unhappy *Siegfried* footnote had to do with Dan Richardson, the Alberich, who fell off the top of Fafner's cave at a rehearsal, breaking both wrists. He performed, however, with a "show must go on" spirit. Suitner's conducting, while not as fully committed as in *Tristan*, was breezy and spirited.

Grace Bumbry having bowed out of *Carmen* several months before the season due to a conflict in dates, the title role fell to Brigitte Fassbaender, a much-praised Munich mezzo and the daughter of Willi Domgraf-Fassbaender, a Glyndebourne Figaro before the War. It was her U.S. debut when she first appeared on Van Ness Avenue September 30. The immensely refreshing thing about her Carmen was that she didn't play it too seriously, too fatalistically. She was almost the girl next door, only one who has gone a little wrong. She was playful in a very natural way, never bogging down into the classic vampish poses thousands of Carmens have struck. The story goes that director Mansouri and Fassbaender had a bet she would pay him a dollar for every time she put her hand on her hip. He obviously didn't collect a dime.

If the young lady from Munich provided the most *natural* (in a different way) Carmen since Gloria Lane, José Van Dam, the Belgian bass-baritone, offered the most elegant Escamillo since Pinza. Guy Chauvet's uptight José was apropos, while Jane Marsh's pretty but weak-toned Micaela caused worry over her vocal estate. Mansouri's handling of that classic stumbling block, the fourth act procession, went Erlo one better: again the processants were invisible, but Mansouri had the populace come up to the footlights and cheer (and hiss) unseen personalities parading, as it were, out in the auditorium.

1970 also saw the return of Stravinsky's *The Rake's Pro-*

gress, evidence this of Adler's policy of keeping his warehouse of contemporary classics alive. Thanks especially to the crisp but warm conducting of Gunther Schuller, it seemed a more human entertainment than before. While caprice and mockery get the upper hand in *Rake*, they do so in an ultimately sublime frame. One doubts if there's a more moving scene on San Francisco record than the one in Bedlam, the demented Tom surrounded by a slowly forward and backward-moving circle of tattered madmen, creatures these who suggest dusty operatic characters assembled from some never-never storehouse, or perhaps the film *The King of Hearts.*

Gregory Dempsey of London's Sadler's Wells returned at short notice to replace the ailing Nolan Van Way in the title role. He gave a moving performance but in terms of pure magnetism of personality the show belonged to William Dooley as Nick Shadow. Made up to suggest a cat, or was it a gargoyle, he moved about in prissy 18th century salon steps, giggling, leering, cajoling—always with impeccable style. *Rake* was performed uncut in 1970; it had been slightly abridged in 1962. The attendance figure, while the lowest of the season, was still an honorable 85%. [10]

There were all manner of fresh bits when *Falstaff* was revived for the fourth time in nine seasons, the direction falling from Hager to the Falstaff himself, Geraint (now Sir Geraint, although he soft-pedalled the title) Evans. Dr. Caius pricked himself on Bardolph's upheld darning needle, Bardolph and Pistol cuddled on a barrel top as Falstaff assailed them, the fat knight wistfully relished the anchovy he found listed on the bill he cannot pay. And so on. Evans moved the Elizabethan set in closer to the audience, and also eliminated the rear projections, all to good effect. His exuberant Falstaff was surrounded by a bright cast vocally dominated by the ideal Nanetta and Fenton of Margaret Price and Stuart Burrows. She floated legato phrases and sustained tones with unsurpassable security and loveliness, and his effortlessly honeyed tones fell on the ear with equal grace. Thanks be, Burrows moved infinitely better than he did at the time of his U.S. debut in San Francisco three years earlier.

Bruno Bartoletti, the Chicago Opera's cultivated musical director, commuted to the Pacific Coast to lead four *Falstaffs* with great warmth and the right mercurialism. Another plus was the Caius of Ulfung, proof that relatively short but important character roles profit from "star" treatment.

If San Francisco's *Falstaff* was better than ever, the Wieland Wagner *Salome* which returned after a season's pause—in an attempt to strike, as it were, while Anja Silja was still hot—seemed more mannered than before. Part of the trouble was that some of the measured struttings about the stage were, or had become, like bad modern dance. The show was best when performers were able to put enough tension into the coiled-spring stances Wieland required. Ulfung's chillingly tormented, convulsive Herod was at an opposite pole from Richard Lewis' relatively playboyish tetrarch of '68, and it showed that Wieland's frame still permitted a fair amount of histrionic latitude. Ulfung kept up the standards in the Herod department very nicely, but Gerd Nienstedt's untidy-sounding Jochanaan fell far short of the smooth, tension-filled product of Franz Mazura two years earlier. Gregor conducted well, but not quite with the long-range intensity of Stein.

The only real dramatic dud of the season was the *Faust*, staged, as a matter of fact, by the brilliant Allen Fletcher who had done the original Spring Opera *Roméo et Juliette* and was reaping laurels for his *Hadrian VII* at San Francisco's American Conservatory Theater. Gounod caught Fletcher in an irreconcilable conflict between his wish to explore dramatic implications in the score (the revellers at the end of the Kermesse, for instance, could be considered to be part of a devilish balletic whirl) and his realistic assessment of the opera as polite middlebrow entertainment. The result, with a cast including some considerably less-than-ideal actors, Alain Vanzo (Faust) and Roger Soyer (Mephistopheles), was disheartening. Meanwhile there was an asset in the warm-voiced Marguerite of Judith Beckman, a 1961 San Francisco Auditions winner contracted in Düsseldorf and Hamburg. Dominic Cossa moved up from Spring Opera to do Valentin.

The *Nabucco* revival introduced Rolf Bjoerling, son of Jussi, as Ismaele in his U.S. opera debut. Frankly, he was disappointing, although he might have made a better impression had not nerves beset him. The voice sounded like a gutty pocket dramatic tenor, rather nasal and more Italianate than that of his father. The German soprano Marion Lippert conquered the demands of Abigaille with relative ease, and Cornell MacNeil (Nabucco) and Giorgio Tozzi (Zaccaria) were in excellent voice, Tozzi perhaps the best in fifteen years. Carlo Felice Cillario conducted engagingly, demonstrating more of an affinity for crisp early Verdi than he had for the romance of Puccini as served up in *Tosca*.

History repeated itself Opening Night of the 1970 season when *Tosca*, that favorite opener, took the stage. Ten years previous Renata Tebaldi had been scheduled to launch the season as Floria but was indisposed. Dorothy Kirsten replaced her. This time Régine Crespin was supposed to sing, but she too cancelled. And who replaced *her?* Dorothy Kirsten, of course. The difference was that in 1960 there was several weeks' notice while in 1970 the indisposition came in the wake of a vocally troubled dress rehearsal.

It took Kirsten an act to spring her voice loose, but she went on to provide a vivid, intense performance. By the third *Tosca*, eight days later, Crespin was able to return, and she offered a performance which had its own remarkable merits. Chief of these was that tender, luxuriant mezzo-forte float of tone which will long be remembered as the Crespin trademark. Some whoopy loud notes elsewhere were much less fortunate. The characterization was elegant, Crespin not fighting Scarpia all the way as Kirsten had. She was, instead, an immensely patrician, feminine Tosca, reluctant to be jealous in the first act and extremely composed at the beginning of the second.

Crespin's second *Tosca*, the fourth of the season, was less successful, and she had to bow out again. So the fifth performance was undertaken by Jeannine Crader, a 1955 San Francisco Auditions winner who was singing at the New York City Opera. She came heralded by a review identifying her Tosca as second only to that of Callas, but the actual thing— displayed under the admittedly adverse circumstances of late arrival—was relatively prosaic.

The sixth and seventh *Toscas* reverted to Kirsten who, toward season's end, officially celebrated the silver anniversary of her company debut. Crespin later cancelled *Tosca* at the Met, and one had to wonder if her bowings out of this opera

287

and *Gioconda* (San Francisco 1967) didn't reflect an inability to handle the full demands of Italianate cantilena roles. The conversational Marschallin, the relatively declamatory Dido and Cassandra—these remained the thoroughly viable Crespin parts.[11]

Tight money put off a projected new production of *Tosca*, but Mansouri brightened up the direction, even scaring some of the customers by having the firing squad shoot toward them (and a Cavaradossi with his back to the audience) in the third act. He also had steps built so the nave of St. Andrea Della Valle could be raised in relation to the central chapel, thus creating a marvelous counterpoint of action on two levels during the Te Deum. Casting in depth brought Capecchi as a simple, tick-racked Sacristan—he had told Adler he'd much rather do Ford in *Falstaff* in addition to his *Cosi* Alfonso but "the boss" persuaded him that "the first five minutes of the season are for me the most critical."

In the final Kirsten performances Cillario's baton was bequeathed to James Levine, a brilliant 27-year-old who had just gone free lance after six years as George Szell's assistant conductor with the Cleveland Orchestra. As a child in Cincinnati he had met Kirsten, told her of his desire to become a conductor, and heard her say: "Maybe we'll do a *Tosca* together someday." Their performing reunion was, to say the least, an exaltedly happy one. But, even without such special motivation, Levine is likely to have conducted with the punch and keen feeling for mood which San Franciscans experienced in November 1970. He was quickly reengaged.

1971

The forty-ninth season of the San Francisco Opera— another strong one—opened with a weekend of performances which, if one overlooks a few passing problems, can be rated as one of the more dreamy three days in the annals. It began with a Tito Capobianco-staged *Manon* bringing Beverly Sills and Nicolai Gedda together for the first time in the U.S. (they had sung Massenet's opera in Buenos Aires, and recorded it, too), continued with a *Rosenkavalier* involving Sena Jurinac as the Marschallin and Christa Ludwig, in her belated San Francisco debut, as Octavian, and went on to a *Madama Butterfly* marking Polish soprano Teresa Kubiak's U.S. stage debut in the title role, with Stuart Burrows taking on his first Pinkerton, and an ex-TV western star, Bruce Yarnell, as Sharpless.

Manon had long been an outcast from the repertoire due to the scarcity of prime protagonists in the interim years between Sayao and Sills, and also because of the cost of a suitable new production. *Manon*, like its heroine, does not come cheap, especially if the important Cours la Reine Scene is included. Thankfully the new tide of corporate support helped get Massenet's charmer back to Van Ness Avenue. The Metropolitan Life Insurance Company made a generous contribution to the cause, and so did Opera Association treasurer James Robertson, a fortyish San Francisco investment man and opera lover who had recently come on the board, without Old Guard credentials.

It was Capobianco's second U.S. production of *Manon*, the first having been an immensely successful effort at the New York City Opera four years earlier. David Mitchell succeeded Marsha Louis Eck as designer, turning out the same sort of rustic realism for the inn scene and powder-puff elegance for Cours la Reine, with a Watteau sky overhead— although less of it was visible in San Francisco's Act 1 because the new set for the inn was built up in the center. Again there were barnyard creatures to be seen, a dog scampered across stage on cue, and Manon was first spied by Des Grieux sitting on a swing, this time on the left instead of the right. At least one observer dubbed this Capobianco's "mirror image" *Manon*.

Capobianco's staging was full of, but not cluttered with, meaningful business, like the ironic touch of an unseeing Guillot appearing, in the midst of a game of blind man's buff, on the balcony of the inn just as Manon and Des Grieux escape beneath him. That ubiquitous young man in Cours la Reine, a Bunthorne-like creature who leisurely, fervently contemplated a flower, subsequently attempting to give it to Manon, was a happy inspiration. The Cours la Reine ballet, devised in collaboration with Lew Christensen, was extremely stuffy and severe, almost petrified, a state of affairs which fits the Lullyesque music and the rather sacred image of the Paris Opera, whose ballet only Guillot could afford to hire for Manon's amusement.

Sills' return to the company after eighteen years (remember

that, in 1953, she sang the fourth maid in *Elektra* and a subsidiary Valkyrie besides Donna Elvira) resulted in six sold out
houses for *Manon*. Those six nice audiences encountered a
superstar capable of so many meaningful shades between
mercurial and plaintive that her voice came forth more as
the servant of a dramatic concept than a simply predictable,
marketable asset. Which is not to forget the expert agility and
panache of her coloratura work in Cours la Reine, during
which she sang, as she had only once or twice before, both
the Gavotte and the alternate Fabliau.

Gedda's second role with the company afforded his listeners a more musically satisfying experience than his entrance
in *Fra Diavolo*. His gloriously ringing tenor, heard in the
meaty part of Des Grieux, confirmed his place on a Tucker-
Bergonzi level of vocal virtuosity, and there was the added
advantage of real acting ability. In more than one performance Sills and Gedda reached a peak of electricity in the St.
Sulpice Scene, he clutching her stole like a security blanket
while her advances gradually melted his reserve.

San Francisco's production had, besides Gedda, another
keen Scandinavian asset in the uniquely ebullient, hilarious
Guillot of Ragnar Ulfung, whose new gallery of inimitable
character portraits (Monostatos, Dr. Caius, Valzacchi, etc.,
not to speak of the larger Mime) was growing rapidly in San
Francisco thanks to the encouragement of Adler. Ulfung's
address to Manon in the first act, decorated with sighs and
the fancy footwork of an elaborate bow, was worthy of the
Comédie Française. In Cours la Reine he was a giddy,
sparkly, twinkly, zippily twitching fop. In fact, he and the
cynical, effeminate Brétigny (Mark Howard, whose voice
was much less fine than his acting) looked like a couple of
preening poodles. Meanwhile, WOT veteran Allan Monk
found one of his most congenial opportunities as a resonant,
fine-toned, moderately bullish Lescaut.

All performed on Opening Night without benefit of
prompter—Capobianco was eager to get rid of such an
operatic convention—and there were no mishaps. But
worriers among the performers brought about the return of
the man in the box at later performances. Out front Jean
Périsson's conducting, suave, sexy and affectionate, reaffirmed his position as the most effective French maestro

working in the U.S. Surely his listeners were hard put to remember a *Manon* conductor who achieved such a sonic sigh when the love music appears in the first act prelude.

Street musicians, those characteristic and delightful San Francisco fantasy ingredients (they'd sprung up all over downtown in 1971) were playing baroque music in excellent style by the steps of the Opera House on the second night of the season. This little concert was a good omen for what went on inside, a performance of *Der Rosenkavalier* which, thanks to very even casting of the principals and tidy, civilized staging by Hager, set a fresh standard.

Obviously much attention centered on Christa Ludwig and she was awarded a standing ovation after the third act. Although she had "graduated" elsewhere to the Marschallin how nice it was to have her superbly aristocratic Octavian. Newly slim of figure, she looked entirely credible as an ardent young gentleman, and she sang throughout with a tastefully creamy, unforced tone. There was immense class in everything she did, and when this Octavian dressed up as Mariandel she was very funny but in a deft, pointed rather than broadly slapstick way. For once the Mariandel dialect wasn't too screechy or squealy—even the impressive Stevens of a generation earlier had been guilty on this score. Adler had been courting Madame Ludwig for years, but scheduling had always been a problem, partly because her husband Walter Berry, from whom she was now divorced, didn't like to fly.

Sena Jurinac—who, by the way, had not by 1971 come to terms with the Met—returned to the scene of her American debut to provide a gracious, good-humored, warmly-sung Marschallin.[12] It was probably the most natural account of the role San Franciscans saw in modern times, which is to say the era of Schwarzkopf and successors. The Sophie of Helen Donath, an American imported from Germany (preceded by the Solti *Rosenkavalier* recording in which she participated) was radiant and cozy. Manfred Jungwirth's extroverted but not too slapstick Ochs was another prime merit, not to mention, in three of the performances, the knockout Italian Tenor of Gedda which continued the "class casting" policy for this role revived with Ilosfalvy in '67. Ulfung's *moto perpetuo* Valzacchi was made up (by Ulfung himself) in a zig-zag face which made him look like an ex-pirate.

The *Rosenkavalier* conductor was Silvio Varviso, absent for ten years. His 1960 *Rosenkavalier* had been one of the best things he did during his years of regular San Francisco service, and his return found him as affectionate a Straussian as ever, with the added advantage of a more concise baton style than that of his youth.

Madama Butterfly, the third opera in Adler's opening weekend wedge, made a sizeable impression thanks to the lovely, polished singing of Burrows as Pinkerton and the im-mensely genial, stalwartly-sung Sharpless of Yarnell, a six-foot-six alumnus of the TV series *The Outlaws*, on which he had presided as Deputy Marshal Chalk Breeson. The Butter-fly herself, Teresa Kubiak, had appeared in New York concert performances of *Queen of Sheba* and *Euryanthe*. She made a warmly sympathetic if hardly fragile heroine. Her sensuous voice, a veritable dramatic soprano, was at times unwieldy, but it was generally agreed that she was a force to be reck-oned with, especially if she returned as Aida or the *Forza* Leonora.

James Levine was back on the podium, offering the same grand, surging style and penetrating dramatic sense ex-perienced in his *Tosca* of the previous year. By this time, inci-dentally, the baton assignments in the Italian wing were being given out to numerous gentlemen of assorted nationali-ties. The last "principal" Italian maestro, Giuseppe Patane, had only been available for *Otello* in 1970, and he disquali-fied himself altogether (at least for awhile) by precipitously cancelling that engagement to go to La Scala. Ah, Milano!

Yarnell turned out to be not only a critic's performing ideal —so often a Sharpless is either thoroughly uncomfortable standing around drinking whisky in a business suit or else he fidgets the role to death—but also a supreme character off-stage. A rumor around the Opera House had it that the hulk-ing baritone in white knit pants, red sportshirt and off-red bandana was a gent from Texas who was going to buy the San Francisco Opera. Actually the behemoth was from Los Angeles, and all he wanted to do was sing with the company, not purchase it, but it turned out he was a collector of original papal bulls, assorted fine pistols, and Empire furniture.

Not to speak of his fancy for Turner paintings. It was absolutely characteristic that he would come to the opera one night dressed in white tie, tails and cape, and with a batch of medals on his breast—medals acquired at a local novelty store!

Die Meistersinger shared with *Manon* the rights of an elaborate full dress new production built especially for San Francisco's 1971 season. There was also a new *Il Tabarro*, but that is simply a one set show. Tchaikovsky's *Eugene Onegin* was hastily put into the schedule with a production purchased from the Mannheim Opera. The *Meistersinger*, which really looked beautiful, was brought out in memory of Robert Watt Miller, who had died in February 1970. A little over $100,000 was raised in his memory to help pay the bill. Erich Leinsdorf was Adler's guest in Box A at the opening—he was in the area, conducting a London Philharmonic tour—and he paid warm tribute to Miller during a broadcast intermission interview heard on KKHI the same evening.[13] Leinsdorf, remember, had been the conductor of *Pelléas* in 1938 when Miller was a young president of the Opera Association—and Reiner was conducting one of Miller's favorite operas, *Die Meistersinger*. Miller had, said the maestro, "a great independence of mind which some people mistakenly interpreted as rudeness." He went on to explain that behind the gruff, aristocratic exterior there resided a deep and warm concern for the company, allied with a vigilance about maintaining challenging standards in repertoire and performance.

Meanwhile Adler recalled that "during performances Mr. Miller's seat was in Box F, subscribed by him at all times. He had a very keen eye; whenever he rushed backstage everyone knew he had noticed something wrong with the scenery or lighting before anyone else had." Talk of rushing backstage, he would sweep in after a performance, complete with cape and cane, to congratulate a singer or director. He cut a truly operatic figure.

The *Meistersinger* sets by Roberto Oswald, a Hager colleague from the Teatro Colon, had a nice woodsy glow and a certain monumentality, too. While the general visual approach was more realistic than abstract, Nürnberg Act 2 was revealed not in the traditional clutter of rather cute operatic dwellings but with a large terrace between Sachs' and Pogner's houses downstage and, beyond a seeming chasm, a towering, cubistic backdrop of intersecting gables suggesting a painting of Feininger or Marc. The effect, while not precisely 16th century, was quintessentially German, and what is *Meistersinger* if not that?

Adler had long had the idea that James King was a logical candidate for Stolzing, and the realization of that idea (later carried to the Met) was a series of performances in which King's dark tenor made a sure, trim and ringing sound. This was just one of the year's numerous "firsts," because Leontyne Price also did her first Giorgetta in *Tabarro*, Gabriel Bacquier his first Michele in the same opera, Burrows his already-noted first Pinkerton *and* his first Lensky in *Onegin*, Luciano Pavarotti his first Riccardo in *Ballo in Maschera* (although he'd recorded the role, as Price had Giorgetta) and Thomas Stewart his first Onegin (it had originally been planned for the Met, only to be cancelled by a strike).

King was joined in the *Meistersinger* lineup by the East German Theo Adam whose Sachs, while vocally lightweight (closer in that respect to Janssen than Schoeffler) was immensely sympathetic, outgoing, flexible. There was, in fact, something unique about it—a floating, arching, compassionate, soft-grained quality, a matter this, of tone and phrasing which, in terms of style and rhythm if not actual sound, reminded of his higher-voiced colleague Jess Thomas. Evans' prissy, oily, agonized, R-rolling, compulsively hand-signalling Beckmesser was as entertaining as ten years earlier. New was the crisp David of John Walker, Spring Opera's *Pasquale* Ernesto graduated to the senior troupe. Arlene Saunders returned as Eva, a congenial assignment.

The same reduction in cuts which had benefited *Tristan* the year before made *Meistersinger*-ites relatively happy in '71. Again Otmar Suitner was the conductor, not quite maintaining equal intensity throughout the run this time (the chief sag came in the third act at the second performance) but most of the time piloting things with great humanity. While his *Tristan* was basically on the slow side, his *Meistersinger* tended to a healthy and fairly boisterous clip, sometimes rather heedless, but not without memorable dalliances like the third act quintet—and a very long fermata at the beginning of the chorus "Wach Auf." In general there was maximum radiance for Eva, impetuosity for Stolzing, impishness for Beckmesser.[14]

If the *Meistersinger* represented an artistic highpoint in terms of scenic values, the revival of the 1965 *Ballo in Maschera* brought special honors in the staging department. Truth to say, this Boston-version *Ballo* had never quite come off before, partly because of imbalanced casting, or singers who could not be persuaded to act. Piero Faggioni, a lyrical young disciple of Jean Vilar, changed all that. A movie actor and stage director—he had played bedroom scenes with Monica Vitti—Faggioni arrived in the U.S. from Italy knowing a thing or two about realism in the theater. He also demonstrated exquisite taste, along with the creative push of a director willing to take chances. The underlying strength of the direction was a continuous line of meaningful action involving not only soloists but choristers who were treated individually. No one was allowed to lag—he even prodded Pavarotti, not the world's greatest rehearser, into a fairly complete characterization.[15]

Probably the most memorable "business" in Faggioni's *Ballo* was a little "Pagliaccio" play put on upstage at the ball by three clowns. It served the purpose of distracting the partygoers from the lovers' confrontation, it suited the delicate music Verdi wrote for this scene, and, most vitally, it scored an ironic point because the playlet involved, as does the basic plot, a love triangle. Perhaps it was too much of a coincidence that the stabbing in the Commedia dell'Arte entertainment came at exactly the same time as the murder of Riccardo, and yet, in terms of dramatic inevitability, how could it be otherwise? In the first act the byplay between a zippy, mocking Oscar and the punctilious judge was especially mercurial and irreverent. And, since Faggioni was working with the "Boston" version, he even had a contingent of Indians paying their respects at the governor's court.

Martina Arroyo made an auspicious company debut as Amelia, pouring out a meltingly sensuous tone, and really sounding like a lovetorn young woman. Helen Donath was an Oscar in the same class as Reri Grist, Irene Dalis an authoritative, neatly musical Ulrica. Ingvar Wixell was the scheduled Renato, but he pleaded illness from Europe and an obscure baritone named Franco Bordoni was brought over from Italy. He turned out to be a small man with a large, well-schooled, decidedly Italianate voice. The projection was sometimes a bit covered rather than ideally magnetic, but he gave much pleasure, never failing at a climax and maintaining good taste throughout. Charles Mackerras was back in the pit, presiding with a great deal of brio. The staccato effects he achieved with the music for Oscar and the conspirators were quite special.

Verdi dominated midseason, *Ballo* running back-to-back with a return of the 1968 *Trovatore*. Leontyne Price was the Leonora of the first (chronologically-speaking) cast, singing with a beauty and refinement perhaps unequalled in her long history of San Francisco performances. Obviously there had been some artistic reappraisal on her part since the blustery Opening Night *Ernani* three years earlier. This time she only used obvious chest tones for very occasional dramatic effect—for instance when Leonora takes the poison. Her less than all-consuming sense of dramatic involvement brought a slight slowing down of Hager's originally intense direction of the principals, but a well-considered deceleration it was. Choral movement, as before, was Wielandesque, with long periods of neat, dutiful immobility giving way to rushes of action.

James King began the procession of Manricos, singing with a crispness and rather massive ring which were only Italianate by secondhand but sometimes exciting. A cold forced him to cancel the second performance and it was taken over by Placido Domingo, who happened to be giving a concert in El Paso when the emergency was declared. Domingo was just about ideal in voice and movement, and people will long talk about the evening of October 26, 1971 as enjoyed in San Francisco's War Memorial Opera House. More news was made in the first four *Trovatores* by Margarita Lilova, whose Azucena had grown somewhat in fine-lined sumptuousness since 1968. And certainly her crawling about that cell in the last scene was in the great tradition of caged dramatic lions. Raymond Wolansky was the di Luna, big-voiced, musical, not special although he came close in "Il Balen" on broadcast night.

By season's end the cast had almost completely changed (there were seven public *Trovatores*, plus three for the students), Ljiljana Molnar-Talajic, the 1969 Aida, returning as Leonora, Irene Dalis taking over Azucena, James McCracken (in bad voice) doing Manrico, and Louis Quilico commuting from New York City Opera dates in Los Angeles for one di Luna. Molnar-Talajic made an interesting foil to Price since her voice, rather than sounding dark and haunting, was more like the sonic equivalent of a calm moonlit sea on a cold northern night. The transparency and "weightlessness" of her bright-timbred tone reminded a bit of Milanov, especially since the acid quality noticed in '69 seemed less in evidence.

New to the repertoire for 1971 were Tchaikovsky's lovely, bittersweet *Eugene Onegin,* and Donizetti's spotty but assuredly viable *Maria Stuarda.* The *Onegin* arrived in the repertoire rather obliquely, since Adler's basic Tchaikovskian plan concerned itself with the long-discussed revival of *Queen of Spades.* A good production of this opera had been reposing in the warehouse following its 1963 success. Back in the mid-60's there'd been mutterings of a revival with Vickers, and then, for the 1971 season, Adler tried to persuade Jean Cox, a first-line American tenor working in Europe, to learn Herman in English. But Cox was not interested. Talk with Richard Cassilly was unproductive, too. So, one night in Germany, Hager received a call from Adler about the possibility of using an *Onegin* production imported from Europe. Hager had done the show with designer Bauer-Ecsy in Vienna and Paul Walter in Mannheim. He preferred the "more realistic" Mannheim production, and this is the one which came to San Francisco. As a matter of fact, the San Francisco Opera purchased it.[16]

The sets betrayed undue tackyness here and a stylistic inconsistency there, but at least the northern lake setting for the duel scene was genuinely beautiful. There was a nice mist for the rejection scene, an old gardener moving slowly about the shrubs while Tatiana heard from Onegin that he liked her a lot but would not marry her.

Mackerras conducted with affection and snap, the rousing peasant dance in the first scene, for instance, going at a more idiomatic clip than the famous Mr. Solti was stirring up at Covent Garden. Mackerras had taken over *Onegin* performances several times in Hamburg, but San Francisco's production was the first he had seen through basic rehearsals. Perhaps the revelation of the cast was Stuart Burrows' brand new Lensky, which was gorgeously, immaculately sung—really, nothing had ever been better *sung* in the house. There was the added advantage that Lensky is a role which motivated him to move well, as Pinkerton did not. Thomas Stewart's Onegin caught well the bored, stale aspect of this Byronic character. He was very strong, perhaps a little too grim. Evelyn Lear had her touching moments as Tatiana but was dry-voiced and deficient in the innocence and wonderment which are so basic to the character. Former chorister Edna Garabedian graduated from a Spring Opera Maddalena to the *Onegin* Olga, making a nice impression, and Donna Petersen, that faithful local mezzo, was an outstandingly good nanny.

Hager's direction was intelligent if not brilliant. Thankfully he kept his expressionistic bent fairly well under control. David Lloyd-Jones' quite comfortable English translation was used—except that Stewart and Lear filled in with a different one they'd learned for the unhatched Met performances.

Maria Stuarda was mounted for Joan Sutherland, and she sang the title role with her accustomed coloratura virtuosity and a magnificent propulsion—even if there was a tinge of fade in her top tones. But it was Huguette Tourangeau, a multifarious-voiced young Canadian mezzo (and part of the "Sutherland company") who provided the dramatic sparks playing Mary's rival Elizabeth I. In red wig and chalk face, and sporting a fancy outfit with butterfly wings, she looked like a regular Bette Davis. Spurred on by Capobianco, she fingered her pearls nervously, quickstepped about the stage, grabbed a pregnant message from a courtier, and was, in general, a person who created living action. Her decisive, vividly colored vocalism, in fact, was almost Callas-like. Burrows sang yet another role for the first time, the Earl of Leicester, and he was again a leading asset. There were even glints of Bjoerling.

Stuarda could be labelled a formula bel canto opera, dutybound to provide vocal fireworks and tears. But, along with occasional breakdowns in appropriateness or urgency, it does boast a number of musical gems, Elizabeth's pressing "Ah, dal ciel," for instance, and the melting, delicate duet for Leicester and Mary in the second act. Best of all is the grand prayer for Mary and the chorus in the last scene with its martial rhythm rather like that of "God Save the Queen," which Donizetti did use in *Roberto Devereux*.

San Francisco could be credited with the U.S. stage premiere,[17] the American Opera Society having done a concert performance in December 1967 with Montserrat Caballe and Shirley Verrett plus an obscure Hispanic tenor miles short of Burrows in quality. Richard Bonynge conducted zippily, and in the right buoyant style, if not necessarily giving that prayer its full breadth.[18] Using, for the first time in the 20th century, a recently-discovered 1835 score, as opposed to the traditional one from 1865, Bonynge uncovered a campy, operetta-type overture which sounded like the lead-in to something on the order of *Fritzi From Lichtenstein*. It began with a Sullivan-esque Zing-Boom of altogether doubtful dramatic value. But there were unscrappable advantages from 1835 in an unsimplified entrance cabaletta and final cavatina for Mary.

Tabarro was another Faggioni show—he and Capobianco kept the dramatic side of things jumping—and his talent for wringing keenly acted performances from famous *prime donne* was again to be noted. Leontyne Price's first stage Giorgetta was a highly intelligent portrayal, true to life and musically sung. As expected, after Faggioni's *Ballo*, there were no loose ends in the direction. A natural realism was the rule, Price hanging her wash on the line in a hard light under a utilitarian Seine bridge—a working-class district bridge—while Bacquier puffed impassively on his pipe in profile.

The new and striking set was by Paolo Bregni, a designer who had done *Tabarro* for a Florence production with Magda Olivero. Adler's original intention was to use the old Agnini set, but it was found to be, as Faggioni put it in an interview, "broken." There was discussion about renting the Florence show, but building a Bregni design in San Francisco proved the most feasible solution. Cyril Magnin, the well-known San Francisco clothier, paid for the production, in memory of his father Joseph. Faggioni suggested a handsome Italian tenor named Aldo Bottion for the part of Luigi the lover and he really looked ideal. While his reedy, ruggedly dulcet verismo tenor was not in itself great it had the right atmosphere and ring for *Tabarro*. Bacquier was a distinguished Michele,

Betty Allen a delightfully busy Frugola, and Nino Sanzogno, a front-line Italian maestro, conducted tautly, if a bit too discreetly at times considering the dimensions of the house.

The companion piece was the old Ponnelle *Carmina Burana*, well-directed by Ghita Hager. The "medieval illustration" backdrops looked fresher than ever, and Sanzogno conducted pointedly, drawing a rich sound from the orchestra. Bruce Brewer, a WOT alumnus graduated to West Berlin's Opera, was an exceptional lead tenor.

This leaves, of the home-produced efforts, a revival of Berg's *Lulu* done as a vehicle for Anja Silja. Since Silja doesn't like to perform in English it was done in German and therefore became an exercise in futility, the music uninteresting on its own and Hager's reverent direction missing the bizarre humor so discernible in the original Wedekind. Call it the only misfire of the season. Adler had had mixed feelings about the project, but evidently not mixed enough. Chicago, also contracted for a Silja event, copped out and decided on *Salome* instead.[19]

Christoph von Dohnanyi, a frequent Silja collaborator of the post-Wieland years, conducted clinically, and John Reardon was a non-magnetic, non-demonic Dr. Schoen, a pale shadow after the Ramon Vinay of 1965. The most interesting characterization was Ulfung's hollow-eyed, scarey, neurasthenic Painter. Granted that Silja was equipped with the right babydoll voice and a gorgeous figure (her derriere was amply displayed through tights under a feathery tutu) but the several high merits of her cold, puppet-like portrayal did not outweigh the boredom factor inherent in non-translation.

No wonder usually well-behaved patrons talked loudly in the interludes, and that an infrequent San Francisco phenomenon, the boo of disenchantment, could be heard.[20]

"Modern opera" was also represented by the reappearance of Britten's charming *A Midsummer Night's Dream*, brought over in toto (except for orchestra) from London by the English Opera Group. Since the EOG is administered by Covent Garden, the program announced that "The Royal Opera, Covent Garden, Limited and the San Francisco Opera Association present..." Quite impressive! The importation happened because a British Week, a trade show if you will, had been arranged for October 1971 in San Francisco. Princess

Alexandra, a cousin of the Queen, was in attendance at the first night, and she was greeted in the foyer by a ceremonial lineup of visiting English businessmen masquerading as uniformed guardsmen. The performance itself was cultured, with James Bowman an unusually positive counter-tenor in the role of Oberon. Meanwhile there was some argument over Jennifer Vyvyan's rather witchlike portrayal of Titania. The socialite crowd at the opening (Tuesdays had been getting more "popular" but royalty brought out the party set) was not hugely receptive, but later audiences were more intrigued, and indeed, the performers made more of a stab at projecting what is, after all, a rather intimate opera into the big house.

The year 1971 also brought news that the Music Center Opera Association in Los Angeles was establishing its own company to produce opera with big stars on stage and the Los Angeles Philharmonic in the pit, that organization's musical director Zubin Mehta conducting a number of the performances. George London, the retired singer, was appointed general director and set about planning an initial season for 1973, one which would include only three operas (informed sources listed them as *Tristan, Otello* and *Daughter of the Regiment*) instead of the ten or so offered in L.A. by the visiting New York City Opera. The City Opera, it was announced, would continue to visit through 1972. And San Francisco music people were advised that Los Angeles had no intention of creating problems of rivalry with its longtime opera-source to the north.

One could well understand Los Angeleans' desire to get back in the "grand opera" fold reminiscent of the San Francisco Opera visits, but it seemed as if there'd be a long pull to develop as interesting a repertoire as the City Opera could offer Los Angeles. In 1971 it included Handel's *Julius Caesar*, Donizetti's *Roberto Devereux* and Janacek's *Makropulos Case*, plus more standard fare, including a new *Carmen* from Capobianco. In any event, the original upbeat announcement from July was followed by another in November wherein London informed the public that the first season of the new venture had been indefinitely postponed due to a shortage of funds. London noted at the time that he was inhibited by the fact that all the resident companies at the Music Center have their funds raised through the Music Center Arts and Education Fund.

Notes

[1] She was able to resume singing in December in a Chicago *Don Pasquale*.

[2] The Tuesday nighters, traditionally more reserved than other subscribers, applauded for five minutes after the second performance.

[3] Louis Quilico took over in *Trovatore* at one performance.

[4] Played by a super who, it developed, had been a maitre d' in a Madison Avenue Schrafft's in New York.

[5] Moratorium Day in protest against the Vietnam War was observed at the dress rehearsal when Phtha, the thirty-foot Egyptian god, wore a black arm band on his left arm.

[6] Capecchi was fighting a cold, and also doing Dandini in *Cenerentola*, early in the *Forza* run. Lamentably for the audience, much of his admirable Melitone had to be cut at the second performance, the one on the Tuesday series.

[7] While only Crocker came through with such a lavish gift, a heightened campaign during Prentis Cobb Hale's period as president (1967–1970) resulted in a 250% increase in corporate contributions.

[8] The score was fifteen minutes less cut than before—only missing were a standard excision in the second act love duet, thirty lines of Tristan's third act leading up to the words "verflucht sei," and, also from the third act, about half of Isolde's penultimate speech.

[9] *distant*

[10] Next up the pole were *Falstaff*, at 88, and *Nabucco*, at 93.

[11] At least one opera administrator suspected that Crespin's *Tosca* experience might have been happier had she not rested from singing all summer.

[12] Adler thought it would be interesting if Jurinac and Ludwig traded roles at the last performance (Jurinac had been a famous Octavian), but he didn't press the point with his leading ladies.

[13] Ten operas were broadcast complete, in stereo, thanks to a grant from Standard Oil of California.

[14] Speaking of impishness, a typical San Francisco thing happened when, at a *Meistersinger* performance, composer Robert Moran, harpsichordist Margaret Fabrizio and engineer Clay Grillo appeared in their "togetherness suit," a three person toga made from a surplus parachute. Certainly this was in better taste than the Nazi dress uniforms sported by a couple of freaks at a Wagner evening the previous year.

[15] Pavarotti was so eager to leave rehearsals early that Faggioni, not a mean man at all, had to read him the riot act. Peace was ultimately made, while a popular columnist muttered about Pavarotti leaving town. In general, Faggioni's resourceful rehearsal technique was not to argue with the stars but find interesting new solutions for them on the spot.

[16] Due to a prolonged dock strike in the U.S., the scenery had to be transported cross-country from a Mexican port.

[17] Presented in minimal sets by Pier Luigi Pizzi rented from Florence.

[18] Bonynge seemed even better after listening to Aldo Ceccato's overly slow (some of the music just can't take it) and self-conscious conducting in the Sills recording.

[19] According to some sources, Chicago's main reasons for not doing *Lulu* were that impresario Carol Fox didn't like the San Francisco production too well and couldn't find another.

[20] Truth to say, the boo department also gave Sanzogno's *Tabarro* a working over.

302

CHAPTER *17*

A Fresh Spring

Spring Opera, newly christened Spring Opera Theater, opened its first Curran Theater season on schedule on March 18, 1971, with Mozart's *Clemenza da Tito*—or *Titus*, as it comes out in English. An insufficiency of volume from the orchestra playing in its unusual behind-the-scenes position, plus shakedown nerves on stage, and a hesitation about cutting the dialogue: all these kept the Opening Night from being more than a rather charming but unfinished adventure. However, on the smoother second night, when a highly irreverent but genuinely affecting *Rigoletto* took to the thrust stage, Spring's new production concept established itself as monumentally successful. Gilbert Moses, a young, black legitimate theater director, went too far out in his zappy interpretation to please all customers, but there was, in any event, a full house. And for those able to run his merry stylistic chase, which included a "collage" of costumes centered in the 1930's, the results were extremely diverting.

As the blackout during the prelude lifted, a smiling "comedian" in horse-blanket suit, sort of a black Stubby Kaye out of *Guys and Dolls*, could be dimly perceived. Then, when the lights went up, someone at the Duke of Mantua's party let a lot of balloons out of a chest. And couples took up amorous positions on the floor by the stairs, left and right, leading into the unusually small fractions of the orchestra pit not covered by the stage. It was not unlike an orgy out of Playboy Magazine. Courtiers popped balloons tied to a serving girl's bikini (the girl, it developed, was Monterone's ruined but comely daughter), and a particularly lecherous fellow chased female prey up the Curran aisle. The courtiers wore tuxedos or tails, but with bare chests and low-slung circusy orange

303

vests. And Moses poked fun at the cuckolded Ceprano by dressing him up in a doorman's uniform. Policemen almost literally *dropped* Monterone into the pit, pointing up in the process the "closed community" aspect of the Duke's palazzo.

When, in the next scene, the Duke visited Gilda disguised as a student, he was gotten up in a mod-hippie bush jacket and granny glasses which really spelled *student*. In the last act he visited Maddalena in a clanking Hell's Angels suit revealing his baser instincts. Gilda's house (as designed by scenic director Robert Darling) was a crazy prison tower in a back alley—does that make the Duke an alley cat?—with a cyclone fence. Her doting nanny Giovanna read like a not quite proper landlady and was full of affection, a dowdy, lower middle-class matron out of a *Rural America in the '30's* photo show. In the second act the courtiers hopped about, ate apples, read comic books, and at times almost suggested the errant politicos in the old Kurt Jooss ballet *The Green Table*. In the last act Sparafucile, the craftsmanly cutthroat, wore a plastic apron. And the storm was done with blinking naked red light bulbs.

Perhaps it *was* too much that Sparafucile, when encountered in the first act, was diligently playing a saw to Verdi's rocking, menacing, (dare one say it) sawing cello line. But the audience didn't have to take this "concert" literally.

By making an upside down cake of tradition, Moses came up with a remarkably valid, forceful, moving evening of opera, capital R Realism brewed with a witch's cauldron of distortion and satire to point up essences. Rarely have so many different images come together so well. And, thanks also to the closeness of the performers and the use of English, Rigoletto's plight was more touching than ever. What on earth will happen to the poor jester when not only wife but daughter are lost to him? Does the audience usually think about that? Robert Mosley's big voice and warm, believable acting helped Moses make his point. So did Dennis Russell Davies' theatrically acute conducting.

The Spring people delivered another memorable original when *Don Pasquale*, also updated, was revived a few evenings later. The show didn't begin with a game of blind man's

304

buff as, by coincidence, *Titus* and *Rigoletto* had. But it did open with an hilarious pantomime to the overture. Director Richard Pearlman, a Zeffirelli disciple, got around the open stage during the overture in an ingenious way: Pasquale is an opera nut, and he puts a record on his ancient gramophone (it's San Francisco 1909), cranking out the cue for the music from behind the scenes. And then, as he sits and fantasizes, vision upon vision in the shapes of famous operatic heroines appear before him—from a trap door leading up through a false-bottom chest. The traffic jam of these ladies, including a gigantic Brünnhilde enacted by Pasquale's heroic-sized maidservant, and a Salome in a natural hairdo who swiped a detachable head off a statue, was positively riotous. Many of the leading ladies were enacted by the "Cockettes," a local collection of female impersonators known for their post-midnight programs at the Palace cinema in North Beach.

The evening's merriment continued at a resolute but not hectic pace, Pasquale's servants handing down pink cotton candy from the stage as the entertainment concluded, little page girls passing the goodies about the audience.

The *Titus* was an extremely interesting production, but there was an inescapable impression of Ingenuity trying to conquer the Untheatrical. Despite some very fine music, especially in the second half of the first act, Mozart's final opera seems to have almost totally escaped modern performance for good reason.[1] The libretto, about a compassionate, forgiving monarch, is terribly wooden, and even when the endless recitativo secco is scrapped, as it was in the Spring production, there still has to be binding material between the arias and ensembles, and what Spring came up with was almost endless spoken dialogue. The dialogue was more human, but not inspiring.

Titus was directed by William Francisco, a young legitimate theater man who, like Gilbert Moses, had never done an opera before. This is not necessarily a detriment, and Francisco did what he could with very difficult material. His slightly cumbersome but rather brilliantly executed stage plan involved two planes of action (the dialogue people and the singing people) moving alternately and simultaneously, sometimes overlapping, sometimes merging.

The premise of the evening was that it was 1791 in Vienna, the year Mozart wrote *Titus*. Leopold II has just been crowned Emperor of the Bohemian Estates (the opera was written for his coronation) and the French Revolution is raging. Some idealistic teenage students join to celebrate a boy's birthday, and they do so by performing a Metastasio play, *The Clemency of Titus*, which strikes them as particularly relevant because it's concerned with the idea of government by trust rather than deceit and force. Sounds like 1972! The teenagers (local high school drama students) carried the spoken lines while the opera, performed by professionals in modern formal dress, unfolded around them.[2] A large baroque mirror permitted *play* to actually reflect *opera* and vice versa.

Director Francisco had it that the teenagers are never aware the opera is going on, but the singers are aware of *them*, perhaps as themselves as children.

The second performance brought some improvement in orchestra volume—slight amplification was carefully employed during the season—and a reduction in the amount of dialogue. The third performance went even better. At all of them the main joy was listening to the Sesto of Frederica von Stade, a young mezzo with a full, milky voice and commanding phrasing who'd been doing smallish parts at the Met. The *Titus* she considered her debut, and it won her deserved ovations, also an invitation to sing Cherubino with the San Francisco Opera in the fall of 1972.

As a cap to the three home-produced shows, Spring brought in a package from the Center Opera in Minneapolis, an avant-garde concoction called *Faust Counter Faust*. It was a lively, swift-moving, virtuoso production, done up all in white with Renaissance or surrealist slide projections atop the set and live and recorded music emitted from various parts of the house. Gounod, Berlioz, Boito *and* John Gessner all got into the sonic act.

The jock-strapped central protagonist in *Faust Counter Faust* is a mental patient, one Marlowe Gurdja (regurdjitate?) who tries to get his fellow inmates to enact his *Revelation of Dr. Faustus*, this being a magic ritual which he hopes will release man from the ruinous Faustian compulsion to know everything. But the others prefer to sing Gounod or Boito, even with comically distorted accompaniments. Gurdja believes the various retellings of the Faust story have been contrived to obscure Faust's real sin: the search for knowledge at any cost. A special target is the Gounod opera in which Faust is shown trading his soul to the devil for youth and love, not knowledge.

By the time the evening is through Gurdja has fallen ten feet backwards off the top of the set and into the arms of four of his fellows. Despite this shaking experience, he's ready, the audience is informed, for Stage Two of his cure. That could be saved for *The Return of Faust Counter Faust.*

On the heels of the Spring season there came a reincarnation of Dollar Opera, the clock-of-inflation turned back by Western Opera Theater thanks to a grant from, appropriately enough, the Golden Grain Macaroni Company. Perhaps WOT's little season at the Palace of Fine Arts Theater should have been dubbed the Macaroni Opera. *Bòheme, Cenerentola* and a double bill of *The Medium* and *Gianni Schicchi* were offered with orchestra, in English, and indubitably at the right price—even if pasta wasn't served in the intermissions.

Spring Opera's 1972 season, opening at the Curran by calendar in winter but in balmy pre-spring weather, found the orchestra improved, and brought out (in two of the three shows) from its perch backstage. Richard Pearlman, director of the previous year's *Pasquale*, delivered a *Barber* with a neat string of surprising, irreverent yet musically apropos business, running aground only on a surfeit of "revolutionary" antics inspired by Beaumarchais. San Francisco found itself, in fact, owning not one but two viable *Barber* productions, this one putting rather more emphasis on movement generated by the cast as opposed to Rennert's performing-fool of a three-story house. Young Alan Titus' Figaro (he juggled oranges, executed a Spanish dance and performed a haircut during the "Largo al Factotum") brought a remarkable combination of dash, grace and sex appeal. Another bit of news: Fiorello's "employer be damned" recitative at the end of the first scene was included, as it almost never is in *Barber* performances.

Monteverdi's *Orfeo* came to life in Gerald Freedman's

magically lit production, a fluid, unpretentious sarabande moving from one rococo stage picture to another. The idea of setting Orfeo-the-artist apart via modern dress worked all right, once a labored introduction was left behind. The Kurt Weill-Bert Brecht *Mahagonny*, quite a rarity in the U.S., climaxed the inventive season in a magnificently salty, batty production, deadpan but compassionate, for which director Francisco and designer Darling can take much credit. It was, in fact the most prized experience of the three good ones offered. Ariel Bybee's Jenny was softer, more haunting, than Lotte Lenya's on the "official" recording, and Richard Kness was a powerful Mahoney. If *Mahagonny* had appeared in an autumn season, as was Adler's original intention, the Mahoney would have been Jon Vickers. Dress rehearsal of the Spring show revealed the first stage nudity under San Francisco Opera auspices, but it was vetoed before performance time. However, there *were* four-letter words.

Notes

[1] Recent productions took place in Munich; in Cologne, staged by Jean-Pierre Ponnelle; and at New York's Juilliard Opera Center.

[2] The girls performing Sesto and Annio, the opera's "pants parts," looked dangerously close to the reverse of female impersonators.

308

Tuesday Night at the Opera, in the War Memorial Opera House.

Backstage at *Die Walküre*, 1936:
Lauritz Melchior, Kirsten
Flagstad, Fritz Reiner.

Two views of Lotte Lehmann:
As Tosca, 1936.

Aged 80, examining memorabilia in
the S.F. Opera Museum, 1968.

Jess Thomas in title role of *Siegfried;* a Ken Howard photo, 1970.

A "Standard Hour" broadcast of *Otello* excerpts:
Set Svanholm, Leonard Warren, Licia Albanese, Claramae Turner.

Renata Tebaldi as Maddalena, *Andrea Chenier*, 1950.

Inge Borkh as Elsa, *Lohengrin*, 1955; a Robert Lackenbach photo.

Leyla Gencer and Gianni Raimondi in *La Traviata*, 1957.

Leonie Rysanek made her U.S. debut as Senta, *The Flying Dutchman*, 1956.

Dorothy Kirsten and Jussi Bjoerling in *Manon Lescaut*, 1956.

Nicola Rossi-Lemeni making up for *Mefistofele*, 1952; photo by, and courtesy of, Paul Tracy.

At a *Sonnambula* rehearsal 1960:
Francesco Molinari-Pradelli
and Dino Yannopoulos

At a *Cenerentola* rehearsal 1969:
Renato Capecchi
and Paolo Montarsolo.

Robert Weede, a San
Francisco regular, as Germont
in *La Traviata*, 1960.

Tito Gobbi as Jack Rance,
La Fanciulla del West,
1960; a portrait by
Carolyn Mason Jones.

Elisabeth Schwarzkopf
as the Countess in
Strauss' *Capriccio*, a
role she sang in very
few cities, 1963.

Giorgio Tozzi's first Don Giovanni was in San Francisco, 1962.

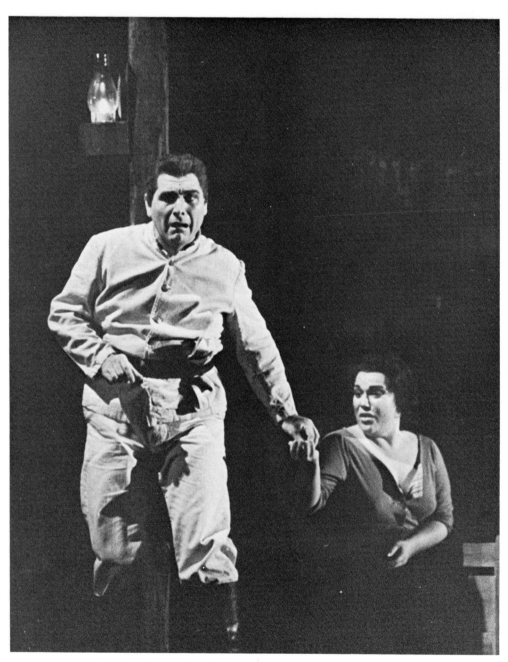

Geraint Evans and Marilyn Horne in his favorite
production of *Wozzeck*, 1960.

It's only red wine: Sesto
Bruscantini and his *Elixir
of Love*, 1967.

Ramon Vinay plays Falstaff,
the master tippler, 1966.

Gregory Dempsey and Sylvia Anderson at
Baba's, *The Rake's Progress*, 1970.

Dan Richardson and Ragnar Ulfung in *Falstaff*, 1970.

Jess Thomas and Irene
Dalis in her first
and only *Tristan and
Isolde*, 1967.

Leontyne Price sang her
first Giorgetta in *Il
Tabarro* in 1971. Gabriel
Bacquier is Michele.

Amy Shuard as Elektra,
1966; photo by
Cecil J. Thompson.

Anja Silja as Salome,
1968; photo by
C.M. Jones.

The late Marie Collier and Chester Ludgin in
The Makropulos Case, 1966.

Joan Sutherland in title role of *Maria Stuarda*, 1971. Costume by José Varona.

Spring Opera Theater's *Mahagonny*, 1972: Richard J. Clark as Alaska Wolf Joe and Ariel Bybee as Jenny.

Finale

As the San Francisco Opera entered its fiftieth anniversary season, a season highlighted by the first *Ring* in the U.S. since 1962 plus the American premiere of Gottfried von Einem's *Visit of the Old Lady* and the company's first Meyerbeer (the first major staging of a Meyerbeer work in America since 1934), a tabulation of newsworthy past statistics included:

U.S. premieres: Britten's *A Midsummer Night's Dream*, Cherubini's *The Portuguese Inn*, Janacek's *Makropulos Case*, Carl Orff's *Die Kluge*, Poulenc's *Dialogues of the Carmelites*, Ravel's *L'Enfant et les Sortilèges*, Shostakovich's *Katerina Ismailova*, Strauss' *Die Frau Ohne Schatten*, and Walton's *Troilus and Cressida*.

U.S. stage premieres: Cherubini's *Medea*, Donizetti's *Maria Stuarda*, Honegger's *Joan of Arc at the Stake*, Milhaud's *Discovery of America*, and Orff's *Carmina Burana*.

All-professional U.S. stage premiere: Berlioz' *Les Troyens*.

First production in America by a U.S. company: Gunther Schuller's *The Visitation*.

World premiere: Norman Dello Joio's *Blood Moon*.

West Coast premieres: Berg's *Wozzeck* and *Lulu*.

Most if not all of these events transpired during the regime of Kurt Herbert Adler begun in 1953. In the 1960's his determined schedule of premieres slowed down slightly (first to balance the repertoire, then the budget!) but this was a decade which saw a great crescendo in the number of new productions of standard repertoire. Another basic Adlerian contribution was to gradually reduce the number of operas in a season, and it became the standard operating procedure for all the casts, of productions new or old, to come together for two or three weeks' rehearsal, a stage director actively in charge in each case. A major Adler achievement, of course, was the gradual lengthening of the senior company's seasons to eleven weeks. (In 1923 the season was finished in two weeks.)

Plotting an historical chart of San Francisco Opera productions in the standard Verdi-Puccini-Wagner repertoire, the archivist discovers that, in most cases, there existed original "Agnini" sets (generally "old school" and often interchangeable) from the '20's and '30's, these succeeded in Adler's regime by "contemporary" productions. For Verdi, for instance, there was a new *Don Carlo* and *Falstaff* in '62, *Forza* in '63, *Ballo* in '65, *Trovatore* in '68, *Aida* and *Traviata* in '69, *Otello* in '70, with *Rigoletto* momentarily left to Spring Opera Theater ('71) and Adler still dreaming of an eventual *Boccanegra*. *Ernani* was once borrowed, and the company has a *Nabucco* and *Macbeth*.

A middle chapter, mostly in the '50's and early '60's, finds interim variations being made on pieces from the Agnini warehouse to give shows a more simplified, up-to-date look. By 1972 Adler had achieved a virtually complete scenic overhauling of essential repertoire, lacking principally a new *Lohengrin* and *Cav and Pag*, plus a really workable *Don Giovanni*.

Adler' initial brisk pace in introducing new voices to the U.S. relented a bit, but not much, after 1960. To the earlier names of sopranos Inge Borkh, Rosanna Carteri, Leyla Gencer, Sena Jurinac, Birgit Nilsson, Leonie Rysanek and Merola's Renata Tebaldi one can add the later ones of the lamented Marie Collier, Pilar Lorengar, Ljiljana Molnar-Talajic, Margaret Price, Graziella Sciutti and Anja Silja. To such earlier tenor debutants from Merola and Adler years as Mario Del Monaco, Sandor Konya, Richard Lewis, Gotthelf Pistor and Cesare Valletti one can add Stuart Burrows, Ryland Davies and Robert Ilosfalvy.

A longer (but incomplete) list of U.S. debuts throughout the half century includes sopranos Janine Micheau and Rosina Torri, mezzos Margarete Klose, Giulietta Simionato and Ebe Stignani, baritones and basses Boris Christoff, Anselmo Colzani, Geraint Evans, Tito Gobbi, Rolando Panerai, Giuseppe Taddei and Ingvar Wixell, not to mention conductor Georg Solti.

310

Adler can be credited with making much use of Mary Costa, Reri Grist, Eileen Farrell, Leontyne Price and Elisabeth Schwarzkopf, not to mention numerous others, before his New York colleague Rudolf Bing got around to them. And the San Francisco Opera, under Merola and Adler, can pride itself (in most cases) on being the scene of Jeritza's first Salome in America, the first *Siegfried* Brünnhilde of Flagstad's career, the only Lehmann-Flagstad Walküre, Leontyne Price's first Donna Elvira, Giorgetta and four Verdi heroines (in *Forza, Aida, Ballo* and *Trovatore*), Albanese's first Desdemona, Kirsten's first Tosca and Louise, Tebaldi's first *Boccanegra*, Irene Dalis' first Klytemnestra and *only* Isolde, Marilyn Horne's first Eboli, Janis Martin's only Ulrica, Marie Collier's first Minnie, Martinelli's first Otello, Bjoerling and Pavarotti's first Riccardos, Vinay's first Tristan *and* Bartolo, Jess Thomas' first Tristan, James King's first Stolzing, Richard Lewis' first Herod, the first Iago of Tibbett, Eberhard Waechter's first Barak, Geraint Evans' first Wozzeck, Pizarro and Kezal, Renato Capecchi's first Sacristan, Giorgio Tozzi's first Don Giovanni, Gurnemanz and King Marke, Pons' first Violetta, Journet's 1000th Mephistopheles, Schorr's 200th Sachs, Lehmann's last Marschallin, and one of the nine Florestans Melchior ever sang (none were at the Met). Other performances reported unavailable in New York include Baccaloni's Falstaff, Lily Djanel's Sieglinde, Sayao's Nedda, etc. etc.

Adler also has a good record of bringing back estimable expatriate American singers like Sylvia Anderson, Thomas Tipton, Judith Beckman and Kieth Engen in leading roles.

As a personality, Kurt Herbert Adler has not achieved the lovability level of his predecessor Merola. A less relaxed but tremendously efficient and marvelously committed general director, he has kept the company in high gear and what might be called a well-functioning fever of activity. Adler has a warm side, but a number of people would rate him as pretty formidable. He does love a good scrap, and he drives a hard bargain, but then again, he balances his budget (or, in operatic parlance, budgeted deficit), putting on a high level quality of opera at a cost somewhat less than that run up for a similar amount of operatic activity by other American companies employing numerous stars. [1]

311

Stage director Paul Hager has observed that the tempo of preparation for performances slows down perceptibly if the usually ubiquitous Adler is away for several hours of the fourteen he's likely to spend in the house. This is one way of noting that the norm is a thoroughgoing concern on Adler's part for producing a show which, right or wrong, good or bad, is a quality product, carefully considered.

"Naturally I make mistakes," he once told an interviewer. "One time when I made a horrible mistake I went to the board and apologized. I told them I was very sorry but I could be expected to make the same sort of mistake again because if I didn't make mistakes they couldn't afford me . . ."

Many pages of this volume attest to his increasingly high batting average in casting, some of it quite daring, and his keen interest in staging and the scenic side. There are lapses, to be sure. Lately he has cut too many corners on the ballet (the San Francisco Ballet itself is partly responsible for cutting ties with the Opera)[2] and he has overexposed his chief stage director. One could ask for more really far-out fall season productions a la Frank Corsaro, but who can argue with the employment of such directors as the Messrs. Rennert, Everding, Rott, Ponnelle, Capobianco, Mansouri, Erlo, etc., not to mention the good achievements of Paul Hager. One can be thankful, too, that the company's common denominator of scenic style has been more in the direction of buoyancy than undue Scala-type massiveness.

In sum, Adler has achieved more than enough to earn the description irreplaceable. Certainly one is hard put to think of someone who could readily take his place. And his achievement quotient goes up considering the logistical problems involved in producing opera in San Francisco. Since many choristers work at other jobs daytimes, they must rehearse at night. Thus most staging rehearsals for the chorus have to be held in the summer, before the casts arrive. Various production elements are grafted together later. Futhermore, since there is no rehearsal stage in the Opera House other than the main stage itself, some of the casts have to do their initial stage preparation in a drafty, acoustic-less armory in the Mission district. Amazingly enough the company's artistic results manage almost invariably to conceal the presence of such problematical features of the preparation periods.

312

Adler has shown that his audience (its core drawing, of course, on an expanding Bay Area population) can be significantly increased. When he took over in 1953 there were twenty-two adult performances, in 1971 there were fifty-six. During the 1971 season the company played to 94% average capacity,[3] thirty-four of those performances being sold out or virtually so. The total gross was $2,015,000, with only $132,-000 worth of seats unsold. This as opposed to $300,000 unsold the season before when there were forty-nine performances. Such a gross does not, of course, cover all expenses. The difference is made up by production gifts from corporations or individuals (*Traviata, Cosi, Meistersinger, Tabarro, Manon*, etc.), an annual fund drive ($550,000 in 1971–72), guarantor fees, and a hotel tax grant ($235,000 is the latest figure).

Meanwhile, the pace of Opera House refurbishment in the wake of the defeated Proposition B has slowed down to a crawl. One dream of Adler's which looks dim of realization is to redo the main floor of the house, putting in new and slightly smaller seats and making a larger pit.

In the future—maybe!—is a third building in the War Memorial complex, one which would include a 2700-seat Symphony Hall and a full-scale rehearsal stage for the Opera, the opera annex part connected to the Opera House via tunnel and/or bridge. The building would be integrated with the existing War Memorial by steps from the present central plaza, these leading to a large elevated plaza in front of the new building. One large money-saving decision in the project is not to dip Franklin Street into a tunnel as previously envisioned. Another improvement over the Proposition B plan is to refrain from digging a garage into the new building but set it apart on the western end of the Gough-Franklin-Grove-Hayes block. A pleasant gastronomic advantage would be a cafe tucked in amongst the steps leading from the present plaza to the new elevated one, and, in the new building itself, a restaurant across the front at a level above the foyer.

Such a new building (more likely to be successfully financed privately than through a bond issue) would naturally relieve pressure on the heavily-booked Opera House. Also, with a separate performing place for the Symphony, which has long used the Opera House, the orchestra could conceivably begin its season during the traditional operatic autumn, and Adler could hire another orchestra for an expanded grand opera season—however, he would have a very difficult time finding as resourceful an opera orchestra as the Symphony-spawned group he's had at his disposal.

Suffice to say that this not the place to answer the questions of the future. The first half-century of the San Francisco Opera constitutes a highly productive and satisfying history. A good tempo is set, and on with the show!

Notes

[1] Chicago fees can be considerably higher than San Francisco's; admitted Met fees are roughly similar.

[2] Hiring of the American Ballet Theater's Cynthia Gregory (a former San Franciscan) for the 1972 Aida signalled a switch in the right direction.

[3] The 1972 figure looked to be 100%!

San Francisco Casts—1923-1971

The designation "Same cast" always refers to the first listed performance of a particular opera.

CASTS—1923 SEASON

September 26: LA BOHÈME (Puccini)
MIMI: Mario, RODOLFO: Martinelli, MARCELLO: Gandolfi, COLLINE: Didur, SCHAUNARD: D'Angelo, MUSETTA: Young, BENOIT: Ananian, ALCINDORO: Ananian, PARPIGNOL: Paltrinieri, SERGEANT: Corral, OFFICER: Alibertini, CONDUCTOR: Merola.

September 27: ANDREA CHENIER (Giordano)
MADELEINE: Saroya, ANDREA CHENIER: Gigli, GERARD: De Luca, MATHIEU: Didur, FLÉVILLE: D'Angelo, ROUCHER: D'Angelo, DUMAS: D'Angelo, ABBÉ: Paltrinieri, SPY: Paltrinieri, SCHMIDT: Ananian, FOUQUIER-TINVILLE: Ananian, COUNTESS: Johnstone, MADELON: Fernanda, BERSI: Lazelle, CONDUCTOR: Merola.

September 29, matinee: IL TABARRO (Puccini)
GIORGETTA: Saroya, LUIGI: Tokatyan, MICHELE: Gandolfi, TINCA: Paltrinieri, TALPA: Didur, SONG VENDOR: Frediani, FRUGOLA: Fernanda, CONDUCTOR: Merola.

followed by: SUOR ANGELICA (Puccini)
SUOR ANGELICA: Saroya, PRINCESS: Fernanda, ABBESS: Johnstone, MISTRESS OF NOVICES: Eybel, ALMS COLLECTOR: Lazelle, SISTER GENEVIEVE: Young, SISTER OSMINA: Christoph, NOVICE: Monotti, CONVERTS: Ferguson, Badger, CONDUCTOR: Merola.

followed by: GIANNI SCHICCHI (Puccini)
GIANNI SCHICCHI: De Luca, RINUCCIO: Tokatyan, LAURETTA: Epton, SIMONE: Didur, BETTO: Ananian, GHERARDO: Paltrinieri, MARCO: D'Angelo, SPINELLOCCIO: Gillette, NOTARY: Frediani, PINELLINO: Corral, GUCCIO: Alibertini, ZITA: Fernanda, NELLA: Young, LA CIESCA: Lazelle, CONDUCTOR: Merola.

September 29: LA BOHÈME (Puccini)
Same cast.

October 1: MEFISTOFELE (Boito)
MEFISTOFELE: Didur, FAUST: Gigli, MARGHERITA: Saroya, ELENA: Saroya, WAGNER: Paltrinieri, MARTHA: Fernanda, PANTALIS: Fernanda, CONDUCTOR: Merola.

October 2: TOSCA (Puccini)
TOSCA: Saroya, CAVARADOSSI: Martinelli, SCARPIA: De Luca, SPOLETTA: Paltrinieri, SACRISTAN: Ananian, ANGELOTTI: D'Angelo, SCIARRONE: Corral, JAILOR: Alibertini, SHEPHERD: Johnstone, CONDUCTOR: Merola.
October 4: ROMEO ÉT JULIETTE (Gounod)
ROMÉO: Gigli, JULIETTE: Mario, MERCUTIO: De Luca, TYBALT: Paltrinieri, CAPULET: Didur, FRIAR LAWRENCE: D'Angelo, GREGORIO: Ananian, BENVOGLIO: Frediani, DUKE OF VERONA: Gillette, STEPHANO: Young, GERTRUDE: Johnstone, CONDUCTOR: Merola.
October 6, matinee: GIANNI SCHICCHI (Puccini)
Same cast except: RINUCCIO: Paltrinieri, GHERARDO: Frediani, NOTARY: Ordini.
                    followed by: I PAGLIACCI (Leoncavallo)
CANIO: Martinelli, TONIO: De Luca, NEDDA: Mario, SILVIO: Gandolfi, BEPPE: Paltrinieri, CONDUCTOR: Merola.
October 6: ANDREA CHENIER (Giordano)
Same cast except: GERARD: Gandolfi.
October 8: RIGOLETTO (Verdi)
GILDA: Mario, DUKE: Gigli, RIGOLETTO: De Luca, MADDALENA: Fernanda, SPARAFUCILE: Didur, MONTERONE: D'Angelo, BORSA: Paltrinieri, MARULLO: Ananian, CEPRANO: Gillette, COUNTESS CEPRANO: Olmsted, GIOVANNA: Monotti, PAGE: Ferguson, CONDUCTOR: Merola.

CASTS—1924 SEASON

September 22: ANDREA CHENIER (Giordano)
MADELEINE: Muzio, ANDREA CHENIER: Gigli, GERARD: De Luca, MATHIEU: Ananian, FLÉVILLE: D'Angelo, ROUCHER: Seri, DUMAS: Gillette, ABBÉ: Oliviero, SPY: Oliviero, SCHMIDT: Gillette, FOUQUIER-TINVILLE: D'Angelo, COUNTESS: Shaffner, MADELON: Eybel, BERSI: De Vol, CONDUCTOR: Merola.
September 24: LA BOHÈME (Puccini)
MIMI: Mario, RODOLFO: Gigli, MARCELLO: Picco, COLLINE: Seri, SCHAUNARD: D'Angelo, MUSETTA: Young, BENOIT: Ananian, ALCINDORO: Ananian, CONDUCTOR: Merola.
September 26: MADAMA BUTTERFLY (Puccini)
CIO-CIO-SAN: Sabanieeva, PINKERTON: Mojica, SHARPLESS: Picco, SUZUKI: Marlowe, GORO: Oliviero, BONZE: Ananian, YAMADORI: D'Angelo, COMMISSIONER: Gillette, KATE PINKERTON: Clifford, CONDUCTOR: Merola.
September 27: RIGOLETTO (Verdi)
GILDA: Mario, DUKE: Gigli, RIGOLETTO: De Luca, MADDALENA: Bruntsch, SPARAFUCILE: Seri, MONTERONE: D'Angelo, BORSA: Oliviero, MARULLO: Ananian, CEPRANO: Gillette, COUNTESS CEPRANO: Olmsted, GIOVANNA: Monotti, PAGE: Ferguson, CONDUCTOR: Merola.
September 28, matinee: LA BOHÈME (Puccini)
Same cast except: MIMI: Donnelly, RODOLFO: Mojica.
September 29: MANON (Massenet)

MANON: Sabanieeva, CHEVALIER DES GRIEUX: Schipa, LESCAUT: Picco, GUILLOT: Ferrier, DE BRÉTIGNY: D'Angelo, COUNT DES GRIEUX: Ananian, POUSETTE: Young, JAVOTTE: Newsom, ROSETTE: Shaffner, SERVANT: Moncla, GUARDS: Frediani, Feduloff, CONDUCTOR: Merola.

September 30: TOSCA (Puccini)
TOSCA: Muzio, CAVARADOSSI: Gigli, SCARPIA: De Luca, SPOLETTA: Oliviero, SACRISTAN: Ananian, ANGELOTTI: Seri, SCIARRONE: D'Angelo, JAILOR: Gillette, SHEPHERD: Eybel, CONDUCTOR: Merola.

October 2: L'AMICO FRITZ (Mascagni)
SUZEL: Sabanieeva, FRITZ: Schipa, RABBINO: De Luca, HANEZO: Ananian, FEDERICO: Oliviero, CATERINA: De Vol, BEPPE: Eybel, CONDUCTOR: Merola.
followed by: GIANNI SCHICCHI (Puccini)
GIANNI SCHICCHI: De Luca, RINUCCIO: Mojica, LAURETTA: Donnelly, SIMONE: Seri, BETTO: Ananian, GHERARDO: Oliviero, MARCO: D'Angelo, SPINELLOCCIO: Gillette, NOTARY: Ferrier, PINELLINO: Frediani, GUCCIO: Alibertini, ZITA: Bruntsch, NELLA: Young, LA CIESCA: Lazelle, GHERARDINO: Olive Jones, CONDUCTOR: Merola.

October 3: Testimonial for Merola. *Madama Butterfly,* love duet, Act 1; *Manon, Act 2; Tosca,* Act 3; *Gianni Schicchi.* (Same casts.)

October 4: LA TRAVIATA (Verdi)
VIOLETTA: Muzio, ALFREDO: Schipa, GERMONT: De Luca, GASTON: Oliviero, BARON DOUPHOL: D'Angelo, MARQUIS D'OBIGNY: Ananian, DR. GRENVIL: Seri, FLORA: Young, ANNINA: Monotti, CONDUCTOR: Merola.

CASTS—1925 SEASON

September 19: MANON (Massenet)
MANON: Torri, CHEVALIER DES GRIEUX: Schipa, LESCAUT: Nicolich, GUILLOT: Oliviero, DE BRÉTIGNY: Argall, COUNT DES GRIEUX: Journet, POUSETTE: Young, JAVOTTE: Newsom, ROSETTE: Cross, INNKEEPER: Vogel, SERGEANT: Frediani, CONDUCTOR: Merola.

September 21: SAMSON AND DELILAH (Saint-Saens)
SAMSON: Ansseau, DELILAH: D'Alvarez, HIGH PRIEST: Journet, ABIMELECH: Nicolich, OLD HEBREW: Vogel, MESSENGER: Oliviero, PHILISTINES: Frediani, Argall, CONDUCTOR: Cimini.

September 24: THE BARBER OF SEVILLE (Rossini)
ROSINA: De Hidalgo, COUNT ALMAVIVA: Schipa, FIGARO: Stracciari, BARTOLO: Trevisan, BASILIO: Journet, FIORELLO: Oliviero, OFFICER: Oliviero, BERTHA: Marlo, CONDUCTOR: Cimini.

September 26, matinee: ANIMA ALLEGRA (Vittadini)
CONSUELO: Torri, PEDRO: Cortis, DON ELIGIO: Trevisan, DONNA SACRAMENTO: Witter, CORALITO: Young, FRASQUITA: Elkus, CARMEN: Monotti, MARIQUITA: Golcher, LUCIO: Attilio Vannucci, TONIO: Oliviero, DIEGO: Nicolich, GYPSY: Argall, YOUNG MAN: Frediani, RAMMIREZ: Alibertini, CANTOR: Regoli, AURORA: Michelini, CONDUCTOR: Merola.

September 26: SAMSON AND DELILAH (Saint-Saens)
Same cast.

September 28: LA TRAVIATA (Verdi) (Auspices Italy America Society)

317

VIOLETTA: De Hidalgo, ALFREDO: Schipa, GERMONT: Stracciari, GASTON: Oliviero, BARON DOUPHOL: Nicolich, MARQUIS D'OBIGNY: Argall, DR. GRENVIL: Trevisan, FLORA: Young, ANNINA: Monotti, CONDUCTOR: Merola.

September 30: MARTHA (Flotow)
LADY HARRIET: De Hidalgo, LIONEL: Schipa, PLUNKETT: Journet, SIR TRISTAN: Trevisan, SHERIFF: Wright, NANCY: Marlo, MOLLY: Badger, POLLY: Ferguson, BETTY: Monotti, FARMER'S WIFE: Darrow, CONDUCTOR: Cimini.

October 1: THE BARBER OF SEVILLE (Rossini) (Testimonial for Merola)
Same cast.

October 2: L'AMORE DEI TRE RE (Montemezzi)
FIORA: Torri, AVITO: Ansseau, MANFREDO: Stracciari, ARCHIBALDO: Journet, FLAMINIO: Oliviero, YOUTH: Frediani, OLD WOMAN: Marlo, YOUNG GIRL: Newsom, SERVANT: Farncroft, CONDUCTOR: Merola.

October 3, matinee: MANON (Massenet)
Same cast.

October 3: AIDA (Verdi)
AIDA: Muzio, AMNERIS: D'Alvarez, RHADAMES: Cortis, AMONASRO: Formichi, RAMFIS: Journet, KING: Nicolich, MESSENGER: Oliviero, PRIESTESS: Eybel, CONDUCTOR: Merola.

October 4, matinee: TOSCA (Puccini)
TOSCA: Muzio, CAVARADOSSI: Ansseau, SCARPIA: Stracciari, SPOLETTA: Oliviero, SACRISTAN: Trevisan, ANGELOTTI: Nicolich, SCIARRONE: Nicolich, JAILOR: Alibertini, SHEPHERD: Eybel, CONDUCTOR: Merola.

CASTS—1926 SEASON

September 21: MARTHA (Flotow)
LADY HARRIET: Macbeth, LIONEL: Schipa, PLUNKETT: Journet, SIR TRISTAN: Trevisan, SHERIFF: Wright, NANCY: Marlo, FARMER'S WIFE: Polidori, CONDUCTOR: Cimini.

September 23: FAUST (Gounod)
MARGUERITE: Donnelly, FAUST: Althouse, MEPHISTOPHELES: Journet, VALENTIN: Defrère, WAGNER: Nicolich, SIEBEL: Badger, MARTHE: Marlo, CONDUCTOR: Merola.

September 25: THE BARBER OF SEVILLE (Rossini)
ROSINA: Macbeth, COUNT ALMAVIVA: Schipa, FIGARO: Bonelli, BARTOLO: Trevisan, BASILIO: Journet, FIORELLO: Oliviero, OFFICER: Oliviero, BERTHA: Marlo, CONDUCTOR: Cimini.

September 27: SAMSON AND DELILAH (Saint-Saens)
SAMSON: Marshall, DELILAH: Homer, HIGH PRIEST: Journet, ABIMELECH: Nicolich, OLD HEBREW: Vogel, MESSENGER: Oliviero, PHILISTINE: Frediani, CONDUCTOR: Cimini.

September 28: MANON LESCAUT (Puccini)
MANON LESCAUT: Muzio, CHEVALIER DES GRIEUX: Cortis, LESCAUT: Defrère, GERONTE: Trevisan, EDMONDO: Oliviero, DANCING MASTER: Oliviero,

LAMPLIGHTER: Oliviero, HAIRDRESSER: Frediani, CAPTAIN: Vogel, MUSICIAN: Fremont, CONDUCTOR: Merola.

September 29: RIGOLETTO (Verdi)
GILDA: Melius, DUKE: Schipa, RIGOLETTO: Bonelli, MADDALENA: Marlo, SPARAFUCILE: Journet, MONTERONE: Nicolich, BORSA: Oliviero, MARULLO: Vogel, CEPRANO: Alibertini, COUNTESS CEPRANO: Smith, GIOVANNA: Farncroft, CONDUCTOR: Cimini.

October 1: AIDA (Verdi)
AIDA: Muzio, AMNERIS: Meisle, RHADAMES: Cortis, AMONASRO: Bonelli, RAMFIS: Journet, KING: Nicolich, MESSENGER: Regoli, PRIESTESS: Knierr, CONDUCTOR: Merola.

October 2: FRA DIAVOLO (Auber)
FRA DIAVOLO: Schipa, ZERLINA: Macbeth, LORD RICHBURG: Trevisan, LADY PAMELA: Marlo, LORENZO: Bulotti, MATTEO: Vogel, BEPPO: Oliviero, GIACOMO: Lazzari, CONDUCTOR: Cimini

October 3, matinee: LA BOHÈME (Puccini)
MIMI: Muzio, RODOLFO: Cortis, MARCELLO: Bonelli, COLLINE: Journet, SCHAUNARD: Nicolich, MUSETTA: Donnelly, BENOIT: Trevisan, ALCINDORO: Trevisan, CONDUCTOR: Merola.

October 4: TOSCA (Puccini)
TOSCA: Muzio, CAVARADOSSI: Cortis, SCARPIA: Journet, SPOLETTA: Oliviero, SACRISTAN: Trevisan, ANGELOTTI: Nicolich, SCIARRONE: Nicolich, JAILOR: Alibertini, SHEPHERD: Huff, CONDUCTOR: Merola.

October 5: LUCIA DI LAMMERMOOR (Donizetti)
LUCIA: Melius, LORD HENRY: Bonelli, EDGARDO: Schipa, LORD ARTHUR: Regoli, RAYMOND: Nicolich, ALICE: Badger, NORMAN: Carcione, CONDUCTOR: Cimini.

October 6: IL TROVATORE (Verdi)
LEONORA: Muzio, AZUCENA: Meisle, MANRICO: Lindi, COUNT DI LUNA: Bonelli, FERRANDO: Nicolich, RUIZ: Messina, OLD GYPSY: Guenter, INEZ: Knierr, CONDUCTOR: Merola.

CASTS—1927 SEASON

September 15: MANON LESCAUT (Puccini)
MANON LESCAUT: Peralta, CHEVALIER DES GRIEUX: Martinelli, LESCAUT: Scotti, GERONTE: D'Angelo, EDMONDO: Bada, DANCING MASTER: Oliviero, CAPTAIN: Sperry, MUSICIAN: Fremont, SERGEANT: Guenter, INNKEEPER: Alibertini, CONDUCTOR: Merola.

September 16: TRISTAN AND ISOLDE (Wagner)
ISOLDE: Alsen, BRANGÄNE: Meisle, TRISTAN: Laubenthal, KING MARKE: Patton, KURWENAL: Amato, MELOT: Picco, SHEPHERD: Oliviero, SAILOR'S VOICE: Bada, STEERSMAN: D'Angelo, CONDUCTOR: Hertz.

September 17: TOSCA (Puccini)
TOSCA: Roselle, CAVARADOSSI: Chamlee, SCARPIA: Scotti, SPOLETTA: Bada, SACRISTAN: Defrère, ANGELOTTI: D'Angelo, SCIARRONE: D'Angelo, JAILOR: Alibertini, SHEPHERD: Huff, CONDUCTOR: Merola.

September 19: TURANDOT (Puccini)

TURANDOT: Roselle, LIU: Donnelly, CALAF: Tokatyan, TIMUR: Pinza, PING: Picco, PANG: Bada, PONG: Oliviero, EMPEROR ALTOUM: Pilcher, MANDARIN: Sperry, PRINCE OF PERSIA: Kostin, MAIDS: Susulich, Chapman, CONDUCTOR: Merola.

September 20: ROMÉO ET JULIETTE (Gounod)
ROMÉO: Chamlee, JULIETTE: Macbeth, MERCUTIO: Defrère, TYBALT: Bada, CAPULET: D'Angelo, FRIAR LAWRENCE: Pinza, GREGORIO: Keaumoku, BENVOGLIO: Carcione, DUKE OF VERONA: Sperry, STEPHANO: Estabrook, GERTRUDE: Ferguson, CONDUCTOR: Merola.

September 22: IL TROVATORE (Verdi)
LEONORA: Roselle, AZUCENA: Meisle, MANRICO: Martinelli, COUNT DI LUNA: Picco, FERRANDO: D'Angelo, RUIZ: Messina, OLD GYPSY: Tulagin, INEZ: Smith, CONDUCTOR: Cimini.

September 24: CAVALLERIA RUSTICANA (Mascagni)
SANTUZZA: Peralta, TURIDDU: Chamlee, ALFIO: Amato, LOLA: Marlo, MAMMA LUCIA: Karkova, CONDUCTOR: Cimini.
    followed by: I PAGLIACCI (Leoncavallo)
CANIO: Martinelli, TONIO: Amato, NEDDA: Roselle, SILVIO: Picco, BEPPE: Bada, CONDUCTOR: Cimini.

September 25, matinee: TRISTAN AND ISOLDE (Wagner)
Same cast.

September 27: FALSTAFF (Verdi)
SIR JOHN FALSTAFF: Scotti, MISTRESS FORD: Peralta, MISTRESS PAGE: Marlo, DAME QUICKLY: Bourskaya, ANNE: Donnelly, FENTON: Tokatyan, FORD: Tibbett, DR. CAIUS: Bada, BARDOLPH: Oliviero, PISTOL: D'Angelo, CONDUCTOR: Merola.

September 28: AIDA (Verdi)
AIDA: Roselle, AMNERIS: Bourskaya, RHADAMES: Martinelli, AMONASRO: Amato, RAMFIS: Pinza, KING: D'Angelo, MESSENGER: Carcione, PRIESTESS: Knierr, CONDUCTOR: Cimini.

September 29: LA CENA DELLE BEFFE (Giordano)
GINEVRA: Peralta, LISABETTA: Donnelly, NERI: Tibbett, GIANNETTO: Tokatyan, GABRIELLO: Bada, TORNAQUINCI: D'Angelo, FAZIO: Picco, TRINCA: Oliviero, DOTTORE: Sperry, CALANDRA: Pisani, LAPO: Dini, LALDOMINE: Deeley, FIAMMETTA: Leo, CINTIA: Marlo, SINGER: Attilio Vannucci, CONDUCTOR: Cimini.

September 30: LA BOHEME (Puccini)
MIMI: Macbeth, RODOLFO: Chamlee, MARCELLO: Picco, COLLINE: Pinza, SCHAUNARD: Defrère, MUSETTA: Seymour, BENOIT: Oliviero, ALCINDORO: Oliviero, SERGEANT: Alibertini, OFFICER: Wright, CONDUCTOR: Cimini.

October 1: CARMEN (Bizet)
CARMEN: Bourskaya, MICAELA: Donnelly, DON JOSE: Martinelli, ESCAMILLO: Defrère, ZUNIGA: D'Angelo, DANCAIRO: Oliviero, REMENDADO: Bada, MORALES: Picco, FRASQUITA: Leo, MERCEDES: Fremont, CONDUCTOR: Merola.

October 2, matinee: TURANDOT (Puccini)
Same cast.

CASTS—1928 SEASON

September 15: AIDA (Verdi)
AIDA: Rethberg, AMNERIS: Telva, RHADAMES: Johnson, AMONASRO: Tibbett, RAMFIS: Pinza, KING: D'Angelo, MESSENGER: Oliviero, PRIESTESS: Knierr, CONDUCTOR: Merola.

September 17: LA CENA DELLE BEFFE (Giordano)
GINEVRA: Vettori, LISABETTA: Donnelly, NERI: Tibbett, GIANNETTO: Tokatyan, GABRIELLO: Bada, TORNAQUINCI: D'Angelo, FAZIO: Picco, TRINCA: Oliviero, DOTTORE: Sperry, CALANDRA: Guenter, LAPO: Dini, LALDOMINE: Elliott, FIAMMETTA: Stadtegger, CINTIA: Forno, SINGER: Attilio Vannucci, CONDUCTOR: Cimini.

September 19: TOSCA (Puccini)
TOSCA: Jeritza, CAVARADOSSI: Tokatyan, SCARPIA: Tibbett, SPOLETTA: Bada, SACRISTAN: Malatesta, ANGELOTTI: D'Angelo, SCIARRONE: D'Angelo, JAILOR: Alibertini, SHEPHERD: Huff, CONDUCTOR: Merola.

September 21: MADAMA BUTTERFLY (Puccini)
CIO-CIO-SAN: Rethberg, PINKERTON: Barra, SHARPLESS: Picco, SUZUKI: Telva, GORO: Oliviero, BONZE: D'Angelo, YAMADORI: Malatesta, COMMISSIONER: Sperry, KATE PINKERTON: Sewall, CONDUCTOR: Cimini.

September 22: TURANDOT (Puccini)
TURANDOT: Jeritza, LIU: Vettori, CALAF: Tokatyan, TIMUR: D'Angelo, PING: Picco, PANG: Bada, PONG: Oliviero, EMPEROR ALTOUM: Attilio Vannucci, MANDARIN: Sperry, PRINCE OF PERSIA: Bonnecaze, CONDUCTOR: Merola.

September 24: L'AMORE DEI TRE RE (Montemezzi)
FIORA: Vettori, AVITO: Johnson, MANFREDO: Tibbett, ARCHIBALDO: Pinza, FLAMINIO: Bada, YOUTH: Frediani, OLD WOMAN: Elliott, YOUNG GIRL: Sewall, SERVANT: Gionas, CONDUCTOR: Pelletier.

September 25: FEDORA (Giordano)
FEDORA: Jeritza, OLGA: Donnelly, LORIS: Johnson, DE SIRIEX: Danise, GRECH: D'Angelo, DESIRE: Oliviero, ROUVEL: Bada, BOROV: Picco, CIRILLO: Mercado, LOREK: Sperry, DIMITRI: Gionas, LITTLE SAVOYARD: Ott, NICOLA: Alibertini, SERGIO: Frediani, CONDUCTOR: Merola.

September 27: ANDREA CHENIER (Giordano)
MADELEINE: Rethberg, ANDREA CHENIER: Barra, GERARD: Danise, MATHIEU: Malatesta, FLÉVILLE: D'Angelo, ROUCHER: Picco, DUMAS: Sperry, ABBÉ: Oliviero, SPY: Bada, SCHMIDT: Sperry, FOUQUIER-TINVILLE: D'Angelo, COUNTESS: Gruninger, MADELON: Telva, BERSI: Post, CONDUCTOR: Merola.

September 29, matinee: TOSCA (Puccini)
Same cast except: CAVARADOSSI: Barra, SCARPIA: Danise.

September 29: FAUST (Gounod)
MARGUERITE: Rethberg, FAUST: Tokatyan, MEPHISTOPHELES: Pinza, VALENTIN: Picco, WAGNER: D'Angelo, SIEBEL: Florence, MARTHE: Ferguson, CONDUCTOR: Cimini.

October 1: CARMEN (Bizet)
CARMEN: Jeritza, DON JOSÉ: Tokatyan, ESCAMILLO: Pinza, MICAELA: Donnelly, ZUNIGA: D'Angelo, DANCAIRO: Picco, REMENDADO: Bada, MOR-

ALES: Mercado, FRASQUITA: Chirot, MERCEDES: Ivey, CONDUCTOR: Pelletier.

October 3: CAVALLERIA RUSTICANA (Mascagni)
SANTUZZA: Vettori, TURIDDU: Barra, ALFIO: Mercado, LOLA: Gruninger, MAMMA LUCIA: Emery, CONDUCTOR: Cimini.

followed by: I PAGLIACCI (Leoncavallo)
CANIO: Johnson, TONIO: Tibbett, NEDDA: Vettori, SILVIO: Mercado, BEPPE: Oliviero, PEASANTS: Dini, Wright, CONDUCTOR: Cimini.

CASTS—1929 SEASON

September 12: RIGOLETTO (Verdi)
GILDA: Mario, DUKE: Lauri-Volpi, RIGOLETTO: De Luca, MADDALENA: Gruninger, SPARAFUCILE: Rothier, MONTERONE: D'Angelo, BORSA: Oliviero, MARULLO: Picco, CEPRANO: Sperry, COUNTESS CEPRANO: Perdue, GIOVANNA: E. Smith, PAGE: M. Smith, CONDUCTOR: Merola.

September 14, matinee: HANSEL AND GRETEL (Humperdinck)
HANSEL: Ivey, GRETEL: Mario, WITCH: Meisle, GERTRUDE: Gruninger, PETER: Sandrini, SANDMAN: Sewall, DEWMAN: Rivero, CONDUCTOR: Riedel.

September 14: THE ELIXIR OF LOVE (Donizetti)
ADINA: Morgana, NEMORINO: Schipa, BELCORE: Picco, DR. DULCAMARA: Malatesta, GIANNETTA: Bruni, CONDUCTOR: Cimini.

September 16: IL TROVATORE (Verdi)
LEONORA: Rethberg, AZUCENA: Meisle, MANRICO: Lauri-Volpi, COUNT DI LUNA: Danise, FERRANDO: Rothier, RUIZ: Oliviero, OLD GYPSY: Alibertini, INEZ: Romaine, CONDUCTOR: Merola.

September 18: THE BARBER OF SEVILLE (Rossini)
ROSINA: Morgana, COUNT ALMAVIVA: Schipa, FIGARO: De Luca, BARTOLO: Malatesta, BASILIO: Rothier, FIORELLO: Sperry, OFFICER: Oliviero, BERTHA: Ivey, CONDUCTOR: Cimini.

September 20: LA BOHÈME (Puccini)
MIMI: Rethberg, RODOLFO: Barra, MARCELLO: Danise, COLLINE: Rothier, SCHAUNARD: Picco, MUSETTA: Young, BENOIT: Sandrini, ALCINDORO: Malatesta, PARPIGNOL: Oliviero, CONDUCTOR: Cimini.

September 21: GIANNI SCHICCHI (Puccini)
GIANNI SCHICCHI: De Luca, RINUCCIO: Barra, LAURETTA: Morgana, SIMONE: D'Angelo, BETTO: Picco, GHERARDO: Oliviero, MARCO: Sandrini, SPINELLOCCIO: Malatesta, NOTARY: Ferrier, PINELLINO: Alibertini, GUCCIO: Germanetti, ZITA: Gruninger, NELLA: Young, LA CIESCA: Ivey, CONDUCTOR: Merola.

followed by: I PAGLIACCI (Leoncavallo)
CANIO: Lauri-Volpi, TONIO: De Luca, NEDDA: Morgana, SILVIO: Picco, BEPPE: Oliviero, CONDUCTOR: Cimini.

September 23: MARTHA (Flotow)
LADY HARRIET: Mario, LIONEL: Schipa, PLUNKETT: De Luca, SIR TRISTAN: Malatesta, SHERIFF: D'Angelo, NANCY: Ivey, MAIDS: Huff, Twigg, Treweck, FARMER: Wright, SERVANT: Sigond, CONDUCTOR: Riedel.

September 25: AIDA (Verdi)

AIDA: Rethberg, AMNERIS: Meisle, RHADAMES: Lauri-Volpi, AMONASRO: Danise, RAMFIS: Rothier, KING: Sandrini, MESSENGER: Oliviero, PRIESTESS: Post, CONDUCTOR: Merola.

September 27: DON PASQUALE (Donizetti)
NORINA: Morgana, ERNESTO: Schipa, DR. MALATESTA: De Luca, DON PAS-QUALE: Malatesta, NOTARY: Oliviero, CONDUCTOR: Dell'Orefice.

September 28: FAUST (Gounod)
MARGUERITE: Rethberg, FAUST: Lauri-Volpi, MEPHISTOPHELES: Rothier, VALENTIN: Danise, WAGNER: Sandrini, SIEBEL: Torres, MARTHE: Ferguson, CONDUCTOR: Pelletier.

September 30: MANON (Massenet)
MANON: Mario, CHEVALIER DES GRIEUX: Schipa, LESCAUT: De Luca, GUIL-LOT: Oliviero, DE BRÉTIGNY: Picco, COUNT DES GRIEUX: Rothier, INN-KEEPER: Ferrier, CONDUCTOR: Merola.

CASTS—1930 SEASON

September 11: MANON (Massenet)
MANON: Mario, CHEVALIER DES GRIEUX: Gigli, LESCAUT: Picco, GUILLOT: Oliviero, DE BRÉTIGNY: Sandrini, COUNT DES GRIEUX: D'Angelo, POU-SETTE: Elmassian, JAVOTTE: Hodge, ROSETTE: Ferguson, SERVANT: Torres, GUARD: Steger, CONDUCTOR: Merola.

September 12: SALOME (Strauss)
SALOME: Jeritza, HEROD: Rayner, JOCHANAAN: Thomas, HERODIAS: Man-ski, NARRABOTH: Riedel, PAGE: Gruninger, SOLDIERS: D'Angelo, Sandrini, NAZARENES: Williams, Horton, JEWS: Paltrinieri, Oliviero, Caravacci, Steger, Picco, CONDUCTOR: Merola.

September 13: LA TRAVIATA (Verdi)
VIOLETTA: Clairbert, ALFREDO: Gigli, GERMONT: Viviani, GASTON: Paltri-nieri, BARON DOUPHOL: D'Angelo, MARQUIS D'OBIGNY: Picco, DR. GRENVIL: Sandrini, FLORA: Bruni, ANNINA: Cioni, CONDUCTOR: Merola.

September 15: LA FANCIULLA DEL WEST (Puccini)
MINNIE: Jeritza, DICK JOHNSON: Jagel, JACK RANCE: Viviani, JAKE WAL-LACE: Williams, NICK: Oliviero, ASHBY: D'Angelo, SONORA: Picco, TRIN: Paltrinieri, SID: Ferrier, HANDSOME: Cozzi, HARRY: Caravacci, JOE: Fadem, HAPPY: Sellon, LARKENS: Sandrini, JOSÉ CASTRO: Sandrini, BILLY JACK-RABBIT: Sandrini, WOWKLE: Marlo, CONDUCTOR: Merola.

September 17: LA BOHÈME (Puccini)
MIMI: Mario, RODOLFO: Gigli, MARCELLO: Viviani, COLLINE: Pinza, SCHAUNARD: Picco, MUSETTA: Farncroft, BENOIT: Sandrini, ALCINDORO: Sandrini, PARPIGNOL: Oliviero, SERGEANT: Alibertini, CONDUCTOR: Dell'-Orefice.

September 19: L'ENFANT ET LES SORTILÈGES (Ravel)
BOY: Mario, FIRE: Farncroft, PRINCESS: Farncroft, LARK: Farncroft, MOTHER: Gruninger, BUTTERFLY: Gruninger, ARMCHAIR: D'Angelo, TREE: D'Angelo, CLOCK: Picco, TOMCAT: Picco, TEAPOT: Oliviero, ARITHMETIC: Ferrier, FROG: Paltrinieri, SHEPHERD: Caravacci, SHEPHERDESSES: Kova-

leff, Torres, SQUIRREL: Torres, LOUIS XV CHAIR: Torres, CAT: Ferguson, BAT: Dimitrieff, OWL: Gionas, CHINESE CUP: Strause, CONDUCTOR: Merola.

followed by: HANSEL AND GRETEL (Humperdinck)
HANSEL: Marlo, GRETEL: Mario, WITCH: Manski, GERTRUDE: Gruninger, PETER: Sandrini, SANDMAN: Zickhardt, DEWMAN: Elmassian, CONDUCTOR: Riedel.

September 20: CAVALLERIA RUSTICANA (Mascagni)
SANTUZZA: Jeritza, TURIDDU: Jagel, ALFIO: Picco, LOLA: Gruninger, MAMMA LUCIA: Gambi, CONDUCTOR: Dell'Orefice.

followed by: I PAGLIACCI (Leoncavallo)
CANIO: Rayner, TONIO: Thomas, NEDDA: Jeritza, SILVIO: Picco, BEPPE: Paltrinieri, PEASANTS: Alibertini, Dini, CONDUCTOR: Dell'Orefice.

September 22: MIGNON (Thomas)
MIGNON: Mario, PHILINE: Clairbert, WILHELM MEISTER: Gigli, LOTHARIO: Pinza, LAERTE: Paltrinieri, ANTONIO: Sandrini, GIARNO: Sandrini, FREDERIC: Marlo, CONDUCTOR: Pelletier.

September 23: TANNHÄUSER (Wagner)
ELISABETH: Jeritza, VENUS: Manski, TANNHÄUSER: Rayner, WOLFRAM: Thomas, LANDGRAVE: Pinza, WALTHER: Paltrinieri, BITEROLF: Sandrini, HEINRICH: Oliviero, REINMAR: D'Angelo, SHEPHERD: Elmassian, CONDUCTOR: Riedel.

September 25: FAUST (Gounod)
MARGUERITE: Hampton, FAUST: Jagel, MEPHISTOPHELES: Pinza, VALENTIN: Thomas, WAGNER: Sandrini, SIEBEL: Torres, MARTHE: Ferguson, CONDUCTOR: Pelletier.

September 27, matinee: SALOME (Strauss)
Same cast.

September 27: LUCIA DI LAMMERMOOR (Donizetti)
LUCIA: Clairbert, LORD HENRY: Viviani, EDGARDO: Gigli, LORD ARTHUR: Oliviero, RAYMOND: D'Angelo, ALICE: Gambi, NORMAN: Paltrinieri, CONDUCTOR: Merola.

CASTS—1931 SEASON

September 10: MÂROUF (Rabaud)
PRINCESS SAAMCHEDDINE: Gall, MÂROUF: Chamlee, FATIMAH: Gruninger, SULTAN: D'Angelo, VIZIER: Sandrini, ALI: Picco, THE FELLAH: Windheim, MERCHANTS: Windheim, Williams, THE KADI: Williams, AHMAD: D'Angelo, DONKEY DRIVER: Oliviero, SEA CAPTAIN: Oliviero, MUZZEINS: Oliviero, Simondet, POLICEMEN: Julian, Radic, CONDUCTOR: Merola.

September 12: AIDA (Verdi)
AIDA: Rethberg, AMNERIS: Petrova, RHADAMES: Martinelli, AMONASRO: Danise, RAMFIS: D'Angelo, KING: Sandrini, MESSENGER: Oliviero, PRIESTESS: Linne, CONDUCTOR: Merola.

September 14: LOHENGRIN (Wagner)
ELSA: Müller, ORTRUD: Petrova, LOHENGRIN: Pistor, TELRAMUND: Schorr, KING HENRY: D'Angelo, HERALD: Gabor, CONDUCTOR: Blechschmidt.

September 16: ANDREA CHENIER (Giordano)

MADELEINE: Rethberg, ANDREA CHENIER: Martinelli, GERARD: Danise,
MATHIEU: Sandrini, FLÉVILLE: D'Angelo, ROUCHER: Picco, DUMAS: Picco,
ABBÉ: Windheim, SPY: Oliviero, SCHMIDT: Sandrini, FOUQUIER-TINVILLE:
D'Angelo, COUNTESS: Gruninger, MADELON: Petrova, BERSI: Ferguson,
CONDUCTOR: Merola.

September 18: MADAMA BUTTERFLY (Puccini)
CIO-CIO-SAN: Müller, PINKERTON: Chamlee, SHARPLESS: De Segurola,
SUZUKI: Petrova, GORO: Oliviero, BONZE: D'Angelo, YAMADORI: Sandrini,
COMMISSIONER: Picco, KATE PINKERTON: Murphy, REGISTRAR: Alibertini,
CONDUCTOR: Pelletier.

September 19: UN BALLO IN MASCHERA (Verdi)
AMELIA: Rethberg, ULRICA: Silva, OSCAR: Farncroft, RICCARDO:Martinelli,
RENATO: Danise, SAM: D'Angelo, TOM: Sandrini, JUDGE: Edmunds,
SERVANT: Julian, CONDUCTOR: Cimini.

September 21: TOSCA (Puccini)
TOSCA: Gall, CAVARADOSSI: Chamlee, SCARPIA: Danise, SPOLETTA: Olivi-
ero, SACRISTAN: Sandrini, ANGELOTTI: D'Angelo, SCIARRONE: Picco,
JAILOR: Picco, SHEPHERD: Gruninger, CONDUCTOR: Cimini.

September 23: TANNHÄUSER (Wagner)
ELISABETH: Rethberg, VENUS: Castleton, TANNHÄUSER: Pistor, WOLFRAM:
Schorr, LANDGRAVE: Pinza, WALTHER: Windheim, BITEROLF: Gabor,
HEINRICH: Oliviero, REINMAR: D'Angelo, SHEPHERD: McLaughlin, CON-
DUCTOR: Blechschmidt.

September 25: LA BOHÈME (Puccini)
MIMI: Müller, RODOLFO: Chamlee, MARCELLO: De Segurola, COLLINE:
Pinza, SCHAUNARD: Picco, MUSETTA: Farncroft, BENOIT: Oliviero, ALCIN-
DORO: Sandrini, PARPIGNOL: Oliviero, SERGEANT: Alibertini, OFFICER:
Miller, CONDUCTOR: Dell'Orefice.

September 26: IL TROVATORE (Verdi)
LEONORA: Rethberg, AZUCENA: Silva, MANRICO: Martinelli, COUNT DI
LUNA: Danise, FERRANDO: D'Angelo, RUIZ: Oliviero, OLD GYPSY: Alibertini,
INEZ: Strause, CONDUCTOR: Merola.

September 28: DIE MEISTERSINGER (Wagner)
EVA: Müller, MAGDALENA: Gruninger, WALTHER: Pistor, HANS SACHS:
Schorr, POGNER: Pinza, DAVID: Windheim, BECKMESSER: Gabor, KOTHNER:
Picco, NIGHT WATCHMAN: Sandrini, VOGELGESANG: Steger, NACHTIGALL:
D'Angelo, ZORN: Horton, EISSLINGER: Oliviero, MOSER: Simondet,
ORTEL: Williams, SCHWARZ: Sellon, FOLTZ: Sandrini, CONDUCTOR:
Blechschmidt.

September 29: CARMEN (Bizet)
CARMEN: Petrova, MICAELA: Farncroft, DON JOSÉ: Martinelli, ESCAMILLO:
Pinza, ZUNIGA: D'Angelo, DANCAIRO: Picco, REMENDADO: Oliviero,
MORALES: Gabor, FRASQUITA: Elmassian, MERCEDES: Gruninger, CONDUC-
TOR: Pelletier.

CASTS—1932 SEASON

October 15: TOSCA (Puccini)
TOSCA: Muzio, CAVARADOSSI: Borgioli, SCARPIA: Gandolfi, SPOLETTA:

Windheim, SACRISTAN: D'Angelo, ANGELOTTI: Argall, SCIARRONE: D'Angelo, JAILOR: Sperry, SHEPHERD: Gruninger, CONDUCTOR: Merola.

October 17: LUCIA DI LAMMERMOOR (Donizetti)
LUCIA: Pons, LORD HENRY: Gandolfi, EDGARDO: Merli, LORD ARTHUR: Marlowe, RAYMOND: D'Angelo, ALICE: Bruni, NORMAN: Lanfranconi, CONDUCTOR: Merola.

October 18: DIE MEISTERSINGER (Wagner)
EVA: Müller, MAGDALENA: MacNevin, WALTHER: Chamlee, HANS SACHS: Schorr, POGNER: Pinza, DAVID: Windheim, BECKMESSER: Gabor, KOTHNER: Gandolfi, NIGHT WATCHMAN: Argall, VOGELGESANG: Marlowe, NACHTIGALL: D'Angelo, ZORN: Horton, EISSLINGER: Argall, MOSER: Simondet, ORTEL: Williams, SCHWARZ: Tibbe, FOLTZ: Eldredge, CONDUCTOR: Blechschmidt.

October 20: RIGOLETTO (Verdi)
GILDA: Pons, DUKE: Borgioli, RIGOLETTO: Bonelli, MADDALENA: Gruninger, SPARAFUCILE: Pinza, MONTERONE: D'Angelo, BORSA: Windheim, MARULLO: Argall, CEPRANO: Alibertini, COUNTESS CEPRANO: Linne, GIOVANNA: Bruni, PAGE: Dimitrieff, CONDUCTOR: Merola.

October 22, matinee: HANSEL AND GRETEL (Humperdinck)
HANSEL: Lothrop, GRETEL: Mario, WITCH: Meisle, GERTRUDE: MacNevin, PETER: Gabor, SANDMAN: Sewall, DEWMAN: Malinoff, CONDUCTOR: Blechschmidt.
         followed by: LA VALSE and BOLERO ballets (Ravel)
THE DANCER (*Bolero*):Reed, CONDUCTOR: Merola.

October 22: CAVALLERIA RUSTICANA (Mascagni)
SANTUZZA: Muzio, TURIDDU: Chamlee, ALFIO: Gandolfi, LOLA: Gruninger, MAMMA LUCIA: Gambi, CONDUCTOR: Merola.
         followed by: I PAGLIACCI (Leoncavallo)
CANIO: MacKenzie, TONIO: Bonelli, NEDDA: Muzio, SILVIO: Argall, BEPPE: Lanfranconi, CONDUCTOR: Cimini.

October 23, matinee: LUCIA DI LAMMERMOOR (Donizetti)
Same cast except: EDGARDO: Borgioli.

October 25: LOHENGRIN (Wagner)
ELSA: Müller, ORTRUD: Meisle, LOHENGRIN: Chamlee, TELRAMUND: Schorr, KING HENRY: D'Angelo, HERALD: Gabor, CONDUCTOR: Blechschmidt.

October 27: FAUST (Gounod)
MARGUERITE: Mario, FAUST: Borgioli, MEPHISTOPHELES: Pinza, VALENTIN: Bonelli, WAGNER: D'Angelo, SIEBEL: Malova, MARTHE: Gruninger, CONDUCTOR: Blechschmidt.

October 29: IL TROVATORE (Verdi)
LEONORA: Muzio, AZUCENA: Meisle, MANRICO: MacKenzie, COUNT DI LUNA: Bonelli, FERRANDO: D'Angelo, RUIZ: Lanfranconi, OLD GYPSY: Alibertini, INEZ: Strause, CONDUCTOR: Cimini.

October 30, matinee: DIE MEISTERSINGER (Wagner)
Same cast.

November 1: LA TRAVIATA (Verdi)
VIOLETTA: Muzio, ALFREDO: Borgioli, GERMONT: Bonelli, GASTON: Wind-

heim, BARON DOUPHOL: Argall, MARQUIS D'OBIGNY: Alibertini, DR. GREN-
VIL: D'Angelo, FLORA: Malova, ANNINA: McLaughlin, CONDUCTOR: Merola.

CASTS—1933 SEASON

November 3: SAMSON AND DELILAH (Saint-Saens)
SAMSON: Martinelli, DELILAH: Van Gordon, HIGH PRIEST: Pinza, ABIMEL-
ECH: D'Angelo, OLD HEBREW: Belarsky, MESSENGER: Oliviero, PHILISTINES:
Simondet, Eldredge, CONDUCTOR: Merola.

November 6: LE COQ D'OR (Rimsky-Korsakoff)
Dance Pantomime with Vocal Accompaniment
Singers: QUEEN: Hardy, KING DODON: Stewart, ASTROLOGER: Marlowe,
GENERAL: Eldredge, AMELFA: Leonard, VOICE OF COCK: Eybel, PRINCE
GUIDON: Frediani, BOYARS: Albert Vannucci, Levi, *Dancers:* QUEEN: Ruiz,
KING DODON: Bolm, ASTROLOGER: Bratoff, GENERAL: Vasilieff, AMELFA:
Paulini, PRINCE GUIDON: Charisse, PRINCE AFRON: Cooke, BOYARS: Kolodin,
Romanoff, CONDUCTOR: Pelletier.

November 8: AIDA (Verdi)
AIDA: Muzio, AMNERIS: Meisle, RHADAMES: Martinelli, AMONASRO: Bonelli,
RAMFIS: Pinza, KING: D'Angelo, MESSENGER: Oliviero, PRIESTESS: Folli,
CONDUCTOR: Merola.

November 10: TRISTAN AND ISOLDE (Wagner)
ISOLDE: Kappel, BRANGÄNE: Meisle, TRISTAN: Althouse, KING MARKE:
Pinza, KURWENAL: Bonelli, MELOT: Gandolfi, SHEPHERD: Oliviero, SAIL-
OR'S VOICE: Marlowe, STEERSMAN: D'Angelo, CONDUCTOR: Hertz.

November 12, matinee: SAMSON AND DELILAH (Saint-Saens)
Same cast.

November 14: MANON (Massenet)
MANON: Bori, CHEVALIER DES GRIEUX: Borgioli, LESCAUT: Gandolfi, GUIL-
LOT: Oliviero, DE BRÉTIGNY: Stewart, COUNT DES GRIEUX: D'Angelo,
POUSETTE: McLaughlin, JAVOTTE: Wayne, ROSETTE: Strause, SERVANT:
Lanz, INNKEEPER: Ferrier, GUARDS: Simondet, Stanton, CONDUCTOR:
Pelletier.

November 17: THE SECRET OF SUZANNE (Wolf-Ferrari)
COUNTESS SUZANNE: Morgana, COUNT GIL: Gandolfi, SANTE: D'Angelo,
CONDUCTOR: Dell'Orefice.
followed by: THE EMPEROR JONES (Gruenberg)
BRUTUS JONES: Tibbett, HENRY SMITHERS: Marlowe, OLD NATIVE WOMAN:
Leonard, PULLMAN PORTER: Anderson, CONGO WITCH DOCTOR: Charisse,
CONDUCTOR: Pelletier.

November 19, matinee: TRISTAN AND ISOLDE (Wagner)
Same cast.

November 21: CAVALLERIA RUSTICANA (Mascagni)
SANTUZZA: Muzio, TURIDDU: Borgioli, ALFIO: Gandolfi, LOLA: Leonard,
MAMMA LUCIA: Strause, CONDUCTOR: Dell'Orefice.
followed by: I PAGLIACCI (Leoncavallo)
CANIO: Martinelli, TONIO: Tibbett, NEDDA: Bori, SILVIO: Gandolfi, BEPPE:
Oliviero, PEASANTS: Alibertini, Frediani, CONDUCTOR: Merola.

327

November 24: LA TRAVIATA (Verdi)
VIOLETTA: Muzio, ALFREDO: Borgioli, GERMONT: Tibbett, GASTON: Oliviero,
BARON DOUPHOL: Gandolfi, MARQUIS D'OBIGNY: Eldredge, DR. GRENVIL:
D'Angelo, FLORA: Eybel, ANNINA: McLaughlin, CONDUCTOR: Merola.
November 26, matinee: LE COQ D'OR (Rimsky-Korsakoff)
Same cast.
November 28: LA BOHÈME (Puccini)
MIMI: Bori, RODOLFO: Borgioli, MARCELLO: Bonelli, COLLINE: Pinza,
SCHAUNARD: Gandolfi, MUSETTA: Hardy, BENOIT: Oliviero, ALCINDORO:
D'Angelo, PARPIGNOL: Oliviero, CONDUCTOR: Merola.
November 30, matinee: THE SECRET OF SUZANNE (Wolf-Ferrari)
          followed by: THE EMPEROR JONES (Gruenberg)
Same casts.
December 1: LA FORZA DEL DESTINO (Verdi)
LEONORA: Muzio, DON ALVARO: Martinelli, DON CARLO: Bonelli, PADRE
GUARDIANO: Pinza, FRA MELITONE: Gandolfi, PREZIOSILLA: Leonard,
MARQUIS OF CALATRAVA: D'Angelo, ALCADE: Eldredge, TRABUCCO: Oli-
viero, CURRA: Strause, SURGEON: D'Angelo, CONDUCTOR: Merola.
December 2: MANON (Massenet)
Same cast.

CASTS—1934 SEASON

November 14: THE BARTERED BRIDE (Smetana)
MARIE: Rethberg, JENIK: Chamlee, KEZAL: D'Angelo, VASHEK: Windheim,
KRUSCHINA: Gandolfi, LUDMILA: Smith, MICHA: Howell, HATA: Gruninger,
SPRINGER: Taenzler, ESMERALDA: Clark, MUFF: Ellis, CONDUCTOR: Hertz.
November 16: TOSCA (Puccini)
TOSCA: Lehmann, CAVARADOSSI: Borgioli, SCARPIA: Gandolfi, SPOLETTA:
Windheim, SACRISTAN: D'Angelo, ANGELOTTI: Howell, SCIARRONE: D'An-
gelo, JAILOR: Alibertini, SHEPHERD: Gruninger, CONDUCTOR: Merola.
November 17: CARMEN (Bizet)
CARMEN: Vallin, MICAELA: Clark, DON JOSÉ: Chamlee, ESCAMILLO: Pinza,
ZUNIGA: D'Angelo, DANCAIRO: Ellis, REMENDADO: Windheim, MORALES:
Howell, FRASQUITA: Smith, MERCEDES: Gruninger, CONDUCTOR: Merola.
November 19: MANON (Massenet)
MANON: Bori, CHEVALIER DES GRIEUX: Crooks, LESCAUT: Gandolfi, GUIL-
LOT: Windheim, DE BRÉTIGNY: Howell, COUNT DES GRIEUX: D'Angelo,
POUSETTE: McLaughlin, JAVOTTE: Strause, ROSETTE: Schiller, SERVANT:
Lanz, INNKEEPER: Ferrier, GUARDS: Simondet, Frediani, CONDUCTOR:
Cimini.
November 22: MADAMA BUTTERFLY (Puccini)
CIO-CIO-SAN: Lehmann, PINKERTON: Borgioli, SHARPLESS: Gandolfi,
SUZUKI: Marlo, GORO: Windheim, BONZE: D'Angelo, YAMADORI: D'Angelo,
COMMISSIONER: Howell, KATE PINKERTON: Glando, REGISTRAR: Alibertini,
CONDUCTOR: Cimini.
November 26: TANNHÄUSER (Wagner)
ELISABETH: Rethberg, VENUS: Eybel, TANNHÄUSER: Melchior, WOLFRAM:

Bonelli, LANDGRAVE: Pinza, WALTHER: Windheim, BITEROLF: Gandolfi, HEINRICH: Marlowe, REINMAR: D'Angelo, SHEPHERD: Clark, CONDUCTOR: Hertz.

November 28: LA TRAVIATA (Verdi)
VIOLETTA: Bori, ALFREDO: Crooks, GERMONT: Bonelli, GASTON: Windheim, BARON DOUPHOL: Gandolfi, MARQUIS D'OBIGNY: Howell, DR. GRENVIL: D'Angelo, FLORA: Badger, ANNINA: McLaughlin, CONDUCTOR: Merola.

November 30: FAUST (Gounod)
MARGUERITE: Vallin, FAUST: Crooks, MEPHISTOPHELES: Pinza, VALENTIN: Bonelli, WAGNER: Howell, SIEBEL: Clark, MARTHE: Gruninger, CONDUCTOR: Merola.

December 1: MANON (Massenet)
Same cast.

December 2, matinee: MADAMA BUTTERFLY (Puccini)
Same cast except: CIO-CIO-SAN: Rethberg, PINKERTON: Chamlee.

December 3: LA RONDINE (Puccini)
MAGDA: Bori, RUGGERO: Borgioli, LISETTE: Clark, PRUNIER: Windheim, RAMBALDO: D'Angelo, PERICHAUD: Howell, GOBIN: Frediani, CREBILLON: Alibertini, YVETTE: Folli, BIANCA: Smith, SUZY: Strause, VOICE: Nostrom, CONDUCTOR: Merola.

December 4: LAKMÉ (Delibes)
LAKMÉ: Hardy, GERALD: Chamlee, FREDERIC: Gandolfi, NILAKANTHA: Pinza, HADJI: Simondet, MALLIKA: Gruninger, MRS. BENSON: J. G. Ferrier, ELLEN: Clark, ROSE: Strause, A SEPOY: Howell, CHINESE VENDOR: Frediani, CONDUCTOR: Merola.

December 5: OTELLO (Verdi)
DESDEMONA: Rethberg, OTELLO: Melchior, IAGO: Bonelli, CASSIO: Marlowe, RODERIGO: Frediani, LODOVICO: D'Angelo, MONTANO: Alibertini, HERALD: Howell, EMILIA: Gruninger, CONDUCTOR: Merola.

December 7: MIGNON (Thomas)
MIGNON: Bori, PHILINE: Hardy, WILHELM MEISTER: Borgioli, LOTHARIO: Pinza, LAERTE: Windheim, GIARNO: D'Angelo, FREDERIC: Marlo, CONDUCTOR: Cimini.

December 8: TANNHÄUSER (Wagner)
Same cast except: WOLFRAM: Eddy, SHEPHERD: McLaughlin.

CASTS—1935 SEASON

November 1: DAS RHEINGOLD (Wagner)
WOTAN: Schorr, DONNER: Gandolfi, FROH: Marlowe, LOGE: Clemens, ALBERICH: Schützendorf, MIME: Windheim, FASOLT: Baromeo, FAFNER: Beattie, FRICKA: Eybel, FREIA: Manski, ERDA: Meisle, WOGLINDE: Omeron, WELLGUNDE: Merrill, FLOSSHILDE: Doe, CONDUCTOR: Bodanzky.

November 4: DIE WALKÜRE (Wagner)
BRÜNNHILDE: Flagstad, SIEGLINDE: Rethberg, FRICKA: Meisle, SIEGMUND: Melchior, WOTAN: Schorr, HUNDING: Baromeo, HELMWIGE: Manski, GERHILDE: Eybel, ORTLINDE: Merrill, SIEGRUNE: Gerdau, ROSSWEISSE: Lean-

dre, WALTRAUTE: Doe, GRIMGERDE: Callahan, SCHWERTLEITE: Gruninger, CONDUCTOR: Bodanzky.

November 6: SIEGFRIED (Wagner)
BRÜNNHILDE: Flagstad, SIEGFRIED: Melchior, WANDERER: Schorr, FAFNER: Baromeo, ALBERICH: Schützendorf, MIME: Windheim, ERDA: Meisle, VOICE OF THE FOREST BIRD: Hardy, CONDUCTOR: Bodanzky.

November 9, at 5 p.m.: GÖTTERDÄMMERUNG (Wagner)
BRÜNNHILDE: Flagstad, SIEGFRIED: Melchior, GUNTHER: Schorr, GUTRUNE: Manski, HAGEN: List, ALBERICH: Schützendorf, WALTRAUTE: Meisle, NORNS: Doe, Meisle, Manski, WOGLINDE: Kroph, WELLGUNDE: Merrill, FLOSSHILDE: Doe, VASSALS: Braunstein, Martin, CONDUCTOR: Bodanzky.

November 11: AIDA (Verdi)
AIDA: Rethberg, AMNERIS: Meisle, RHADAMES: Martinelli, AMONASRO: Eddy, RAMFIS: Pinza, KING: Beattie, MESSENGER: Windheim, PRIESTESS: Watt, CONDUCTOR: Merola.

November 13: DIE WALKÜRE (Wagner)
Same cast except: HUNDING: List.

November 16: MARTHA (Flotow)
LADY HARRIET: Jepson, LIONEL: Schipa, PLUNKETT: Shefoff, SIR TRISTAN: D'Angelo, SHERIFF: Beattie, NANCY: Glade, MAIDS: Ferguson, Nostrom, Isariotis, FARMER: Baldacci, FARMER'S WIFE: Callahan, CONDUCTOR: Lert.

November 18: LA JUIVE (Halévy)
RACHEL: Rethberg, ELEAZAR: Martinelli, CARDINAL: Pinza, LEOPOLD: Clemens, EUDOXIA: Hardy, RUGGIERO: Howell, TOWN CRIER: Howell, EXECUTIONER: Guenter, ALBERT: Wright, CONDUCTOR: Lert.

November 22: WERTHER (Massenet)
CHARLOTTE: Glade, WERTHER: Schipa, SOPHIE: Young, ALBERT: Gandolfi, BAILIFF: D'Angelo, SCHMIDT: Marlowe, JOHANN: Howell, BRUHLMANN: Albert Vannucci, KATCHEN: Lanz, CONDUCTOR: Merola.

November 23: AIDA (Verdi)
Same cast except: AMNERIS: Glade, AMONASRO: Bonelli.

November 25: THE BARBER OF SEVILLE (Rossini)
ROSINA: Tumminia, COUNT ALMAVIVA: Schipa, FIGARO: Bonelli, BARTOLO: D'Angelo, BASILIO: Pinza, FIORELLO: Howell, OFFICER: Windheim, BERTHA: Gruninger, CONDUCTOR: Merola.

November 27: LA BOHÈME (Puccini)
MIMI: Jepson, RODOLFO: Martinelli, MARCELLO: Bonelli, COLLINE: Pinza, SCHAUNARD: Gandolfi, MUSETTA: Smith, BENOIT: D'Angelo, ALCINDORO: D'Angelo, PARPIGNOL: Mennucci, CONDUCTOR: Lert.

November 29: RIGOLETTO (Verdi)
GILDA: Hardy, DUKE: Schipa, RIGOLETTO: Bonelli, MADDALENA: Gruninger, SPARAFUCILE: Pinza, MONTERONE: Beattie, BORSA: Rossini, MARULLO: Howell, CEPRANO: Alibertini, COUNTESS CEPRANO: Sholl, GIOVANNA: Callahan, PAGE: Giragossiantz, CONDUCTOR: Merola.

December 2, matinee: MARTHA (Flotow)
Same cast except: NANCY: Gruninger.

December 2: SUOR ANGELICA (Puccini)

SUOR ANGELICA: Gahagan, PRINCESS: O'Dea, ABBESS: Hartman, MISTRESS OF NOVICES: Steed, SISTER GENEVIEVE: Young, NOVICES: Callahan, Fremont, CONVERTS: Schiller, Ferguson, CONDUCTOR: Merola.
    followed by: LE COQ D'OR (Rimsky-Korsakoff)
Dance Pantomime with Vocal Accompaniment
Singers: QUEEN: Hardy, KING DODON: Beattie, ASTROLOGER: Marlowe, GENERAL: Jones, AMELFA: Gruninger, VOICE OF COCK: Eybel, PRINCE GUIDON: Friberg, BOYERS: Albert Vannucci, Alibertini, *Dancers:* QUEEN: Ruiz, KING DODON: Bolm, ASTROLOGER: Bratoff, GENERAL: Vasilieff, AMELFA: Lauche, PRINCE GUIDON: Romanoff, PRICE AFRON: Block, CONDUCTOR: Merola.

CASTS—1936 SEASON

REGULAR SERIES

October 30: LA JUIVE (Halévy)
RACHEL: Rethberg, ELEAZAR: Martinelli, CARDINAL: Pinza, LEOPOLD: Clemens, EUDOXIA: Boerner, RUGGIERO: Howell, TOWN CRIER: Burr, EXECUTIONER: Guenter, ALBERT: Wright, CONDUCTOR: Merola.
November 2: TRISTAN AND ISOLDE (Wagner)
ISOLDE: Flagstad, BRANGÄNE: Meisle, TRISTAN: Melchior, KING MARKE: List, KURWENAL: Schorr, MELOT: Gabor, SHEPHERD: Clemens, SAILOR'S VOICE: Oliviero, STEERSMAN: D'Angelo, CONDUCTOR: Reiner.
November 4: CARMEN (Bizet)
CARMEN: Castagna, MICAELA: Tumminia, DON JOSÉ: Kullman, ESCAMILLO: Pinza, ZUNIGA: D'Angelo, DANCAIRO: Russell, REMENDADO: Oliviero, MORALES: Howell, FRASQUITA: Kroph, MERCEDES: Doe, CONDUCTOR: Papi.
November 6: RIGOLETTO (Verdi)
GILDA: Tumminia, DUKE: Kullman, RIGOLETTO: Tibbett, MADDALENA: Gruninger, SPARAFUCILE: Pinza, MONTERONE: Cordon, BORSA: Oliviero, MARULLO: Howell, CEPRANO: Jones, COUNTESS CEPRANO: Green, GIOVANNA: Hackett, PAGE: Lawlor, CONDUCTOR: Papi.
November 7, at 5 p.m.: GÖTTERDÄMMERUNG (Wagner)
BRÜNNHILDE: Flagstad, SIEGFRIED: Melchior, GUNTHER: Schorr, GUTRUNE: Manski, HAGEN: List, ALBERICH: Gabor, WALTRAUTE: Meisle, NORNS: Doe, O'Dea, Manski, WOGLINDE: Kroph, WELLGUNDE: Merrill, FLOSSHILDE: Doe, CONDUCTOR: Reiner.
November 9: THE MARRIAGE OF FIGARO (Mozart)
SUSANNA: Boerner, COUNTESS: Rethberg, CHERUBINO: Vanna, FIGARO: Pinza, COUNT: Askam, BARTOLO: D'Angelo, BASILIO: Clemens, MARCELLINA: Callahan, BARBARINA: Monte, ANTONIO: Jones, CONDUCTOR: Lert.
November 11: I PAGLIACCI (Leoncavallo)
CANIO: Martinelli, TONIO: Tibbett, NEDDA: Vanna, SILVIO: Howell, BEPPE: Oliviero, CONDUCTOR: Papi.
    followed by: GIANNI SCHICCHI (Puccini)
GIANNI SCHICCHI: Tibbett, RINUCCIO: Kullman, LAURETTA: Tumminia,

SIMONE: Cordon, BETTO: Gabor, GHERARDO: Oliviero, MARCO: D'Angelo, SPINELLOCCIO: Oliver Jones, NOTARY: Gandolfi, PINELLINO: Sherrill, GUCCIO: Wright, ZITA: Doe, NELLA: Green, LA CIESCA: Merrill, GHERARDINO: Lawlor, CONDUCTOR: Papi.

November 13: DIE WALKÜRE (Wagner)
BRÜNNHILDE: Flagstad, SIEGLINDE: Lehmann, FRICKA: Meisle, SIEGMUND: Melchior, WOTAN: Schorr, HUNDING: List, HELMWIGE: Manski, GERHILDE: Glando, ORTLINDE: Merrill, SIEGRUNE: Watt, ROSSWEISSE: Green, WALTRAUTE: Doe, GRIMGERDE: Callahan, SCHWERTLEITE: Gruninger, CONDUCTOR: Reiner.

November 16: LA FORZA DEL DESTINO (Verdi)
LEONORA: Rethberg, DON ALVARO: Martinelli, DON CARLO: Morelli, PADRE GUARDIANO: Pinza, FRA MELITONE: Gandolfi, PREZIOSILLA: Doe, MARQUIS OF CALATRAVA: D'Angelo, ALCADE: Howell, TRABUCCO: Oliviero, CURRA: Callahan, SURGEON: Burr, CONDUCTOR: Papi.

November 18: TOSCA (Puccini)
TOSCA: Lehmann, CAVARADOSSI: Kullman, SCARPIA: Tibbett, SPOLETTA: Oliviero, SACRISTAN: D'Angelo, ANGELOTTI: Cordon, SCIARRONE: Howell, JAILOR: Burr, SHEPHERD: Fremont, CONDUCTOR: Papi.

November 20: OTELLO (Verdi)
DESDEMONA: Rethberg, OTELLO: Martinelli, IAGO: Tibbett, CASSIO: Clemens, RODERIGO: Russell, LODOVICO: D'Angelo, MONTANO: Howell, HERALD: Burr, EMILIA: Gruninger, CONDUCTOR: Merola.

POPULAR SERIES

October 31: THE BARBER OF SEVILLE (Rossini)
ROSINA: Tumminia, COUNT ALMAVIVA: Kullman, FIGARO: Morelli, BARTOLO: D'Angelo, BASILIO: Pinza, FIORELLO: Oliviero, OFFICER: Jones, BERTHA: Gruninger, CONDUCTOR: Merola.

November 14, matinee: IL TROVATORE (Verdi)
LEONORA: Rethberg, AZUCENA: Castagna, MANRICO: Martinelli, COUNT DI LUNA: Morelli, FERRANDO: D'Angelo, RUIZ: Oliviero, OLD GYPSY: Burr, INEZ: Maschio, CONDUCTOR: Papi.

November 21: DAS RHEINGOLD (Wagner)
WOTAN: Schorr, DONNER: Gandolfi, FROH: George, LOGE: Clemens, ALBERICH: Gabor, MIME: Oliviero, FASOLT: Cordon, FAFNER: List, FRICKA: Manski, FREIA: Merrill, ERDA: O'Dea, WOGLINDE: Kroph, WELLGUNDE: Merrill, FLOSSHILDE: Doe, CONDUCTOR: Riedel.

EXTRA PERFORMANCES

November 15, matinee: CARMEN (Bizet)
Same cast.

November 17: TRISTAN AND ISOLDE (Wagner)
Same cast except: BRANGÄNE: Doe.

November 22, matinee: DIE WALKÜRE (Wagner)
Same cast.

CASTS—1937 SEASON

REGULAR SERIES

October 15: AIDA (Verdi)
AIDA: Cigna, AMNERIS: Castagna, RHADAMES: Martinelli, AMONASRO: Bonelli, RAMFIS: List, KING: Cordon, MESSENGER: Oliviero, PRIESTESS: Balfour, CONDUCTOR: Merola.

October 18: LA BOHÈME (Puccini)
MIMI: Bovy, RODOLFO: Kullman, MARCELLO: Bonelli, COLLINE: Pinza, SCHAUNARD: Cehanovsky, MUSETTA: Boerner, BENOIT: Oliviero, ALCINDORO: Oliver Jones, PARPIGNOL: Mancini, SERGEANT: Alibertini, OFFICER: Lorenzini, CONDUCTOR: Papi.

October 20: UN BALLO IN MASCHERA (Verdi)
AMELIA: Cigna, ULRICA: Castagna, OSCAR: Boerner, RICCARDO: Martinelli, RENATO: Bonelli, SAM: List, TOM: Cordon, SILVANO: Cehanovsky, JUDGE: Oliviero, CONDUCTOR: Papi.

October 25: TRISTAN AND ISOLDE (Wagner)
ISOLDE: Flagstad, BRANGÄNE: Meisle, TRISTAN: Melchior, KING MARKE: Hofmann, KURWENAL: Huehn, MELOT: Cehanovsky, SHEPHERD: Clemens, SAILOR'S VOICE: Clemens, STEERSMAN: Cordon, CONDUCTOR: Reiner.

October 27: MADAMA BUTTERFLY (Puccini)
CIO-CIO-SAN: Tentoni, PINKERTON: Kullman, SHARPLESS: Huehn, SUZUKI: Cornish, GORO: Oliviero, BONZE: Cordon, YAMADORI: Howell, COMMISSIONER: Lorenzini, KATE PINKERTON: Hackett, REGISTRAR: Alibertini, CONDUCTOR: Papi.

October 29: LAKMÉ (Delibes)
LAKMÉ: Pons, GERALD: Maison, FREDERIC: Cehanovsky, NILAKANTHA: Pinza, HADJI: Ferrier, MALLIKA: Beatty, MRS. BENSON: Callahan, ELLEN: Kroph, ROSE: Hackett, CONDUCTOR: Cimini.

November 1: ROMÉO ET JULIETTE (Gounod)
ROMÉO: Maison, JULIETTE: Bovy, MERCUTIO: Askam, TYBALT: Russell, CAPULET: Cordon, FRIAR LAWRENCE: List, GREGORIO: Howell, BENVOGLIO: Oliviero, DUKE OF VERONA: Shefoff, STEPHANO: Green, GERTRUDE: Cornish, CONDUCTOR: Merola.

November 5: LOHENGRIN (Wagner)
ELSA: Flagstad, ORTRUD: Meisle, LOHENGRIN: Melchior, TELRAMUND: Huehn, KING HENRY: Hofmann, HERALD: Cehanovsky, CONDUCTOR: Reiner.

November 8: FIDELIO (Beethoven)
LEONORE: Flagstad, FLORESTAN: Maison, ROCCO: List, DON PIZARRO: Hofmann, DON FERNANDO: Huehn, MARZELLINE: Boerner, JACQUINO: Clemens, PRISONERS: George, Sherrill, CONDUCTOR: Reiner.

November 10: MANON (Massenet)
MANON: Bovy, CHEVALIER DES GRIEUX: Maison, LESCAUT: Bonelli, GUILLOT: Oliviero, DE BRÉTIGNY: Cehanovsky, COUNT DES GRIEUX: Cordon, POUSETTE: Kroph, JAVOTTE: Landan, ROSETTE: Luscombe, INNKEEPER: Ferrier, SERVANT: Robert, GUARDS: Loughery, Bernhard, CONDUCTOR: Cimini.

November 13: NORMA (Bellini)

NORMA: Cigna, ADALGISA: Castagna, POLLIONE: Martinelli, OROVESO: Pinza, FLAVIO: Oliviero, CLOTILDE: Cornish, CONDUCTOR: Merola.

POPULAR SERIES

October 23: FAUST (Gounod)
MARGUERITE: Boerner, FAUST: Martinelli, MEPHISTOPHELES: Pinza, VALENTIN: Askam, WAGNER: Howell, SIEBEL: Beatty, MARTHE: Callahan, CONDUCTOR: Cimini.
October 30: LA TRAVIATA (Verdi)
VIOLETTA: Cigna, ALFREDO: Kullman, GERMONT: Bonelli, GASTON: Oliviero, BARON DOUPHOL: Cehanovsky, MARQUIS D'OBIGNY: Howell, DR. GRENVIL: Cordon, FLORA: Kroph, ANNINA: Hathaway, CONDUCTOR: Merola.
November 6: RIGOLETTO (Verdi)
GILDA: Tumminia, DUKE: Kullman, RIGOLETTO: Bonelli, MADDALENA: Cornish, SPARAFUCILE: Cordon, MONTERONE: Shefoff, BORSA: Oliviero, MARULLO: Cehanovsky, CEPRANO: Alibertini, COUNTESS CEPRANO: Wishart, GIOVANNA: Hackett, PAGE: Cozzens, CONDUCTOR: Papi.

REPEAT SERIES

October 26: AIDA (Verdi)
Same cast except: RAMFIS: Pinza.
October 31, matinee: TRISTAN AND ISOLDE (Wagner)
Same cast.
November 3: LAKMÉ (Delibes)
Same cast.
November 11: LOHENGRIN (Wagner)
Same cast.

CASTS—1938 SEASON

REGULAR SERIES

October 7: ANDREA CHENIER (Giordano)
MADELEINE: Rethberg, ANDREA CHENIER: Gigli, GERARD: Bonelli, MATHIEU: D'Angelo, FLÉVILLE: Howell, ROUCHER: Cehanovsky, DUMAS: Cordon, ABBÉ: Oliviero, SPY: Oliviero, SCHMIDT: Gabor, FOUQUIER-TINVILLE: Gabor, COUNTESS: Doe, MADELON: Doe, BERSI: Kroph, CONDUCTOR: Merola.
October 10: DON GIOVANNI (Mozart)
DONNA ANNA: Rethberg, DONNA ELVIRA: Jessner, ZERLINA: Favero, DON GIOVANNI: Pinza, LEPORELLO: Baccaloni, DON OTTAVIO: Borgioli, COMMENDATORE: Cordon, MASETTO: D'Angelo, CONDUCTOR: Reiner.
October 12: MARTHA (Flotow)
LADY HARRIET: Favero, LIONEL: Gigli, PLUNKETT: D'Angelo, SIR TRISTAN: Baccaloni, SHERIFF: Cordon, NANCY: Doe, MAIDS: Allison, Lawlor, Browne, FARMER: Palumbo, FARMER'S WIFE: Gambi, CONDUCTOR: Papi.
October 14: DIE MEISTERSINGER (Wagner)
EVA: Jessner, MAGDALENA: Thorborg, WALTHER: Kullman, HANS SACHS:

Schorr, POGNER: Gauld, DAVID: Laufkötter, BECKMESSER: Gabor, KOTH-
NER: Huehn, NIGHT WATCHMAN: Cehanovsky, VOGELGESANG: Clemens,
NACHTIGALL: D'Angelo, ZORN: George, EISSLINGER: Oliviero, MOSER:
Hague, ORTEL: Cehanovsky, SCHWARZ: Cordon, FOLTZ: Howell, CONDUC-
TOR: Reiner.

October 17: CAVALLERIA RUSTICANA (Mascagni)
SANTUZZA: Stignani, TURIDDU: Ziliani, ALFIO: Tagliabue, LOLA: Doe,
MAMMA LUCIA: Votipka, CONDUCTOR: Merola.
followed by: DON PASQUALE (Donizetti)
NORINA: Favero, ERNESTO: Borgioli, DR. MALATESTA: Bonelli, DON PASQUALE:
Baccaloni, NOTARY: Oliviero, CONDUCTOR: Papi.

October 19: PELLÉAS ET MÉLISANDE (Debussy)
MÉLISANDE: Micheau, PELLÉAS: Cathelat, GOLAUD: Gauld, ARKEL: D'An-
gelo, GENEVIÈVE: Doe, YNIOLD: Jamison, DOCTOR: Ferrier, CONDUCTOR:
Leinsdorf.

October 21: LUCIA DI LAMMERMOOR (Donizetti)
LUCIA: Pons, LORD HENRY: Tagliabue, EDGARDO: Masini, LORD ARTHUR:
George, RAYMOND: Cordon, ALICE: Votipka, NORMAN: Oliviero, CONDUC-
TOR: Papi.

October 24: ELEKTRA (Strauss)
ELEKTRA: Pauly, CHRYSOTHEMIS: Jessner, KLYTEMNESTRA: Thorborg, AEGIS-
THUS: Laufkötter, ORESTES: Huehn, ORESTES' TUTOR: Cordon, CONFIDANTE:
Markham, TRAINBEARER: Lawlor, YOUNG SERVANT: Clemens, OLD SERVANT:
Youngs, OVERSEER: Ponitz, MAIDSERVANTS: Doe, Kroph, Avakian, Votipka,
Cornish, CONDUCTOR: Reiner.

October 28: LA FORZA DEL DESTINO (Verdi)
LEONORA: Rethberg, DON ALVARO: Gigli, DON CARLO: Bonelli, PADRE
GUARDIANO: Pinza, FRA MELITONE: Baccaloni, PREZIOSILLA: Doe, MARQUIS
OF CALATRAVA: D'Angelo, ALCADE: Howell, TRABUCCO: Oliviero, CURRA:
Votipka, SURGEON: D'Angelo, CONDUCTOR: Papi.

October 31: LA BOHÈME (Puccini)
MIMI: Favero, RODOLFO: Masini, MARCELLO: Tagliabue, COLLINE: Pinza,
SCHAUNARD: Cehanovsky, MUSETTA: Jamison, BENOIT: Oliviero, ALCINDORO:
D'Angelo, PARPIGNOL: Walti, CONDUCTOR: Papi.

November 3: LE COQ D'OR (Rimsky-Korsakoff)
QUEEN: Pons, KING DODON: Pinza, ASTROLOGER: Massue, GENERAL: Cordon,
AMELFA: Doe, VOICE OF COCK: Votipka, CONDUCTOR: Papi.

POPULAR SERIES

October 15: ANDREA CHENIER (Giordano)
Same cast except: GERARD: Tagliabue.
October 22: CAVALLERIA RUSTICANA (Mascagni)
Same cast except: TURIDDU: Masini.
followed by: DON PASQUALE (Donizetti)
Same cast.
October 29: LUCIA DI LAMMERMOOR (Donizetti)
Same cast.

EXTRA PERFORMANCES

October 20: DON GIOVANNI (Mozart)
Same cast.
October 23, matinee: THE BARBER OF SEVILLE (Rossini)
ROSINA: Micheau, COUNT ALMAVIVA: Borgioli, FIGARO: Tagliabue, BARTOLO:
Baccaloni, BASILIO: Cordon, FIORELLO: Oliviero, OFFICER: Oliviero, BERTHA:
Gruninger, CONDUCTOR: Merola.
October 26: DIE MEISTERSINGER (Wagner)
Same cast.
October 30, matinee: ELEKTRA (Strauss)
Same cast.
November 1: LA FORZA DEL DESTINO (Verdi)
Same cast except: DON CARLO: Tagliabue.

CASTS—1939 SEASON

REGULAR SERIES

October 13: MANON (Massenet)
MANON: Sayao, CHEVALIER DES GRIEUX: Schipa, LESCAUT: Bonelli, GUILLOT:
Ferrier, DE BRÉTIGNY: Cehanovsky, COUNT DES GRIEUX: Cordon, GUARDS:
Edwards, Noonan, MAID: Ritter, CONDUCTOR: Merola.
October 17: DIE WALKÜRE (Wagner)
BRÜNNHILDE: Lawrence, SIEGLINDE: Flagstad, FRICKA: Meisle, SIEGMUND:
Melchior, WOTAN: Huehn, HUNDING: Cordon, HELMWIGE: Sharpe, GER-
HILDE: Votipka, ORTLINDE: Ponitz, SIEGRUNE: Paulee, ROSSWEISSE: Browne,
WALTRAUTE: Glaz, GRIMGERDE: Avakian, SCHWERTLEITE: Cornish, CON-
DUCTOR: Leinsdorf.
October 18: MADAMA BUTTERFLY (Puccini)
CIO-CIO-SAN: Novotna, PINKERTON: Bartlett, SHARPLESS: Huehn, SUZUKI:
Glaz, GORO: Oliviero, BONZE: Shiffeler, YAMADORI: Harvey, COMMISSIONER:
Noonan, KATE PINKERTON: Hackett, REGISTRAR: Alibertini, CONDUCTOR:
Papi.
October 20: TRISTAN AND ISOLDE (Wagner)
ISOLDE: Flagstad, BRANGÄNE: Meisle, TRISTAN: Melchior, KING MARKE:
Kipnis, KURWENAL: Huehn, MELOT: Cehanovsky, SHEPHERD: Oliviero,
SAILOR'S VOICE: George, STEERSMAN: D'Angelo, CONDUCTOR: McArthur.
October 23: RIGOLETTO (Verdi)
GILDA: Pons, DUKE: Jagel, RIGOLETTO: Tibbett, MADDALENA: Glaz, SPARA-
FUCILE: Cordon, MONTERONE: Shiffeler, BORSA: Oliviero, MARULLO: Ce-
hanovsky, CEPRANO: Wellman, COUNTESS CEPRANO: Chinn, GIOVANNA:
Votipka, PAGE: Lawlor, CONDUCTOR: Papi.
October 25: LUCIA DI LAMMERMOOR (Donizetti)
LUCIA: Pons, LORD HENRY: Ballarini, EDGARDO: Schipa, LORD ARTHUR:
George, RAYMOND: Cordon, ALICE: Votipka, NORMAN: Oliviero, CONDUC-
TOR: Papi.
October 27: OTELLO (Verdi)

DESDEMONA: Rethberg, OTELLO: Martinelli, IAGO: Tibbett, CASSIO: Oliviero, RODERIGO: Walti, LODOVICO: D'Angelo, MONTANO: Cehanovsky, HERALD: Navarro, EMILIA: Votipka, CONDUCTOR: Merola.

October 30: LA TRAVIATA (Verdi)
VIOLETTA: Novotna, ALFREDO: Martini, GERMONT: Tibbett, GASTON: Oliviero, BARON DOUPHOL: Cehanovsky, MARQUIS D'OBIGNY: Noonan, DR. GRENVIL: D'Angelo, FLORA: Votipka, ANNINA: Ritter, CONDUCTOR: Merola.

November 1: THE BARBER OF SEVILLE (Rossini)
ROSINA: Pons, COUNT ALMAVIVA: Martini: FIGARO: Bonelli, BARTOLO: D'Angelo, BASILIO: Cordon, FIORELLO: Oliviero, OFFICER: Oliviero, BERTHA: Glaz, CONDUCTOR: Papi.

November 3: FIDELIO (Beethoven)
LEONORE: Flagstad, FLORESTAN: Melchior, ROCCIO: Kipnis, DON PIZARRO: Destal, DON FERNANDO: Huehn, MARZELLINE: Boerner, JACQUINO: Clemens, PRISONERS: Walti, Garden, CONDUCTOR: Leinsdorf.

POPULAR SERIES

October 21: I PAGLIACCI (Leoncavallo)
CANIO: Stinson, TONIO: Bonelli, NEDDA: Boerner, SILVIO: Cehanovsky, BEPPE: Oliviero, CONDUCTOR: Merola.
followed by: CAVALLERIA RUSTICANA (Mascagni)
SANTUZZA: Giannini, TURIDDU: Jagel, ALFIO: Cehanovsky, LOLA: Avakian, MAMMA LUCIA: Votipka, CONDUCTOR: Papi.

October 24: DIE WALKÜRE (Wagner)
Same cast except: BRÜNNHILDE: Flagstad, SIEGLINDE: Lawrence, FRICKA: Glaz, WOTAN: Destal, CONDUCTOR: McArthur.

October 29, matinee: RIGOLETTO (Verdi)
Same cast except: MADDALENA: Gaihle.

November 4: IL TROVATORE (Verdi)
LEONORA: Rethberg, AZUCENA: Meisle, MANRICO: Martinelli, COUNT DI LUNA: Bonelli, FERRANDO: Cordon, RUIZ: Oliviero, OLD GYPSY: Alibertini, INEZ: Votipka, CONDUCTOR: Papi.

EXTRA PERFORMANCES

October 31: I PAGLIACCI (Leoncavallo)
Same cast.
followed by: COPPELIA ballet (Delibes)
SWANHILDA: Reed, FRANTZ: W. Christensen, COPPELIUS: Riggins, BURGOMEISTER: Crockett, CONDUCTOR: Van Den Burg.

November 2: TRISTAN AND ISOLDE (Wagner)
Same cast except: BRANGÄNE: Glaz.

YOUNG PEOPLE'S PERFORMANCE

November 3, matinee: MADAMA BUTTERFLY (Puccini)
Same cast except: SHARPLESS: Cehanovsky.

CASTS—1940 SEASON

October 12: THE MARRIAGE OF FIGARO (Mozart)
SUSANNA: Sayao, COUNTESS: Rethberg, CHERUBINO: Stevens, FIGARO: Pinza, COUNT: Brownlee, BARTOLO: Pechner, BASILIO: De Paolis, MARCELLINA: Petina, BARBARINA: Monte, ANTONIO: Cehanovsky, DON CURZIO: Ballagh, CONDUCTOR: Leinsdorf.

October 14: LAKMÉ (Delibes)
LAKMÉ: Pons, GERALD: Jobin, FREDERIC: Cehanovsky, NILAKANTHA: Kipnis, HADJI: Ferrier, MALLIKA: Petina, MRS. BENSON: Votipka, ELLEN: Andreotti, ROSE: Paulee, CONDUCTOR: Merola.

October 16: DER ROSENKAVALIER (Strauss)
MARSCHALLIN: Lehmann, BARON OCHS: Kipnis, OCTAVIAN: Stevens, SOPHIE: Bokor, FANINAL: Olitzki, TENOR: Naya, MARIANNE: Ponitz, VALZACCHI: De Paolis, ANNINA: Sten, POLICE COMMISSIONER: Alvary, NOTARY: Lorenz, LANDLORD: George, MILLINER: Simpson, ANIMAL VENDOR: Lieber, MARSCHALLIN'S MAJORDOMO: George, FANINAL'S MAJOR-DOMO: Walti, ORPHANS: Lawlor, Hackett, Ward, CONDUCTOR: Leinsdorf.

October 18: LA BOHÈME (Puccini)
MIMI: Sayao, RODOLFO: Bjoerling, MARCELLO: Brownlee, COLLINE: Pinza, SCHAUNARD: Cehanovsky, MUSETTA: Bokor, BENOIT: De Paolis, ALCINDORO: Alvary, PARPIGNOL: Walti, SERGEANT: Alibertini, OFFICER: Lorenzini, CONDUCTOR: Papi.

October 21: DON GIOVANNI (Mozart)
DONNA ANNA: Rethberg, DONNA ELVIRA: Zebranska, ZERLINA: Bokor, DON GIOVANNI: Pinza, LEPORELLO: Kipnis, DON OTTAVIO: De Paolis, COMMENDATORE: Alvary, MASETTO: Cehanovsky, CONDUCTOR: Leinsdorf.

October 23: UN BALLO IN MASCHERA (Verdi)
AMELIA: Rethberg, ULRICA: Sten, OSCAR: Bokor, RICCARDO: Bjoerling, RENATO: Bonelli, SAM: Alvary, TOM: Sellon, SILVANO: Cehanovsky, JUDGE: Walti, SERVANT: Garden, CONDUCTOR: Papi.

October 25: CARMEN (Bizet)
CARMEN: Lawrence, MICAELA: Osborne, DON JOSÉ: Jobin, ESCAMILLO: Pinza, ZUNIGA: Alvary, DANCAIRO: Cehanovsky, REMENDADO: De Paolis, MORALES: Noonan, FRASQUITA: Votipka, MERCEDES: Avakian, CONDUCTOR: Merola.

October 28: RIGOLETTO (Verdi)
GILDA: Pons, DUKE: Naya, RIGOLETTO: Weede, MADDALENA: Avakian, SPARAFUCILE: Alvary, MONTERONE: Shiffeler, BORSA: De Paolis, MARULLO: Cehanovsky, CEPRANO: Wellman, COUNTESS CEPRANO: Wishart, GIOVANNA: Votipka, PAGE: Lawlor, CONDUCTOR: Papi.

October 29: AIDA (Verdi)
AIDA: Rethberg, AMNERIS: Sten, RHADAMES: Jagel, AMONASRO: Weede, RAMFIS: Pinza, KING: Alvary, MESSENGER: Walti, PRIESTESS: Ponitz, CONDUCTOR: Papi.

November 1: MANON (Massenet)
MANON: Sayao, CHEVALIER DES GRIEUX: Schipa, LESCAUT: Brownlee,

338

GUILLOT: De Paolis, DE BRÉTIGNY: Cehanovsky, COUNT DES GRIEUX: Alvary, SERVANT: Ritter, GUARDS: Ballagh, Noonan, CONDUCTOR: Merola.

POPULAR SERIES

October 20, matinee: LAKMÉ (Delibes)
Same cast.
October 27, matinee: DER ROSENKAVALIER (Strauss)
Same cast.
October 29: LA BOHÉME (Puccini)
Same cast.
November 2: CARMEN (Bizet)
Same cast.

YOUNG PEOPLE'S PERFORMANCES

October 31, matinee: CARMEN (Bizet)
Same cast.
November 1, matinee: AIDA (Verdi)
Same cast except: AMNERIS: Zebranska, RHADAMES: Stinson.

CASTS—1941 SEASON

REGULAR SERIES

October 13: DON PASQUALE (Donizetti)
NORINA: Sayao, ERNESTO: Perulli, DR. MALATESTA: Brownlee, DON PASQUALE: Baccaloni, NOTARY: Marlowe, CONDUCTOR: Papi.
October 14: DER ROSENKAVALIER (Strauss)
MARSCHALLIN: Lehmann, BARON OCHS: Kipnis, OCTAVIAN: Stevens, SOPHIE: Bokor, FANINAL: Olitzki, TENOR: George, MARIANNE: Ponitz, VALZACCHI: Laufkötter, ANNINA: Petina, POLICE COMMISSIONER: Alvary, NOTARY: Lorenz, LANDLORD: George, MILLINER: Simpson, ANIMAL VENDOR: Lieber, MARSCHALLIN'S MAJOR DOMO: Schoen, FANINAL'S MAJOR DOMO: Walti, ORPHANS: Lawlor, Hersch, Hackett, CONDUCTOR: Leinsdorf.
October 16: THE DAUGHTER OF THE REGIMENT (Donizetti)
MARIE: Pons, TONIO: Jobin, SULPICE: Baccaloni, MARQUISE DE BIRKENFELD: Petina, HORTENSIUS: Alvary, CORPORAL: Cehanovsky, NOTARY: Riggins, PEASANT: Schoen, DUCHESSE DE KRAKENTHORP: Spence, YOUNG DUKE: Thompson, CONDUCTOR: Papi.
October 18: TOSCA (Puccini)
TOSCA: Roman, CAVARADOSSI: Kullman, SCARPIA: Brownlee, SPOLETTA: Marlowe, SACRISTAN: Baccaloni, ANGELOTTI: Alvary, SCIARRONE: Cehanovsky, JAILOR: Lorenz, SHEPHERD: Ritter, CONDUCTOR: Merola.
October 20: MADAMA BUTTERFLY (Puccini)
CIO-CIO-SAN: Albanese, PINKERTON: Jagel, SHARPLESS: Brownlee, SUZUKI: Petina, GORO: Windheim, BONZE: Alvary, YAMADORI: Cehanovsky, COMMISSIONER: Wellman, KATE PINKERTON: Ritter, REGISTRAR: Alibertini, CONDUCTOR: Papi.
October 22: THE BARBER OF SEVILLE (Rossini)
ROSINA: Sayao, COUNT ALMAVIVA: Perulli, FIGARO: Tibbett, BARTOLO: Bac-

caloni, BASILIO: Pinza, FIORELLO: Cehanovsky, OFFICER: Marlowe, BERTHA: Petina, CONDUCTOR: Merola.

October 24: TANNHAÜSER (Wagner)
ELISABETH: Roman, VENUS: Branzell, TANNHAÜSER: Melchior, WOLFRAM: Huehn, LANDGRAVE: Kipnis, WALTHER: Walti, BITEROLF: Hines, HEINRICH: Marlowe, REINMAR: Strelkoff, SHEPHERD: Carroll, PAGES: Spence, Carroll, Avakian, Hopkins, CONDUCTOR: Leinsdorf.

October 27: CARMEN (Bizet)
CARMEN: Swarthout, MICAELA: Albanese, DON JOSÉ: Jobin, ESCAMILLO: Weede, ZUNIGA: Alvary, DANCAIRO: Cehanovsky, REMENDADO: Laufkötter, MORALES: Cehanovsky, FRASQUITA: Votipka, MERCEDES: Avakian, CONDUCTOR: Leinsdorf.

October 29: L'AMORE DEI TRE RE (Montemezzi)
FIORA: Moore, AVITO: Kullman, MANFREDO: Weede, ARCHIBALDO: Pinza, FLAMINIO: Marlowe, YOUTH: Walti, OLD WOMAN: Avakian, YOUNG GIRL: Jurs, SERVANT: Votipka, VOICE: Ritter, CONDUCTOR: Montemezzi.

November 1: SIMON BOCCANEGRA (Verdi)
SIMON BOCCANEGRA: Tibbett, AMELIA: Roman, FIESCO: Pinza, ADORNO: Jagel, PAOLO: Brownlee, PIETRO: Alvary, CAPTAIN: Marlowe, MAIDSERVANT: Votipka, CONDUCTOR: Leinsdorf.

POPULAR SERIES

October 19, matinee: RIGOLETTO (Verdi)
GILDA: Pons, DUKE: Peerce, RIGOLETTO: Tibbett, MADDALENA: Petina, SPARACUFILE: Alvary, MONTERONE: Hines, BORSA: Marlowe, MARULLO: Cehanovsky, CEPRANO: Wellman, COUNTESS CEPRANO: Markham, GIOVANNA: Votipka, PAGE: Lawlor, CONDUCTOR: Papi.

October 23: MADAMA BUTTERFLY (Puccini)
Same cast.

October 28: THE DAUGHTER OF THE REGIMENT (Donizetti)
Same cast.

October 30: TANNHAÜSER (Wagner)
Same cast.

YOUNG PEOPLE'S PERFORMANCES

October 24, 31, matinees: THE BARBER OF SEVILLE (Rossini)
Same cast except: FIGARO: Weede.

CASTS—1942 SEASON

REGULAR SERIES

October 9: AIDA (Verdi)
AIDA: Roman, AMNERIS: Castagna, RHADAMES: Jagel, AMONASRO: Weede, RAMFIS: Pinza, KING: Alvary, MESSENGER: Walti, PRIESTESS: Votipka, CONDUCTOR: Merola.

October 12: THE DAUGHTER OF THE REGIMENT (Donizetti)
MARIE: Pons, TONIO: Jobin, SULPICE: Baccaloni, MARQUISE DE BIRKENFELD:

Petina, HORTENSIUS: Alvary, CORPORAL: Cehanovsky, NOTARY: Riggins, PEASANT: Walti, DUCHESSE DE KRAKENTHORP: Hopkins, YOUNG DUKE: Krauter, CONDUCTOR: Cimara.

October 14: LA TRAVIATA (Verdi)
VIOLETTA: Sayao, ALFREDO: Peerce, GERMONT: Bonelli, GASTON: De Paolis, BARON DOUPHOL: Cehanovsky, MARQUIS D'OBIGNY: Alvary, DR. GRENVIL: Beattie, FLORA: Votipka, ANNINA: Ritter, CONDUCTOR: Cleva.

October 16: THE BARTERED BRIDE (Smetana)
MARIE: Antoine, JENIK: Kullman, KEZAL: Beattie, VASHEK: Windheim, KRUS-CHINA: Cehanovsky, LUDMILA: Votipka, MICHA: Alvary, HATA: Wysor, SPRINGER: Shiffeler, ESMERALDA: Engel, MUFF: Harvey, CONDUCTOR: Herbert.

October 19: CARMEN (Bizet)
CARMEN: Petina, MICAELA: Albanese, DON JOSÉ: Jobin, ESCAMILLO: Brownlee, ZUNIGA: Alvary, DANCAIRO: Cehanovsky, REMENDADO: De Paolis, MORALES: Cehanovsky, FRASQUITA: Votipka, MERCEDES: Carroll, CONDUCTOR: Merola.

October 21: FAUST (Gounod)
MARGUERITE: Albanese, FAUST: Kullman, MEPHISTOPHELES: Pinza, VALENTIN: Brownlee, WAGNER: Cehanovsky, SIEBEL: Osborne, MARTHE: Votipka, CONDUCTOR: Cleva.

October 23: L'AMORE DEI TRE RE (Montemezzi)
FIORA: Tennyson, AVITO: Kullman, MANFREDO: Weede, ARCHIBALDO: Pinza, FLAMINIO: De Paolis, YOUTH: Walti, OLD WOMAN: Wysor, YOUNG GIRL: Lawlor, SERVANT: McCarthy, VOICE: Turner, CONDUCTOR: Montemezzi.

October 26: DIE FLEDERMAUS (Johann Strauss)
ROSALINDA: Bokor, ADELE: Antoine, PRINCE ORLOFSKY: Petina, ALFRED: Marshall, EISENSTEIN: Windheim, FRANK: Beattie, DR. FALKE: Brownlee, DR. BLIND: Alvary, FROSCH: Lockhart, MOLLY: Carroll, IVAN: Marvin, CONDUCTOR: Herbert.

October 28: UN BALLO IN MASCHERA (Verdi)
AMELIA: Roman, ULRICA: Castagna, OSCAR: Bokor, RICCARDO: Jagel, RENATO: Bonelli, SAM: Alvary, TOM: Beattie, SILVANO: Cehanovsky, JUDGE: Walti, SERVANT: Wellman, CONDUCTOR: Cleva.

October 30: LE COQ D'OR (Rimsky-Korsakoff)
QUEEN: Antoine, KING DODON: Baccaloni, ASTROLOGER: De Paolis, GENERAL: Beattie, AMELFA: Wysor, VOICE OF COCK: Votipka, PRINCE GUIDON: Walti, PRINCE AFRON: Palumbo, CONDUCTOR: Merola.

POPULAR SERIES

October 18, matinee: LUCIA DI LAMMERMOOR (Donizetti)
LUCIA: Pons, LORD HENRY: Bonelli, EDGARDO: Peerce, LORD ARTHUR: De Paolis, RAYMOND: Alvary, ALICE: Votipka, NORMAN: Walti, CONDUCTOR: Cimara.

October 25, matinee: AIDA (Verdi)
Same cast.

October 27: THE BARBER OF SEVILLE (Rossini)
ROSINA: Sayao, COUNT ALMAVIVA: Kullman, FIGARO: Brownlee, BARTOLO:

Baccaloni, BASILIO: Pinza, FIORELLO: Cehanovsky, OFFICER: De Paolis, BERTHA: Petina, CONDUCTOR: Cleva.
October 31: FAUST (Gounod)
Same cast.

EXTRA PERFORMANCE
October 22: THE DAUGHTER OF THE REGIMENT (Donizetti) (Auspices France Forever)
Same cast.

CASTS—1943 SEASON

October 7: SAMSON AND DELILAH (Saint-Saens)
SAMSON: Jobin, DELILAH: Thorborg, HIGH PRIEST: Warren, ABIMELECH: Cehanovsky, OLD HEBREW: Alvary, MESSENGER: De Paolis, PHILISTINES: Garris, Wellman, CONDUCTOR: Merola.
October 11: LA FORZA DEL DESTINO (Verdi)
LEONORA: Milanov, DON ALVARO: Jagel, DON CARLO: Warren, PADRE GUARDIANO: Pinza, FRA MELITONE: Baccaloni, PREZIOSILLA: Petina, MARQUIS OF CALATRAVA: Alvary, ALCADE: Alvary, TRABUCCO: De Paolis, CURRA: Votipka, SURGEON: Cehanovsky, CONDUCTOR: Merola.
October 13: CAVALLERIA RUSTICANA (Mascagni)
SANTUZZA: Giannini, TURIDDU: Kullman, ALFIO: Cehanovsky, LOLA: Johnson, MAMMA LUCIA: Votipka, CONDUCTOR: Adler.
followed by: I PAGLIACCI (Leoncavallo)
CANIO: Jobin, TONIO: Thomas, NEDDA: Albanese, SILVIO: Valentino, BEPPE: De Paolis, PEASANTS: Wellman, Mennucci, CONDUCTOR: Cimara.
October 15: LA FANCIULLA DEL WEST (Puccini)
MINNIE: Kirk, DICK JOHNSON: Jagel, JACK RANCE: Weede, JAKE WALLACE: Alexander, NICK: De Paolis, ASHBY: Alvary, SONORA: Cehanovsky, TRIN: Garris, SID: Lorenzini, HANDSOME: Wellman, HARRY: Evans, JOE: Oliver, HAPPY: Lourenzo, LARKENS: Thompson, JOSÉ CASTRO: Goodwin, BILLY JACKRABBIT: Goodwin, WOWKLE: Johnson, CONDUCTOR: Cleva.
October 18: LUCIA DI LAMMERMOOR (Donizetti)
LUCIA: Pons, LORD HENRY: Warren, EDGARDO: Peerce, LORD ARTHUR: Garris, RAYMOND: Alvary, ALICE: Votipka, NORMAN: Evans, CONDUCTOR: Cimara.
October 20: LA BOHÈME (Puccini)
MIMI: Albanese, RODOLFO: Kullman, MARCELLO: Valentino, COLLINE: Pinza, SCHAUNARD: Cehanovsky, MUSETTA: Osborne, BENOIT: Baccaloni, ALCINDORO: Baccaloni, SERGEANT: Alibertini, OFFICER: Lorenzini, CONDUCTOR: Merola.
October 22: IL TROVATORE (Verdi)
LEONORA: Milanov, AZUCENA: Thorborg, MANRICO: Baum, COUNT DI LUNA: Weede, FERRANDO: Silva, RUIZ: Garris, OLD GYPSY: Guenter, INEZ: Votipka, CONDUCTOR: Cleva.
October 25: RIGOLETTO (Verdi)

GILDA: Pons, DUKE: Peerce, RIGOLETTO: Petroff, MADDALENA: Johnson, SPARAFUCILE: Alvary, MONTERONE: London (Burnson), BORSA: De Paolis, MARULLO: Cehanovsky, CEPRANO: Wellman, COUNTESS CEPRANO: Markham, GIOVANNA: Votipka, PAGE: Lawlor, CONDUCTOR: Cimara.

October 27: DON GIOVANNI (Mozart)
DONNA ANNA: Milanov, DONNA ELVIRA: Kirk, ZERLINA: Albanese, DON GIOVANNI: Pinza, LEPORELLO: Baccaloni, DON OTTAVIO: Kullman, COMMENDATORE: Silva, MASETTO: Alvary, CONDUCTOR: Beecham.

October 29: DON PASQUALE (Donizetti)
NORINA: Albanese, ERNESTO: Garris, DR. MALATESTA: Petroff, DON PASQUALE: Baccaloni, NOTARY: De Paolis, CONDUCTOR: Cimara.

POPULAR SERIES

October 10, matinee: LA TRAVIATA (Verdi)
VIOLETTA: Albanese, ALFREDO: Kullman, GERMONT: Valentino, GASTON: De Paolis, BARON DOUPHOL: Cehanovsky, MARQUIS D'OBIGNY: Lorenzini, DR. GRENVIL: Alvary, FLORA: Votipka, ANNINA: Lawlor, CONDUCTOR: Cleva.

October 17, matinee: LA FORZA DEL DESTINO (Verdi)
Same cast except: DON ALVARO: Baum.

October 24: CARMEN (Bizet)
CARMEN: Petina, MICAELA: Gonzales, DON JOSÉ: Jobin, ESCAMILLO: Pinza, ZUNIGA: Alvary, DANCAIRO: Cehanovsky, REMENDADO: De Paolis, MORALES: Cehanovsky, FRASQUITA: Votipka, MERCEDES: Johnson, CONDUCTOR: Beecham.

October 28: RIGOLETTO (Verdi)
Same cast except: RIGOLETTO: Thomas.

October 30: CAVALLERIA RUSTICANA (Mascagni)
Same cast except: TURIDDU: Baum.
    followed by: I PAGLIACCI (Leoncavallo)
Same cast except: TONIO: Weede.

EXTRA PERFORMANCES

October 24, matinee: LA BOHÈME (Puccini)
Same cast except: COLLINE: Silva.

October 26: SAMSON AND DELILAH (Saint-Saens)
Same cast except: ABIMELECH: Silva.

CASTS—1944 SEASON

REGULAR SERIES

September 29: AIDA (Verdi)
AIDA: Roman, AMNERIS: Harshaw, RHADAMES: Jagel, AMONASRO: Warren, RAMFIS: Pinza, KING: Alvary, MESSENGER: De Paolis, PRIESTESS: Votipka, CONDUCTOR: Merola.

October 3: MARTHA (Flotow)
LADY HARRIET: Albanese, LIONEL: Landi, PLUNKETT: Alvary, SIR TRISTAN: Baccaloni, SHERIFF: Goodwin, NANCY: Glaz, MAIDS: Gianopulos, Lawlor,

Levon, FARMER: Martin, FARMER'S WIFE: Gambi, LACKEYS: Wahlin, Guenter, Doan, Albert Vannucci, CONDUCTOR: Merola.

October 6: LAKMÉ (Delibes)
LAKMÉ: Pons, GERALD: Jobin, FREDERIC: Cehanovsky, NILAKANTHA: Silva, HADJI: Garris, MALLIKA: Glaz, MRS. BENSON: Votipka, ELLEN: Karpelenia, ROSE: Avakian, A SEPOY: De Lugg, CHINESE VENDOR: Tallone, ASTROLOGER: Martin, CONDUCTOR: Cimara.

October 10: MANON (Massenet)
MANON: Albanese, CHEVALIER DES GRIEUX: Kullman, LESCAUT: Valentino, GUILLOT: De Paolis, DE BRÉTIGNY: Cehanovsky, COUNT DES GRIEUX: Alvary, SERVANT: Levon, GUARDS: Bernhard, Wellman, CONDUCTOR: Cimara.

October 13: THE SECRET OF SUZANNE (Wolf-Ferrari)
COUNTESS SUZANNE: MacWatters, COUNT GIL: Thompson, SANTE: De Paolis, CONDUCTOR: Adler.

followed by: SALOME (Strauss)
SALOME: Djanel, HEROD: Jagel, JOCHANAAN: Shafer, HERODIAS: Harshaw, NARRABOTH: Garris, PAGE: Glaz, SOLDIERS: Cehanovsky, Wellman, NAZARENES: Alvary, Nelson, JEWS: Garris, Berton, De Paolis, Tissier, Goodwin, SLAVE: Heitman, CAPPADOCIAN: Sanders, HENCHMAN: Anderson, CONDUCTOR: Sebastian.

October 16: FALSTAFF (Verdi)
SIR JOHN FALSTAFF: Baccaloni, MISTRESS FORD: Della Chiesa, MISTRESS PAGE: Glaz, DAME QUICKLY: Harshaw, ANNE: Albanese, FENTON: Landi, FORD: Petroff, DR. CAIUS: Garris, BARDOLPH: De Paolis, PISTOL: Alvary, CONDUCTOR: Steinberg.

October 18: FAUST (Gounod)
MARGUERITE: Della Chiesa, FAUST: Jobin, MEPHISTOPHELES: Pinza, VALENTIN: Warren, WAGNER: Cehanovsky, SIEBEL: Glaz, MARTHE: Votipka, CONDUCTOR: Steinberg.

October 20: UN BALLO IN MASCHERA (Verdi)
AMELIA: Roman, ULRICA: Harshaw, OSCAR: MacWatters, RICCARDO: Peerce, RENATO: Warren, SAM: Alvary, TOM: Goodwin, SILVANO: Cehanovsky, JUDGE: Tallone, SERVANT: Lorenzini, CONDUCTOR: Steinberg.

October 24: THE TALES OF HOFFMANN (Offenbach)
HOFFMANN: Jobin, OLYMPIA: MacWatters, GIULIETTA: Djanel, ANTONIA: Albanese, COPPELIUS: Pinza, DAPERTUTTO: Valentino, DR. MIRACLE: Pinza, NICKLAUSSE: Glaz, VOICE OF ANTONIA'S MOTHER: Turner, SPALANZANI: De Paolis, SCHLEMIL: Cehanovsky, CRESPEL: Alvary, FRANTZ: De Paolis, COCHENILLE: Garris, PITICHINACCIO: Garris, NATHANAEL: Tissier, HERMANN: Wellman, LUTHER: Sanders, CONDUCTOR: Merola.

October 27: CARMEN (Bizet)
CARMEN: Stevens, MICAELA: MacWatters, DON JOSÉ: Kullman, ESCAMILLO: Valentino, ZUNIGA: Alvary, DANCAIRO: Cehanovsky, REMENDADO: De Paolis, MORALES: Cehanovsky, FRASQUITA: Votipka, MERCEDES: Avakian, CONDUCTOR: Sebastian.

POPULAR SERIES

October 5: LA BOHÈME (Puccini)
MIMI: Albanese, RODOLFO: Kullman, MARCELLO: Valentino, COLLINE: Pinza,

344

SCHAUNARD: Cehanovsky, MUSETTA: MacWatters, BENOIT: Baccaloni, AL-CINDORO: Baccaloni, SERGEANT: Alibertini, OFFICER: Lorenzini, CONDUC-TOR: Merola.

October 11: LUCIA DI LAMMERMOOR (Donizetti)
LUCIA: Pons, LORD HENRY: Petroff, EDGARDO: Peerce, LORD ARTHUR: Garris, RAYMOND: Alvary, ALICE: Votipka, NORMAN: Tissier, CONDUCTOR: Cimara.

October 15, matinee: AIDA (Verdi)
Same cast.

October 19: THE SECRET OF SUZANNE (Wolf-Ferrari)
Same cast.

followed by: SALOME (Strauss)

Same cast.

October 26: FALSTAFF (Verdi)
Same cast.

EXTRA PERFORMANCES

October 1, matinee: LA FORZA DEL DESTINO (Verdi)
LEONORA: Roman, DON ALVARO: Jagel, DON CARLO: Warren, PADRE GUAR-DIANO: Pinza, FRA MELITONE: Baccaloni, PREZIOSILLA: Glaz, MARQUIS OF CALATRAVA: Alvary, ALCADE: Alvary, TRABUCCO: De Paolis, CURRA: Votipka, SURGEON: Cehanovsky, CONDUCTOR: Merola.

October 8, matinee: MARTHA (Flotow)
Same cast, CONDUCTOR: Riedel.

October 17: RIGOLETTO (Verdi)
GILDA: Pons, DUKE: Peerce, RIGOLETTO: Warren, MADDALENA: Glaz, SPAR-AFUCILE: Silva, MONTERONE: Alvary, BORSA: De Paolis, MARULLO: Cehanovsky, CEPRANO: Wellman, COUNTESS CEPRANO: Markham, GIOVANNA: Votipka, PAGE: Lawlor, CONDUCTOR: Cimara.

October 22, matinee: MANON (Massenet)
Same cast.

October 28: THE TALES OF HOFFMANN (Offenbach)
Same cast.

CASTS—1945 SEASON

REGULAR SERIES

September 25: CARMEN (Bizet)
CARMEN: Stevens, MICAELA: Steber, DON JOSÉ: Jobin, ESCAMILLO: Harrell, ZUNIGA: Olitzki, DANCAIRO: Cehanovsky, REMENDADO: De Paolis, MORALES: Cehanovsky, FRASQUITA: Votipka, MERCEDES: Turner, CONDUCTOR: Merola.

September 28: LA BOHÈME (Puccini)
MIMI: Albanese, RODOLFO: Kullman, MARCELLO: Harrell, COLLINE: Pinza, SCHAUNARD: Cehanovsky, MUSETTA: Conner, BENOIT: Baccaloni, ALCIN-DORO: Baccaloni, SERGEANT: Alibertini, OFFICER: Lorenzini, CONDUCTOR: Merola.

October 2: DER ROSENKAVALIER (Strauss)

MARSCHALLIN: Lehmann, BARON OCHS: Alvary, OCTAVIAN: Stevens, SO-
PHIE: Steber, FANINAL: Olitzki, TENOR: Landi, MARIANNE: Votipka, VAL-
ZACCHI: De Paolis, ANNINA: Glaz, POLICE COMMISSIONER: Harrell, NOTARY:
Goodwin, LANDLORD: Garris, MILLINER: King, ANIMAL VENDOR: Lieber,
MARSCHALLIN'S MAJOR DOMO: Tissier, FANINAL'S MAJOR DOMO: Tallone,
ORPHANS: Lawlor, Hersch, Sanderson, FOOTMEN: Guenter, Tallone, Mac-
Kay, Williams, CONDUCTOR: Sebastian.

October 5: TRISTAN AND ISOLDE (Wagner)

ISOLDE: Traubel, BRANGÄNE: Glaz, TRISTAN: Melchior, KING MARKE: Alvary,
KURWENAL: Janssen, MELOT: Olitzki, SHEPHERD: Garris, SAILOR'S VOICE:
Garris, STEERSMAN: Goodwin, CONDUCTOR: Steinberg.

October 9: DIE WALKÜRE (Wagner)

BRÜNNHILDE: Traubel, SIEGLINDE: Djanel, FRICKA: Harshaw, SIEGMUND:
Melchior, WOTAN: Janssen, HUNDING: Alvary, HELMWIGE: Ragusa, GER-
HILDE: Votipka, ORTLINDE: Demers, SIEGRUNE: Glaz, ROSSWEISSE: Ander-
son, WALTRAUTE: Calcagno, GRIMGERDE: Turner, SCHWERTLEITE: Harshaw,
CONDUCTOR: Steinberg.

October 12: BORIS GODOUNOFF (Moussorgsky)

BORIS: Pinza, DIMITRI: Jagel, MARINA: Della Chiesa, PIMEN: Alvary, SHOU-
ISKY: De Paolis, VARLAAM: Baccaloni, MISSAIL: Nystrom, TCHELKALOFF:
Cehanovsky, FEODOR: Glaz, XENIA: Castellani, NURSE: Harshaw, INN-
KEEPER: Turner, SIMPLETON: Garris, POLICE OFFICER: Mills, FRONTIER
GUARD SERGEANT: Spelvinski, BOYAR-IN-WAITING: Tissier, LOVITZKY: Good-
win, TCHERNIAKOVSKY: Mills, BOYAR: Lieber, PEASANTS: Bruni, Calcagno,
Martin, Lourenzo, CONDUCTOR: Sebastian.

October 16: DON GIOVANNI (Mozart)

DONNA ANNA: Roman, DONNA ELVIRA: Della Chiesa, ZERLINA: Albanese,
DON GIOVANNI: Pinza, LEPORELLO: Baccaloni, DON OTTAVIO: Landi, COM-
MENDATORE: Mills, MASETTO: Harrell, CONDUCTOR: Steinberg.

October 19: LUCIA DI LAMMERMOOR (Donizetti)

LUCIA: Pons, LORD HENRY: Petroff, EDGARDO: Peerce, LORD ARTHUR:
Garris, RAYMOND: Alvary, ALICE: Votipka, NORMAN: Tallone, CONDUCTOR:
Cimara.

October 23: THE SPANISH HOUR (Ravel)

CONCEPCION: Albanese, GONZALVE: Garris, TORQUEMADA: De Paolis,
RAMIRO: Harrell, DON INIGO GOMEZ: Baccaloni, CONDUCTOR: Merola.

followed by: SALOME (Strauss)

SALOME: Djanel, HEROD: Jagel, JOCHANAAN: Janssen, HERODIAS: Harshaw,
NARRABOTH: Garris, PAGE: Glaz, SOLDIERS: Cehanovsky, Mills, NAZARENES:
Alvary, Nelson, JEWS: Tallone, Nystrom, De Paolis, Tissier, Goodwin,
SLAVE: Heitman, CAPPADOCIAN: Sanders, HENCHMAN: Galt, CONDUCTOR:
Sebastian.

October 26: RIGOLETTO (Verdi)

GILDA: Pons, DUKE: Peerce, RIGOLETTO: Petroff, MADDALENA: Glaz, SPARA-
FUCILE: Alvary, MONTERONE: Mills, BORSA: De Paolis, MARULLO: Cehanov-
sky, CEPRANO: Nelson, COUNTESS CEPRANO: Calcagno, GIOVANNA: Ragusa,
PAGE: Lawlor, CONDUCTOR: Cimara.

POPULAR SERIES

October 4: THE TALES OF HOFFMANN (Offenbach)
HOFFMANN: Jobin, OLYMPIA: Corvello, GIULIETTA: Djanel, ANTONIA: Albanese, COPPELIUS: Pinza, DAPERTUTTO: Valentino, DR. MIRACLE: Pinza, NICKLAUSSE: Glaz, VOICE OF ANTONIA'S MOTHER: Turner, SPALANZANI: De Paolis, SCHLEMIL: Olitzki, CRESPEL: Alvary, FRANTZ: De Paolis, COCHENILLE: Garris, PITICHINACCIO: Garris, NATHANAEL: Tissier, HERMANN: Mills, LUTHER: Sanders, CONDUCTOR: Merola.
October 11: CARMEN (Bizet)
Same cast.
October 18: DER ROSENKAVALIER (Strauss)
Same cast except: SOPHIE: Conner.
October 22: BORIS GODOUNOFF (Moussorgsky)
Same cast.
October 25: DON GIOVANNI (Mozart)
Same cast except: DONNA ELVIRA: Steber, ZERLINA: Conner, MASETTO: Alvary.

EXTRA PERFORMANCES

September 30, matinee: LA TRAVIATA (Verdi)
VIOLETTA: Albanese, ALFREDO: Kullman, GERMONT: Valentino, GASTON: De Paolis, BARON DOUPHOL: Cehanovsky, MARQUIS D'OBIGNY: Olitzki, DR. GRENVIL: Goodwin, FLORA: Ragusa, ANNINA: Lawlor, CONDUCTOR: Merola.
October 7, matinee: CAVALLERIA RUSTICANA (Mascagni)
SANTUZZA: Della Chiesa, TURIDDU: Kullman, ALFIO: Petroff, LOLA: Glaz, MAMMA LUCIA: Votipka, CONDUCTOR: Adler.
   followed by: I PAGLIACCI (Leoncavallo)
CANIO: Jobin, TONIO: Valentino, NEDDA: Albanese, SILVIO: Harrell, BEPPE: De Paolis, PEASANTS: Sanders, Tallone, CONDUCTOR: Adler.
October 14, matinee: TRISTAN AND ISOLDE (Wagner)
Same cast except: BRANGÄNE: Harshaw.
October 17: LA TRAVIATA (Verdi)
Same cast, CONDUCTOR: Cimara.
October 21, matinee: THE BARBER OF SEVILLE (Rossini)
ROSINA: Reggiani, COUNT ALMAVIVA: Landi, FIGARO: Valentino, BARTOLO: Baccaloni, BASILIO: Pinza, FIORELLO: De Paolis, OFFICER: Tallone, BERTHA: Turner, CONDUCTOR: Cimara.
October 24: LA BOHÈME (Puccini)
Same cast except: MIMI: Della Chiesa, MARCELLO: Valentino.
October 27: AIDA (Verdi)
AIDA: Roman, AMNERIS: Harshaw, RHADAMES: Jagel, AMONASRO: Petroff, RAMFIS: Pinza, KING: Alvary, MESSENGER: De Paolis, PRIESTESS: Votipka, CONDUCTOR: Kritz.

CASTS—1946 SEASON

REGULAR SERIES

September 17: LOHENGRIN (Wagner)

ELSA: Varnay, ORTRUD: Harshaw, LOHENGRIN: Svanholm, TELRAMUND: Czaplicki, KING HENRY: Moscona, HERALD: Harrell, PAGES: Zubiri, Connors, Sanderson, Hessling, CONDUCTOR: Steinberg.

September 20: LA TRAVIATA (Verdi)
VIOLETTA: Albanese, ALFREDO: Peerce, GERMONT: Valentino, GASTON: De Paolis, BARON DOUPHOL: Cehanovsky, MARQUIS D'OBIGNY: Olitzki, DR. GRENVIL: Ligeti, FLORA: Votipka, ANNINA: Lawlor, CONDUCTOR: Merola.

September 24: ROMÉO ET JULIETTE (Gounod)
ROMÉO: Jobin, JULIETTE: Sayao, MERCUTIO: Brownlee, TYBALT: De Paolis, CAPULET: Schon, FRIAR LAWRENCE: Moscona, GREGORIO: Harvey, BENVOGLIO: Tissier, DUKE OF VERONA: Ligeti, STEPHANO: Knapp, GERTRUDE: Votipka, CONDUCTOR: Breisach.

September 27: BORIS GODOUNOFF (Moussorgsky)
BORIS: Pinza, DIMITRI: Berini, MARINA: Glaz, PIMEN: Alvary, SHOUISKY: De Paolis, VARLAAM: Baccaloni, MISSAIL: Tissier, TCHELKALOFF: Cehanovsky, FEODOR: Knapp, XENIA: Demers, NURSE: Harshaw, INNKEEPER: Repp, SIMPLETON: Garris, POLICE OFFICER: Ligeti, FRONTIER GUARD SERGEANT: Schon, BOYAR-IN-WAITING: Tallone, LOVITZKY: Ligeti, TCHERNIAKOVSKY: Olitzki, BOYAR: Rooney, PEASANTS: Bruni, Calcagno, Martin, Lourenzo, CONDUCTOR: Sebastian.

October 1: LAKMÉ (Delibes)
LAKMÉ: Pons, GERALD: Jobin, FREDERIC: Cehanovsky, NILAKANTHA: Moscona, HADJI: Garris, MALLIKA: Glaz, MRS. BENSON: Votipka, ELLEN: Zubiri, ROSE: Knapp, A SEPOY: Doan, CHINESE VENDOR: Tallone, ASTROLOGER: Martin, CONDUCTOR: Cimara.

October 3: LA FORZA DEL DESTINO (Verdi)
LEONORA: Roman, DON ALVARO: Baum, DON CARLO: Valentino, PADRE GUARDIANO: Pinza, FRA MELITONE: Baccaloni, PREZIOSILLA: Glaz, MARQUIS OF CALATRAVA: Alvary, ALCADE: Ligeti, TRABUCCO: De Paolis, CURRA: Votipka, SURGEON: Cehanovsky, CONDUCTOR: Merola.

October 8: DER ROSENKAVALIER (Strauss)
MARSCHALLIN: Lehmann, BARON OCHS: Alvary, OCTAVIAN: Novotna, SOPHIE: Conner, FANINAL: Olitzki, TENOR: Baum, MARIANNE: Votipka, VALZACCHI: De Paolis, ANNINA: Glaz, POLICE COMMISSIONER: Harrell, NOTARY: Harvey, LANDLORD: Garris, MILLINER: King, ANIMAL VENDOR: Daneluz, MARSCHALLIN'S MAJOR DOMO: Tissier, FANINAL'S MAJOR DOMO: Tallone, ORPHANS: Lawlor, Sanderson, Calcagno, FOOTMEN: Guenter, Tallone, Lawrence, E. Vannucci, CONDUCTOR: Sebastian.

October 11: FIDELIO (Beethoven)
LEONORE: Resnik, FLORESTAN: Berini, ROCCO: Alvary, DON PIZARRO: Schon, DON FERNANDO: Harrell, MARZELLINE: Conner, JACQUINO: Garris, PRISONERS: Nesbitt, Harvey, CONDUCTOR: Breisach.

October 15: MADAMA BUTTERFLY (Puccini)
CIO-CIO-SAN: Albanese, PINKERTON: Kullman, SHARPLESS: Brownlee, SUZUKI: Glaz, GORO: De Paolis, BONZE: Alvary, YAMADORI: Cehanovsky, COMMISSIONER: Olitzki, KATE PINKERTON: Eloise Farrell, REGISTRAR: Harvey, CONDUCTOR: Merola.

October 18: THE MARRIAGE OF FIGARO (Mozart)

SUSANNA: Sayao, COUNTESS: Roman, CHERUBINO: Novotna, FIGARO: Pinza, COUNT: Brownlee, BARTOLO: Baccaloni, BASILIO: De Paolis, MARCELLINA: Glaz, BARBARINA: Zubiri, ANTONIO: Ligeti, DON CURZIO: Garris, PEASANT GIRLS: Demers, Viti, CONDUCTOR: Steinberg.

POPULAR SERIES

September 19: CARMEN (Bizet)
CARMEN: Djanel, MICAELA: Conner, DON JOSÉ: Jobin, ESCAMILLO: Czaplicki, ZUNIGA: Alvary, DANCAIRO: Cehanovsky, REMENDADO: De Paolis, MORALES: Cehanovsky, FRASQUITA: Votipka, MERCEDES: Glaz, CONDUCTOR: Breisach.
September 26: LA BOHÈME (Puccini)
MIMI: Sayao, RODOLFO: Kullman, MARCELLO: Valentino, COLLINE: Pinza, SCHAUNARD: Cehanovsky, MUSETTA: Sa Earp, BENOIT: Baccaloni, ALCIN-DORO: Baccaloni, SERGEANT: Lorenzini, OFFICER: E. Vannucci, CONDUCTOR: Merola.
October 2: LOHENGRIN (Wagner)
Same cast.
October 10: LUCIA DI LAMMERMOOR (Donizetti)
LUCIA: Pons, LORD HENRY: Petroff, EDGARDO: Peerce, LORD ARTHUR: Tissier, RAYMOND: Alvary, ALICE: Votipka, NORMAN: Tallone, CONDUCTOR: Cimara.
October 17: FIDELIO (Beethoven)
Same cast.

EXTRA PERFORMANCES

September 22, matinee: DON PASQUALE (Donizetti)
NORINA: Albanese, ERNESTO: Garris, DR. MALATESTA: Brownlee, DON PAS-QUALE: Baccaloni, NOTARY: De Paolis, CONDUCTOR: Kritz.
September 29, matinee: CARMEN (Bizet)
Same cast except: MICAELA: George, ESCAMILLO: Harrell, ZUNIGA: Olitzki.
September 30: LA TRAVIATA (Verdi)
Same cast except: GERMONT: Harrell.
October 6, matinee: LAKMÉ (Delibes)
Same cast.
October 7: BORIS GODOUNOFF (Moussorgsky)
Same cast.
October 13, matinee: DER ROSENKAVALIER (Strauss)
Same cast except: TENOR: Nesbitt, LANDLORD: Tallone.
October 14: LA BOHÈME (Puccini)
Same cast except: MIMI: Roman, RODOLFO: Bjoerling, MARCELLO: Harrell, COLLINE: Moscona, CONDUCTOR: Cimara.
October 16: IL TROVATORE (Verdi)
LEONORA: Roman, AZUCENA: Harshaw, MANRICO: Bjoerling, COUNT DI LUNA: Valentino, FERRANDO: Moscona, RUIZ: Tissier, OLD GYPSY: E. Vannucci, INEZ: Viti, CONDUCTOR: Adler.
October 19: RIGOLETTO (Verdi)
GILDA: Pons, DUKE: Peerce, RIGOLETTO: Tibbett, MADDALENA: Knapp, SPARAFUCILE: Alvary, MONTERONE: Ligeti, BORSA: Tissier, MARULLO:

Cehanovsky, CEPRANO: Harvey, COUNTESS CEPRANO: Heitman, GIOVANNA: Calcagno, PAGE: Lawlor, CONDUCTOR: Cimara.
October 20, matinee: MADAMA BUTTERFLY (Puccini)
Same cast.

YOUNG PEOPLE'S PERFORMANCES

October 4, matinee: CARMEN (Bizet)
Same cast except: MICAELA: George, ZUNIGA: Olitzki, MERCEDES: Knapp.
October 11, matinee: DON PASQUALE (Donizetti)
Same cast except: DR. MALATESTA: Valentino.

CASTS—1947 SEASON

REGULAR SERIES

September 16: LA TRAVIATA (Verdi)
VIOLETTA: Albanese, ALFREDO: Peerce, GERMONT: Warren, GASTON: De Paolis, BARON DOUPHOL: Cehanovsky, MARQUIS D'OBIGNY: Olitzki, DR. GRENVIL: Ligeti, FLORA: Votipka, ANNINA: Lawlor, CONDUCTOR: Merola.
September 19: DON GIOVANNI (Mozart)
DONNA ANNA: Roman, DONNA ELVIRA: Quartararo, ZERLINA: Albanese, DON GIOVANNI: Pinza, LEPORELLO: Baccaloni, DON OTTAVIO: Kullman, COMMENDATORE: Ligeti, MASETTO: Alvary, CONDUCTOR: Breisach.
September 22: MADAMA BUTTERFLY (Puccini)
CIO-CIO-SAN: Albanese, PINKERTON: Peerce, SHARPLESS: Valentino, SUZUKI: Glaz, GORO: De Paolis, BONZE: Alvary, YAMADORI: Cehanovsky, COMMISSIONER: Olitzki, KATE PINKERTON: Votipka, REGISTRAR: Harvey, CONDUCTOR: Cimara.
September 26: GÖTTERDÄMMERUNG (Wagner)
BRÜNNHILDE: Traubel, SIEGFRIED: Svanholm, GUNTHER: Czaplicki, GUTRUNE: Resnik, HAGEN: Alvary, ALBERICH: Olitzki, WALTRAUTE: Harshaw, NORNS: Glaz, Turner, Votipka, WOGLINDE: Hartzell, WELLGUNDE: Popper, FLOSSHILDE: Glaz, VASSALS: Guenter, Benson, Daneluz, CONDUCTOR: Steinberg.
September 30: LA GIOCONDA (Ponchielli)
LA GIOCONDA: Roman, LAURA: Thebom, LA CIECA: Harshaw, ENZO: Baum, BARNABA: Warren, ALVISE: Moscona, ZUANE: Benson, ISEPO: Tallone, PILOT: Nelson, MONK: Ligeti, CANTOR: McVey, VOICES: Alibertini, Tallone, CONDUCTOR: Marzollo.
October 3: LOUISE (Charpentier)
LOUISE: Kirsten, JULIEN: Jobin, MOTHER: Turner, FATHER: Pinza, RAGPICKER: Lazzari, JUNKMAN: Ligeti, YOUNG RAGPICKER: Baldwin, STREET SWEEPER: Turnbull, NEWSPAPER GIRL: Hessling, MILKWOMAN: Browne, COALPICKER: Spry, STREET ARAB: Zubiri, BIRDFOOD VENDOR: Bish, ARTICHOKE VENDOR: Votipka, WATERCRESS VENDOR: Popper, CHAIR MENDER: Popper, OLD CLOTHES MAN: Tallone, GREEN PEA VENDOR: Daneluz, CARROT VENDOR: Nesbitt, RAG VENDOR: Cehanovsky, POLICEMEN: Harvey, Lorenzini, NOCTAMBULIST: De Paolis, KING OF FOOLS: De Paolis, SONG WRITER: Cehanovsky, PHILOSOPHERS: Olitzki, Martin, PAINTER: Davis,

SCULPTOR: McVey, POET: Lawrence, STUDENT: Schmidling, IRMA: Hartzell, CAMILLE: Gray, GERTRUDE: Popper, APPRENTICE: Zubiri, ELISE: Coryell, BLANCHE: Phillips, SUZANNE: Lawlor, FOREWOMAN: Heitman, MAR-
GUERITE: Campbell, MADELEINE: Harper, CONDUCTOR: Breisach.

October 7: OTELLO (Verdi)
DESDEMONA: Albanese, OTELLO: Svanholm, IAGO: Tibbett, CASSIO: De
Paolis, RODERIGO: Chabay, LODOVICO: Lazzari, MONTANO: Cehanovsky,
HERALD: Nelson, EMILIA: Votipka, CONDUCTOR: Steinberg.

October 10: PELLÉAS ET MÉLISANDE (Debussy)
MÉLISANDE: Sayao, PELLÉAS: Singher, GOLAUD: Tibbett, ARKEL: Alvary,
GENEVIÈVE: Harshaw, YNIOLD: Zubiri, DOCTOR: Ligeti, CONDUCTOR: Pelle-
tier.

October 14: L'AMORE DEI TRE RE (Montemezzi)
FIORA: Kirsten, AVITO: Kullman, MANFREDO: Weede, ARCHIBALDO: Pinza,
FLAMINIO: De Paolis, YOUTH: Nesbitt, OLD WOMAN: Turner, YOUNG
GIRL: Lawlor, SERVANT: Turnbull, VOICE: Baldwin, CONDUCTOR: Mon-
temezzi.

October 17: LUCIA DI LAMMERMOOR (Donizetti)
LUCIA: Tumminia, LORD HENRY: Valentino, EDGARDO: Peerce, LORD AR-
THUR: Chabay, RAYMOND: Alvary, ALICE: Votipka, NORMAN: Tallone, CON-
DUCTOR: Cimara.

POPULAR SERIES

September 18: ROMÉO ET JULIETTE (Gounod)
ROMÉO: Jobin, JULIETTE: Sayao, MERCUTIO: Singher, TYBALT: De Paolis,
CAPULET: Ligeti, FRIAR LAWRENCE: Moscona, GREGORIO: Harvey, BEN-
VOGLIO: Tallone, DUKE OF VERONA: Cehanovsky, STEPHANO: Glaz, GER-
TRUDE: Turner, CONDUCTOR: Pelletier.

September 25: AIDA (Verdi)
AIDA: Roman, AMNERIS: Thebom, RHADAMES: Baum, AMONASRO: Warren,
RAMFIS: Moscona, KING: Alvary, MESSENGER: Chabay, PRIESTESS: Votipka,
CONDUCTOR: Breisach.

October 2: TRISTAN AND ISOLDE (Wagner)
ISOLDE: Traubel, BRANGÄNE: Thebom, TRISTAN: Svanholm, KING MARKE:
Alvary, KURWENAL: Czaplicki, MELOT: Olitzki, SHEPHERD: Chabay, SAIL-
OR'S VOICE: Chabay, STEERSMAN: Ligeti, CONDUCTOR: Steinberg.

October 9: GÖTTERDÄMMERUNG (Wagner)
Same cast.

October 16: LA GIOCONDA (Ponchielli)
Same cast except: LA GIOCONDA: Resnik.

EXTRA PERFORMANCES

September 21, matinee: FAUST (Gounod)
MARGUERITE: Claudia Pinza, FAUST: Jobin, MEPHISTOPHELES: Pinza, VALEN-
TIN: Valdengo, WAGNER: Cehanovsky, SIEBEL: Glaz, MARTHE: Turner,
CONDUCTOR: Pelletier.

September 28, matinee: LA BOHÈME (Puccini)
MIMI: Sayao, RODOLFO: Peerce, MARCELLO: Valentino, COLLINE: Moscona,

SCHAUNARD: Cehanovsky, MUSETTA: Hartzell, BENOIT: Baccaloni, ALCIN-
DORO: Baccaloni, PARPIGNOL: Tallone, SERGEANT: Lorenzini, OFFICER:
E. Vannucci, CONDUCTOR: Merola.

October 5, matinee: THE MARRIAGE OF FIGARO (Mozart)
SUSANNA: Sayao, COUNTESS: Quartararo, CHERUBINO: Thebom, FIGARO:
Pinza, COUNT: Singher, BARTOLO: Baccaloni, BASILIO: De Paolis, MAR-
CELLINA: Glaz, BARBARINA: Zubiri, ANTONIO: Ligeti, DON CURZIO: Chabay,
PEASANT GIRLS: Phillips, Gray, CONDUCTOR: Steinberg.

October 12, matinee: RIGOLETTO (Verdi)
GILDA: Pons, DUKE: Peerce, RIGOLETTO: Tibbett, MADDALENA: Turner,
SPARAFUCILE: Lazzari, MONTERONE: Ligeti, BORSA: Chabay, MARULLO:
Cehanovsky, CEPRANO: Harvey, COUNTESS CEPRANO: Heitman, GIO-
VANNA: Votipka, PAGE: Lawlor, CONDUCTOR: Cimara.

October 19, matinee: LOUISE (Charpentier)
Same cast.

ADDED PERFORMANCES

September 24: ROMÉO ET JULIETTE (Gounod)
Same cast.

October 4, matinee: LA TRAVIATA (Verdi)
Same cast except: ALFREDO: Kullman, CONDUCTOR: Adler.

October 6: FAUST (Gounod)
Same cast except: VALENTIN: Weede.

October 8: DON GIOVANNI (Mozart)
Same cast except: DONNA ELVIRA: Resnik, ZERLINA: Conner.

October 13: TRISTAN AND ISOLDE (Wagner)
Same cast except: BRANGÄNE: Harshaw.

October 15: LA BOHÈME (Puccini)
Same cast except: COLLINE: Lazzari.

October 18: MADAMA BUTTERFLY (Puccini)
Same cast except: PINKERTON: Kullman.

YOUNG PEOPLE'S PERFORMANCES

October 10, matinee: LA TRAVIATA (Verdi)
Same cast except: VIOLETTA: Conner, ALFREDO: Kullman, GERMONT: Valentino.

October 17, matinee: LA TRAVIATA (Verdi)
Same cast except: VIOLETTA: Conner, ALFREDO: Kullman, GERMONT: Tibbett, CONDUCTOR: Adler.

CASTS—1948 SEASON

REGULAR SERIES

September 14: FALSTAFF (Verdi)
SIR JOHN FALSTAFF: Baccaloni, MISTRESS FORD: Resnik, MISTRESS PAGE:
Glaz, DAME QUICKLY; Stignani, ANNE: Albanese, FENTON: Lichtegg, FORD:
Weede, DR. CAIUS: Garris, BARDOLPH: De Paolis, PISTOL: Alvary, CONDUC-
TOR: Steinberg.

September 17: MANON (Massenet)

MANON: Sayao, CHEVALIER DES GRIEUX: Jobin, LESCAUT: Valentino, GUIL-
LOT: De Paolis, DE BRÉTIGNY: Cehanovsky, COUNT DES GRIEUX: Alvary,
POUSETTE: Hartzell, JAVOTTE: Zubiri, ROSETTE: Sanderson, SERVANT:
Alver, INNKEEPER: Olitzki, GUARDS: Curzi, Lorenzini, CONDUCTOR:
Breisach.

September 21: DIE MEISTERSINGER (Wagner)

EVA: Varnay, MAGDALENA: Glaz, WALTHER: Kullman, HANS SACHS: Jans-
sen, POGNER: Moscona, DAVID: Garris, BECKMESSER: Olitzki, KOTHNER:
Duno, NIGHT WATCHMAN: Sharretts, VOGELGESANG: Walti, NACHTIGALL:
Uppman, ZORN: De Paolis, EISSLINGER: Chabay, MOSER: Schwabacher,
ORTEL: Cehanovsky, SCHWARZ: Ligeti, FOLTZ: Ford, CONDUCTOR: Stein-
berg.

September 24: LA FORZA DEL DESTINO (Verdi)

LEONORA: Menkes, DON ALVARO: Baum, DON CARLO: Warren, PADRE
GUARDIANO: Pinza, FRA MELITONE: Baccaloni, PREZIOSILLA: Turner, MAR-
QUIS OF CALATRAVA: Alvary, ALCADE: Ford, TRABUCCO: De Paolis, CURRA:
Baldwin, SURGEON: Cehanovsky, CONDUCTOR: Merola.

September 28: CAVALLERIA RUSTICANA (Mascagni)

SANTUZZA: Stignani, TURIDDU: Binci, ALFIO: Valentino, LOLA: Glaz, MAM-
MA LUCIA: Turner, CONDUCTOR: Marzollo.

followed by: I PAGLIACCI (Leoncavallo)

CANIO: Baum, TONIO: Weede, NEDDA: Albanese, SILVIO: Cehanovsky,
BEPPE: Chabay, PEASANTS: Benson, Curzi, CONDUCTOR: Cimara.

October 1: BORIS GODOUNOFF (Moussorgsky)

BORIS: Pinza, DIMITRI: Kullman, MARINA: Heidt, PIMEN: Alvary, SHOUISKY:
De Paolis, RANGONI: Duno, VARLAAM: Baccaloni, MISSAIL: Chabay, TCHEL-
KALOFF: Cehanovsky, FEODOR: Zubiri, XENIA: Hartzell, NURSE: Turner,
INNKEEPER: Beal, SIMPLETON: Garris, POLICE OFFICER: Ford, FRONTIER
GUARD SERGEANT: Ligeti, BOYAR-IN-WAITING: Walti, LOVITZKY: Olitzki,
TCHERNIAKOVSKY: Ford, BOYAR: Rooney, CONDUCTOR: Leinsdorf.

October 5: CARMEN (Bizet)

CARMEN: Heidt, MICAELA: Conner, DON JOSÉ: Kullman, ESCAMILLO: Val-
dengo, ZUNIGA: Alvary, DANCAIRO: Cehanovsky, REMENDADO: De Paolis,
MORALES: Uppman, FRASQUITA: Hartzell, MERCEDES: Turner, CONDUCTOR:
Leinsdorf.

October 8: MADAMA BUTTERFLY (Puccini)

CIO-CIO-SAN: Kirsten, PINKERTON: Peerce, SHARPLESS: Valdengo, SUZUKI:
Glaz, GORO: De Paolis, BONZE: Alvary, YAMADORI: Cehanovsky, COMMIS-
SIONER: Olitzki, KATE PINKERTON: Gray, REGISTRAR: Harvey, CONDUC-
TOR: Cimara.

October 11: THE ELIXIR OF LOVE (Donizetti)

ADINA: Sayao, NEMORINO: Tagliavini, BELCORE: Gobbi, DR. DULCAMARA:
Baccaloni, GIANNETTA: Hartzell, CONDUCTOR: Breisach.

October 14: SIEGFRIED (Wagner)

BRÜNNHILDE: Varnay, SIEGFRIED: Svanholm, WANDERER: Janssen, FAFNER:
Ligeti, ALBERICH: Olitzki, MIME: Garris, ERDA: Beal, VOICE OF THE FOREST
BIRD: Hartzell, CONDUCTOR: Leinsdorf.

POPULAR SERIES

September 16: LA TRAVIATA (Verdi)
VIOLETTA: Albanese, ALFREDO: Peerce, GERMONT: Valdengo, GASTON: De Paolis, BARON DOUPHOL: Cehanovsky, MARQUIS D'OBIGNY: Olitzki, DR. GRENVIL: Ligeti, FLORA: Gray, ANNINA: Lawlor, CONDUCTOR: Cimara.

September 23: LA BOHÈME (Puccini)
MIMI: Sayao, RODOLFO: Peerce, MARCELLO: Valentino, COLLINE: Tajo, SCHAUNARD: Cehanovsky, MUSETTA: Hartzell, BENOIT: Baccaloni, ALCINDORO: Baccaloni, PARPIGNOL: Curzi, SERGEANT: Lorenzini, OFFICER: Benson, CONDUCTOR: Merola.

September 30: IL TROVATORE (Verdi)
LEONORA: Menkes, AZUCENA: Elmo, MANRICO: Baum, COUNT DI LUNA: Warren, FERRANDO: Moscona, RUIZ: Chabay, OLD GYPSY: Benson, INEZ; Baldwin, CONDUCTOR: Marzollo.

October 7: FALSTAFF (Verdi)
Same cast except: DAME QUICKLY: Elmo, ANNE: Warenskjold.

October 16: OTELLO (Verdi)
DESDEMONA: Albanese, OTELLO: Svanholm, IAGO: Warren, CASSIO: De Paolis, RODERIGO: Chabay, LODOVICO: Ligeti, MONTANO: Cehanovsky, HERALD: Nelson, EMILIA: Turner, CONDUCTOR: Steinberg.

NON-SUBSCRIPTION PERFORMANCES

September 19, matinee: DON GIOVANNI (Mozart)
DONNA ANNA: Resnik, DONNA ELVIRA: Claudia Pinza, ZERLINA: Sayao, DON GIOVANNI: Pinza, LEPORELLO: Baccaloni, DON OTTAVIO: Lichtegg, COMMENDATORE: Ligeti, MASETTO: Alvary, CONDUCTOR: Breisach.

September 22: THE BARBER OF SEVILLE (Rossini)
ROSINA: Conner, COUNT ALMAVIVA: Garris, FIGARO: Valdengo, BARTOLO: Baccaloni, BASILIO: Tajo, FIORELLO: De Paolis, OFFICER: Chabay, BERTHA: Turner, CONDUCTOR: Breisach.

September 26, matinee: RIGOLETTO (Verdi)
GILDA: Conner, DUKE: Peerce, RIGOLETTO: Warren, MADDALENA: Glaz, SPARAFUCILE: Alvary, MONTERONE: Ligeti, BORSA: De Paolis, MARULLO: Cehanovsky, CEPRANO: Harvey, COUNTESS CEPRANO: Heitman, GIOVANNA: Baldwin, PAGE: Lawlor, CONDUCTOR: Adler.

September 29: DON GIOVANNI (Mozart)
Same cast except: LEPORELLO: Tajo.

October 2, matinee: THE BARBER OF SEVILLE (Rossini)
Same cast except: FIGARO: Gobbi, FIORELLO: Cehanovsky.

October 3, matinee: LA GIOCONDA (Ponchielli)
LA GIOCONDA: Varnay, LAURA: Stignani, LA CIECA: Turner, ENZO: Baum, BARNABA: Valentino, ALVISE: Moscona, ZUANE: McVey, ISEPO: Curzi, PILOT: Nelson, MONK: Ligeti, CANTOR: Benson, VOICES: Alibertini, Attarian, CONDUCTOR: Marzollo.

October 4: MANON (Massenet)
Same cast except: COUNT DES GRIEUX: Moscona.

October 6: LA FORZA DEL DESTINO (Verdi)
Same cast except: DON CARLO: Weede, CONDUCTOR: Marzollo.

October 10, matinee: DIE MEISTERSINGER (Wagner)
Same cast except: WALTHER: Svanholm.
October 12: LA BOHÈME (Puccini)
Same cast except: MIMI: Albanese, RODOLFO: Bjoerling, MARCELLO: Gobbi.
October 13: BORIS GODOUNOFF (Moussorgsky) (Portola Festival performance)
Same cast.
October 15: LA TRAVIATA (Verdi)
Same cast except: VIOLETTA: Kirsten, ALFREDO: Tagliavini, GERMONT: Weede, GASTON: Chabay, FLORA: Zubiri.
October 17, matinee: CARMEN (Bizet)
Same cast except: MICAELA: Warenskjold, DON JOSÉ: Jobin.

YOUNG PEOPLE'S PERFORMANCES
October 8, matinee: LA BOHÈME (Puccini)
Same cast except: MIMI: Albanese, RODOLFO: Kullman, MARCELLO: Gobbi, BENOIT: Olitzki, ALCINDORO: Olitzki.
October 15, matinee: LA BOHÈME (Puccini)
Same cast except: RODOLFO: Bjoerling, MUSETTA: Zubiri, CONDUCTOR: Kritz.

CASTS—1949 SEASON

REGULAR SERIES
September 20: TOSCA (Puccini)
TOSCA: Barbato, CAVARADOSSI: Bjoerling, SCARPIA: Tibbett, SPOLETTA: De Paolis, SACRISTAN: Baccaloni, ANGELOTTI: Ligeti, SCIARRONE: Cehanovsky, JAILOR: Guenter, SHEPHERD: Walker, CONDUCTOR: Cleva.
September 22: FAUST (Gounod)
MARGUERITE: Albanese, FAUST: Jobin, MEPHISTOPHELES: Tajo, VALENTIN: Mascherini, WAGNER: McVey, SIEBEL: Glaz, MARTHE: Turner, CONDUCTOR: Merola.
September 27: DON GIOVANNI (Mozart)
DONNA ANNA: Bampton, DONNA ELVIRA: Novotna, ZERLINA: Albanese, DON GIOVANNI: Tajo, LEPORELLO: Baccaloni, DON OTTAVIO: Peerce, COMMENDATORE: Ligeti, MASETTO: Cehanovsky, CONDUCTOR: Breisach.
September 30: TRISTAN AND ISOLDE (Wagner)
ISOLDE: Flagstad, BRANGÄNE: Thebom, TRISTAN: Svanholm, KING MARKE: Szekely, KURWENAL: Janssen, MELOT: Cehanovsky, SHEPHERD: Chabay, SAILOR'S VOICE: Chabay, STEERSMAN: McVey, CONDUCTOR: Steinberg.
October 4: AIDA (Verdi)
AIDA: Barbato, AMNERIS: Thebom, RHADAMES: Svanholm, AMONASRO: Weede, RAMFIS: Moscona, KING: Ligeti, MESSENGER: Chabay, PRIESTESS: Graf, CONDUCTOR: Steinberg.
October 7: MANON LESCAUT (Puccini)
MANON LESCAUT: Albanese, CHEVALIER DES GRIEUX: Bjoerling, LESCAUT: Mascherini, GERONTE: Baccaloni, EDMONDO: Curzi, DANCING MASTER:

De Paolis, LAMPLIGHTER: Chabay, CAPTAIN: Ligeti, MUSICIAN: Glaz, INN-KEEPER: Harvey, CONDUCTOR: Cleva.

October 11: DIE WALKÜRE (Wagner)
BRÜNNHILDE: Flagstad, SIEGLINDE: Bampton, FRICKA: Thebom, SIEGMUND: Svanholm, WOTAN: Sharretts, HUNDING: Szekely, HELMWIGE: Wilcox, GERHILDE: Spry, ORTLINDE: Chauveau, SIEGRUNE: Glaz, ROSSWEISSE: Baldwin, WALTRAUTE: Ostrowski, GRIMGERDE: Thornbury, SCHWERT-LEITE: Walker, CONDUCTOR: Steinberg.

October 14: THE TALES OF HOFFMANN (Offenbach)
HOFFMANN: Jobin, OLYMPIA: Graf, GIULIETTA: Novotna, ANTONIA: Albanese, COPPELIUS: Baccaloni, DAPERTUTTO: Tibbett, DR. MIRACLE: Tibbett, NICKLAUSSE: Glaz, VOICE OF ANTONIA'S MOTHER: Walker, SPALANZANI: De Paolis, SCHLEMIL: Cehanovsky, CRESPEL: Ligeti, FRANTZ: De Paolis, COCHENILLE: Chabay, PITICHINACCIO: Chabay, NATHANAEL: Curzi, HER-MANN: Trevor, LUTHER: Harvey, LINDORF: Cehanovsky, ANDRES: Chabay, STELLA: Lagorio, CONDUCTOR: Breisach.

October 18: SAMSON AND DELILAH (Saint-Saens)
SAMSON: Jobin, DELILAH: Thebom, HIGH PRIEST: Weede, ABIMELECH: Cehanovsky, OLD HEBREW: Ligeti, MESSENGER: Peters, PHILISTINE: Nelson, CONDUCTOR: Cleva.

October 21: LUCIA DI LAMMERMOOR (Donizetti)
LUCIA: Pons, LORD HENRY: Valentino, EDGARDO: Tagliavini, LORD ARTHUR: Chabay, RAYMOND: Ligeti, ALICE: Zubiri, NORMAN: Curzi, CONDUCTOR: Merola.

POPULAR MATINEE SERIES

September 25: LA BOHÈME (Puccini)
MIMI: Albanese, RODOLFO: Bjoerling, MARCELLO: Mascherini, COLLINE: Moscona, SCHAUNARD: Cehanovsky, MUSETTA: Hartzell, BENOIT: Baccaloni, ALCINDORO: Baccaloni, PARPIGNOL: Curzi, SERGEANT: Lorenzini, OF-FICER: Harvey, CONDUCTOR: Kritz.

October 2: FAUST (Gounod)
Same cast except: MARGUERITE: Quartararo, FAUST: Bjoerling, MEPHIS-TOPHELES: Moscona, MARTHE: Ostrowski, CONDUCTOR: Adler.

October 9: DON GIOVANNI (Mozart)
Same cast.

October 16: MANON LESCAUT (Puccini)
Same cast except: LESCAUT: Valentino.

October 23: DIE WALKÜRE (Wagner)
Same cast except: WOTAN: Janssen.

POPULAR EVENING SERIES

September 24: CARMEN (Bizet)
CARMEN: Heidt, MICAELA: Graf, DON JOSÉ: Vinay, ESCAMILLO: Valentino, ZUNIGA: Ligeti, DANCAIRO: Cehanovsky, REMENDADO: De Paolis, MORALES: Cehanovsky, FRASQUITA: Hartzell, MERCEDES: Turner, CONDUCTOR: Brei-sach.

September 29: TOSCA (Puccini)
Same cast except: CAVARADOSSI: Tagliavini.
October 6: TRISTAN AND ISOLDE (Wagner)
Same cast except: BRANGÄNE: Glaz.
October 13: AIDA (Verdi)
Same cast except: RAMFIS: Szekely.
October 20: THE TALES OF HOFFMANN (Offenbach)
Same cast except: OLYMPIA: O'Connell, GIULIETTA: Thebom, ANTONIA: Warenskjold.

EXTRA PERFORMANCES

October 8: TOSCA (Puccini)
Same cast except: CAVARADOSSI: Tagliavini.
October 15: TRISTAN AND ISOLDE (Wagner)
Same cast.
October 19: LA BOHÈME (Puccini)
Same cast except: RODOLFO: Tagliavini, MARCELLO: Valentino.

YOUNG PEOPLE'S PERFORMANCES

October 6, matinee: FAUST (Gounod)
Same cast except: MARGUERITE: Quartararo, VALENTIN: Weede, SIEBEL: Hartzell, MARTHE: Ostrowski, CONDUCTOR: Adler.
October 13, matinee: FAUST (Gounod)
Same cast except: MARGUERITE: Quartararo, FAUST: Bjoerling, MEPHISTOPHELES: Moscona, MARTHE: Glaz, CONDUCTOR: Adler.

CASTS—1950 SEASON

REGULAR SERIES

September 26: AIDA (Verdi)
AIDA: Tebaldi, AMNERIS: Nikolaidi, RHADAMES: Del Monaco, AMONASRO: Weede, RAMFIS: Tajo, KING: Ligeti, MESSENGER: Curzi, PRIESTESS: Graf, CONDUCTOR: Cleva.
September 29: THE MARRIAGE OF FIGARO (Mozart)
SUSANNA: Sayao, COUNTESS: Quartararo, CHERUBINO: Glaz, FIGARO: Tajo, COUNT: Brownlee, BARTOLO: Baccaloni, BASILIO: De Paolis, MARCELLINA: Turner, BARBARINA: Chauveau, ANTONIO: Cehanovsky, DON CURZIO: Norville, PEASANT GIRLS: Lanyon, Brubaker, CONDUCTOR: Perlea.
October 3: TRISTAN AND ISOLDE (Wagner)
ISOLDE: Flagstad, BRANGÄNE: Glaz, TRISTAN: Vinay, KING MARKE: Ernster, KURWENAL: Sigurd Bjoerling, MELOT: Cehanovsky, SHEPHERD: Schwabacher, SAILOR'S VOICE: Norville, STEERSMAN: Ford, CONDUCTOR: Perlea.
October 6: ANDREA CHENIER (Giordano)
MADELEINE: Albanese, ANDREA CHENIER: Del Monaco, GERARD: Weede, MATHIEU: Herbert, FLÉVILLE: Sze, ROUCHER: Cehanovsky, DUMAS: Sze, ABBÉ: Norville, SPY: De Paolis, SCHMIDT: Ford, FOUQUIER-TINVILLE: Ligeti, COUNTESS: Turner, MADELON: Walker, BERSI: Ostrowski, CONDUCTOR: Cleva.

357

October 10: OTELLO (Verdi)
DESDEMONA: Tebaldi, OTELLO: Vinay, IAGO: Valdengo, CASSIO: De Paolis, RODERIGO: Schwabacher, LODOVICO: Ligeti, MONTANO: Cehanovsky, HERALD: R. Nelson, EMILIA: Ostrowski, CONDUCTOR: Cleva.

October 13: THE MAGIC FLUTE (Mozart)
PAMINA: Warenskjold, QUEEN OF THE NIGHT: Barabas, TAMINO: Kullman, PAPAGENO: Brownlee, SARASTRO: Ernster, SPEAKER: Sze, PAPAGENA: Williams, MONOSTATOS: Norville, PRIESTS: Ford, Schwabacher, LADIES: Lauppe, Chauveau, Turner, SLAVES: Harvey, Bond, Louw, GUARDS: Curzi, Ligeti, YOUTHS: O'Connell, Sanderson, Baldwin, CONDUCTOR: Breisach.

October 17: THE BARBER OF SEVILLE (Rossini)
ROSINA: Pons, COUNT ALMAVIVA: Conley, FIGARO: Mascherini, BARTOLO: Baccaloni, BASILIO: Tajo, FIORELLO: Cehanovsky, OFFICER: De Paolis, BERTHA: Turner, AMBROSIO: Harvey, CONDUCTOR: Rescigno.

October 20: SUOR ANGELICA (Puccini)
SUOR ANGELICA: Albanese, PRINCESS: Turner, ABBESS: Thornbury, MISTRESS OF NOVICES: Walker, ALMS COLLECTOR: Baldwin, SISTER GENEVIEVE: Chauveau, SISTER OSMINA: Throndson, SISTER MONITOR: Ostrowski, SISTER DOLCINA: Hurd, NURSING SISTER: Stephens, NOVICES: Pappas, Lanyon, LAY SISTERS: Welton, G. Nelson, SISTERS: Barbano, Bruni, Andreatta, CONDUCTOR: Adler.

followed by: SALOME (Strauss)
SALOME: Lewis, HEROD: Jagel, JOCHANAAN: Sigurd Bjoerling, HERODIAS: Turner, NARRABOTH: Fredericks, PAGE: Glaz, SOLDIERS: Cehanovsky, Ford, NAZARENES: Ligeti, Peters, JEWS: Norville, Curzi, De Paolis, Schwabacher, Sze, SLAVE: Baldwin, CAPPADOCIAN: R. Nelson, HENCHMAN: Louw, CONDUCTOR: Breisach.

October 24: MANON LESCAUT (Puccini)
MANON LESCAUT: Kirsten, CHEVALIER DES GRIEUX: Del Monaco, LESCAUT: Valdengo, GERONTE: Herbert, EDMONDO: Curzi, DANCING MASTER: De Paolis, LAMPLIGHTER: Norville, CAPTAIN: Ford, MUSICIAN: Glaz, INNKEEPER: Harvey, SERGEANT: McVey, CONDUCTOR: Cleva.

October 27, at 5 p.m.: PARSIFAL (Wagner)
KUNDRY: Flagstad, PARSIFAL: Kullman, AMFORTAS: Sigurd Bjoerling, GURNEMANZ: Ernster, KLINGSOR: Herbert, TITUREL: Ligeti, VOICE: Walker, KNIGHTS: Curzi, Ford, ESQUIRES: Graf, Glaz, Norville, Schwabacher, FLOWER MAIDENS: Graf, Chauveau, Glaz, O'Connell, Stephens, Ostrowski, CONDUCTOR: Perlea.

SUNDAY MATINEE SERIES

October 1: AIDA (Verdi)
Same cast except: KING: Sze.

October 8: LA BOHÈME (Puccini)
MIMI: Sayao, RODOLFO: Di Stefano, MARCELLO: Mascherini, COLLINE: Tajo, SCHAUNARD: Cehanovsky, MUSETTA: Graf, BENOIT: Baccaloni, ALCINDORO: Baccaloni, PARPIGNOL: Curzi, SERGEANT: Lorenzini, OFFICER: Harvey, CONDUCTOR: Kritz.

358

October 15: ANDREA CHENIER (Giordano)
Same cast.
October 22: THE BARBER OF SEVILLE (Rossini)
Same cast.
October 29: PARSIFAL (Wagner)
Same cast.

MIDWEEK EVEINING SERIES

September 28: LUCIA DI LAMMERMOOR (Donizetti)
LUCIA: Pons, LORD HENRY: Mascherini, EDGARDO: Di Stefano, LORD AR-
THUR: Curzi, RAYMOND: Ligeti, ALICE: Chauveau, NORMAN: Norville, CON-
DUCTOR: Breisach.
October 4: THE MARRIAGE OF FIGARO (Mozart)
Same cast except: CHERUBINO: Warenskjold.
October 12: TRISTAN AND ISOLDE (Wagner)
Same cast except: KING MARKE: Ligeti.
October 19: OTELLO (Verdi)
Same cast.
October 26: SUOR ANGELICA (Puccini)
Same cast.
                   followed by: SALOME (Strauss)
Same cast except: JOCHANAAN: Herbert.

EXTRA PERFORMANCES

October 2: LUCIA DI LAMMERMOOR (Donizetti)
Same cast except: LORD HENRY: Valentino, EDGARDO: Conley.
October 11: THE MAGIC FLUTE (Mozart) (California Masonic Cen-
tennial performance)
Same cast except: PAMINA: Graf.
October 28: LA BOHÈME (Puccini)
Same cast except: MARCELLO: Valentino.

YOUNG PEOPLE'S PERFORMANCES

October 19, matinee: MADAMA BUTTERFLY (Puccini)
CIO-CIO-SAN: Kirsten, PINKERTON: Conley, SHARPLESS: Valentino, SUZUKI:
Glaz, GORO: De Paolis, BONZE: Sze, YAMADORI: Cehanovsky, COMMIS-
SIONER: Ford, KATE PINKERTON: Chauveau, REGISTRAR: Harvey, CONDUC-
TOR: Rescigno.
October 26, matinee: MADAMA BUTTERFLY (Puccini)
Same cast except: SUZUKI: Ostrowski.

CASTS—1951 SEASON

REGULAR SERIES

September 18: OTELLO (Verdi)
DESDEMONA: Nelli, OTELLO: Vinay, IAGO: Valdengo, CASSIO: Schwaba-
cher, RODERIGO: Curzi, LODOVICO: Ligeti, MONTANO: Cehanovsky, HER-
ALD: Trevor, EMILIA: Ostrowski, CONDUCTOR: Cleva.

September 21: ROMÉO ET JULIETTE (Gounod)
ROMÉO: Bjoerling, JULIETTE: Sayao, MERCUTIO: Herbert, TYBALT: Schwabacher, CAPULET: Ligeti, FRIAR LAWRENCE: Moscona, GREGORIO: Harvey, BENVOGLIO: Curzi, DUKE OF VERONA: Ernster, STEPHANO: Glaz, GERTRUDE: Ostrowski, CONDUCTOR: Breisach.

September 25: DER ROSENKAVALIER (Strauss)
MARSCHALLIN: Roman, BARON OCHS: Alvary, OCTAVIAN: Thebom, SOPHIE: Graf, FANINAL: Herbert, TENOR: Conley, MARIANNE: Chauveau, VALZACCHI: De Paolis, ANNINA: Glaz, POLICE COMMISSIONER: Ligeti, NOTARY: Harvey, LANDLORD: Curzi, MILLINER: Brubaker, ANIMAL VENDOR: Thomson, MARSCHALLIN'S MAJOR DOMO: Andersen, FANINAL'S MAJOR DOMO: Schwabacher, ORPHANS: Lanyon, Baldwin, Lagorio, FOOTMEN: Miller, Guenter, Rossi, Trevor, CONDUCTOR: Leinsdorf.

September 28: LA FORZA DEL DESTINO (Verdi)
LEONORA: Nelli, DON ALVARO: Baum, DON CARLO: Weede, PADRE GUARDIANO: Moscona, FRA MELITONE: Baccaloni, PREZIOSILLA: Turner, MARQUIS OF CALTRAVA: Alvary, ALCADE: Sze, TRABUCCO: De Paolis, CURRA: Baldwin, SURGEON: Cehanovsky, CONDUCTOR: Adler.

October 2: BORIS GODOUNOFF (Moussorgsky)
BORIS: Rossi-Lemeni, DIMITRI: Fredericks, MARINA: Thebom, PIMEN: Moscona, SHOUISKY: De Paolis, RANGONI: Ligeti, VARLAAM: Baccaloni, MISSAIL: Curzi, TCHELKALOFF: Cehanovsky, FEODOR: Chauveau, XENIA: Hartzell, NURSE: Wilkins, INNKEEPER: Ostrowski, SIMPLETON: Schwabacher, POLICE OFFICER: Sze, FRONTIER GUARD SERGEANT: Porta, BOYAR-IN-WAITING: Lawrence, LOVITZKY: Sze, TCHERNIAKOVSKY: Cehanovsky, BOYAR: White, PEASANTS: McIntosh, Eloise Farrell, Guenter, Novi, CONDUCTOR: Leinsdorf.

October 5: LA TRAVIATA (Verdi)
VIOLETTA: Pons, ALFREDO: Peerce, GERMONT: Valdengo, GASTON: De Paolis, BARON DOUPHOL: Cehanovsky, MARQUIS D'OBIGNY: Sze, DR. GRENVIL: Ligeti, FLORA: Chauveau, ANNINA: Baldwin, CONDUCTOR: Cleva.

October 8: LA BOHÈME (Puccini)
MIMI: Sayao, RODOLFO: Bjoerling, MARCELLO: Valdengo, COLLINE: Moscona, SCHAUNARD: Cehanovsky, MUSETTA: Graf, BENOIT: Baccaloni, ALCINDORO: Baccaloni, PARPIGNOL: Curzi, SERGEANT: Lorenzini, OFFICER: Harvey, CONDUCTOR: Breisach.

October 12: TOSCA (Puccini)
TOSCA: Kirsten, CAVARADOSSI: Bjoerling, SCARPIA: Weede, SPOLETTA: De Paolis, SACRISTAN: Baccaloni, ANGELOTTI: Ligeti, SCIARRONE: Cehanovsky, JAILOR: Sze, SHEPHERD: Throndson, CONDUCTOR: Cleva.

October 16: MANON (Massenet)
MANON: Sayao, CHEVALIER DES GRIEUX: Vroons, LESCAUT: Valentino, GUILLOT: De Paolis, DE BRÉTIGNY: Cehanovsky, COUNT DES GRIEUX: Alvary, POUSETTE: Hartzell, JAVOTTE: Chauveau, ROSETTE: Baldwin, SERVANT: Lanyon, GUARDS: Andersen, Lorenzini, TRAVELERS: Hurd, Knapp, CONDUCTOR: Cleva.

October 19: FIDELIO (Beethoven)
LEONORE: Varnay, FLORESTAN: Svanholm, ROCCO: Ernster, DON

PIZARRO: Janssen, DON FERNANDO: Ligeti, MARZELLINE: Graf, JACQUINO: Schwabacher, PRISONERS: Lawrence, Sze, CONDUCTOR: Wallenstein.

SUNDAY MATINEE SERIES

September 23: OTELLO (Verdi)
Same cast.
September 30: DER ROSENKAVALIER (Strauss)
Same cast except: SOPHIE: Warenskjold, TENOR: Fredericks.
October 7: BORIS GODOUNOFF (Moussorgsky)
Same cast except: MARINA: Turner, PIMEN: Alvary, FRONTIER GUARD SERGEANT: Ligeti.
October 14: LA BOHÈME (Puccini)
Same cast except: COLLINE: Rossi-Lemeni, MUSETTA: Hartzell.
October 21: MANON (Massenet)
Same cast except: COUNT DES GRIEUX: Moscona.

THURSDAY EVENING SERIES

September 20: CARMEN (Bizet)
CARMEN: Thebom, MICAELA: Warenskjold, DON JOSÉ: Vinay, ESCAMILLO: Valdengo, ZUNIGA: Alvary, DANCAIRO: Cehanovsky, REMENDADO: De Paolis, MORALES: Andersen, FRASQUITA: Hartzell, MERCEDES: Ostrowski, CONDUCTOR: Breisach.
September 27: ROMÉO ET JULIETTE (Gounod)
Same cast except: JULIETTE: Anna Lisa Bjoerling, FRIAR LAWRENCE: Alvary.
October 4: LA FORZA DEL DESTINO (Verdi)
Same cast except: PADRE GUARDIANO: Rossi-Lemeni.
October 11: LA TRAVIATA (Verdi)
Same cast except: ALFREDO: Conley.
October 18: TOSCA (Puccini)
Same cast except: CAVARADOSSI: Peerce, SCARPIA: Herbert.

EXTRA PERFORMANCES

September 29: MADAMA BUTTERFLY (Puccini)
CIO-CIO-SAN: Kirsten, PINKERTON: Conley, SHARPLESS: Valentino, SUZUKI: Glaz, GORO: De Paolis, BONZE: Sze, YAMADORI: Cehanovsky, COMMISSIONER: Trevor, KATE PINKERTON: Chauveau, REGISTRAR: Harvey, CONDUCTOR: Rescigno.
October 13: PARSIFAL (Wagner)
KUNDRY: Varnay, PARSIFAL: Svanholm, AMFORTAS: Janssen, GURNEMANZ: Ernster, KLINGSOR: Herbert, TITUREL: Ligeti, VOICE: Turner, KNIGHTS: Curzi, Sze, ESQUIRES: Graf, Glaz, Lawrence, Schwabacher, FLOWER MAIDENS: Graf, Chauveau, Glaz, Hartzell, Stephens, Ostrowski, CONDUCTOR: Leinsdorf.
October 20: RIGOLETTO (Verdi)
GILDA: Pons, DUKE: Bjoerling, RIGOLETTO: Weede, MADDALENA: Glaz, SPARAFUCILE: Alvary, MONTERONE: Ligeti, BORSA: De Paolis, MARULLO: Cehanovsky, CEPRANO: Harvey, COUNTESS CEPRANO: Chauveau, GIOVANNA: Baldwin, PAGE: Lanyon, CONDUCTOR: Cimara.

YOUNG PEOPLE'S PERFORMANCES

October 4, matinee: CARMEN (Bizet)
Same cast except: MICAELA: Graf, ESCAMILLO: Herbert, ZUNIGA: Ligeti.
October 11, matinee: CARMEN (Bizet)
Same cast except: MICAELA: Graf, DON JOSÉ: Svanholm, ESCAMILLO: Herbert.
October 18, matinee: CARMEN (Bizet)
Same cast except: CARMEN: Turner, DON JOSÉ: Baum, CONDUCTOR: Kritz.

CASTS—1952 SEASON

REGULAR SERIES

September 16: TOSCA (Puccini)
TOSCA: Kirsten, CAVARADOSSI: Del Monaco, SCARPIA: Weede, SPOLETTA: De Paolis, SACRISTAN: Baccaloni, ANGELOTTI: Ligeti, SCIARRONE: Cehanovsky, JAILOR: Andersen, SHEPHERD: Throndson, CONDUCTOR: Cleva.
September 20: MEFISTOFELE (Boito)
MEFISTOFELE: Rossi-Lemeni, FAUST: Tagliavini, MARGHERITA: Sayao, ELENA: Fenn, WAGNER: Assandri, MARTHA: Votipka, PANTALIS: Roggero, NEREO: Curzi, CONDUCTOR: Cleva.
September 23: AIDA (Verdi)
AIDA: Curtis, AMNERIS: Thebom, RHADAMES: Del Monaco, AMONASRO: Valdengo, RAMFIS: Tajo, KING: Ligeti, MESSENGER: Schwabacher, PRIESTESS: Roggero, CONDUCTOR: Adler.
September 26: IL TABARRO (Puccini)
GIORGETTA: Lewis, LUIGI: Del Monaco, MICHELE: Weede, TINCA: Assandri, TALPA: Moscona, SONG VENDOR: Curzi, FRUGOLA: Turner, LOVERS: Chauveau, Schwabacher, CONDUCTOR: Curiel.
followed by: SUOR ANGELICA (Puccini)
SUOR ANGELICA: Curtis, PRINCESS: Turner, ABBESS: Throndson, MISTRESS OF NOVICES: Walker, ALMS COLLECTORS: Andreatta, Baldwin, SISTER GENEVIEVE: Roggero, SISTER OSMINA: Sherry Stevens, SISTER MONITOR: Votipka, SISTER DOLCINA: Johanson, NURSING SISTER: Oliver, NOVICES: Marion, Larsen, LAY SISTERS: Kantor, Hoots, SISTERS: Brubaker, Barbano, Knapp, CONDUCTOR: Adler.
followed by: GIANNI SCHICCHI (Puccini)
GIANNI SCHICCHI: Tajo, RINUCCIO: Conley, LAURETTA: Warenskjold, SIMONE: Alvary, BETTO: Cehanovsky, GHERARDO: De Paolis, MARCO: Gbur, SPINELLOCCIO: Louw, NOTARY: Ligeti, PINELLINO: Harvey, GUCCIO: Andersen, ZITA: Turner, NELLA: Chauveau, LA CIESCA: Votipka, GHERARDINO: Andreatta, CONDUCTOR: Kritz.
September 30: DER ROSENKAVALIER (Strauss)
MARSCHALLIN: Lewis, BARON OCHS: Alvary, OCTAVIAN: Thebom, SOPHIE: Warenskjold, FANINAL: Herbert, TENOR: Lawrence, MARIANNE: Votipka, VALZACCHI: De Paolis, ANNINA: Roggero, POLICE COMMISSIONER: Gbur, NOTARY: Harvey, LANDLORD: Curzi, MILLINER: Brubaker, ANIMAL

VENDOR: Daneluz, MARSCHALLIN'S MAJOR DOMO: Andersen, FANINAL'S MAJOR DOMO: Schwabacher, ORPHANS: Marion, Hoots, Baldwin, FOOTMEN: Miller, Guenter, Rossi, Ford, CONDUCTOR: Breisach.

October 3: IL TROVATORE (Verdi)
LEONORA: Nelli, AZUCENA: Turner, MANRICO: Del Monaco, COUNT DI LUNA: Guarrera, FERRANDO: Moscona, RUIZ: Assandri, OLD GYPSY: Lovasich, INEZ: Votipka, CONDUCTOR: Breisach.

October 7: THE DAUGHTER OF THE REGIMENT (Donizetti)
MARIE: Pons, TONIO: Lawrence, SULPICE: Baccaloni, MARQUISE DE BIRKENFELD: Turner, HORTENSIUS: Alvary, CORPORAL: Cehanovsky, NOTARY: Harvey, PEASANT: Schwabacher, DUCHESSE DE KRAKENTHORP: Chauveau, CONDUCTOR: Cimara.

October 10: LA BOHÈME (Puccini)
MIMI: Sayao, RODOLFO: Peerce, MARCELLO: Valentino, COLLINE: Tajo, SCHAUNARD: Cehanovsky, MUSETTA: Fenn, BENOIT: Baccaloni, ALCINDORO: Baccaloni, PARPIGNOL: Curzi, SERGEANT: Lorenzini, OFFICER: Harvey, CONDUCTOR: Merola.

October 14: DON GIOVANNI (Mozart)
DONNA ANNA: Curtis, DONNA ELVIRA: Lewis, ZERLINA: Sayao, DON GIOVANNI: Rossi-Lemeni, LEPORELLO: Tajo, DON OTTAVIO: Peerce, COMMENDATORE: Ligeti, MASETTO: Alvary, CONDUCTOR: Breisach.

October 17: L'AMORE DEI TRE RE (Montemezzi)
FIORA: Kirsten, AVITO: Sullivan, MANFREDO: Weede, ARCHIBALDO: Rossi-Lemeni, FLAMINIO: Assandri, YOUTH: Curzi, OLD WOMAN: Votipka, YOUNG GIRL: Larsen, SERVANT: Knapp, VOICE: Baldwin, CONDUCTOR: Cleva.

SUNDAY MATINEE SERIES

September 21: TOSCA (Puccini)
Same cast except: CAVARADOSSI: Conley.

September 28: AIDA (Verdi)
Same cast except: AIDA: Nelli, KING: Gbur.

October 5: DER ROSENKAVALIER (Strauss)
Same cast except: TENOR: Fredericks.

October 12: THE DAUGHTER OF THE REGIMENT (Donizetti)
Same cast.

October 19: DON GIOVANNI (Mozart)
Same cast except: DON OTTAVIO: Conley, MASETTO: Herbert.

WEDNESDAY EVENING SERIES

September 17: RIGOLETTO (Verdi)
GILDA: Pons, DUKE: Peerce, RIGOLETTO: Valdengo, MADDALENA: Turner, SPARAFUCILE: Moscona, MONTERONE: Gbur, BORSA: De Paolis, MARULLO: Cehanovsky, CEPRANO: Harvey, COUNTESS CEPRANO: Chauveau, GIOVANNA: Baldwin, PAGE: Brubaker, CONDUCTOR: Cimara.

September 24: MEFISTOFELE (Boito)
Same cast.

October 1: IL TABARRO (Puccini)
Same cast except: LUIGI: Fredericks.
          followed by: SUOR ANGELICA (Puccini)
Same cast.
          followed by: GIANNI SCHICCHI (Puccini)
Same cast.
October 8: IL TROVATORE (Verdi)
Same cast except: LEONORA: Curtis, AZUCENA: Barbieri.
October 15: LA BOHÈME (Puccini)
Same cast except: MIMI: Warenskjold, RODOLFO: Tagliavini, MARCELLO: Valdengo, COLLINE: Moscona, MUSETTA: Lewis, CONDUCTOR: Kritz.

EXTRA PERFORMANCES

October 4: LA TRAVIATA (Verdi)
VIOLETTA: Pons, ALFREDO: Conley, GERMONT: Weede, GASTON: De Paolis, BARON DOUPHOL: Cehanovsky, MARQUIS D'OBIGNY: Gbur, DR. GRENVIL: Ligeti, FLORA: Chauveau, ANNINA: Baldwin, CONDUCTOR: Cimara.
October 11, matinee: MEFISTOFELE (Boito)
Same cast except: FAUST: Del Monaco.
October 16: CAVALLERIA RUSTICANA (Mascagni)
SANTUZZA: Barbieri, TURIDDU: Peerce, ALFIO: Herbert, LOLA: Roggero, MAMMA LUCIA: Votipka, CONDUCTOR: Adler.
          followed by: I PAGLIACCI (Leoncavallo)
CANIO: Del Monaco, TONIO: Guarrera, NEDDA: Sayao, SILVIO: Valentino, BEPPE: Assandri, PEASANTS: Harvey, Frost, CONDUCTOR: Kritz.
October 18: AIDA (Verdi)
Same cast except: AIDA: Nelli, AMNERIS: Barbieri, RAMFIS: Moscona, KING: Gbur.

YOUNG PEOPLE'S PERFORMANCES

October 1, matinee: CAVALLERIA RUSTICANA (Mascagni)
Same cast except: SANTUZZA: Nelli, LOLA: Chauveau.
          followed by: I PAGLIACCI (Leoncavallo)
Same cast except: TONIO: Valentino, NEDDA: Fenn, SILVIO: Cehanovsky.
October 8, matinee: CAVALLERIA RUSTICANA (Mascagni)
Same cast except: TURIDDU: Conley, LOLA: Chauveau.
          followed by: I PAGLIACCI (Leoncavallo)
Same cast except: CANIO: Fredericks, TONIO: Valentino, SILVIO: Cehanovsky, BEPPE: Curzi.
October 15, matinee: CAVALLERIA RUSTICANA (Mascagni)
Same cast except: TURIDDU: Conley.
          followed by: I PAGLIACCI (Leoncavallo)
Same cast except: CANIO: Fredericks, NEDDA: Fenn.

CASTS—1953 SEASON

REGULAR SERIES

September 15: MEFISTOFELE (Boito)

MEFISTOFELE: Rossi-Lemeni, FAUST: Peerce, MARGHERITA: Albanese, ELENA: Sills, WAGNER: Assandri, MARTHA: Wilkins, PANTALIS: Roggero, NEREO: Curzi, CONDUCTOR: Cleva.

September 19: WERTHER (Massenet)
CHARLOTTE: Simionato, WERTHER: Valletti, SOPHIE: Warenskjold, ALBERT: Lombardi, BAILIFF: Alvary, SCHMIDT: Curzi, JOHANN: Cehanovsky, BRUHLMANN: Andersen, KATCHEN: Roehr, CONDUCTOR: Serafin.

September 22: LA TRAVIATA (Verdi)
VIOLETTA: Kirsten, ALFREDO: Poleri, GERMONT: Mascherini, GASTON: De Paolis, BARON DOUPHOL: Cehanovsky, MARQUIS D'OBIGNY: Gbur, DR. GRENVIL: Ligeti, FLORA: Chauveau, ANNINA: Currier, CONDUCTOR: Cleva.

September 25: THE CREATURES OF PROMETHEUS ballet (Beethoven)
PROMETHEUS: Paxman, FIRE: V. Johnson, ZEUS: Feinberg, WOMAN: N. Johnson, MAN: Barallobre, ATHENA: Johnston, APOLLO: Mallozzi, TERPSICHORE: Arnold, APHRODITE: Bailey, MELPOMENE: Bering, QUEEN: Shore, KING: Sage, THALIA: Coler, BACCHUS: Ludlow, CONDUCTOR: Curiel.

followed by: ELEKTRA (Strauss)
ELEKTRA: Borkh, CHRYSOTHEMIS: Faull, KLYTEMNESTRA: Klose, AEGISTHUS: Suthaus, ORESTES: Schoeffler, ORESTES' TUTOR: Ligeti, CONFIDANTE: Eloise Farrell, TRAINBEARER: Roehr, OLD SERVANT: Gbur, OVERSEER: Chauveau, MAIDSERVANTS: Roggero, Wilkins, Moudry, Sills, Hartzell, CONDUCTOR: Solti.

September 29: BORIS GODOUNOFF (Moussorgsky)
BORIS: Rossi-Lemeni, DIMITRI: Sullivan, MARINA: Simionato, PIMEN: Alvary, SHOUISKY: De Paolis, RANGONI: Bardelli, VARLAAM: Baccaloni, MISSAIL: Curzi, TCHELKALOFF: Cehanovsky, FEODOR: Chauveau, XENIA: Hartzell, NURSE: Wilkins, INNKEEPER: Moudry, SIMPLETON: Mason, POLICE OFFICER: Gbur, FRONTIER GUARD SERGEANT: Ligeti, BOYAR-IN-WAITING: Assandri, LOVITZKY: Gbur, TCHERNIAKOVSKY: Cehanovsky, BOYAR: White, CONDUCTOR: Serafin.

October 2: TRISTAN AND ISOLDE (Wagner)
ISOLDE: Grob-Prandl, BRANGÄNE: Klose, TRISTAN: Suthaus, KING MARKE: Ernster, KURWENAL: Schoeffler, MELOT: Cehanovsky, SHEPHERD: Mason, SAILOR'S VOICE: Curzi, STEERSMAN: Gbur, CONDUCTOR: Solti.

October 6: TURANDOT (Puccini)
TURANDOT: Borkh, LIU: Albanese, CALAF: Turrini, TIMUR: Tajo, PING: Lombardi, PANG: Assandri, PONG: Curzi, EMPEROR ALTOUM: De Paolis, MANDARIN: Gbur, PRINCE OF PERSIA: Daneluz, MAIDS: Gotelli, Petersen, CONDUCTOR: Cleva.

October 9: THE BARBER OF SEVILLE (Rossini)
ROSINA: Simionato, COUNT ALMAVIVA: Valletti, FIGARO: Guarrera, BARTOLO: Baccaloni, BASILIO: Rossi-Lemeni, FIORELLO: De Paolis, OFFICER: Assandri, BERTHA: Moudry, CONDUCTOR: Serafin.

October 13: DIE WALKÜRE (Wagner)
BRÜNNHILDE: Grob-Prandl, SIEGLINDE: Borkh, FRICKA: Klose, SIEGMUND: Suthaus, WOTAN: Schoeffler, HUNDING: Ernster, HELMWIGE: Faull, GERHILDE: Sills, ORTLINDE: Chauveau, SIEGRUNE: Moudry, ROSSWEISSE: Rog-

gero, WALTRAUTE: Eloise Farrell, GRIMGERDE: Petersen, SCHWERTLEITE: Wilkins, CONDUCTOR: Solti.

October 16: UN BALLO IN MASCHERA (Verdi)
AMELIA: Grob-Prandl, ULRICA: Klose, OSCAR: B. Gibson, RICCARDO: Turrini, RENATO: Mascherini, SAM: Alvary, TOM: Ligeti, SILVANO: Cehanovsky, JUDGE: Assandri, SERVANT: Lorenzini, CONDUCTOR: Serafin.

SUNDAY MATINEE SERIES

September 20: MEFISTOFELE (Boito)
Same cast.
September 27: MADAMA BUTTERFLY (Puccini)
CIO-CIO-SAN: Albanese, PINKERTON: Sullivan, SHARPLESS: Bardelli, SUZUKI: Roggero, GORO: De Paolis, BONZE: Alvary, YAMADORI: Cehanovsky, COMMISSIONER: Gbur, KATE PINKERTON: Chauveau, REGISTRAR: Harvey, CONDUCTOR: Adler.
October 4: BORIS GODOUNOFF (Moussorgsky)
Same cast.
October 11: TURANDOT (Puccini)
Same cast except: LIU: Warenskjold.
October 18: DIE WALKÜRE (Wagner)
Same cast.

WEDNESDAY EVENING SERIES

September 16: LA BOHÈME (Puccini)
MIMI: Kirsten, RODOLFO: Poleri, MARCELLO: Bardelli, COLLINE: Tajo, SCHAUNARD: Cehanovsky, MUSETTA: Hartzell, BENOIT: Baccaloni, ALCINDORO: Baccaloni, SERGEANT: Lorenzini, OFFICER: Harvey, CONDUCTOR: Curiel.
September 23: DON GIOVANNI (Mozart)
DONNA ANNA: Faull, DONNA ELVIRA: Sills, ZERLINA: B. Gibson, DON GIOVANNI: Rossi-Lemeni, LEPORELLO: Tajo, DON OTTAVIO: Peerce, COMMENDATORE: Ernster, MASETTO: Alvary, CONDUCTOR: Serafin.
September 30: THE CREATURES OF PROMETHEUS ballet (Beethoven)
Same cast.
              followed by: ELEKTRA (Strauss)
Same cast.
October 7: TRISTAN AND ISOLDE (Wagner)
Same cast except: KING MARKE: Ligeti.
October 14: LA TRAVIATA (Verdi)
Same cast exept: VIOLETTA: Albanese, ALFREDO: Peerce.

EXTRA PERFORMANCES

September 26: CARMEN (Bizet)
CARMEN: Turner, MICAELA: Warenskjold, DON JOSÉ: Poleri, ESCAMILLO: Guarrera, ZUNIGA: Alvary, DANCAIRO: Cehanovsky, REMENDADO: De

Paolis, MORALES: Andersen, FRASQUITA: Hartzell, MERCEDES: Roggero, CONDUCTOR: Cleva.

October 17: LA BOHÈME (Puccini)
Same cast except: MIMI: Albanese, RODOLFO: Peerce, MARCELLO: Mascherini.

YOUNG PEOPLE'S PERFORMANCES

September 30, matinee: THE BARBER OF SEVILLE (Rossini)
Same cast except: ROSINA: B. Gibson, FIGARO: Mascherini, BASILIO: Tajo, BERTHA: Wilkins, CONDUCTOR: Kritz.
October 7, matinee: THE BARBER OF SEVILLE (Rossini)
Same cast except: ROSINA: B. Gibson, FIGARO: Mascherini, BASILIO: Tajo, BERTHA: Wilkins, CONDUCTOR: Kritz.
October 14, matinee: THE BARBER OF SEVILLE (Rossini)
Same cast except: BASILIO: Tajo, CONDUCTOR: Kritz.

CASTS—1954 SEASON

REGULAR SERIES

September 17: RIGOLETTO (Verdi)
GILDA: Robin, DUKE: Tucker, RIGOLETTO: Warren, MADDALENA: Turner, SPARAFUCILE: Moscona, MONTERONE: Palangi, BORSA: De Paolis, MARULLO: Cehanovsky, CEPRANO: Harvey, COUNTESS CEPRANO: Hall, GIOVANNA: Warren, PAGE: Currier, CONDUCTOR: Cleva.
September 21: LA FORZA DEL DESTINO (Verdi)
LEONORA: Martinis, DON ALVARO: Tucker, DON CARLO: Warren, PADRE GUARDIANO: Siepi, FRA MELITONE: Baccaloni, PREZIOSILLA: Turner, MARQUIS OF CALATRAVA: Ligeti, ALCADE: Palangi, TRABUCCO: De Paolis, CURRA: Warren, SURGEON: Andersen, CONDUCTOR: Cleva.
September 24: THE PORTUGUESE INN (Cherubini)
RODRIGO: Alvary, DONNA GABRIELA: Carteri, ROSELBO: Herbert, DON CARLOS: Curzi, PEDRILLO: Cehanovsky, INIGO: De Paolis, INES: Caselle, CONDUCTOR: Curiel.
followed by: SALOME (Strauss)
SALOME: Borkh, HEROD: Kullman, JOCHANAAN: Welitsch, HERODIAS: Turner, NARRABOTH: B. Sullivan, PAGE: Nadell, SOLDIERS: Cehanovsky, Palangi, NAZARENES: Ligeti, Andersen, JEWS: Curzi, Assandri, De Paolis, Mason, Harvey, SLAVE: Scott, CAPPADOCIAN: Enns, CONDUCTOR: Szenkar.
September 28: MANON (Massenet)
MANON: Kirsten, CHEVALIER DES GRIEUX: Prandelli, LESCAUT: Herbert, GUILLOT: De Paolis, DE BRÉTIGNY: Cehanovsky, COUNT DES GRIEUX: Alvary, POUSETTE: Caselle, JAVOTTE: Warren, ROSETTE: Nadell, SERVANT: Pappas, INNKEEPER: Harvey, GUARDS: Andersen, Lorenzini, CONDUCTOR: Monteux.
October 1: TOSCA (Puccini)
TOSCA: Kirsten, CAVARADOSSI: Peerce, SCARPIA: Weede, SPOLETTA: De

Paolis, SACRISTAN: Baccaloni, ANGELOTTI: Ligeti, SCIARRONE: Cehanovsky, JAILOR: Palangi, SHEPHERD: Rosenblatt, CONDUCTOR: Cleva.

October 5: THE FLYING DUTCHMAN (Wagner)
DUTCHMAN: Hotter, SENTA: Borkh, ERIC: B. Sullivan, DALAND: Alvary, STEERSMAN: Curzi, MARY: Warren, CONDUCTOR: Szenkar.

October 8: TURANDOT (Puccini)
TURANDOT: Martinis, LIU: Albanese, CALAF: Turrini, TIMUR: Moscona, PING: Guarrera, PANG: Assandri, PONG: Curzi, EMPEROR ALTOUM: De Paolis, MANDARIN: Palangi, PRINCE OF PERSIA: Bruce, MAIDS: Gotelli, D. Petersen, CONDUCTOR: Cleva.

October 12: THE MARRIAGE OF FIGARO (Mozart)
SUSANNA: Carteri, COUNTESS: Albanese, CHERUBINO: Warenskjold, FIGARO: Siepi, COUNT: Hotter, BARTOLO: Baccaloni, BASILIO: De Paolis, MARCELLINA: Warren, BARBARINA: Caselle, ANTONIO: Cehanovsky, DON CURZIO: Curzi, CONDUCTOR: Szenkar.

October 15: IL TABARRO (Puccini)
GIORGETTA: Martinis, LUIGI: B. Sullivan, MICHELE: Weede, TINCA: Assandri, TALPA: Moscona, SONG VENDOR: Curzi, FRUGOLA: Turner, LOVERS: Currier, W. Petersen, CONDUCTOR: Curiel.

  followed by: JOAN OF ARC AT THE STAKE (Honegger)
JOAN: McGuire, FRIAR DOMINIC: Marvin, PORCUS: Kullman, VIRGIN: Duval, ST. MARGARET: Hall, ST. CATHERINE: Nadell, HERALDS: Mason, Herbert, Palangi, CLERIC: Curzi, JUDGE: Ligeti, MONK: Assandri, VOICE IN THE PROLOGUE: Hall, VOICES: Andersen, Flynn, CHILD: Ursino, ASS: Walker, DUKE OF BEDFORD: Sage, JOHN OF LUXEMBOURG: Paxman, REYNOLD OF CHARTRES: Carvajal, WILLIAM OF FLAVY: Ross, GRINDER TRUSTY: Ross, MOTHER OF BARRELS: McDonald, YOUNG PEASANT: Franklyn, OLD PEASANT: Hagopian, PERROT: Hatch, JAILORS: J. Sullivan, Verdell, CONDUCTOR: Monteux.

October 19: FIDELIO (Beethoven)
LEONORE: Borkh, FLORESTAN: Turrini, ROCCO: Alvary, DON PIZARRO: Hotter, DON FERNANDO: Welitsch, MARZELLINE: Warenskjold, JACQUINO: Curzi, PRISONERS: Millar, Enns, CONDUCTOR: Monteux.

SUNDAY MATINEE SERIES

September 19: LA BOHÈME (Puccini)
MIMI: Carteri, RODOLFO: Peerce, MARCELLO: Guarrera, COLLINE: Moscona, SCHAUNARD: Cehanovsky, MUSETTA: Duval, BENOIT: Baccaloni, ALCINDORO: Baccaloni, PARPIGNOL: Assandri, SERGEANT: Lorenzini, OFFICER: Harvey, CONDUCTOR: Mueller.

September 26: RIGOLETTO (Verdi)
Same cast except: DUKE: B. Sullivan, MADDALENA: Nadell, SPARAFUCILE: Ligeti, COUNTESS CEPRANO: Roehr, CONDUCTOR: Kritz.

October 3: MANON (Massenet)
Same cast except: MANON: Carteri.

October 10: THE FLYING DUTCHMAN (Wagner)
Same cast.

368

October 17: THE MARRIAGE OF FIGARO (Mozart)
Same cast.

THURSDAY EVENING SERIES

September 23: LUCIA DI LAMMERMOOR (Donizetti)
LUCIA: Robin, LORD HENRY: Guarrera, EDGARDO: Peerce, LORD ARTHUR: Curzi, RAYMOND: Moscona, ALICE: Warren, NORMAN: Assandri, CONDUCTOR: Barbini.
September 30: LA FORZA DEL DESTINO (Verdi)
Same cast except: DON ALVARO: Turrini.
October 7: THE PORTUGUESE INN (Cherubini)
Same cast.
              followed by: SALOME (Strauss)
Same cast.
October 14: TURANDOT (Puccini)
Same cast except: TURANDOT: Borkh, LIU: Warenskjold.
October 21: IL TABARRO (Puccini)
Same cast.
              followed by: JOAN OF ARC AT THE STAKE (Honegger)
Same cast.

EXTRA PERFORMANCES

September 18: MADAMA BUTTERFLY (Puccini)
CIO-CIO-SAN: Albanese, PINKERTON: Prandelli, SHARPLESS: Herbert, SUZUKI: Nadell, GORO: De Paolis, BONZE: Ligeti, YAMADORI: Cehanovsky, COMMISSIONER: Palangi, KATE PINKERTON: Hall, REGISTRAR: Harvey, CONDUCTOR: Kritz.
October 16: A GALA NIGHT AT THE OPERA
I Pagliacci, PROLOGUE: Weede, *La Bohème,* ACT 1: Carteri, Tucker, Guarrera, Siepi, Cehanovsky, Baccaloni, *Forza Del Destino,* OVERTURE AND MONASTERY SCENE: Martinis, Moscona, Baccaloni, *Manon,* COURS LA REINE SCENE: Kirsten, Herbert, De Paolis, Cehanovsky, Alvary, Caselle, Warren, Nadell, *Rigoletto,* ACT 3: Robin, Tucker, Warren, Palangi, Assandri, Cehanovsky, Harvey, Currier, CONDUCTORS: Mueller, Cleva, Monteux, Kritz.
October 20: TOSCA (Puccini)
Same cast except: TOSCA: Albanese, CAVARADOSSI: Tucker.

YOUNG PEOPLE'S PERFORMANCES

October 7, matinee: RIGOLETTO (Verdi)
Same cast except: DUKE: Prandelli, RIGOLETTO: Weede, MADDALENA: Nadell, BORSA: Assandri, COUNTESS CEPRANO: Roehr, CONDUCTOR: Kritz.
October 14, matinee: RIGOLETTO (Verdi)
Same cast except: DUKE: Prandelli, MADDALENA: Nadell, SPARAFUCILE: Alvary, BORSA: Assandri, COUNTESS CEPRANO: Roehr, CONDUCTOR: Kritz.
October 18, matinee: RIGOLETTO (Verdi)
Same cast except: DUKE: Prandelli, RIGOLETTO: Weede, MADDALENA: Nadell, BORSA: Assandri, COUNTESS CEPRANO: Roehr, CONDUCTOR: Kritz.

CASTS—1955 SEASON

REGULAR SERIES

September 15: AIDA (Verdi)
AIDA: Tebaldi, AMNERIS: Turner, RHADAMES: Turrini, AMONASRO: Warren, RAMFIS: Tozzi, KING: Ligeti, MESSENGER: Assandri, PRIESTESS: Roggero, CONDUCTOR: Cleva.

September 20: DER ROSENKAVALIER (Strauss)
MARSCHALLIN: Schwarzkopf, BARON OCHS: Edelmann, OCTAVIAN: Bible, SOPHIE: Warenskjold, FANINAL: Herbert, TENOR: Manton, MARIANNE: Roehr, VALZACCHI: De Paolis, ANNINA: Roggero, POLICE COMMISSIONER: Palangi, NOTARY: Harvey, LANDLORD: Lachona, MILLINER: McArt, ANIMAL VENDOR: Assandri, MARSCHALLIN'S MAJOR DOMO: Segale, FANINAL'S MAJOR DOMO: Hague, ORPHANS: Crader, Walker, Hilgenberg, FOOTMEN: Frost, Booth, Guenter, Toolatjan, CONDUCTOR: Leinsdorf.

September 23: LOUISE (Charpentier)
LOUISE: Kirsten, JULIEN: Sullivan, MOTHER: Turner, FATHER: Herbert, RAGPICKER: Alvary, JUNKMAN: Ligeti, YOUNG RAGPICKER: Roggero, STREET SWEEPER: Walker, NEWSPAPER GIRL: Ronec, MILKWOMAN: West, COAL-PICKER: Roehr, STREET ARAB: McArt, BIRDFOOD VENDOR: Scott, ARTI-CHOKE VENDOR: Karras, WATERCRESS VENDOR: Bible, CHAIR MENDER: Bible, OLD CLOTHES MAN: De Paolis, CARROT VENDOR: Assandri, RAG VENDOR: Cehanovsky, POLICEMEN: Blankenburg, Palangi, NOCTAMBULIST: Lachona, KING OF FOOLS: Lachona, SONG WRITER: Cehanovsky, PHILOS-OPHERS: Andersen, Harvey, PAINTER: Taylor, SCULPTOR: Booth, POET: Petit, STUDENT: Segale, IRMA: Crader, CAMILLE: Gordon, GERTRUDE: Hil-genberg, APPRENTICE: McArt, ELISE: Allen, BLANCHE: Garnier, SUZANNE: Knapp, FOREWOMAN: Avery, MARGUERITE: Gotelli, MADELEINE: Coving-ton, CONDUCTOR: Morel.

September 27: MACBETH (Verdi)
LADY MACBETH: Borkh, MACBETH: Weede, BANQUO: Tozzi, MACDUFF: Fredericks, MALCOLM: Assandri, LADY-IN-WAITING: Roehr, MEDIC: Palangi, SERVANT: Andersen, ASSASSIN: Blankenburg, HERALD: Turner, APPARI-TIONS: Murphy, Gotelli, Moore, CONDUCTOR: Cleva.

September 30: DON GIOVANNI (Mozart)
DONNA ANNA: Albanese, DONNA ELVIRA: Schwarzkopf, ZERLINA: Carteri, DON GIOVANNI: Siepi, LEPORELLO: Alvary, DON OTTAVIO: Peerce, COM-MENDATORE: Ligeti, MASETTO: Herbert, CONDUCTOR: Leinsdorf.

October 4: ANDREA CHENIER (Giordano)
MADELEINE: Tebaldi, ANDREA CHENIER: Tucker, GERARD: Warren, MA-THIEU: Alvary, FLÉVILLE: Cehanovsky, ROUCHER: Blankenburg, DUMAS: Palangi, ABBÉ: Assandri, SPY: De Paolis, SCHMIDT: Harvey, FOUQUIER-TINVILLE: Ligeti, COUNTESS: Hilgenberg, MADELON: Roggero, BERSI: Rog-gero, CONDUCTOR: Cleva.

October 7: TROILUS AND CRESSIDA (Walton)
TROILUS: Lewis, CRESSIDA: Kirsten, DIOMEDE: Weede, CALKAS: Tozzi, PANDARUS: McChesney, ANTENOR: Palangi, EVADNE: Bible, HORASTE: Blankenburg, PRIESTS: Hammons, Andersen, TROJAN LADIES: Gor-

don, San Miguel, Gotelli, WATCHMEN: Toolatjan, Manning, W. Petersen, SOLDIERS: Daneluz, Mayock, CONDUCTOR: Leinsdorf.

October 11: LE COQ D'OR (Rimsky-Korsakoff)
QUEEN: Dobbs, KING DODON: Alvary, ASTROLOGER: Manton, GENERAL: Tozzi, AMELFA: Roggero, VOICE OF COCK: Roehr, PRINCE GUIDON: Fredericks, PRINCE AFRON: Blankenburg, BOYARS: Frost, Andersen, CONDUCTOR: Leinsdorf.

followed by: I PAGLIACCI (Leoncavallo)
CANIO: Turrini, TONIO: Warren, NEDDA: Albanese, SILVIO: MacNeil, BEPPE: Assandri, PEASANTS: Mayock, Hammons, CONDUCTOR: Barbini.

October 14: LOHENGRIN (Wagner)
ELSA: Borkh, ORTRUD: Rankin, LOHENGRIN: Sullivan, TELRAMUND: Welitsch, KING HENRY: Edelmann, HERALD: MacNeil, PAGES: Crader, McArt, Roehr, Hilgenberg, CONDUCTOR: Cleva.

October 18: FAUST (Gounod)
MARGUERITE: Carteri, FAUST: Peerce, MEPHISTOPHELES: Siepi, VALENTIN: MacNeil, WAGNER: Palangi, SIEBEL: Bible, MARTHE: Hilgenberg, CONDUCTOR: Morel.

SATURDAY EVENING SERIES

September 17: CARMEN (Bizet)
CARMEN: Rankin, MICAELA: Carteri, DON JOSÉ: Lewis, ESCAMILLO: MacNeil, ZUNIGA: Alvary, DANCAIRO: Cehanovsky, REMENDADO: De Paolis, MORALES: Blankenburg, FRASQUITA: Roehr, MERCEDES: Roggero, CONDUCTOR: Morel.

September 24: DER ROSENKAVALIER (Strauss)
Same cast except: TENOR: Fredericks.

October 1: MACBETH (Verdi)
Same cast except: THIRD APPARITION: Ursino.

October 8: ANDREA CHENIER (Giordano)
Same cast.

October 15: LE COQ D'OR (Rimsky-Korsakoff)
Same cast.

followed by: I PAGLIACCI (Leoncavallo)
Same cast except: TONIO: Weede, SILVIO: Blankenburg.

THURSDAY EVENING SERIES

September 22: AIDA (Verdi)
Same cast except: AMNERIS: Rankin.

September 29: LOUISE (Charpentier)
Same cast.

October 6: DON GIOVANNI (Mozart)
Same cast.

October 13: TROILUS AND CRESSIDA (Walton)
Same cast.

October 20: LOHENGRIN (Wagner)
Same cast.

EXTRA PERFORMANCES

October 16, matinee: AIDA (Verdi)
Same cast.
October 19: TOSCA (Puccini)
TOSCA: Tebaldi, CAVARADOSSI: Tucker, SCARPIA: Weede, SPOLETTA: De Paolis, SACRISTAN: Cehanovsky, ANGELOTTI: Ligeti, SCIARRONE: Palangi, JAILOR: Blankenburg, SHEPHERD: Roggero, CONDUCTOR: Curiel.

YOUNG PEOPLE'S PERFORMANCES

October 6, matinee: CARMEN (Bizet)
Same cast except: MICAELA: Warenskjold, DON JOSÉ: Fredericks, ZUNIGA: Palangi, CONDUCTOR: Mueller.
October 13, matinee: CARMEN (Bizet)
Same cast except: CARMEN: Turner, DON JOSÉ: Fredericks, ESCAMILLO: Herbert, CONDUCTOR: Mueller.
October 17, matinee: CARMEN (Bizet)
Same cast except: MICAELA: Warenskjold, ESCAMILLO: Herbert, CONDUCTOR: Mueller.

CASTS—1956 SEASON

REGULAR SERIES

September 13: MANON LESCAUT (Puccini)
MANON LESCAUT: Kirsten, CHEVALIER DES GRIEUX: Bjoerling, LESCAUT: Quilico, GERONTE: Alvary, EDMONDO: Curzi, DANCING MASTER: De Paolis, LAMPLIGHTER: Assandri, CAPTAIN: Palangi, MUSICIAN: Roggero, SERGEANT: Andersen, CONDUCTOR: De Fabritiis.
September 18: THE FLYING DUTCHMAN (Wagner)
DUTCHMAN: Hotter, SENTA: Rysanek, ERIC: Suthaus, DALAND: Alvary, STEERSMAN: Curzi, MARY: Hilgenberg, CONDUCTOR: Steinberg.
September 21: FALSTAFF (Verdi)
SIR JOHN FALSTAFF: Warren, MISTRESS FORD: Schwarzkopf, MISTRESS PAGE: Roggero, DAME QUICKLY: Dominguez, ANNE: Schuh, FENTON: Campora, FORD: Guarrera, DR. CAIUS: Assandri, BARDOLPH: De Paolis, PISTOL: Moscona, CONDUCTOR: Steinberg.
September 25: BORIS GODOUNOFF (Moussorgsky)
BORIS: Christoff, DIMITRI: Lewis, MARINA: Dominguez, PIMEN: Moscona, SHOUISKY: Curzi, RANGONI: Hotter, VARLAAM: Alvary, MISSAIL: Lachona, TCHELKALOFF: Cehanovsky, FEODOR: Nadell, XENIA: Crader, NURSE: Wilkins, INNKEEPER: Hilgenberg, SIMPLETON: Manton, POLICE OFFICER: Palangi, FRONTIER GUARD SERGEANT: Ligeti, LOVITZKY: Kenig, TCHERNIAKOVSKY: Quilico, BOYAR: Assandri, PEASANTS: Covington, Eloise Farrell, Lovasich, CONDUCTOR: Steinberg.
September 28: FRANCESCA DA RIMINI (Zandonai)
FRANCESCA: Gencer, PAOLO: Martell, GIOVANNI: Colzani, MALATESTINO: Curzi, SAMARITANA: Crader, BIANCOFIORE: Gray, GARSENDA: McArt, ALTICHIARA: Roggero, DONELLA: Nadell, OSTASIO: Palangi, SER TOLDO

BERARDENGO: De Paolis, JESTER: Blankenburg, BOWMAN: Lachona, TOWER WARDEN: Kenig, SMARAGDI: Hilgenberg, VOICE OF A PRISONER: Assandri, CONDUCTOR: De Fabritiis.

October 2: COSI FAN TUTTE (Mozart)
FIORDILIGI: Schwarzkopf, DORABELLA: Rankin, DESPINA: Munsel, FERRANDO: Lewis, GUGLIELMO: Guarrera, DON ALFONSO: Alvary, CONDUCTOR: Schwieger.

October 5: DIE WALKÜRE (Wagner)
BRÜNNHILDE: Nilsson, SIEGLINDE: Rysanek, FRICKA: Rankin, SIEGMUND: Suthaus, WOTAN: Hotter, HUNDING: Moscona, HELMWIGE: Velsir, GERHILDE: Ronson, ORTLINDE: Althof, SIEGRUNE: Hilgenberg, ROSSWEISSE: Roggero, WALTRAUTE: Krooskos, GRIMGERDE: Petersen, SCHWERTLEITE: Nadell, CONDUCTOR: Schwieger.

October 9: SIMON BOCCANEGRA (Verdi)
SIMON BOCCANEGRA: Warren, AMELIA: Tebaldi, FIESCO: Christoff, ADORNO: Turrini, PAOLO: Blankenburg, PIETRO: Palangi, CAPTAIN: Assandri, MAIDSERVANT: Krooskos, CONDUCTOR: De Fabritiis.

October 12: THE ELIXIR OF LOVE (Donizetti)
ADINA: Munsel, NEMORINO: Campora, BELCORE: Quilico, DR. DULCAMARA: Tajo, GIANNETTA: McArt, CONDUCTOR: Curiel.

October 16: LA BOHÈME (Puccini)
MIMI: Albanese, RODOLFO: Peerce, MARCELLO: Quilico, COLLINE: Tajo, SCHAUNARD: Blankenburg, MUSETTA: Gray, BENOIT: Cehanovsky, ALCINDORO: De Paolis, PARPIGNOL: Assandri, CONDUCTOR: Kritz.

SATURDAY EVENING SERIES

September 15: TOSCA (Puccini)
TOSCA: Tebaldi, CAVARADOSSI: Martell, SCARPIA: Warren, SPOLETTA: De Paolis, SACRISTAN: Cehanovsky, ANGELOTTI: Palangi, SCIARRONE: Cehanovsky, JAILOR: Harvey, SHEPHERD: Hilgenberg, CONDUCTOR: Curiel.

September 22: THE FLYING DUTCHMAN (Wagner)
Same cast.

September 29: BORIS GODOUNOFF (Moussorgsky)
Same cast.

October 6: COSI FAN TUTTE (Mozart)
Same cast.

October 13: SIMON BOCCANEGRA (Verdi)
Same cast.

THURSDAY EVENING SERIES

September 20: MANON LESCAUT (Puccini)
Same cast.

September 27: FALSTAFF (Verdi)
Same cast.

October 4: FRANCESCA DA RIMINI (Zandonai)
Same cast.

October 11: DIE WALKÜRE (Wagner)
Same cast except: HUNDING: Alvary.

October 18: THE ELIXIR OF LOVE (Donizetti)
Same cast.

EXTRA PERFORMANCES

September 16, matinee: IL TROVATORE (Verdi)
LEONORA: Farrell, AZUCENA: Dominguez, MANRICO: Bjoerling, COUNT DI
LUNA: Colzani, FERRANDO: Moscona, RUIZ: Assandri, OLD GYPSY: Lovasich, INEZ: Krooskos, CONDUCTOR: De Fabritiis.
September 23, matinee: TOSCA (Puccini)
Same cast except: CAVARADOSSI: Bjoerling, SCARPIA: Colzani, SCIARRONE:
Blankenburg.
October 7, matinee: MADAMA BUTTERFLY (Puccini)
CIO-CIO-SAN: Albanese, PINKERTON: Campora, SHARPLESS: Quilico, SUZUKI: Roggero, GORO: De Paolis, BONZE: Ligeti, YAMADORI: Cehanovsky,
COMMISSIONER: Palangi, KATE PINKERTON: Covington, REGISTRAR: Harvey,
CONDUCTOR: Kritz.
October 14, matinee: COSI FAN TUTTE (Mozart)
Same cast.
October 17: AIDA (Verdi)
AIDA: Rysanek, AMNERIS: Rankin, RHADAMES: Martell, AMONASRO: Colzani, RAMFIS: Moscona, KING: Ligeti, MESSENGER: Assandri, PRIESTESS:
Hilgenberg, CONDUCTOR: De Fabritiis.

YOUNG PEOPLE'S PERFORMANCES

October 10, matinee: MADAMA BUTTERFLY (Puccini)
Same cast except: PINKERTON: Lewis, SHARPLESS: Colzani.
October 11, matinee: MADAMA BUTTERFLY (Puccini)
Same cast except: CIO-CIO-SAN: Kirsten, PINKERTON: Curzi, SHARPLESS:
Guarrera, SUZUKI: Nadell.
October 16, matinee: MADAMA BUTTERFLY (Puccini)
Same cast except: CIO-CIO-SAN: Kirsten, PINKERTON: Lewis, SHARPLESS:
Guarrera, GORO: Assandri.

CASTS—1957 SEASON

REGULAR SERIES

September 17: TURANDOT (Puccini)
TURANDOT: Rysanek, LIU: Albanese, CALAF: Tobin, TIMUR: Moscona,
PING: Blankenburg, PANG: Assandri, PONG: Curzi, EMPEROR ALTOUM:
Fried, PRINCE OF PERSIA: Malone, MAIDS: Cadwallader, Petersen, CONDUCTOR: Molinari-Pradelli.
September 20: THE DIALOGUES OF THE CARMELITES (Poulenc)
BLANCHE: Kirsten, PRIORESS: Turner, NEW PRIORESS: Price, MOTHER MARIE: Thebom, SISTER CONSTANCE: Stahlman, MARQUIS DE LA FORCE: Herbert, CHEVALIER: Crain, MOTHER JEANNE: Hilgenberg, SISTER MATHILDE:
Petersen, FATHER CONFESSOR: Curzi, COMMISSIONERS: Fried, Palangi,
JAILOR: Presnell, GOVERNESS: West, THIERRY: Kenig, M. JAVELINOT: Enns,

374

FIRST OFFICER: Reitan, FANATIC WOMAN: Knapp, WOMEN: Berrar, Johnson, OLD MAN: Wagner, CONDUCTOR: Leinsdorf.

September 24: UN BALLO IN MASCHERA (Verdi)
AMELIA: Rysanek, ULRICA: Turner, OSCAR: Stahlman, RICCARDO: Peerce, RENATO: Merrill, SAM: Alvary, TOM: Moscona, SILVANO: Blankenburg, JUDGE: Fried, SERVANT: Kenig, CONDUCTOR: Steinberg.

September 27: LUCIA DI LAMMERMOOR (Donizetti)
LUCIA: Gencer, LORD HENRY: Borghi, EDGARDO: Raimondi, LORD ARTHUR: Curzi, RAYMOND: Alvary, ALICE: Burlingham, NORMAN: Assandri, CONDUCTOR: Molinari-Pradelli.

October 1: DER ROSENKAVALIER (Strauss)
MARSCHALLIN: Schwarzkopf, BARON OCHS: Edelmann, OCTAVIAN: Bible, SOPHIE: Streich, FANINAL: Herbert, TENOR: Crain, MARIANNE: Andrew, VALZACCHI: Fried, ANNINA: Hilgenberg, POLICE COMMISSIONER: Presnell, NOTARY: Harvey, LANDLORD: Curzi, MILLINER: McArt, ANIMAL VENDOR: Assandri, MARSCHALLIN'S MAJOR DOMO: Kenig, FANINAL'S MAJOR DOMO: Thomas, ORPHANS: Hoffman, San Miguel, Petersen, FOOTMEN: Hubbard, Booth, Guenter, Woellhaf, CONDUCTOR: Leinsdorf.

October 8: ARIADNE AUF NAXOS (Strauss)
ARIADNE, PRIMA DONNA: Rysanek, BACCHUS, TENOR: Lewis, COMPOSER: George, ZERBINETTA: Streich, MUSIC TEACHER: Herbert, MAJOR DOMO: Louw, ARLECCHINO: Blankenburg, SCARAMUCCIO: Manton, TRUFFALDINO: Alvary, BRIGHELLA: Curzi, NAIAD: Stahlman, DRYAD: Turner, ECHO: Gibson, DANCING MASTER: Fried, WIGMAKER: Kenig, LACKEY: Palangi, OFFICER: Presnell, CONDUCTOR: Steinberg.

October 11: MACBETH (Verdi)
LADY MACBETH: Rysanek, MACBETH: Taddei, BANQUO: Alvary, MACDUFF: Crain, MALCOLM: Thomas, LADY-IN-WAITING: Burlingham, MEDIC: Enns, SERVANT: Andersen, ASSASSIN: Kenig, HERALD: Lovasich, APPARITIONS: Murphy, Covington, Fernandez, CONDUCTOR: Molinari-Pradelli.

October 15: TOSCA (Puccini)
TOSCA: Kirsten, CAVARADOSSI: Peerce, SCARPIA: Taddei, ANGELOTTI: Palangi, SPOLETA: Assandri, SACRISTAN: Herbert, SCIARRONE: Presnell, JAILOR: Enns, SHEPHERD: Fernandez, CONDUCTOR: Leinsdorf.

October 18: AIDA (Verdi)
AIDA: Price, AMNERIS: Thebom, RHADAMES: Tobin, AMONASRO: Merrill, RAMFIS: Moscona, KING: Palangi, MESSENGER: Fried, PRIESTESS: Andrew, CONDUCTOR: Molinari-Pradelli.

October 22: COSI FAN TUTTE (Mozart)
FIORDILIGI: Schwarzkopf, DORABELLA: Merriman, DESPINA: Streich, FERRANDO: Lewis, GUGLIELMO: Blankenburg, DON ALFONSO: Alvary, CONDUCTOR: Leinsdorf.

SATURDAY EVENING SERIES

September 21: TURANDOT (Puccini)
Same cast.
September 28: UN BALLO IN MASCHERA (Verdi)
Same cast except: AMELIA: Nelli.

October 5: LUCIA DI LAMMERMOOR (Donizetti)
Same cast except: EDGARDO: Peerce, RAYMOND: Moscona
October 12: ARIADNE AUF NAXOS (Strauss)
Same cast.
October 19: TOSCA (Puccini)
Same cast except: CAVARADOSSI: Crain.

THURSDAY EVENING SERIES

September 19: LA TRAVIATA (Verdi)
VIOLETTA: Gencer, ALFREDO: Raimondi, GERMONT: Merrill, GASTON: Assandri, BARON DOUPHOL: Kenig, MARQUIS D'OBIGNY: Presnell, DR. GRENVIL: Palangi, FLORA: McArt, ANNINA: Hilgenberg, CONDUCTOR: Curiel.
September 26: THE DIALOGUES OF THE CARMELITES (Poulenc)
Same cast.
October 3: DER ROSENKAVALIER (Strauss)
Same cast except: TENOR: Tobin.
October 10: MADAMA BUTTERFLY (Puccini)
CIO-CIO-SAN: Albanese, PINKERTON: Raimondi, SHARPLESS: Borghi, SUZUKI: Hilgenberg, GORO: Assandri, BONZE: Palangi, YAMADORI: Blankenburg, COMMISSIONER: Enns, KATE PINKERTON: Howe, REGISTRAR: Harvey, CONDUCTOR: Kritz.
October 17: MACBETH (Verdi)
Same cast.

EXTRA PERFORMANCES

October 13, matinee: DER ROSENKAVLIER (Strauss)
Same cast except: SOPHIE: Stahlman, TENOR: Manton.
October 16: THE DIALOGUES OF THE CARMELITES (Poulenc)
    (special performance for International Industrial Development
        Conference under Time-Life auspices)
Same cast.
October 20, matinee: LA TRAVIATA (Verdi)
Same cast except: VIOLETTA: Albanese.
October 21: AIDA (Verdi)
Same cast except: AIDA: Rysanek, AMNERIS: Turner.
October 23: AIDA (Verdi)
Same cast except: AMNERIS: Turner
October 24: COSI FAN TUTTE (Mozart)
Same cast.

YOUNG PEOPLE'S PERFORMANCES

October 4, matinee: LA TRAVIATA (Verdi)
Same cast except: VIOLETTA: Albanese, ALFREDO: Crain, GERMONT: Borghi.
October 10, matinee: LA TRAVIATA (Verdi)
Same cast except: ALFREDO: Curzi.
October 17, matinee: LA TRAVIATA (Verdi)
Same cast except: ALFREDO: Curzi, GERMONT: Borghi.

376

CASTS—1958 SEASON

REGULAR SERIES

September 12: MEDEA (Cherubini)
MEDEA: Farrell, JASON: Lewis, CREON: Modesti, GLAUCE: Stahlman, NERIS: Turner, CAPTAIN: Enns, HANDMAIDENS: Moynagh, Blum, CONDUCTOR: Fournet.

September 16: DON CARLO (Verdi)
ELISABETH: Gencer, EBOLI: Dalis, DON CARLO: Ferraro, RODRIGO: Guarrera, PHILIP II: Tozzi, GRAND INQUISITOR: Modesti, FRIAR: Elyn, COUNTESS OF MONDECAR: Moynagh, COUNT LERMA: Assandri, ROYAL HERALD: R. Thomas, COUNTESS OF AREMBERG: Broughton, CELESTIAL VOICE: Daniel, CONDUCTOR: Sebastian.

September 19: LA BOHÈME (Puccini)
MIMI: Della Casa, RODOLFO: Raimondi, MARCELLO: Panerai, COLLINE: Alvary, SCHAUNARD: Gillaspy, MUSETTA: Ratti, BENOIT: Wentworth, ALCINDORO: Assandri, PARPIGNOL: R. Thomas, SERGEANT: Lorenzini, OFFICER: Harvey, CONDUCTOR: Fournet.

September 26: IL TROVATORE (Verdi)
LEONORA: Price, AZUCENA: Turner, MANRICO: Bjoerling, COUNT DI LUNA: Quilico, FERRANDO: Elyn, RUIZ: Assandri, OLD GYPSY: Enns, INEZ: Blum, CONDUCTOR: Sebastian.

September 30: THE BARTERED BRIDE (Smetana)
MARIE: Schwarzkopf, JENIK: Lewis, KEZAL: Tozzi, VASHEK: Fried, KRUSCHINA: Green, LUDMILA: Ward, MICHA: Wentworth, HATA: Hilgenberg, SPRINGER: Hager, ESMERALDA: Moynagh, MUFF: Harvey, CONDUCTOR: Ludwig.

October 3: THE WISE MAIDEN (Orff)
KING: Winters, PEASANT'S DAUGHTER: Price, PEASANT: Alvary, JAILOR: Wagner, MAN WITH DONKEY: Manton, MAN WITH MULE: Green, TRAMPS: R. Thomas, Gillaspy, Wentworth, CONDUCTOR: Ludwig.

followed by: CARMINA BURANA (Orff)
BURGUNDIAN TROUBADOUR: Guarrera, OLD POET: Guarrera, DRINKERS: Guarrera, Manton, BURGUNDIAN LADY: Malbin, YOUNG COUPLE IN LOVE: Blum, Green, COQUETTES: Oldt, Ward, Moynagh, FRIENDS OF TROUBADOUR: R. Thomas, Fried, Gillaspy, Green, Elyn, Enns, PAGES OF THE LADY: Carilli, Cherney, Dong, Fromer, Kattge, Wong, CONDUCTOR: Ludwig.

October 7: LA FORZA DEL DESTINO (Verdi)
LEONORA: Rysanek, DON ALVARO: Ferraro, DON CARLO: Weede, PADRE GUARDIANO: Modesti, FRA MELITONE: Wentworth, PREZIOSILLA: Ward, MARQUIS OF CALATRAVA: Elyn, ALCADE: Enns, TRABUCCO: Assandri, CURRA: Hilgenberg, SURGEON: Harvey, CONDUCTOR: Sebastian.

October 10: GIANNI SCHICCHI (Puccini)
GIANNI SCHICCHI: Taddei, RINUCCIO: Miller, LAURETTA: Stahlman, SIMONE: Alvary, BETTO: Wentworth, GHERARDO: Assandri, MARCO: Gillaspy, SPINELLOCCIO: Green, NOTARY: Elyn, PINELLINO: Harvey, GUCCIO: Enns, ZITA: Hilgenberg, NELLA: Moynagh, LA CIESCA: Ward, GHERARDINO:

Fromer, CONDUCTOR: Curiel.

followed by: ELEKTRA (Strauss)
ELEKTRA: Goltz, CHRYSOTHEMIS: Della Casa, KLYTEMNESTRA: Turner, AEGISTHUS: Feiersinger, ORESTES: Van Mill, ORESTES' TUTOR: Elyn, CONFIDANTE: Blum, TRAINBEARER: Oldt, YOUNG SERVANT: R. Thomas, OLD SERVANT: Enns, OVERSEER: Ward, MAIDSERVANTS: Taylor, Groves, Hilgenberg, Moynagh, Daniel, CONDUCTOR: Ludwig.

October 14: TANNHÄUSER (Wagner)
ELISABETH: Rysanek, VENUS: Hoffman, TANNHÄUSER: Feiersinger, WOLFRAM: Winters, LANDGRAVE: Van Mill, WALTHER: Miller, BITEROLF: Elyn, HEINRICH: Fried, REINMAR: Enns, SHEPHERD: Stahlman, CONDUCTOR: Ludwig.

October 17: MANON (Massenet)
MANON: Gencer, CHEVALIER DES GRIEUX: Lewis, LESCAUT: Quilico, GUILLOT: Fried, DE BRÉTIGNY: Gillaspy, COUNT DES GRIEUX: Alvary, POUSETTE: Stahlman, JAVOTTE: Moynagh, ROSETTE: Blum, INNKEEPER: Green, SERVANT: Pappas, GUARDS: R. Thomas, Enns, SERGEANT: Andersen, ATTENDANT: Lorenzini, CONDUCTOR: Fournet.

October 21: THE MARRIAGE OF FIGARO (Mozart)
SUSANNA: Ratti, COUNTESS: Schwarzkopf, CHERUBINO: Ward, FIGARO: Panerai, COUNT: Modesti, BARTOLO: Wentworth, BASILIO: Fried, MARCELLINA: Hilgenberg, BARBARINA: Moynagh, ANTONIO: Green, DON CURZIO: Manton, PEASANT GIRLS: Oldt, Blum, CONDUCTOR: Adler.

SATURDAY EVENING SERIES

September 13: THE BARBER OF SEVILLE (Rossini)
ROSINA: Ratti, COUNT ALMAVIVA: Miller, FIGARO: Panerai, BARTOLO: Baccaloni, BASILIO: Tozzi, FIORELLO: Gillaspy, OFFICER: Assandri, BERTHA: Hilgenberg, CONDUCTOR: Curiel.

September 20: DON CARLO (Verdi)
Same cast.

September 27: LA BOHÈME (Puccini)
Same cast.

October 4: THE BARTERED BRIDE (Smetana)
Same cast.

October 11: IL TROVATORE (Verdi)
Same cast except: AZUCENA: Dalis, INEZ: Groves.

October 18: TÄNNHAUSER (Wagner)
Same cast.

THURSDAY EVENING SERIES

September 18: MEDEA (Cherubini)
Same cast.

September 25: RIGOLETTO (Verdi)
GILDA: Gencer, DUKE: Raimondi, RIGOLETTO: Weede, MADDALENA: Ward, SPARAFUCILE: Alvary, MONTERONE: Elyn, BORSA: Assandri, MARULLO: Enns, CEPRANO: Gillaspy, COUNTESS CEPRANO: Blum, GIOVANNA: Hilgenberg, PAGE: Moynagh, CONDUCTOR: Fournet.

October 2: LA BOHÈME (Puccini)
Same cast except: RODOLFO: Bjoerling, COLLINE: Tozzi.
October 9: THE WISE MAIDEN (Orff)
Same cast.
        followed by: CARMINA BURANA (Orff)
Same cast.
October 16: GIANNI SCHICCHI (Puccini)
Same cast.
        followed by: ELEKTRA (Strauss)
Same cast except: KLYTEMNESTRA: Dalis.
October 23: THE MARRIAGE OF FIGARO (Mozart)
Same cast.

EXTRA PERFORMANCES

October 12, matinee: THE BARTERED BRIDE (Smetana)
Same cast.
October 19, matinee: DON CARLO (Verdi)
Same cast except: ELISABETH: Goltz, EBOLI: Hoffman, PHILIP II: Van Mill, GRAND INQUISITOR: Alvary, FRIAR: Enns.
October 20: RIGOLETTO (Verdi) (East Bay Night)
Same cast except: MADDALENA: Turner.
October 22: TANNHÄUSER (Wagner)
Same cast.

YOUNG PEOPLE'S PERFORMANCES

October 2, matinee: LA BOHÈME (Puccini)
Same cast except: MIMI: Moynagh, MARCELLO: Quilico, MUSETTA: Stahlman, CONDUCTOR: Kritz.
October 16, matinee: LA BOHÈME (Puccini)
Same cast except: MIMI: Malbin, RODOLFO: Ferraro, MARCELLO: Guarrera, COLLINE: Elyn, ALCINDORO: Green.
October 22, matinee: LA BOHÈME (Puccini)
Same cast except: MARCELLO: Quilico, MUSETTA: Stahlman, ALCINDORO: Green.

CASTS—1959 SEASON

REGULAR SERIES
September 11: AIDA (Verdi)
AIDA: Price, AMNERIS: Dalis, RHADAMES: Vickers, AMONASRO: Weede, RAMFIS: Tozzi, KING: Palangi, MESSENGER: R. Thomas, PRIESTESS: Hilgenberg, CONDUCTOR: Molinari-Pradelli.
September 15: ORFEO (Gluck)
ORFEO: Thebom, EURIDICE: Amara, AMOR: Moynagh, CONDUCTOR: Varviso.
September 17: DIE FRAU OHNE SCHATTEN (Strauss)
EMPRESS: Lang, EMPEROR: Feiersinger, BARAK: Yahia, BARAK'S WIFE: Schech, NURSE: Dalis, SPIRIT MESSENGER: Elyn, GUARDIAN OF TEMPLE GATES: Costa, ONE-ARMED MAN: Alvary, ONE-EYED MAN: Green, HUNCH-

BACK: Manton, FALCON'S VOICE: Moynagh, YOUTH: R. Thomas, SPIRITS: Hilgenberg, Winden, NIGHT WATCHMEN: Quilico, Andersen, McGuckin, SERVANTS: Foster, Moynagh, Blum, SOLO VOICES: Foster, Costa, Moynagh, E. Evans, Blum, Hilgenberg, CONDUCTOR: Ludwig.

September 22: MADAMA BUTTERFLY (Puccini)
CIO-CIO-SAN: Jurinac, PINKERTON: Zampieri, SHARPLESS: Zanasi, SUZUKI: E. Evans, GORO: Assandri, BONZE: Elyn, YAMADORI: Fried, COMMISSIONER: Green, KATE PINKERTON: Blum, REGISTRAR: Harvey, CONDUCTOR: Basile.

September 25: ANDREA CHENIER (Giordano)
MADELEINE: Tucci, ANDREA CHENIER: Del Monaco, GERARD: Weede, MATHIEU: Alvary, FLÉVILLE: Elyn, ROUCHER: Quilico, DUMAS: Palangi, ABBÉ: R. Thomas, SPY: Assandri, SCHMIDT: Woellhaf, FOUQUIER-TINVILLE: Green, COUNTESS: Taylor, MADELON: Hilgenberg, BERSI: E. Evans, CONDUCTOR: Molinari-Pradelli.

September 29: CARMEN (Bizet)
CARMEN: Lane, MICAELA: Amara, DON JOSÉ: Vickers, ESCAMILLO: Guarrera, ZUNIGA: Alvary, DANCAIRO: Fried, REMENDADO: R. Thomas, MORALES: Green, FRASQUITA: Moynagh, MERCEDES: E. Evans, CONDUCTOR: Basile.

October 6: DIE MEISTERSINGER (Wagner)
EVA: Jurinac, MAGDALENA: Hilgenberg, WALTHER: Feiersinger, HANS SACHS: Schoeffler, POGNER: Tozzi, DAVID: Curzi, BECKMESSER: G. Evans, KOTHNER: Winters, NIGHT WATCHMAN: Elyn, VOGELGESANG: Manton, NACHTIGALL: Green, ZORN: R. Thomas, EISSLINGER: Dal Poggetto, MOSER: Fried, ORTEL: McGuckin, SCHWARZ: Palangi, FOLTZ: Elyn, CONDUCTOR: Ludwig.

October 9: L'AMORE DEI TRE RE (Montemezzi)
FIORA: Kirsten, AVITO: Zampieri, MANFREDO: Guarrera, ARCHIBALDO: Tozzi, FLAMINIO: R. Thomas, YOUTH: Fried, OLD WOMAN: E. Evans, YOUNG GIRL: Cann, SERVANT: Blum, CONDUCTOR: Molinari-Pradelli.

October 13: DANSES CONCERTANTES ballet (Stravinsky)
PRINCIPALS: N. Johnson, Drew, Fuerstner, Herrin, Bailey, Stowell, Vollmar, Carter, V. Johnson, Smuin, CONDUCTOR: Murray.
followed by: ARIADNE AUF NAXOS (Strauss)
ARIADNE, PRIMA DONNA: Farrell, BACCHUS, TENOR: Lewis, COMPOSER: Jurinac, ZERBINETTA: Streich, MUSIC TEACHER: G. Evans, MAJOR DOMO: Symonds, ARLECCHINO: Uppman, SCARAMUCCIO: Manton, TRUFFALDINO: Alvary, BRIGHELLA: Curzi, NAIAD: Alarie, DRYAD: Hilgenberg, ECHO: Moynagh, DANCING MASTER: Fried, WIGMAKER: Assandri, LACKEY: Palangi, OFFICER: R. Thomas, CONDUCTOR: Ludwig.

October 16: OTELLO (Verdi)
DESDEMONA: Tucci, OTELLO: Del Monaco, IAGO: Zanasi, CASSIO: Zampieri, RODERIGO: Fried, LODOVICO: Yahia, MONTANO: Elyn, HERALD: Green, EMILIA: Hilgenberg, CONDUCTOR: Molinari-Pradelli.

October 20: DON GIOVANNI (Mozart)
DONNA ANNA: Jurinac, DONNA ELVIRA: Price, ZERLINA: Alarie, DON GIOVANNI: London, LEPORELLO: Alvary, DON OTTAVIO: Lewis, COMMENDATORE: Yahia, MASETTO: Uppman, CONDUCTOR: Ludwig.

SATURDAY EVENING SERIES

September 12: MADAMA BUTTERFLY (Puccini)
Same cast exept: CIO-CIO-SAN: Kirsten, PINKERTON: Gismondo.
September 19: I PAGLIACCI (Leoncavallo)
CANIO: Vickers, TONIO: Weede, NEDDA: Amara, SILVIO: Quilico, BEPPE: Fried, PEASANTS: Green, R. Thomas, CONDUCTOR: Basile.
          followed by: CARMINA BURANA (Orff)
BURGUNDIAN TROUBADOUR: Guarrera, OLD POET: Guarrera, DRINKERS: Guarrera, Manton, BURGUNDIAN LADY: Costa, YOUNG COUPLE IN LOVE: Winden, Elyn, THREE COQUETTES: Foster, Blum, Moynagh, FRIENDS OF TROUBADOUR: R. Thomas, Fried, Dal Poggetto, Green, Elyn, Palangi, PAGES OF THE LADY: Carilli, Dong, Fromer, Goodwin, Murphy, Waring, CONDUCTOR: Varviso.
September 26: ORFEO (Gluck)
Same cast.
October 3: DON GIOVANNI (Mozart)
Same cast except: DON GIOVANNI: Yahia, COMMENDATORE: Tozzi.
October 10: ANDREA CHENIER (Giordano)
Same cast.
October 17: DANSES CONCERTANTES ballet (Stravinsky)
Same cast.
          followed by: ARIADNE AUF NAXOS (Strauss)
Same cast.

THURSDAY EVENING SERIES

September 17: L'AMORE DEI TRE RE (Montemezzi)
Same cast.
September 24: AIDA (Verdi)
Same cast except: AMONASRO: Winters, RAMFIS: Yahia.
October 1: CARMEN (Bizet)
Same cast except: MICAELA: Costa, ESCAMILLO: Zanasi.
October 8: DIE MEISTERSINGER (Wagner)
Same cast except: POGNER: Yahia.
October 15: DIE FRAU OHNE SCHATTEN (Strauss)
Same cast.
October 22: OTELLO (Verdi)
Same cast.

EXTRA PERFORMANCES

October 2: AIDA (Verdi)
Same cast except: AIDA: Amara, RHADAMES: Del Monaco, AMONASRO: Quilico, KING: Elyn.
October 19: LA BOHÈME (Puccini)
MIMI: Albanese, RODOLFO: Gismondo, MARCELLO: Uppman, COLLINE: Alvary, SCHAUNARD: G. Evans, MUSETTA: Costa, BENOIT: Baccaloni, ALCINDORO: Baccaloni, PARPIGNOL: Assandri, SERGEANT: Lorenzini, OFFICER: Harvey, CONDUCTOR: Varviso.

October 21: DIE MEISTERSINGER (Wagner)
Same cast except: POGNER: Yahia.

YOUNG PEOPLE'S PERFORMANCES

October 15, matinee: I PAGLIACCI (Leoncavallo)
Same cast except: TONIO: Winters, NEDDA: Mari, SILVIO: Uppman, BEPPE: Curzi, CONDUCTOR: Martin.
October 19, matinee: I PAGLIACCI (Leoncavallo)
Same cast except: CANIO: Feiersinger, TONIO: Winters, NEDDA: Mari, SILVIO: Guarrera, BEPPE: Curzi, CONDUCTOR: Martin.
October 20, matinee: I PAGLIACCI (Leoncavallo)
Same cast except: NEDDA: Mari, SILVIO: Guarrera, BEPPE: Manton, CONDUCTOR: Basile.

CASTS—1960 SEASON

REGULAR SERIES

September 16: TOSCA (Puccini)
TOSCA: Kirsten, CAVARADOSSI: Zampieri, SCARPIA: Gobbi, SPOLETTA: Fried, SACRISTAN: Baccaloni, ANGELOTTI: Foldi, SCIARRONE: Romero, JAILOR: Standard, SHEPHERD: Waring, CONDUCTOR: Varviso.
September 20: DIE FRAU OHNE SCHATTEN (Strauss)
EMPRESS: Rysanek, EMPEROR: Parly, BARAK: Schoeffler, BARAK'S WIFE: Schech, NURSE: Dalis, SPIRIT MESSENGER: Anderson, GUARDIAN OF TEMPLE GATES: Costa, ONE-ARMED MAN: Alvary, ONE-EYED MAN: Wentworth, HUNCHBACK: Manton, FALCON'S VOICE: McCann, YOUTH: Russell, SPIRITS: Martin, Blum, NIGHT WATCHMEN: Drain, Standard, Romero, SERVANTS: Starr, McCann, Blum, SOLO VOICES: Starr, Costa, McCann, Martin, Blum, Hilgenberg, CONDUCTOR: Ludwig.
September 23: LA FANCIULLA DEL WEST (Puccini)
MINNIE: Kirsten, DICK JOHNSON: Konya, JACK RANCE: Gobbi, JAKE WALLACE: Standard, NICK: Fried, ASHBY: Alvary, SONORA: Romero, TRIN: Manton, SID: Harvey, HANDSOME: Drain, HARRY: Russell, JOE: Hoskinson, HAPPY: Foldi, LARKENS: Andersen, JOSÉ CASTRO: Anderson, BILLY JACKRABBIT: Wentworth, WOWKLE: Hilgenberg, CONDUCTOR: Molinari-Pradelli.
September 27: SIMON BOCCANEGRA (Verdi)
SIMON BOCCANEGRA: Gobbi, AMELIA: Amara, FIESCO: Tozzi, ADORNO: Zampieri, PAOLO: Evans, PIETRO: Anderson, CAPTAIN: Russell, MAIDSERVANT: Martin, CONDUCTOR: Ludwig.
October 4: WOZZECK (Berg)
WOZZECK: Evans, MARIE: Horne, CAPTAIN: Lewis, DOCTOR: Alvary, DRUM MAJOR: Parly, ANDRES: Manton, MARGRET: Blum, ARTISANS: Wentworth, Romero, FOOL: Fried, SOLDIERS: Booth, Pierre, CHILD: Garay, CONDUCTOR: Ludwig.
October 7: DER ROSENKAVALIER (Strauss)
MARSCHALLIN: Schwarzkopf, BARON OCHS: Boehme, OCTAVIAN: Toepper, SOPHIE: Stahlman, FANINAL: Wentworth, TENOR: Manton, MARIANNE:

McCann, VALZACCHI: Fried, ANNINA: Hilgenberg, POLICE COMMISSIONER: Foldi, NOTARY: Harvey, LANDLORD: Hoskinson, MILLINER: Curatilo, ANIMAL VENDOR: Caperello, MARSCHALLIN'S MAJOR DOMO: Andersen, FANINAL'S MAJOR DOMO: Russell, ORPHANS: Liagre, Blum, Martin, FOOT-MEN: Hoskinson, Drain, Booth, Standard, CONDUCTOR: Varviso.

October 11: LA SONNAMBULA (Bellini)
AMINA: Moffo, ELVINO: Monti, RODOLFO: Tozzi, LISA: Stahlman, TERESA: Martin, ALESSIO: Foldi, NOTARY: Manton, CONDUCTOR: Molinari-Pradelli.

followed by: VARIATIONS DE BALLET (Glazounoff)
PRINCIPALS: Vollmar, Bailey, Drew, Herrin, CONDUCTOR: De Rosa.

October 14: LA BOHÈME (Puccini)
MIMI: Amara, RODOLFO: Konya, MARCELLO: Zanasi, COLLINE: Alvary, SCHAUNARD: Romero, MUSETTA: Costa, BENOIT: Baccaloni, ALCINDORO: Baccaloni, PARPIGNOL: Russell, SERGEANT: Standard, OFFICER: Drain, CONDUCTOR: Varviso.

October 18: COSI FAN TUTTE (Mozart)
FIORDILIGI: Schwarzkopf, DORABELLA: Hilgenberg, DESPINA: Costa, FERRANDO: Lewis, GUGLIELMO: Guarrera, DON ALFONSO: Schoeffler, CONDUCTOR: Adler.

October 21: LOHENGRIN (Wagner)
ELSA: Bjoner, ORTRUD: Dalis, LOHENGRIN: Konya, TELRAMUND: Anderson, KING HENRY: Boehme, HERALD: Wentworth, PAGES: Liagre, Curatilo, Blum, Martin, CONDUCTOR: Molinari-Pradelli.

October 25: LA TRAVIATA (Verdi)
VIOLETTA: Moffo, ALFREDO: Peerce, GERMONT: Weede, GASTON: Russell, BARON DOUPHOL: Romero, MARQUIS D'OBIGNY: Standard, DR. GRENVIL: Foldi, FLORA: Blum, ANNINA: Martin, CONDUCTOR: Varviso.

SATURDAY EVENING SERIES

September 17: CARMEN (Bizet)
CARMEN: Madeira, MICAELA: Costa, DON JOSÉ: Vickers, ESCAMILLO: Zanasi, ZUNIGA: Alvary, DANCAIRO: Fried, REMENDADO: Manton, MORALES: Romero, FRASQUITA: McCann, MERCEDES: Hilgenberg, CONDUCTOR: Molinari-Pradelli.

September 24: DIE FRAU OHNE SCHATTEN (Strauss)
Same cast.

October 1: LA FANCIULLA DEL WEST (Puccini)
Same cast.

October 8: WOZZECK (Berg)
Same cast.

October 15: COSI FAN TUTTE (Mozart)
Same cast.

October 22: LA BOHÈME (Puccini)
Same cast except: RODOLFO: Peerce.

THURSDAY EVENING SERIES

September 22: TOSCA (Puccini)
Same cast except: TOSCA: Amara, SCARPIA: Zanasi.

September 29: DER ROSENKAVALIER (Strauss)
Same cast except: OCTAVIAN: Bible.
October 6: SIMON BOCCANEGRA (Verdi)
Same cast.
October 13: LA SONNAMBULA (Bellini)
Same cast.
        followed by: VARIATIONS DE BALLET (Glazounoff)
Same cast.
October 20: LA TRAVIATA (Verdi)
Same cast except: VIOLETTA: Costa, ALFREDO: Zampieri.
October 27: LOHENGRIN (Wagner)
Same cast.

EXTRA PERFORMANCES

September 30: AIDA (Verdi)
AIDA: Rysanek, AMNERIS: Dalis, RHADAMES: Vickers, AMONASRO: Weede, RAMFIS: Tozzi, KING: Foldi, MESSENGER: Russell, PRIESTESS: Martin, CONDUCTOR: Molinari-Pradelli.
October 16: DER ROSENKAVALIER (Strauss)
Same cast except: TENOR: Parly.
October 24: AIDA (Verdi)
Same cast except: AIDA: Cavalli, RHADAMES: Konya, AMONASRO: Zanasi, RAMFIS: Anderson.
October 26: WOZZECK (Berg)
Same cast.

YOUNG PEOPLE'S PERFORMANCES

October 18, matinee: GIANNI SCHICCHI (Puccini)
GIANNI SCHICCHI: Evans, RINUCCIO: Parly, LAURETTA: Stahlman, SIMONE: Alvary, BETTO: Wentworth, GHERARDO: Manton, MARCO: Romero, SPINELLOCCIO: Foldi, NOTARY: Anderson, PINELLINO: Harvey, GUCCIO: Standard, ZITA: Horne, NELLA: McCann, LA CIESCA: Martin, CONDUCTOR: Schaefer.
        followed by: CON AMORE ballet (Rossini)
CAPTAIN: Bailey, THIEF: Drew, MISTRESS: Lawler, MASTER: Herrin, DANDY: Ohman, SAILOR: Smuin, STUDENT: Orr, AMOR: Wallace, CONDUCTOR: De Rosa.
October 25, 26, matinees: GIANNI SCHICCHI (Puccini)
Same cast except: ZITA: Hilgenberg.
        followed by: CON ARMORE ballet (Rossini)
Same cast.

CASTS—1961 SEASON

REGULAR SERIES
September 15: LUCIA DI LAMMERMOOR (Donizetti)

384

LUCIA: Moffo, LORD HENRY: Ruzdak, EDGARDO: Cioni, LORD ARTHUR: Handt, RAYMOND: Engen, ALICE: Cole, NORMAN: Fried, CONDUCTOR: Molinari-Pradelli.

September 18: BLOOD MOON (Dello Joio)
NINETTE: Costa, CLEO LAFONT: Dalis, RAYMOND BARDAC: Lance, ALEXANDRE DUMAS: Engen, TOM HENNEY: Heater, MR. PARKER: Foldi, MADAME BARDAC: Cole, EDMÉE LE BLANC: Gignac, BLIND WANDERER: Hecht, SISTER ANNE: Martin, POLICEMEN: Riffel, Leonetti, YOUNG MEN: Drain, Nilsson, Andersen, BUTLER: Harvey, CONDUCTOR: Ludwig.

September 22: MADAMA BUTTERFLY (Puccini)
CIO-CIO-SAN: Price, PINKERTON: Konya, SHARPLESS: Ruzdak, SUZUKI: Miller, GORO: Fried, BONZE: Hecht, YAMADORI: Nilsson, COMMISSIONER: Drain, REGISTRAR: Harvey, KATE PINKERTON: Blum, CONDUCTOR: Adler.

September 26: TURANDOT (Puccini)
TURANDOT: Udovick, LIU: Price, CALAF: Konya, TIMUR: Clabassi, PING: Heater, PANG: Manton, PONG: Thaw, EMPEROR ALTOUM: Fried, MANDARIN: Leonetti, PRINCE OF PERSIA: Riffel, MAIDS: Curatilo, Martin, CONDUCTOR: Molinari-Pradelli.

September 29: MARRIAGE OF FIGARO (Mozart)
SUSANNA: Sciutti, COUNTESS: Della Casa, CHERUBINO: Miller, FIGARO: Evans, COUNT: Engen, BARTOLO: Foldi, BASILIO: Handt, MARCELLINA: Hilgenberg, BARBARINA: Curatilo, ANTONIO: Drain, DON CURZIO: Manton, PEASANT GIRLS: Cadwallader, Blum, CONDUCTOR: Varviso.

October 6: NABUCCO (Verdi)
NABUCCO: MacNeil, ABIGAILLE: Udovick, ZACCARIA: Tozzi, ISMAELE: Zampieri, FENENA: Bence, HIGH PRIEST: Hecht, ANNA: Martin, ABDALLO: Fried, CONDUCTOR: Molinari-Pradelli.

October 10: A MIDSUMMER NIGHT'S DREAM (Britten)
BOTTOM: Evans, TITANIA: Costa, OBERON: Oberlin, LYSANDER: Thaw, HERMIA: Horne, DEMETRIUS: Heater, HELENA: Gignac, QUINCE: Engen, FLUTE: Handt, SNUG: Foldi, SNOUT: Manton, STARVELING: Drain, PUCK: Coghill, THESEUS: Hecht, HIPPOLYTA: Blum, COBWEB: Strubing, MUSTARDSEED: Olson, PEASEBLOSSOM: Schaffer, MOTH: Garay, CONDUCTOR: Varviso.

October 13: BORIS GODOUNOFF (Moussorgsky)
BORIS: Tozzi, DIMITRI: Lance, MARINA: Horne, PIMEN: Hecht, SHOUISKY: Handt, RANGONI: Clabassi, VARLAAM: Engen, MISSAIL: Fried, TCHELKALOFF: Heater, FEODOR: Blum, XENIA: Curatilo, NURSE: Martin, INNKEEPER: Hilgenberg, SIMPLETON: Manton, POLICE OFFICER: Leonetti, FRONTIER GUARD SERGEANT: Foldi, LOVITZKY: Drain, TCHERNIAKOVSKY: Leonetti, BOYAR: Nilsson, CONDUCTOR: Ludwig.

October 17: DIE MEISTERSINGER (Wagner)
EVA: Della Casa, MAGDALENA: Hilgenberg, WALTHER: Uhl, HANS SACHS: Schoeffler, POGNER: Tozzi, DAVID: Thaw, BECKMESSER: Evans, KOTHNER: Engen, NIGHT WATCHMAN: Foldi, VOGELGESANG: Manton, NACHTIGALL: Drain, ZORN: Nilsson, EISSLINGER: Riffel, MOSER: Fried, ORTEL: McGuckin, SCHWARZ: Hecht, FOLTZ: Foldi, CONDUCTOR: Ludwig.

October 20: UN BALLO IN MASCHERA (Verdi)
AMELIA: Brouwenstijn, ULRICA: Bence, OSCAR: Sciutti, RICCARDO:

Zampieri, RENATO: Bastianini, SAM: Clabassi, TOM: Foldi, SILVANO: Drain, JUDGE: Nilsson, SERVANT: Andersen, CONDUCTOR: Molinari-Pradelli.

October 24: FIDELIO (Beethoven)
LEONORE: Brouwenstijn, FLORESTAN: Uhl, ROCCO: Von Rohr, DON PIZARRO: Schoeffler, DON FERNANDO: Engen, MARZELLINE: Horne, JACQUINO: Thaw, PRISONERS: Manton, Foldi, CONDUCTOR: Ludwig.

SATURDAY EVENING SERIES

September 16: TURANDOT (Puccini)
Same cast.
September 23: LUCIA DI LAMMERMOOR (Donizetti)
Same cast except: LUCIA: Sutherland.
September 30: RIGOLETTO (Verdi)
GILDA: Costa, DUKE: Cioni, RIGOLETTO: MacNeil, MADDALENA: Bence, SPARAFUCILE: Clabassi, MONTERONE: Hecht, BORSA: Nilsson, MARULLO: Drain, CEPRANO: Foldi, COUNTESS CEPRANO: Blum, GIOVANNA: Martin, PAGE: Curatilo, CONDUCTOR: Varviso.
October 7: BLOOD MOON (Dello Joio)
Same cast.
October 14: THE MARRIAGE OF FIGARO (Mozart)
Same cast.
October 21: DIE MEISTERSINGER (Wagner)
Same cast except: POGNER: Von Rohr.

THURSDAY EVENING SERIES

September 21: BORIS GODOUNOFF (Moussorgsky)
Same cast except: MARINA: Dalis.
September 28: MADAMA BUTTERFLY (Puccini)
Same cast.
October 5: FIDELIO (Beethoven)
Same cast except: ROCCO: Wildermann.
October 12: UN BALLO IN MASCHERA (Verdi)
Same cast.
October 19: NABUCCO (Verdi)
Same cast except: ISMAELE: Cioni.
October 26: A MIDSUMMER NIGHT'S DREAM (Britten)
Same cast.

EXTRA PERFORMANCES

October 18: RIGOLETTO (Verdi)
Same cast except: DUKE: Zampieri, RIGOLETTO: Bastianini, MADDALENA: Miller, CEPRANO: Leonetti.
October 23: NABUCCO (Verdi)
Same cast except: NABUCCO: Bastianini, ISMAELE: Cioni, FENENA: Martin, ANNA: Curatilo.
October 25: LUCIA DI LAMMERMOOR (Donizetti)
Same cast except: LUCIA: Sutherland, LORD HENRY: Heater, RAYMOND: Tozzi.

YOUNG PEOPLE'S PERFORMANCES

October 18, matinee: RIGOLETTO (Verdi)
Same cast except: GILDA: Gignac, DUKE: Lance, RIGOLETTO: Ruzdak, SPARAFUCILE: Hecht, MONTERONE: Leonetti, CONDUCTOR: Lawner.

October 19, matinee: RIGOLETTO (Verdi)
Same cast except: GILDA: Gignac, DUKE: Handt, RIGOLETTO: Ruzdak, MADDALENA: Miller, MONTERONE: Leonetti, CONDUCTOR: Lawner.

October 23, matinee: RIGOLETTO (Verdi)
Same cast except: DUKE: Zampieri, RIGOLETTO: Ruzdak, MADDALENA: Hilgenberg, MONTERONE: Leonetti, CONDUCTOR: Lawner.

October 25, matinee: RIGOLETTO (Verdi)
Same cast except: GILDA: Gignac, DUKE: Lance, SPARAFUCILE: Hecht, MONTERONE: Leonetti, CONDUCTOR: Lawner.

CASTS—SPRING OPERA 1961

May 2: ROMÉO ET JULIETTE (Gounod)
ROMÉO: Verreau, JULIETTE: Venora, MERCUTIO: Fredricks, TYBALT: Schmorr, CAPULET: Rayson, FRIAR LAWRENCE: Macurdy, GREGORIO: Drain, BENVOGLIO: Caperello, DUKE OF VERONA: McGuckin, STEPHANO: Blum, GERTRUDE: Martin, PARIS: Andersen, CONDUCTOR: Rosenstock.

May 5: LA BOHÈME (Puccini)
MIMI: Venora, RODOLFO: Shirley, MARCELLO: Pelayo, COLLINE: Malas, SCHAUNARD: Fredricks, MUSETTA: De Sett, BENOIT: Giosso, ALCINDORO: Schmorr, PARPIGNOL: Frost, SERGEANT: Harvey, GUARD: Andersen, CONDUCTOR: Lewis.

May 9: MARTHA (Flotow)
LADY HARRIET: Gray, LIONEL: Nilsson, PLUNKETT: Malas, SIR TRISTAN: Drain, SHERIFF: Harvey, NANCY: Blum, MAIDS: Dakin, Knyiados, Cadwallader, FARMER: Lysell, FARMER'S WIFE: Scott, SERVANTS: Fairley, Andersen, Lawrence, CONDUCTOR: Salgo.

May 13: LA TRAVIATA (Verdi)
VIOLETTA: Gray, ALFREDO: Verreau, GERMONT: Rayson, GASTON: Schmorr, BARON DOUPHOL: Drain, MARQUIS D'OBIGNY: McGuckin, DR. GRENVIL: Giosso, FLORA: Martin, ANNINA: Petersen, CONDUCTOR: Lewis.

May 16: THE MAGIC FLUTE (Mozart)
PAMINA: Yarick, QUEEN OF THE NIGHT: De Sett, TAMINO: Shirley, PAPAGENO: Drain, SARASTRO: Macurdy, SPEAKER: Malas, PAPAGENA: Curatilo, MONOSTATOS: Schmorr, PRIESTS: Andersen, Harvey, LADIES: Cann, Blum, Martin, ARMORED MEN: Caperello, McGuckin, YOUTHS: Goodchild, Schaffer, Cramer, CONDUCTOR: Rosenstock.

May 19: CARMEN (Bizet)
CARMEN: Horne, MICAELA: Yarick, DON JOSÉ: King, ESCAMILLO: Pelayo, ZUNIGA: McGuckin, DANCAIRO: Gallegos, REMENDADO: Schmorr, MORALES: Andersen, FRASQUITA: Curatilo, MERCEDES: Martin, CONDUCTOR: Rosenstock.

CASTS—1962 SEASON

REGULAR SERIES

September 14: LA BOHÈME (Puccini)
MIMI: Kirsten, RODOLFO: Cioni, MARCELLO: Tipton, COLLINE: Tozzi, SCHAUNARD: Christopher, MUSETTA: Costa, BENOIT: Baccaloni, ALCINDORO: Baccaloni, PARPIGNOL: Fried, SERGEANT: Andersen, GUARD: Harvey, CONDUCTOR: Molinari-Pradelli.

September 18: DON CARLO (Verdi)
ELISABETH: Rubio, EBOLI: Dalis, DON CARLO: Konya, RODRIGO: Stewart, PHILIP II: Tozzi, GRAND INQUISITOR: Langdon, FRIAR: Macurdy, COUNTESS OF MONDECAR: Curatilo, COUNT LERMA: Riffel, COUNTESS OF AREMBERG: Stalley, CELESTIAL VOICE: Todd, CONDUCTOR: Molinari-Pradelli.

September 21: WOZZECK (Berg)
WOZZECK: Evans, MARIE: Horne, CAPTAIN: Lewis, DOCTOR: Langdon, DRUM MAJOR: Sullivan, ANDRES: Manton, MARGRET: Martin, ARTISANS: Tipton, Christopher, FOOL: Fried, SOLDIERS: Budzinski, Gomez, CHILD: Robb, CONDUCTOR: Ludwig.

September 25: FAUST (Gounod)
MARGUERITE: Costa, FAUST: Lance, MEPHISTOPHELES: Tozzi, VALENTIN: Stewart, WAGNER: Drain, SIEBEL: Meyer, MARTHE: Cole, CONDUCTOR: De Fabritiis.

October 2: IL TROVATORE (Verdi)
LEONORA: Ross, AZUCENA: Simionato, MANRICO: McCracken, COUNT DI LUNA: Bastianini, FERRANDO: Hecht, RUIZ: Riffel, OLD GYPSY: Drain, INEZ: Cole, CONDUCTOR: Molinari-Pradelli.

October 5: CARMEN (Bizet)
CARMEN: Cervena, MICAELA: Lipp, DON JOSÉ: Del Monaco, ESCAMILLO: Stewart, ZUNIGA: Hecht, DANCAIRO: Fried, REMENDADO: Manton, MORALES: Christopher, FRASQUITA: Todd, MERCEDES: Martin, CONDUCTOR: Ferencsik.

October 9: OTELLO (Verdi)
DESDEMONA: De Los Angeles, OTELLO: McCracken, IAGO: Gobbi, CASSIO: Peterson, RODERIGO: Riffel, LODOVICO: Macurdy, MONTANO: Christopher, HERALD: Drain, EMILIA: Martin, CONDUCTOR: Molinari-Pradelli.

October 12: DER ROSENKAVALIER (Strauss)
MARSCHALLIN: Schwarzkopf, BARON OCHS: Langdon, OCTAVIAN: Meyer, SOPHIE: Lipp, FANINAL: Tipton, TENOR: Peterson, MARIANNE: Curatilo, VALZACCHI: Fried, ANNINA: Martin, POLICE COMMISSIONER: Hecht, NOTARY: Harvey, LANDLORD: Manton, MILLINER: Todd, ANIMAL VENDOR: Fairley, MARSCHALLIN'S MAJOR DOMO: Andersen, FANINAL'S MAJOR DOMO: Riffel, ORPHANS: Krikorian, Moore, Leonard, FOOTMEN: Gomez, Wagner, Budzinski, Woellhaf, CONDUCTOR: Ferencsik.

October 16: DON GIOVANNI (Mozart)
DONNA ANNA: De Los Angeles, DONNA ELVIRA: Schwarzkopf, ZERLINA: Meneguzzer, DON GIOVANNI: Tozzi, LEPORELLO: Evans, DON OTTAVIO: Lewis, COMMENDATORE: Langdon, MASETTO: Hecht, CONDUCTOR: Ludwig.

October 19: THE RAKE'S PROGRESS (Stravinsky)

388

TOM RAKEWELL: Lewis, ANNE TRULOVE: Costa, NICK SHADOW: Tipton, FATHER TRULOVE: Macurdy, BABA THE TURK: Meyer, MOTHER GOOSE: Cervena, SELLEM: Fried, WARDEN: Drain, CONDUCTOR: Ludwig.
October 23: FALSTAFF (Verdi)
SIR JOHN FALSTAFF: Evans, MISTRESS FORD: Lipp, MISTRESS PAGE: Meyer, DAME QUICKLY: Simionato, ANNE: Meneguzzer, FENTON: Peterson, FORD: Stewart, DR. CAIUS: Fried, BARDOLPH: Manton, PISTOL: Langdon, CONDUCTOR: Ferencsik.

SATURDAY EVENING SERIES

September 15: WOZZECK (Berg)
Same cast.
September 22: DON CARLO (Verdi)
Same cast.
September 29: LA BOHÈME (Puccini)
Same cast except: COLLINE: Macurdy, MUSETTA: Horne.
October 6: IL TROVATORE (Verdi)
Same cast.
October 13: I PAGLIACCI (Leoncavallo)
CANIO: Del Monaco, TONIO: Bastianini, NEDDA: Horne, SILVIO: Christopher, BEPPE: Manton, PEASANTS: Drain, Riffel, CONDUCTOR: De Fabritiis.
        followed by: CAVALLERIA RUSTICANA (Mascagni)
SANTUZZA: Dalis, TURIDDU: Cioni, ALFIO: Tipton, LOLA: Martin, MAMMA LUCIA: Cole, CONDUCTOR: De Fabritiis.
October 20: DON GIOVANNI (Mozart)
Same cast.

THURSDAY EVENING SERIES

September 20: CARMEN (Bizet)
Same cast.
September 27: DER ROSENKAVALIER (Strauss)
Same cast.
October 4: THE DAUGHTER OF THE REGIMENT (Donizetti)
MARIE: Meneguzzer, TONIO: Cioni, SULPICE: Baccaloni, MARQUISE DE BIRKENFELD: Cervena, HORTENSIUS: Hecht, CORPORAL: Drain, NOTARY: Harvey, PEASANT: Riffel, DUCHESSE DE KRAKENTHORP: Cole, CONDUCTOR: De Fabritiis.
October 11: FALSTAFF (Verdi)
Same cast.
October 18: OTELLO (Verdi)
Same cast except: DESDEMONA: Kabaiwanska.
October 25: THE RAKE'S PROGRESS (Stravinsky)
Same cast.

EXTRA PERFORMANCES

September 28: FAUST (Gounod)
Same cast.

389

October 22: LA BOHÈME (Puccini)
Same cast except: MIMI: De Los Angeles, COLLINE: Macurdy, MUSETTA: Horne.
October 24: I PAGLIACCI (Leoncavallo)
Same cast except: NEDDA: Lipp.
        followed by: CAVALLERIA RUSTICANA (Mascagni)
Same cast except: SANTUZZA: Simionato, TURIDDU: Sullivan.

YOUNG PEOPLE'S PERFORMANCES

October 4, matinee: THE DAUGHTER OF THE REGIMENT (Donizetti)
Same cast except: MARIE: Horne, TONIO: Peterson, MARQUISE DE BIRKEN-FELD: Meyer.
October 18, matinee: THE DAUGHTER OF THE REGIMENT (Donizetti)
Same cast.
October 22, matinee: THE DAUGHTER OF THE REGIMENT (Donizetti)
Same cast except: TONIO: Peterson, MARQUISE DE BIRKENFELD: Meyer.
October 23, matinee: THE DAUGHTER OF THE REGIMENT (Donizetti)
Same cast except: MARIE: Horne.

CASTS—SPRING OPERA 1962

May 8: MANON (Massenet)
MANON: Venora, CHEVALIER DES GRIEUX: Verreau, LESCAUT: Fredricks, GUILLOT: Hoskinson, DE BRÉTIGNY: Dunlap, COUNT DES GRIEUX: Macurdy, POUSETTE: Power, JAVOTTE: Langee, ROSETTE: Petersen, INNKEEPER: Drain, GUARDS: Gomez, Andersen, CONDUCTOR: Alessandro.
May 11: THE BARBER OF SEVILLE (Rossini)
ROSINA: Horne, COUNT ALMAVIVA: Manton, FIGARO: Fredricks, BARTOLO: Beattie, BASILIO: Macurdy, FIORELLO: Drain, OFFICER: Hoskinson, BERTHA: Cole, AMBROSIO: Harvey, CONDUCTOR: Kritz.
May 12: THE BARBER OF SEVILLE (Rossini)
Same cast.
May 15: THE PEARL FISHERS (Bizet)
LEILA: Venora, NADIR: Verreau, ZURGA: Ludgin, NOURABAD: Macurdy, CONDUCTOR· Alessandro.
May 17: THE ABDUCTION FROM THE SERAGLIO (Mozart)
CONSTANZE: Carron, BLONDE: Scovotti, BELMONTE: Walker, PEDRILLO: Lopez, OSMIN: Beattie, PASHA: Drain, CONDUCTOR: Kritz.
May 18: THE ABDUCTION FROM THE SERAGLIO (Mozart)
Same cast.
May 19: THE PEARL FISHERS (Bizet)
Same cast.
May 22: TOSCA (Puccini)
TOSCA: Barrera, CAVARADOSSI: Di Giuseppe, SCARPIA: Ludgin, ANGELOTTI:

Drain, SPOLETTA: Hoskinson, SACRISTAN: Beattie, SCIARRONE: Dunlap, JAILOR: Harvey, SHEPHERD: Strubing, CONDUCTOR: Lewis.
May 25: LA TRAVIATA (Verdi)
VIOLETTA: Carron, ALFREDO: Manton, GERMONT: Maero, GASTON: Lopez, BARON DOUPHOL: Drain, MARQUIS D'OBIGNY: Dunlap, DR. GRENVIL: Matthes, FLORA: Langee, ANNINA: Petersen, CONDUCTOR: Lewis.
May 26: TOSCA (Puccini)
Same cast.

CASTS—1963 SEASON

REGULAR SERIES

September 13: AIDA (Verdi)
AIDA: Price, AMNERIS: Resnik, RHADAMES: Konya, AMONASRO: Shaw, RAMFIS: Tozzi, KING: Hecht, MESSENGER: Riffel, PRIESTESS: Todd, CONDUCTOR: Molinari-Pradelli.
September 17: LA SONNAMBULA (Bellini)
AMINA: Sutherland, ELVINO: Cioni, RODOLFO: Cross, LISA: Meneguzzer, TERESA: Cole, ALESSIO: Hecht, NOTARY: Manton, CONDUCTOR: Bonynge.
September 20: THE BARBER OF SEVILLE (Rossini)
ROSINA: Grist, COUNT ALMAVIVA: Valletti, FIGARO: Prey, BARTOLO: Esparza, BASILIO: Van Der Bilt, FIORELLO: Christopher, OFFICER: McCaughna, BERTHA: Cervena, AMBROSIO: Harvey, CONDUCTOR: Ferencsik.
September 24: MEFISTOFELE (Boito)
MEFISTOFELE: Tozzi, FAUST: Konya, MARGHERITA: Costa, ELENA: Costa, WAGNER: Fried, MARTHA: Cole, PANTALIS: Martin, NEREO: Riffel, CONDUCTOR: Molinari-Pradelli.
October 1: THE QUEEN OF SPADES (Tchaikovsky)
HERMANN: McCracken, LISA: Kirsten, COUNTESS: Resnik, TOMSKY: Shaw, YELETSKY: Stewart, PAULINE: Martin, MASCHA: Todd, TCHEKALINSKY: Peterson, SOURIN: Hecht, MASTER OF CEREMONIES: Riffel, TCHAPLITSKY: Fried, NARUMOFF: McCaughna, MAIDS: Nenova, Liagre, Leonard, San Miguel, CONDUCTOR: Ludwig.
October 4: LA TRAVIATA (Verdi)
VIOLETTA: Costa, ALFREDO: Cioni, GERMONT: Stewart, GASTON: Riffel, BARON DOUPHOL: Esparza, MARQUIS D'OBIGNY: Christopher, DR. GRENVIL: Van Der Bilt, FLORA: Cervena, ANNINA: Todd, CONDUCTOR: Molinari-Pradelli.
October 8: LA FORZA DEL DESTINO (Verdi)
LEONORA: Price, DON ALVARO: McCracken, DON CARLO: Haas, PADRE GUARDIANO: Kreppel, FRA MELITONE: Esparza, PREZIOSILLA: Martin, MARQUIS OF CALATRAVA: Hecht, ALCADE: Van Der Bilt, TRABUCCO: Fried, CURRA: Cole, SURGEON: McCaughna, CONDUCTOR: Molinari-Pradelli.
October 11: SAMSON AND DELILAH (Saint-Saens)
SAMSON: McCracken, DELILAH: Warfield, HIGH PRIEST: Haas, ABIMELECH: Hecht, OLD HEBREW: Van Der Bilt, MESSENGER: Manton, PHILISTINES: Riffel, Christopher, CONDUCTOR: Prêtre.
October 15: DIE WALKÜRE (Wagner)

BRÜNNHILDE: Shuard, SIEGLINDE: Ericsdotter, FRICKA: Resnik, SIEGMUND: Vickers, WOTAN: Wolovsky, HUNDING: Kreppel, HELMWIGE: Todd, GERHILDE: Parker, ORTLINDE: Warden, SIEGRUNE: Chronis, ROSSWEISSE: Cervena, WALTRAUTE: Martin, GRIMGERDE: Petersen, SCHWERTLEITE: Cole, CONDUCTOR: Ludwig.

October 22: THE DIALOGUES OF THE CARMELITES (Poulenc)
BLANCHE: Venora, PRIORESS: Resnik, NEW PRIORESS: Ericsdotter, MOTHER MARIE: Warfield, SISTER CONSTANCE: Grist, MARQUIS DE LA FORCE: Shaw, CHEVALIER: Peterson, MOTHER JEANNE; Cole, SISTER MATHILDE: Todd, FATHER CONFESSOR: Nilsson, COMMISSIONERS: Fried, Esparza, JAILOR: Van Der Bilt, GOVERNESS: Null, THIERRY: Andersen, M. JAVELINOT: Christopher, FIRST OFFICER: McCaughna, WOMEN: Hemmingsen, Bradley, OLD MAN: Wagner, CONDUCTOR: Ludwig.

October 25: CAPRICCIO (Strauss)
COUNTESS: Schwarzkopf, LA ROCHE: Wolovsky, FLAMAND: Valletti, OLIVIER: Prey, COUNT: Stewart, CLAIRON: Cervena, M. TAUPE: Fried, ITALIAN SINGERS: Meneguzzer, Peterson, MAJOR DOMO: Van Der Bilt, BALLERINA: Gregory, HER PARTNER: Gladstein, SERVANTS: Christopher, Eitze, Glover, Harvey, Hecht, Manton, McCaughna, Riffel, CONDUCTOR: Prêtre.

October 29: COSI FAN TUTTE (Mozart)
FIORDILIGI: Schwarzkopf, DORABELLA: Vanni, DESPINA: Grist, FERRANDO: Valletti, GUGLIELMO: Prey, DON ALFONSO: Wolovsky, CONDUCTOR: Ferencsik.

SATURDAY EVENING SERIES

September 14: LA SONNAMBULA (Bellini)
Same cast.
September 21: AIDA (Verdi)
Same cast.
September 28: THE BARBER OF SEVILLE (Rossini)
Same cast.
October 5: THE QUEEN OF SPADES (Tchaikovsky)
Same cast.
October 12: FALSTAFF (Verdi)
SIR JOHN FALSTAFF: Evans, MISTRESS FORD: Costa, MISTRESS PAGE: Martin, DAME QUICKLY: Cervena, ANNE: Meneguzzer, FENTON: Peterson, FORD: Stewart, DR. CAIUS: Fried, BARDOLPH: Manton, PISTOL: Van Der Bilt, CONDUCTOR: Ferencsik.
October 19: COSI FAN TUTTE (Mozart)
Same cast.
October 26: THE DIALOGUES OF THE CARMELITES (Poulenc)
Same cast.

THURSDAY EVENING SERIES

September 19: MEFISTOFELE (Boito)
Same cast.

September 26: SAMSON AND DELILAH (Saint-Saens)
Same cast.
October 3: TOSCA (Puccini)
TOSCA: Price, CAVARADOSSI: Konya, SCARPIA: Shaw, SPOLETTA: Fried,
SACRISTAN: Esparza, ANGELOTTI: Hecht, SCIARRONE: Christopher, JAILOR:
McCaughna, SHEPHERD: Hethcoat, CONDUCTOR: Prêtre.
October 10: DIE WALKÜRE (Wagner)
Same cast.
October 17: LA TRAVIATA (Verdi)
Same cast.
October 24: LA FORZA DEL DESTINO (Verdi)
Same cast.
October 31: CAPRICCIO (Strauss)
Same cast.

SUNDAY MATINEE SERIES

September 22: LA SONNAMBULA (Bellini)
Same cast.
October 6: THE BARBER OF SEVILLE (Rossini)
Same cast.
October 13: TOSCA (Puccini)
Same cast except: CAVARADOSSI: Cioni, SCARPIA: Haas.
October 27: THE QUEEN OF SPADES (Tchaikovsky)
Same cast.

EXTRA PERFORMANCES

September 27: TOSCA (Puccini)
Same cast.
October 18: AIDA (Verdi)
Same cast except: AMNERIS: Warfield, RHADAMES: McCracken, AMONASRO:
Haas, RAMFIS: Kreppel.

YOUNG PEOPLE'S PERFORMANCES

October 15, 24, 29, 31, matinees: FALSTAFF (Verdi)
Same cast.

CASTS—SPRING OPERA 1963

April 30: THE TALES OF HOFFMANN (Offenbach)
HOFFMANN: Moulson, OLYMPIA: Toscano, GIULIETTA: Wolff, ANTONIA:
Todd, LINDORF, COPPELIUS, DAPERTUTTO, DR. MIRACLE: Ristow, NICK-
LAUSSE: Williams, VOICE OF ANTONIA'S MOTHER: Wilkins, SPALANZANI:
Klebe, SCHLEMIL: Giosso, CRESPEL: West, FRANTZ, COCHENILLE, PITICHINA-
CCIO: Detwiler, NATHANAEL: Budzinski, HERMANN: Wagner, LUTHER: Har-
vey, STELLA: Hobson, CONDUCTOR: Kritz.
May 3: THE TALES OF HOFFMANN (Offenbach)
Same cast.
May 7: RIGOLETTO (Verdi)

GILDA: Yarick, DUKE: Deis, RIGOLETTO: Ludgin, MADDALENA: Baldwin, SPARAFUCILE: Paul, MONTERONE: Jones, BORSA: Lopez, MARULLO: Smith, CEPRANO: Klebe, COUNTESS CEPRANO: Harden, GIOVANNA: Petersen, PAGE: Hethcoat, CONDUCTOR: Kritz.
May 10: RIGOLETTO (Verdi)
Same cast.
May 14: THE MAGIC FLUTE (Mozart)
PAMINA: Yarick, QUEEN OF THE NIGHT: Raina, TAMINO: Walker, PAPAGENO: Fredricks, SARASTRO: West, SPEAKER: Paul, PAPAGENA: Curatilo, MONOSTATOS: Lopez, PRIESTS: Silva, Harvey, LADIES: Todd, Williams, Petersen, ARMORED MEN: Detwiler, Jones, YOUTHS: Steele, Gordon, Martin, CONDUCTOR: Lewis.
May 21: DON PASQUALE (Donizetti)
NORINA: Venora, ERNESTO: Bressler, DR. MALATESTA: Fredricks, DON PASQUALE: Beattie, NOTARY: Harvey, CONDUCTOR: Lewis.
May 25: THE MAGIC FLUTE (Mozart)
Same cast.
May 28: MADAMA BUTTERFLY (Puccini)
CIO-CIO-SAN: Carron, PINKERTON: Deis, SHARPLESS: Wright, SUZUKI: Baldwin, GORO: Hata, BONZE: Giosso, YAMADORI: Klebe, COMMISSIONER: Smith, KATE PINKERTON: Harden, REGISTRAR: Harvey, CONDUCTOR: Popper.
June 4: THE SPANISH HOUR (Ravel)
CONCEPCION: Venora, GONZALVE: Bressler, TORQUEMADA: Lopez, RAMIRO: Fredricks, DON INIGO: Beattie, CONDUCTOR: Popper.
        followed by: BLUEBEARD'S CASTLE (Bartok)
JUDITH: Wolff, BLUEBEARD: Harrower, CONDUCTOR: Popper.
June 8: MADAMA BUTTERFLY (Puccini)
Same cast.

CASTS—1964 SEASON

REGULAR SERIES

September 11: OTELLO (Verdi)
DESDEMONA: Lorengar, OTELLO: McCracken, IAGO: Gobbi, CASSIO: Peterson, RODERIGO: Riffel, LODOVICO: Menci, MONTANO: McCaughna, HERALD: Giosso, EMILIA: Martin, CONDUCTOR: Molinari-Pradelli.
September 14: CARMEN (Bizet)
CARMEN: Resnik, MICAELA: Costa, DON JOSÉ: Martell, ESCAMILLO: Hecht, ZUNIGA: West, DANCAIRO: Fried, REMENDADO: Manton, MORALES: McCaughna, FRASQUITA: Todd, MERCEDES: Martin, CONDUCTOR: Prêtre.
September 18: PARSIFAL (Wagner)
KUNDRY: Dalis, PARSIFAL: Konya, AMFORTAS: Waechter, GURNEMANZ: Tozzi, KLINGSOR: Hecht, TITUREL: West, VOICE: Martin, KNIGHTS: Riffel, Menci, ESQUIRES: Todd, Martin, Fried, Glover, FLOWER MAIDENS: Venora, Todd, Curatilo, Gordon, Martin, Wien, CONDUCTOR: Prêtre.
September 22: DER ROSENKAVALIER (Strauss)

MARSCHALLIN: Schwarzkopf, BARON OCHS: Edelmann, OCTAVIAN: Seefried, SOPHIE: Grist, FANINAL: Ludgin, TENOR: Montal, MARIANNE: Curatilo, VALZACCHI: Fried, ANNINA: Martin, POLICE COMMISSIONER: Menci, NOTARY: Harvey, LANDLORD: Manton. MILLINER: Todd, ANIMAL VENDOR: Glover, MARSCHALLIN'S MAJOR DOMO: Andersen, FANINAL'S MAJOR DOMO: Riffel, ORPHANS: Hall, Gordon, White, FOOTMEN: Eitze, Wagner, Grace, Styles, CONDUCTOR: Leitner.

September 29: IL TROVATORE (Verdi)
LEONORA: Lee, AZUCENA: Resnik, MANRICO: McCracken, COUNT DI LUNA: Wolansky, FERRANDO: Hecht, RUIZ: Riffel, OLD GYPSY: Giosso, INEZ: White, MESSENGER: Glover, CONDUCTOR: Molinari-Pradelli.

October 2: GIANNI SCHICCHI (Puccini)
GIANNI SCHICCHI: Gobbi, RINUCCIO: Peterson, LAURETTA: Venora, SIMONE: Foldi, BETTO: McCaughna, GHERARDO: Fried, MARCO: Menci, SPINELLOCCIO: Giosso, NOTARY: West, PINELLINO: Harvey, GUCCIO: Andersen, ZITA: Wien, NELLA: Todd, LA CIESCA: Martin, GHERARDINO: Waddell, CONDUCTOR: Leitner.

followed by: CARMINA BURANA (Orff)
BURGUNDIAN TROUBADOUR: Wolansky, OLD POET: Wolansky, DRINKERS: Wolansky, Montal, BURGUNDIAN LADY: Grist, YOUNG COUPLE IN LOVE: White, West, COQUETTES: Todd, White, Curatilo, FRIENDS OF TROUBADOUR: Glover, Fried, Riffel, McCaughna, Giosso, West, PAGES OF THE LADY: Demers, Gilchrist, Krings, Martin, Van Leeuwen, Waddell, CONDUCTOR: Leitner.

October 6: NABUCCO (Verdi)
NABUCCO: Gobbi, ABIGAILLE: Kuchta, ZACCARIA: Tozzi, ISMAELE: Franco Tagliavini, FENENA: Martin, HIGH PRIEST: Menci, ANNA: Todd, ABDALLO: Riffel, CONDUCTOR: Molinari-Pradelli.

October 13: FIDELIO (Beethoven)
LEONORE: Nilsson, FLORESTAN: Vickers, ROCCO: Foldi, DON PIZARRO: Evans, DON FERNANDO: Ludgin, MARZELLINE: Venora, JACQUINO: Peterson, PRISONERS: Montal, Giosso, CONDUCTOR: Ludwig.

October 20: TURANDOT (Puccini)
TURANDOT: Nilsson, LIU: Lorengar, CALAF: Franco Tagliavini, TIMUR: Tozzi, PING: Wolansky, PANG: Manton, PONG: Montal, EMPEROR ALTOUM: Fried, MANDARIN: West, PRINCE OF PERSIA: Glover, MAIDS: White, Curatilo, CONDUCTOR: Molinari-Pradelli.

October 23: KATERINA ISMAILOVA (Shostakovich)
KATERINA: Collier, BORIS TIMOFEYEVICH: Ludgin, SERGEI: Vickers, ZINOVY: Martell, OLD CONVICT: Tozzi, AKSINYA: White, SONYETKA: Wien, DRUNK: Manton, PRIEST: Foldi, POLICE INSPECTOR: Hecht, MILL HAND: McCaughna, COACHMAN: Mayer, PORTER: West, STEWARD: Giosso, WORKMEN: Riffel, Glover, SENTRY: McCaughna, FEMALE CONVICT: Todd, SERGEANT: Andersen, CONDUCTOR: Ludwig.

October 30: DIE FRAU OHNE SCHATTEN (Strauss)
EMPRESS: Lee, EMPEROR: Martell, BARAK: Waechter, BARAK'S WIFE: Kuchta, NURSE: Dalis, SPIRIT MESSENGER: Hecht, GUARDIAN OF TEMPLE GATES: Venora, ONE-ARMED MAN: Foldi, ONE-EYED MAN: Menci, HUNCHBACK:

Manton, FALCON'S VOICE: Todd, YOUTH: Montal (mimed by Gladstein), SPIRITS: Wien, White, NIGHT WATCHMEN: Riffel, McCaughna, West, SERVANTS: Hall, Curatilo, Petersen, SOLO VOICES: Hall, Curatilo, Todd, Petersen, Wien, White, CONDUCTOR: Ludwig.
November 3: LA TRAVIATA (Verdi)
VIOLETTA: Sutherland, ALFREDO: Ilosfalvy, GERMONT: Waechter, GASTON: Riffel, BARON DOUPHOL: Hecht, MARQUIS D'OBIGNY: McCaughna, DR. GRENVIL: West, FLORA: Wien, ANNINA: Todd, CONDUCTOR: Bonynge.

SATURDAY EVENING SERIES

September 12: PARSIFAL (Wagner)
Same cast.
September 19: OTELLO (Verdi)
Same cast.
September 26: DIE FRAU OHNE SCHATTEN (Strauss)
Same cast.
✓ *October 3:* THE MARRIAGE OF FIGARO (Mozart)
SUSANNA: Grist, COUNTESS: Lorengar, CHERUBINO: Venora, FIGARO: Evans, COUNT: Waechter, BARTOLO: Foldi, BASILIO: Fried, MARCELLINA: Wien, BARBARINA: Curatilo, ANTONIO: Menci, DON CURZIO: Manton, CONDUCTOR: Leitner.
October 10: GIANNI SCHICCHI (Puccini)
Same cast.
         followed by: CARMINA BURANA (Orff)
Same cast except: BURGUNDIAN LADY: Costa.
October 17: FIDELIO (Beethoven)
Same cast.
October 24: IL TROVATORE (Verdi)
Same cast except: AZUCENA: Warfield.
October 31: KATERINA ISMAILOVA (Shostakovich)
Same cast.

THURSDAY EVENING SERIES

September 17: THE MARRIAGE OF FIGARO (Mozart)
Same cast.
September 24: DER ROSENKAVALIER (Strauss)
Same cast.
October 1: CARMEN (Bizet)
Same cast except: MICAELA: Lorengar, CONDUCTOR: Leitner.
✓ *October 8:* THE BARTERED BRIDE (Smetana)
MARIE: Costa, JENIK: Peterson, KEZAL: Evans, VASHEK: Fried, KRUSCHINA: Ludgin, LUDMILA: White, MICHA: West, HATA: Wien, SPRINGER: Resnick, ESMERALDA: Venora, COMEDIAN: Harvey, CONDUCTOR: Ludwig.
October 15: NABUCCO (Verdi)
Same cast.
October 22: TURANDOT (Puccini)
Same cast.
October 29: IL TROVATORE (Verdi)

Same cast except: AZUCENA: Warfield.
November 5: LA TRAVIATA (Verdi)
Same cast.

SUNDAY MATINEE SERIES

September 20: PARSIFAL (Wagner)
Same cast.
September 27: DER ROSENKAVALIER (Strauss)
Same cast.
October 11: THE BARTERED BRIDE (Smetana)
Same cast.
October 25: TURANDOT (Puccini)
Same cast.
November 1: LA TRAVIATA (Verdi)
Same cast.

EXTRA PERFORMANCES

September 25: OTELLO (Verdi)
Same cast.
October 9: CARMEN (Bizet)
Same cast except: MICAELA: Lorengar, DON JOSÉ: Vickers, CONDUCTOR:
Leitner.
October 16: IL TROVATORE (Verdi)
Same cast.
✓ *October 27:* I PAGLIACCI (Leoncavallo)
CANIO: McCracken, TONIO: Weede, NEDDA: Costa, SILVIO: Wolansky,
BEPPE: Montal, PEASANTS: Glover, Giosso, CONDUCTOR: Molinari-Pradelli.
                followed by: CARMINA BURANA (Orff)
Same cast.

YOUNG PEOPLE'S PERFORMANCES

October 26, matinee: THE BARTERED BRIDE (Smetana)
Same cast except: MARIE: Collier.
October 29, matinee: THE BARTERED BRIDE (Smetana)
Same cast.
November 3, matinee: THE BARTERED BRIDE (Smetana)
Same cast.
November 4, matinee: THE BARTERED BRIDE (Smetana)
Same cast.

CASTS—SPRING OPERA 1964

May 6: DER FREISCHÜTZ (Weber)
MAX: Cassilly, AGATHE: Mosher, CASPAR: Smith, AENNCHEN: Curatilo,
SAMIEL: Giosso, KILIAN: Turner, CUNO: Forbes, PRINCE OTTOKAR: McCaugh-
na, HERMIT: West, HUNTERS: Andersen, Harvey, CONDUCTOR: Popper.
May 13: SUSANNAH (Floyd)

SUSANNAH: Venora, OLIN BLITCH: Treigle, SAM POLK: Cassilly, LITTLE BAT: Kraus, MRS. GLEATON: Shipley, MRS. HAYES: Parker, MRS. MCLEAN: Petersen, MRS. OTT: Campagna-Pinto, ELDER MCLEAN: Forbes, ELDER HAYES: Glover, ELDER OTT: Giosso, ELDER GLEATON: Daugherty, TWO MEN: Andersen, Wagner, CONDUCTOR: Grossman.
May 16: SUSANNAH (Floyd)
Same cast.
May 20: LA BOHÈME (Puccini)
MIMI: Venora, RODOLFO: Di Giuseppe, MARCELLO: Fredricks, COLLINE: Paul, SCHAUNARD: McCaughna, MUSETTA: Pavek, BENOIT: Turner, ALCINDORO: Giosso, PARPIGNOL: Glover, SERGEANT: Andersen, GUARD: Harvey, CONDUCTOR: Kritz.
May 23: LA BOHÈME (Puccini)
Same cast except: RODOLFO: Lo Monaco.
May 26: THE PEARL FISHERS (Bizet)
LEILA: Pracht, NADIR: Verreau, ZURGA: Ludgin, NOURABAD: Paul, CONDUCTOR: Lawner.
June 2: FAUST (Gounod)
MARGUERITE: Todd, FAUST: Verreau, MEPHISTOPHELES: Voketaitis, VALENTIN: Ludgin, WAGNER: Turner, SIEBEL: Williams, MARTHE: Petersen, CONDUCTOR: Kritz.
June 5: THE ABDUCTION FROM THE SERAGLIO (Mozart)
CONSTANZE: Pracht, BLONDE: Brooks, BELMONTE: Montal, PEDRILLO: Lopez, OSMIN: Beattie, PASHA: Giosso, CONDUCTOR: Popper.
June 6: FAUST (Gounod)
Same cast.
June 9: THE ITALIAN GIRL IN ALGIERS (Rossini)
ISABELLA: Horne, LINDORO: Montal, ELVIRA: Brooks, MUSTAPHA: Beattie, TADDEO: Malas, HALY: McCaughna, ZULMA: Williams, CONDUCTOR: Lewis.
June 13: THE ITALIAN GIRL IN ALGIERS (Rossini)
Same cast.

CASTS—1965 SEASON

REGULAR SERIES

September 10: ANDREA CHENIER (Giordano)
MADELEINE: Tebaldi, ANDREA CHENIER: Tucker, GERARD: Bastianini, MATHIEU: Hecht, FLÉVILLE: West, ROUCHER: Fredricks, DUMAS: Menci, ABBÉ: Whitesides, SPY: Fried, SCHMIDT: Giosso, FOUQUIER-TINVILLE: Fazah, COUNTESS: Cervena, MADELON: Turner, BERSI: Bessel, CONDUCTOR: Molinari-Pradelli.
September 14: DIE FLEDERMAUS (Johann Strauss)
ROSALINDA: Costa, ADELE: Grist, PRINCE ORLOFSKY: Cervena, ALFRED: Sullivan, EISENSTEIN: Lewis, FRANK: Wolansky, DR. FALKE: Stewart, DR. BLIND: Foldi, FROSCH: Beach, IDA: Ray, IVAN: Menci, CONDUCTOR: Ludwig.
September 17: DIE MEISTERSINGER (Wagner)
EVA: Lorengar, MAGDALENA: Turner, WALTHER: Thomas, HANS SACHS:

Imdahl, POGNER: O'Leary, DAVID: Young, BECKMESSER: Blankenheim, KOTHNER: Ludgin, NIGHT WATCHMAN: Foldi, VOGELGESANG: Whitesides, NACHTIGALL: Fredricks, ZORN: Glover, EISSLINGER: Manton, MOSER: Fried, ORTEL: Fazah, SCHWARZ: Hecht, FOLTZ: West, CONDUCTOR: Ludwig.

September 21: LA FANCIULLA DEL WEST (Puccini)
MINNIE: Collier, DICK JOHNSON: Gibin, JACK RANCE: Ludgin, JAKE WALLACE: West, NICK: Fried, ASHBY: Hecht, SONORA: Fredricks, TRIN: Manton, SID: Harvey, HANDSOME: Andersen, HARRY: Whitesides, JOE: Glover, HAPPY: Giosso, LARKENS: Fazah, JOSÉ CASTRO: Menci, BILLY JACKRABBIT: Foldi, WOWKLE: White, CONDUCTOR: Molinari-Pradelli.

September 28: LA FORZA DEL DESTINO (Verdi)
LEONORA: Price, DON ALVARO: Konya, DON CARLO: Wolansky, PADRE GUARDIANO: Trama, FRA MELITONE: Blankenburg, PREZIOSILLA: Bessel, MARQUIS OF CALATRAVA: Hecht, ALCADE: West, TRABUCCO: Fried, CURRA: White, SURGEON: Fazah, CONDUCTOR: Molinari-Pradelli.

October 1: LULU (Berg)
LULU: Lear, DR. SCHOEN: Vinay, ALWA: Lewis, PAINTER: Sullivan, ANIMAL TRAINER: Resnick, SCHIGOLCH: Foldi, COUNTESS GESCHWITZ: Cervena, RODRIGO: Ludgin, PRINCE: Fried, DR. GOLL: Beach, WARDROBE MISTRESS: White, STAGE DIRECTOR: O'Leary, STUDENT: Bessel, SERVANT: Giosso, JACK THE RIPPER: Landry, CONDUCTOR: Ludwig.

October 8: THE BARBER OF SEVILLE (Rossini)
ROSINA: Grist, COUNT ALMAVIVA: Young, FIGARO: Fredricks, BARTOLO: Vinay, BASILIO: Trama, FIORELLO: Fazah, OFFICER: Glover, BERTHA: Cervena, AMBROSIO: Harvey, CONDUCTOR: Bellugi.

October 12: LOHENGRIN (Wagner)
ELSA: Hillebrecht, ORTRUD: Bessel, LOHENGRIN: Thomas, TELRAMUND: Ludgin, KING HENRY: O'Leary, HERALD: Fredricks, CONDUCTOR: Stein.

October 15: DON GIOVANNI (Mozart)
DONNA ANNA: Price, DONNA ELVIRA: Amara, ZERLINA: Meneguzzer, DON GIOVANNI: Stewart, LEPORELLO: Trama, DON OTTAVIO: Lewis, COMMENDATORE: O'Leary, MASETTO: West, CONDUCTOR: Molinari-Pradelli.

October 19: UN BALLO IN MASCHERA (Verdi)
AMELIA: Price, ULRICA: Turner, OSCAR: Meneguzzer, RICCARDO: Konya, RENATO: Wolansky, SAM: Hecht, TOM: West, SILVANO: Fredricks, JUDGE: Whitesides, CONDUCTOR: Molinari-Pradelli.

October 26: ARIADNE AUF NAXOS (Strauss)
ARIADNE, PRIMA DONNA: Hillebrecht, BACCHUS, TENOR: Thomas, COMPOSER: Vanni, ZERBINETTA: Grist, MUSIC MASTER: Ludgin, MAJOR DOMO: Beach, ARLECCHINO: Fredricks, SCARAMUCCIO: Manton, TRUFFALDINO: West, BRIGHELLA: Young, NAIAD: Meneguzzer, DRYAD: Bessel, ECHO: Curatilo, DANCING MASTER: Whitesides, WIGMAKER: Fried, LACKEY: Giosso, OFFICER: Eitze, CONDUCTOR: Stein.

October 29: PELLÉAS ET MÉLISANDE (Debussy)
MÉLISANDE: Lorengar, PELLÉAS: A. Jobin, GOLAUD: Stewart, ARKEL: O'Leary, GENEVIÈVE: Turner, YNIOLD: Kailer, DOCTOR: West, CONDUCTOR: Martinon.

SATURDAY EVENING SERIES

September 11: DIE MEISTERSINGER (Wagner)
Same cast.
September 18: DIE FLEDERMAUS (Johann Strauss)
Same cast.
September 25: LULU (Berg)
Same cast.
October 2: ANDREA CHENIER (Giordano)
Same cast except: ANDREA CHENIER: Gibin.
October 9: LA FORZA DEL DESTINO (Verdi)
Same cast.
October 16: TOSCA (Puccini)
TOSCA: Collier, CAVARADOSSI: Konya, SCARPIA: Vinay, SPOLETTA: Fried,
SACRISTAN: Foldi, ANGELOTTI: Hecht, SCIARRONE: Fazah, JAILOR: Giosso,
SHEPHERD: Di Francesco, CONDUCTOR: Bellugi.
October 23: ARIADNE AUF NAXOS (Strauss)
Same cast.
October 30: DON GIOVANNI (Mozart)
Same cast except: DONNA ANNA: Lorengar, LEPORELLO: Blankenburg.

THURSDAY EVENING SERIES

September 16: ANDREA CHENIER (Giordano)
Same cast.
September 23: LA BOHÈME (Puccini)
MIMI: Tebaldi, RODOLFO: Konya, MARCELLO: Wolansky, COLLINE: Hecht,
SCHAUNARD: Fredricks, MUSETTA: Meneguzzer, BENOIT: Foldi, ALCINDORO:
Fried, PARPIGNOL: Eitze, SERGEANT: Andersen, OFFICER: Harvey, CONDUC-
TOR: Bellugi.
September 30: DIE FLEDERMAUS (Johann Strauss)
Same cast.
October 7: THE BARBER OF SEVILLE (Rossini)
Same cast.
October 14: LOHENGRIN (Wagner)
Same cast.
October 21: TOSCA (Puccini)
Same cast except: CAVARADOSSI: Thomas.
October 28: UN BALLO IN MASCHERA (Verdi)
Same cast.
November 3 (Wednesday): PELLÉAS ET MÉLISANDE (Debussy)
Same cast.

SUNDAY MATINEE SERIES

September 19: LA BOHÈME (Puccini)
Same cast.
September 26: LA FANCIULLA DEL WEST (Puccini)
Same cast.
October 3: DIE MEISTERSINGER (Wagner)

Same cast except: EVA: Amara.

October 10: DIE FLEDERMAUS (Johann Strauss)
Same cast with CONDUCTOR: Stein.

October 24: THE BARBER OF SEVILLE (Rossini)
Same cast except: ROSINA: Meneguzzer, FIGARO: Blankenburg, BERTHA: Turner.

October 31: UN BALLO IN MASCHERA (Verdi)
Same cast except: OSCAR: Grist.

EXTRA PERFORMANCES

September 24: DIE FLEDERMAUS (Johann Strauss)
Same cast.

September 29: LA BOHÈME (Puccini)
Same cast except: RODOLFO: Cioni, MUSETTA: Collier.

October 22: DON GIOVANNI (Mozart)
Same cast.

YOUNG PEOPLE'S PERFORMANCES

October 6, matinee: THE BARBER OF SEVILLE (Rossini)
Same cast.

October 7, matinee: THE BARBER OF SEVILLE (Rossini)
Same cast except: ROSINA: Meneguzzer, COUNT ALMAVIVA: Whitesides, FIGARO: Blankenburg, BARTOLO: Foldi, BASILIO: Hecht.

October 11, matinee: THE BARBER OF SEVILLE (Rossini)
Same cast except: ROSINA: Meneguzzer, FIGARO: Blankenburg, BARTOLO: Foldi, BASILIO: Hecht, BERTHA: Turner.

October 25, matinee: THE BARBER OF SEVILLE (Rossini)
Same cast except: ROSINA: Meneguzzer, BARTOLO: Foldi, BERTHA: Turner.

CASTS—SPRING OPERA 1965

May 25: BLUEBEARD'S CASTLE (Bartok)
JUDITH: Wolff, BLUEBEARD: Berberian, CONDUCTOR: Samuel.
followed by: THE SPANISH HOUR (Ravel)
CONCEPCION: Todd, GONZALVE: Montal, TORQUEMADA: Glover, RAMIRO: Patrick, DON INIGO GOMEZ: Beattie, CONDUCTOR: Lawner.

June 1: MADAMA BUTTERFLY (Puccini)
CIO-CIO-SAN: Todd, PINKERTON: Craig, SHARPLESS: Bottcher, SUZUKI: Hirst, GORO: Glover, BONZE: Berberian, YAMADORI: Remo, COMMISSIONER: Turner, KATE PINKERTON: Hall, REGISTRAR: Harvey, CONDUCTOR: Grossman.

June 4: MADAMA BUTTERFLY (Puccini)
Same cast.

June 8: COSI FAN TUTTE (Mozart)
FIORDILIGI: Coulter, DORABELLA: Friedrich, DESPINA: Bogard, FERRANDO: Montal, GUGLIELMO: Patrick, DON ALFONSO: Beattie, CONDUCTOR: Kritz.

June 11: COSI FAN TUTTE (Mozart)
Same cast.

✓*June 15:* RIGOLETTO (Verdi)
GILDA: Newman, DUKE: Craig, RIGOLETTO: Ludgin, MADDALENA: Hirst, SPARAFUCILE: Macurdy, MONTERONE: Bottcher, BORSA: Remo, MARULLO: Turner, CEPRANO: Giosso, COUNTESS CEPRANO: Hall, GIOVANNA: Petersen, PAGE: Waddell, CONDUCTOR: Kritz.
June 18: RIGOLETTO (Verdi)
Same cast with CONDUCTOR: Rosekrans.
June 22: THE CRUCIBLE (Ward)
JOHN PROCTOR: Ludgin, ELIZABETH PROCTOR: Bible, REV. JOHN HALE: Macurdy, MARY WARREN: Newman, JUDGE DANFORTH: Nagy, BETTY PARRIS: White, REV. SAMUEL PARRIS: Remo, TITUBA: Patton, ABIGAIL WILLIAMS: Wheeler, ANN PUTNAM: Curatilo, THOMAS PUTNAM: Turner, REBECCA NURSE: Petersen, FRANCIS NURSE: Giosso, GILES COREY: Glover, EZEKIEL CHEEVER: Eitze, SARAH GOOD: Liagre, RUTH PUTNAM: Hall, SUSANNA WAL-COTT: Graber, MERCY LEWIS: Bradley, MARTHA SHELDON: Corsale, BRIDGET BOOTH: Talbot, CONDUCTOR: Grossman.

CASTS—1966 SEASON

REGULAR SERIES

September 20: I PURITANI (Bellini)
ELVIRA: Sutherland, ARTURO: Kraus, RICCARDO: Wolansky, GIORGIO: Ghiuselev, ENRICHETTA: Cole, BRUNO: Clements, WALTON: Grant, CONDUC-TOR: Bonynge.
✓*September 27:* DON CARLO (Verdi)
ELISABETH: Watson, EBOLI: Horne, DON CARLO: Vickers, RODRIGO: Glos-sop, PHILIP II: Tozzi, GRAND INQUISITOR: Ludgin, FRIAR: Berberian, COUNTESS OF MONDECAR: Curatilo, COUNT LERMA: Clements, COUNTESS OF AREMBERG: De Heurtaumont, CELESTIAL VOICE: Stevenson, CONDUC-TOR: Molinari-Pradelli.
September 30: ELEKTRA (Strauss)
ELEKTRA: Shuard, CHRYSOTHEMIS: Tarrés, KLYTEMNESTRA: Resnik, AEGISTHUS: Cassilly, ORESTES: Stewart, ORESTES' TUTOR: Berberian, CON-FIDANTE: Davis, TRAINBEARER: Corsale, YOUNG SERVANT: Thaw, OLD SER-VANT: Grant, OVERSEER: Cole, MAIDSERVANTS: Petersen, Wiench, Kirkpat-rick, Curatilo, Stevenson, CONDUCTOR: Stein.
October 4: L'AMORE DEI TRE RE (Montemezzi)
FIORA: Kirsten, AVITO: Campora, MANFREDO: Wolansky, ARCHIBALDO: Ghiuselev, FLAMINIO: Thaw, YOUTH: Clements, OLD WOMAN: Cole, YOUNG GIRL: Stevenson, SERVANT: Kirkpatrick, CONDUCTOR: Molinari-Pradelli.
October 11: BORIS GODOUNOFF (Moussorgsky)
BORIS: Ludgin, DIMITRI: Cassilly, MARINA: Martin, PIMEN: Berberian, SHOUISKY: Fried, RANGONI: Meredith, VARLAAM: Vinay, MISSAIL: Man-ton, TCHELKALOFF: Fazah, FEODOR: Krebill, XENIA: Curatilo, NURSE: Cole, INNKEEPER: Cervena, SIMPLETON: Thaw, POLICE OFFICER: Grant, FRONTIER GUARD SERGEANT: Grant, LOVITZKY: Giosso, TCHERNIAKOVSKY: Grant,

BOYAR: Clements, PEASANTS: Moore, Andersen, CONDUCTOR: Stein.

October 18: TANNHÄUSER (Wagner)
ELISABETH: Crespin, VENUS: Martin, TANNHÄUSER: Thomas, WOLFRAM: Stewart, LANDGRAVE: Kreppel, WALTHER: Thaw, BITEROLF: Berberian, HEINRICH: Clements, REINMAR: Grant, SHEPHERD: Christensen, CONDUCTOR: Stein.

October 25: MADAMA BUTTERFLY (Puccini)
CIO-CIO-SAN: Stratas, PINKERTON: Garaventa, SHARPLESS: Ludgin, SUZUKI: Krebill, GORO: Fried, BONZE: Davia, YAMADORI: Glover, COMMISSIONER: Fazah, KATE PINKERTON: Kirkpatrick, REGISTRAR: Harvey, CONDUCTOR: Molinari-Pradelli.

November 1: THE MARRIAGE OF FIGARO (Mozart)
SUSANNA: Grist, COUNTESS: Watson, CHERUBINO: Venora, FIGARO: Evans, COUNT: Stewart, BARTOLO: Vinay, BASILIO: Thaw, MARCELLINA: Cervena, BARBARINA: Curatilo, ANTONIO: Giosso, DON CURZIO: Manton, PEASANT GIRLS: Christensen, Kirkpatrick, CONDUCTOR: Horenstein.

✓ *November 8:* LES TROYENS (Berlioz)
DIDO: Crespin, CASSANDRA: Crespin, AENEAS: Vickers, NARBAL: Berberian, ANNA: Cervena, ASCANIUS: Krebill, IOPAS: Thaw, PANTHEAS: Grant, HYLAS: Clements, GHOST OF PRIAM: Giosso, GHOST OF CHOREBUS: Grant, GHOST OF CASSANDRA: Kirkpatrick, GHOST OF HECTOR: Fazah, CONDUCTOR: Périsson.

✓ *November 11:* FALSTAFF (Verdi)
SIR JOHN FALSTAFF: Vinay, MISTRESS FORD: Kabaiwanska, MISTRESS PAGE: Martin, DAME QUICKLY: Cervena, ANNE: Venora, FENTON: Garaventa, FORD: Guarrera, DR. CAIUS: Fried, BARDOLPH: Manton, PISTOL: Davia, CONDUCTOR: Molinari-Pradelli.

November 15: CARMEN (Bizet)
CARMEN: Bumbry, MICAELA: Todd, DON JOSÉ: Vickers, ESCAMILLO: Guarrera, ZUNIGA: Davia, DANCAIRO: Fried, REMENDADO: Manton, MORALES: Fazah, FRASQUITA: Christensen, MERCEDES: Krebill, CONDUCTOR: Périsson.

November 22: THE MAKROPULOS CASE (Janacek)
EMILIA MARTY: Collier, ALBERT GREGOR: Dempsey, PRUS: Ludgin, DR. KOLENATY: Lishner, CHRISTA: Todd, JANEK: Thaw, HAUK: Fried, CHARWOMAN: Kirkpatrick, STAGEHAND: Giosso, CHAMBERMAID: Curatilo, CONDUCTOR: Horenstein.

SATURDAY EVENING SERIES

September 24: ELEKTRA (Strauss)
Same cast.
October 1: DON CARLO (Verdi)
Same cast.
October 8: I PURITANI (Bellini)
Same cast.
October 15: L'AMORE DEI TRE RE (Montemezzi)
Same cast.
October 22: TANNHÄUSER (Wagner)

Same cast.
✓ *October 29:* THE MARRIAGE OF FIGARO (Mozart)
Same cast except: ANTONIO: Davia.
November 5: RIGOLETTO (Verdi)
GILDA: Venora, DUKE: Garaventa, RIGOLETTO: Ludgin, MADDALENA: Martin, SPARAFUCILE: Davia, MONTERONE: Grant, BORSA: Clements, MARULLO: Fazah, CEPRANO: Giosso, GIOVANNA: Petersen, PAGE: Graber, CONDUCTOR: Molinari-Pradelli.
November 12: LES TROYENS (Berlioz)
Same cast.
November 19: THE MAKROPULOS CASE (Janacek)
Same cast.
November 26: MADAMA BUTTERFLY (Puccini)
Same cast except: CIO-CIO-SAN: Kirsten, SUZUKI: Martin, BONZE: Grant.

THURSDAY EVENING SERIES

September 22: DON CARLO (Verdi)
Same cast.
September 29: I PURITANI (Bellini)
Same cast.
October 6: ELEKTRA (Strauss)
Same cast.
October 13: RIGOLETTO (Verdi)
Same cast except: GILDA: Grist, DUKE: Kraus, RIGOLETTO: Glossop, MADDALENA: Blackham, SPARAFUCILE: Kreppel.
October 20: BORIS GODOUNOFF (Moussorgsky)
Same cast.
October 27: TANNHÄUSER (Wagner)
Same cast.
November 3: MADAMA BUTTERFLY (Puccini)
Same cast except: BONZE: Grant.
November 10: THE MARRIAGE OF FIGARO (Mozart)
Same cast.
November 17: FALSTAFF (Verdi)
Same cast.
November 24: CARMEN (Bizet)
Same cast except: ZUNIGA: Grant.

SUNDAY MATINEE SERIES

October 2: I PURITANI (Bellini)
Same cast.
October 16: RIGOLETTO (Verdi)
Same cast except: GILDA: Grist, DUKE: Kraus, RIGOLETTO: Glossop, MADDALENA: Blackham, SPARAFUCILE: Kreppel.
October 23: BORIS GODOUNOFF (Moussorgsky)
Same cast.
October 30: TANNHÄUSER (Wagner)
Same cast.

November 6: THE MARRIAGE OF FIGARO (Mozart)
Same cast.
November 13: MADAMA BUTTERFLY (Puccini)
Same cast except: CIO-CIO-SAN: Kirsten, SUZUKI: Martin, BONZE: Grant.
November 20: FALSTAFF (Verdi)
Same cast.
November 27: CARMEN (Bizet)
Same cast.

FRIDAY EVENING SERIES

September 23: I PURITANI (Bellini)
Same cast.
October 7: L'AMORE DEI TRE RE (Montemezzi)
Same cast.
October 14: BORIS GODOUNOFF (Moussorgsky)
Same cast.
✓ *October 21:* RIGOLETTO (Verdi)
Same cast except: GILDA: Grist, DUKE: Kraus, RIGOLETTO: Glossop,
MADDALENA: Blackham, SPARAFUCILE: Kreppel.
October 28: MADAMA BUTTERFLY (Puccini)
Same cast except: BONZE: Grant.
November 4: LES TROYENS (Berlioz)
Same cast.
November 18: CARMEN (Bizet)
Same cast except: ZUNIGA: Grant.
November 25: THE MAKROPULOS CASE (Janacek)
Same cast.

YOUNG PEOPLE'S PERFORMANCES

October 31, matinee: RIGOLETTO (Verdi)
Same cast.
November 7, matinee: RIGOLETTO (Verdi)
Same cast except: GILDA: Christensen, MADDALENA: Krebill.
November 21, matinee: RIGOLETTO (Verdi)
Same cast except: GILDA: Christensen, MADDALENA: Krebill.
November 22, matinee: RIGOLETTO (Verdi)
Same cast except: RIGOLETTO: Guarrera.

CASTS—SPRING OPERA 1966

May 24: MIGNON (Thomas)
MIGNON: Vanni, PHILINE: Nixon, WILHELM MEISTER: Porretta, LOTHARIO:
Boatwright, LAERTE: Glover, GIARNO: Giosso, FREDERIC: Kova, CONDUC-
TOR: Lawner.
May 27: MIGNON (Thomas)
Same cast.
✓ *May 31:* LUCIA DI LAMMERMOOR (Donizetti)
LUCIA: Newman, LORD HENRY: Clatworthy, EDGARDO: Di Virgilio, LORD

ARTHUR: Price, RAYMOND: Enns, ALICE: Kirkpatrick, NORMAN: Eitze, CONDUCTOR: Samuel.
June 3: LUCIA DI LAMMERMOOR (Donizetti)
Same cast.
June 7: THE ITALIAN GIRL IN ALGIERS (Rossini)
ISABELLA: Vanni, LINDORO: Sevilla, MUSTAPHA: Beattie, ELVIRA: Armstrong, TADDEO: Beni, HALY: Turner, ZULMA: Petersen, CONDUCTOR: Whallon.
June 10: THE ITALIAN GIRL IN ALGIERS (Rossini)
Same cast.
June 14: CARRY NATION (Moore)
CARRY NATION: Wolff, CHARLES: Fredricks, CARRY'S MOTHER: Faull, CARRY'S FATHER: Smith, FIRST MAN: Andersen, SECOND MAN: Eitze, MARSHAL: Harvey, BEN: Glover, PREACHER: Turner, EDNA MAUD: Kirkpatrick, BOY AT HOEDOWN: Gomez, PARTICIPANTS IN HOEDOWN: San Miguel, Bland, Andersen, Lawrence, FIRST WOMAN: Petersen, SECOND WOMAN: Bradley, THIRD WOMAN: Graber, BOY IN SALOON: Massay, MEN IN SALOON: Eitze, Mayer, Styles, Lawrence, CARETAKER: Turner, CONDUCTOR: Grossman.
June 17: CARRY NATION (Moore)
Same cast.
June 21: IL TROVATORE (Verdi)
LEONORA: Todd, AZUCENA: Allen, MANRICO: Dal Ponte, COUNT DI LUNA: Boatwright, FERRANDO: Enns, RUIZ: Glover, OLD GYPSY: Harvey, INEZ: Kirkpatrick, CONDUCTOR: Rosekrans.
June 24: THE TURN OF THE SCREW (Britten)
GOVERNESS: Neway, QUINT: Nilsson, MILES: Martinez, FLORA: Lantz, MISS JESSEL: Curatilo, MRS. GROSE: Patton, PROLOGUE: Glover, CONDUCTOR: Grossman.
June 25: IL TROVATORE (Verdi)
Same cast.
June 28: THE TURN OF THE SCREW (Britten)
Same cast.

CASTS—1967 SEASON

REGULAR SERIES

September 19: LA GIOCONDA (Ponchielli)
LA GIOCONDA: Gencer, LAURA: Bumbry, LA CIECA: Forrester, ENZO: Cioni, BARNABA: Ludgin, ALVISE: Berberian, ZUANE: Monk, ISEPO: Clements, PILOT: Styles, MONK: Grant, SINGERS: Beauchamp, Booth, VOICES: Huie, Lawrence, CONDUCTOR: Patane.
September 26: THE MAGIC FLUTE (Mozart)
PAMINA: Marsh, QUEEN OF THE NIGHT: Scovotti, TAMINO: Burrows, PAPAGENO: Evans, SARASTRO: O'Leary, SPEAKER: Berberian, PAPAGENA: Davis, MONOSTATOS: Glover, PRIESTS: Clements, Monk, LADIES: Marks, Kirkpatrick, Petersen, ARMORED MEN: MacWherter, Grant, GENII: Bales, Aird, Yamamoto, CONDUCTOR: Stein.

October 3: LOUISE (Charpentier)
LOUISE: Saunders, JULIEN: Alexander, MOTHER: Cervena, FATHER: Rossi-Lemeni, RAGPICKER: Berberian, JUNKMAN: Grant, YOUNG RAGPICKER: Tede, STREET SWEEPER: Kirkpatrick, NEWSPAPER GIRL: Corsale, MILKWOMAN: Gunn, COALPICKER: Strong, STREET ARAB: Kova, BIRDFOOD VENDOR: Davis, ARTICHOKE VENDOR: Marks, WATERCRESS VENDOR: Petersen, CHAIR MENDER: Graber, OLD CLOTHES MAN: Manton, CARROT VENDOR: Glover, RAG VENDOR: MacWherter, POLICEMEN: Monk, Beauchamp, NOCTAMBULIST: Burrows, KING OF THE FOOLS: Burrows, SONG WRITER: Clements, PHILOSOPHERS: Andersen, Styles, PAINTER: Tarantino, SCULPTOR: Lawrence, POET: Tredway, STUDENT: Booth, IRMA: Stevenson, CAMILLE: Davis, GERTRUDE: Petersen, APPRENTICE: Kova, ELISE: Graber, BLANCHE: Liagre, SUZANNE: Bruzzone, FOREWOMAN: Bradley, MARGUERITE: Winnington, MADELEINE: San Miguel, CONDUCTOR: Périsson.

✓ *October 10:* DER ROSENKAVALIER (Strauss)
MARSCHALLIN: Crespin, BARON OCHS: Greindl, OCTAVIAN: Sylvia Anderson, SOPHIE: Grist, FANINAL: Modenos, TENOR: Ilosfalvy, MARIANNE: Kirkpatrick, VALZACCHI: Fried, ANNINA: Kova, POLICE COMMISSIONER: Davia, NOTARY: Harvey, LANDLORD: Manton, MILLINER: Stevenson, ANIMAL VENDOR: Glover, MARSCHALLIN'S MAJOR DOMO: Andersen, FANINAL'S MAJOR DOMO: Clements, ORPHANS: Marks, Davis, Petersen, FOOTMEN: MacWherter, Tenbrook, Serbo, Beauchamp, CONDUCTOR: Stein.

October 17: MACBETH (Verdi)
LADY MACBETH: Bumbry, MACBETH: Ludgin, BANQUO: O'Leary, MACDUFF: Barioni, MALCOLM: Clements, LADY-IN-WAITING: Kirkpatrick, MEDIC: Beauchamp, SERVANT: Andersen, ASSASSIN: Monk, APPARITIONS: MacWherter, Marks, Lindstedt, CONDUCTOR: Patane.

October 24: MANON LESCAUT (Puccini)
MANON LESCAUT: Kirsten, CHEVALIER DES GRIEUX: Ilosfalvy, LESCAUT: Bryn-Jones, GERONTE: Davia, EDMONDO: Burrows, DANCING MASTER: Clements, LAMPLIGHTER: Manton, CAPTAIN: Grant, MUSICIAN: Kova, SERGEANT: Monk, CONDUCTOR: Grossman.

✓ *October 31:* TRISTAN AND ISOLDE (Wagner)
ISOLDE: Dalis, BRANGÄNE: Dunn, TRISTAN: Thomas, KING MARKE: Greindl, KURWENAL: Ludgin, MELOT: MacWherter, SHEPHERD: Glover, SAILOR'S VOICE: Burrows, STEERSMAN: Grant, CONDUCTOR: Stein.

November 3: THE VISITATION (Schuller)
CARTER JONES: Estes, CHUCK: Ulfung, CLAIBORNE: Bryn-Jones, TEENA: Weathers, MISS HAMPTON: Scovotti, HELD: Wixell, PULISI: Crofoot, PREACHER: Hinton, BILL: Modenos, FRANK: O'Leary, JOE: Monk, INSPECTOR: Berberian, LANDLADY: Kirkpatrick, MATTIE: Klebe, GIRL: Arrieta, DRUG ADDICT: Kersh, COPS: Rubino, Bergman, DEPUTIES: Grant, Beauchamp, PRESIDING OFFICER: Ludgin, ASSOCIATES: Glover, Harvey, COMPANIONS: Serbo, Tenbrook, Urquhart, WOMAN: Cervena, BOY: David Anderson, GIRL: Virginia Anderson, COPS: Lardner, Nissi, WHIPPER: Chester Russelle, UNCLE ALBERT: Holmes, PATTERSON: MacWherter, CLEANING WOMAN: Cleodel Russelle, DEACON: Wendt, DANCING GIRLS: De Heurtaumont, Smith, De Vere, Arrieta, COUPLES: De Heurtaumont,

Engstrom, De Vere, Johnson, Smith, McFall, CONDUCTOR: Schuller.

✓*November 7:* FAUST (Gounod)
MARGUERITE: Saunders, FAUST: Kraus, MEPHISTOPHELES: Ghiaurov, VALENTIN: Wixell, WAGNER: Monk, SIEBEL: Sylvia Anderson, MARTHE: Cervena, CONDUCTOR: Périsson.

✓ *November 14:* UN BALLO IN MASCHERA (Verdi)
AMELIA: Price, ULRICA: Dunn, OSCAR: Grist, RICCARDO: Ulfung, RENATO: MacNeil, SAM: Berberian, TOM: Davia, SILVANO: Monk, JUDGE: Clements, SERVANT: Beauchamp, CONDUCTOR: Bernardi.

November 17: DAS RHEINGOLD (Wagner)
WOTAN: Ward, DONNER: Bryn-Jones, FROH: MacWherter, LOGE: Thomas, ALBERICH: Modenos, MIME: Glover, FASOLT: O'Leary, FAFNER: Greindl, FRICKA: Dalis, FREIA: Saunders, ERDA: Dunn, WOGLINDE: Marks, WELLGUNDE: Kova, FLOSSHILDE: Sylvia Anderson, CONDUCTOR: Ludwig.

November 21: LA BOHÈME (Puccini)
MIMI: Freni, RODOLFO: Pavarotti, MARCELLO: Wixell, COLLINE: Estes, SCHAUNARD: Bryn-Jones, MUSETTA: Scovotti, BENOIT: Davia, ALCINDORO: Crofoot, SERGEANT: Andersen, OFFICER: Harvey, CONDUCTOR Bernardi.

SATURDAY EVENING SERIES

September 23: THE MAGIC FLUTE (Mozart)
Same cast.
September 30: LOUISE (Charpentier)
Same cast.
October 7: DER ROSENKAVALIER (Strauss)
Same cast.
October 14: MANON LESCAUT (Puccini)
Same cast.

✓ *October 21:* THE ELIXIR OF LOVE (Donizetti)
ADINA: Grist, NEMORINO: Kraus, BELCORE: Wixell, DR. DULCAMARA: Bruscantini, GIANNETTA: Kova, CONDUCTOR: Patane.
October 28: THE VISITATION (Schuller)
Same cast.
November 4: FAUST (Gounod)
Same cast.
November 11: LA BOHÈME (Puccini)
Same cast.
November 18: UN BALLO IN MASCHERA (Verdi)
Same cast.
November 25: DAS RHEINGOLD (Wagner)
Same cast.

WEDNESDAY EVENING SERIES

September 20: THE MAGIC FLUTE (Mozart)
Same cast.
September 27: LA GIOCONDA (Ponchielli)
Same cast.

October 4: DER ROSENKAVALIER (Strauss)
Same cast.
October 11: MACBETH (Verdi)
Same cast.
October 18: TRISTAN AND ISOLDE (Wagner)
Same cast.
October 25: THE ELIXIR OF LOVE (Donizetti)
Same cast.
November 1: FAUST (Gounod)
Same cast.
November 8: THE VISITATION (Schuller)
Same cast.
November 15: LA BOHÈME (Puccini)
Same cast.
November 22: DAS RHEINGOLD (Wagner)
Same cast.

SUNDAY AFTERNOON SERIES

October 1: LA GIOCONDA (Ponchielli)
Same cast.
October 8: THE MAGIC FLUTE (Mozart)
Same cast.
October 15: DER ROSENKAVALIER (Strauss)
Same cast.
October 29: THE ELIXIR OF LOVE (Donizetti)
Same cast.
November 5: TRISTAN AND ISOLDE (Wagner)
Same cast.
November 12: FAUST (Gounod)
Same cast.
November 19: LA BOHÈME (Puccini)
Same cast.
November 26: UN BALLO IN MASCHERA (Verdi)
Same cast.

FRIDAY EVENING SERIES

September 22: LA GIOCONDA (Ponchielli)
Same cast.
September 29: THE MAGIC FLUTE (Mozart)
Same cast.
October 6: MACBETH (Verdi)
Same cast.
October 13: LOUISE (Charpentier)
Same cast.
October 20: MANON LESCAUT (Puccini)
Same cast.
October 27: TRISTAN AND ISOLDE (Wagner)
Same cast.

November 10: FAUST (Gounod)
Same cast.
November 24: LA BOHÈME (Puccini)
Same cast.

YOUNG PEOPLE'S PERFORMANCES

October 20, 25, November 7, 21, matinees: THE MAGIC FLUTE
(Mozart)
Same cast except: PAMINA: Stevenson, PAPAGENO: Bryn-Jones, CONDUC-
TOR: Grossman.

CASTS—SPRING OPERA 1967

✔ *June 2:* LA TRAVIATA (Verdi)
VIOLETTA: Brooks, ALFREDO: Wyatt, GERMONT: Schwartzman, GASTON:
Hageman, BARON DOUPHOL: Monk, MARQUIS D'OBIGNY: Beauchamp,
DR. GRENVIL: Giosso, FLORA: Kirkpatrick, ANNINA: Petersen, CONDUC-
TOR: Kritz.
June 6: THE PEARL FISHERS (Bizet)
LEILA: Malbin, NADIR: Kolk, ZURGA: Cossa, NOURABAD: Enns, CONDUCTOR:
Samuel.
June 9: THE PEARL FISHERS (Bizet)
Same cast.
June 10: LA TRAVIATA (Verdi)
Same cast.
June 13: CAVALLERIA RUSTICANA (Mascagni)
SANTUZZA: Roberto, TURIDDU: Di Virgilio, ALFIO: Cossa, LOLA: Kirkpat-
rick, MAMMA LUCIA: Petersen, CONDUCTOR: Grossman.
        followed by: I PAGLIACCI (Leoncavallo)
CANIO: Olvis, TONIO: Schwartzman, NEDDA: Niska, SILVIO: Cossa, BEPPE:
Serbo, PEASANTS: Lawrence, Huie, CONDUCTOR: Grossman.
June 16: CAVALLERIA RUSTICANA (Mascagni)
        followed by: I PAGLIACCI (Leoncavallo)
Same casts.
✔ *June 20:* THE TALES OF HOFFMANN (Offenbach)
HOFFMANN: Di Virgilio, OLYMPIA: Toscano, GIULIETTA: Kirkpatrick, AN-
TONIA: Davis, LINDORF, COPPELIUS, DAPERTUTTO, DR. MIRACLE: Estes,
NICKLAUSSE: Serbo, A COURTESAN: Petersen, VOICE OF ANTONIA'S MOTHER:
Petersen, SPALANZANI: Klebe, SCHLEMIL: Giosso, CRESPEL: Beauchamp,
COCHENILLE, PITICHINACCIO, FRANTZ, ANDRES: Glover, NATHANAEL: Silva,
HERMANN: Andersen, LUTHER: Harvey, STELLA: De Heurtaumont, CON-
DUCTOR: Grossman.
June 23: THE TALES OF HOFFMANN (Offenbach)
Same cast.

CASTS—1968 SEASON

REGULAR SERIES
✔ *September 13:* ERNANI (Verdi)

410

ELVIRA: Price, ERNANI: Cioni, DON CARLO: Glossop, SILVA: Flagello, DON RICCARDO: Glover, IAGO: Clark, GIOVANNA: Nadler, CONDUCTOR: Patane.

✓ *September 17:* THE BARBER OF SEVILLE (Rossini)
ROSINA: Berganza, COUNT ALMAVIVA: Bottazzo, FIGARO: Wixell, BARTOLO: Capecchi, BASILIO: Rossi-Lemeni, FIORELLO: Monk, OFFICER: Glover, BERTHA: Cervena, AMBROSIO: Harvey, CONDUCTOR: Faldi.

✓ *September 24:* LES TROYENS (Berlioz)
DIDO: Crespin, CASSANDRA: Crespin, AENEAS: Chauvet, NARBAL: Berberian, ANNA: Lilova, ASCANIUS: Anderson, IOPAS: Serbo, PANTHEAS: Clark, HYLAS: Khanzadian, PRIAM: Monk, HECUBA: Nadler, GHOST OF PRIAM: Monk, GHOST OF CASSANDRA: Nadler, GHOST OF HECTOR: Janzen CONDUCTOR: Périsson.

✓ *September 30:* DIE WALKÜRE (Wagner)
BRÜNNHILDE: Kniplova, SIEGLINDE: Crespin, FRICKA: Lilova, SIEGMUND: Thomas, WOTAN: Hofmann, HUNDING: Wildermann, HELMWIGE: Todd, GERHILDE: Matsumoto, ORTLINDE: Marks, SIEGRUNE: Anderson, ROSSWEISSE: Cervena, WALTRAUTE: White, GRIMGERDE: Petersen, SCHWERTLEITE: Nadler, CONDUCTOR: Ludwig.

October 4: MADAMA BUTTERFLY (Puccini)
CIO-CIO-SAN: Pilou, PINKERTON: Di Virgilio, SHARPLESS: Wixell, SUZUKI: Anderson, GORO: Crofoot, BONZE: Grant, YAMADORI: Fried, COMMISSIONER: Janzen, KATE PINKERTON: Nadler, REGISTRAR: Harvey, CONDUCTOR: Faldi.

October 8: ROYAL PALACE (Weill-Schuller)
DANCERS: Mehl, Sullivan, Kersh, Borden, Thompson, SINGERS: Todd, Janzen, Berberian, Crofoot, Grant, Marks, Khanzadian, CONDUCTOR: Schuller.

followed by: ERWARTUNG (Schoenberg)
WOMAN: Collier, CONDUCTOR: Schuller.

followed by: CHRISTOPHER COLUMBUS [THE DISCOVERY OF AMERICA] (Milhaud)
COLUMBUS I: Tipton, COLUMBUS II: Monk, EXPLICATOR: Wildermann, PROSECUTOR: Beattie, SOPRANO VOICE: Matsumoto, DEFENDERS: Fried, Malone, Grant, SERVANT: Nilsson, INNKEEPER: Matthes, QUEEN ISABELLA: Todd, GUITAR PLAYERS: Manton, Fleck, Barker, CREDITORS: Crofoot, Clark, Janzen, MAJOR DOMO OF THE KING OF SPAIN: Glover, YOUNG SOLDIER: Khanzadian, WISE MAN: Berberian, RECRUITING OFFICER: Le Page, RECRUITER: Tenbrook, HANGMAN: Gettys, DELEGATE OF THE SAILORS: Drake, OFFICER: Nolen, CONDUCTOR: Schuller.

✓ *October 15:* IL TROVATORE (Verdi)
LEONORA: Bakocevic, AZUCENA: Lilova, MANRICO: Ilosfalvy, COUNT DI LUNA: Braun, FERRANDO: Berberian, RUIZ: Glover, OLD GYPSY: Janzen, INEZ: Nadler, MESSENGER: Eitze, CONDUCTOR: Patane.

✓ *October 22:* WOZZECK (Berg)
WOZZECK: Evans, MARIE: Lear, CAPTAIN: Lewis, DOCTOR: Beattie, DRUM MAJOR: Parly, ANDRES: Khanzadian, MARGRET: Anderson, ARTISANS: Drake, Monk, FOOL: Fried, SOLDIERS: Booth, Eitze, CHILD: Renton, CONDUCTOR: Ludwig.

411

October 29: LUCIA DI LAMMERMOOR (Donizetti)
LUCIA: Rinaldi, LORD HENRY: Braun, EDGARDO: Pavarotti, LORD AR-
THUR: Khanzadian, RAYMOND: Grant, ALICE: Nadler, NORMAN: Glover,
CONDUCTOR: Patane.

November 5: SALOME (Strauss)
SALOME: Silja, HEROD: Lewis, JOCHANAAN: Mazura, HERODIAS: Cervena,
NARRABOTH: Di Virgilio, PAGE: Nadler, SOLDIERS: Clark, Grant, NAZA-
RENES: Berberian, Barker, JEWS: Fried, Glover, Crofoot, Khanzadian,
Drake, SLAVE: Matsumoto, CAPPADOCIAN: Fleck, CONDUCTOR: Stein.

November 12: DON GIOVANNI (Mozart)
DONNA ANNA: Tarrés, DONNA ELVIRA: Zylis-Gara, ZERLINA: Pilou,
DON GIOVANNI: Siepi, LEPORELLO: Trama, DON OTTAVIO: Holley, COM-
MENDATORE: Mazura, MASETTO: Monk, CONDUCTOR: Stein.

November 19: TURANDOT (Puccini)
TURANDOT: Shuard, LIU: Marsh, CALAF: Spiess, TIMUR: Berberian, PING:
Wixell, PANG: Manton, PONG: Crofoot, EMPEROR ALTOUM: Fried, MAN-
DARIN: Grant, PRINCE OF PERSIA: Eitze, MAIDS: Matsumoto, Nadler,
CONDUCTOR: Patane.

November 26: FRA DIAVOLO (Auber)
FRA DIAVOLO: Gedda, ZERLINA: Costa[1], LORD PLIMPTON: Beattie, LADY
PAMELA: Anderson, LORENZO: Khanzadian, MATTEO: Grant, BEPPO:
Manton, GIACOMO: Drake, CONDUCTOR: Bernardi.

SATURDAY EVENING PERFORMANCES

September 14: THE BARBER OF SEVILLE (Rossini)
Same cast.

September 21: LES TROYENS (Berlioz)
Same cast.

September 28: ERNANI (Verdi)
Same cast.

October 5: ROYAL PALACE (Weill-Schuller)
       followed by: ERWARTUNG (Schoenberg)
       followed by: CHRISTOPHER COLUMBUS
       [THE DISCOVERY OF AMERICA] (Milhaud)
Same casts.

October 12: DIE WALKÜRE (Wagner)
Same cast.

October 19: MADAMA BUTTERFLY (Puccini)
Same cast.

October 26: WOZZECK (Berg)
Same cast.

November 2: IL TROVATORE (Verdi)
Same cast except: COUNT DI LUNA: Quilico.

November 9: LUCIA DI LAMMERMOOR (Donizetti)
Same cast.

November 16: SALOME (Strauss)
Same cast.

412

November 23: DON GIOVANNI (Mozart)
Same cast.
November 30: TURANDOT (Puccini)
Same cast.

WEDNESDAY EVENING PERFORMANCES

September 18: ERNANI (Verdi)
Same cast.
September 25: THE BARBER OF SEVILLE (Rossini)
Same cast.
October 9: DIE WALKÜRE (Wagner)
Same cast.
October 23: IL TROVATORE (Verdi)
Same cast.
November 6: LUCIA DI LAMMERMOOR (Donizetti)
Same cast except: EDGARDO: Di Virgilio.
November 20: DON GIOVANNI (Mozart)
Same cast.
November 27: TURANDOT (Puccini)
Same cast.

SUNDAY MATINEE PERFORMANCES

September 15: LES TROYENS (Berlioz)
Same cast.
September 22: ERNANI (Verdi)
Same cast.
September 29: THE BARBER OF SEVILLE (Rossini)
Same cast.
October 13: ROYAL PALACE (Weill-Schuller)
        followed by: ERWARTUNG (Schoenberg)
        followed by: CHRISTOPHER COLUMBUS
        [THE DISCOVERY OF AMERICA] (Milhaud)
Same casts.
October 20: IL TROVATORE (Verdi)
Same cast.
October 27: MADAMA BUTTERFLY (Puccini)
Same cast.
November 3: LUCIA DI LAMMERMOOR (Donizetti)
Same cast.
November 10: SALOME (Strauss)
Same cast.
November 17: DON GIOVANNI (Mozart)
Same cast.
November 24: TURANDOT (Puccini)
Same cast.
December 1: FRA DIAVOLO (Auber)
Same cast.

FRIDAY EVENING PERFORMANCES

September 20: THE BARBER OF SEVILLE (Rossini)
Same cast.
September 27: DIE WALKÜRE (Wagner)
Same cast.
October 11: IL TROVATORE (Verdi)
Same cast.
October 18: WOZZECK (Berg)
Same cast.
October 25: LUCIA DI LAMMERMOOR (Donizetti)
Same cast.
November 1: SALOME (Strauss)
Same cast.
November 8: DON GIOVANNI (Mozart)
Same cast.
November 15: TURANDOT (Puccini)
Same cast.
November 22: FRA DIAVOLO (Auber)
Same cast.
November 29: MADAMA BUTTERFLY (Puccini)
Same cast.

EXTRA PERFORMANCE

November 9, matinee: MADAMA BUTTERFLY (Puccini)
Same cast except: CIO-CIO-SAN: Kirsten.

YOUNG PEOPLE'S PERFORMANCES

October 23, matinee: MADAMA BUTTERFLY (Puccini)
Same cast.
October 30, matinee: MADAMA BUTTERFLY (Puccini)
Same cast except: CIO-CIO-SAN: Bakocevic.
November 6, matinee: MADAMA BUTTERFLY (Puccini)
Same cast except: CIO-CIO-SAN: Bakocevic.
November 13, matinee: MADAMA BUTTERFLY (Puccini)
Same cast except: CIO-CIO-SAN: Bakocevic.
November 26, matinee: MADAMA BUTTERFLY (Puccini)
Same cast.

CASTS—SPRING OPERA 1968

April 9: THE ABDUCTION FROM THE SERAGLIO (Mozart)
CONSTANZE: Carron, BLONDE: Belling, BELMONTE: Bullard, PEDRILLO: Vrenios, OSMIN: Beattie, PASHA: Harris, CONDUCTOR: Whallon.
April 13: THE ABDUCTION FROM THE SERAGLIO (Mozart)
Same cast.
April 16: CARMEN (Bizet)
CARMEN: Krebill, MICAELA: Tyler, DON JOSÉ: Theyard, ESCAMILLO:

Palmer, ZUNIGA: Drake, DANCAIRO: Cosindas, REMENDADO: Hoskinson, MORALES: Tenbrook, FRASQUITA: Gibson, MERCEDES: Curry, CONDUCTOR: Reimuller.

April 19: CARMEN (Bizet)
Same cast.

April 23: LA RONDINE (Puccini)
MAGDA: Todd, RUGGERO: Khanzadian, LISETTE: Belling, PRUNIER: Fitch, RAMBALDO: Drake, PERICHAUD: Metlenko, GOBIN: Andersen, CREBILLON: Lawrence, YVETTE: Howe, BIANCA: Corsale, SUZY: San Miguel, SINGER: Graber, GIRLS: Woodburn, Pfandl, MAJOR DOMO: McEachern, CONDUCTOR: Coppola.

April 26: LA RONDINE (Puccini)
Same cast.

April 30: RIGOLETTO (Verdi)
GILDA: Elgar, DUKE: Theyard, RIGOLETTO: Schwartzman, MADDALENA: Curry, SPARAFUCILE: Mundt, MONTERONE: Clark, BORSA: Eitze, MARULLO: Monk, CEPRANO: Malone, COUNTESS CEPRANO: Szymkun, GIOVANNA: Hinson, PAGE: Aird, CONDUCTOR: Coppola.

May 3: RIGOLETTO (Verdi)
Same cast.

CASTS—1969 SEASON

REGULAR SERIES

September 16: LA TRAVIATA (Verdi)
VIOLETTA: Pilou, ALFREDO: Bonisolli, GERMONT: Wixell, GASTON: Paige, BARON DOUPHOL: Esparza, MARQUIS D'OBIGNY: Gilbert, DR. GRENVIL: Clark, FLORA: Cervena, ANNINA: Nadler, CONDUCTOR: Patane.

September 23: LA BOHÈME (Puccini)
MIMI: Kirsten, RODOLFO: Pavarotti, MARCELLO: Bruscantini, COLLINE: Berberian, SCHAUNARD: Blankenburg, MUSETTA: Boky, BENOIT: Esparza, ALICINDORO: Gilbert, PARPIGNOL: Nilsson, SERGEANT: Lawrence, OFFICER: Harvey, CONDUCTOR: Coppola.

September 26: ARIADNE AUF NAXOS (Strauss)
ARIADNE, PRIMA DONNA: Dvorakova, BACCHUS, TENOR: J. Thomas, COMPOSER: Martin, ZERBINETTA: Boky, MUSIC MASTER: Monk, MAJOR DOMO: Matthes, ARLECCHINO: Blankenburg, SCARAMUCCIO: Manton, TRUFFALDINO: Esparza, BRIGHELLA: Paige, NAIAD: Marks, DRYAD: Nadler, ECHO: Matsumoto, DANCING MASTER: Paige, WIGMAKER: Nolen, LACKEY: Gilbert, OFFICER: Nilsson, CONDUCTOR: Schuller.

September 30: FIDELIO (Beethoven)
LEONORE: Jones, FLORESTAN: King, ROCCO: Lagger, DON PIZARRO: Mazura, DON FERNANDO: Berberian, MARZELLINE: Marks, JACQUINO: E. Thomas, PRISONERS: Nilsson, Clark, CONDUCTOR: Ehrling.

October 7: THE ELIXIR OF LOVE (Donizetti)
ADINA: Grist, NEMORINO: Pavarotti, BELCORE: Wixell, DR. DULCAMARA: Bruscantini, GIANNETTA: Matsumoto, CONDUCTOR: Patane.

415

✓ *October 14:* GÖTTERDÄMMERUNG (Wagner)
BRÜNNHILDE: Shuard, SIEGFRIED: J. Thomas, GUNTHER: Mazura, GUT-
RUNE: Martin, HAGEN: Lagger, ALBERICH: Esparza, WALTRAUTE: Lilova,
NORNS: Cervena, Nadler, Anderson, WOGLINDE: Marks, WELLGUNDE:
Anderson, FLOSSHILDE: Nadler, CONDUCTOR: Suitner.

October 21: AIDA (Verdi)
✓ AIDA: Jones, AMNERIS: Lilova, RHADAMES: Chauvet, AMONASRO: Farrar, RAM-
FIS: Berberian, KING: Grant, MESSENGER: Herrnkind, PRIESTESS: Nadler,
CONDUCTOR: Périsson.

October 28: THE MAGIC FLUTE (Mozart)
PAMINA: M. Price, QUEEN OF THE NIGHT: Deutekom, TAMINO: Burrows,
PAPAGENO: Evans, SARASTRO: Ward, SPEAKER: Mazura, PAPAGENA: Mat-
sumoto, MONOSTATOS: Ulfung, PRIESTS: Monk, Nilsson, LADIES: Marks,
Anderson, Nadler, ARMORED MEN: Herrnkind, Grant, GENII: Aird,
Brookie, Hunt, CONDUCTOR: Mackerras.

✓ *November 4:* LA FORZA DEL DESTINO (Verdi)
LEONORA: Tatum, DON ALVARO: Bergonzi, DON CARLO: Wixell, PADRE
GUARDIANO: Tozzi, FRA MELITONE: Capecchi, PREZIOSILLA: Anderson,
MARQUIS OF CALATRAVA: Berberian, ALCADE: Grant, TRABUCCO: Fried,
CURRA: Nadler, SURGEON: Clark, CONDUCTOR: Patane.

✓ *November 11:* LA CENERENTOLA (Rossini)
CENERENTOLA: Berganza, DON RAMIRO: Bottazzo, DANDINI: Capecchi,
DON MAGNIFICO: Montarsolo, ALIDORO: Grant, CLORINDA: Marks, TISBE:
Cervena, CONDUCTOR: Mackerras.

✓ *November 18:* PELLÉAS ET MÉLISANDE (Debussy)
MÉLISANDE: Pilou, PELLÉAS: Gui, GOLAUD: Petri, ARKEL: Tozzi, GENE-
VIÈVE: Lilova, YNIOLD: Moser, DOCTOR: Clark, CONDUCTOR: Périsson.

✓ *November 25:* JENUFA (Janacek)
JENUFA: Weathers, KOSTELNICKA: Dalis, LACA: Peterson, STEVA: Ulfung,
STARENKA: Cervena, STAREK: Berberian, MAYOR: Grant, MAYOR'S WIFE:
Petersen, KAROLKA: Matsumoto, PASTUCHYNA: Tede, BARENA: Marks, JANO:
Stull, AUNT: Bick, CONDUCTOR: Gregor.

SATURDAY EVENING PERFORMANCES

September 20: LA BOHÈME (Puccini)
Same cast.
September 27: FIDELIO (Beethoven)
Same cast.
October 4: LA TRAVIATA (Verdi)
Same cast.
October 11: GÖTTERDÄMMERUNG (Wagner)
Same cast.
October 18: AIDA (Verdi)
Same cast.
October 25: THE MAGIC FLUTE (Mozart)
Same cast.
November 1: LA FORZA DEL DESTINO (Verdi)
Same cast.

November 8: LA CENERENTOLA (Rossini)
Same cast.
November 22: PELLÉAS ET MÉLISANDE (Debussy)
Same cast.
November 29: JENUFA (Janacek)
Same cast.

WEDNESDAY EVENING PERFORMANCES

September 17: ARIADNE AUF NAXOS (Strauss)
Same cast except: ZERBINETTA: Grist.
September 24: LA TRAVIATA (Verdi)
Same cast.
October 1: LA BOHÈME (Puccini)
Same cast except: MARCELLO: Wixell, SCHAUNARD: Monk, MUSETTA: Moser.
October 8: FIDELIO (Beethoven)
Same cast.
October 15: THE ELIXIR OF LOVE (Donizetti)
Same cast.
October 22: THE MAGIC FLUTE (Mozart)
Same cast.
October 29: AIDA (Verdi)
Same cast.
November 5: LA CENERENTOLA (Rossini)
Same cast.
November 12: LA FORZA DEL DESTINO (Verdi)
Same cast.

SUNDAY AFTERNOON PERFORMANCES

September 21: ARIADNE AUF NAXOS (Strauss)
Same cast except: BACCHUS: King, ZERBINETTA: Grist.
September 28: LA TRAVIATA (Verdi)
Same cast.
October 12: LA BOHÈME (Puccini)
Same cast except: MARCELLO: Wixell, SCHAUNARD: Monk, MUSETTA: Moser.
October 19: THE ELIXIR OF LOVE (Donizetti)
Same cast.
October 26: GÖTTERDÄMMERUNG (Wagner)
Same cast.
November 9: LA FORZA DEL DESTINO (Verdi)
Same cast.
November 16: LA CENERENTOLA (Rossini)
Same cast.
November 30: AIDA (Verdi)
Same cast except: AIDA: Molnar-Talajic, RHADAMES: Vickers, PRIESTESS: Marks.

417

FRIDAY EVENING PERFORMANCES

September 19: LA TRAVIATA (Verdi)
Same cast.
October 3: FIDELIO (Beethoven)
Same cast.
October 10: THE ELIXIR OF LOVE (Donizetti)
Same cast.
October 17: GÖTTERDÄMMERUNG (Wagner)
Same cast.
October 24: AIDA (Verdi)
Same cast.
October 31: THE MAGIC FLUTE (Mozart)
Same cast except: SARASTRO: Lagger.
November 7: LA FORZA DEL DESTINO (Verdi)
Same cast.
November 14: PELLÉAS ET MÉLISANDE (Debussy)
Same cast.
November 21: JENUFA (Janacek)
Same cast.
November 28: LA BOHÈME (Puccini)
Same cast except: RODOLFO: Alexander, MARCELLO: Farrar, SCHAUNARD:
Monk, MUSETTA: Moser, CONDUCTOR: Périsson.

EXTRA PERFORMANCES

November 15: LA BOHÈME (Puccini)
Same cast except: MIMI: Amara, RODOLFO: Domingo, MARCELLO: Far-
rar, SCHAUNARD: Monk, MUSETTA: Moser, CONDUCTOR: Périsson.
November 26: AIDA (Verdi)
Same cast except: AIDA: Molnar-Talajic, RHADAMES: Vickers, PRIEST-
ESS: Marks.

YOUNG PEOPLE'S PERFORMANCES

November 7, 12, 19, 24, 25, matinees: THE ELIXIR OF LOVE (Donizetti)
Same cast except: ADINA: Moser, NEMORINO: Burrows, BELCORE: Monk,
DR. DULCAMARA: Esparza, CONDUCTOR: Minde.

CASTS—SPRING OPERA 1969

June 3: LA RONDINE (Puccini)
MAGDA: Todd, RUGGERO: Khanzadian, LISETTE: Armstrong, PRUNIER:
Fitch, RAMBALDO: Drake, PERICHAUD: Lawrence, GOBIN: Andersen,
CREBILLON: Metlenko, YVETTE: Matsumoto, BIANCA: Lindsey, SUZY:
Wilson, SINGER: Graber, GIRLS: Corsale, Woodburn, MAJOR DOMO:
McEachern, GABRIELLE: Noble, LOLETTE: San Miguel, YOUNG MAN:
Martorano, CONDUCTOR: Guadagno.
June 6: LA RONDINE (Puccini)
Same cast.

June 10: THE CONSUL (Menotti)
MAGDA SOREL: Crader, JOHN SOREL: Schwartzman, THE MOTHER: Krooskos, SECRET POLICE AGENT: Hecht, THE SECRETARY: Davidson, MR. KOFNER: Clark, THE FOREIGN WOMAN: Schneider, ANNA GOMEZ: Lindsey, VERA BORONEL: Petersen, THE MAGICIAN: Manton, ASSAN: Barker, CONDUCTOR: Wilson.
June 13: THE CONSUL (Menotti)
Same cast.
June 17: THE MARRIAGE OF FIGARO (Mozart)
SUSANNA: Mandac, COUNTESS: Marks, CHERUBINO: Forst, FIGARO: Monk, COUNT: Patrick, BARTOLO: Drake, BASILIO: Manton, MARCELLINA: Petersen, BARBARINA: Matsumoto, ANTONIO: Clark, DON CURZIO: Jameson, PEASANT GIRLS: Corsale, Graber, CONDUCTOR: Minde.
June 20: THE MARRIAGE OF FIGARO (Mozart)
Same cast.
June 24: ROMÉO ET JULIETTE (Gounod)
ROMÉO: Kolk, JULIETTE: Patenaude, MERCUTIO: Goodloe, TYBALT: Boyll, CAPULET: Monk, FRIAR LAWRENCE: Enns, GREGORIO: Nolen, BENVOGLIO: Janzen, DUKE OF VERONA: Clark, STEPHANO: Forst, GERTRUDE: Petersen, PARIS: Andersen, CONDUCTOR: Kritz.
June 27: ROMÉO ET JULIETTE (Gounod)
Same cast.

CASTS—1970 SEASON

September 18: TOSCA (Puccini)
TOSCA: Kirsten, CAVARADOSSI: Spiess, SCARPIA: MacNeil, SPOLETTA: Fried, SACRISTAN: Capecchi, ANGELOTTI: Van Dam, SCIARRONE: Nolen, JAILOR: Lombardi, SHEPHERD: Shoenfeld, CONDUCTOR: Cillario.
September 22: SIEGFRIED (Wagner)
BRÜNNHILDE: Lindholm, SIEGFRIED: Thomas, WANDERER: Stewart, FAFNER: Berberian, ALBERICH: Richardson, MIME: Ulfung, ERDA: Nadler, VOICE OF THE FOREST BIRD: Lewis, CONDUCTOR: Suitner.
September 29: FALSTAFF (Verdi)
SIR JOHN FALSTAFF: Evans, MISTRESS FORD: Costa, MISTRESS PAGE: Anderson, DAME QUICKLY: Chookasian, ANNE: M. Price, FENTON: Burrows, FORD: Richardson, DR. CAIUS: Ulfung, BARDOLPH: Manton, PISTOL: Berberian, CONDUCTOR: Bartoletti.
October 6: CARMEN (Bizet)
CARMEN: Fassbaender, MICAELA: Marsh, DON JOSÉ: Chauvet, ESCAMILLO: Van Dam, ZUNIGA: Grant, DANCAIRO: Fried, REMENDADO: Manton, MORALES: Nolen, FRASQUITA: Matsumoto, MERCEDES: Nadler, CONDUCTOR: Périsson.
October 13: NABUCCO (Verdi)
NABUCCO: MacNeil, ABIGAILLE: Lippert, ZACCARIA: Tozzi, ISMAELE: R. Bjoerling, FENENA: Anderson, HIGH PRIEST: Grant, ANNA: Bybee, ABDALLO: Fried, CONDUCTOR: Cillario.
October 20: COSI FAN TUTTE (Mozart)

FIORDILIGI: M. Price, DORABELLA: Berganza, DESPINA: Sciutti, FERRANDO: Davies, GUGLIELMO: Rinaldi, DON ALFONSO: Capecchi, CONDUCTOR: Pritchard.

October 27: SALOME (Strauss)
SALOME: Silja, HEROD: Ulfung, JOCHANAAN: Nienstedt, HERODIAS: Cervena, NARRABOTH: Peterson, PAGE: Nadler, SOLDIERS: Monk, Grant, NAZARENES: Van Dam, Nolen, JEWS: Fried, Janzen, Manton, Hall-Sundquist, Magary, SLAVE: Matsumoto, CAPPADOCIAN: Lombardi, CONDUCTOR: Gregor.

November 3: FAUST (Gounod)
MARGUERITE: Beckman, FAUST: Vanzo, MEPHISTOPHELES: Soyer, VALENTIN: Cossa, WAGNER: Lombardi, SIEBEL: Anderson, MARTHE: Cervena, CONDUCTOR: Périsson.

November 10: TRISTAN AND ISOLDE (Wagner)
ISOLDE: Nilsson, BRANGÄNE: Martin, TRISTAN: Windgassen, KING MARKE: Tozzi, KURWENAL: Dooley, MELOT: Monk, SHEPHERD: Hall-Sundquist, SAILOR'S VOICE: Davies, STEERSMAN: Grant, CONDUCTOR: Suitner.

November 17: THE RAKE'S PROGRESS (Stravinsky)
TOM RAKEWELL: Dempsey, ANNE TRULOVE: Marsh, NICK SHADOW: Dooley, FATHER TRULOVE: Grant, BABA THE TURK: Anderson, MOTHER GOOSE: Petersen, SELLEM: Fried, WARDEN: Lombardi, CONDUCTOR: Schuller.

November 24: OTELLO (Verdi)
DESDEMONA: Kabaiwanska, OTELLO: McCracken, IAGO: Paskalis, CASSIO: Davies, RODERIGO: Hall-Sundquist, LODOVICO: Grant, MONTANO: Nolen, HERALD: Lombardi, EMILIA: Nadler, CONDUCTOR: Gregor.

SATURDAY EVENING PERFORMANCES

September 19: FALSTAFF (Verdi)
Same cast.

September 26: TOSCA (Puccini)
Same cast except: TOSCA: Crespin.

October 3: CARMEN (Bizet)
Same cast.

October 10: NABUCCO (Verdi)
Same cast.

October 17: COSI FAN TUTTE (Mozart)
Same cast.

October 24: SALOME (Strauss)
Same cast.

October 31: TRISTAN AND ISOLDE (Wagner)
Same cast.

November 7: OTELLO (Verdi)
Same cast.

November 14: THE RAKE'S PROGRESS (Stravinsky)
Same cast.

November 21: FAUST (Gounod)
Same cast except: SIEBEL: Castle.

420

November 28: TOSCA (Puccini)
Same cast except: CAVARADOSSI: Domingo, SCARPIA: Quilico, SACRISTAN: Grant, ANGELOTTI: Monk, CONDUCTOR: Levine.

WEDNESDAY EVENING PERFORMANCES

September 23: TOSCA (Puccini)
Same cast.
September 30: CARMEN (Bizet)
Same cast.
October 7: FALSTAFF (Verdi)
Same cast.
October 21: NABUCCO (Verdi)
Same cast.
October 28: COSI FAN TUTTE (Mozart)
Same cast except: DORABELLA: Elias.
November 11: OTELLO (Verdi)
Same cast.
November 18: TRISTAN AND ISOLDE (Wagner)
Same cast.
November 25: FAUST (Gounod)
Same cast.

SUNDAY AFTERNOON PERFORMANCES

September 27: SIEGFRIED (Wagner)
Same cast.
October 4: TOSCA (Puccini)
Same cast except: TOSCA: Crespin.
October 11: CARMEN (Bizet)
Same cast.
October 18: NABUCCO (Verdi)
Same cast.
November 8: FAUST (Gounod)
Same cast.
November 15: TRISTAN AND ISOLDE (Wagner)
Same cast.
November 22: TOSCA (Puccini)
Same cast except: CAVARADOSSI: Domingo, SCARPIA: Quilico, SACRISTAN: Grant, ANGELOTTI: Monk, CONDUCTOR: Levine.
November 29: OTELLO (Verdi)
Same cast.

FRIDAY EVENING PERFORMANCES

September 25: FALSTAFF (Verdi)
Same cast.
October 2: SIEGFRIED (Wagner)
Same cast.
October 9: TOSCA (Puccini)
Same cast except: TOSCA: Crader.

October 16: CARMEN (Bizet)
Same cast.
October 23: COSI FAN TUTTE (Mozart)
Same cast except: DORABELLA: Elias.
October 30: SALOME (Strauss)
Same cast.
November 6: TRISTAN AND ISOLDE (Wagner)
Same cast.
November 13: FAUST (Gounod)
Same cast.
November 20: OTELLO (Verdi)
Same cast.
November 27: THE RAKE'S PROGRESS (Stravinsky)
Same cast.

EXTRA PERFORMANCE

November 26: CARMEN (Bizet)
Same cast except: CARMEN: Davidson, DON JOSÉ: Domingo, ESCAMILLO: Monk.

YOUNG PEOPLE'S PERFORMANCES

October 13, matinee: CARMEN (Bizet)
Same cast.
October 21, matinee: CARMEN (Bizet)
Same cast except: CARMEN: Davidson, DON JOSÉ: Peterson, CONDUCTOR: Beckman.
November 13, matinee: CARMEN (Bizet)
Same cast except: CARMEN: Davidson, MICAELA: Matsumoto, DON JOSÉ: Peterson, ESCAMILLO: Monk, FRASQUITA: Lewis.
November 20, matinee: CARMEN (Bizet)
Same cast except: CARMEN: Anderson, DON JOSÉ: Peterson, ESCAMILLO: Monk, CONDUCTOR: Beckman.
November 24, matinee: CARMEN (Bizet)
Same cast except: CARMEN: Anderson, MICAELA: Matsumoto, DON JOSÉ: Peterson, ESCAMILLO: Monk, FRASQUITA: Lewis, CONDUCTOR: Beckman.

CASTS—1971 SEASON

REGULAR SERIES

✓ *September 10:* MANON (Massenet)
MANON: Sills, CHEVALIER DES GRIEUX: Gedda, LESCAUT: Monk, GUILLOT: Ulfung, DE BRÉTIGNY: Howard, COUNT DES GRIEUX: Berberian, POUSETTE: Lewis, JAVOTTE: Jones, ROSETTE: Bush, INNKEEPER: Fleck, SERVANT: Corsale, GUARDS: Pinedo, Sullivan, SERGEANT: Miller, ATTENDANT: Tredway, CONDUCTOR: Périsson.
🖊 *September 14:* DER ROSENKAVALIER (Strauss)

MARSCHALLIN: Jurinac, BARON OCHS: Jungwirth, OCTAVIAN: Ludwig, SOPHIE: Donath, FANINAL: Wolansky, TENOR: Riegel, MARIANNE: Emoed-Wallace, VALZACCHI: Ulfung, ANNINA: Garabedian, POLICE COMMISSIONER: Monk, NOTARY: Fleck, LANDLORD: Pinedo, MILLINER: A. Adams, ANIMAL VENDOR: Hoskinson, MARSCHALLIN'S MAJOR DOMO: Van Derick, FANINAL'S MAJOR DOMO: Atherton, ORPHANS: Lewis, Jones, Bush, FOOTMEN: Glenister, Styles, Naham, Lawrence, CONDUCTOR: Varviso.

September 21: MADAMA BUTTERFLY (Puccini)
CIO-CIO-SAN: Kubiak, PINKERTON: Burrows, SHARPLESS: Yarnell, SUZUKI: Vanni, GORO: Atherton, BONZE: Mundt, YAMADORI: Manton, COMMISSIONER: Howard, KATE PINKERTON: Jones, REGISTRAR: Harvey, CONDUCTOR: Levine.

October 5: A MIDSUMMER NIGHT'S DREAM (Britten) [English Opera Group] (British Week Gala attended by Princess Alexandra)
BOTTOM: Brannigan, TITANIA: Vyvyan, OBERON: Bowman, LYSANDER: Tear, HERMIA: Maia, DEMETRIUS: Luxon, HELENA: Cantelo, QUINCE: Lumsden, FLUTE: Dickerson, SNUG: Holmes, SNOUT: Allum, STARVELING: Leeming, PUCK: Molloy, THESEUS: Morgan, HIPPOLYTA: J. Adams, COBWEB: West, MUSTARDSEED: Dance, PEASEBLOSSOM: Beeby, MOTH: Marsland, CONDUCTOR: Bedford.

October 12: DIE MEISTERSINGER (Wagner)
EVA: Saunders, MAGDALENA: Vanni, WALTHER: King, HANS SACHS: Adam, POGNER: Flagello, DAVID: Walker, BECKMESSER: Evans, KOTHNER: Wolansky, NIGHT WATCHMAN: Berberian, VOGELGESANG: Atherton, NACHTIGALL: Howard, ZORN: Hoskinson, EISSLINGER: Manton, MOSER: Pinedo, ORTEL: Monk, SCHWARZ: Berberian, FOLTZ: Mundt, CONDUCTOR: Suitner.

October 19: EUGENE ONEGIN (Tchaikovsky)
TATIANA: Lear, OLGA: Garabedian, ONEGIN: Stewart, LENSKY: Burrows, GREMIN: Berberian, FILIPYEVNA: Petersen, MADAME LARINA: Vanni, TRIQUET: Walker, ZARETZKY: Booth, CAPTAIN: Sullivan, CHORUS LEADER: Van Derick, CONDUCTOR: Mackerras.

October 26: IL TROVATORE (Verdi)
LEONORA: Price, AZUCENA: Lilova, MANRICO: Domingo, COUNT DI LUNA: Wolansky, FERRANDO: Mundt, RUIZ: Pinedo, OLD GYPSY: Lawrence, INEZ: Petersen, CONDUCTOR: Cillario.

November 2: UN BALLO IN MASCHERA (Verdi)
AMELIA: Arroyo, ULRICA: Dalis, OSCAR: Donath, RICCARDO: Pavarotti, RENATO: Bordoni, SAM: Mundt, TOM: Booth, SILVANO: Monk, JUDGE: Pinedo, SERVANT: Sullivan, CONDUCTOR: Mackerras.

November 9: LULU (Berg)
LULU: Silja, DR. SCHOEN: Reardon, ALWA: Hopferweiser, PAINTER: Ulfung, ANIMAL TRAINER: Yarnell, SCHIGOLCH: Alvary, COUNTESS GESCHWITZ: Cervena, RODRIGO: Yarnell, PRINCE: Walker, DR. GOLL: Yarnell, JACK THE RIPPER: Yarnell, WARDROBE MISTRESS: Petersen, STAGE DIRECTOR: Mundt, STUDENT: Jones, SERVANT: Sullivan, CONDUCTOR: von Dohnanyi.

November 16: MARIA STUARDA (Donizetti)
MARY STUART: Sutherland, ELIZABETH I: Tourangeau, LEICESTER: Burrows,

TALBOT: Opthof, CECIL: Berberian, ANNE: Bybee, HERALD: Sullivan, CON-
DUCTOR: Bonynge.

✓ *November 23:* IL TABARRO (Puccini)
GIORGETTA: Price, LUIGI: Bottion, MICHELE: Bacquier, TINCA: Manton,
TALPA: Fleck, SONG VENDOR: Pinedo, FRUGOLA: Allen, LOVERS: Bybee,
Covington, VOICES: Lewis, Covington, CONDUCTOR: Sanzogno.
followed by: CARMINA BURANA (Orff)
BURGUNDIAN TROUBADOUR: Wolansky, OLD POET: Wolansky, DRINKERS:
Wolansky, Brewer, BURGUNDIAN LADY: Matsumoto, YOUNG COUPLE IN
LOVE: Jones, Booth, FRIENDS OF TROUBADOUR: Covington, Pinedo, Jan-
zen, Sullivan, Fleck, Booth, CONDUCTOR: Sanzogno.

SATURDAY EVENING PERFORMANCES

✓ *September 11:* DER ROSENKAVALIER (Strauss)
Same cast except: TENOR: Gedda.
September 18: MADAMA BUTTERFLY (Puccini)
Same cast.
September 25: MANON (Massenet)
Same cast.
October 2: MADAMA BUTTERFLY (Puccini)
Same cast.
October 9: DIE MEISTERSINGER (Wagner)
Same cast.
October 16: EUGENE ONEGIN (Tchaikovsky)
Same cast.
✓ *October 23:* IL TROVATORE (Verdi)
Same cast except: MANRICO: King. ~~FERRANDO: BOLS~~
October 30: UN BALLO IN MASCHERA (Verdi)
Same cast.
November 6: LULU (Berg)
Same cast.
November 13: IL TROVATORE (Verdi)
Same cast except: LEONORA: Molnar-Talajic, AZUCENA: Dalis, MANRICO:
King, FERRANDO: Berberian, INEZ: Jones.
November 20: IL TABARRO (Puccini)
followed by: CARMINA BURANA (Orff)
Same casts.
November 27: MARIA STUARDA (Donizetti)
Same cast.

WEDNESDAY EVENING PERFORMANCES

September 15: MADAMA BUTTERFLY (Puccini)
Same cast.
September 22: DER ROSENKAVALIER (Strauss)
Same cast except: TENOR: Gedda.
September 29: MANON (Massenet)
Same cast.
October 6: DIE MEISTERSINGER (Wagner)

Same cast.
October 13: EUGENE ONEGIN (Tchaikovsky)
Same cast.
October 27: UN BALLO IN MASCHERA (Verdi)
Same cast.
November 3: IL TROVATORE (Verdi)
Same cast except: MANRICO: King, FERRANDO: Michalski.
November 17: IL TABARRO (Puccini)
　　　　　followed by: CARMINA BURANA (Orff)
Same casts.
November 24: MARIA STUARDA (Donizetti)
Same cast.

SUNDAY AFTERNOON PERFORMANCES

September 12: MADAMA BUTTERFLY (Puccini)
Same cast.
September 19: MANON (Massenet)
Same cast.
September 26: DER ROSENKAVALIER (Strauss)
Same cast.
October 3: MANON (Massenet)
Same cast.
October 10: A MIDSUMMER NIGHT'S DREAM (Britten)
Same cast except: HERMIA: Morelle, HIPPOLYTA: Maia.
October 17: DIE MEISTERSINGER (Wagner)
Same cast.
October 24: MADAMA BUTTERFLY (Puccini)
Same cast.
October 31: EUGENE ONEGIN (Tchaikovsky)
Same cast.
November 7: UN BALLO IN MASCHERA (Verdi)
Same cast.
*November 14:*LULU (Berg)
Same cast.
November 21: MARIA STUARDA (Donizetti)
Same cast.
November 28: IL TROVATORE (Verdi)
Same cast except: LEONORA: Molnar-Talajic, AZUCENA: Dalis, MANRICO: McCracken, FERRANDO: Berberian, INEZ: Jones, CONDUCTOR: Wilson.

FRIDAY EVENING PERFORMANCES

September 17: DER ROSENKAVALIER (Strauss)
Same cast except: TENOR: Gedda.
September 24: MADAMA BUTTERFLY (Puccini)
Same cast.
October 1: DIE MEISTERSINGER (Wagner)
Same cast.
October 8: MANON (Massenet)

Same cast.

October 15: A MIDSUMMER NIGHT'S DREAM (Britten)
Same cast except: LYSANDER: Williams, HERMIA: Morelle, HIPPOLYTA: Maia.

October 22: EUGENE ONEGIN (Tchaikovsky)
Same cast.

October 29: IL TROVATORE (Verdi)
Same cast except: MANRICO: King, FERRANDO: Michalski.

November 5: UN BALLO IN MASCHERA (Verdi)
Same cast.

November 12: MARIA STUARDA (Donizetti)
Same cast.

November 19: LULU (Berg)
Same cast.

November 26: IL TABARRO (Puccini)
         followed by: CARMINA BURANA (Orff)
Same casts.

EXTRA PERFORMANCE

November 25: IL TROVATORE (Verdi)
Same cast except: LEONORA: Molnar-Talajic, AZUCENA: Dalis, MANRICO: McCracken, COUNT DI LUNA: Quilico, FERRANDO: Berberian, INEZ: Jones, CONDUCTOR: Wilson.

YOUNG PEOPLE'S PERFORMANCES

October 7, 8, matinees: A MIDSUMMER NIGHT'S DREAM (Britten)
Same cast except: HERMIA: Morelle, HIPPOLYTA: Maia.

October 26, matinee: IL TROVATORE (Verdi)
Same cast except: LEONORA: Molnar-Talajic, AZUCENA: Dalis, MANRICO: McCray, COUNT DI LUNA: Opthof, FERRANDO: Michalski, INEZ: Jones, CONDUCTOR: Wilson.

October 29, matinee: IL TROVATORE (Verdi)
Same cast except: LEONORA: Molnar-Talajic, AZUCENA: Dalis, MANRICO: McCray, COUNT DI LUNA: Opthof, INEZ: Jones, CONDUCTOR: Wilson.

November 3, matinee: IL TROVATORE (Verdi)
Same cast except: LEONORA: Molnar-Talajic, AZUCENA: Allen, MANRICO: McCray, COUNT DI LUNA: Opthof, FERRANDO: Berberian, INEZ: Jones, CONDUCTOR: Wilson.

CASTS—SPRING OPERA 1971

March 18, 20 and 26: TITUS (Mozart)
TITUS: McDonald, VITELLIA: Cooper, SEXTUS: von Stade, SERVILIA: Benner, ANNIUS: Jones, PUBLIUS: Monk, CONDUCTOR: Meier.

March 19, 21 (matinee), 27: RIGOLETTO (Verdi)
GILDA: Toscano, DUKE: Danner, RIGOLETTO: Mosley, MADDALENA: Garabedian, SPARAFUCILE: Mundt, MONTERONE: Monk, BORSA: Hall-Sundquist,

MARULLO: Lombardi, CEPRANO: Sullivan, COUNTESS CEPRANO: Emoed-Wallace, GIOVANNA: Petersen, PAGE: Schoenfeld, CONDUCTOR: Davies.

March 25, 28 (matinee), April 2: DON PASQUALE (Donizetti)
NORINA: Matsumoto, ERNESTO: J. Walker, DR. MALATESTA: Justus, DON PASQUALE: Best, NOTARY: Micheletti, CONDUCTOR: Lee.

April 1, 3, 4 (matinee): FAUST COUNTER FAUST (Gessner) [Center Opera of Minneapolis]
JOHN FAUSTUS: Sutton, HENRI FAUST: Neill, GRETCHEN: Brandt, MARGUERITE: Roche, LIESCHEN: Hardy, MEPHISTOPHELES: Lehr, LUCIFER: C. P. Walker, MARTHA: Erickson, VALENTINE: Peterson, WAGNER: Hansen, CONDUCTOR: Brunelle.

Note

[1]At this performance the indisposed Costa mimed the role while Sheila Marks sang it from the pit.

Index of Conductors 1923-1971

at home and on tour

The letter S *before a date refers to a season of Spring Opera, produced by the San Francisco Opera; when a performer appeared only in a Southern California season, the date is preceded by* LA

Adler, Kurt Herbert: 1943–53, 1958, 1960–61
Alessandro, Victor: S1962
Barbini, Ernesto: 1954–55
Bartoletti, Bruno: 1970
Basile, Arturo: 1959
Beckman, Irving: 1970
Bedford, Steuart: 1971 (MND)[1]
Beecham, Sir Thomas: 1943
Bellugi, Piero: 1965
Bernardi, Mario: 1967–68
Blechschmidt, Hans: 1931–32
Bodanzky, Artur: 1935
Bonynge, Richard: 1963–64, 1966, 1971
Breisach, Paul: 1946–52
Brunelle, Philip: S1971 (FCF)[2],
Cillario, Carlo Felice: 1970–71
Cimara, Pietro: 1942–48, 1951–52
Cimini, Pietro: 1925–29, 1931–32, 1934, 1937
Cleva, Fausto: 1942–43, 1949–55
Coppola, Anton: 1969/S1968
Curiel, Glauco: 1952–58
Davies, Dennis Russell: S1971
De Fabritiis, Oliviero: 1956, 1962
Dell 'Orefice, Antonio: 1929–31, 1933

Di Rosa, Ottavio: 1960
Dohnanyi, Christoph von: 1971
Ehrling, Sixten: 1969
Faldi, Aldo: 1968
Ferencsik, Janos: 1962–63
Fournet, Jean: 1958
Gregor, Bohumil: 1969–70
Grossman, Herbert: 1967/S1964–67
Guadagno, Anton: S1969
Herbert, Walter: 1942
Horenstein, Jascha: 1966
Karp, Richard: LA 1950
Kritz Karl: 1945–46, 1949–54, 1956–58/S1962–65, S1967, S1969
Lawner, George: 1961/S1964–66
Lee, Everett: S1971
Leinsdorf, Erich: 1938–41, 1948, 1951, 1955, 1957
Leitner, Ferdinand: 1964
Lert, Richard: 1935–36
Levine, James: 1970–71
Lewis, Henry: S1961–64
Ludwig, Leopold: 1958–65, 1967–68
Mackerras, Charles: 1969, 1971
Martin, Wolfgang: 1959
Martinon, Jean: 1965
Marzollo, Dick: 1947–48

McArthur, Edwin: 1939
Meier, Gustav: S1971
Merola, Gaetano: 1923–49, 1952/ LA 1951 (plus Stanford season 1922)
Minde, Stefan: S1969
Molinari-Pradelli, Francesco: 1957, 1959–66
Montemezzi, Italo: 1941–42, 1947
Monteux, Pierre: 1954
Morel, Jean: 1955
Mueller, Leo: 1954
Murray, Earl: 1959
Papi, Gennaro: 1936–41
Patane, Giuseppe: 1967–69
Pelletier, Wilfred: 1928–31, 1933, 1947
Périsson, Jean: 1966–71
Perlea, Jonel: 1950
Popper, Jan: S1963–64
Prêtre, Georges: 1963–64
Pritchard, John: 1970
Reimuller, Ross: S1968
Reiner, Fritz: 1936–38

Rescigno, Nicola: 1950–51
Riedel, Karl: 1929–30, 1936, 1944
Rosekrans, Charles: S1965–66
Rosenstock, Joseph: S1961
Salgo, Sandor: S1961
Samuel, Gerhard: S1965
Sanzogno, Nino: 1971
Schaefer, Hans George: 1960
Schuller, Gunther: 1967–70
Schwieger, Hans: 1956
Sebastian, Georges: 1944–46, 1958
Serafin, Tullio: 1953
Solti, Georg: 1953
Stein, Horst: 1965–68
Steinberg, William: 1944–49, 1956–57
Suitner, Otmar: 1969–71
Szenkar, Eugen: 1954
Van Den Burg, Willem: 1939
Varviso, Silvio: 1959–61, 1971
Wallenstein, Alfred: 1951
Whallon, Evan: S1966, S1968
Wilson, Charles: 1971/S1969

Notes

[1] MND refers to English Opera Group production of Britten's *A Midsummer Night's Dream*.

[2] FCF refers to Center Opera Company of Minneapolis' production of *Faust Counter Faust*.

Roster of Solo Singers (and Dancers)

at home and on tour—1923-71, plus the Stanford season of 1922

The letter S before a date refers to a season of Spring Opera; when a performer appeared only in a Southern California season, the date is preceded by LA; *Stanford season listings are preceded by an* St.

Adams, Arlene: 1971
Adams, Josephine: 1971 (MND)[1]
Agni, R.: St.
Aird, Brooke: 1969/S1968
Alarie, Pierrette: 1959
Albanese, Licia: 1941–50, 1953–57, 1959/LA 1961
Alexander, John: 1967, 1969
Alexander, Nicolai: 1943
Alibertini, Evaristo: 1923–35, 1937–41, 1943–45, 1947–48
Allen, Betty: 1971/S1966
Allen, Janette: 1955
Allison, Catherine: 1938/LA 1937
Allum, Graham: 1971 (MND)
Alsen, Elsa: 1927
Althof, Phyllis: 1956
Althouse, Paul: 1926, 1933
Alvary, Lorenzo: 1940–48, 1951–60, 1971
Alver, Sheril: 1948
Amara, Lucine: 1959–60, 1965, 1969
Amato, Pasquale: 1927
Ananian, Paolo: 1923–24
Andersen, Winther: 1951–67/ S1961–62, S1964, S1966–69
Anderson, Britta: 1945

Anderson, David: 1967
Anderson, Eugene: 1933
Anderson, Geary: 1944
Anderson, Robert: 1960
Anderson, Sylvia: 1967–70
Anderson, Virginia: 1967
Andreatta, Carmen: 1950, 1952
Andreotti, Norma: 1940
Andrew, Milla: 1957
Ansseau, Fernand: 1925
Antoine, Josephine: 1942
Argall, Marsden: St., 1925, 1932
Armstrong, Karan: S1966, S1969
Arnold, Bene: 1953
Arrieta, Rosa: 1967
Arroyo, Martina: 1971
Askam, Perry: 1936–37
Assandri, Virginio: 1952–59
Atherton, James: 1971
Attarian, James: 1948
Avakian, Alice: 1938–41, 1944
Avery, Eleanor: 1955
Baccaloni, Salvatore: 1938, 1941–54, 1958–60, 1962
Bada, Angelo: 1927–28
Badger, Flossita: 1923, 1925–26, 1934
Bacquier, Gabriel: 1971

430

Bailey, Sally: 1953, 1959–60
Bakocevic, Radmila: 1968
Baldacci, Otello: 1935
Baldwin, Eileen: 1947–52
Baldwin, Marcia: S1963
Bales, Tom: 1967
Balfour, Jean: 1937
Ballagh, Robert: 1940
Ballarini, Stefan: 1939
Ballester, Vincente: St.
Bampton, Rose: 1949
Barabas, Sari: 1950
Barallobre, Ray: 1953
Barbano, Josephine: 1950, 1952
Barbato, Elisabetta: 1949
Barbieri, Fedora: 1952
Bardelli, Cesare: 1953
Barioni, Daniele: 1967
Barker, Sean: 1968/S1969
Baromeo, Chase: 1935
Barra, Gennaro: 1928–29
Barrera, Giulia: S1962
Bartlett, Michael: 1939
Bastianini, Ettore: 1961–62, 1965
Baum, Kurt: 1943, 1946–48, 1951
Beach, Scott: 1965
Beal, Eula: 1948
Beattie, Douglas: 1935, 1942
Beattie, Herbert: 1968/S1962–66,
   S1968
Beatty, Helen: 1937
Beckman, Judith: 1970
Beeby, Marc: 1971 (MND)
Belarsky, Sidor: 1933
Bell, Marion: LA 1941
Belling, Susan: S1968
Bence, Margarethe: 1961
Beni, Gimi: S1966
Benner, Joan: S1971
Benson, Norman: 1947–48
Berberian, Ara: 1966–71/S1965
Berganza, Teresa: 1968–70
Bergman, Alan: 1967
Bergonzi, Carlo: 1969
Bering, Christine: 1953
Berini, Mario: 1946
Bernhard, Alton: 1937, 1944
Berrar, Carol: 1957

Berton, Anthony: 1944
Bessel, Annamaria: 1965
Best, Richard: S1971
Bible, Frances: 1955, 1957, 1960/
   S1965
Bick, Mary Jane: 1969
Binci, Mario: 1948
Bish, Dora: 1947
Bjoerling, Anna Lisa: 1951
Bjoerling, Jussi: 1940, 1946, 1948–
   49, 1951, 1956, 1958
Bjoerling, Rolf: 1970
Bjoerling, Sigurd: 1950
Bjoner, Ingrid: 1960
Bland, George: S1966
Blankenburg, Heinz: 1955–57, 1965,
   1969
Blankenheim, Toni: 1965
Block, Arnold: 1935
Blum, Margot: 1958–60/S1961
Boatwright, McHenry: S1966
Boehme, Kurt: 1960
Boerner, Charlotte: 1936–37, 1939
Bogard, Carole: S1965
Bogart, Dorothy: 1971
Bokor, Margit: 1940–42
Boky, Colette: 1969
Bolm, Adolph: 1933, 1935
Bond, William: 1950
Bonelli, Richard: 1926, 1932–35,
   1937–40, 1942
Bonisolli, Franco: 1969
Bonnecaze, Joseph: 1928
Booth, Philip: 1971
Booth, William: 1955, 1957, 1967–
   68
Borden, Lemuel: 1968
Bordoni, Franco: 1971
Borghi, Umberto: 1957
Borgioli, Dino: 1932–34, 1938
Bori, Lucrezia: 1933–34
Borkh, Inge: 1953–55
Bose, Martin: LA 1938
Bottazzo, Pietro: 1968–69
Bottcher, Ron: S1965
Bottion, Aldo: 1971
Bourskaya, Ina: St., 1927
Bovy, Vina: 1937

Bowman, James: 1971 (MND)
Boyll, Lawrence: S1969
Bradley, Walda: 1963, 1967/S1965–66
Brandt, Barbara: S1971 (FCF)[2]
Brannigan, Owen: 1971 (MND)
Branzell, Karin: 1941
Bratoff, George: 1933, 1935
Braun, Victor: 1968
Braunstein, Louis: 1935
Bressler, Charles: S1963
Brewer, Bruce: 1971
Brookie, Scott: 1969
Brooks, Patricia: S1964, S1967
Broughton, Marjorie: 1958
Brouwenstijn, Gré: 1961
Brown, Robert: 1933
Browne, Eileen: 1947
Browne, Sue Bell: 1938–39
Brownlee, John: 1940–42, 1946, 1950
Brubaker, John: 1950–52
Bruce, Robert Gordon: 1950
Bruni, Bianca: 1929–30, 1932, 1945–46, 1950
Bruntsch, Margareta: 1924
Bruscantini, Sesto: 1967, 1969
Bruzzone, Norma 1967
Bryn-Jones, Delme: 1967/LA 1968 ('68 repertoire in March '69)
Budzinski, Jan: 1962/S1963
Bullard, Gene: S1968
Bulotti, Charles: 1926
Bumbry, Grace: 1966–67
Burlingham, Jean: 1957
Burr, John: 1936
Burrows, Stuart: 1967, 1969–71
Bush, Sandra: 1971
Bybee, Ariel: 1970–71
Cadwallader, Yvonne: 1957
Calcagno, Lorraine: 1945–46
Callahan, Olga: 1935–37
Campagna-Pinto, Marjorie: S1964
Campbell, Beverly: 1947
Campora, Giuseppe: 1956, 1966
Cann, Patricia: 1959/S1961
Cantelo, April: 1971 (MND)
Capecchi, Renato: 1968–70
Caperello, Thomas: 1960/S1961

Caravacci, Nullo: 1930
Carcione, Giuseppe: 1926–27
Carilli, Anthony: 1958–59
Carroll, Christina: 1941–42
Carron, Elisabeth: S1962–63, S1968
Carter, Richard: 1959
Carteri, Rosanna: 1954–55
Carvajal, Carlos: 1954
Caselle, Yola: 1954
Cassilly, Richard: 1966/S1964
Castagna, Bruna: 1936–37, 1942
Castellani, Frances: 1945
Castle, Joyce: 1970
Castleton, Maxine: 1931
Cathelat, Georges: 1938
Cavalli, Floriana: 1960
Cehanovsky, George: 1937–56
Cervena, Sona: 1962–63, 1965–71
Chabay, Leslie: 1947–49
Chamlee, Mario: 1927, 1931–32, 1934
Chapman, Lulu Mae: 1927
Charisse, Nico: 1933
Chauveau, Yvonne: 1949–53
Chauvet, Guy: 1968–70
Cherney, David: 1958
Chinn, Laurran: 1939
Chirot, Armanda: 1928
Christensen, Catherine: 1966
Christensen, Willam: 1939
Christoff, Boris: 1956
Christoph, K.: 1923
Christopher, Russell: 1962–63
Chronis, Olga: 1963
Cigna, Gina: 1937
Cioni, Laura: 1930
Cioni, Renato: 1961–63, 1965, 1967–68
Clabassi, Plinio: 1961
Clairbert, Clara: 1930
Clark, Lillian: 1934
Clark, Richard J.: 1968–69/S1968–69
Clatworthy, David: S1966
Clemens, Hans: 1935–39
Clements, David: 1966–67
Clifford, Glen: 1924
Cochran, William: LA 1968

Coghill, Joy: 1961
Cole, Dorothy: 1961–63, 1966/
   S1962
Coler, Constance: 1953
Collier, Marie: 1964–66, 1968
Colzani, Anselmo: 1956
Conley, Eugene: 1950–52
Conner, Nadine: 1945–48
Connors, Mary Lou: 1946
Cook, Jeanne: LA 1968
Cooke, Allan: 1933
Cooper, Sylvia: S1971
Cordon, Norman: 1936–39
Cornish, Dorothy: 1937–39
Corral, José: 1923
Corsale, Louise: 1966–67, 1971/
   S1965, S1968–69
Cortis, Antonio: 1925–26
Corvello, Evelynn: 1945
Coryell, Eleanor: 1947
Cosindas, Nicholas: S1968
Cossa, Dominic: 1970/S1967
Costa, Mary: 1959–65, 1968, 1970
Coulter, Dorothy: S1965
Covington, Peggy: 1955–57
Covington, Steve: 1971
Cozzens, Jayne: 1937
Cozzi, Carlo: 1930
Crader, Jeannine: 1955–56, 1970/
   S1969
Craig, John: S1965
Crain, Jon: 1957
Cramer, Ken: S1961
Crespin, Régine: 1966–68, 1970
Crockett, Deane: 1939
Crofoot, Alan: 1967–68
Crooks, Richard: 1934
Cross, Elsie: 1925
Cross, Richard: 1963
Curatilo, Gwen: 1960–62, 1964–66/
   S1961, S1963–66
Currier, Sharon: 1952
Curry, Corinne: S1968
Curtis, Mary (Curtis-Verna): 1952/
   LA 1960
Curzi, Cesare: 1948–54, 1956–57,
   1959
Czaplicki, George: 1946–47

Dakin, Alice: S1961
Dalis, Irene: 1958–62, 1964, 1967,
   1969, 1971
Dal Ponte, Baldo: S1966
D'Alvarez, Marguerite: 1925
Dance, Andrew: 1971 (MND)
Daneluz, Galliano: 1946–47, 1952–
   53, 1955
D'Angelo, Louis: 1923–24, 1927–36,
   1938–39
Daniel, Ruth: 1958
Danise, Giuseppe: 1928–29, 1931
Danner, Harry: S1971
Darrow, Lois Viola: 1925
Daugherty, Patrick: S1964
Davia, Federico: 1966–67
Davidson, Joy: 1970/S1969
Davies, Ryland: 1970
Davis, Floyd: 1947
Davis, Sylvia: 1966–67/S1967
Deeley, Ellen: 1927
Defrère, Désiré: 1926–27
De Heurtaumont, Illana: 1966–67/
   S1967
De Hidalgo, Elvira: 1925
Deis, Jean: S1963
Della Casa, Lisa: 1958
Della Chiesa, Vivian: 1944–45
Del Monaco, Mario: 1950, 1952,
   1959, 1962
De Los Angeles, Victoria: 1962
De Luca, Giuseppe: 1923–24, 1929
De Lugg, Harry: 1944
Demers, Mike: 1964
Demers, Muriel: 1945–46
Dempsey, Gregory: 1966, 1970
De Paolis, Alessio: 1940, 1942–56
De Segurola, Andres: 1931
De Sett, Luisa: S1961
Destal, Fred: 1939
Detwiler, Lynn: S1963
Deutekom, Cristina: 1969
De Vere, Joan: 1967
De Vol, Eva: 1924
Dickerson, Bernard: 1971 (MND)
Didur, Adamo: 1923
Di Francesco, Michael: 1965
Di Giuseppe, Enrico: S1962, S1964

Dimitrieff, Zoia: 1930, 1932
Dini, Adolfo: 1927–28, 1930
Di Stefano, Giuseppe: 1950
Di Virgilio, Nicholas: 1968/S1966–67
Djanel, Lily: 1944–46
Doan, Philip: 1944, 1946
Dobbs, Mattiwilda: 1955
Doe, Doris: 1935–36, 1938
Domingo, Placido: 1969–71
Dominguez, Oralia: 1956
Donath, Helen: 1971
Dong, Galen: 1958–59
Donnelly, Myrtle: 1924, 1926–28
Dooley, William: 1970
Drain, Donald: 1960–62/S1961–62
Drake, Archie: 1968/S1968–69
Drake, Bryan: 1971 (MND)
Drew, Roderick: 1959–60
Dunlap, John Robert: S1962
Dunn, Mignon: 1967
Duno, Daniel: 1948
Duval, Franca: 1954
Dvorakova, Ludmila: 1969
Eddy, Nelson: 1934–35
Edelmann, Otto: 1955, 1957, 1964/ LA 1963
Edmunds, Robert: 1931
Edwards, Max: 1939
Eitze, James: 1964–65, 1968/ S1965–66, S1968
Eldredge, George: 1932–33
Elgar, Anne: S1968
Elias, Rosalind: 1970
Elkus, Miriam: 1925
Elliott, Mary Taylor: 1928
Ellis, John: 1934
Elmassian, Zaruhi: 1930–31
Elmo, Cloe: 1948
Elyn, Mark: 1958–59
Emery, Marie DeForest: 1928
Emoed-Wallace, Julia: 1971/S1971
Engel, Peggy: 1942
Engen, Kieth: 1961
Engstrom, Jon: 1967
Enns, Harold: 1954, 1957–58/ S1966–67, S1969
Epton, Merle: 1923

Erickson, Judith: S1971 (FCF)
Ericsdotter, Siw: 1963
Ernster, Dezso: 1950–51, 1953
Esparza, Elfego: 1963, 1969
Estabrook, Winifred: 1927
Estes, Simon: 1967/S1967
Evans, Edith: 1959
Evans, Sir Geraint: 1959–64, 1966–71
Evans, Randall: 1943
Eybel, Querita: 1923–25, 1933–35
Fadem, Edward: 1930
Fairley, William: 1962/S1961
Farncroft, Audrey: 1925–26, 1930–31
Farrar, James: 1969
Farrell, Eileen: 1956, 1958–59
Farrell, Eloise: 1946, 1951, 1953, 1956
Faull, Ellen: 1953/S1966
Favero, Mafalda: 1938
Fazah, Adib: 1965–66
Feduloff, N.: 1924
Feiersinger, Sebastian: 1958–59
Feinberg, Ronald: 1953
Fenn, Jean: 1952
Ferguson, DuBlois: 1923–24, 1927–31, 1935
Fernanda, Doria: St., 1923
Fernandez, Alfredo: 1957
Ferraro, Piero Miranda: 1958
Ferrier, André: 1924, 1929–30, 1933–34, 1937–40
Ferrier, Jeanne Gustin: 1934
Fitch, Bernard: S1968–69
Flagello, Ezio: 1968, 1971
Flagstad, Kirsten: 1935–37, 1939, 1949–50
Fleck, William: 1968, 1971
Florence, Rose: 1928
Flynn, John: 1954
Foldi, Andrew: 1960–61, 1964–65
Folli, Ester: 1933–34
Forbes, Graham: S1964
Ford, John: 1948, 1950
Ford, Lloyd: 1952
Formichi, Cesare: 1925
Forno, Fedela: 1928

Forrester, Maureen: 1967
Forst, Judith: S1969
Foster, Nancy: 1959
Franklyn, Roy: 1954
Fredericks, Walter: 1950–52, 1955
Frediani, Amerigo: 1923–26, 1928, 1933–34
Fredricks, Richard: 1965/S1961–64, S1966
Fremont, Irene: 1926–27, 1935–36
Freni, Mirella: 1967
Friberg, C. Martin: 1935
Fried, Howard: 1957–70
Friedrich, Sylvia: S1965
Fromer, Jonathan: 1958–59
Frost, Willis: 1952, 1955/S1961
Fuerstner, Fiona: 1959
Gabor, Arnold: 1931–32, 1936, 1938
Gahagan, Helen: 1935
Gaihle, Sandra: 1939
Gall, Yvonne: 1931
Gallegos, Ronald: S1961
Galt, Leo: 1945
Gambi, Lelia: 1930, 1938, 1944
Gandolfi, Alfredo: 1923, 1932–36
Garabedian, Edna: 1971/S1971
Garaventa, Ottavio: 1966
Garay, Philip: 1960–61
Garden, Roy: 1939–40
Garnier, Elizabeth: 1955
Garris, John: 1943–46, 1948
Gauld, Carlton: 1938
Gbur, Jan: 1952–53
Gedda, Nicolai: 1968, 1971
Gencer, Leyla: 1956–58, 1967
George, Florence: 1946
George, Helen: 1957
George, Leslie: 1936–41
Germanetti, Giovanni: 1929
Gettys, James: 1968
Ghiaurov, Nicolai: 1967
Ghiuselev, Nicola: 1966
Giannini, Dusolina: 1939, 1943
Gianopoulos, Georgia: 1944
Gibin, Giovanni: 1965
Gibson, Barbara: 1953
Gibson, Marie: 1957/S1968

Gigli, Beniamino: 1923–24, 1930, 1938
Gignac, Marguerite: 1961
Gilbert, Alan: 1969
Gilchrist, David 1964
Gillaspy, John: 1958
Gillette, Albert: 1923–24
Gionas, Fannetta: 1928, 1930
Giosso, David: 1960, 1964–66/S1961, S1963–67
Giragossiantz, Rubsie: 1935
Gismondo, Giuseppe: 1959
Glade, Coe: 1935
Gladstein, Robert: 1963
Glando, Bernice: 1934, 1936
Glaz, Hertha: 1939, 1944–51
Glenister, John: 1971
Glossop, Peter: 1966, 1968
Glover, Robert: 1964–68/S1964–67
Gobbi, Tito: 1948, 1960, 1962, 1964
Golcher, Elise: 1925
Goltz, Christel: 1958
Gomez, John: 1962/S1962, S1966
Gonzales, Irma: 1943
Goodchild, Randy: S1961
Goodloe, Robert: S1969
Goodwin, Charles: 1943–45
Goodwin, Ronald: 1959
Gordon, Betty: 1959
Gordon, Leona: 1964
Gordon, Paul: S1963
Gotelli, Yvonne: 1953–55
Graber, Ann: 1967/S1965–66, S1968–69
Grace, Neil: 1964
Graf, Uta: 1949–51
Grant, Clifford: 1966–70
Gray, Mary: 1947–48, 1956/S1961
Green, Esther: 1936–37
Green, Eugene: 1958–59
Greindl, Josef: 1967
Grist, Reri: 1963–67, 1969
Grob-Prandl, Gertrud: 1953
Groves, Frances: 1958
Gruninger, Eva: 1928–32, 1934–36
Guarrera, Frank: 1952–54, 1956, 1958–60, 1966/LA 1962

Guenter, Paul: 1926–28, 1935–36, 1943–47, 1949, 1951–52, 1955, 1957
Gui, Henri: 1969
Gunn, Willene: 1967
Haas, Julien: 1963
Hackett, Elizabeth: 1936–37, 1939–41
Hageman, Thomas: S1967
Hagopian, Robert: 1954
Hague, Carl: 1938, 1955
Hall, Joyce: 1964/S1965
Hall, Marilynn: 1954
Hall-Sundquist, David: 1970/S1971
Hammons, Raymond: 1955
Hampton, Hope: 1930
Handt, Herbert: 1961
Hansen, Lloyd: S1971 (FCF)
Harden, Gretta: S1963
Hardy, Emily: 1933–35
Hardy, Janis: S1971 (FCF)
Harper, Thora: 1947
Harrell, Mack: 1945–46
Harris, Mercer: S1968
Harrower, Peter: S1963
Harshaw, Margaret: 1944–47
Hartman, Jean: 1935
Hartzell, Lois: 1947–49, 1951, 1953
Harvey, Colin: 1939, 1941–42, 1946–71/S1961, S1963–68
Hata, Kuniaka: S1963
Hatch, Stephen: 1954
Hathaway, Frances: 1937
Heater, Claude: 1961
Hecht, Joshua: 1961–65/S1969
Heidt, Winifred: 1948–49
Heitman, Elma: 1944–48
Hemmingsen, Betty: 1963
Herbert, Ralph: 1950–52, 1954–55, 1957
Herrin, Julien: 1959–60
Herrnkind, Edward: 1969
Hersch, Rose Agnes: 1941, 1945
Hessling, Esther: 1946–47
Hilgenberg, Katherine: 1955–61
Hillebrecht, Hildegard: 1965/LA 1964
Hines, Jerome: 1941
Hinson, Nina: S1968

Hinton, Walter: 1967
Hipp, Martha: 1927
Hirst, Darlene: S1965
Hobson, Saramarie: S1963
Hodge, Charlotte: 1930
Hoffman, Grace, 1958
Hoffman, Mary Louise: 1957
Hofmann, Hubert: 1968
Hofmann, Ludwig: 1937
Holley, William: 1968
Holmes, Brian: 1971 (MND)
Holmes, Eugene: 1967
Homer, Louise: 1926
Hoots, Barbara: 1952
Hopferweiser, Josef: 1971
Hopkins, Jeanette: 1941–42
Horne, Marilyn: 1960–62, 1966/S1961–62, S1964
Horton, Russell: 1930–32
Hoskinson, Orva: 1960, 1971/S1962, S1968
Hotter, Hans: 1954, 1956
Howard, Mark: 1971
Howe, Francesca: 1957/S1968
Howell, John: 1934–38
Hubbard, Victor: 1957
Huehn, Julius: 1937–39, 1941
Huff, Hazel: 1926–29
Huie, Jonathan: 1967/S1967
Hunt, Paul: 1969
Hurd, Leona: 1950–51
Ilosfalvy, Robert: 1964, 1967–68
Imdahl, Heinz: 1965
Isariotis, Katina: 1935
Ivey, Lenore: 1928–29
Jagel, Frederick: 1930, 1939–45, 1950
Jameson, Edward: S1969
Jamison, Anne: 1938
Janssen, Herbert: 1945, 1948–49, 1951
Janzen, Stephen: 1968, 1970–71/S1969
Jepson, Helen: 1935
Jeritza, Maria: 1928, 1930/LA1937
Jessner, Irene: 1938
Jobin, André: 1965
Jobin, Raoul: 1940–49
Johansen, Barbara: 1952

Johnson, Barbara: 1957
Johnson, Christine: 1943
Johnson, Edward: 1928
Johnson, Nancy: 1953, 1959
Johnson, Virginia: 1953, 1959
Johnson, William: 1967
Johnston, Patricia: 1953
Johnstone, Lela: 1923
Jones, Eugene: S1963
Jones, Gwen: 1971/S1971
Jones, Gwyneth: 1969
Jones, Olive: 1924
Jones, Oliver: 1935–37
Journet, Marcel: 1925–26
Julian, Alexandre: 1931
Jungwirth, Manfred: 1971
Jurinac, Sena: 1959, 1971
Jurs, Evelyn: 1941
Justus, William: S1971
Kabaiwanska, Raina: 1962, 1966, 1970
Kailer, Lucille: 1965
Kantor, Mary: 1952
Kappel, Gertrude: 1933
Karkova, Anna: 1927
Karpelenia, Helen: 1944
Karras, Sophie: 1955
Kattge, Gary: 1958
Keaumoku, Louis: 1927
Kenig, Murray: 1956–57
Kersh, Henry: 1967–68
Khanzadian, Vahan: 1968/S1968–69
King, James: 1969, 1971/S1961
King, Marilynn: 1945–46
Kipnis, Alexander: 1939–41
Kirk, Florence: 1943
Kirkpatrick, Carol: 1966–67/S1966–67
Kirsten, Dorothy: 1947–48, 1950–57, 1959–60, 1962–63, 1966–70/LA1945, LA1958, LA1965
Klebe, Marvin: 1967/S1963, S1967
Klose, Margarete: 1953
Knapp, Eleanor: 1946
Knapp, Sybil Louise: 1951–52, 1955, 1957
Knierr, Marcella: 1926–28
Kniplova, Nadezda: 1968

Knoll, Rudolf: LA 1968
Knyiadas, Athena: S1961
Kolk, Stanley: S1967, S1969
Kolodin, Michael: 1933
Konya, Sandor: 1960–65
Kostin, Feodor: 1927
Kova, Marija: 1967/S1966
Kovaleff, Alexandra: 1930
Kraus, Alfredo: 1966–67
Kraus, Herbert: S1964
Krauter, Marvin: 1942
Krebill, Dorothy: 1966/S1968
Kreppel, Walter: 1963, 1966
Krikorian, Melina: 1962
Krings, Ted: 1964
Krooskos, Christine: 1956/S1969
Kroph, Lina: 1935–38
Kubiak, Teresa: 1971
Kuchta, Gladys: 1964
Kullman, Charles: 1936–38, 1941–48, 1950, 1954
Lachona, Chris: 1955–56
Lagger, Peter: 1969
Lagorio, Valerie: 1949, 1951
Lance, Albert: 1961–62
Landan, Charlotte: 1937
Landi, Bruno: 1944–45
Landry, Jules: 1965
Lane, Gloria: 1959
Lanfranconi, Terry: 1932
Lang, Edith: 1959
Langdon, Michael: 1962
Langee, Jacqueline: S1962
Lantz, Elizabeth: S1966
Lanyon, Sherrill: 1950–51
Lanz, Madelaine: 1933–35
Lardner, Geoffrey: 1967
Larsen, Karen: 1952
Laubenthal, Rudolf: 1927
Lauche, Clare: 1935
Laufkötter, Karl: 1938, 1941
Lauppe, Barbara: 1950
Lauri-Volpi, Giacomo: 1929
Lawler, Louise: 1960
Lawlor, Kathleen: 1936, 1938–48
Lawrence, Erich: 1946–47
Lawrence, Ernest: 1951–52
Lawrence, Eugene: 1969, 1971/S1968–69, S1971

Lawrence, Marjorie: 1939-40
Lazelle, Rena: 1923-24
Lazzari, Virgilio: 1926, 1947
Leandre, Marie: 1935
Lear, Evelyn: 1965, 1968, 1971
Lee, Ella: 1964
Leeming, Peter: 1971 (MND)
Lehmann, Lotte: 1934, 1936, 1940-41, 1945-46
Lehr, LeRoy: S1971 (FCF)
Leo, Cecile: 1927
Leonard, Gail: 1962-63
Leonard, Myrtle: 1933
Leonetti, Gino: 1961
Le Page, Don: 1968
Levi, Alfred: 1933
Levon, Nevart: 1944
Lewis, Brenda: 1950, 1952
Lewis, Richard: 1955-60, 1962, 1965, 1968
Liagre, Jeannine: 1960, 1963, 1967/ S1965
Lichtegg, Max: 1948
Lieber, Paul: 1940-41, 1945
Ligeti, Desire: 1946-56
Likova, Eva: LA1961
Lilova, Margarita: 1968-69, 1971
Lindholm, Berit: 1970
Lindi, Aroldo: 1926
Lindsey, Claudia: S1969
Lindstedt, Erik: 1967
Linne, Charlotte: 1931-32
Lipp, Wilma: 1962
Lippert, Marion: 1970
Lishner, Leon: 1966
List, Emanuel: 1935-37
Lockhart, Gene: 1942
Lombardi, John: 1953
Lombardi, Richard: 1970/S1971
Lo Monaco, Jerry: S1964
London, George (Burnson, George): 1943, 1959
Lopez, Nathaniel: S1963-64
Lorengar, Pilar: 1964-65
Lorenz, Walter: 1940-41
Lorenzini, Max: 1937-38, 1940, 1943-54, 1958
Lothrop, Marie: 1932

Loughery, Edward: 1937
Lourenzo, August: 1943, 1945-46
Louw, Allan: 1950, 1952, 1957
Lovasich, Edward: 1952, 1956-57
Ludgin, Chester: 1964-67/S1962-65
Ludlow, Conrad: 1953
Ludwig, Christa: 1971
Lumsden, Norman: 1971 (MND)
Luscombe, Grace: 1937
Luxon, Benjamin: 1971 (MND)
Lysell, Eric: S1961
Macbeth, Florence: 1926-27
MacKay, Margery: 1969
MacKenzie, Tandy: 1932
MacNeil, Cornell: 1955, 1961, 1967, 1970
MacNevin, Evelyn: 1932
Macurdy, John: 1962/S1961-62, S1965
MacWatters, Virginia: 1944
Maia, Carolyn: 1971 (MND)
Maison, René: 1937
Malas, Spiro: S1961, S1964
Malatesta, Pompilio: 1928-29
Malbin, Elaine: 1958/S1967
Malinoff, Bascha: 1932
Mallozzi, John: 1953
Malone, Dale: 1957
Malone, Richard: 1968/S1968
Malova, Katerina: 1932
Mancini, Gino: 1937
Manning, Dave: 1955
Manski, Dorothee: 1930, 1935-36
Manton, Raymond: 1955-71/ S1962, S1969
Mari, Dolores: 1959
Mario, Queena: 1923-24, 1929-30, 1932
Marion, Doris: 1952
Markham, Mary Helen: 1938, 1941, 1943-44
Marks, Sheila: 1967-69/S1969
Marlo, Elinor: 1925-27, 1930, 1934
Marlowe, Anthony: 1941
Marlowe, Irene: 1924
Marlowe, Raymond: 1932-35
Marsh, Jane: 1967-68, 1970

Marshall, Charles: 1926
Marshall, Robert: 1942
Marsland, Peter: 1971 (MND)
Martell, Richard: 1956, 1964
Martin, Benjamin: 1935, 1944–47
Martin, Gerald: 1964/S1963
Martin, Janis: 1960–64, 1966, 1969–70/S1961
Martinelli, Giovanni: St., 1923, 1927, 1931, 1933, 1935–37, 1939
Martinez, Raymond: S1966
Martini, Nino: 1939
Martinis, Carla: 1954
Martorano, Salvatore: S1969
Marvin, Lee: 1954
Mascherini, Enzo: 1949–50, 1953
Maschio, Jeanette: 1936
Masini, Galliano: 1938
Mason, Lawrence: 1953–54
Massay, Kevin: S1966
Massue, Nicholas: 1938
Matsumoto, Shigemi: 1968–71/ S1969, S1971
Matthes, Walter: 1968–69/S1962
Mayer, Hugo: 1964/S1966
Mayock, Douglas: 1955
Mazura, Franz: 1968–69
Mazzoli, Ferruccio: LA1960
McArt, Jan: 1955–57
McCann, Frances: 1960
McCarthy, Marjorie: 1942
McCaughna, Daniel: 1963–64/ S1964
McChesney, Ernest: 1955
McCracken, James: 1962–64, 1970–71
McCray, James: 1971
McDonald, Betty: 1954
McDonald, William: S1971
McEachern, Thomas: S1968–69
McFall, John: 1967
McGuckin, Henry: 1959, 1961/ S1961
McGuire, Dorothy: 1954
McIntosh, Arlene: 1951
McLaughlin, Myrtle: 1931–34
McVey, Patrick: 1947–50
Mehl, Charlene: 1968

Meisle, Kathryn: 1926–27, 1929, 1932–33, 1935–37, 1939
Melchior, Lauritz: 1934–37, 1939, 1941, 1945
Melius, Luella: 1926
Menci, Pietro: 1964–65
Meneguzzer, Jolanda: 1962–63, 1965
Menkes, Sara: 1948
Mennucci, Carlo: 1933, 1943
Mercado, José: 1928
Meredith, Morley: 1966
Merli, Francesco: 1932
Merrill, Jean: 1935–36
Merrill, Robert: 1957
Merriman, Nan: 1957
Messina, Salvatore: 1926–27
Metlenko, Henry: S1968–69
Meyer, Kerstin: 1962
Michalski, Raymond: 1971
Micheau, Janine: 1938
Micheletti, Carlo: S1971
Michelini, Alma: 1925
Milanov, Zinka: 1943
Millar, Gregory: 1954
Miller, George: 1931
Miller, Mildred: 1961
Miller, John: 1971
Miller, Richard: 1958
Miller, Thomas: 1951–52
Mills, Robert: 1945
Modenos, John: 1967
Modesti, Giuseppe: 1958
Moffo, Anna: 1960–61
Mojica, José: 1924
Molloy, Clive: 1971 (MND)
Molnar-Talajic, Ljiljana: 1969, 1971
Moncla, Constance: 1924
Monk, Allan: 1967–71/S1967–69, S1971
Monotti, Teresina: 1923–25
Montal, Andre: 1964/S1964–65
Montarsolo, Paolo: 1969
Monte, Mari: 1936, 1940
Monti, Nicola: 1960
Moore, Ann: 1962, 1966
Moore, Grace: 1941

Moore, Robert: 1955
Morelle, Maureen: 1971 (MND)
Morelli, Carlo: 1936
Morgan, Gerwyn: 1971 (MND)
Morgana, Nina: 1929, 1933
Moscona, Nicola: 1946–49, 1951–52, 1954, 1956–57
Moser, Margot: 1969
Mosher, Elisabeth: S1964
Mosley, Robert: S1971
Moudry, Janice: 1953
Moulson, Robert: S1963
Moynagh, Joan Marie: 1958–59
Müller, Maria: 1931–32
Mundt, Richard: 1971/S1968, S1971
Munsel, Patrice: 1956
Murphy, Delphine: 1931
Murphy, Pierce: 1955, 1957
Murphy, Ralph: 1959
Muzio, Claudia: 1924–26, 1932–33
Nadell, Rosalind: 1954, 1956
Nadler, Sheila: 1968–70
Nagy, Robert: S1965
Naham, Eugene: 1971
Navarro, Juan: 1939
Naya, Francisco: 1940
Neill, William: S1971 (FCF)
Nelli, Herva: 1951–52, 1957
Nelson, Greta: 1950
Nelson, Robin: 1944–45, 1947–50
Nenova, Pepi: 1963
Neri, Aristide: St.
Nesbitt, Kayton: 1946–47
Neway, Patricia: S1966
Newman, Linda: S1965–66
Newsom, Mary: 1924–25
Nicolich, Antonio: 1925–26
Nienstedt, Gerd: 1970
Nikolaidi, Elena: 1950
Nilsson, Birgit: 1956, 1964, 1970
Nilsson, Raymond: 1961, 1963, 1968–69/S1961, S1966
Niska, Maralin: S1967
Nissi, Eric: 1967
Nixon, Marni: S1966
Noble, Luana: S1969
Nolen, Timothy: 1968–70/S1969

Noonan, Stanley: 1939–40
Norville, Hubert: 1950
Nostrom, Helen: 1934–35
Novi, Edward: 1951
Novotna, Jarmila: 1939, 1946, 1949
Null, Neysa: 1963
Nystrom, Herbert: 1945
Oberlin, Russell: 1961
O'Connell, Jo Ann: 1949–50
O'Dea, Margaret: 1935–36
Ohman, Frank: 1960
Oldt, Louise: 1958
O'Leary, Thomas: 1965, 1967
Olitzki, Walter: 1940–41, 1945–48
Oliver, Frances: 1952
Oliver, Francis: 1943
Oliviero, Lodovico: 1924–31, 1933, 1936–39
Olmsted, Anita: 1923–24
Olson, Tim: 1961
Olvis, William: S1967
Omeron, Grace: 1935
Opthof, Cornelis: 1971
Ordini, G.: 1923
Orr, Terry: 1960
Osborne, Verna: 1940, 1942–43
Ostrowski, Alice: 1949–51
Ott, Hildegarde: 1928
Palangi, Carl: 1954–57, 1959
Paltrinieri, Giordano: 1923, 1930
Palumbo, Frank: 1938, 1942
Panerai, Rolando: 1958
Pappas, Pauline: 1950, 1954
Parker, Jeanne: 1963/S1964
Parly, Ticho: 1960, 1968
Patrick, Julian: S1965, S1969
Patton, Barbara: S1965–66
Patton, Fred: 1927
Paul, Thomas: S1963–64
Paulee, Mona: 1939–40
Paulini, Philippa: 1954
Pauly, Rose: 1938
Pavarotti, Luciano: 1967–69, 1971
Pavek, Janet: S1964
Paxman, Gordon: 1953–54
Pechner, Gerhard: 1940
Peerce, Jan: 1941–49, 1951–57, 1960

Pelayo, Hernan: S1961
Peralta, Frances: 1927
Perdue, Lola: 1929
Perulli, Franco: 1941
Peters, Arthur: 1949–50
Petersen, Donna: 1953–54, 1956–57, 1963, 1966–71/S1961–67, S1969, S1971
Petersen, William: 1954–55
Peterson, Glade: 1962–64, 1969–70/LA1968
Peterson, LeRoy: S1971 (FCF)
Petina, Irra: 1940–43
Petit, Joseph: 1955
Petri, Frantz: 1969
Petroff, Ivan: 1943–46
Petrova, Faina: 1931
Pfandl, Jeanne: S1968
Phillips, Delphia: 1947
Picco, Millo: 1924, 1927–31
Pilcher, William: 1927
Pilou, Jeannette: 1968–69
Pinedo, Joe: 1971
Pinza, Claudia: 1947–48
Pinza, Ezio: 1927–28, 1930–38, 1940–48
Pisani, Gioacchino: 1927
Pistor, Gotthelf: 1931
Poleri, David: 1953
Polidori, Violetta: 1926
Ponitz, Olive: 1938–41
Pons, Lily: 1932, 1937–47, 1949–52
Popper, Beta: 1947
Porta, Enrico: 1951
Post, Valeria: 1928–29
Power, Margot: S1962
Prandelli, Giacinto: 1954
Presnell, Harve: 1957
Prey, Hermann: 1963
Price, Leontyne: 1957–59, 1961, 1963, 1965, 1967–68, 1971/LA1960
Price, Margaret: 1969–70
Price, Perry: S1966
Quartararo, Florence: 1947, 1949–50
Quilico, Louis: 1956, 1958–59, 1968, 1970–71

Radic, John: 1931
Ragusa, Anita: 1945
Raimondi, Gianni: 1957–58
Raina, Elena: S1963
Rankin, Nell: 1955–56/LA1963
Ratti, Eugenia: 1958
Ray, Marguerite: 1965
Rayner, Sydney: 1930
Rayson, Benjamin: S1961
Reardon, John: 1971
Reed, Estelle: 1932
Reed, Janet: 1939
Reese, Constance: St.
Reggiani, Hilde: 1945
Regoli, Nazareth: 1925–26
Reitan, Roald: 1957
Reiter, Prosper: 1926
Remo, Ken: S1965
Renton, Jeremy: 1968
Repp, Ellen: 1946
Resnick, Sam: 1964–65
Resnik, Regina: 1946–48, 1963–64, 1966
Rethberg, Elisabeth: 1928–29, 1931, 1934–36, 1938–40
Richardson, Dan: 1970
Riedel, Johann: 1930
Riffel, Richard: 1961–64
Riggins, Earl: 1939, 1941–42
Rinaldi, Alberto: 1970
Rinaldi, Margherita: 1968
Ristow, Roderick: S1963
Ritter, Margaret: 1939–42
Rivero, Adeline: 1929
Robb, Peter: 1962
Robert, Josephine: 1937
Roberto, Francesca: S1967
Robin, Mado: 1954
Roche, Sarita: S1971 (FCF)
Roehr, Ruth: 1953–55
Roggero, Margaret: 1952–53, 1955–56
Romaine, Hilda: 1929
Roman, Stella: 1941–42, 1944–47, 1951
Romanoff, Dimitri: 1933, 1935
Romero, Ned: 1960
Ronec, Olga: 1955

Ronson, Annabell: 1956
Rooney, William: 1946, 1948
Roselle, Anne: 1927
Rosenblatt, Robert: 1954
Ross, Elinor: 1962/LA1961
Ross, Ron: 1954
Rossi, Attilio: 1951–52
Rossi-Lemeni, Nicola: 1951–53, 1967–68
Rossini, Angelo: 1935
Rothier, Léon: St., 1929
Rovere, U.: St.
Rubino, Michael: 1967
Rubio, Consuelo: 1962
Ruiz, Maclovia: 1933, 1935
Russell, Gilbert: 1960
Russell, Roy: 1936–37
Russelle, Chester: 1967
Russelle, Cleodel: 1967
Ruzdak, Vladimir: 1961
Rysanek, Leonie: 1956–58, 1960
Sabanieeva, Thalia: 1924
Sa Earp, Maria: 1946
Sage, Russell: 1953–54
Sanders, W. Vernon: 1944–45
Sanderson, Bettie: 1945–47
Sandrini, Eugenio: 1929–31
San Miguel, Dolores: 1955, 1957, 1963, 1967/S1966, S1968–69
Saroya, Bianca: St., 1923
Saunders, Arlene: 1967, 1971
Sayao, Bidu: 1939–42, 1946–48, 1950–52
Schaffer, Evan: 1961/S1961
Schech, Marianne: 1959–60
Schiller, Georgette: 1934–35
Schipa, Tito: 1924–26, 1929, 1935, 1939–40
Schmidling, Allen: 1947
Schmorr, Robert: S1961
Schneider, Jacklyn: S1969
Schoeffler, Paul: 1953, 1959–61
Schoen, Ernest: 1941
Schoenfeld, Ted: S1971
Schon, Kenneth: 1946
Schorr, Friedrich: 1931–32, 1935–36, 1938
Schuh, Audrey: 1956

Schützendorf, Gustav: 1935
Schwabacher, James: 1948, 1950–52
Schwartzman, Seymour: S1967–69
Schwarzkopf, Elisabeth: 1955–58, 1960, 1962–64
Sciutti, Graziella: 1961, 1970
Scott, Eileen: 1954–55/S1961
Scotti, Antonio: 1927
Scovotti, Jeanette: 1967/S1962
Seefried, Irmgard: 1964
Segale, John: 1955
Sellon, Robert: 1930–31, 1940
Serbo, Rico: 1967–68/S1967
Seri, Francesco: 1924
Sevilla, Rafael: S1966
Sewall, May: 1928–29, 1932
Seymour, Katherine: 1927
Shafer, John: 1944
Shaffner, Ruth: 1924
Sharpe, Marion: 1939
Sharretts, Richard: 1948–49
Shaw, John: 1963
Shefoff, Henri: 1935, 1937
Sherrill, Lawrence: 1936–37
Shiffeler, Charles: 1939–40, 1942
Shipley, Kay: S1964
Shirley, George: S1961
Shoenfeld, Ted: 1970/S1971
Sholl, Jeanette: 1935
Shore, Sharon: 1953
Shuard, Amy: 1963, 1966, 1968–69
Siepi, Cesare: 1954–55, 1968
Sigond, Marguerite: 1929
Silja, Anja: 1968, 1970–71
Sills, Beverly: 1953, 1971
Silva, Delbert: S1963, S1967
Silva, Luisa: 1931
Silva, Roberto: 1943–44
Simionato, Giulietta: 1953, 1962
Simondet, Georges: 1931–34
Simpson, Gladys: 1940–41
Singher, Martial: 1947
Smith, Cary Archer: S1963
Smith, Edna: 1926–27, 1929, 1934–35
Smith, Kenneth: S1966
Smith, Malcolm: S1964

Smith, Maudelene: 1929
Smith, Salicia: 1967
Smuin, Michael: 1959–60
Sordello, Enzo: LA1968
Soyer, Roger: 1970
Spence, Wilma: 1941
Sperry, Austin: 1927–29, 1932
Spiess, Ludovic: 1968, 1970
Spry, Mary Jane: 1947, 1949
Stadtegger, Eleanor: 1928
Stahlman, Sylvia: 1957–58, 1960
Stalley, Suzanne: 1962
Standard, James: 1960
Stanton, Robert: 1933
Starr, Virginia: 1960
Steber, Eleanor: 1945
Steele, James: S1963
Steger, Dan: 1930–31
Sten, Suzanne: 1940
Stephens, Joyce: 1950–51
Stevens, Risë: 1940–41, 1944–45
Stevens, Sherry: 1952
Stevenson, Delcina: 1966–67
Stewart, Nathan: 1933
Stewart, Thomas: 1962–63, 1965–66, 1970–71
Stignani, Ebe: 1938, 1948
Stinson, George: 1939–40
Stowell, Kent: 1959
Stracciari, Riccardo: 1925
Stratas, Teresa: 1966
Strause, Helene: 1930–34
Strauss, Georgianna: St.
Streich, Rita: 1957, 1959
Strelkoff, Serafim: 1941
Strong, Marcelle Minot: 1967
Strubing, James: 1961/S1962
Stull, Susanne: 1969
Styles, Richard: 1964, 1967, 1971/S1966
Sullivan, Brian: 1952–55, 1962, 1965
Sullivan, Daniel: 1971/S1971
Sullivan, John: 1954
Sullivan, John: 1968
Susulich, Lina: 1927
Suthaus, Ludwig: 1953, 1956
Sutherland, Joan: 1961, 1963–64, 1966, 1971

Sutton, Vern: S1971 (FCF)
Svanholm, Set: 1946–49, 1951
Swarthout, Gladys: 1941
Sze, Yi-Kwei: 1950–51
Szekely, Mihaly: 1949
Szymkun, Giovanna: S1968
Taddei, Giuseppe: 1957–58
Taenzler, Hans: 1934
Tagliabue, Carlo: 1938
Tagliavini, Ferruccio: 1948–49, 1952
Tagliavini, Franco: 1964
Tajo, Italo: 1948–50, 1952–53, 1956
Talbot, Sharon: S1965
Tallone, George: 1944–47
Tarantino, James: 1967
Tarrés, Enriqueta: 1966, 1968
Tatum, Nancy: 1969
Taylor, Alice: 1959
Taylor, John: 1955
Tear, Robert: 1971 (MND)
Tebaldi, Renata: 1950, 1955–56, 1965
Tede, Margery: 1967, 1969
Telva, Marion: 1928
Tenbrook, David: 1967–68/S1968
Tennyson, Jean: 1942
Tentoni, Rosa: 1937
Thaw, David: 1961, 1966
Thebom, Blanche: 1947, 1949, 1951–52, 1957, 1959/LA1963
Theyard, Harry: S1968
Thomas, Evan: 1969
Thomas, Jess: 1957, 1965–70
Thomas, John Charles: 1930, 1943
Thomas, Robert: 1958–59
Thompson, Hugh: 1944
Thompson, Norman: 1941
Thompson, Truman: 1943
Thompson, Zack: 1968
Thomson, Austin: 1951
Thorborg, Kerstin: 1938, 1943
Thornbury, Destal: 1949–50
Throndson, Dorothy: 1950–52
Tibbe, Cuthbert: 1932
Tibbett, Lawrence: 1927–28, 1933, 1936, 1939, 1941, 1946–47, 1949
Tipton, Thomas: 1962, 1968

Tissier, Joseph: 1944–46
Tobin, Eugene: 1957
Todd, Carol: 1962–64, 1966, 1968/ S1963–66, S1968–69
Toepper, Hertha: 1960
Tokatyan, Armand: 1923, 1927–28
Toolatjan, Vahan: 1955
Torres, Suzanne: 1929–30
Torri, Rosina: 1925
Toscano, Carol: S1963, S1967, S1971
Tourangeau, Huguette: 1971
Tozzi, Giorgio: 1955, 1958–64, 1966, 1969–70/LA1968
Trama, Ugo: 1965, 1968
Traubel, Helen: 1945, 1947
Tredway, William: 1967, 1971
Treigle, Norman: S1964
Trevisan, Vittorio: 1925–26
Trevor, Demy: 1949, 1951
Treweck, Ruth: 1929
Tucci, Gabriella: 1959
Tucker, Richard: 1954–55, 1965
Tulajin, J.: 1927
Tumminia, Josephine: 1935–37, 1947
Turnbull, Mary Jane: 1947
Turner, Albert: 1955
Turner, Brian: S1964–66
Turner, Claramae: 1942, 1944–45, 1947–55, 1957–58, 1965
Turrini, Roberto: 1953–56
Twigg, Ethel: 1929
Tyler, Veronica: S1968
Udovick, Lucille: 1961
Uhl, Fritz: 1961
Ulfung, Ragnar: 1967, 1969–71
Urquhart, Deems: 1967
Ursino, James: 1954–55
Valdengo, Giuseppe: 1947–48, 1950–52
Valentino, Francesco: 1943–52
Valletti, Cesare: 1953, 1963
Vallin, Ninon: 1934
Van Dam, José: 1970
Van Der Bilt, Peter: 1963
Van Derick, Peter: 1971
Van Gordon, Cyrena: 1933

Van Leeuwen, David: 1964
Van Mill, Arnold: 1958
Vanna, Gina: 1936
Vanni, Helen: 1963, 1965, 1971/ S1966
Vannucci, Albert: 1933, 1935, 1944
Vannucci, Attilio: 1925, 1927–28
Vannucci, Edwin: 1946–47
Vanzo, Alain: 1970
Varnay, Astrid: 1946, 1948, 1951
Vasilieff, Nikolai: 1933, 1935
Velsir, Patricia: 1956
Venora, Lee: 1963–64, 1966/S1961– 64
Verdell, Anthony: 1954
Verreau, Richard: S1961–62, S1964
Vettori, Elda: 1928
Vickers, Jon: 1959–60, 1963–64, 1966, 1969–70/LA1968
Vinay, Ramon: 1949–51, 1965–66/ LA1968
Viti, Geraldine: 1946
Viviani, Gaetano: 1930
Vogel, Victor: 1925–26
Voketaitis, Arnold: S1964
Vollmar, Jocelyn: 1959–60
Von Rohr, Otto: 1961
Von Stade, Frederica: S1971
Votipka, Thelma: 1938–47, 1952
Vrenios, Anastasios: S1968
Vroons, Frans: 1951
Vyvyan, Jennifer: 1971 (MND)
Waddell, Brad: 1964/S1965
Wade, Paul: 1971 (MND)
Wagner, James: 1957–58
Wahlin, Fred: 1944
Walker, Clyde P.: S1971 (FCF)
Walker, Donna: 1949–50, 1952, 1955
Walker, John: 1971/S1971
Walker, Mallory: S1962–63
Walker, Sidney: 1954
Wallace, Mimi: 1960
Walti, Paul: 1938–42, 1948
Ward, Barbara: 1940
Ward, Cecilia: 1958
Ward, David: 1967, 1969/LA1968
Warden, Georgia: 1963

444

Warenskjold, Dorothy: 1948–55
Warfield, Sandra: 1963–64
Waring, James: 1959
Warren, Elinor: 1954
Warren, Leonard: 1943–44, 1947–48, 1954–56
Watson, Claire: 1966
Wayne, Letha: 1933
Weathers, Felicia: 1967, 1969
Weede, Robert: 1940–43, 1947–52, 1954–55, 1958–60, 1964
Welitsch, Alexander: 1954–55
Wellman, Edward: 1939–44
Welton, Joan: 1950
Wendt, Allan: 1967
Wentworth, Richard: 1958, 1960
West, John: 1964–65/S1963–64
West, Leslie: 1971 (MND)
West, Maria: 1955, 1957
Wheeler, Janice: S1965
White, Claudia: 1964–65, 1968/S1965
White, Harold: 1951, 1953
Whitesides, William: 1965
Wien, Erika: 1964
Wiench, Nancy: 1968
Wilcox, Virginia: 1949
Wildermann, William: 1961, 1968
Wilkins, June: 1951, 1953, 1956/S1963
Williams, Frederick: 1945
Williams, Geraldine: 1950
Williams, Nancy: S1963–64
Williams, Neville: 1971 (MND)

Williams, Tudor: 1930–32
Wilson, Karen: S1969
Winden, Joan: 1959
Windgassen, Wolfgang: 1970
Windheim, Marek: 1931–32, 1934–35, 1941–42
Winnington, Sally: 1967
Winters, Lawrence: 1958–59
Wishart, Edith: 1937, 1940
Wixell, Ingvar: 1967–69
Woellhaf, Karl: 1957, 1959
Wolansky, Raymond: 1964–66, 1971
Wolff, Beverly: S1963, S1965–66
Wolovsky, Leonardo: 1963
Wong, Marston: 1958
Woodburn, Arlene: S1968–69
Wright, Richard: S1963
Wyatt, Keith: S1967
Wysor, Elisabeth: 1942
Yahia, Mino: 1959
Yamamoto, Alan: 1967
Yarick, Doris: S1961, S1963
Yarnell, Bruce: 1971
Young, Alexander: 1965
Young, Anna: 1923–25, 1929, 1935
Youngs, Malcolm: 1938
Zampieri, Giuseppe: 1959–61
Zanasi, Mario: 1959–60
Zebranska, Elsa: 1940
Zickhardt, Joice: 1930
Ziliani, Alessandro: 1938
Zubiri, Martina: 1946–49
Zylis-Gara, Teresa: 1968

Notes

[1]MND refers to English Opera Group production of Britten's *A Midsummer Night's Dream.*

[2]FCF refers to Center Opera Company of Minneapolis' production of *Faust Counter Faust.*

Repertoire 1923–1972

The letter S *before a date refers to a season of Spring Opera.*

AUBER
Fra Diavolo: 1926, 1968
BARTOK
Bluebeard's Castle: S1963, S1965
BEETHOVEN
Fidelio: 1937, 1939, 1946, 1951, 1954, 1961, 1964, 1969
BELLINI
Norma: 1937, 1972
I Puritani: 1966
La Sonnambula: 1960, 1963
BERG
Lulu: 1965, 1971
Wozzeck: 1960, 1962, 1968
BERLIOZ
Les Troyens: 1966, 1968
BIZET
Carmen: 1927–28, 1931, 1934, 1936, 1940–46, 1948–49, 1951, 1953, 1955, 1959–60, 1962, 1964, 1966, 1970/S1961, S1968
The Pearl Fishers: S1962, S1964, S1967
BOITO
Mefistofele: 1923, 1952–53, 1963
BRITTEN
A Midsummer Night's Dream: 1961, 1971
The Turn of the Screw: S1966
CHARPENTIER
Louise: 1947, 1955, 1967

CHERUBINI
Medea: 1958
The Portuguese Inn: 1954
DEBUSSY
Pelléas et Melísande: 1938, 1947, 1965, 1969
DELIBES
Lakmé: 1934, 1937, 1940, 1944, 1946
DELLO JOIO
Blood Moon: 1961
DONIZETTI
The Daughter of the Regiment: 1941–42, 1952, 1962
Don Pasquale: 1929, 1938, 1941, 1943, 1946/S1963, S1971
The Elixir of Love: 1929, 1948, 1956, 1967, 1969
Lucia di Lammermoor: 1926, 1930, 1932, 1938–39, 1942–47, 1949–50, 1954, 1957, 1961, 1968, 1972/S1966/LA1940.
Maria Stuarda: 1971
EINEM
The Visit of the Old Lady: 1972
FLOTOW
Martha: 1925–26, 1929, 1935, 1938, 1944/S1961
FLOYD
Susannah: S1964

446

GESSNER
Faust Counter Faust: S1971
GIORDANO
Andrea Chenier: 1923–24, 1928, 1931, 1938, 1950, 1955, 1959, 1965
La Cena Delle Beffe: 1927–28
Fedora: 1928
GLUCK
Orfeo: 1959
GOUNOD
Faust: 1926, 1928–30, 1932, 1934, 1937, 1942, 1944, 1947, 1949, 1955, 1962, 1967, 1970/S1964
Roméo et Juliette: 1923, 1927, 1937, 1946–47, 1951/S1961, S1969
GRUENBERG
The Emperor Jones: 1933
HALÉVY
La Juive: 1935–36
HONEGGER
Joan of Arc at the Stake: 1954
HUMPERDINCK
Hansel and Gretel: 1929–30, 1932
JANACEK
Jenufa: 1969
The Makropulos Case: 1966
LEONCAVALLO
I Pagliacci: 1923, 1927–30, 1932–33, 1936, 1939, 1943, 1945, 1948, 1952, 1955, 1959, 1962, 1964/S1967
MASCAGNI
L'Amico Fritz: 1924
Cavalleria Rusticana: 1927–28, 1930, 1932–33, 1938–39, 1943, 1945, 1948, 1952, 1962/S1967
MASSENET
Manon: 1924–25, 1929–30, 1933–34, 1937, 1939–40, 1944, 1948, 1951, 1954, 1958, 1971/S1962/Portland-Seattle 1941.
Werther: 1935, 1953
MENOTTI
The Consul: S1969
MEYERBEER
L'Africaine: 1972

MILHAUD
Christopher Columbus (The Discovery of America): 1968
MONTEMEZZI
L'Amore dei Tre Re: 1925, 1928, 1941–42, 1947, 1952, 1959, 1966
MONTEVERDI
Orfeo: S1972
MOORE
Carry Nation: S1966
MOUSSORGSKY
Boris Godounoff: 1945–46, 1948, 1951, 1953, 1956, 1961, 1966
MOZART
The Abduction from the Seraglio: S1962, S1964, S1968
Cosi Fan Tutte: 1956–57, 1960, 1963, 1970/S1965
Don Giovanni: 1938, 1940, 1943, 1945, 1947–49, 1952–53, 1955, 1959, 1962, 1965, 1968
The Magic Flute: 1950, 1967, 1969/S1961, S1963
The Marriage of Figaro: 1936, 1940, 1946–47, 1950, 1954, 1958, 1961, 1964, 1966, 1972/S1969
Titus: S1971
OFFENBACH
The Tales of Hoffmann: 1944–45, 1949/S1963, S1967
ORFF
Carmina Burana: 1958–59, 1964, 1971
The Wise Maiden: 1958
PONCHIELLI
La Gioconda: 1947–48, 1967
POULENC
The Dialogues of the Carmelites: 1957, 1963
PUCCINI
La Bohème: 1923–24, 1926–27, 1929–31, 1933, 1935, 1937–38, 1940, 1943–54, 1956, 1958–60, 1962, 1965, 1967, 1969/S1961, S1964/LA1963
La Fanciulla Del West: 1930, 1943, 1960, 1965

447

34, 1937, 1939, 1942–43, 1945–48, 1951–53, 1957, 1960, 1963–64, 1969/S1961–62, S1967
Il Trovatore: 1926–27, 1929, 1931–32, 1936, 1939, 1943, 1946, 1948, 1952, 1956, 1958, 1962, 1964, 1968, 1971/S1966
VITTADINI
Anima Allegra: 1925
WAGNER
The Flying Dutchman: 1954, 1956
Götterdämmerung: 1935–36, 1947, 1969, 1972
Lohengrin: 1931–32, 1937, 1946, 1955, 1960, 1965
Die Meistersinger: 1931–32, 1938, 1948, 1959, 1961, 1965, 1971
Parsifal: 1950–51, 1964
Das Rheingold: 1935–36, 1967, 1972
Siegfried: 1935, 1948, 1970, 1972

Tannhäuser: 1930–31, 1934, 1941, 1958, 1966
Tristan and Isolde: 1927, 1933, 1936–37, 1939, 1945, 1947, 1949–50, 1953, 1967, 1970
Die Walküre: 1935–36, 1939, 1945, 1949, 1953, 1956, 1963, 1968, 1972
WALTON
Troilus and Cressida: 1955
WARD
The Crucible: S1965
WEBER
Der Freischütz: S1964
WEILL
Mahagonny: S1972
Royal Palace: 1968
WOLF-FERRARI
The Secret of Suzanne: 1933, 1944
ZANDONAI
Francesca da Rimini: 1956

BALLETS

BEETHOVEN
The Creatures of Prometheus: 1953
DELIBES
Coppelia: 1939
GLAZOUNOFF
Variations de Ballet: 1960

RAVEL
Bolero: 1932
La Valse: 1932
ROSSINI
Con Amore: 1960
STRAVINSKY
Danses Concertantes: 1959

As this volume went to press, leading contenders for addition to the repertoire were Britten's *Peter Grimes*, Donizetti's *La Favorita*, and Massenet's *Don Quichotte*.

Operas Given at the Hearst
Greek Theater, Berkeley

1957: *Turandot*
1958: *Medea*
1959: *Aida*
1960: *Carmen*
1961: *Fidelio*
1962: *Il Trovatore*
1963: *Falstaff*
1964: *Nabucco*
1965: *Lohengrin*
1966: *Elektra*
1967: *Macbeth*
1968: *Les Troyens*
1969: *The Magic Flute*